The Illustrated Encyclopedia of
TRUCKS
AND BUSES

The Illustrated Encyclopedia of
TRUCKS
AND BUSES

Denis Miller

Quantum
Books

A QUANTUM BOOK

This book is produced by
Quantum Publishing Ltd.
6 Blundell Street
London N7 9BH

Copyright ©MCMLXXXII
Quarto Ltd.

This edition printed 2002

ISBN 1-86160-603-6

QUMT&B

Typeset in Hong Kong by
Everbest Printing Co. Ltd
Colour Separation in England by
Rodney Howe
Printed in China by
Leefung-Asco Printers Ltd.

Opposite page: A heavy-duty Scammell truck on the road. After the Second World War, the
heavy vehicle industry continued the dramatic expansion that had been a feature of the war
years.

Contents

An idea is born

THE MAN generally credited with developing the world's first practical self-propelled vehicle in 1769 is Captain Nicolas Joseph Cugnot, of the Artillerie Française, although there were numerous other experiments prior to this time. The earliest recorded attempt was made by the German, Johann Hautach, who, in the sixteenth century, constructed a horseless carriage apparently propelled by a system of coiled springs. One century later, two Englishmen, Ramsay and Wildgoose, patented another design. Both types were purely experimental, however, and it is unlikely that they ever ran on a public highway.

Cugnot worked hard, first building a model steam carriage to illustrate his ideas. The French government was favourably impressed and ordered him to construct a full-size model, which was demonstrated in front of the French Minister of War. Although the demonstration proved that the design was not quite as reliable as it could have been, a second machine was ordered with a 4½-ton payload capable of hauling field artillery on level ground at a speed of 6km/h. In spite of being crude and clumsy, this vehicle was a comparative success.

In 1784, while working for the Cornish steam engine manufacturers Boulton and Watt, William Murdock, a young Scottish mechanic, built his first steam carriage, but this was not particularly successful, and again appears never to have run on the public highway. Meanwhile, Oliver Evans, a Welsh inventor living in the United States, was investigating the possibility of applying steam power to a road-going carriage, and in 1787 was granted the exclusive right to develop such a machine in the State of Maryland. No actual wagon appears to have materialized, although in 1804 he fitted wheels to a 20-ton steam dredger and drove it under its own power to the River Schuylkill, along which he sailed to Delaware. This was undoubtedly the world's first self-propelled amphibious vehicle, and Evans's ideas also formed the first US patent for a self-propelled steam road vehicle in 1789. A year later, Charles Dalley, of Amiens, France, constructed a rela-

Above The world's oldest surviving self-propelled vehicle is Cugnot's 1770 artillery tractor. *Left* In 1833 Dr F. Church designed a very ornate machine, which even had springs supporting the simple front wheel. *Opposite left* One year after the success of Trevithick's first self-propelled steam carriage in 1801, he constructed a new model *Opposite top right* This replica of William Murdock's steam vehicle of 1784 shows steam propulsion at its simplest. *Opposite bottom right* Goldsworthy steam carriages were reminiscent of the stage coach, this example was used on Sir Charles Dance's Gloucester-Cheltenham run.

tively successful steam carriage, while in America both Apollo Kinsley of Hartford, Connecticut, and Nathan Read, of Eden, Massachusetts, developed vehicles of this type.

In the United Kingdom, Richard Trevithick, who already held the distinction of building the world's first steam railway locomotive, constructed the world's first self-propelled steam carriage to run successfully on public roads. It appeared in 1801. One year later Trevithick's second steam carriage was completed, but lack of finance curtailed further development. It was the lack of funds which also hampered other early experiments in the field, particularly in the United Kingdom, where many financiers already had a vested interest in other forms of transport, such as canals and railways, and were unlikely to show

much enthusiasm for a competitive activity. It may well have been this lack of financial backing that led to an economy of design which precipitated serious, and often fatal, accidents involving early self-propelled vehicles such as boiler explosions, and steering and brake failures, none of which did anything to instil enthusiasm for this new mode of transport.

Goldsworthy Gurney was quick to realize that safety had to come first if the public was to have any confidence in mechanical road transport, and by 1827, following experiments with three alternative types of boiler, he had constructed his first steam coach. Having perfected a "safe" boiler, he then looked for other improvements, deciding to use coke, which was smokeless, for fuel, rather than coal. Within a year he had perfected his de-

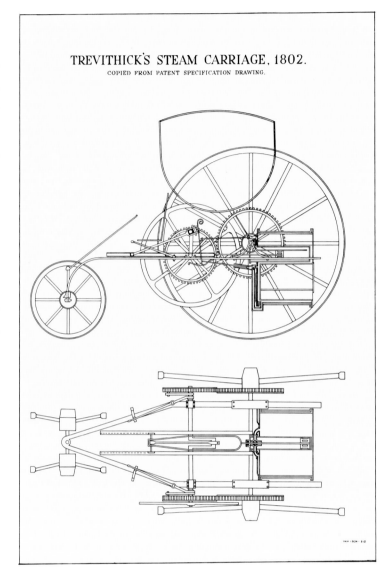

TREVITHICK'S STEAM CARRIAGE, 1802.
COPIED FROM PATENT SPECIFICATION DRAWING.

sign with one machine completing a 135-km run between Melksham, Wilts, and Cranford, Middx, in just ten hours. Sir Charles Dance was a Gurney customer who improved the specification still further and, in 1831, inaugurated a service which ran four times a day along a 14-km route between Gloucester and Cheltenham at an average speed, including stops, of 16 to 19km/h. Other routes followed, but both official and unofficial opposition forced him to close down.

One of the most successful of all United Kingdom steam carriage builders was Walter Hancock, who built his first machine in 1827. Again, safety was of prime consideration, and the first Hancock coach embodied a chain transmission and tight metal boiler joints to withstand high pressures. In 1828 the French engineer

Onesiphore Pecqueur designed and patented a 4-ton steam truck, but construction is not recorded.

Opposition to steam-powered road vehicles in the United Kingdom grew rapidly, with many influential people being against the project. As a result, in 1831 a series of prohibitive bills were passed by the British government to discourage the development of steam vehicles.

The world's first automotive publication, *The Journal of Elemental Locomotion*, was founded by Alexander Gordon in 1832. Sir Goldsworthy Gurney did much to reverse the government's attitude and an attempt was made to form the United Kingdom's first public passenger transport company. This was the London, Holyhead & Liverpool Steam Coach & Road Co, with a capital of £350,000.

Although it failed, at least the company showed the country's growing awareness of the commercial possibilities of mechanical road transport.

As a result of these moves by the government, the development of steam road propulsion stagnated for thirty years, during which time many pioneers turned to the railways and steam shipping.

While the development of self-propelled road vehicles had been largely halted, there were numerous developments on the agricultural front, where portable steam engines, previously hauled by horses, were now being converted to self-propulsion.

By the 1850s, some of the more intrepid inventors were again looking at road vehicles and, despite their being illegal in the United Kingdom, demonstrations frequently took place on

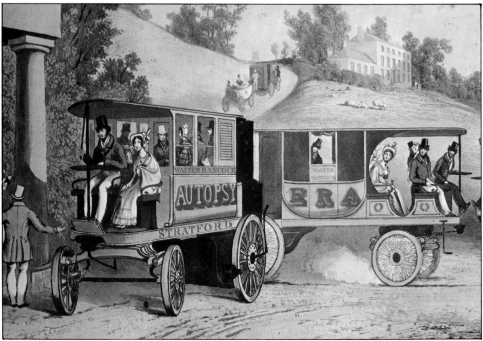

the public highways. This unfortunately led to the crippling Locomotive Acts of 1861 and 1865, and to the Highways & Locomotives (Amendment) Act of 1878. Thus, as Continental and American inventors raced ahead, so their British counterparts were left behind.

While this was taking place in the United Kingdom, in France, Joseph Ravel had taken out a patent in 1868 for "a steam generator heated by mineral oils supplied to steam locomotives on ordinary roads and to all industrial purposes", which was later developed into a petroleum-fuelled steamer. An Englishman, Joseph Wilkinson, is also said to have developed such a system and J H Knight, of Farnham, Surrey, had built a 1½-ton steam carriage. Another French development was the gas engine invented by Etienne Lenoir in 1860, in which gas was mixed with air and ignited by electricity. This was used in the inventor's first horseless carriage two years later. By 1872 the first engine to use fuel oil rather than gas was patented in the United Kingdom by George Brayton, and three years later what may have been the world's first self-propelled load-carrier was created – a 4-ton steam wagon constructed by Brown & May, of Devizes, Wilts. Unfortunately, Brayton's idea was developed into designs for a complete vehicle by George Baldwin Selden, Rochester, New York, in 1879 and led ultimately to a US patent being granted in 1895, in which anyone else using an internal-combustion engine in a road vehicle had to pay royalties to Selden. This arrangement held until 1911 and did much to stunt motor industry growth in the United States.

However, the greatest advances were about to be made in Germany, and were to be crucial to the development of heavy trucks and buses.

Karl Benz was the son of an engine driver, and attended an engineering course at the Karlsruhe Polytechnic before joining a local railway locomotive builder. He became fascinated with the theories of Professor Redtenbacher at the Polytechnic, and as a result turned his attention to the development of the internal-combus-

8

tion engine for road vehicles. Soon Benz had set up his own business, as a manufacturer of stationary gas engines and in 1885, at his Mannheim premises, his first motor car, a 3-wheeler, began to take shape. This was the world's first internal-combustion engined passenger car and set numerous precedents for the future. Drive was transmitted to a countershaft and then by chain and sprocket to the rear wheels, while other features included liquid cooling and an electric ignition system.

Another German pioneer was Gottlieb Daimler, who worked in many parts of Europe before settling in Germany and developing oil engines with Dr Nickolaus August Otto and Eugen Langen. Neither of the latter saw much future in the use of the internal-

combustion engine to provide power for road vehicles, so, in 1882, Daimler resigned and was joined at an experimental workshop in Cannstatt by Wilhelm Maybach, another ex-employee of Otto and Langen. Their first gas engine was a single-cyl air-cooled horizontal unit which was followed, in 1883, by a fully-enclosed design with tube ignition which, by 1885, was being used to power a motorized bicycle. Daimler's first car appeared in 1886. This was a converted horse-drawn carriage powered by a 1½hp single-cyl air-cooled unit with 2-speed transmission via a friction clutch to the rear wheels. An improved model, with differential gear and a 4-speed transmission, appeared in 1889, this having a rear-mounted single-cyl vertical water-cooled engine and all-gear final

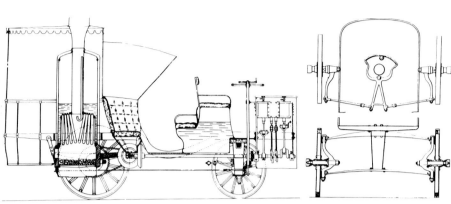

Opposite top Richard Dudgeon, of New York, constructed a passenger steam road vehicle in 1850 which ran successfully for nearly ten years. *Opposite bottom* The most successful steam carriage inventor of the period was Walter Hancock who built and operated 'Autopsy', 'Era' and 'Infant'. *Above* Amédée Bollée Snr who constructed this carriage in 1873 was a leading French advocate of steam-propulsion. *Top right* A front-mounted vertical-twin engine was combined with a rear-mounted vertical boiler in this Amédée Bollée design of 1878. *Right* The Grenville steam carriage was built in Britain in 1875 employing a rear-mounted vertical boiler.

drive. Daimler's third attempt incorporated belt transmission and a 'V'-twin engine, and was one of the most important landmarks in the early days of motoring. Simultaneously, Benz was improving his self-propelled 3-wheeler, but it was in 1891 that his first 4-wheeled passenger car was built.

While these ideas were taking shape in Germany, the French were also hard at work. In 1890 Léon Serpollet took a significant step in the development of steam propulsion for road vehicles by inventing the "flash" boiler. Meanwhile, Panhard et Levassor, Paris, which had been appointed an agent for Daimler gas and oil engines, was soon developing in 1891 the world's first "real" passenger car, using a ladder-type chassis frame and full working drawings. Powered by a 'V'-twin Daimler engine mounted vertically at the front, this had a clutch and sliding 3-speed pinion transmission and marked the dawn of the motor car.

The first self-propelled vehicle to be exported from the United States was a steam carriage built by R E Olds which was delivered to the Francis Times Co, Bombay, India. In the United Kingdom, Hornsby & Son developed its first oil engine the following year. The Germans, however, were in the forefront of internal-combustion engine developments, and were now regularly supplying such units to other road vehicle builders throughout the Western world.

For the time being, however, Maurice LeBlant's 1892 steam vans, with Serpollet boilers and 3-cyl engines with steersman at the front and stoker at the rear, were about the only self-propelled load-carriers in Europe. One was entered in the world's first motor vehicle trial between Paris and Rouen in 1894, but was only marginally successful. Also in 1894, an experimental 5-ton steam wagon was built at Leyland, Lancs, by the young James Sumner, forming the foundations of the world-renowned commercial vehicle manufacturer, Leyland Vehicles.

The first light commercials were also French, derived from Panhard et Levassor and Peugeot passenger car designs and there were also battery-electric types such as those built by Jeantaud and Krieger. The next two years, however, were to see the dawn of the internal-combustion engined commercial vehicle.

Fire engines

The lure of the fire engine is universal. From small boys to grown men, the sound of the siren stops all in their tracks just as the clanging bell and clattering hooves did at the turn of the century. When originally developed, the fire engine was a means of combating fire but can now handle a multitude of diverse tasks the most important of which is rescue. Thus, a host of special machinery has been designed, often mounted on specially developed reliable chassis capable of high-speed operation. While many truck manufacturers have, from time to time, offered a fire engine chassis, it is the specialist companies such as American LaFrance, Dennis, Merryweather, Seagrave and Ward LaFrance that have become world famous in this field.

1

2

3

7 6

4

5

8

9

10

1 In 1903 Merryweather & Sons Ltd supplied the world's first petrol-engined chemical appliance to the Tottenham Fire Brigade. 2 The Dependable Truck & Tractor Co, Illinois, built this chemical appliance around 1921. 3 As early as 1907, Gobron-Brillié had combined a petrol-engined chassis with a steam-powered pump. 4 The Dennis was the most popular British appliance of the 1920s and 30s. 5 In 1952 the Dennis F8 appliance appeared. It was used as a motor pump. 6 This American LaFrance has an artic aerial ladder truck. 7 Comparatively rare as a fire appliance, this Bedford RMA was fitted with a hydraulic watertower. 8 In 1977 the 6x6 Oshkosh 'M'-Series was launched for special use on airfields. 9 Daimler-Benz offers the 4x4 Unimags with chemical foam equipment for industrial use. 10 The White 'Road Xpeditor 2'.

The experimental years

HORSELESS CARRIAGE FEVER was now rife throughout Europe, the United States, and the United Kingdom. By the mid-1890s there were many entrepreneurs in road vehicle development, but one man in particular got things underway in the United Kingdom. He was Sir David Salomons who, as a skilled engineer and Mayor of Tunbridge Wells, Kent, organized what was probably the world's first horseless carriage exhibition, on the Tunbridge Wells Agricultural Showground in 1895. Although only five vehicles (including a Daimler-engined Panhard et Levassor motor fire pump and a De Dion-Bouton "steam horse") were present, the event attracted much attention.

One month later, the inaugural meeting of the Self-Propelled Traffic Association (SPTA) was held in London, again organized by Sir David, but with the assistance of Frederick Richard Simms, another motoring pioneer who was a director of Daimler Motoren Gesellschaft. He had been responsible for establishing Daimler products in the United Kingdom and had developed an automatic fuel feed system for carburettors. The idea behind the SPTA was to put pressure on the government to repeal the Highways & Locomotives (Amendment) Act of 1878, in order to clear the way for new developments in the automotive field. A deputation was to meet the President of the Board of Agriculture.

With restrictions still in force, there was little hope for the British motor industry, whereas on the Continent, inventors were moving ahead with revolutionary ideas. Some of these were quickly taken up by manufacturers in other countries. Richard F Stewart, New York, United States, for example, used a 2hp Daimler engine and internal-gear drive in his prototype 1895 wagon.

As a prelude to the repeal of the 1878 Act, the Daimler Motor Co was registered in England early in 1896. Chairman was Harry J Lawson, and other directors included such notables as the Hon Evelyn Ellis, Gottlieb Daimler, William Wright, Henry Sturmey, J H Mace, H E Sherwin

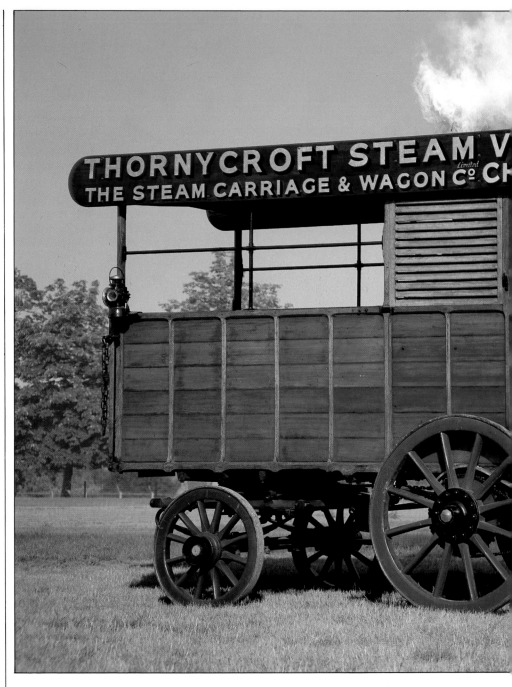

Holt and J S Bradshaw. Frederick Simms was Consulting Engineer and J S Critchley was Works Manager. The new company acquired a disused cotton mill in Coventry and was soon in business as the United Kingdom's first motor manufacturer. Lawson also set up the Great Horseless Carriage Co and organized a petition to the House of Commons requesting that the 1878 Act be repealed.

Another Lawson enterprise was the formation of the Motor Car Club (MCC), which was described as "a society for the protection, encourage-

ment and development of the motor car industry". However, it is more likely that it was set up to serve its founder's own ends. One of the first tasks of the MCC was to put on an exhibition of horseless carriages at London's Imperial Institute, opening to the public in May 1896. Every conceivable type of vehicle was present, including a Peugeot-built Daimler bus. While this event was in progress, a Bill repealing the 1878 Act was in preparation.

One of the first production load-carriers in the United States was a pe-

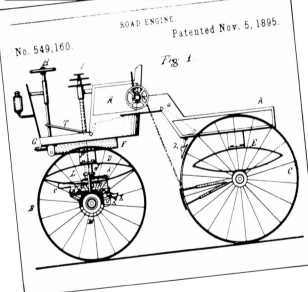

ROAD ENGINE.
Patented Nov. 5, 1895.
No. 549,160.
Fig 1.

Far left John I Thornycroft's 1-ton steam van had front-wheel drive and near wheel steer layout. *Left and above* Selden's steam vehicle which was constructed in the 1870s. In spite of this, it was not patented until 1895 and the patent was worded in such a way that it held back US motor industry development until 1911.

trol-engined wagon entered by the Langert Co, Philadelphia, Pennsylvania, in the 1896 Cosmopolitan Race from New York to Irvington-on-the-Hudson and back. At the same time, a horse-drawn van was converted into a steam wagon by the Cruickshank Engineering Works, Providence, Rhode Island; Charles Woods, Chicago, was alleged to have built the first practical battery-electric commercial; and C S Fairfield, Portland, Oregon, built a kerosene-engined passenger model. In Germany, Daimler Motoren Gesellschaft had built the first purpose-built Daimler truck – a 2-tonner which, like the company's passenger cars, had the driver at the front and engine at the rear.

The 1878 Act was withdrawn with the introduction of the Locomotives on Highways Act in 1896. This stipulated the speeds at which vehicles could travel. This also stipulated that motor vehicles weighing up to 1½ tons unladen could now travel at up to 18km/h, those weighing between 1½ and 2 tons could travel at up to 12km/h and any vehicle exceeding 2 tons was restricted to 7km/h.

The first commercial load-carrying vehicle in the United Kingdom was a 1-ton steam van with front-wheel drive and rear-wheel steering built by John Isaac Thornycroft, Chiswick, West London. Powered by a Strickland vertical twin marine engine, this was shown at the 1896 Crystal Palace Motor Show organized by Sir David Salomons. It was quickly followed by a 1½-ton steamer built by the Lancashire Steam Motor Co, successor to James Sumner's small business in Leyland, Lancs. In Germany, meanwhile, the Daimler internal-combustion en-

Above **By 1898 German Daimler trucks had adapted a front-engined layout and they had a tube radiator and pinion drive.**
Right **Completed in 1898, just in time for the Liverpool Heavy Vehicle Trials, this Thornycroft was the world's first artic steam lorry.**

gined truck range was being expanded to include models from 1½ to 5 tons capacity with power outputs of up to 10hp.

Petrol, diesel or steam?

ALTHOUGH REGARDED as a modern means of propulsion, the pioneer work of the diesel was undertaken at the turn of the century, when "heavy" loads were moved by steam. The 1½-ton steam wagon built by the Lancashire Steam Motor Co in 1896 won a Silver Medal at the Royal Agricultural Society's Manchester Trials in 1897. Later that year, the first petrol-engined commercial to be sold in the United Kingdom was a Daimler. At about the same time, MAN of Germany announced the world's first heavy oil engine, and before the end of the year, Daimler adopted a front-engined layout for all commercial models, with the driver positioned on top to provide greater load-carrying area than bonneted types of the same wheelbase. This layout was also used by other manufacturers in the years leading up to 1900, although Daimler himself settled on the bonneted style in 1899, following driver complaints of excessive vibration and difficulty in reaching the vehicle's lofty perch.

In 1898 the American inventor Alexander Winton introduced the first United States petrol-engined load-carrier built in any quantity. A L Riker perfected his design for a series of heavy battery-electric commercials, exemplified by a 1315-kg payload vehicle propelled by batteries weighing 45,359kg, which he exhibited at Madison Square Gardens. It was in the United States that the battery-electric commercial was to have its greatest following during these formative years.

In Germany, Daimler had started to use Bosch magneto ignitions, developed jointly by Robert Bosch and Frederick Simms, which began to woo customers away from steam propulsion. This movement did not, how-

Left One of London's first motor-buses was a vulgar-looking Daimler that ran between Oxford Circus and South Kensington. *Below left* Built in 1902, this 3-ton Thornycroft steamer had a vertical water-tube boiler and a compound "undertype" engine. *Below* This steam-powered mail van was shipped to Ceylon in 1901. It was the Lancashire Steam Motor Co's first export order.

THORNYCROFT

ever, apply to the American market, where oil was plentiful and steam had never figured greatly.

Prompted by the repeal of the 1878 Act, the Liverpool Branch of the Self-Propelled Traffic Association, by then affiliated to the Automobile Club of Great Britain and Ireland, organized the first of a series of heavy vehicle trials in 1898, the second taking place in 1899 and the third in 1901. These were held at the instigation of the Liverpool Branch's Honorary Secretary, Mr E Shrapnell-Smith, a great enthusiast for mechanical commercial transport, who succeeded in his wish of encouraging the manufacture of such vehicles.

By 1899 Thornycroft's steam wagons were becoming popular as tippers and refuse collectors, as well as seeing active service in the Boer War. The same company had also completed work on the world's first steam-powered articulated lorry. Generally, however, there was no standard mode of propulsion, the choice ranging through steam, petrol, kerosene and electricity.

The heavy oil or diesel engine should not be forgotten, as eventually it would become almost universally accepted for use in heavy commercials. Despite Rudolf Diesel's pioneering work in Germany (his main achievement being the development of an automatic ignition system using compressed air) it was two Englishmen, Priestman and Ackroyd Stuart, who developed the heavy oil engine as we know it today. Priestman adopted a system whereby fuel was injected into a cylinder-held pocket of air at maximum pressure and he had the world's first oil-engined lorry on the road by 1897. Meanwhile, Ackroyd Stuart developed the hot bulb ignition system, which replaced the external method used by Priestman and others.

Steam vehicles excepted, commercial load-carrying development paralleled that of the passenger car, which was more noticeable in the lighter designs. Steamers were especially popular in the United Kingdom, where plentiful supplies of comparatively cheap coal and coke were readily available. Such machines were normally of "undertype" layout, with engine slung beneath the chassis frame and a vertical boiler located ahead of, or behind, the driver, thereby providing maximum load space. Engine accessibility was poor, and boilers were often inefficient, but the solutions to these problems were to be found in the United Kingdom by 1901.

The last year of the nineteenth century saw some bus operators experimenting with self-propelled vehicles, but it was still to be some time before these ousted the ever-faithful horse. From 1900 onwards, however, the development of the self-propelled commercial load-carrier was to become even more fascinating than that of the passenger motor car.

The truck revolution

THE COMMERCIAL VEHICLE was by no means a European idea, because it was at this time that the United States began vehicle trials, thereby increasing the interest in such vehicles in the country.

With the turn of the century, the internal-combustion engine had yet to prove itself. Unreliability continued to be a major obstacle to commercial acceptance and business people generally regarded it as more for the mad motoring public than as being reliable for goods delivery. Horse-drawn or steam vehicles were accepted as the ideal choice for work of this nature. In an attempt to counteract this attitude and establish the internal-combustion engined vehicle in business circles, the British Automobile Club set up the Motor Van, Wagon & Omnibus Users' Association, which subsequently provided much of the impetus required.

By 1900 Daimler had built the world's first charabanc, and the German Army was undertaking field trials with a Daimler lorry. In 1901 the world's first mechanical street sweeper was built by the American, John Collins, of Connecticut, and an American subsidiary of the German

Top Leyland Motors Ltd received one of the first Royal Warrants granted to a British Motor manufacturer for a shooting van which they built in 1910 for King George V. The warrant is shown above the van together with the Leyland logo. *Above* Affectionately known as "The Pig", the first petrol-engined Leyland was a 1½-ton truck. *Left* While petrol-engined vehicles were now dealing with the lighter loads, a 6 ton steamer, such as this Leyland, was used for larger consignments.

Right The Manhattan sight-seeing bus of 1904 was one of the earliest production vehicles built in the United States by the Mack brothers.　　By 1910 Reliant trucks were reaching the end of the line as a marque in their own right, having already been taken over by General Motors. *Below* Early Daimler ideas were now being reflected in other marques such as this three ton Bussing made in 1902.

Daimler organization set up what is believed to have been the world's first truck service and tow-in scheme. On the steam front, the British firm of Fodens Ltd introduced the efficient loco-type horizontal boiler and "over-type" engine on a new wagon, which was quickly copied, despite the fact that it occupied more load space. In 1902 the first petrol-engined Thornycroft commercial appeared, a 2-ton lorry, relying upon experience gained from the manufacture of internal-combustion engined passenger cars. This company did not forsake its steam wagons, and later developed a demountable body system for its municipal steamers. In 1904, the John S Muir Syndicate announced a steam-powered sweeper/sprinkler which was another first in the municipal field.

America's first truck contest was organized in May 1903 by the newly formed Automobile Club of America, using a two-stage course starting from the club's headquarters in New York's Fifth Avenue. It was a two-day event, with entries divided into two classes, delivery wagons and heavy trucks, the former having to complete 64km a day and the latter 48km. All entries had to be fully laden, the winners on both days being a Knox-Waterless and a Herschmann steamer. As in the United Kingdom, this event encouraged the growth of vehicle manufacture. A specialist journal, *The Horseless Age*, commented that delivery wagons had now "arrived".

On the passenger vehicle scene, London witnessed numerous experiments with mechanically-propelled vehicles of this type, many being steam-powered and a frightening experience to the many horse-drawn vehicles still in operation. The first fleet of self-propelled buses to be used appears to have been that of the London General Omnibus Co, which had a number of vehicles in service by 1904. Among early experiments were those of the London Road Car Co, which introduced a few Maudslay buses as early as 1902. The Maudslay Motor Co Ltd, Coventry, was a pioneer in the development of the British commercial vehicle industry, using many advanced features in its designs.

One such was the single-piece axle; another was removable inspection plates in the engine crankcase to facilitate big-end inspection and the removal of damaged connecting rods or pistons.

By this time, United Kingdom speed restrictions had been relaxed and the Lancashire Steam Motor Co announced its first internal-combustion engined commercial – a 1½-ton model affectionately known as "The Pig". A new type of passenger vehicle which became popular at this time was the charabanc, with each row of seats being slightly higher than the one in front, to provide all passengers with a good view of the road ahead. Until the passenger car became a viable proposition for the working classes, the charabanc took pride of place in many fleets, particularly those based in coastal and tourist areas.

On the other side of the Atlantic, another commercial vehicle test was held in New York in April 1904, to encourage more firms to build such vehicles. Many were of driver-over-engine layout, as in the case of the first Daimlers, and by the end of 1904 the first power-assisted steering system had been developed. A year later petrol-engined buses ran for the first time on New York's fashionable Fifth Avenue.

For city deliveries, the heavy battery-electric wagon was coming into its own but was restricted to a particular operating base, where its batteries could be re-charged. The battery-electric had both advantages and disadvantages. One advantage was that it was comparatively easy to maintain, while, on the negative side, the batteries were exceptionally heavy – until Thomas Edison discovered the iron-nickel-alkaline battery in 1908. Such machines were also ponderously slow, often necessitating the use of two or even four traction motors, usually mounted in the vehicle's wheels.

In the United Kingdom, in March 1905, the first edition of *Commercial Motor* appeared (later to become one of the most important heavy automotive journals in the world) with E Shrapnell-Smith as Editor, joined three months later by *Motor Traction*.

The trade paper 'The Commercial Motor' first came out on 16 March, 1905. It was priced at one penny and included advertisements for truck parts as well as for trucks.

Top left The VCPL bus was unique in having two engines slung beneath the vehicle. Each of these engines supplied current to an electric motor at each rear wheel. *Next row extreme left* C A Tilt's first truck, a 1½-ton Diamond T which he built in 1911. He quickly introduced other models with capacities up to 5 tons. *Left* This 5-ton "overtype" wagon was a rarity, built by "undertype" pioneer Alley and McLellon Ltd. *Below and bottom* While Adolph Sauerer AG, Switzerland was exporting ambulances to Russia, a plant was being set up in the USA and a US-built 4-tonner was sent on a transcontinental publicity run. The Saurer logo is shown to the right of the picture.

САНИТАРНЫЙ АВТОМОБИЛЬ
ЗАУРЕРЪ

SAURER MOTOR TRUCK
OCEAN TO OCEAN. PIONEER FREIGHTER
AGENTS
MOTOR SALES OF CAL.
346 GOLDEN GATE AVE.

ÖSTERR.
SAURER
WERKE

Meanwhile, in Lavender Hill, South London, Commercial Motors Ltd had been set up to pursue the commercial possibilities of the Linley pre-select gearbox. A 4-ton iron-wheeled lorry called the CC was constructed, which was to become the Commer. The development of the new transmission systems occupied a great deal of thought at this time. Some, such as Panhard, used a sliding-tooth system, and others, such as DeDion, left the gears in mesh, with gear-changing effected by the use of expanding friction clutches. There were also planetary or constant-mesh systems, and the German inventor, Dr H Föttinger, even developed an automatic system.

The first American motor truck show was held in Chicago in 1907, and the world's first steam vacuum cesspool emptier, developed by Merryweather & Sons Ltd, appeared in 1908. The latter made the self-propelled vehicle more important than it had been in local authorities. The Chicago event attracted attention on both sides of the Atlantic, due to the publicity surrounding a 489-km test run accomplished by a 3-ton petrol-engined Reliance in less than four days. A 1609-km commercial vehicle trial for 19 petrol-engined 3-tonners and 10 petrol- and steam-powered 5-tonners was organized by the Automobile Club in 1907. The first British Commercial Motor Show was held at Olympia, London, in the same year, under the jurisdiction of the Society of Motor Manufacturers & Traders. These events finally set the commercial vehicle on the map.

Some manufacturers were now turning from steam to petrol, although few completely abandoned the former. Thus, the Lancashire Steam Motor Co became Leyland Motors Ltd, and two petrol-engined lorries were the first internal-combustion engined Thornycrofts to receive a War Office diploma. The Swiss Saurer company was now converting 4-cyl Safir petrol engines into diesel units, and developed an engine brake which compressed air inside the engine, converting it into a retarder. This same company was soon exporting petrol-engined trucks worldwide. Other sig-

nificant advances included the first closed-top double-deck bus and trolleybus experiments were held in North London.

Elsewhere, the first production articulated lorry was seen, namely the unusual 3-wheeled Knox, built in Springfield, Massachusetts, United States. A major development of 1909 was Sven Winquist's ball-race system for commercial vehicle wheels, successfully tested in a new Scania truck between Malmo and Stockholm in Sweden.

The London General Omnibus Co Ltd (LGOC) had meanwhile been busy acquiring various independent operators, but was finding its motley collection of self-propelled buses none too reliable. Accordingly, the Associated Equipment Co, which was responsible for the LGOC's maintenance facilities, began constructing its own vehicles in Walthamstow. The first was the AEC 'X'-Type, followed before the end of 1910 by the most advanced open-top double-decker seen so far – the famous 'B'-Type with ultra-lightweight chassis and body, conforming to police regulations limiting the gross weight to 3½ tons. Instead of the more popular channel-steel frame, the 'B'-Type was of ash wood with nickel-steel flitch plates, apparently used to counteract vibration.

Another model which was gaining popularity was the Tilling-Stevens pe-

Top left The 24-seat Thames coach, resembling a motorized stage coach, was another oddity of the pre-World War II days. *Far left top* George A Brockway's first truck was this bonneted high-wheeler, a design typical of many US manufacturers of the period. *Far left bottom* The Reo 'Democrat' wagon introduced in 1911 by R E Old's Reo Motor Car Co was another vehicle which followed the high-wheeler principle. *Left* The LGOC's 'B'-Type double decker revolutionized London's public transport system and during the war it provided transport to the Front. *Right* Despite the general acceptance of a bonneted layout, there were still a few strange designs around in 1911 when this French Berliet 'CAT'-Type was built.

trol-electric, which eliminated gear-changing, making a driver's transition from horse to internal-combustion driving that much easier. Another vehicle which used a similar system was the KPL, built by the Daimler Motor Co Ltd, Coventry. This was even more revolutionary, being of integral construction with two Knight sleeve-valve petrol engines coupled to two traction motors which, in turn, were connected to each rear wheel. Four-wheel brakes were another unusual feature.

Following the country's first War Department vehicle trials, Britain's first "subsidy" scheme was devised, whereby an operator buying a lorry conforming to a particular specifica-tion was entitled to an annual subsidy of £110, provided the vehicle was available to the military authorities, within 72 hours, in an emergency. By 1911 both Leeds and Bradford were running the first British trolleybus fleets. The "subsidy" scheme did much to establish conformity amongst British vehicle manufacturers.

The world's first tiltcab truck was the American-built Pope-Hartford of 1912, and in 1913 an even more unusual design, the 2/3-ton Austin twin-shaft lorry, was announced. The inauguration of the world's first true motor truck assembly line at the Ford Motor Co plant, Dearborn, Michigan, took place in 1914, resulting in the United States becoming a world lead-er in truck production. Meanwhile, Sydney Guy, formerly of Sunbeam, unveiled his first commercial, a 1½-ton design with one of the first over-drive transmissions, a road speed gov-ernor and, even rarer, detachable overhead valves.

By the time World War I broke out, there had been many other advances in the commercial vehicle field. Steam wagons, for example, were now shod with solid rubber tyres instead of the noisy steel units fitted to earlier mod-els, and internal-combustion engined commercials were rapidly replacing the horse. New bus services were be-ing established in most countries and, because of the competitiveness of op-erators, advances were rapid.

Buses

Road passenger transport in the early 1900s was undertaken by goods chassis fitted with passenger-carrying bodies. Bus services were maintained by single- and double-deckers, the latter open-topped, with very high floor levels and it was not unusual for some operators to run a single chassis with two bodies – one for goods, the other for passengers. By the 1920s this attitude was changing and lower-loading passenger chassis were appearing. Greater comfort came about through the introduction of pneumatic tyres, covering in top decks and general weather-proofing of bus bodies, while developments of the 1930s brought about greater carrying capacities through the use of multi axles. Chassisless and even articulated types now prevail.

The bus is the workhorse of the road passenger transport industry and the coach is its somewhat upstage sister, with more luxurious accommodation and often capable of higher speeds. The first true coaches were the toas-tracks and charabancs of the pre World War I era. These were invariably trucks during the week but re-bodied at weekends to take parties of trippers to the coast. Many firms up to the 1950s built both buses and coaches, some have since specialised in one or the other and certain European manufacturers are now renowned for their coach models.

1 The earliest motorbuses followed German designs, this open-topped bus, of c.1914, was a British-built Daimler. 2 A Tilling-Stevens with petrol-electric transmission. 3 Glasgow Corporation took delivery of its first batch of BUT single-deck trolleybuses around 1953. These were unique to Glasgow and had 36-seat centre-entrance standee bodies. 4 LGOC brought in their S-Type, a 54-seat double decker bus which they launched on London. 5 This Bristol K5G was originally delivered to the Hants and Dorset Motor Services Ltd in 1940. In 1954 it was rebodied and used as an open-topper sea front bus. 6 These 1948 MCI 'Courier' single-deckers lined up at Windsor, Ontario, were typical of North American and Canadian passenger models of the late 1940s and early '50s. 7 The first two Birmingham-built Metrobuses to be used in London ran on the number 16 route between Cricklewood Garage and Victoria. 8 The most common Swiss postal coach was the Saurer. For many years the postal coach was unique to Switzerland but it is now familiar in a number of countries. 9 This Leyland 'Tiger Cub' operated by Watt Bros City Coast Buses, Queensland, Australia is similar to the MCI Courier.

The great war

AN IMMEDIATE DEMAND for mechanical military transport following the declaration of war in Europe was partly solved by a considerable influx of well-engineered cross-country trucks from the United States. Those countries that had prepared in advance by introducing "subsidy" schemes soon found they were in a far superior position to those that had not. Despite this, problems abounded.

Steam-powered vehicles such as traction engines had been used on a small scale in earlier situations, but the internal-combustion engined truck had never been used in war conditions, and weaknesses in design were soon apparent. These included insufficient power, lack of ground clearance, and poor protection of mechanical units from the ravages of water and mud, for which the Flanders battlefields were soon renowned. There was, however, another major problem that few had foreseen. Both sides in the conflict used many components supplied by firms on the opposing side: German-manufactured Bosch magnetos were used almost exclusively by the Allies, while German forces relied largely upon British- and French-manufactured Dunlop and Michelin tyres. Luckily, the Bosch magneto had been developed jointly by Robert Bosch and the American Frederick Simms, and German supplies were replaced by magnetos from the Simms Magneto Co factory, Watsersing, New Jersey.

At this stage it is worth looking in depth at some of the "subsidy" schemes operating at the time. The instigators of this idea were the Germans who, in the years prior to 1914, had been building up their military reserves. The German scheme is understood to have applied to any truck which an operator was prepared to release to the military upon mobilization. The operator received an initial grant of £150 towards the purchase of the vehicle, followed by a subsidy of £60 for each of the next four years. By the time war was declared, some 825 "subsidy" trucks had been released to the German Armed Forces.

A similar scheme was organized by the French government, and the British system, in which there were two classes of load-carrying vehicle – a 1½-tonner and a 3-tonner – brought about the first signs of standardization in the

Above Leyland's 'RAF'-Type 3-tonner was one of the best known British 'subsidy' types. *Right* After the war many of these vehicles were resold onto the civilian market, like this Chivers' van.

Left Many "Tommies", such as these members of the 2nd Battalion Royal Warwickshire Regiment, made their last journeys in London's 'B'-Type buses. *Below* Many British industries could not spare their lorries; this 1915 Fiat 18BL was one of many similar types that remained on the Home Front. *Below centre* Even a 1-ton Studebaker found itself involved in hostilities. Its headlamps were masked so as to make it less of an obvious target. *Bottom* Many vehicles were adapted for military use including this Swiss Saurer 5-tonner.

commercial vehicle industry. The British government offered the purchaser of an approved vehicle a subsidy. However, the vehicle had to be handed over to the authorities within 72 hours of mobilization.

One of the most advanced British "subsidy" types was the 3½-ton Dennis 'A'-Type, although the 'L' or 'RAF'-Type Leyland was certainly the best known. The Dennis had considerable influence on British truck design after the war, its most striking feature being a rear axle with removable upper casing containing the worm shaft, worm wheel, differential and bearings, thus enabling the entire final-drive mechanism to be inspected or replaced without disturbing either the chassis or the wheels. Leyland Motors, on the other hand, built both a 1½-tonner and the 3-ton 'RAF'-Type, while Albion supplied 6000 "subsidy" vehicles, and the Associated Equipment Co Ltd over 10,000. Many of their London General Omni-

bus Co 'B'-Type open-top double-deck buses were also commandeered and ordered to the Front. The standardization of models and components required by the British "subsidy" scheme enabled so-called cannibalization to take place to keep transport moving, whereas the adoption of any suitable vehicle by the French and German forces gave no such advantage.

As the war progressed, so British forces began to take delivery of new American-built trucks designed specifically for arduous work. Amongst these was the Mack 'AC', nicknamed the "Bulldog" because of its snub nose and rugged construction. Ultimately, this became so well-known by its nickname that the bulldog was adopted as the Mack logo, which it remains to this day. Some American manufacturers, such as General Motors, were now concentrating almost exclusively on the construction of military vehicles, while certain European manufacturers,

Below In 1915 a new series of Internationals were launched. These introduced the 'coal-scuttle' bonnet to the US market. The radiator was carried behind the engine. *Below centre* Large numbers of US-built Peerless 5-tonners were also shipped to Europe. *Bottom left* With increasing competition between manufacturers, publicity stunts such as the GMC milk run from Seattle to New York, became all the rage. *Bottom right* This 1-ton 4x4 built in 1917 by the Wisconsin Duplex Auto Co was the ancestor of the modern Oshkosh range.

Left The Mack 'Bulldog', which was a chain-drive model, saw war service in Europe. Its name was apparently coined by British troops who thought that the pugnacious styling of the steel hood resembled a bulldog. The bulldog was quickly adopted as the company symbol. *Below* This early drawbar model of the 'Bulldog' series was produced in America. Even today examples of it can be found in various parts of the world.

such as MAN, Magirus in Germany or Société d'Outillage Mécanique et d'Usinage d'Artilleries (Somua) in France, were building their first trucks in an attempt to turn the tide. Indeed, Somua was established for the sole purpose of building army trucks.

Throughout the Western world, factories not involved in the manufacture of military trucks were turned over to the production of armaments such as shells, firearms and aero engines, while others manufactured both military vehicles and also armaments.

Many American-built trucks saw service not only in Europe but also in the Mexican border campaign of 1916, when the United States government waged war against the Mexican bandit Pancho Villa. This served as a proving ground for these trucks, many of which were later shipped to Europe

for military service. At this time, few US-built military trucks were standardized, and it was not until the development of the US Quartermaster Corps's 'B'-Class heavy truck, known as the "Liberty", that proper standardization occurred.

On the civilian front, producer-gas was used to combat the lack of petrol, and in the United States the 1916 Federal Aid Road Act was instrumental in establishing a new interstate highway system which contributed greatly to the development of American commercial vehicles. With a rubber tyre shortage, particularly in Germany where manufacturers had relied upon British- and French-made supplies, unconventional steel-wheeled vehicles, sometimes incorporating metal plates backed by small leaf springs, appeared for a short while, but these were mainly for heavy tractors used

for hauling artillery. Developments in commercial vehicle design, such as the use of shaft-drive, glass windscreens and electric rather than acetylene lighting, were now creeping in from the passenger car side and, although apparent in many light commercials, it was some years before these were adopted for the heavy commercial market. Pneumatic tyres were also becoming commonplace on lighter types but, again, were to remain a rarity on "heavies" for some time.

While the war did much to establish new standards for commercial vehicles, military vehicle requirements were far different from those used on the public highway. High payloads and economy were more important to civilian operators than high ground clearance or all-wheel drive. Thus, with a return to peace, much re-organization was necessary.

Peacetime development

WHILE the end of the war in 1918 opened the field to new manufacturers, it also presented new problems to the existing commercial motor industry. Some German armament producers, such as Krupp, were not allowed to continue production, and had to turn to the manufacture of trucks instead. However, vast quantities of ex-military vehicles were already being released into the civilian market and snapped up by both operators and thousands of servicemen anxious to set up in the expanding goods and passenger haulage business. In France alone there were thousands of American, British and German trucks scattered around, and although there were only some 400 licensed road hauliers in the United Kingdom at this time, by 1923 these had expanded to 2400, many of the vehicles being shipped into the country through ex-army dealers. Thus, demand for new vehicles was relatively low and sales suffered badly. Some manufacturers, such as Leyland Motors, established a re-conditioning plant for ex-WD trucks, while some dealers concentrated on particular makes such as the American Peerless and FWD, ultimately constructing vehicles of similar design and using the same identity.

By this time production equipment was out-of-date, and existing manufacturers were often faced with considerable re-tooling before new models could be introduced. Most, however, continued to concentrate on existing designs until 1923, due to a considerable slump in trade whereby those manufacturers which also built passenger cars found themselves with quantities of unsold cars. Another result of war-surplus trucks flooding the market was the effect on the road-going steamer, which was pushed further into the background by legislation and, ultimately, by the development of the diesel engine.

By 1919 the American, Malcolm Loughhead, had developed the 4-wheel Lockheed hydraulic braking system, and both Dunlop and Goodyear had announced their first pneumatic tyres. There was also increasing interest in large-capacity passenger vehicles.

Left Special facilities, such as the roof-mounted sleeper compartment on this 3-ton White, were needed for long-distance hauls in the USA. *Centre and bottom left* Specialist British municipal vehicles were led by the 3-wheeled Lacre roadsweeper; the French market was led by the DeDion 4-wheeler. *Right* Steam was still popular and even Leyland Motors offered an "undertype" wagon until 1926. *Bottom right* Vast numbers of ex-military trucks were now rapidly replacing the horse, particularly for transporting fuel.

Such change in social conditions resulted in the gradual development of vehicles built specifically to carry passengers. Some manufacturers which had been less fortunate during the war and had concentrated on the manufacture of armaments, were forced to start again with a small selection of lightweight commercials for passengers or payloads of up to 2½ tons. Existing passenger models, such as the 34-seat AEC 'B'-Type, were replaced by designs of even greater capacity, in this instance by the 46-seat 'K'-Type, and soon after by the 54-seat 'S'-Type. By 1923 the first of the famous 'NS'-Type, with its futuristic low-loading entrance, had appeared.

By the mid-1920s, road transport was becoming established and new ideas were plentiful. Forward-control or cab-over-engine layout were popular ways of increasing the load-carrying space, and Scammell Lorries Ltd, founded in 1921, built a 7½-ton 6-wheeled articulated lorry designed by Lt Col A G Scammell, DSO, which quickly led to other vehicles of similar layout. By 1925 a new 5/6-ton Dennis load-carrier had become the first Dennis to be powered by a monobloc engine with four integrally-cast cylinders and two detachable heads. The earlier charabanc was now being replaced by the sedate motor coach, one excellent example being the Albion 'Viking' of 1923. In 1924, Thornycroft built its first unit-construction vehicle, the A1 1½-tonner with engine, clutch and gearbox mounted as one unit at three points in the chassis frame. The old leather-to-metal clutch was now replaced by a single-plate unit and pneumatic tyres fitted. Pneumatics had been regarded with some scepticism by the authorities, as had 4-wheel brakes which were not permitted in London until 1926, when a suitably equipped Dennis 'E'-Type was tested on a hard surface with a coating of soft soap.

As a contrast to the European manufacturer, where each marque had an individual identity, and many parts were manufactured by the one company, the majority of American companies built vehicles which were purely assembled, using components which were available to anybody. It was not until the 1930s that this pattern began to change.

The rigid multi-wheeler

THE DEVELOPMENT of pneumatic tyres led to the construction of the first multi-wheeled goods and passenger models. Among the first rigid 6-wheelers were single- and double-drive conversions of the US Army's "Liberty" truck, followed by a new double-drive 4-wheel braked bogie developed by Hendrickson Mfg, of America, in 1924. With larger payloads, pneumatic-tyred 4-wheelers suffered increasingly from punctures, leading to the idea that the load should be distributed over two rear axles, with manufacturers adopting different layouts and drive systems. It was also discovered that 2-axle pneumatic-tyred bogies caused less damage to road surfaces than those of single-axle design.

Varying drive layouts were adopted for such bogies. The German Büssing organization drove each rear axle separately from an auxiliary gearbox located behind the main box, while the Scottish-built Caledon 6-wheeler had one "live" axle driving two "dead" ones by roller chain. Karrier was another British marque that was early on the 6-wheeled scene, using two under-worm axles. Guy Motors delivered the world's first 6-wheeled trolleybus to the Wolverhampton Corp in 1926, fitting a double-deck body and regenerative control. This company also built the world's first double-deck motorbus, as well as a small fleet of 6-wheeled double-deckers in 1927.

Another notable 6-wheeler was the Thornycroft A3, developed from the A1 "subsidy" lorry of 1924 and intended for cross-country operation. This was actually a military vehicle, but quickly caught on overseas where its worm-drive axles and auxiliary transmission established it as a worthwhile machine for both on- and off-road work. In military guise, the A3 could handle 1½-ton loads and, for civilian work, loads of up to 2½ tons could be managed. Cross-country tracks could be fitted over the rear wheels as required.

Meanwhile, on the passenger vehicle front, the Associated Daimler Co, formed from a short-lived liaison between Associated Equipment Co Ltd and Daimler Co Ltd, developed the

RUGBY TRUCKS are Engineered by Experts to Cut Haulage Costs

RUGBY
A GOOD TRUCK BUILT BY DURANT

Above The bonneted 4-wheeled arrangement was still preferred in Europe as on this 1922 Austrian-built Steyr street-washer. *Top* Rugby Trucks catered for the smaller end of the light-weight truck market. *Centre* Articulation meant greater capacity, an ideal solution for household removals, this operator is using a Magiruz-hauled outfit. *Above right and right* Multi-wheeled rigids were gaining in popularity on both sides of the Atlantic, demonstrated here by a 1929 Scammell 'Rigid-6' and in 1924 by a Mack "Bulldog". *Far right* Breweries were among the last strongholds of steam, this 6-ton Foden was delivered to the Openshaw Brewery Ltd in 1928.

massive Model 802 or "London Six", using a double-reduction worm bogie similar to that used in a 10-ton goods model produced by Brozincevic & Co, Zürich. The "London Six" was a breakthrough in that engine vibration was minimized by mounting the 6-cyl sleeve-valve unit in a subframe which was supported in the main chassis frame by a series of cushion pads, with final-drive effected by a central underslung worm-gear for each wheel and each axle's own differential.

By this time, the bonneted layout was the most popular for both goods and passenger models, and while some truck manufacturers shifted their allegiance to passenger cars, so others switched from cars to trucks, or added trucks to their product lines. One such was Morris Cars Ltd, which set up Morris Commercial Cars Ltd in 1924 to build a new 1-tonner, adding 1½- and 2-ton double-drive 6-wheelers within three years.

Many countries, such as Japan and the Soviet Union, were new to commercial vehicle manufacture, but were quick to develop reliable new models, often based on existing British or American designs. Indeed, it was Britain and America which set the example to many other countries, particularly with operating commercials, for in Britain alone, between 1919 and 1929, the number of operational goods vehicles rose from 62,000 to 330,000, and in America these figures were even higher.

Six-cyl petrol engines were now making their mark, the first 6-cyl Leyland commercial being the 'Titan' double-decker announced in 1927. The 'Titan' was also one of the first lowbridge double-deckers, with a sunken gangway in each saloon and an overall height of less than 4m. One of the most talked-about exhibits in 1927 was the Thornycroft 'Lightning' motor coach with a new side-valve

6-cyl petrol engine producing 70bhp. Some argued it was well ahead of its time, having vacuum-assisted 4-wheel brakes, but it merely pointed the way for other manufacturers.

Advances in these fields precipitated other changes. At Tilling-Stevens, petrol-electric propulsion was replaced by petrol power, with the introduction of the lightweight 4-cyl 'Express' passenger model, and by 1926 the world's first frameless tank semi-trailer had been pioneered by Scammell Lorries Ltd, Watford, Herts. By the end of the 1920s, the military lorry was rapidly disappearing in passenger and goods haulage circles. In 1928 the first oil-engined truck to enter service in the United Kingdom was a Mercedes-Benz, and one year later the Kerr-Stuart, the first all-British diesel lorry, arrived. Also in 1929, two of the world's heaviest vehicles, 100-ton Scammells, were constructed for heavy haulage work.

The depression

THE 1930s dawned with the Depression hanging over the world. Its influence meant that manufacturers and operators were beginning to use the diesel engine for motor vehicles, because it was more economical.

Diesel engines had been fitted experimentally in certain commercials from the mid-1920s, one of the first British examples being fitted to a London bus in 1928, but it was on the Continent that such developments grew, with Berliet of France fitting its first diesel in 1930, Renault in 1931, and Fiat of Italy in 4- and 6-tonners in 1931. Leyland Motors was also experimenting with diesel, and the Tilling-Stevens Express bus was offered with a 4-cyl diesel engine, but the first complete diesel-engined bus built in the United Kingdom was a 1931 Crossley.

Many of these engines were constructed along similar lines, but there were exceptions. Klockner-Humboldt-Deutz was looking at air-cooled units, but these were not fitted in any quantity until 1940. In the United States, both Cummins and General Motors (GM) were experimenting, the former fitting its first diesel, the Model 'H', to a truck in 1932, while GM pondered on the development of a 2-stroke/diesel which did not go into full production until 1937.

While it was apparent that the diesel engine was the answer to the economic problem, many operators were still prejudiced as it was largely an unknown quantity.

Although some American manufacturers were developing diesel engines, there were others concentrating on the development of more powerful petrol units, as the United States had a plentiful supply of cheap home-produced petrol. Thus, the petrol engine dominated the field in the United States until the 1960s, when increasing dependency upon imported fuels led to an increased use of automotive diesels. Similarly, Germany relied upon imported fuel, and Hitler was quick to realize the importance of developing the country's own fuel source. Thus, diesel came to the fore.

Generally, there were two types of diesel engine – direct and indirect injection – although most were of the in-

direct type, as this was quieter and more economical. The advent of the diesel engine brought new-found wealth to many established concerns.

Fodens Ltd, of Sandbank, Cheshire, also went through considerable re-organization at this time with E R Foden and his son leaving the company to set up the diesel vehicle manufacturer ERF Ltd in 1933. Meanwhile Fodens itself continued vehicle building, changing from steam to diesel propulsion. Dennis Bros Ltd, of Guildford, Surrey, moved into the diesel field in 1935, with a version of its Lancet II passenger model powered by a Dennis Big Four petrol engine or a Dennis-Lanova low-compression diesel. One of the earliest diesel engine builders in Britain was W H Dorman & Co Ltd, whose first design was a 4-cyl job developing 20bhp at 1000rpm. This company built

Above The early 1930s were a crucial time for the California-based Fageol Motors Co, despite the production of short bonneted trucks with a low centre of gravity. *Left* When this Type 85 Alfa-Romeo was built in 1934 even bonneted trucks were beginning to reflect more modern styling. *Bottom left* The first passenger vehicle to carry the Bedford name was the 14-seater WHB built in 1931. *Top right* The 2½-ton FN was built in Belgium, powered by a straight 8 petrol engine. *Above middle right* The spoked wheels on this 1932 Kenworth were unusual for a vehicle operating on the west side of the US at this time. *Above bottom right* The Sentinel was one of the most advanced steam vehicles and the most famous was the multi-wheeled 58 of 1934. *Right* 'Commercial Car Journal' was now the leading road transport publication in the USA.

both the Dorman-Ricardo high-speed airless injection type and the direct-injection type, but in recent years has concentrated on the manufacture of industrial diesels rather than those for automotive use. Another firm which is synonymous with the production of automotive diesels is F Perkins Ltd, Peterborough, which was founded in 1932 to produce the P6 diesel, again popular as a conversion.

However, it was not just diesel developments which accelerated during the 1930s, as commercial bodywork was improving rapidly, particularly on the passenger vehicle side. Motor coach bodies throughout Europe and America were following passenger car styling, particularly in Germany, and ventilation and other comforts were much improved. Many coaches had sunshine roofs which could be folded back for all-weather

Right The Latil 'Traulier' was a French design combining the manouevrability of 4-wheel steering with the go-anywhere characteristics of 4-wheel drive. *Below right* Morris-Commercial's 3-ton C9/60, although of bonneted layout, had its engine protruding into the cab giving it a "snub-nosed" appearance. *Below* Legislation was now forcing breweries to change from steam to diesel, by going with this trend manufacturers such as Foden (whose logo appears below) managed to retain their customers.

operation, and both buses and coaches were far more comfortable.

By the mid-1930s, with the exception of trolleybuses, 6-wheeled passenger models were vanishing while 4-axle rigid goods models were offered by most British diesel-engined goods vehicle manufacturers. The use of articulated load-carriers was catching on, and in the United States, the first "double bottoms" – articulated vehi-

cles with an extra drawbar trailer – were beginning to appear on the longer inter-state routes. In urban areas, there was the "mechanical horse", a strange 3-wheeled tractor replacing the horse and cart, built mainly in Britain by Scammell and Karrier. This vehicle was specially devised to hitch up to horse-drawn carts, particularly used by railway companies to speed deliveries. A derivative of

this was the 3-wheeled Ford Tug of 1935, which had a Model 'Y' van body.

A bonneted layout was still the norm for heavy commercials but forward-control was becoming increasingly popular, due to the fact that more load-carrying space was now available.

However, a generally conservative attitude ensured that the bonnet-

Top left German manufacturers were now well ahead, both in vehicle design and in the development of new propulsion systems. This Magirus-Deutz had an underfloor engine running on producer gas. *Middle left above* The Czechoslovakian Tatra T82 6-wheeler of 1936 had an air-cooled diesel engine. *Above* Aerodynamic styling became the vogue in North America and Canada at this time. Labart's Canadian brewery took delivery of this spectacular White in 1937. *Left* The ERF C1561 6-wheeler had a 5-cylinder Gardner diesel engine and was popular with many British hauliers during the 1930s and 1940s.

ed arrangement would continue for some time. As the distance between delivery points increased, so the use of sleeper cabs grew, mainly on the Continent and in the United States, and to make the driver's job even easier, power-steering began to appear. Suspensions were improved, some incorporating rubber units, and brake systems were up-dated to make the heavier trucks, buses and coaches safer.

Hydraulic braking was offered on many 4-wheeled rigids, although multi-wheeled rigids and artics were still without brakes on some axles. In Switzerland, Italy and France, the first exhaust brakes, suited to mountainous terrains, began to appear, and in America particularly, automatic or semi-automatic transmissions were being fitted.

In common with passenger body-

work, truck bodies were beginning to be constructed of light-alloy, and some American manufacturers were even building truck and van bodies on line-flow principles. Also in America, increasing use was being made of lightweight materials, even in chassis manufacture, and by the end of the 1930s most of the present-day leading truck and bus manufacturers were in business.

World war II

THROUGHOUT the latter half of the 1930s, the world was relentlessly moving towards another war. The German Schell Programme of 1938 called for the standardization of military truck production, segregating vehicles into light-, medium- and heavy-duty types from 1 to 6½ tons payload with engines of a given minimum output. These ideas were later reflected in the commercial truck boom of the 1950s and 1960s when German-built trucks had to have a minimum of 8bhp per ton of a vehicle's gross weight.

By 1939 the German forces were prepared for hostilities. While many hard lessons had been learned during World War I, some countries were still lagging behind in vehicle production. In Britain, production of military vehicles and equipment was stepped up towards the end of the 1930s, although many military trucks were merely militarized versions of commercial models. The larger manufacturers, such as Leyland Motors, moved into armaments production, while others, such as Austin and Morris-Commercial, concentrated on trucks and artillery tractors.

Weight did not matter as much as the vehicle's ability to go anywhere, and sturdily constructed 4 x 4, 6 x 4 and 6 x 6 trucks were rushed off the production lines. One British manufacturer which was prepared was Guy Motors, Wolverhampton, which had abandoned civilian in favour of government contracts in the mid-1930s, concentrating on production of the 4-wheel drive 'Quad-Ant', an 8 x 8 load-carrier, and, after 1941, a civilian version of the 'Quad-Ant' known as the 'Vixen'. The best known 3-ton army trucks were to be the Bedford QL 4 x 4 and 'OY'-Series 4 x 2, of which, at the time, nearly 1000 a week were being built. Both Commer and Karrier also built 4 x 4s, but perhaps the most well remembered of the period were the 4 x 4 AEC Matador medium artillery tractor and the massive Scammell Pioneer range of artillery, tank recovery and vehicle breakdown models based on Scammell Lorries' pre-war oilfield and heavy haulage tractor.

Although British and American forces moved their tanks by road on

Above The Morris-Commercial C8 was one of the most profilic field artillery tractors on the Allied side.
Left German Forces were great users of the hybrid half-truck. This was the 2-ton Magirus-Deutz 53000/SSM.
Left bottom: A 1943 Bedford QL, which was one of the most familiar 3-ton 4 x 4's in the British Services.

Top and extreme right Two US truck advertisements. The competitive nature of many US truck advertisements turned to propaganda at the end of the 1930s as World War II got under way. *Right* Diamond T production lines, showing part of the "Six-by-Six" and "Tank-hauler" production. Diamond T's war truck production exceeds the normal peacetime heavy-truck output of the entire automotive industry.

The Marines Grab a Foothold!

Just a foothold—that's all they ask. Tropic mud or arctic snow—they are all the same to the Marines.

Like the Marines, the motorized equipment used by them usually has a strictly "off-the-highway" job. A typical unit is this rugged, 2½-ton truck, fittingly named the "Marine 6 by 6." It is noteworthy for its lower silhouette, its husky power plant and, above all, for its tremendous tractive ability.

THORNTON
Automatic-Locking
DIFFERENTIAL

in both rear driving axles eliminates wheel-spin and gives positive traction in mud, sand, snow or ice.

These THORNTON qualities that serve the Marines so well . . . sturdiness, tractive ability, dependability . . . fit equally well into other military vehicles.

The THORNTON
full driving torque to e
or mud.

Thus there is no u
under conditions wh

THORNTON TA
8711-8779 GRINNELL AVE.
Manufacturers also of the THORNTON Fou
"When you need TRACTION you

Another Fleet of Locomotive-Sized Federals
GOES ON THE WAR PATH TO VICTORY

★ The operation pictured above is somewhere in the Canadian Northwest, where airfields, coast artillery, gun emplacements and military roads have become vital in the defense of America. These works—now completed —or being rushed to completion—are important to our protective strategy. They serve to illustrate how hundreds of fleets of husky Federal Trucks have been doing legion work, aiding in the all important job of protecting the Arsenals of Democracy from land, air or sea invasion— hastening the day of Victory.

Many months before Pearl Harbor, Federal Trucks were in wide use with our own and the United Nations' Armed Forces. Today Federal Trucks are operating in the combat and defensive areas of the Middle East, Alaska, the Canal Zone, India, Russia, China, Britain, Canada, Australia and the U. S. A.

Hundreds of uses, in thousands of jobs, as armored tank haulers, giant aircraft rescue trucks, road builders, airfield construction units, fire fighters and heavy transport carriers, are proving over and over again how Federal's "all-truck", balanced design is recognized for long-lived dependability and consistent, top flight performance. That's why those in important positions on both our work fronts and war fronts demand Federal's huskier, heavy duty reliability. They're tossing the tough jobs to Federal because they know they'll deliver!

FEDERAL MOTOR TRUCK COMPANY, DETROIT, MICHIGAN

The Army and Navy "E" was awarded to Federal—"For Excellence in War Production"—building thousands of heavy duty trucks for our Armed Forces.

FEDERAL TRUCKS
Since 1910 . . . Known in Every Country—Sold on Every Continent

Top right The austere Fiat 626N
3-tonner of 1939 was used by
civilians as well as by the Armed
Forces. *Far right middle* The
Model 1506 cab fitted to civvy
GMC's in 1941 was plain to say the
least. *Extreme far right middle* Due
to the vast numbers of vehicles
needed, many US manufacturers
built vehicles of standard design.
This Mormon-Herrington
H-542-11 5-ton tractor was based
on International Harvester
designs. *Far bottom right* This
AEC 'Mammoth Major III' was
supplied in 1941 for essential
civilian use. *Right* An Austin K4
(16) which was used in peacetime
as a coal truck.

transporters, thereby causing them much wear and tear, the Germans preferred to use rail. The Allies also perfected the movement of other heavy loads and, with a return to peace, adapted these methods to the haulage and construction industries, often using ex-military equipment. Articulation was used, particularly for hauling aircraft components such as wings and fuselages, and Scammell Lorries again came to the fore in the supply of general cargo or tank semi-trailers with automatic couplings.

One American-built truck worthy of special mention was the 6 x 6 GMC of which more than 600,000 were built. This became a real army work-horse and was adopted for a surprising number of tasks. There were many much heavier types as well, such as those produced by Autocar, Diamond T, Kenworth, Oshkosh, Reo and White, as well as numerous lighter types.

Although much of the world's truck production was given over to military types, civilian models were still being built. In France, for example, Berliet was producing wood-burning trucks which ran on the gas resulting from the combustion process but this ended with the Occupation, when manufacturers were forced to supply vehicles to the German forces. However, it was the French heavy vehicle industry that was hardest hit by World War II, although Allied bombers also left little of the German truck plants standing.

By 1941 fuel shortages were a serious problem throughout Europe. Even bus operators could not obtain sufficient supplies, and many of these vehicles were withdrawn, while others were converted to operate with producer-gas trailers. Some single-deckers even ran on town gas stored in huge tent-like structures mounted on the roof. A year later certain manufacturers, such as Guy Motors, were authorized to build austerity versions of their passenger models to replace pre-war vehicles wrecked or damaged. To clear bomb damage or haul heavy machinery, traction engines and other extinct types were moved into service.

Off road & construction vehicles

Following World War I many hundreds of all-wheel drive and other heavy specification military trucks came onto the civilian market and were quickly snapped up by the construction industry and others requiring heavy-duty vehicles. New civilian versions were soon developed for on/off-road working and even larger strictly off-road types gradually developed, principally for mining and quarrying. The most common off-road types are now dump trucks. There are other designs which have been developed specifically for the building and construction industries; these include drilling rigs, lorry-mounted cranes and concrete mixers.

3

1

2

8

9

1 The twin-engined rotary snowplough built around 1920 by the Winther Motor Truck Co, Wisconsin was unusual for its day. 2 A 1919 Walker Model 'K' 1-ton battery-electric integral van. 3 The front-discharge unit is an increasingly popular feature. In the case of the 'B'-Series Oshkosh it incorporated a rear-mounted engine, a centrally placed one-man cab and a 6x6 layout. 4 Off-highway dump trucks such as this rear-wheel drive Terex 33-11B are the real construction giants. 5 This 6x6 Autocar construction truck, made by the White Motor Corp. can cope with very heavy work. 6/7 The 'Lowline' crane carrier is of almost universal appeal, it is exemplified here by the Mitsubishi Fuso K600 60-tonner.

8/9 An early prototype Scammell 'Pioneer' equipped with all-over tracks shows off its capabilities while Scammell's first tank transporter recovers a disabled truck. 10 The British-built AIM 'Stalwart' 6x6 with full independent suspension and steering on all but the last two wheels was adopted by the military authorities of many countries as a standard amphibious land-carrier. 11 The US-built NOZ Mack of the 1940s was a 7½-ton 6x6 with double-reduction gearing in the steering ends of the front axle which provided a higher front axle than the vehicle's hubs.

The post-war years

THE WESTERN WORLD of 1945 was far different from that of 1919. Not only was there a shortage of materials (the most important being steel), but also monetary restrictions out-of-date equipment, and a lack of skilled labour. In the United Kingdom, the government decided to increase exports, and insisted that sixty percent of total vehicle exports should comprise commercial vehicles. By 1946 the government's seemingly impossible sales figures had been reached, simply by selling more vehicles abroad than before the war.

British manufacturers continued mainly with pre-war ranges, such as the bonneted Commer 'Superpoise', launched in 1939, and the Bedford 'O'-Type, also a normal-control design. This gave firms sufficient breathing space to introduce totally new models like the forward-control underfloor-engined Commer of 1948, and the 'Big Bedford' of 1950. This had a 4.9-litre 6-cyl petrol engine, regarded by many as the best petrol engine ever fitted in a commercial.

The 1947 British Transport Act led to the nationalization of road haulage, which in turn resulted in fleet standardization and other improvements. By 1948, United Kingdom commercial vehicle exports were five times higher than in 1938, and British expertise led

the world. Leyland engines and other components were used in the first DAF trucks and many United Kingdom manufacturers, particularly the premium truck and bus builders like Fodens, Atkinson, ERF and Leyland, concentrated on Commonwealth markets, such as Northern and Southern Rhodesia, South Africa and Australia. Mergers became commonplace in an effort to consolidate activities, with AEC acquiring Crossley in 1948 and Maudslay in 1949, while Leyland bought Albion in 1951, and Scammell in 1955.

The Japanese now have one of the world's largest vehicle industries, certainly as far as exports are concerned, but in 1946 it was still in its infancy. Hino's first truck was a 15-ton capacity artic announced in 1946, followed one year later by an air-braked articulated bus. Volume production did not get underway until 1949, the company's heaviest model being a 6 x 6 10-tonner introduced in 1951. During these early days of the Japanese motor industry there were close ties with European manufacturers such as Renault and Rootes, but once established in their own right, these ties were quickly broken.

The immediate post-war period was the heyday of the American truck-building industry, with products being

Far left and top left For countries that had been involved in the war, many post-war models were the same as pre-war types. Both the Foden DG6/15 and the Belford 'M'-type fall into this category. *Bottom left* After the war Leyland developed a number of all-steel cabs with forward-control such as this 'Beaver'. *Above* The 'KB'-Line International of 1947 was a much modified and improved version of the pre-war 'K'-Series. *Right* In 1950 GMC announced a new "weight-saving" diesel tractor which used much more light alloy than before.

Far right The WF800 Freightliner "cabover", designed by a truck operator became the White Freightliner when White took over Freightliner sales and service in 1951. Meanwhile, the White Motor Co's own idea of a medium-weight "cabover" was the tiltcab '3000' series. *Right and below* Peterbilt and Kenworth were custom-building their heavy-duty "conventionals".

sold worldwide. It was at this time that American manufacturers set the trend for heavy "cabover" articulated tractor units for long-distance haulage, employing many ideas gleaned from the war years and, in particular, from aircraft production. Aluminium alloy was being used in increasing quantities, not only for components but also for body sections and framing. Some of the larger manufacturers were even acquiring individual body-building concerns, so that vehicle bodies, such as light- and mediumweight panel vans, could be produced by that manufacturer.

Since World War II there have been two major innovations in the commercial vehicle field. One is the almost universal adoption of articulation, and the other the use of forward-control tilt-cabs. Articulation has now developed furthest in the United States where, since the 1950s, "double-bottom" outfits comprising one tractor, a dolly and two semi-trailers, have become common. In Europe a drawbar configuration is still the most popular, whilst articulation rates as the most popular method in the United Kingdom.

The use of forward-control tilt-cabs in the United States only really caught on in the 1950s, before which time bonneted tractors were more popular. However, the "cabover" layout permits longer semi-trailers to be used, thereby making vehicle operations more economical.

New technology

WITH A WORLDWIDE INCREASE in prosperity, the accent was placed on vehicle design, although great advances were still being made in other aspects of vehicle manufacture, particularly their efficiency. At the 1948 Commercial Motor Show, Fodens Ltd exhibited a new 4-cyl 2-stroke diesel engine which was to herald a new technological age for the commercial vehicle. It was a particularly efficient design, followed in 1955 by a 3-cyl Rootes 2-stroke for diesel or multi-fuel applications. Turbocharged diesels were first used in trucks by Volvo of Sweden, where gross weights are

Far right top **A 1953 Volvo L375 4/5 ton truck.** *Middle top* In spite of being functional, the bonneted French Willème was a decidedly ugly vehicle. *Right top* Built in France in 1955 this Latil was unlikely to be seen outside France. *Right* The 1956 bonneted Bedford was a very versatile truck that did much to boost Britain's export figures. *Below* This crew-cabbed petrol-engined Dennis was typical of the vehicles operated by many British local authorities at the time.

the highest in Europe. Instead of building larger engines to produce greater power, Volvo fitted a turbo compressor which enabled as much as fifty percent more power to be produced by each engine. This system was announced in 1954 and, as well as giving increased power output, offers low fuel consumption and quiet running.

Petrol engines were still popular in the United States after World War II, but as the 1950s progressed, the use of diesels in heavy trucks became the norm. Mack Trucks announced its 'Thermodyne' diesel in 1953, and by the early 1960s many British-built Perkins diesels were being fitted in even light- and mediumweight delivery models, and high-speed 'V'-form diesels were being used both in the United States and Europe. Agreements were signed between the American-owned Cummins Engine Co, Jaguar in the United Kingdom, and Krupp in Germany, to manufacture Cummins engines in Europe under the Jaguar-Cummins and Krupp-Cummins brand names. These agreements, however, were later cancelled and Cummins 'V' engines built in quantity in the company's British plant. While some, such as Cummins and Scania, have developed successful 'V' diesels, others have not. AEC, Southall, Middx, developed its own V8 unit, known as the '800'-Series, but this was unsuccessful.

The new era

During the 1960s there was considerable interest in the use of gas-turbine power for both trucks and buses, and a number of prototypes were built. Many of the leading American manufacturers investigated this source of power and in the United Kingdom, British Leyland developed four vehicles. However, with the exception of the massive Lectra-Haul dump truck, which is powered by an 1100bhp Saturn gas-turbine, none of these reached production stage and the cost of fuel is now prohibitive.

Recent years have seen the opening up of large areas of the world to long-distance trucking largely due to the construction of motorways and other major routes. The Asian Highway was just one example, having a considerable effect on European road haulage and, eventually, on the design of vehicles operating over long distances. Many manufacturers began offering a special "Middle East" package on heavier trucks and tractor units, with features which provided maximum driver comfort. Vehicle braking systems and tyres have improved as distances and speeds have increased, so that the modern long-haul artic unit invariably relies upon full air brakes, while intermediate types have adopted air/hydraulic systems. More recently, exhaust brakes and other forms of engine retarder have appeared more frequently.

Left Scammell's 'Highwayman' was particularly popular as an artic tanker, special versions of it were frequently sold abroad. This one was sold to Venezuela. *Bottom far left* The Mercedes-Benz artic truck was popular in the UK in the 60s.

It was a bonneted model and had forward-control. *Bottom centre* A mini revolution in the UK cab design resulted in some very pleasing models. ERF's 'LV' cab was a case in point. *Bottom right* This mass-produced Ford Thames 'Trader' was now a familiar sight on British roads.

Truck transmissions have also changed. It is only since the war that synchromesh transmissions have appeared in large numbers, and by the early 1960s range-change transmissions and 2-speed axles were increasingly popular. Automatic or semi-automatic transmissions also have their place, but have never gained much popularity in the truck field. On the suspension front, air systems have become commonplace on passenger models but are still comparatively rare on trucks, being more popular for vehicles carrying bulk liquids than on those for general goods.

A further revolution in road trans-port has been created by the movement of containers on an international scale and the use of special pallets to aid mechanical handling. As recently as the 1960s, truck drivers had to load, sheet and rope their own vehicles, and some still do, but in the main the loads are now containerized or palletized, simplifying the operation considerably. In some countries, such as France, even the semi-trailers are specially built to be carried on "Kangaroo" rail wagons, thereby eliminating long trips by road, but in the main, containers of standard dimensions are used internationally, enabling complete interchangeability.

Left British trucks for the Australian market were very different from their UK counterparts, roadtrains such as this AEC 'Mammoth Major' hauled outfit being commonplace in the outback. *Centre left* Concentrating on custom-built trucks, the Hendrickson Mfg. Co. Illinois, offered its Model 'B' tipper to virtually any specification. *Centre right* At the heavier end of the UK market was the Thorneycroft 'Antor' C6T. It sold to military and heavy haulage customers, this example being exported to Argentina. *Bottom left* By the end of the decade AB Volvo was expanding rapidly in export fields. Despite the dated appearance of this bonetted range it was well suited for this market. *Bottom centre* The Hino 'T.E.' – F series tipper of 1966 was another very straightforward design. *Bottom right* American regulations permit the use of double and triple-bottom long-haul outfits such as this GMC 'Astro' machine.

The present and the future

THE 1970s could be truly termed the technological age as far as the commercial vehicle is concerned. We have already seen how the gas-turbine was seriously considered at the end of the previous decade as an alternative to petrol or diesel power for the heavier vehicle and how this possibility was brought to an abrupt halt by the fuel crisis. Meanwhile, in a further attempt to produce an economical substitute fuel for use in road vehicles, experiments got under way in most countries into the feasibility of battery-electric propulsion, the major obstacle being that of weight. Leaders in this field are General Motors in the USA and the Lucas-Chloride partnership in the UK, although a recent announcement from British Rail's Technical Centre in Derby suggests that they may at last have developed a lightweight sodium-sulphur battery suitable for road use.

The last decade has also seen increasing interest in the protection of the environment which has frequently backfired on the road transport operator in the form of lorry cordons and other restrictive legislation. From the bureaucratic angle, the EEC (Common Market) has also had much effect throughout Europe, making the tachograph ('spy in the cab') compulsory in member countries and reducing permissible driving hours. Connected both with this and the environmentalists' attitude, there have also been attempts, largely unsuccessful, to transfer goods from road to rail. Certain European countries no longer permit heavy trucks to operate on Sundays, substituting instead a railway service on which all lorries are carried.

In many countries the weights and size of vehicles has gradually increased and in Britain experiments are being conducted with American-style double-bottom outfits, comprising tractor, semi-trailer, drawbar dolly and second semi-trailer, for motorway operation. Abnormal and indivisible loads have also become heavier, with some European specialists now offering a transport service for individual loads in excess of 500 tons.

There have been even more changes in the manufacturing side of

Above left By the early 1970s "Big Red", Ford of America's gas-turbine prototype, was becoming a thing of the past rather than the future. *Above* The EEC introduced UK truckers to tachographs. These record drivers' hours and the vehicle operations. They were phased in gradually towards the end of the 70s. *Left* MAN's giant X-90 project with roof-mounted sleeping compartments looks to the future. *Below* The oil crisis of the mid-1970s inspired this prototype of a wedge-shaped Paymaster. It was designed by an Oregon trucker. *Right* Chevrolet's 'Turbo Titan III', a gas-turbine powered aerodynamically styled vehicle whose low silhouette provided low wind resistance.

the business, with some old-established concerns taken over and sometimes even closed down completely. A classic example is that of British Leyland which had already acquired the manufacturing plants for AEC, Albion, Bristol, Guy, Scammell and Thornycroft, discontinuing all except Bristol and Scammell, by the end of the 1970s. In America, meanwhile, Daimler-Benz AG of Germany has acquired the Freightliner Corp and, subject to confirmation, AB Volvo of Sweden has purchased the huge White Motor Corp, taking over assembly of

Top The cab on the Berlet-derived TR305 is also used by Ford on its 'Transcontinental' model. *Above* As continental manufacturers moved in on the British market so new models gradually emerged to please UK operators. A DAF offering is the rigid-8 2300. *Right* Volvos have been built to survive the arduous weather conditions of Scandinavia, so it is not surprising that the heavier models with their rugged specifications have carved a niche for themselves in long-haul transport operations in other parts of the world. European operators using the F88 and F89 ranges led the field in the race to North Africa, the Middle East, and beyond in the mid-1970s.

Custom rigs

Originating mainly in the United States, the custom rig is gradually spreading throughout the Western World, particularly among owner drivers. Special paint jobs and the fitting of chromed accessories are essential to the custom rig operator who, through these means, is able to express his individuality. There is now such a demand for this that virtually all US truck manufacturers now offer special paint schemes, following the lead set by companies such as Freightliner, Kenworth, Mack and Peterbilt, many of whose sales are aimed at the owner driver. Custom paint shops now also cater for trucks.

Top An imaginative 'cowboy' image is carried by this White Western Star. *Above* These two White Western Star tractors show just how far some manufacturers are prepared to go. *Far left* This fancy Kenworth ''conventional'' is definitely not ex-factory. *Left* These Kenworth paint jobs were specially developed for the owner-operator.

White, Autocar and Western Star trucks. These moves have been brought about by the search for still wider markets by European manufacturers.

Passenger transportation has also altered in the last decade, particularly in Britain. By the end of the 1960s the familiar half-cab double-decker which had been the mainstay of British bus operations for many years, was no longer in production, being superseded by mainly rear-engined full-front models easily adapted for one-man operation. As in the truck business, Britain's bus fleets were gradually infiltrated by similar vehicles of Continental origin, notably the Metro-Scania and Volvo 'Ailsa'.

For many years the articulated single-decker for fast urban operation had been popular in Europe and Scandinavia, especially in Germany and Sweden, and as in the case of the double-bottom goods vehicle, the British authorities permitted experiments with these on public roads. Similar arrangements were made in the USA, again using imported European models, and the idea is now being adopted almost worldwide with MAN, Scania and Volvo in the forefront.

In common with most other manufacturing industries, the world's commercial vehicle industry has suffered badly from the economic recession of the last few years. Some new marques, such as Ginaf, Stonefield, Terberg and Titan, have appeared during this time but even some of these have experienced financial problems. There is little doubt that the recession will have a continuing effect upon both commercial vehicle manufacturing and operating and some will find their only course is to close down. While this situation prevails, significant developments are likely to be few unless in the cause of economy. In the face of the gradual erosion of the world's oil resources, the search for new fuels will certainly continue, but there remains much development work to be done in this field.

The quest for fuel economy and more power has seen various developments in the engine field. In the USA, where petrol-engined trucks were the norm at the end of the 1960s, the diesel now reigns supreme, the cost of petrol being largely prohibitive. American truck operations have also been affected by a blanket 55mph speed limit, again in the interests of economy. In Europe, meanwhile, the fixed-head diesel engine gained brief popularity as a maintenance-free unit, only to fall down on length of operational life, but turbocharging, largely pioneered by AB Volvo, is obviously here to stay. 'V'-configuration engines are particularly popular in Germany where Mercedes and Magirus are the leaders.

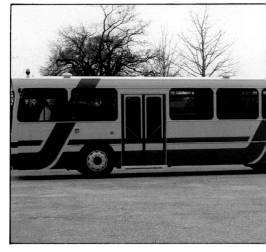

Top far left The Scottish-built Ailsa double-decker, with Volvo components, illustrated the British approach to urban transit operations. *Top centre left* The 'juggernaut' syndrome of the 1970s encouraged Mercedes to develop a less imposing heavy truck cab without sacrificing its capabilities. *Left* This early model of Leyland's 'Roadtrain' (built in 1980), the 16-28 incorporated many components that can be adapted for virtually any size or weight of vehicle. *Centre far left* The Maxeter 'Flexibus' which uses Mercedes running gears. *Centre left* For basic ruggedness Scammell's 'Crusader' became the general haulage vehicle of the early 1970s, often carrying a sleeper car which makes it suitable for long-distance work. *Bottom far left* The 1978 Fiat truck range illustrates the marque's design similarities which could lead to more economic production. *Bottom centre* West coast styling from General Motors in this GMC 'General'. *Below* Kenworth continued to build West coach types, both ''cabovers'' and ''conventionals''.

Golden oldies

Because of the numerous changes in truck and bus safety legislation over the years the 'oldie' in its original form is often unacceptable as a roadworthy vehicle. However, these vehicles can be adapted to meet new regulations and have often been successfully modified.

Vehicle recovery specialists and travelling showmen are among those who have appreciated the potential of the 'oldie', often through necessity rather than choice. They have converted ex-military and cheap commercially operated designs and adapted them, for their own use to today's standards. Through working and caring for their vehicle they will have found out a great deal about it.

1 After World War II the ex-Service AEC 'Matador' 0853 4x4 became one of the best known recovery vehicles in Europe. 2 A 1950 Freightliner (foreground) and a 1940 'E'-Series Mack (behind) still in use in 1963. 3 Even this semi forward-control Mack is now in the 'oldie' class.

4 A fleet of AEC's, some of them Maudslays in disguise used by fairground people in the early 1960's. **5** With its custom paint job this ex-Services Mack NOZ 6x6 carried a fairground organ inside its restored timber body. **6** In 1952 a typical East coast offering was the 'conventional' Diamond T, another type that outlived many of its competitors. **7** The Gardner-engined Foden 'DG' range, typified by this 1939 DG6/15, survived longer than most types.

Pioneers

AUSTIN, Herbert *(1866-1941)*
Herbert Austin was born at Little Missenden, Bucks, in November 1866 and by 1883 had emigrated to Australia where he became an engineering manager. In 1890 he returned to the British Isles and took up an appointment as Director of the Wolseley Sheep-Shearing Co, Birmingham, designing this company's first motorcar, a 3-wheeler, in 1895. The first 4-wheeler, also designed by Austin, appeared in 1900 and by 1906 he had set up his own production facility in the Longbridge Works, Birmingham, developing this into the huge Austin Motor Co Ltd.

Knighted in 1917 and a Conservative MP from 1919 until 1924, Austin became a baron in 1936. He died at Bromsgrove, Worcs, in May 1941.

Carl F. Benz

BENZ, Carl F *(1844-1929)*
Carl Friedrich Benz was born in 1844 at Karlsruhe, Germany, and his early career was as a mechanical engineer. In 1883 he founded Benz & Cie at Mannheim to build stationary internal combustion engines, designing and constructing the world's first practical internal combustion engined motor car which first ran early in 1885 and was patented in January 1886.

In 1893 Benz built his first 4-wheeled car and introduced the first of a series of racing cars in 1899. By 1906 he had left the firm to set up C Benz Söhne, Laden burg, with sons Eugen and Richard. He died on 4 April 1929.

BOLLEE, Amédée père *(1844-1917)*
Amédée Bollée Snr, born in 1844, ran the family bell-founding business in Le Mans, France, but was inspired by certain steam-powered exhibits at the Paris World Exhibition in 1867 to construct a fast private carriage, establishing a motor vehicle workshop in a corner of the foundry. The machine was far in advance

Amédée Bollée Snr

of anything that had gone before, following its own design parameters rather than those of horse-drawn or rail-borne vehicles.

He next constructed two 4-wheel drive 4-wheel steer tramcars with independent suspension and followed these with a new steam carriage with engine ahead of the driver and boiler at the rear. This he exhibited at the 1878 Paris World Exhibition, setting up a new workshop outside the family bell foundry, but a royalty agreement with a German manufacturer was unsuccessful and the collapse of this business led to Bollée's gradual disinterest in vehicle-building. He reverted to bell-founding, passing all vehicle enquiries to his eldest son, also Amédée Bollée.

BOLLEE, Amédée *fils (1868-1926)*
Amédée Bollée Jnr was just 18 when his father passed a steam carriage order to him. He had already built a light 2-seater for himself but this new project was a 16-seat double mail coach for the Marquis de Brox. He was not very successful in the steam sphere but opted instead for the petrol-driven motor car, the first of which he constructed in 1896, his designs being built under licence by De Dietrich.

He regularly took part in speed trials and this experience taught him the importance of aerodynamics. He built a number of machines with unusual torpedo-shaped bodies which led to numerous orders. By 1900 he had withdrawn from speed events and was concentrating instead on the construction of refined limited-production vehicles.

BOLLEE, Leon *(1870-1913)*
Amédée Bollée Jnr's younger brother, Léon, concentrated on the development of automatic machinery until the age of 26, showing one of the earliest automatic calculating machines at the 1889 Paris Exhibition. However, 1896 saw a new 3-wheeled motorcar which was the first vehicle to

be sold with pneumatic tyres as standard. Examples were built in England as well as France but within three years a new Léon Bollée design was under construction in the Darracq factory.

From 1903 Léon started to manufacture his own vehicles, backed financially and thus securely by the Vanderbilt family. Although he died in 1913, the Léon Bollée range continued for some years.

CHRYSLER, Walter P *(1875-1940)*
Walter Percy Chrysler was born at Wamego, Kansas, in 1875 and was later apprenticed to the Union Pacific Railroad machine shop. Joining the American Locomotive Co, he worked up to the position of Plant Manager but seeing opportunities elsewhere became Works Manager at the Buick Motor Co for half the salary. By 1916 he was President, building the Buick operation into the strongest of all General Motors subsidiaries by the time he left in 1919.

Six months later he took over the helm of both the Willys-Overland Co and the Maxwell Motor Co. These formed the basis of the Chrysler Corp, founded in 1925, which quickly introduced his own design of high-compression engined car. This became so successful that Maxwell production was discontinued.

In 1928 Chrysler purchased the Dodge Bros Manufacturing Co from the bank that had controlled it since the Dodge brothers' deaths, enabling him to launch the Plymouth range in 1928 as a new competitor for both Ford and Chevrolet.

Amédée Bollée Jnr

CITROEN, Andre G *(1878-1935)*
André Gustave Citroën, born in Paris on 5 February 1878, was both an engineer and an industrialist who was strongly in favour of Henry Ford's mass-production techniques, himself boosting Mors car and commercial production from 125 to 1200 units per year. He even convinced the French

Army that mass-production of munitions was essential during World War I and he set up a factory to do just this, later converting the plant into an automotive works. Refusing to admit defeat during the Depression, he introduced the only popular front-wheel drive car of the day. The company was made bankrupt in 1934 and Citroën lost control, dying in July 1935.

DAIMLER, Gottlieb W *(1834-1900)*
Gottlieb Wilhelm Daimler was born at Schorndorf, Württemburg, in 1834, and like Carl Benz became a mechanical engineer and inventor. At 38 he joined Eugen Langen and Nikolaus Otto at the Deutz Works in Cologne to assist with the development of a 4-stroke petrol engine. He soon became a leading figure in automotive development, setting up a workshop at Canstatt with Wilhelm Maybach in 1882 and pat-

Léon Bollée

enting one of the world's first high-speed internal combustion engines in December 1883, following this with a new design of carburettor.

In 1885 Daimler developed one of the world's first motorcycles, a 4-wheeled self-propelled carriage in 1886, a boat in 1887 and a 4-wheeled motorcar in 1889. The French rights to his engine patents were sold to Panhard et Levassor and in 1890 he founded Daimler-Motoren-Gesellschaft, again at Canstatt, to produce more motor vehicles, one of which was the Mercedes car, named after Co-Director Émile Jellinek's daughter. Daimler died in Canstatt on 6 March 1900.

DURANT, William C *(1861-1947)*
William Crapo Durant was born at Boston, Massachusetts, on 8 December 1861, and by 1886 had set up a carriage-building business in Michigan. After taking over another firm he began to construct Buick cars, merging this

Walter P. Chrysler

operation with those of several other manufacturers to form the General Motors Co in 1908. Due to financial wheeler-dealing, he lost control in 1910 but established the Chevrolet Motor Co with ex-racing driver Louis Chevrolet.

By manipulating shares, Durant placed this operation in a position where it was able to take over the General Motors Co in 1915 to form the General Motors Corp, with Durant as President. Business expanded well but the post World War I sales slump forced him out again in 1920. Undeterred, he founded Durant Motors Inc, again taking over various smaller organizations to diversify operations but neither this nor later ventures were very successful. He died in New York City in 1947.

FODEN, Edwin R *(1870-1950)*
Edwin Richard Foden was born on 28 March 1870 and followed in his father's footsteps with a great interest in things mechanical. His father ran the Foden traction engine and threshing machine business in Sandbach, Cheshire, and young Edwin was soon advising him on points of design. One of these was to construct a 2-cylinder machine that was both easier to start and smoother-running, thus leading to many new orders.

Edwin Richard's father died in 1911 and he took over the reins of the firm. He was the first to use pneumatic tyres on a steam wagon and developed a number of very advanced designs but the authorities were anti-steam and he began to investigate diesel power at the end of the 1920s. His colleagues on the board were not interested and so, for both business and health reasons, he retired to Blackpool in 1930. He was not inactive, however, and pondered deeply on the possibilities of diesel. Then, in 1932, he began to construct his own prototype diesel lorry in a rented shed back at Sandbach with the assistance of

former Foden colleagues and son Dennis. Carrying the legend 'E R Foden & Son Diesel', the first ERF, as it was soon known, was well ahead of its time and a new factory was set up almost immediately with E R Foden as Managing Director.

Business built up rapidly and E R Foden remained an active participant until his death in 1950.

FORD, Henry *(1863-1947)*
Born the son of Irish immigrants in Wayne County, Michigan, on 30 July 1863, Henry Ford started his working life as a machinist's apprentice in Detroit at the age of 15. He soon moved back to the family farm and set up a small machine shop and sawmill, determined to make farm work a lot easier.

His persistence won him the post of Chief Engineer to the Edison Co, Detroit, which he held until 1899 when he set up the Detroit Automobile Co with some colleagues but left soon after to construct racing cars. This led to the formation of the Ford Motor Co in 1903 and the introduction of the immortal Model 'T' five years later. Ford soon earned himself a reputation for revolutionizing production techniques, his philosophy being to produce as many vehicles as possible and by so doing cut the price to the customer. By 1913 the Model 'T' was selling at just $500 and when discontinued in 1927 was replaced by the Model 'A'. A V8 petrol engine was developed in 1932 and gradually the company opened plants throughout the world, all employing mass-production techniques.

LEVASSOR, Emile *(1844-1897)*
Emile Levassor was a French inventor who, with René Panhard, took over a manufacturer of woodworking machinery in 1886 and began building his own version of the Daimler petrol engine for the French market on behalf

Gottlieb W. Daimler

of a Belgian entrepreneur. Unfortunately, this gentleman died suddenly so Levassor married his widow to whom the French Daimler rights had passed. He developed a revolutionary new car layout with horizontal engine ahead of the driver to provide good front wheel adhesion and a pinion-and-gearwheel transmission providing several alternative speeds. Such a layout was to become the norm for both cars and commercials of the immediate future.

Edwin R. Foden

MORRIS, William R *(1877-1963)*
Born in Worcestershire in October 1877, William Richard Morris was forced to give up his hopes of a medical career through his father's ill-health, beginning work at 15 by setting up a cycle repair shop behind his home. He also built cycles to order and raced them, later moving on to motorcycles and finally to cars. In 1903 he took a partner into the business but was soon bankrupt.

With a set of tools and a £50 debt, he established a small workshop at Cowley, Oxford, where he constructed the first Morris 'Oxford' 2-seater in 1913. Prosperity followed and he soon introduced the Morris 'Cowley', assembling this along Ford's mass-production lines. Morris Motors Ltd was founded in 1919 and in order to survive during 1920/1 all prices were slashed drastically. In 1923 his Morris Garages operation constructed the first MG and in the same year he formed Morris Commercial Cars Ltd to introduce mass-production techniques into the British truck industry.

In 1952 his vehicle-building activities were merged with those of the Austin Motor Co Ltd to form the British Motor Corp, which at the time was the third largest vehicle manufacturer in the world.

OLDS, Ransom E *(1864-1950)*
Claimed to be the first successful American vehicle manufacturer,

Ransom Eli Olds was born at Geneva, Ohio, in 1864 and as a young man quickly established a reputation as a first-rate inventor. His first 3hp curved-dash Olds appeared in the 1890s and in 1899 he established the Olds Motor Works, backed financially by Samuel L Smith, in Lansing, Michigan, to construct Oldsmobile cars on one of the world's first automotive assembly lines.

Unfortunately, a disagreement with Smith led to Old's resignation in 1904 after which he found the Reo Motor Car Co, the descendant of which was to become world-famous as a heavy truck producer.

SELDEN, George B *(1846-1922)*
Fully qualified as a lawyer, George Baldwin Selden, born 1846, was granted a patent for a revolutionary road engine in 1895 and sold the rights to this only on a royalty basis. For a while he had the entire American motor industry eating out of his hand but his monopoly was brought to an end by Henry Ford who stubbornly refused to pay. Selden took him to court and in a 1911 decision it was decreed that the Ford design was fundamentally different and royalties did not have to be paid.

SIMMS, Frederick R *(1863-1935)*
Frederick Richard Simms, born in 1863, was one of the great pioneers of the British motor industry, founding Simms & Co, consulting engineers, in 1890, which pioneered the use of low-tension

Frederick R. Simms

ignitions and the manufacture of motorboat engines and aerial cableways.

In 1901 Simms founded the Society of Motor Manufacturers & Traders, and was elected its first President. As well as building both cars and commercials in the early days, Simms's company concentrated on the manufacture of vehicle ignition systems and fuel-injection equipment during the 1930s but he resigned his position of Managing Director in 1935 and died nine years later.

A-Z

OF THE WORLD'S TRUCKS AND BUSES

Opposite A powerful GMC Astro hauls a heavy
load on one of the many super-highways
of the USA.

A

AAA (1)/*France 1919-1921*
Ateliers d'Automobile et d'Aviation, Paris, built battery-electric goods vehicles. There was no connection with AAA of Germany.

AAA (2)/*Germany 1919-1922*
AG für Akkumulatoren und Automobilbau, of Berlin, offered AAA battery-electric delivery-models up to 2 tons capacity.

AARBURG/*Switzerland c1959*
Aarburg built a large mobile shop, powered by a front-mounted Ford V8 petrol engine. Entrance doors were air-operated and a pay desk was situated at the front.

A & B/*USA 1914-1922*
The American & British Mfg Co, Bridgeport, Connecticut, introduced a single-axle petrol-electric tractor known as the A & B, or Hoadley, for hauling former horse-drawn fire-fighting equipment. Powered by a 4-cyl engine driving an electric motor in each wheel, this was joined by short-lived 3- and 5-ton trucks before production was transferred to Providence, Rhode Island.

ABC/*Scotland 1906-1908*
Established in Glasgow by George Johnston, who also founded Arrol-Johnston Ltd, the All-British Car Co Ltd built ABC light commercials and a prototype underfloor-engined bus, which was fitted with a 44hp 4-cyl vertical petrol engine, 2-speed chain gearbox and chain-drive. It ran experimentally.

ABENDROTH & ROOT/*USA 1912-1913*
Abendroth & Root commercials were of forward-control chain-drive layout with capacities of between 3 and 5 tons. Previously sold as Frontenac, they were built by the Abendroth & Root Mfg Co, Newburgh, New York State, but marketed as A & R from the year 1913.

ABOAG/*Germany 1897, 1913-17*
Berlin bus operator Allgemeine Berliner Omnibus AG, trading as ABOAG, entered the bus-building field by converting a horse-bus into an experimental battery-electric vehicle in 1897, constructing bus bodies on various chassis from 1911, and complete vehicles from 1913. The latter was a double-decker known as the 'RK-Car', which remained in production until 1917. Production resumed in 1928 as BVG.

ABRESCH/*USA 1910-1912*
The Charles Abresch Co, Milwaukee, Wisconsin, marketed assembled trucks often as the Abresch-Kremers but sometimes incorrectly referred to as the Abresch-Cramer or Abresch-Cremer.

ACASON/*USA 1915-1925*
Utilizing semi-elliptic leaf springs and Timken worm-drive rear axle, most Acason stakeside trucks were sold as 2- and 3½-tonners by the Acason Motor Truck Co, Detroit, Michigan. Power came from 4-cyl Waukesha engines of between 22 and 40hp.

ACE/*USA 1918-1927*
Ace commercials were assembled by the American Motor Truck Co, Newark, Ohio, and were occasionally known as American. Starting with a Buda-engined 2½-tonner, the line was quickly expanded to include models from 1½- to 3-ton capacity, a unique feature being headlamps which turned with the steering! Passenger models from 20- to 32-seaters were also offered, some with low-loading chassis and underslung axles, one of these forming the basis of a special passenger model which was built by the Royal Coach Co during the years of the 1920s.

ACF/*USA 1927-1942*
In 1925 the Fageol Motors Co, Kent, Ohio, and J G Brill Co, Philadelphia, Pennsylvania, were taken over by the American Car & Foundry Co, Detroit, Michigan. Fageol production was transferred to Detroit in 1926 but the following year powerful new ACF models replaced them and the Fageol brothers left to set up the Twin Coach Co, Kent, Ohio, although certain models still carried the Fageol name in 1929. In 1928 the ACF 'Metropolitan' petrol or petrol-electric underfloor-engined passenger model was launched but was largely unsuccessful, although listed until 1932. Six-cyl Hall-Scott petrol engines were standard but a small front-engined model introduced in 1930 had a Hercules unit. Some 25 trucks and tractors, all with Hall-Scott engines, were built in the next two years, and a new generation of underfloor-engined buses launched toward the end of 1932. By 1937 this range included models for up to 45 passengers, some with automatic transmission but production halted in 1942 to cope with wartime requirements, eventually resuming as the ACF-Brill.

ACF-BRILL/*USA 1945-1953*
The ACF-Brill name was used for an underfloor-engined, Hall-Scott-powered passenger design with optional Spicer hydraulic transmissions, built by the ACF-Brill Motors Co, a subsidiary of the American Car & Foundry Motors Co, Detroit, Michigan.

ACLO/*England 1948-1962*
From the inception of Associated Commercial Vehicles Ltd, all AEC, Crossley and Maudslay goods and passenger models supplied to Spanish-speaking countries were known as ACLO. From 1962, in common with Leyland Group policy, these were often marketed as Leyland.

ACME (1)/*USA 1915-1932*
The Cadillac Auto Truck Co, Cadillac, Michigan, assembled commercial models under the Acme and Acme-Detroit names, using proprietary components. In 1917 the company was re-formed as the Acme Motor Truck Co, using such proprietary items as Continental engines, Gray & Davis electrics, Detroit springs, Timken axles, Cotta transmissions and Borg & Beck clutches. The 'C' and 'E' 3½- and 4-tonners were powered by 4-cyl Continental petrol engines and by 1919 the 3.30-m wheelbase 'B' 1-tonner, 3.75-m wheelbase 'A' 2-tonner, new 4.27-m wheelbase 'C' 3½-tonner and 4.57-m wheelbase version of the 'E', now up-rated to 5 tons, were offered. A brand new range, using model numbers rather than letters, was launched in March 1925, the heaviest being a 6-ton rigid. In 1927 the United Motors Products Co, Grand Rapids, Michigan, was acquired, but by the end of the 1920s, vehicle assembly had been moved to Anderson, Indiana.

1962 ACLO 'Regal VI'

ACME (2)/*USA 1916-1921*
The Acme Wagon Co, Emingsville, Pennsylvania, assembled a 1-ton truck aimed at farming communities. This had a 17hp 4-cyl petrol engine, dry-plate clutch, 3-speed gearbox and bevel final-drive.

ACORN/*USA 1923-1930*
The Acorn Motor Truck Co, Chicago, offered load-carriers from 1- to 5-ton capacity powered by 4- or 6-cyl Buda engines.

ADAMS (1)/*England c1907-1913*
The Adams Mfg Co Ltd, Bedford, built various mediumweight Adams and Adams-Hewitt commercials, including a 1½-tonner with a 2.1-litre 2-cyl petrol engine located under the bonnet, and a larger 25hp model with a 4.8-litre 4-cyl petrol engine. By 1908, these were powered respectively by 14/16 and 18hp 4-cyl petrol engines, the latter being one of the most advanced of its day, but by 1913, only light commercials were offered.

ADAMS (2)/*USA 1911-1916*
The Findlay, Ohio-based Adams Bros Co offered a number of mediumweight commercials, starting with a 4-cyl engined 1-tonner and quickly joined by 1½- and 2-tonners. A bottom-dump was listed in 1915 but, in 1916, when the company was re-constituted as the Adams Truck, Foundry & Machine Co, the line-up comprised just 1-, 2- and 2½-tonners.

ADC/*England 1926-1928*
The Associated Daimler Co Ltd was a short-lived fusion of interests between the Associated Equipment Co Ltd and the Daimler Motor Co Ltd, the first true ADCs, or Associated Daimlers, being the ultra-lightweight 423 and 424 models, with a choice between 4-cyl AEC poppet-valve or 6-cyl Daimler sleeve-valve petrol engines. Other models included the half-cab semi-bonneted 419; the 802 (also known as the 'London Six'), which was the first 3-axle chassis

1927 ADC 'Ramillies'

to be built by the company, and possibly the first vehicle with double-drive bogie and 3rd differential; and a range of trolleybuses based on earlier AEC designs but with 55hp Bull traction motors, Westinghouse air brakes, and pneumatic tyres. The only single-decker 802 was very unusual in that it had petrol-electric transmission. Goods models included a 3½-tonner, a 5-tonner and the 'Ramillies' 6-tonner. One incorporated many passenger features, such as a half-cab and engine accessories on the left-hand side, with drive via a cone clutch and shaft to a chain gearbox located amidships and thence by another shaft to an overhead-worm rear axle. The brakes acted only on the rear wheels which were suspended on semi-elliptic leaf springs with rubber helper units. A special double-decker, using a 6-wheeled chassis, carried 104 seats but was used only to transport the company's own staff. When the company ceased trading, operations returned to the original constituent companies.

1928 ADC Model 802

ADLER/*Germany 1902-1939*
Initially, Adler Fahrradwerke vorm Heinrich Kleyer AG, Frankfurt, built commercials on car chassis. A 25hp 3-tonner was listed in 1910, a 5-tonner added in 1921 and, later, a 40bhp 2-tonner also introduced. By 1928 the company had been re-named Adlerwerke vorm Heinrich Kleyer AG and only a 1-tonner was built. The company's last commercials were again based on car chassis.

AEBI/*Switzerland 1964 to date*
Originally an agricultural equipment manufacturer, Aebi & Co AG Maschinenfabrik, Burgdorf, has produced cross-country trucks in the 1500 to 3300kg payload bracket for some years, starting with the open-cabbed 'Transporter' TP2000 with tubular backbone chassis. Specially designed

for use on steep Swiss hillside farms, all have full synchromesh gearboxes with six forward and two reverse speeds, hydraulic braking and a drive system that can be disengaged at either front or rear. The lightest models have either a single-cyl diesel or twin-cyl petrol engine, while the intermediate design has a Deutz air-cooled unit

AEG/*Germany 1903-1905 1935-1939*
Electrical equipment manufacturer Allgemeiner Elektrizitats AG, Berlin, originally built AEG trolleybuses but did not return to vehicle manufacture until 1935 with a series of 3- and 6-ton battery-electric trucks and fire appliances. Similar electric models were built by a subsidiary, Neue Automobil AG, but marketed as NAG.

1927 ADC Model 416

AEC (1)/*England 1912-1979*
The Associated Equipment Co Ltd was set up to manufacture passenger vehicles for the London General Ombibus Co Ltd and other buyers. Based in London E17, the company continued production of the 34-seat double-deck open-top LGOC 'B'-Type bus with flitched wood/steel chassis frame and worm-drive, offering a 32.7hp 4-cyl alternative to the original 28.9hp petrol engine. Some single-deck 'B'-Types. with experimental all-steel chassis, appeared in 1915, followed by the all-steel chassised 'Y'-Type, constructed on the first moving-track commercial vehicle assembly line in Europe. Over 10,000 3/4-ton "subsidy" trucks were supplied on this chassis during World War I, making AEC the largest British supplier of "subsidy" models at that time.

The first forward-control AEC was the 301 or 'K'-Type, announced in 1919 with single- or double-deck bodywork but still the old wood/steel chassis frame. LGOC-operated versions, as for the later 'S' and 'NS'-Types, had the 'GENERAL' name cast into the radiator top tank. The 35bhp wood/steel-chassised 'S'-Type of 1920 was also known as the 401, increasing double-deck capacity from 46 for the 301 to 54, and in 1922 the new 'NS' or 405 model, with 'S'-Type engine and low-loading pressed-steel chassis frame, enabled bodies of lower overall height to be fitted. The first AEC trolleybuses, of which only six were built in 1922, had Dick Kerr traction equipment mounted on an 'S'-Type chassis.

The 'Y'-Type had now become a 5-tonner known as the 501, powered by a 45bhp 4-cyl petrol engine, while 1923 saw the introduction of the first true AEC goods model – the 2-ton 201 with 28bhp 'L'-head petrol engine. There was also a heavy articulated tractor with 65bhp petrol engine and turntable coupling mounted direct on the rear axle rather than on the chassis itself. Although a few vehicles were now being sold outside the capital, most still went to London operators and in an effort to improve this situation there was a brief fusion of marketing and production facilities between AEC and the British Daimler concern in 1926. Apart from the bulk of LGOC deliveries, all new vehicles carried the Associated Daimler or ADC names, although one or two carried the Associated Equipment or AEC Ltd names. To improve production, the company moved to a 63-acre site at Southall, Middx, in 1927, taking the moving-track assembly line with it and in July 1928 the Asso-

1960 AEC (2) bonneted 'Mammoth Major'

ciated Daimler Co Ltd ceased trading and AEC and Daimler again became rivals, the former continuing production of the ultra-lightweight forward control ADC 423, now with a detachable-head version of the 'S'-Type engine, as its 426 and 427 models, later replaced by the stop-gap 'Reliance' 660 with cone clutch, gate-change transmission, servo brakes and a 37.2hp 6-cyl overhead-valve petrol engine. Before the end of 1929 this was replaced by the 'Regal' 662, using the same engine, a single dry-plate clutch and semi-floating rear axle. A double-deck version of shorter wheelbase was known as the 'Regent' 661, while the 'Renown' 6-wheeler was listed as the 663 double- and 664 single-decker. From October 1928 Four Wheel Drive Motors Ltd and Hardy Rail Motors Ltd entered into an agreement with AEC whereby they would use AEC components for all cross-country models, marketing these as FWD-England or, from 1931, as Hardy, to avoid confusion with the American-built FWD. In 1930 the bonneted 'Ranger' passenger model appeared, and also the first AEC diesel engine – a lightweight high-speed design – became optional for most models from 1931, possibly the first diesel engine to be built by a British commercial vehicle manufacturer. The 3½-ton 'Mercury' and 4-ton 'Monarch' goods chassis were also new for 1930 and new heavier trucks included the bonneted 6-ton 'Majestic' and the 7/8-ton 'Mammoth'. A trolleybus version of the 'Renown' – the 663T – also appeared, followed in 1931 by the 661T, a 'Regent' equivalent.

The revolutionary 'Q'-Type appeared as a 4- or 6-wheeled double- or 4-wheeled single-

decker in 1932 with a unique side-engined layout. Powered by a 7.4-litre petrol or, from 1935, by a 7.7-litre diesel engine, both of which were mounted vertically behind the offside front wheel, this had a rear axle at the very end of the chassis to maintain a straight drive-line. It also had a fluid fly-wheel and Wilson pre-select gearbox. In July 1933 the company went public and two particularly unusual vehicles were constructed. One was a 30-ton gross 3-trailer road-train hauled by a 8 x 8 tractor developed from earlier FWD-England and Hardy vehicles, and the other a low-loading rigid 8 x 4 machinery carrier called the 'Crocodile' which resembled another new model of 1934 – the rigid 8-wheeled 'Mammoth Major', claimed to be the second production rigid 8-wheeler built in Britain.

In 1935 some 6-wheeled passenger models known as NGTs were built to the design of the Northern General Transport Co Ltd, and working in conjunction with the London Passenger Transport Board the company developed a prototype double-decker in 1938 to replace the original 'Re-

gent'. Designated the A185, this became London's standard passenger model – the world-famous 'RT' – the last of which was not withdrawn until 1979.

Civilian production ceased in 1941 to concentrate on military equipment. Most famous was the 10-ton 4 x 4 'Matador' gun tractor developed from the old Hardy 4 x 4 and there was also a 6 x 6 version which was used by Coles Cranes Ltd as a basis for its lorry-mounted cranes. Civilian production resumed in 1945 and in 1946 the company combined resources with arch-rival Leyland Motors Ltd to form British United Traction Ltd to construct trolleybuses previously built by both firms. Between 1948 and 1949 AEC acquired Crossley Motors Ltd and the Maudslay Motor Co Ltd as well as bodybuilders Park Royal Vehicles Ltd and Charles H Roe Ltd, registering Associated Commercial Vehicles Ltd as the holding company. Both Crossleys and Maudslays were soon badge-engineered AECs, while Park Royal was to work closely with AEC Ltd in the manufacture of chassisless passenger models. At about this time, vehicles exported to Spain

1961 AEC (1) Dumptruk 1100 and 1948 AEC 'Regent III' 0961

and other Spanish-speaking countries became known as ACLO.

The first British production underfloor-engined single-deck passenger model – the 'Regal IV' – appeared in 1949 following trials of a prototype shipped to Canada in 1939, but was succeeded in 1953 by a new version of the 'Reliance', a double-deck prototype being the 'Regent IV'. Also new was the 8-ton 'Mercury', joined in 1955 by a MK II version for 14 tons GVW. Diversification was reflected by Maudslay-built fire appliance chassis supplied to Merryweather & Sons Ltd and the first 'Dumptruck', a 6 x 4 half-cab version of the 'Mammoth Major' with 10 cu m scow-end body announced in 1957. Within two years this had been joined by a bonneted 'Dumptruk' called the 690, production of which was later transferred to Aveling-Barford Ltd. There was also a massive 18 cu m 2-axle machine, the 1100, with a 340bhp 6-cyl turbo-charged diesel engine and 10-speed transmission. A bonneted 'Mogul' for the export market also appeared in 1959, followed by a similar 'Ma-

1932 AEC (1) 'Mercury' 640

jestic' 6-wheeler, and in 1961 agreement was reached with Barreiros Diesel SA which led to the manufacture of Barreiros-AEC passenger models in Madrid and with SIAM Di Tella Automotores SA, of Buenos Aires, permitting licence manufacture of AECs in Argentina. Meanwhile, a new range of chassisless passenger models was developed in conjunction with NV Autoindustrie Verheul in the Netherlands.

Transport Equipment (Thornycroft) Ltd was acquired in 1961 and by 1962 a merger between Associated Commercial Vehicles Ltd and Leyland Motors Ltd had been agreed. The fruits of this were to be seen in 1964 in the form of the Leyland-designed 'Ergomatic' tiltcab which, simultaneously, became available on certain

AEC and Leyland trucks. The original moving-track assembly line had been scrapped earlier in the year to accommodate the new range and a new rear-engined passenger model – the single-deck 'Swift' – was introduced for operators requiring a Bus Grant specification. Another rear-engined single-deck chassis – the 'Merlin' – was announced in 1967 followed, in 1968, by the unique 'Sabre' with '800'-Series 247bhp V8 diesel engine, again rear-mounted and common to the 'Mandator V8' tractor for up to 56 tons GCW. Unfortunately, this engine was to prove a complete disaster.

The Leyland Motor Group merged with the British Motor Corp Ltd in 1968 to form the British Leyland Motor Corp Ltd with AEC as part of its Truck & Bus Divn. Southall-built vehicles still carried the AEC badge but gradually the marque's demise was approaching as production of the Leyland 'Marathon' tractor, developed from US-style AEC prototypes, took over part of the plant. AEC models were withdrawn and by 1979 the plant closed.

AEC (2)/*Australia/South Africa 1961-1968*
The first South African-built AEC was the rugged 'Kudu' front-engined passenger chassis constructed in Johannesburg by Associated Commercial Vehicles Ltd, and quickly joined by heavy-duty bonneted goods models such as the 6 x 4 'Super Mammoth', also available in Australia. Other vehicles for these markets were imported either complete or in CKD form, but no other purely South African or Australian types were built after the formation of the British Leyland Motor Corp Ltd in 1968.

AEC-EEC/*England 1931-c1938*
Agreement was reached between the Associated Equipment Co Ltd and the English Electric Co Ltd whereby the two would combine

1954 AEC-PRV 'Monocoach' prototype single-deck bus

resources to construct trolleybuses under the AEC-EEC brand name. Using English Electric traction equipment, the new range was built at the AEC plant while English Electric's Preston, Lancs, factory produced the traction equipment.

AEC-MCW/*England 1938-1940, c1956 & 1965*
Metropolitan-Cammell-Weymann Motor Bodies Ltd, with plants in Birmingham, and Addlestone, Surrey, built a prototype all-metal-bodied chassisless double-deck trolleybus known as the AEC-MCW in 1938, incorporating 6-wheeled AEC running units. This marked the first large-scale attempt at chassisless vehicle construction in Britain and was followed by a number of production models. The company's successor, Metropolitan-Cammell-Weymann Ltd, was later called upon to construct one of four prototype integral-construction 'Routemaster' buses. The only other known AEC-MCW chassisless types were a series of half-cab low-height double-deckers supplied on 'Renown' running gear in 1965.

1939 AEC-MCW chassisless double-deck trolleybus

AEC-PRV/*England 1953-1967*
Park Royal Vehicles Ltd, London NW10, entered the integral-construction field with the single-deck 'Monocoach', using engine and running units common to AEC's 'Reliance' passenger model. A year later the second prototype for London Transport's famous 'Routemaster' chassisless double-decker was also built, and in 1959 full-scale 'Routemaster' production got underway. This was a half-cab rear-entrance model using AEC mechanical units, coil spring suspension with air suspension at the rear on some later models, and an AEC or Leyland diesel engine. When production came to an end in 1967 both 8.38-m and 9.14-m versions had been built, some with front entrances. A prototype front-entrance rear-engined model, again using an AEC engine and running gear, was built in 1966 and became the model for a new London bus of the 1980s – the XRM. Development of this was later shelved. Other double-deckers from the Park Royal stable have included the 'Renown' and its successor the 'Bridgemaster', both traditional half-cab models combining chassisless construction and low height bodywork.

AEC-VERHEUL/*Netherlands 1960-1964*
When old-established Dutch bodybuilder NV Autoindustrie Verheul, Waddinxveen, was acquired by AEC Ltd most subsequent passenger models embodied AEC engines, transmissions and running units, and were marketed as AEC-Verheul. A rear-engined design announced at the 1964 Amsterdam Show was the VBA10 single-deck transit bus. The arrangement came to an end following a merger between Associated Commercial Vehicles Ltd and the Leyland Motor Corp Ltd, when the company was re-named Leyland-Verheul Nederland NV.

AERFER/*Italy c1952-1965*
Industrie Meccaniche Aeronautiche Meridionali, Naples, was a former aircraft manufacturer that built chassisless Aerfer buses. Of light-alloy construction, the largest was a 150-passenger double-decker with a 150bhp horizontal Fiat diesel engine and automatic transmission which was located at the rear.

AERMACCHI/*Italy 1947-1970*
Three-wheeled commercials known as Aermacchi or Macchi went into production in the Soc Commerciale Aeronautica Macchi SpA aircraft factory at Varese, comprising both light- and mediumweight models. Using a tubular backbone chassis and shaft-drive, the most popular model had a 750cc flat-twin engine and an 8 forward and 2 reverse gearbox. A 4-wheeled version, with front wheel-drive and torsion-bar independent suspension, appeared in the 1950s, followed in 1957 by a new 3-wheeler with 18bhp 973cc 2-cyl air-cooled diesel engine. The company was acquired by Harley-Davidson in 1960, being re-named Aermacchi Harley-Davidson SpA, but in 1969 Harley-Davidson was itself taken over and the firm re-named AMF-Harley-Davidson Varese SpA. Later, manufacturing rights were acquired by Fratelli Brenna who sold the design as the Bremach.

AERO/*Czechoslovakia 1946-1951*
Passenger car and light commercial manufacturer Aero Tovarna Letadel, Prague, resumed production after World War II with the 1½-ton L-150 truck based on the Skoda 933 model. This had a 52bhp 2.09-litre 4-cyl overhead-valve petrol engine, but by 1951 had been re-designated the Praga A-150.

AEROCOACH/*USA 1940-1952*
The bus-building operation of Gar Wood Industries Inc, Detroit, Michigan, passed to the General American Transportation Corp, Chicago, Illinois, and the General American Aerocoach Co was formed to continue some of the lightweight Gar Wood designs until 1943, when the war brought production to a temporary halt. Larger 29- and 33-seat vehicles of similar construction, with International engines and Clark 5-speed transmissions, were quickly added to the range. In 1948, 36- and 45-passenger rapid transit models with fully automatic heating and ventilation systems also went into production, but these were unsuccessful.

AETNA/*USA 1914-1916*
A few 1½- and 2½-ton goods models were built by the Aetna Motor Truck Co, Detroit, Michigan. These had worm-drive axles and ¾-elliptic underslung leaf springs.

AGRICOLA/*Greece 1975 to date*
Built in Salonica since 1975 and intended for agricultural use, the Agricola is a 4 x 4 agricultural vehicle powered by a Mercedes 180D diesel engine driving both axles via a Mercedes gearbox. Other features include all-steel construction and a full-power take-off system.

1927 Ahrens-Fox pumper and hose car fire appliance

AHRENS-FOX/*USA 1912-1956*
The Ahrens-Fox Fire Engine Co was founded in 1911 in Cincinnati, Ohio. The company's first motor fire engine, with 80hp 6-cyl Herschell-Spillman engine and 2-cyl 750gpm pump, was supplied in 1912 as was its last steam pumper, connected to an electric front-wheel drive unit. In 1915 a new pumper with a distinctive 4-cyl double-acting pump surmounted by a spherical brass air chamber located ahead of the engine made identification of Ahrens-Fox appliances simple until 1951. Other machines included tractors for motorizing horse-drawn appliances, articulated aerial ladder trucks with rear-wheel steering, chemical appliances and hose trucks, with much of the specialist fire-fighting equipment supplied by another fire engine builder – the Peter Pirsch Co, Kenosha, Wisconsin. Six-cyl pumps were also built, the 1921 Model 'P' having a capacity of 1300gpm, and from 1920 shaft-drive became an option to the chain-drive system. Continental engines were used from 1927 and within five years Hercules and Waukesha units were also listed. With the Depression, production slumped dramatically, leading to a merger with the LeBlond-Schacht Truck Co in 1936, an arrangement which continued until 1951 when a local businessman bought the Ahrens-Fox operation. It was sold a year later to C D Beck & Co,

who transferred fire truck manufacture to its Sydney, Ohio, plant, existing models continuing until 1956 when a revolutionary new design, with the cab mounted forward of the front axle, was announced. Later, C D Beck & Co sold out to Mack Trucks Inc, Allentown, Pennsylvania, and all appliances were re-named Mack. By 1961 all assets, machinery and components from the old Ahrens-Fox operation had been acquired by former employee Richard C Nepper.

AIC/*USA 1913-1914*
A 5-ton capacity truck was built by the American Ice Mfg Co, New York, as the AIC or American Ice. It was powered by a 4-cyl petrol engine beneath the driver. *Qv* American Ice.

1977 Ailsa Mk II

AILSA/*Scotland 1968 & 1973-1979*
The first Ailsa was a prototype tipper for 16 tons GVW constructed by Ailsa Trucks Ltd, Glasgow-based concessionaire for Volvo commercials. It had a Motor Panels cab and diesel engine common to Volvo's F86 range, the motive being to offer a Volvo-powered, 16-tonner on the British market. Later, the company offered the first British-built front-engined double-deck bus since 1969. Prototypes appeared in 1973 and a new types announced in 1974 led to a

company, Ailsa Bus Ltd, formed to market the production model. With the exception of one low-height vehicle, all Ailsa double-deckers were of normal height, powered by a 6.75-litre 6-cyl turbocharged diesel engine, driving the rear axle via a 5-speed SCG automatic transmission. Production increased significantly when a new plant was opened at Irvine, Ayrshire, but in 1979 it was decided to market all passenger models in the UK as British Volvo.

AIR-O-FLEX/*USA 1919-1920*
The Air-o-Flex was a goods model built by the Air-o-Flex Automobile Corp, Detroit, Michigan, originally as a 2-tonner but joined later by a 1½-tonner, with a 4-cyl Buda petrol engine, 4-speed gearbox and shaft-drive.

AJS/*England 1927-1931*
A J Stevens & Co (1914) Ltd, Wolverhampton, Staffs, began development work on a range of passenger-carrying commercials in 1927. The first AJS bus was the 24/26-seat, low-loading 'Pilot' with forward- or normal-control, a 70bhp 3.3-litre, 6-cyl Coventry Climax petrol engine, 4-speed gearbox, worm-drive and 4-wheel vacuum brakes. This was joined by the semi-forward-control 'Commodore' for 26-seat coach or 32-seat bus operation, the driver sitting alongside a 100bhp 5.8-litre 6-cyl petrol engine, also of Coventry Climax manufacture. A few chassis were sold, but the company was soon in liquidation.

AKRON MULTI-TRUCK/*USA 1920-1922*
The Akron Multi-Truck was a 3.38-m wheelbase, 1-tonner built by the Thomart Motor Co, Kent, Ohio, and fitted with a rare 4-cyl Hinkley petrol engine, a 3-speed gearbox and bevel-drive. The last few examples are believed to have been sold as Thomart.

ALBANY/*England 1973 to date*
The Albany Motor Carriage Co, Christchurch, Dorset, was established to construct a replica vintage car using modern running units. A replica London General open-top double-deck bus was also built, the prototype employing a Ford 'D'-Series truck chassis. The first production model, using a Leyland Redline 'Terrier' chassis, was constructed in 1976 and others are planned.

ALBION/*Scotland ?-1972*
The first commercials built by the Albion Motor Car Co, Glasgow, for payloads in excess of 1 ton were variations of the company's ¾-ton A3, powered by a 16hp ver-

1976 Albany 'B'-Type replica

tical twin-cyl petrol engine. Up to 1914, this was listed for payloads of up to 2 tons, a special feature which was to become standard Albion practice for some years being an adjustable governor controlling air, throttle and ignition timing through a single lever.

One of the company's most famous trucks, introduced in 1910, was the chain-drive 32hp 4-cyl A10, which was built until 1926. This had a single-plate clutch and a high-tension magneto. The first "live" axle Albion arrived the following year, another new model being a 25hp chassis for 2-ton payloads, a 25-seat charabanc version of which was exhibited at the 1913 Scottish Motor Show. Later, the A10 was adopted by the Armed Forces as a 3-ton load-carrier and some 6000 examples saw service during World War I.

Albion A10 c1916

A new 24hp "subsidy" model, rated at 1½ tons capacity, was announced in 1923 and a number of 20-seat passenger bodies successfully mounted on it. A new low-loading passenger model called the Model 26, later known as the 'Viking', was introduced the following year for 30-seat bodies, one accomplishing a non-stop run from Glasgow to London and

back in just over 24 hours in 1925. The first Albion to carry a model name was the 'Viking-Six', a 90hp 6-cyl passenger design, announced in 1926 and joined in 1927 by a un-named forward-control 4-tonner known simply as the Model 35, in which day-to-day servicing was undertaken from within the cab. By removing a few bolts, the cab could be raised by block and tackle to provide clearer access. A bonneted military 6-wheeler with double-drive bogie, worm-reduction axles, single-plate clutch and four-speed box with optional splitter, was announced the following year, the chassis being specially unusual in that it had a dropped forward section to provide for cab and bonnet.

The company was re-named Albion Motors Ltd in 1930, new models for 1931 including the 6-cyl 'Valiant' 32-seater and its 4-cyl sister, the 'Valkyrie'; the 'Victor' 20-seater; and a new 2-tonner. The Model 127 5½-tonner, under 2½ tons unladen and thus able to operate legally in the UK at up to 48 km/h, appeared in 1935 along with a 13-ton double-drive 6-wheeler and a 6-wheeled version of the 'Valkyrie'. Later that year, Halley Industrial Motors Ltd was acquired, its premises at nearby Yoker proving most useful during World War II and many of the old

1940 Albion CX7N

Halley model names were revived as Albions after the war. During the mid-1930s Gardner diesel engines were options to the Albion petrol range but an Albion diesel was soon developed and by 1937 a rigid 8-wheeled goods model called the CX7, with Albion petrol or Gardner diesel engine, had been announced, followed in 1938 by the CX27 "Chinese Six" – the first British goods model for an 11-ton gross load conforming to maximum axle loading and minimum length restrictions.

Thousands of 3-ton 4 x 4s, 10-ton 6 x 4s and bonneted tractors were produced during World War II, other types including a twin-engined 8 x 8 prototype and the FT15N low-silhouette 6 x 6 artillery tractor. The 'Chieftain' truck was the first post-war civilian model, followed by the 'Clansman' and, in 1950, the 'Clydesdale', the names of the first two originating at Halley. Leyland Motors Ltd acquired the business in 1951, bringing development of a 39-seat single-deck bus with flat underfloor 8-cyl diesel engine to a halt and leading to all Albions employing an increased percentage of Leyland components.

By 1955 the 4/5-ton underfloor-engined 'Claymore' for goods or passenger work had been announced and was soon to become Britain's most popular underfloor-engined commercial. The 8-wheeled 'Caledonian', looking deceptively like Leyland's 'Octopus', arrived in 1958 for a payload of 16½ tons, incorporating a double-drive bogie, rocking-beam suspension, 8-wheel brakes and a Leyland 0.680 diesel engine. By 1960 the Leyland 'Vista-Vue' cab was common to a number of Albions and was even retained on certain 6-wheeled 'Reiver' models long after Leyland's 'Ergomatic' tiltcab had appeared on the 'Super Clydesdale' in 1964. The use of hub-reduction axles with virtually unbreakable half-shafts was popular with Albion customers, particularly those involved in site work, and these were still fitted to both 'Reiver' and 'Clydesdale' long after the Albion name was replaced by Leyland in 1972.

The front-engined 'Lowlander' double-decker of 1961 was merely a variation on the Leyland 'Titan' PD3 with a low-loading chassis frame, while the 1966 Commercial Motor Show saw a special 4 x 4 version of the 'Chieftain' developed in association with Scammell Lorries Ltd. From 1969 turbocharged Leyland diesel engines were available in certain 'Reiver' and 'Clydesdale' models, but from 1972 all Albions carried the Leyland brand name but were marketed variously as Leyland Scotstoun and Leyland Clydeside.

ALBION/MANN-EGERTON
England 1956
This was a 14 tons GVW lightweight chassisless truck developed by the British Aluminium Co Ltd and Mann-Egerton Ltd, Norwich. Similar to the earlier Dennis/Mann-Egerton, it had a front-mounted engine and was constructed almost entirely of light-alloy. Only one was built.

ALCO/*USA 1910-1913*
The American Locomotive Co, Providence, Rhode Island, listed 2-, 3½-, 5- and 6½-ton chain-drive trucks. All were rugged "cabovers" with 4-cyl petrol engines of up to 7718cu cm capacity and 40hp output. Despite one of these vehicles hauling a 3-ton load 6670km in 94 days at a top speed of 24km/h, vehicle production was discontinued in favour of railway locomotives.

ALFA-ROMEO/*Italy 1930 to date*
Specializing in the manufacture of high-performance passenger cars until 1930, SA Alfa-Romeo, Milan, built a high-speed lightweight truck with a 3-litre, 6-cyl petrol engine and within a year, diesel engines were standard for this model and for new 5- and 6-ton goods and passenger models developed from the German Büssing range. In 1934 the company's first articulated bus was launched and by 1937 trucks from 3 to 10 tons capacity were listed, the heaviest being of forward-control layout with 8-speed transmissions. Standard passenger chassis was the ALR, a 6.1-litre, 6-cyl engined design with 4-speed box and air-hydraulic brakes. In 1942 the company became Alfa-Romeo SpA and after 1945 all bonneted models vanished, the pre-war 800 developing into the 8-ton 900 with 9.5-litre 130bhp diesel engine and a smaller 4/5-tonner being equipped with air-hydraulic brakes. Independent torsion-bar front suspension arrived in 1948 but this proved totally unsuccessful and normal axles were fitted from 1950.

1955 Alfa-Romeo Model 955 prototype truck

A new passenger series, with transverse, rear-mounted engines, had been introduced in 1948, a development of this being a fleet of 157-passenger articulated buses and, even more unusual, a 1954 variant with central driving position. The 1950s also saw a number of single-deck trolleybuses, delivered to both home and overseas operators, and the signing of a licence agreement with Fabrica National de Motores SA, Rio de Janeiro, Brazil, whereby this company would produce commercials of Alfa-Romeo design. The 'Romeo Autotutto', an independent suspension 1-ton truck or van, appeared in 1954, with a 1.2-litre, 2-stroke, twin-cyl diesel or de-tuned 1.3-litre, twin-cam petrol engine producing 35bhp. A new forward-control 8-tonnner, the 'Mille', arrived in 1957, having an 11-litre, 6-cyl diesel engine, air-assisted clutch, 8-speed box and full air braking, while a passenger version had a rear-mounted horizontal engine. In 1967 agreement was reached with SA de Vehicules Industriels et Equipements Mécaniques, manufacturer of Saviem commercials, whereby certain of their light models would be assembled by Alfa-Romeo as Alfa-Romeo Saviem, an arrangement which continued well into the 1970s when the Saviem suffix was dropped. In 1978 a brand-new range of semi-forward control models for payloads of between 1½ and 2¼ tons was developed jointly by Alfa-Romeo, Fiat and Saviem. These have the Fiat 'Daily' cab structure and a new 2.4-litre, 4-cyl, Sofim diesel engine. Torsion-bar independent front suspension is again standard as are disc brakes and a 5-speed box with twin rear wheels on the heavier models.

ALFA-ROMEO SAVIEM/*Italy 1967-c1975*
Agreement was reached in 1967 between Alfa-Romeo SpA, and SA de Vehicules Industriels et Equipements Mécaniques, the French builder of Saviem commercials, whereby the latter's 'Goelette' and 'Galion' lightweights would be assembled in Italy as Alfa-Romeo Saviem, often with Alfa-Romeo engines. This arrangement continued well into the 1970s, the 6300kg GVW A 38 being the heaviest.

ALL-AMERICAN/*USA 1918-1923*
Known overseas as the AA, the All-American truck was built by the All-American Truck Co, Chicago, Illinois. Particularly popular was a 3.30-m wheelbase 1-tonner, with 4-cyl Herschell-Spillman petrol engine and 3-speed transmission. In 1922 production passed to the Fremont Motors Corp, Fremont, Ohio, who had previously built the short-lived Panther commercial.

ALL-POWER/*USA 1918-1924*
The All Power Truck Co, Detroit, Michigan, built the SV4, 3½-ton, 4 x 4 truck under the All-Power brand name.

ALLAN TAYLOR/*England 1927-1959*
The Allan Taylor Engineering & Machinery Co Ltd, London SW18, concentrated on the assembly of light golf course, park and sports ground tractors, the majority of which employed Ford Model 'T', 'A' or 'B' components. The design came about because the standard agricultural tractor of the day was far too heavy and powerful for such work. The Allan Taylor, or AT, as it was some-

times called, was much lighter, and often incorporated paraffin starting, switching to petrol for normal running. From about 1929 the company also built 1½/2- and 2½-ton low-loading commercials carried on 510- or 590-mm wheels and solid tyres, using Ford 'AA' components.

1932 Allan Taylor tipper

ALLCHIN/*England 1905-1931*
William Allchin & Co Ltd, Northampton, introduced the first of a series of steam wagons in 1905, selling these as Allchins or Globes. The first was shown in 1906, having a side-fired, loco-style boiler with extended smokebox supplying steam at 200psi to a compound "undertype" engine which drove the rear wheels by roller chain. A pedal-operated, 3-way valve was fitted for doubling the pressure in emergencies. Designed for a 5-ton payload, traction engine influence was clearly illustrated in that the rear wheels were larger than those at

the front. Only seven "under-types" were sold when an "over-type" layout was adopted, making many moving parts more accessible. The first was not satisfactory, because the channel-section frame was attached direct to the boiler in an attempt not to infringe certain Foden patents. Twin underslung water tanks were another unusual feature. The second "overtype" had re-designed framing, while the third used outside valves. Although the company offered models from 3 to 6 tons capacity, and even built three 7-ton payload artics in 1924, each with Westinghouse power brakes, Allchin never survived the Depression.

ALLDAYS/*England 1911-1918*
The Matchless Works, Birmingham, of the Alldays & Onions Pneumatic Engineering Co Ltd, began to turn out light Alldays commercials in 1906, introducing larger trucks with capacities of up to 5 tons in 1911, using a 40hp petrol engine. Although the Railless Electric Traction Co Ltd supplied both vehicles and installations for the first regular British trolleybus systems, the vehicles were actually built by Alldays & Onions.

Entering service in 1911, each vehicle carried two series-wound Siemens motors located side by side beneath the floor, each driving a rear wheel via worm gearing, countershaft and sprocket and chain. A combined output of 40hp was controlled by a tram-type controller with five running positions and reverse, and there were two braking systems. The 28-seat transverse-seat bodies were by Hurst Nelson & Co Ltd, Motherwell, Scotland, the Leeds vehicles having front-entrance bodies for one-man operation (quickly abandoned) and Bradford vehicles slightly larger bodies with rear entrance platforms. Commercial vehicle production came to a halt in 1918, following a merger with the Enfield Autocar Co, thereby establishing Enfield-Allday Motors Ltd being established, Motors Ltd.

ALLEN/*England c1958-1972*
John Allen & Sons Ltd, Oxford, was established in 1913. Towards the end of the 1950s the company launched a range of truck-cranes employing special 4- and 6-wheeled chassis with full, divided or half-cabs. By the end of the decade, the firm had become John Allen & Sons (Oxford) Ltd, the lighter lorry-mounted cranes featuring hydraulic telescopic booms built under licence from the Grove Mfg Co of America, with 30-tonners employing the old lattice jib layout. Eventually, only hydraulic boom machines were built, marketed as Grove Allen.

Alley & McLellan c1910

ALLEY & McLELLAN/*Scotland 1906-1917*
The first 'Sentinel' steam wagon, a 5-tonner with vertical cross-tube boiler, single-coil superheater and 2-cyl "undertype" engine was built by Glasgow marine engineers Alley & McLellan Ltd. The boiler was located beside the driver but behind the front axle, the engine had camshaft-operated poppet valves as used in internal combustion engines of the period, and Ackermann-type steering was employed. An improved model, with boiler in front of the driver, quickly followed; this arrangement being used in all subsequent 'Sentinel' wagons until 1932. Fuel was carried in a bunker at the back of the cab, and water in a tank slung beneath the rear of the chassis frame. A double-coil, superheater, providing 51°C superheat, was also fitted. Generally known as the 'Standard Sentinel' during this period, 3/4- and 6-ton wagons

were offered with respective wheelbases of 2.97 and 3.17m. When production moved to Shrewsbury in 1917 the company was re-named the Sentinel Waggon Works Ltd and wagons sold afterwards as Sentinel.

ALLIS-CHALMERS/*USA 1915-1918*
The Allis-Chalmers Mfg Co, Milwaukee, Wisconsin, built a few 5-ton trucks with half-track rear bogie and engine ahead of the driver. The majority were used for timber haulage.

ALM/*France c1964 to date*
Ateliers Legueu Meaux offers a series of custom-built, medium- and heavy-duty trucks for both on and off-highway use, known as the ALM. These have Ford petrol or Perkins diesel engines, 5-speed gearboxes with 2-speed auxiliary, 4- or 6-wheel drive and fibreglass

1906 Alley & McLellan

cabs and front ends. Popular in the construction industry, some 2½-ton 4 x 4s are also used by the military. One or two tractors were also built. In the early 1970s the company was re-named Les Ateliers de Construction Mécanique de l'Atlantique, but vehicles are still called ALM.

1962 Alvis 'Stalwart' C

ALMA/*USA 1911-1914*
Previously known as the Hercules Motor Truck Co, the Alma Mfg Co, Alma, Michigan, built Alma trucks until the company was re-named the Alma Motor Truck Co in 1914. Models were then sold as Republic.

ALUSUISSE/*Switzerland 1976*
As a supplier of aluminium components to the vehicle construction industry, Schweizerische Aluminium AG have a special interest in vehicle design, assembling a complete vehicle as a promotional exercise, using the Saurer/Berna 5DF/5VF chassis as a model. The 16 tons GVW Alusuisse had numerous aluminium components, thereby achieving a saving of 497kg or 38.7% over the comparable steel-built model. Total unladen weight was 5685kg.

ALVIS/*England 1952-1971*
Having previously built Alvis-Straussler military vehicles, Alvis Ltd, Coventry, introduced the FV600 6 x 6 range in 1952, including the 'Stalwart' load-carrier and 'Salamander' fire appliance. A 5-ton capacity amphibious civilian version of the 'Stalwart', known as the 'Stalwart' C, was shown at the Commercial Motor Show in 1962, having 4-wheel steering at the front, equi-spaced wheels and a 64km/h maximum land speed (5 knots maximum in water). It had a Rolls-Royce B81 8-cyl in-line petrol engine but only military versions were subsequently sold. In 1964, reciprocal agreement was reached between this company and the French manufacturer of Berliet trucks, whereby selected Alvis models were to be sold in Europe as Auroch, and certain Berliet designs in the UK as Alvis-Berliet.

ALVIS-BERLIET/*England 1964-c1968*
Agreement was reached between Alvis Ltd, Coventry, and Auto-

mobiles M Berliet SA, whereby selected Alvis vehicles were to be sold in Europe as Auroch and certain Berliets in the UK as Alvis-Berliet. Only two 6-ton, 6 x 6 heavy wreckers based on the Berliet TBU 15CLD chassis are believed to have carried this name, the arrangement being brought to an end by the takeover of Alvis by British Leyland.

ALVIS-STRAUSSLER/*England c1935-c1939*
In the late 1930s, Alvis Ltd, Coventry, constructed a number of specialist land vehicles designed by cross-country pioneer Nicholas Straussler. These included the 4 x 4 'Hefty' tractor with tubular backbone frame and independent pivoting rear axle and body as used by the Royal Air Force.

AM/*Belgium 1951-1952 & 1960-1961*
Ateliers Metallurgiques, Nivelles, assembled AM integral buses with Leyland or Büssing underfloor engines between 1951 and 1952 but these were not popular. In 1960, as La Brugeoise & Nivelles, the compay again entered the bus market, utilizing components such as Detroit Diesel engines and Allison transmissions, but within a year this project had also ceased, all patents and materials being transferred to the American-owned Bus & Car Co who later introduced the Silver Eagle.

AM GENERAL/*USA 1971 to date*
The AM General Corp, Marshall, Texas, is a wholly-owned subsidiary of the American Motors Corp, which, in the mid-1960s, began to develop pollution-free, electrically-powered delivery vehicles and dual-mode machines powered both by electric motors and low-pollution internal combustion engines. Agreement was reached with Flyer Industries Ltd, Winnipeg, Canada, whereby AM Gen-

1974 AM General 'Flyer' prototype single-deck bus

eral was to have world manufacturing rights for Flyer diesel and electric city transit buses and diesel-powered inter-city buses, making AM General the first manufacturer of complete electric transit buses in the USA. First of the series was a 53-seat diesel transit bus, production of which got underway at South Bend, Indiana, in 1972. Body shells were supplied by Flyer Industries while AM General added the air-conditioning and transverse 6- or 8-cyl Detroit Diesel 'V' engines and Allison automatic transmissions. In 1978 production moved to Marshall where standard transit buses include 11- and 12-m units and a new range of articulated city buses introduced in 1979 with MAN body shells and engines. These are 17 and 18m long and are the first articulated passenger vehicles to operate in the USA. Trolleybuses and a 5-ton multi-fuel 6 x 6 military truck (usually referred to simply as the AM and previously built by the Kaiser Jeep Corp) are also built under the AM General name, although assembly of the latter is often sub-contracted to the Crane Carrier Corp.

AMERICAN (1)/*USA 1906-1912*
The American Motor Truck Co, Lockport, New York State, built a series of heavy-duty trucks with 4-cyl petrol engines from 20 to 60hp output and double chain-drive, sometimes referred to as American Standard to avoid confusion with other vehicles carrying the American name. In 1911 the operation moved to Findlay, Ohio, the firm was re-named the Findlay Motor Co but merged with the Ewing Motor Co in 1912, forming the Ewing-American Motor Co.

AMERICAN (2)/*USA 1910-1912*
The American Motor Truck Co, Detroit, Michigan, manufactured

an unusual 4-wheel drive, 4-wheel steer 5-tonner under the American and American Motor Truck brand names. Of forward-control layout, it had a 4-cyl petrol engine under the driver's 'seat, with chain-drive to both axles. This company was in no way connected with any other manufacturer of the same name.

AMERICAN (3)/*USA 1913-1918*
Another American Motor Truck Co, Detroit, Michigan, began with a 4-cyl, Continental-engined, 1-tonner with a wheelbase of 2.74m, a 3-speed Brown-Lipe gearbox and double-reduction rear axle. A 3½-tonner, with 4-speed Covert transmission and worm-drive, replaced it briefly from 1917.

AMERICAN (4)/*USA 1916-1917*
In Hartford, Connecticut, yet another American Motor Truck Co built a 2-tonner powered by a 4-cyl petrol engine. A 3-speed transmission, worm-drive rear axle and electric lighting and starting were other features.

AMERICAN CARRIER/*USA 1971 to date*
American Carrier Equipment, Fresno, California, supplied three, 100-passenger, open-top, double-deck buses to the Yosemite National Park in 1971. Fitted with 6-cyl Ford engines running on propane gas, these had fully-automatic Allison transmissions and have since been joined by others of similar type.

AMERICAN COLEMAN/*USA 1943-1949 & 1952 to date*
Marketed as American Coleman, specialist trucks built by the American Coleman Co, Littleton, Colorado, are known as Coleman, the name they carried when originally built by the Coleman Four Wheel Drive Co, from 1925 to

1943 in Denver, Colorado. When the firm was re-organized in 1943, production was concentrated upon the 4 x 4 G55A bonneted crane-carrier for the Armed Forces, manufacture of which continued until 1944. Other 4 x 4s were built after World War II but all activities were curtailed between 1949 and 1952 by a bitter labour dispute. Production resumed with a contract for 4-wheel drive 4-wheel steer 'Mule' aircraft towing tractors for the USAF. Since 1954, the company has concentrated on the conversion of other chassis makes to all-wheel drive with only one or two excursions into vehicle-building, most interesting of which was the 1968 'Space Star', a 4-wheel drive 4-wheel steer "cabover" tractor, with semi-trailer coupled rigidly to it. Remaining at prototype stage, this had a 318bhp Detroit Diesel V8, and in-built cab roll-bar and adjustable air suspension, allowing the floor to match varying loading heights. Other models are built to special order only and are popular as snow-clearance, road maintenance or aircraft towing vehicles.

AMERICAN COULTHARD/
USA 1905-1906
The Model 'K' 5-ton steam wagon of T Coulthard & Co Ltd, Preston, Lancs, formed the basis of the American Coulthard, built by the American Coulthard Co, Boston, Massachusetts. A number of these were also constructed by the Corwin Mfg Co of nearby Peabody. Also known as the Coulthard, it was a 30hp machine with 2-cyl compound engine and vertical boiler. By mid-1905 animosity towards steam propulsion had brought about the company's closure but production was continued briefly by the Vaughn Machine Co, also of Peabody.

AMERICAN EAGLE/USA
1911-1912
The American Eagle Motor Car Co, New York, offered a 1½-ton, 2.74-m wheelbase truck powered by a 25hp, 4-cyl petrol engine.

AMERICAN ELECTROMOBILE/USA 1906-1907
Built by the American Electromobile Co, Detroit, Michigan, this was a short-lived, battery-electric, 3-tonner sometimes referred to as the Electromobile.

AMERICAN LaFRANCE/USA
1905 to date
Founded in 1903, the American LaFrance Fire Engine Co, Elmira, New York State, began to experiment with steam and petrol propulsion, exhibiting its first self-propelled steam combination appliance at the 1905 Fire Chiefs' Conference. By 1909, petrol-engined appliances were becoming far more popular and the company fitted a specially designed 4-cyl Simplex petrol engine into a combination hose and chemical appliance, followed in 1910 by a petrol-engined combination which could operate at up to 80km/h. The company also attempted to develop its own 6-cyl petrol engine as well as a front-

1927 American LaFrance pumper and chemical engine fire appliance

drive conversion unit for horse-drawn equipment, known as the Type 31, and developed along the lines of the Front Drive Motor Co's Christie unit. This was in production until 1929 but a 5-ton commercial truck chassis, sometimes also referred to as a LaFrance, lasted for just four years. The company was re-formed in 1913 as the American LaFrance Fire Engine Co Inc, and in 1914 the firm's last steamer and first self-propelled hook and ladder truck were built. Known as the Type 16, the latter had a 10-m wheelbase in its longest form with rear steering controlled by a crew-

1955 American LaFrance '700'-Series pumper fire appliance

man seated high at the back. A DC petrol-electric drive system supplied power to four electric motors each mounted in a wheel. Four-wheel steering and braking were also featured. In 1915, S F Hayward & Co, one of the largest manufacturers of fire-fighting equipment in the USA, was taken over and by 1916, attempts to build a 6-cyl petrol engine had borne fruit, and a new range of 750, 900 and 1000gpm pumpers was shown at the Fire Chiefs' Convention. These had centrifugal, piston or gear pumps and were to form the backbone of the company's range until 1930, when the piston pump was discontinued. In the years after World War I the company undertook many experiments, including the use of Manly hydraulic and electric-drive systems. Commercial trucks were once again available but were now sold as LaFrance, production being transferred to Bloomfield, New Jersey, in 1923 as the American LaFrance Truck Co, before merging with the Republic Motor Truck Co Inc, Alma, Michigan, in 1929 to form the LaFrance-Republic Corp. Meantime, the rival Foamite-Childs Corp, Utica, New York State, manufacturer of the Kearns-Dughie-based Childs Thoroughbred appliance, had been taken over in 1927 and a new company – the American LaFrance & Foamite Corp – introduced the 4-wheel braked 'Master' series at

the 1929 Fire Chiefs' Convention. The American LaFrance-GMC Type 199 medium-duty appliance had now been introduced in association with General Motors and by 1931, a 240bhp V12 petrol engine had been announced, while pumpers were now available with capacities of up to 1500gpm. The V12 unit took the company into the role of engine supplier, this being used in certain Greyhound buses and Brockway trucks. The '400'-Series of 1933 featured a bevel-gear rear axle in place of chain-drive and a new parallel-series 2-stage pump. Another landmark in 1933 was two special pumpers ordered by the New York Fire Dept, each capable of delivering 250gpm to the top of the Empire State Building through a 4-stage pump with a discharge pressure of 600psi. In 1938 four special pumpers were produced, each with two V12 engines – one for motive power and front-mounted pumping, the other solely for the rear pump – for Los Angeles. These were 'Metropolitan Duplex Pumpers' and were the most powerful pumpers built by anyone before World War II. In 1941 the country's first 38-m aerial ladder of bonneted articulated layout went to Boston, Massachusetts, while 1938 had seen the first forward-cabbed aerial ladders and the streamlined '500'-Series firefighter with 3-man cab. Appliance manufacture continued through-

out World War II, culminating in 1945 with the introduction of the 'Tripleflow' pump with ball-bearing mounting of the impeller and the first full range of appliances, known as the '700'-Series, with cab ahead of engine. By 1950 the USAF had ordered its first specialist, airfield fire crash tenders, these being the 0-10 and 0-11 models with remote-controlled roof-mounted foam turrets. The '800'-Series, with new 'Twinflow' pump, replaced the '700' in 1956, followed in 1958 by the re-styled '900'-Series, and in 1960 by three gas turbine-powered machines marketed as the 'Turbo-Chief'. This machine was not successful and all three were converted to petrol. A new range of airfield fire crash trucks, based on 4 x 4 versions of the '900'-Series, soon entered production, and the first mobile aerial platform designed specifically for fire service use was introduced. In 1964 the square-cabbed 'Pioneer' pumper was anounced, and 2-stroke diesel engines were made available from 1965, and in 1966 the company became a division of A-T-O Inc. In 1968 the first 'Ladder Chief' rear-mounted aerial ladder on a rigid, 4-wheeled chassis and a 2000gpm '900'-Series pumper with 'Twinflow' pump powered by a V8 diesel appeared. The '1000'-Series, with 2-stroke diesels as standard, arrived in 1970 and in 1973 was joined by the 'Century' range of pumpers, aerial ladders and snorkel units of 4 x 2 and 6 x 4 layouts.

AMERICAN LaFRANCE-GMC/USA 1928-?
The Buick-engined, American LaFrance-GMC Type 199, medium-duty fire appliance for use as a chemical engine, hose wagon or pumper, was built by the American LaFrance & Foamite Corp, Elmira, New York State, in collaboration with General Motors.

AMERICAN MOTOR BUS/USA 1920-1923
A re-organization of the Chicago

Motor Bus Co, operator and builder of passenger vehicles, led to the formation of the American Motor Bus Co to handle vehicle-building. In 1922 the company constructed 23 fully-enclosed double-deckers followed by a prototype open-top 67-seater, of which 71 were subsequently built before the business was transferred to the Yellow Coach Mfg Co.

AMERICAN PANHARD/USA 1918-1919
The Hamilton Motors Co, Grand Haven, Michigan, built 1-ton 'A' and 1½-ton 'B' trucks carrying the Panhard name on the radiator top tank, but to avoid confusion with imported French-built Panhards were sold as American Panhard. These were assembled trucks with 4-cyl Gray petrol engines, 3-speed Fuller transmissions and Torbensen rear axles. At the end of 1918 the company was re-named the Panhard Motors Co.

AMERICAN STEAM/USA 1912-1913
The American Steam Truck Co, Lansing, Michigan, developed a heavy haulage unit called the American Steam. It had an 8-cyl, quadruple-expansion engine producing 53hp from 300psi of steam.

AMO/Soviet Union 1924-1933
The first Soviet truck to be built after the Revolution, the AMO, was assembled in the Moscow plant of Automobilnoe Moskovskoe Obshchestvo, the first being the F-15 1500kg capacity model, with 4-cyl 35bhp engine, based on the Type 15 Fiat 1½-tonner. This was succeeded in 1931 by the 2500kg AMO-2 which was the first Soviet vehicle to employ hydraulic brakes. It was replaced by the AMO-3, a 2500kg capacity chassis, of more rugged construction, in 1932. One year later, the factory was re-named Zavod Imieni, and a few months later the AMO-3 became the ZIS-3, all subsequent types being produced as ZIS.

1939 American LaFrance artic aerial ladder truck fire appliance

AMOSKEAG/*USA 1867-1908*
The Amoskeag Mfg Co, Manchester, New Hampshire, was the most famous of all horse-drawn steam fire appliance manufacturers in the United States. It also built 22 heavy self-propelled steam pumpers, each using a vertical copper-tube boiler, 2-cyl horizontal engine, single chain final-drive, and 1450gpm pump. Apart from the use of double roller chains in later machines, the specification varied little.

ANDERSEN/*Denmark c1973-?*
It is believed that Albert Andersen's Maskinfabrik A/S, of Industrikvarter Nord, Svenstrup, constructed a series of commercials under the Andersen brand name, but little information can be found.

ANDERSON (1)/*USA 1909-1910*
This was an archaic light goods wagon built by the Anderson Carriage Mfg Co, Anderson, Indiana. It was a 1.78-m wheelbase high-wheeler with obsolete reach-frame and two 2-cyl petrol engines inter-connected by a planetary-drive system with double chain final-drive.

ANDERSON (2)/*USA 1909-1912*
The Anderson Coupling and Fire Supply Co specialized in the manufacture of fire-fighting equipment and is said to have built a number of appliances under the Anderson brand name.

ANDREAS/*Germany 1900-1901*
The unusual Andreas battery-electric delivery van was developed by Sachsische Accumulatorenwerke AG, Dresden, each of its front wheels being driven by a separate electric motor, with bogie steering effected by altering the speed of one or other of the motors.

ANGLO-DANE/*Denmark 1903-1918*
Light- and heavy-duty Anglo-Dane trucks were built by H C Frederikson & Son, Copenhagen, before the company merged with Automobilfabbriken Thrige, Odense, to form Die Forenede Automobili Fabriken A/S, manufacturer of Triangel commercials.

ANNIS/*England 1958-1959*
Heavy hauliers Annis & Co Ltd, Hayes, Middlesex, constructed two special 6 x 4 tractors based on Diamond T Model 980 6 x 4 tractor chassis with Gardner 8LW diesel engines. The first retained its original ballast box body but received a coachbuilt cab and 'ANNIS' radiator. The second was intended for extra heavy loads, having a crew-cab taken from a Foden

heavy haulage outfit and a specially constructed ballast box body.

ANSAIR/*Australia 1958 to date*
Ansair 'Transette' rear-engined city and inter-city buses were announced by Ansair Pty Ltd, North Essendon, Victoria, using 83bhp Perkins diesel or 103bhp US-built,

1958 Annis 6 x 4

Ford V8 petrol engines. In 1960, the company entered into an agreement with the Flxible Co, of America, to build the latter's 'Clipper' model as the Ansair-Flxible until 1965. And new rear-engined Ansair, known as the 'Scenicruiser', replaced the 'Transette' in the late 1960s.

ANSAIR-FLXIBLE/*Australia 1960-1965*
Following agreement between Ansair Pty Ltd, North Essendon, Victoria, manufacturer of Ansair passenger vehicles, and the Flxible Co, of America, the 'Clipper' passenger model was assembled under licence at the North Essendon plant, as the Ansair-Flxible.

ANSALDO (1)/*Italy 1930-1932*
A 2-ton truck introduced by Ansaldo Automobili, Turin, had a 4-cyl petrol engine common to certain passenger cars, while a 3-tonner was powered by a 4.9-litre 6-cyl petrol unit. Both had 4-speed transmissions and double-reduction axles.

ANSALDO (2)/*Italy c1946-1949*
SA Italiano Giovani Ansaldo e Cia, Genoa, was a descendent of the previous firm, introducing single-deck trolleybuses under the same name.

ANSBACH/*Germany 1906-1918, 1926-1930*
Founded in 1906, Fahrzeugfabrik Ansbach GmbH, Ansbach, built trucks up to 6 tons capacity until 1918 when they merged with Nürnberger Feuerloschgerate und Fahrzeug-Fabrik Karl Schmidt and all subsequent models became

known as Faun. This arrangement ended in 1926 when the former Ansbach factory was re-named Fahrzeugfabrik Ansbach AG and the old name re-appeared on a number of Faun trucks, a Maybach-engined passenger model also being introduced. Later, the Faun name was re-introduced.

APE CAR/*Italy 1973 to date*
Soc Piaggio, Genoa already built light scooter-based Ape commercials when it introduced the 1½-ton Ape Car. This has an enclosed 2-man cab, rubber swing-arm suspension at the rear, and wheel steering. It is also built under licence in Yugoslavia.

APEX/*USA 1918-1921*
As well as the American Panhard range, the Hamilton Motors Co, Grand Haven, Michigan, built 1-, 1½- and 2½-ton Apex trucks, with 3-speed Fuller transmissions and Torbensen rear axles.

ARBENZ/*Switzerland 1904-1928*
The first Arbenz truck was a 14/16hp 2-cyl petrol-engined 1½-tonner built by Motorwagenfabrik Eugen Arbenz & Cie, Zurich, an example of which was shown at the 1905 Olympia Show under the Straker-McConnell name. Numerous chain-drive goods and passenger models were soon offered, using 2- or 4-cyl petrol engines of between 12 and 40hp. The company was re-formed as Arbenz AG in 1907. The first shaft-drive Arbenz was a 30hp 4-cyl petrol engined 3-tonner launched in 1913. Production rocketed during World War I but declined immediately after, leading to the company's collapse in 1922. A year later Oetiker & Cie took the company over, still building vehicles under the Arbenz name. In 1924 3-ton shaft- and 5-ton chain-drive models were announced, followed by new 4-cyl engined, 3-, 4- and 5-tonners in 1927. After 1928 models were sold under the name of Oetiker.

ARGO/*USA 1911-1917*
Argo shaft-drive battery-electric, 1-tonners were built by the Argo Electric Vehicle Co, Saginaw, Michigan, until 1914 when the company merged with the Borland-Grannis Co and the Broc Carriage & Wagon Co to form the American Electric Car Co, continuing to build vehicles under the Argo brand name.

ARGOSY/*USA 1976 to date*
The Argosy Mfg Co, Versailles, Ohio, offers 7.3- and 7.6-m Argosy midibuses for capacities of between 25 and 29 seated passengers, for use in areas where normal-capacity vehicles are uneconomical.

ARGUS/*Germany 1902-1910*
Argus 6-cyl light- and medium-weight goods and passenger models were built by Internat Automobil-Centrale KG Jeannin & Co, Berlin. In 1907 the company became Argus Motoren Gesselschaft Jeannin & Co KG.

ARGYLE/*Scotland 1970-c1973*
The Argyle Motor Mfg Co Ltd was registered in 1968 by Argyle Diesel Electronics Ltd, East Kilbride, Lanarks, to manufacture a 16-ton GVW rigid goods model called the 'Christina', aimed exclusively at Scottish operators, using the company's own chassis frame, a Perkins 6.354 diesel engine and a Motor Panels cab. The 'Christina' also had a single-dry plate Borg & Beck clutch, 5-speed Eaton gearbox, 2-speed Eaton bevel-and-pinion rear axle, and a Kirkstall front axle. Later, this 5.28-m wheelbase load-carrier was joined by a 3.8-m wheelbase tipper version, while plans were drawn up for an articulated model to be known as the 'Linsay' and a 24-ton GVW 6-wheeler called the 'Karen', but neither saw the light of day. In 1973 a giant solid-tyred molten steel hauler called the 'Trilby' was delivered to the British Steel Corp for use in South Wales, making this the only non-Scottish customer for the Argyle. Capable of hauling 120 tons, this had a Cummins diesel engine.

ARGYLL/*Scotland 1906-1914*
A product of Argyll Motors Ltd, Glasgow, the Argyll was listed as a forward- or normal-control truck with a payload of 1½ to 3 tons, a 4-cyl Aster petrol engine and worm-drive and joined one year later by a 1-tonner fitted with a 2.2-litre 2-cyl petrol engine. By 1910 an unusual 3-cyl goods model with automatic inlet valves and a side-valve exhaust was listed. This had a semi-hydraulic Hele-Shaw clutch connected to a 3-

1970 Argyle 'Christina' truck

speed sliding gate-change transmission.

From 1911, Argyll fire appliances were fitted as standard with a massive 85hp, 13.3-litre, 6-cyl petrol engine which had dual ignition and a pneumatic starting mechanism

ARIES/*France 1904-1934*
The first Ariès goods model was a forward-control, 2.4-litre, 2-cyl engined 3-tonner built by SA Ariès, Courbevoie, Seine. It had a timber frame, cone clutch, 3-speed transmission and chain-drive, models of this type continuing for nearly ten years but joined in 1910 by a bonneted 3-tonner, with 3.8-litre Aster petrol engine and 4-speed box, some 3000 of which were delivered to the French Armed Forces. This, and a 4.7-litre 5/7-tonner, remained on the company's lists until 1930, joined in 1926 by a 40bhp, 6-tonner which also sold briefly in the UK. Specification included a 4-cyl petrol engine, separate 4-speed box, chain-drive and also a wood-lined, hand-actuated band brake.

ARMLEDER/*USA 1909-1936*
The Otto Armleder Co, Cincinnati, Ohio, turned from horse-drawn wagons to self-propelled trucks in 1909, early models being offered in capacities of up to 136lkg, but by 1917 a 3½-tonner was also listed. Most were assembled designs with Buda, Continental or Hercules petrol engines, Timken worm-and-bevel axles and Brown-Lipe transmissions. Six-cyl engines were introduced in 1927. In 1928 the Armleder Truck Co, as it was then known, was acquired by the LeBlond-Schacht Truck Co, also of Cincinnati, and gradually the Armleder was merged with Schacht production, some of the former being sold as Schacht while others continued as Armleder.

ARMSTRONG-SAURER/*England 1931-1937*
In 1931, Sir W G Armstrong-Whitworth & Co Ltd took over

1934 Armstrong-Saurer 'Samson'

manufacture under licence of the Swiss Saurer truck range, establishing Armstrong-Saurer Commercial Vehicles Ltd, Newcastle-upon-Tyne, to assemble these and develop new models for the UK market. The first were displayed at the 1931 Commercial Motor Show, comprising 4- and 6-wheeled rigid chassis with petrol or diesel engines. By 1933 only 6-cyl diesel vehicles were listed, ranging from the 4 x 2 'Defiant' to the 12-ton 6-wheeled 'Dominant', which had a pressed-steel rear bogie conforming to UK weight restrictions. The 'Dominant' was replaced by the lightweight, 8-ton payload 'Dynamic' 4-wheeler in 1933. Later, this was joined by the 'Active' 4-wheeler for 7/8-ton payloads and the 'Effective' 4-wheeler for drawbar work. Passenger models were not listed, so the company gave Dennis Bros sole rights to fit Armstrong-Saurer diesels in theirs. Most famous of all Armstrong-Saurers, however, was the 22-ton GVW 'Samson' rigid 8-wheeler, announced in 1934. This was very advanced,

having a full air braking system acting on all wheels, and a fully-floating double-reduction spiral-bevel third axle with trailing fourth, drive being via a 4-speed crash box with optional 2-speed auxiliary. In 1935 the company began experimenting with an unusual dual-turbulance 3.62-litre diesel engine with the intention of fitting this in a medium weight truck. Additional finance was needed if this was to be successful, but none was forthcoming and the company went out of business.

ARMSTRONG-SIDDELEY-PAVESI/*England 1927-1932*
Armstrong Siddeley Motors Ltd, Coventry, built a 4-wheel drive, heavy road tractor to Italian Pavesi design under the name of Armstrong-Siddeley-Pavesi. It had a 4-cyl, air-cooled, Armstrong-Siddeley petrol engine and an articulat-

1931 Armstrong-Saurer 'Defiant'

ed frame for steering. In 1930 another Pavesi design was converted to 8 x 8 drive with dual tyres for military and other cross-country applications.

ARMSTRONG-WHITWORTH/*England 1906-1914*
Sir W G Armstrong of Whitworth & Co Ltd, Newcastle-upon-Tyne, embarked on bus construction with chassis specially ordered by Motor Omnibus Construction Ltd, North-East London, a bus-building subsidiary of the London Motor Omnibus Co. Sir W G Armstrong was a director of both the Newcastle firm and the London Motor Omnibus Co, supplying not only a number of finished Armstrong-Whitworth chassis, but also a quantity of other components so that Motor Omnibus Construction Ltd could assemble its own vehicles under the MOC brand name. Specifications for both the Armstrong-Whitworth and the MOC were therefore strikingly similar, the former having a 4-cyl 32hp petrol engine, 4-speed gearbox and chain-drive. Unfortunately, Motor Omnibus Construction Ltd did not need all the chassis ordered so that the excess were disposed of as 4-ton goods chassis and some used by Sir W G Armstrong, Whitworth & Co Ltd itself. Further batches were built in 1910, some being sold to the Lowcock Commercial Motor Co, Manchester, who resold them under the Locomo or Lowcock names. By 1912 dual-ignition had been introduced and a car-based 1-tonner was built for a short time from 1913.

ARO/*Rumania 1966 to date*
Previously known as the MICM, the ARO was built by Uzina Mecanica Muscel, at Muscel, Cimpa-lung. Up to 1970 production was concentrated on a Soviet-designed 4 x 4 utility, but then the 240 was announced. This had an 80bhp, 4-cyl petrol engine, an auxiliary gearbox and coil front suspension. Examples are sold in numerous countries, often under a different name. In Portugal it is known as the Portaro, whilst in the UK it is sold as the Tudor. Recently many components common to the TV, which is another Rumanian-built 4 x 4, have been included in the specification.

1934 Arran 'Dieselet'

ARRAN/*England 1934-1937*

The Arran 'Dieselet' bonneted 4-tonner launched by Arran Motors Ltd, Welwyn Garden City, Herts was one of the UK's first medium-weight trucks powered by a diesel engine. Features included a 48hp Perkins 'Wolf' power unit, a spiral-bevel rear axle, hydraulic brakes and a 4-speed box. It was soon joined by a forward-control version with a larger 4-litre Perkins and by 1936 a 7½-tonner with 4-cyl Gardner and a petrol-engined 4-tonner with 3.5-litre, 6-cyl Austin engine were also listed. In 1937 the company was bought out by Wm Hurlock Jnr Ltd, London SW9, who moved production to its own plant. A few more Arrans were built, but the last two trucks were called HACs.

ARROL-JOHNSTON/*Scotland 1905-1915*

The first true Arrol-Johnston commercial was a 12hp chain-drive 2-ton van exhibited at the Crystal Palace in 1905, by the Mo-Car Syndicate Ltd, Glasgow. The same engine was used in a fleet of 16-seat charabancs supplied to a Fleetwood operator later that year, and the company was quickly re-organized as the New Arrol-Johnston Car Co Ltd. Commercials of up to 3 tons capacity were now listed, powered by 16 or 20hp 3-cyl petrol engines, another new model being a bus chassis with a 5.1-litre 24hp 4-cyl petrol engine with magneto ignition located alongside the driver. Although cars were the company's main product, various new commercials continued to appear. Amongst these was a special load-carrying vehicle for Sir Ernest Shackleton's Antarctic Expedition of 1908, using a 12/15hp, Simms 4-cyl, overhead-valve vertical, air-cooled petrol engine, one set of wooden and one of pneumatic tyres, detachable skis for the front wheels, a snow-melter box over the exhaust and a special non-freeze oil. By the end of 1908 models of 1 to 5

capacity were listed and in 1909 vertical engines became standard. Both single- and double-deck buses were built, including a number for the Great Eastern Railway, but by 1911 the only commercial was a light delivery van and in 1913 production moved to Heathhall, Dumfries, and the company was re-named Arrol-Johnston Ltd. The last Arrol-Johnston truck was a 2½/3-tonner with 3.7-litre, 4-cyl petrol engine.

ARROW/*USA c1964 to date*

The Arrow Mfg Co, Denver, Colorado, specializes in the design and construction of terminal tractors with one-man, half-cabs and lifting fifth wheel couplings for handling a variety of semi-trailers.

A S (1)/*France 1926-1933*

Ets Paul Lavigne, Marseilles, constructed AS goods models until production was transferred to Courbevoie, Seine, and models re-named Lavigne.

A S (2)/*Netherlands 1928-1939 & c1948-1969*

Nederlandsche Automobielfabriek Schmidt NV Amsterdam imported US-built Republic trucks and buses until 1927 when it realized that a home-built equivalent could be sold at a lower price. The first of these, known as the AS, appeared the following year, its specification being similar to the original Republic. It was offered with Continental, Hercules, or Lycoming petrol engines, Timken axles and Spicer transmissions. In 1932 a forward-control, diesel-engined truck, powered by what was claimed to be one of the first Cummins diesel engines fitted in a European vehicle, was announced but no trucks were built during World War II. Production got underway again in the late 1940s, although on a much smaller scale than before. By the 1960s vehicles were built only to special order.

ATKINSON (1)/*England 1916-1970*

Atkinson & Co, Preston, Lancs, sold Alley & McLellan's 'Sentinel' wagon until this company moved to Shrewsbury and took over its own sales. Not to be beaten, the Preston firm designed its own wagon, incorporating the best features of the 'Sentinel' and other types it had experience of, as a steam wagon repairer. The first was a 6-ton "undertype" with a vertical boiler containing inclined water tubes, expanded rather than screwed into position, and with a 2-section boiler shell. A tubular superheater and a 2-cyl compound engine were also used, and speed and power were regulated by a steam throttle. By 1919 a Stumpf-type "uniflow" engine was fitted, admitting steam through ball valves at one end of the cylinder and exhausting at the other. A site at nearby Frenchwood was taken over at the end of World War I to build what was

1920 Atkinson (1) Type 6T "undertype"

now known as the 'Uniflow' wagon, incorporating 2-speed epicyclic gearing. The 'Uniflow' range covered capacities from 5 to 8 tons by 1920, but was joined in 1921 by an uneconomical 2½-tonner with mechanical stoking and in 1923 by a 12-ton artic – making the Atkinson range the largest available from any British manufacturer at that time. By 1924 the company was also building municipal equipment to boost sales but much of the workforce had to be laid off and in 1925 a loan from engineers Walker Bros (Wigan) Ltd, manufacturer of Pagefield vehicles, provided capital to finance new model development and led to new work for the Wigan firm's machine shops. As a result, Atkinson-Walker Waggons Ltd was founded. Under Walker's influence, light railway locomotives went into production but competition was fierce and in another attempt at a revival the company

purchased the remains of the Leyland Motor Co Ltd's steam interests in 1926, but this only served as another nail in the coffin. In 1927 a new 6-wheeled model was pipped at the post by a 'Sentinel' of similar design and by 1928 serious wagon production had come to an end, and only a few railway locos and steam plants kept the company in business. The following year a few wagons of Mann design were assembled using spares acquired from the old Mann Patent Steam Cart Co, Leeds, but later that year, unable to return Walker Bros' financial hospitality, Atkinson-Walker Waggons Ltd returned to the original Preston premises where it again took up wagon repair. A receiver was appointed in 1930 and three local businessmen acquired an interest in the firm, which now became Atkinson & Co Ltd. Axle conversion work was now the company's speciality but in 1931 it was announced that vehicle production was to resume with a range of oil-engined trucks. Three prototypes – a bonneted Dorman-engined 6-ton 4-wheeler, a forward-control Blackstone-engined 6-tonner and a similarly-engined 12-ton 6-wheeler – were constructed in 1932 and within a year Atkinson Lorries (1933) Ltd had been formed, production being transferred to a new plant in 1935. The company was soon standardizing on Gardner engines, David Brown gearboxes and Kirkstall axles, and an entirely new range of 4-wheeled 7- and 7½-tonners and 6-wheeled 10- and 12-tonners was announced. Even the new factory had limited facilities, however, and only six vehicles were built in 1935, the grand total up to the outbreak of war being fifty trucks, including some 15-ton 8-wheelers introduced from 1937. World War II brought the company its largest orders so far, comprising sixty Gardner-engined 6-

1954 Atkinson (1) PL745H

wheelers for the Ministry of Supply in 1940, 100 more in 1941 and 100 8-wheelers at about the same time. The sheer size of these orders resulted in the last 200 vehicles having 7.7-litre AEC engines instead of Gardners. Peacetime brought new enthusiasm. Gardner engines were in short supply as were David Brown boxes, so in 1946 the company announced its own 5-speed box. By 1948 the company had moved to Walton-le-dale, near Preston, where the same basic range was built. The Gardner-engined 'Alpha' passenger chassis appeared in 1952 and in 1954 the company was re-registered as Atkinson Vehicles Ltd. A year later two double-deck bus chassis were built. In 1957 the bonneted 'Omega' on/off-highway heavy haulage tractor was announced, the first being a 100-ton 6 x 6 with 275bhp Rolls-Royce diesel engine, followed by four examples with Cummins and supercharged Rolls-Royce diesels of up to 335bhp output. Other specialist types included both 4- and 6-wheeled Cummins-engined half-cab dump trucks called the 'Hy-Lode', a few 8 x 6 gritter/snow-ploughs and a subsequent fleet of some 400 6 x 6 gritter/snow-

been developed in association with Pickfords Heavy Haulage Ltd for operation at 25 tons GCW, followed by a heavier 6-wheeled version in 1963, the same year that normal haulage models were optionally available without exposed radiators. In 1964 the 'Guardsman' cab was advertised for use on Cummins V8-engined tractors, while a speciality of the company's overseas subsidiaries was a 300bhp Rolls-Royce engined 100-ton heavy haulage tractor based loosely on full-width cab versions of the 6-wheeled dump truck chassis. In 1966 a Perkins V8-engined low-line crane-carrier

el, brought about by changes in UK Construction and Use Regulations, was the 6-wheeled 'Leader' tractor, one of the first British commercials to be powered by Gardner's 8LXB 8-cyl diesel. Also at the Show was the very last bonneted 'Omega' – a 100-ton heavy haulage machine for Pickfords. A series of takeover bids by ERF Ltd and Fodens Ltd in 1970 failed to find favour with shareholders but placed the company in a most vulnerable position. A further bid, by Seddon Diesel Vehicles Ltd, was accepted and later that year the Walton-le-Dale operation became Seddon's Atkinson Divn. New models were well overdue and the parent company developed an entirely new range which was shown both at Brussels and Earls Court, soon after the new company's takeover by International Harvester, as the Seddon, but re-named the Seddon-Atkinson for its production launch. Although patriotic Atkinson operators regularly fitted the familiar Atkinson motif to this model, there were no more true Atkinsons.

1959 Atkinson (1) 8 x 4

ploughs for the Ministry of Transport and for its successor, the Dept of Transport. By 1958 the 4-, 6- and 8-wheeled general haulage range had a fibreglass cab with wrap-round screens, AEC, Cummins, Gardner and Rolls-Royce diesel engines being specially popular, although Perkins units were used in the lighter models. Other changes included optional 2F gearboxes and a few Fuller units, plus one or two examples of the Detroit Diesel engine, even on the home market. By 1962 a semi-bonneted 4-wheeled tractor had

and the amazing 'Viewline' cab on a double-drive tractor chassis appeared at the Commercial Motor Show. This was to prove popular

1964 Atkinson (1) T 3048C

1950 Atkinson (1) 6 x 4

only on 4- and 6-wheeled heavy haulage tractors. By 1967 the company's first production 6-wheeled twin-steer tractors, with air-sprung second steering axle just ahead of the drive axle, had also been launched. The 1968 Commercial Motor Show saw 4 x 2 tractors named 'Borderer', 6-wheeled rigids 'Searcher' and 8-wheelers 'Defender'. A new mod-

ATKINSON (2)/*Netherlands*
1969
Using cabs purchased from the discontinued lorry-building activities of the German Krupp empire, NV Atkinson Vehicles (Europe) SA briefly marketed a range of 4- and 6-wheeled tractors based on the standard Atkinson chassis in Holland and also in the Benelux countries.

Atkinson (1) 'Borderer' c1973

ASEA/*Sweden 1927 to date*
Allemaenna Svenska Elektriska AB, of Vasteras, built Asea trolley-buses, using numerous Volvo components. By 1939 the first Scania-Vabis trolleybuses also used Asea equipment which was standard for such models until the 1950s. Current Asea models comprise both medium- and heavy-duty battery-electric goods vehicles built in a factory at Ludvika.

change of country boundaries in 1918, the company being renamed the Rumanian Wagon & Motor Factory Ltd. Previously building Marta trucks and buses under a licencing arrangement with Westinghouse of France, the plant introduced Astra commercials including fire trucks, trailer pumps, goods and passenger models. Larger designs had a 4-cyl German Bayer petrol engine and

Ashok Leyland 'Comet' c1971

ASHOK LEYLAND/*India 1948 to date*
Ashok Motors Ltd and its successor, Ashok Leyland Ltd, both of Ennore, Madras, have assembled trucks and buses based on outdated Leyland models for some years. These are sold as Ashok Leyland, incorporate cabs and bodies of local design, and are specially engineered to cope with local requirements. One of the most popular current models for general haulage work is the 'Comet', long since discontinued in the UK. Other types include a 4 x 4 military derivative and the 6 x 4 'Hippo'.

ASTRA (1)/*Rumania 1918-c1940*
The factory of Magyar Automobil RT, Arad, Transylvania, found itself in Rumania following a

smaller types an Astra-built 32bhp unit. The city of Arad became the city of Brasov after World War II and in 1954, as Uzina Steagul Rosu, the same factory introduced the SR truck range.

ASTRA (2)/*Italy 1954 to date*
Founded in 1946 to recondition war-surplus vehicles, Astra Costruzioni Veicoli Speciali, of Piacenza, became the Italian concessionaire for Detroit Diesel engines and Allison transmissions in 1952, introducing its first dump trucks in 1954 featuring both products. Later re-named Astra SpA, the company now uses Detroit Diesel, Fiat and Mercedes-Benz engines of up to 465bhp in a range of heavy-duty, 4 x 4, 6 x 4 and 6 x 6 on- and off-highway trucks of up to 38 tons GVW.

AUSTIN (1)/*England 1910-1968*
The Austin Motor Co Ltd's first true commercial was a unique prototype which employed two propeller shafts to achieve a loading height of just 74cm, each shaft transmitting the drive from a common differential behind the 4-speed gearbox via lattice-section sidemembers to each rear wheel, the rear axle being "dead". The 20hp, 4-cyl 'T'-head engine with individual cylinder pots bolted to a cast-aluminium crankcase was angled down towards the rear, thereby keeping the crankshaft in

1950 Austin (1) 'Loadstar' K4 Series II

line with the shafts, while the radiator was located behind the engine and a distinctive "coal-scuttle" bonnet fitted. Other interesting features included dual springing, centrally-positioned gear-change, and complete lack of front dumbirons. World War I led to some 2000 twin-shaft Austins joining the Armed Forces between 1914 and 1917 but numerous mechanical problems brought about its downfall. By September 1917 a number of modifications had been made, but although a 3½-ton twin-shaft was announced in 1919, the problems were never overcome and until 1922 the company was still tying to dispose of its stock. As well as the 3½-ton twin-shaft, 1919 also saw the launch of Austin's first agricultural tractor, also offered as a road haulage machine in 1925 with solid rubber tyres, engine, side panels and other road-going features. To overcome French import levies, a road haulage version was also built in a new tractor plant at Liancourt, Paris. The only true Austin commercial in 1924 was a solid-tyred, 1½-ton worm-drive model based on the 20bhp car of 1919, but from then until 1932 only light car-derived commercials were built. Shortly before World War II the company announced a 26-seat passenger chassis and load-carriers for payloads of between 1½ and 3 tons. These were the first Austins with 3.5-litre, 6-cyl petrol engines re-

maining in modified 4-litre form until the very end of heavy truck production. World War II saw the company again catering for the military, producing 115,000 4- and 6-wheeled lorries, including hundreds of auxiliary towing vehicles, based on the pre-war K2 1½-tonner. Because of styling similarities, this was often referred to as the "Birmingham Bedford". There were also the 3-ton K3 4 x 2 and K6 6 x 4 and the 3-ton K5 4 x 4 which did not appear until 1945 and was thus produced in only small numbers. Peacetime saw the

debut of the famous 1¼-ton 'Three-Way Loader' in 1946, quickly joined by a new 5-tonner. Meanwhile, the company had acquired a 50% interest in the battery-electric vehicle business of A E Morrison & Sons in 1948. In 1950 the bonneted Series II 'Loadstar' range of 2-, 3- and 5-tonners with 3-man cabs was announced, joined in 1952 by a 4 x 4, 1-ton variant, in March 1955 by Series III forward-control, 3- and 5-tonners and by a 4-tonner in 1956. From 1952 most Austin commercials could also be had as BMCs following the merger of the Austin Motor Co Ltd and the Nuf-

1966 Austin (2) 'VA'-Series

field Organization (Morris & Morris-Commercial) to form the British Motor Corp. Commercial rationalization occured quickly under this arrangement, normal-control models being based on Austin designs and forward-con-

1965 Austin (2) FG K150

trol types on Morris-Commercials. A new series of BMC diesel engines from a 3.4-litre, 58bhp, 4-cyl to a 5.1-litre, 90bhp 6-cyl unit was available and an entirely new model, the 701 7-tonner (later known as the 'FF'-Series), appeared in 1957. In 1959 the strange 'FG', 2-, 3- and 4-ton models for multi-stop delivery work were introduced (this series was still listed by Leyland Vehicles Ltd in 1979). A new truck factory was opened at Bathgate, West Lothian, in 1961 and all commercial vehicle production with the exception of certain light and car-derived models, transferred there. In 1967 the 1.1-ton 250JU, marketed as Austin or Morris, replaced Morris' old forward-control LD van range. In 1968, at the instigation of Prime Minister Harold Wilson, the British Motor Corp was merged with the Leyland Motor Corp to form the British Leyland Motor Corp Ltd. Light- and mediumweight commercials were re-named Austin-Morris.

AUSTIN (2)/*Scotland 1961-1968*
A new truck factory, opened by the British Motor Corp Ltd at Bathgate, West Lothian, in 1961 enabled production of all Austin and Morris commercials, apart from light and car-derived models, to be transferred there on a badge-engineered basis as Austin, Morris or BMC. The early 1960s saw the introduction of the forward-control 'FH'-Series, an improved version of the old 'FF', using an inclined underfloor engine, and in 1965 it was joined by a tilt-

cab successor, the 'FJ', with 5-speed transmission, air-hydraulic brakes and air-assisted handbrake. This was also the first Austin to have optional power-steering. The merging of the British Motor Corp Ltd and Leyland Motor Corp to form the British Leyland Motor Corp Ltd in 1968 led to the re-naming of the Scottish-built range as Leyland, Leyland Redline and Leyland Scotland.

AUSTIN (3)/*Turkey 1968 to date*
Using bonneted 'WE'-Series Austin trucks, the BMC Sanayi ve Ticaret AS tractor factory, İzmir, is still building trucks, using a locally-designed, angular, all-steel cab and 105 or 120bhp BMC diesel engines. Other types are built under the Morris name.

AUSTIN-ELECTRICAR/*England 1948-1968*
The Austin Motor Co Ltd acquired a 50% interest in the battery-electric vehicle business of A E Morrison & Sons, South Wigston, Leics, in 1948, forming Austin Crompton Parkinson Electric Vehicles Ltd. Models continued to be sold as Morrison-Electricar except those for export, which were marketed as Austin-Electricar, until the merger of the British Motor Corp Ltd with the Leyland Motor Corp Ltd resulted in models being known as Crompton Leyland Electricar or Morrison-Electricar.

AUSTIN-MORRIS/*England 1970-c1978*
The formation of the British Leyland Motor Corp Ltd in 1968 led to the founding of British Leyland (Austin-Morris) Ltd two years later, assembling light commercials at Longbridge, Birmingham. Previously marketed as Austin, Morris or BMC, these included the 250JU and EA ranges. In 1977 the company became the Austin-Morris Divn of British Leyland (UK) Ltd.

AUSTIN UTILITY COACH/*USA 1933-1934*
Early in the 1930s, Dwight E Austin, of the Pickwick Corp's bus-building division, patented an angled drive system that made use of a transverse rear engine far more practical than it had been. The Pickwick Motor Coach Works went into receivership in 1932, so Austin opened his own Austin System business in El Segundo, California, developing the Austin Utility Coach – a 21-seat transit bus – using his earlier patent. Few were built, as in 1934 Austin joined the Yellow Truck & Coach Mfg Co of Pontiac, Michigan, taking his patent with him.

1944 Austin (1) K6

ATCO/*USA 1920-1923*
The American Truck & Trailer Corp, Kankakee, Illinois, developed the 2-ton Atco truck with 4-cyl Buda petrol engine, 3-speed gearbox and worm final-drive. A 1-tonner soon joined it, both models being re-rated briefly as 1½- and 2½-tonners before production ceased.

ATKEY-GIMSON/*England 1905-1908*
A R Atkey & Co Ltd, Nottingham, designed a truck, construction of which was sub-contracted to Gimson & Co, from 1905. Thus, it was marketed as the Atkey-Gimson, the first example being a 24hp 3-cyl model running on petrol or kerosene and equipped with a 4-speed transmission, and chain- and gear-drive. A new model, with 30hp, 4-cyl petrol engine, was announced in 1907 but few were built.

ATLANTIC/*USA 1912-1921*
The first Atlantic battery-electrics were 3½- and 5-tonners built by the Atlantic Electric Vehicles Co, Newark, New Jersey, the smallest having a range of up to 96km per charge and the largest having 44 cells of lead-acid batteries. By 1914, 1- and 2-tonners had also been developed, both having chain final-drive. By 1921, 1-, 2-, 3½-, 5- and 6½-ton models were also listed.

ATLAS (1)/*USA 1905-1913*
The Knox Motor Truck Co, Springfield, Massachusetts, was an offshoot of the Knox Automobile Co, and as such also marketed its trucks under the Knox brand name. To avoid confusion, the Knox Motor Truck Co's products were re-named Atlas, the first being a 2.44-m wheelbase Type 'A' 2-tonner with 24hp 2-cyl petrol engine and shaft-drive. This was joined by the 3-ton Type 'B' of 2.89-m wheelbase and in 1907 by the 1½-ton Type 'C' and a passenger version called the Type 'D'.

ATLAS (2)/*England 1910*
This Atlas was a 3-ton bus or lorry chassis, with 30hp, 4-cyl petrol engine, built by Martins Motors Ltd, North London. It had a flitch-plated ash frame, semi-elliptic leaf springs and an overhead-worm axle. A pressed-steel engine sump incorporated a pressed-metal grid supporting the crankshaft.

ATLAS (3)/*USA 1912*
The Atlas Motor Car Co, Springfield, Massachusetts, briefly built a 2-ton delivery van. There appears to be no connection between this and the previous entry even though the name is the same.

ATLAS (4)/*USA 1920-1923*
Developed from a range of light delivery vehicles built by its predecessor, the Martin Truck & Body Co, York, Pennsylvania, the Buda-engined Atlas 1-tonner was built by the Martin Parry Corp. Later in 1920 this firm was again re-organized, this time as the Atlas Motor Truck Co, introducing a new 2-tonner in 1922 when the original Atlas was withdrawn. By the end of that year the company had merged with the Selden Motor Vehicle Co to form the Industrial Motors Corp.

ATTERBURY/*USA 1910-1935*
The Buffalo Auto-Car Mfg Co, Buffalo, New York State, was re-named the Atterbury Motor Car Co, offering a series of bonneted trucks in 1-, 2-, 3- and 5-ton capacities, the heaviest of which was chain-driven. All had 4-cyl Continental petrol engines, Brown-Lipe transmissions and Timken axles. Lycoming engines were offered from 1926, when the 26-B, a 6-cyl, 1/1¼-tonner also known as the 'Speedy Six', was introduced. A new 1½/2-tonner called the 'Highway Express Junior', with a wheelbase of 3.68 or 4.06m, 6-cyl petrol engine and 2-wheel brakes, was announced in 1928. It was joined the following year by a new 26-G with single-piece screen, 2-wheel braking and vacuum booster, also known as the 'Silver Anniversary' model. By 1930 all types were powered by 6-cyl Lycoming or Continental petrol engines, while capacities ranged from 1 to 4 tons. After 1931 the range included models from 2 to 5 tons capacity.

ATTILA/*England 1905*
The Attila, or Hunslet, was a 4-ton capacity, shaft-drive lorry built by the Hunslet Engine Co Ltd, Leeds, West Yorks, with a 3-cyl in-line engine of 20hp rating, providing a maximum speed of about 16km/h.

AUDI/*Germany 1913-c1918*
Audi Automobilwerke GmbH, Zwickau, built passenger cars and car-derived commercials along with a heavier truck which it supplied to the military during World War I. This had numerous car components but employed a more rugged chassis.

AULTMAN/*USA 1901-1902*
A few 5-ton steam wagons were built by the Aultman Co, Canton, Ohio. The design was most unusual, employing a 16hp twin-cyl engine, friction transmission and 4-wheel drive, the latter being effected by running double chains to the rear axle and shaft and bevel gears to the front.

1910 Atlas (2) 3-ton chassis

AUSTRO-DAIMLER/*Austria 1900-1920, c1935-c1942*
Oesterreichische Daimler-Motoren-Gesellschaft Bierenz, Fischer & Co, was set up by Daimler-Motoren-Gesellschaft to produce Austro-Daimler trucks. The first was far from satisfactory and improved designs appeared only after Daimler's son Paul had taken over as chief designer. He designed and constructed two 4 x 4 vehicles and in 1902 the firm was re-named Oesterreichische Daimler-Motoren-Gesellschaft Daimler. In 1905 Paul Daimler was replaced by Ferdinand Porsche who, in collaboration with Emile Jellineck of Mercedes, developed battery- and petrol-electric vehicles along Lohner-Porsche lines, selling these as Mercedes Electrique and Mercedes Mixte, these having electric motors mounted in the rear wheels. Although Jellineck had left by 1908, the company continued to build vehicles of this type, mainly as passenger chassis and fire appliances, adding the Lohner-Stoll trolleybus range, also called the Mercedes-Electrique-Stoll. In 1910, the company was re-named Oesterreichische Daimler-Motoren AG. The company's commercial vehicle production closed down in 1920 but, following the merging of Steyr-Werke AG and Puchwerke AG in 1934, a few 6 x 6 cross-country trucks were built until about 1942.

Although marketed as Steyr they were more frequently referred to as Austro-Daimlers.

AUSTRO-FIAT/*Austria 1911-45*
Founded in 1907, Oesterreichische Fiat Werke AG was established in Vienna to assemble Fiat cars and commercials for the Austrian and Hungarian markets. Actual production did not get underway until 1911, some models being almost identical to their Fiat counterparts. All were marketed as Austro-Fiat but actually carried AF or AFA marque letters. Models definitely not of Fiat design, although incorporating a number of Fiat ideas, included 2-, 3- and 4-ton chain-drive "subsidy" trucks with long-stroke 4-cyl side-valve petrol engines and 4-speed transmissions. The Fiat arrangement came to an end in 1925 when the company was re-named Oesterreichische Automobil-Fabriks AG, introducing a new 1½-tonner with pneumatic tyres, 2.8-litre 36bhp 4-cyl side-valve petrol engine, 4-speed gearbox and spiral-bevel rear axle. Later versions resembled the 618 Fiat but had a 2.2-litre 5-bearing petrol engine. By the mid-1930s, this model had been joined by vehicles in the 2½- to 4-ton class, powered by the company's own 3.8-litre 4-cyl petrol engine and optional 4.5-litre 4-cyl MAN diesel for the lightest or 6.8-litre 4-cyl MAN for the heaviest types. In 1938 Maschinenfabrik Augsburg-Nürnberg AG acquired a share in the business, leading to the use of Austro-Fiat axles and other components in the MAN range and the construction by the Austrian firm of the bonneted 4-ton 4 x 4 MAN for the German Armed Forces during World War II. In 1945 the plant was taken over by the Russians, there being no vehicle production until 1948, when, as Oesterreichische Automobilfabrik AG, AFN trucks were produced for a short time.

1928 Austro-Fiat motor pump fire appliance

Autarquia c1945

AUTARQUIA/*Spain 1940-1945*
Using a Model 51 chassis supplied by Ford Motor Iberica, the 3-ton Autarquia battery-electric was built in Barcelona by Vehiculos Electricos Autarquia SA. Sometimes incorrectly referred to as the Autoquia, van, truck and bus versions were offered, each capable of a 32km/h maximum speed and with a range per charge of approximately 72km.

AUTO CAMION/*France 1905-1906*
Soc l'Auto-Camion Levallois-Perret, Seine, built a 4-ton truck fitted with a 18/22hp, 4-cyl petrol engine located beneath the footboard, 3-speed box, and double chain-drive. A smaller model, with 14hp, twin-cyl engine, joined it briefly in 1906.

AUTO UNION/*Germany 1942-?*
Formed in 1932 following the merger of Audi, DKW, Horch and Wanderer, Auto Union GmbH, Zwikau, built a series of prototype forward-control 1½-ton, 4 x 4 trucks, using a 2.7-litre Wanderer engine located behind the front axle, during World War II. No other mediumweight types were built.

AUTO-CAR (1)/*USA 1904-1908*
Starting with a 2-ton, battery-electric truck, a 24-seat bus, a trolleybus and two delivery vans with 2-cyl petrol engines, the Auto-Car Equipment Co established a plant at Buffalo, New York State. A forward-control 3-tonner, with a 35hp, 4-cyl petrol engine, was announced in 1906 and 1907 saw a 4-cyl forward-control 5-tonner, a 20-seat passenger model, and a 12-seat battery-electric bus also announced. A battery-electric 24-seat bus, an ambulance and a 6-ton load carrier were built in 1908, but later that year the company

was reconstituted as the Buffalo Auto-Car Mfg Co and all models were re-named Buffalo to avoid confusion with the products of the Autocar Co, Ardmore, Pennsylvania.

AUTO-CAR (2)/*Italy 1907-1911*
Although every type of vehicle was advertised by Soc Italiana Auto-Cars, only buses were actually built and these were strictly assembled models, using Malicet et Blin chassis frames and Aster petrol engines.

AUTO-MIXTE/*Belgium 1905-1910*
SA Auto-Mixte, Herstal-lez-Lieége, constructed petrol-electric light- and medium-duty goods and passenger models using Henri Pieper's petrol-electric transmission system, which itself was

developed from the American Fischer system. The British Daimler Motor Co Ltd incorporated it in the unique KPL bus of 1910-1911.

AUTO-TRACTION/*Belgium 1920-1940*
SA Auto-Traction, Antwerp, acquired licences to construct the 6-ton payload Chenard-Walcker road tractor as the Auto-Traction. This had a 3.6-litre, 4-cyl Minerva sleeve-valve petrol engine and from 1923 ran on pneumatics. The company was acquired by Minerva Motors SA in 1925, the fifth wheel coupling Auto-Traction continuing as part of this company's line-up.

AUTO-TRACTOR/*England 1933-1947*
The Auto-Mower Engineering Co Ltd, Norton St Philip, Bath, Somerset, developed a road-going timber tractor known as the Type 'T' as a replacement for the many steam tractors still being used in this field but now faced with crippling taxation. Powered by a transverse 24bhp 4-cyl Ford petrol engine located amidships with the driver positioned behind, drive was via a 4-speed and a reverse gearbox with chain-drive to a countershaft carrying gearing for a front-mounted winch and a roller chain to the rear axle. A cab was optional and three late examples had longitudinally-mounted engines. Three examples of the Type 'H' were produced in 1934, powered by 4-cyl Meadows and 5- or 6-cyl Gardner diesel engines, all transversely-mounted with chain-drive. These formed the basis for the Type 'V', the first of

which also appeared in 1934. This had a 30bhp Ford V8 petrol engine, located either transversely or longitudinally, and was listed until 1947, after which timber handling equipment was invariably mounted on proprietary chassis.

AUTOAR/*Argentina 1950-1961*
In 1950, Automotores Argentinos SAIC, Tigre, introduced the Autoar 1½-ton payload van or minibus, with a choice between a 1.9-litre Fiat, 4-cyl or 2.35-litre Simca V8 petrol engine. Throughout the production period, the company also assembled chassis frames for the light Rastrojero truck.

AUTOBIANCHI/*Italy 1955-1968*
Autobianchi SpA was founded in Milan as a result of an agreement between Fabbrica Automobili e Velocipedi Eduardo Bianchi, Fiat SpA, and Pirelli, with commercial vehicle production centred upon light- and mediumweight trucks employing Fiat components. These included 3- and 4½-tonners and a 28-seat coach. The last new Autobianchi appears to have been the 4½-ton 'Scaligero' forward-control truck.

AUTOCAR-KROMHOUT/*Netherlands 1938-1939*
As well as Kromhout commercials, Kromhout Motoren Fabriek D Goedkoop Jnr NV, Amsterdam, assembled both "conventional" and "cabover" US-designed Autocar trucks as Autocar-Kromhouts. Popular as fire appliances or municipal vehicles, these were powered by Hercules petrol engines.

1915 Autocar Type XXI 1½-ton truck

1970 Autocar 6 x 4 artic tractor

AUTOCAR/*USA 1907 to date*
The first Autocar truck built by the Autocar Co, Ardmore, Pennsylvania, was a 1½-ton 2-cyl model with a horizontally-opposed 18hp petrol engine located beneath the driver's seat. Known as the Type XXI, this had a 3-speed transmission and shaft-drive, and was later developed into a 1½/2-tonner. This series was joined in 1919 by various forward-control models from 2 to 5 tons capacity, headed by the Model 26-B, 5-tonner powered by the company's first 4-cyl petrol engine. The early 1920s saw the debut of the company's first electric commercials – a range of 1-, 2- and 3-tonners – but, like all other models, these were discontinued in 1926 to make way for new bonneted trucks of 1½- to 5-ton capacity, with 4- or 6-cyl petrol engines, a 7½-tonner being added later. The smallest was a panel delivery van with 4-wheel braking, while at the heavy end was a 6-cyl 5-tonner. Another new model was the 3-ton 'Trail Blazer', also with a 6-cyl engine but of "cabover" layout. In

the 1930s there was further expansion into the heavy vehicle field with the "conventional" models 'C' and 'S', popular with the construction business. Bonneted long-distance tractors were gaining popularity and, in 1937, a new series of flamboyant panel vans, designated Types 'RM' and 'RL', were announced, followed by a short-wheelbase "cabover" range. By the end of that year there were no fewer than fifty different Autocars, while some models were built in Amsterdam as Autocar-Kromhout by Kromhout Motoren Fabriek D Goedkoop Jnr NV. During World War II, production was concentrated upon heavy "conventionals", particularly 4 x 4 and 6 x 4 tractors, powered by 6-cyl Autocar, Hercules or Cummins engines (petrol and diesel) of up to 150bhp output. Peacetime saw new "cabovers", not unlike pre-war designs, fitted with an easily-removed cab to facilitate engine maintenance. The 1950s heralded an increase in the use of lightweight aluminium and the old rivetted assembly was replaced by

1940 Autocar C-30 pantechnicon

nuts and bolts to ease servicing. Acquired by the White Motor Co in 1953, the Autocar operation eventually became the Autocar Trucks Divn of the White Motor Corp. The company was by now concentrating upon custom-building, offering White petrol, Caterpillar, Cummins or Detroit diesels and a multitude of gearboxes and axles to provide trucks of virtually

any specification. By 1962 aluminium was used extensively, such as in the lightweight 'A' range, typified by the A-10264, a "conventional" 6 x 4 with 220bhp, 6-cyl diesel engine, 4-speed main and 3-speed auxiliary transmissions. Current production includes both "cabover" and "conventional" types of 4 x 2, 6 x 4 and 6 x 6 configuration.

AUTO FORE CARRIAGE/*USA 1907-?*
The Auto Fore Carriage was a motor-driven 2-wheeled tractor of unknown origin designed for converting horse-drawn hook and ladder fire appliances to self-propulsion.

AUTOHORSE/*USA/England 1917-1922*
The US-built Autohorse was an unusual single-wheeled road tractor for motorizing horse-drawn vehicles. It was built by the One Wheel Truck Co, St Louis, Missouri, but proved unstable at high speeds and in icy conditions, no doubt due to an imbalance resulting from the 22½hp 4-cyl Continental petrol engine being located

to one side, although this was supposedly counter-balanced by a 254-litre water tank. Other features included a Borg & Beck clutch, Warner three-speed box and internal gear final-drive. Shortly before production was discontinued, plans were laid for the Autohorse to be marketed in Britain, but only a few were actually delivered.

AUTOMOTIVE SYNDICATE/*USA 1927-1929*
The Automotive Syndicate was formed in Indianapolis, Indiana to develop a steam-powered bus along similar lines to the British-built Clarkson. A prototype 6-wheeler was built, using a patented flash boiler and control system

developed by the Electrol Corp for use in the unsuccessful Standard Steam Truck. The bus was a 40-seat single-decker of modern appearance and all-steel construction. Further development was curtailed by the Depression.

AUTOSAN/*Poland 1973 to date*
Previously sold as the Sanok, integrally-constructed Autosan passenger models are built by Sanocha Fabryka Autobusow, Sanock, using a rear-mounted 125bhp Wola-Leyland diesel engine.

AVAILABLE/*USA 1914-1962*
The first mediumweight truck built by the Available Truck Co, Chicago, Illinois, was a 1-tonner, with underseat 32hp 4-cyl petrol

engine, but by 1915 1- and 2-ton bonneted types with 3-speed transmissions and overhead-worm rear axles had replaced them. Continental-powered vehicles for up to 5 tons payload were listed by 1917 and in 1920 the heavy-duty 'Invincible' – a 7-tonner with 50bhp Waukesha petrol engine was announced. The first pneumatic-tyred Available was a 1½-tonner in 1926 and the first 6-cyl engined trucks were listed from the late 1920s. Production in the 1930s was relatively low, although new "cabovers", a 6-wheeler and various passenger models were introduced in 1936. During World War II 6 x 4 wreckers and crane-carriers were supplied to the Services, and a fire truck chassis announced afterwards was used by custom fire appliance manufacturers as a basis for their own models. By 1950 ten models were listed, from 6804-, to 17,150kg gross, with Waukesha petrol or Cummins diesel engines, Fuller, Spicer or Warner transmissions, and Lockheed hydraulic brakes. Certain passenger chassis had Ford V8 petrol engines at the rear or under the driver and in 1955 a special terminal tractor and a new 6 x 4 crane-carrier was introduced. By 1957 the company had been acquired by the Crane Carrier Corp of Tulsa, Oklahoma, and with one or two exceptions all subsequent vehicles were known as Crane Carrier or CCC.

AVELING/*England 1908*
The firm of TC Aveling & Co, Birmingham, took over manufacture of Broom & Wade paraffin-engined 3- and 4-ton lorries when the original manufacturer decided to concentrate on other projects. Production was short-lived.

AVELING & PORTER/*England 1909-1925*
The first steam wagon built by Aveling & Porter Ltd, Rochester, Kent, was a 3-ton "overtype" with loco-type boiler generating steam at 200psi and a compound engine with outside valve chests and Stephenson's link motion. A manually-operated steam tipper was constructed in 1913, and later that year the first 3/4-ton internal combustion-engined trucks with 4-cyl Aveling & Porter petrol engines appeared, only to vanish again three years later. In 1919 the company combined with Charles Burrel & Sons Ltd and Richard Garrett & Sons to form the ill-fated Agricultural & General Engineers combine, whereby steam wagon production was to be undertaken only at Garrett's Leiston, Suffolk, factory. Twelve Aveling & Porters were constructed there before a final five (one with a Leiston-built boiler) were assembled back at Rochester. The company then concentrated on the manufacture of road rollers and the development of its 'Invicta' diesel engine, eventually merging with Barfords to form construction and mining equipment company Aveling-Barford Ltd.

AVELING-BARFORD/*England 1939 to date*
Aveling-Barford Ltd was formed at Grantham, Lincs, in 1933 following the merger of Aveling & Porter Ltd and the Barford organization, quickly developing a series of site dumpers based on Fordson tractor engine/transmission units, and adding its first shuttle dumper with reversible seat and

1969 Aveling-Barford 690

controls in 1939. This was joined in 1947 by a 12-ton capacity 6-wheeled version with 128bhp 6-cyl Dorman diesel engine. The 10-ton 'SL'-Series 4-wheeled dump truck, with 6-cyl Leyland diesel and reversible controls, appeared in 1957, later developed into a 17-tonner with 201bhp diesel engine, 5 forward and 3 reverse speeds. The giant 'SN'-Series appeared in 1958, being the company's first bonneted model. This had a 450bhp Rolls-Royce V8 or 335bhp Cummins 6-cyl diesel engine and 6-speed transmission. The largest was a 30-tonner but a 35-ton machine with either the Rolls-Royce V8 or a 476bhp Detroit Diesel 2-stroke was announced later. Smaller machines were built by an associate company, Barfords of Belton Ltd, and known as Barford or Barfords, but in 1968, both companies became part of British Leyland's Special Products Divn, and Aveling-Barford inherited the former AEC 690 6-wheeled bonneted 'Dumptruk' which was later built at Scammell Motor's Watford plant and also marketed as the Thornycroft or Leyland LD55 'Bush Tractor' for the export market. The 'SN'-Series was replaced in 1970 by the even larger 'Centaur', offered in five sizes from 25 to 50 tons capacity, and the company was transferred to the Truck & Bus Divn of British Leyland soon after. Now part of Leyland Vehicles Ltd, Aveling-Barford's future is uncertain as it is now up for sale in accordance with Leyland's policy of cutbacks.

AVERY/*USA 1910-1923*
The Avery Co, Peoria, Illinois, was an agricultural equipment manufacturer that also built petrol-engined trucks. These were variously described as combination farm wagons, general farm power machines, tractors and even trucks. Identifying features included extra-wide wheels for soft ground and a front crankshaft extension as power take-off. At

1971 Aveling-Barford 'Centaur' 50

first, these were of 1-ton capacity with 4-cyl petrol engines and chain-drive, but by 1912 there were also 2- and 3-tonners and by 1917 even a "cabover" version.

AVIA (1)/*Czechoslovakia 1956-1957, 1968 to date*
Aircraft manufacturer Avia np, Prague, was established in 1919 building its first vehicles after World War II when it commenced licence production of Skoda goods and passenger models, an arrangement which ended in 1951. Praga and Tatra designs were licence-built from 1961, but the first true Avias appeared in 1968 following agreement with Regie Nationale des Usines Renault, France, whereby certain Renault-Saviem light commercials would be built under licence as Avias. These comprised the A15 and A30 for 1500 and 3000kg payloads respectively, both powered by a 3.3-litre 4-cyl diesel engine. The 7-ton S7T, believed to be entirely Avia-designed, was launched in 1970, having an 8.1-litre 6-cyl air-cooled diesel engine.

AVIA (2)/*Spain c1956-1970*
Aircraft repairer Aeronautica Industrial SA, Madrid, introduced a 4-wheeled Perkins-engined truck for operation within the 1500 to 11,000kg gross weight category or as an 18- to 28-seat bus during the late 1950s. Motor Iberica SA, manufacturer of the Ebro, acquired the company in 1970, all subsequent vehicles being known as Avia Ebro.

AVIA EBRO/*Spain 1970 to date*
Aeronautica Industrial SA Mad-

rid was acquired by Motor Iberica SA, Barcelona, in 1970, all subsequent Avia vehicles being known as Avia Ebro. Production is now undertaken in Barcelona.

AVONSIDE/*England 1913*
The Avonside Engine Co Ltd, Bristol, was a popular builder of small industrial railway locomotives when it announced a range of petrol-engined lorries and a massive 200hp road tractor powered by a 2-stroke semi-diesel or heavy oil engine capable of hauling loads of up to 500 tons GCW. These vehicles were frequently incorrectly described as Avondales.

AVS/*England 1975 to date*
Advanced Vehicle Systems Ltd was set up in Welwyn Garden City, Herts, to find new solutions to the battery-electric vehicle problem. A prototype 1-ton van was based on a Bedford 'CF' model with a torque-converter transmission which improved both the operating range and performance over rival battery-electrics. Developed for experimental use with the Electricity Council, it has an EDC 40/50hp traction motor,

1975 AVS 1-tonner

maintaining equal current discharge by switching batteries in cyclic sequence via a battery scanner. This gives a 64km range when using ordinary lead-acid lorry batteries. Experiments are proceeding.

AWD/*England 1958-c1966*
During the 1950s and early 1960s, the All-Wheel Drive Co Ltd, Camberley, Surrey, became well known for all-wheel drive conversions of proprietary goods chassis. Later, the company constructed a few 4- and 6-wheel drive crane-carriers, with one-man half-cabs, which were adopted by numerous British crane manufacturers. The business was acquired by the Vickers engineering organization in 1962.

BABCOCK DIESEL/*Spain 1950-1955*

After the Civil War and World War II, Spanish hauliers experienced an acute shortage of modern vehicles and, partly to answer this requirement, the engineering plant of Soc Espanola de Construcciones Babcock & Wilcox SA, Bilbao, produced a 5-ton bonneted truck known as the Babcock Diesel. Power came from the company's own 4.9-litre 70bhp 4-cyl engine.

BACKUS/*USA 1925-1927*

Called the 'Speed Truck', the Backus was a bonneted goods model in the 1½ to 6 tons capacity range built by the Backus Motor Truck Co, East Rutherford, New Jersey. The lightest model had a 27.34hp 6-cyl Waukesha petrol engine while heavier models had a larger 4-cyl unit. Brown-Lipe transmissions and Timken axles were used.

BADC/*England 1905-1907*

The British Automobile Development Co Ltd, South London, was a subsidiary of the Brush Electrical Engineering Co, Loughborough, Leics. The first BADC bus, a bonneted 36-seat open-top double-decker, was also offered as a 3-ton truck, with a 30hp 4-cyl petrol engine, 4-speed gearbox and shaft-drive. A forward-control version appeared in 1907 under the Brush brand name.

BAETEN/*Belgium to date*

Baeten NV, Melle, are commercial bodybuilders specializing in mobile shops. These are sold under the Baeten brand name, despite their being mounted on extended Citroën, Saviem and Renault truck chassis.

BAICO/*England ?-c1938*

The British-American Import Co Ltd undertook the conversion of US-built Ford Model 'T' chassis and later, its British-built counterpart to long-wheelbase, often adding an extra axle, strengthening the frame, converting to chain-drive and fitting alternative suspension systems. Some were even converted into tractor units for articulated operation. These were marketed as Baico or Baico-Ford.

BAILEY/*USA 1910*

The Bailey Motor Truck Co was founded in Detroit, Michigan. Before the first truck, a chain-drive 1-tonner appeared, the company had been reconstituted as the Federal Motor Truck Co, and the Federal name was applied to all vehicles built.

BAKER (1)/*England 1907-1909*

Food processing equipment manufacturer Joseph Baker & Sons Ltd constructed a prototype forward-control 3-tonner in its North London factory. It was powered by the company's own 16hp flat-4 petrol engine with shaft-drive via a 4-speed epicyclic box.

BAKER (2)/*USA 1908-1916*

The Cleveland, Ohio-based Baker Motor Vehicle Co offered petrol-engined and battery-electric commercials as Baker and Baker Electric. These were forward-control with chain-drive and load capacities of up to 5080kg. From 1916 models were sold as Baker R & L.

BAKER (3)/*USA 1926*

A prototype steam passenger chassis with 5-cyl rotary engine was developed by the Baker Steam Motor Car & Mfg Co, Pueblo, Colorado. The following year, the Steam Appliance Corp of America – the Cleveland, Ohio-based consortium that had taken over the Baker patents – announced a similar vehicle usually referred to as the Steamline.

BAKER R & L/*USA 1916-1923*

Previously marketed as Baker or Baker Electric, Baker R & L battery-electric and petrol-engined goods models were manufactured by the Baker, Rauch & Lang Co.

BALACHOWSKY & CAIRE/*France 1912-1914*

Balachowsky et Caire, Paris, built 2- and 4-wheel drive petrol-electric vehicles. These had 4-cyl engines supplying current to hub-mounted ACEC electric motors, production being concentrated on underseat-engined load-carriers, military tractors and trolleybuses.

BALDWIN/*USA 1899-1901*

Previously sold as Cruickshank, Baldwin steam wagons were built by the Baldwin Motor Wagon Co, Providence, Rhode Island.

BARBER/*USA 1917-1918*

The Barber Motors Corp, New York, built heavy road tractors powered by 4-cyl Buda petrol engines. For handling a 12-ton load, these were of forward-control layout with worm final-drive without differential.

BARBER-BUCHANAN/*England 1905-1906*

Sometimes referred to as the Buchanan, the Barber-Buchanan was designed for use in the colonies. A 5-tonner, it was built in James Buchanan & Son's Caledonian Foundry, Liverpool, with two compound engines located side by side driving their respective rear wheels by chains. The vertical boiler was cantilevered ahead of the front axle, with fuel feed by gravity, jolted down the inclined plane of firebars by the wagon's own motion. Each wheel hub was segregated into outer and inner portions with small cushioning springs between. Still more unusual features included a fan-cooled condenser and internal-expanding brakes. Numerous orders were claimed but few were actually met.

BARDON/*France 1904*

Automobiles Bardon, Puteaux, Seine, briefly built an under-powered forward-control 3-tonner with 8hp petrol engine and single chain-drive.

1964 Barkas B1000 1-ton van

BARKAS/*East Germany 1954 to date*

The Framo F9 light delivery van was marketed as the Barkas from 1954 and the company re-named VEB Barkas-Werke in 1957. The B1000, a new 1-tonner with 3-cyl petrol engine, replaced this in 1961 and is still current, albeit in up-dated form as van, pick-up, minibus or ambulance.

BARKER (1)/*USA 1912-1917*

Built by the C L Barker Co, Norwalk, Connecticut, the early Barker truck range included a variety of chain-drive trucks with capacities of up to 5080kg. By 1914 these had been replaced by a worm-drive 1-tonner, joined later by a 2-ton model.

BARKER (2)/*USA 1913-1920*

Three- and 5-ton trucks were based on the same 3.81-m wheelbase chassis built by the Barker Motors Co, North Los Angeles, California. Both had a 40hp 4-cyl petrol engine and were offered with van, open or stakeside bodies.

BARON/*England 1957-1969*

Baron Motors Ltd was founded at Borehamwood, Herts, to develop a series of economical commercial chassis aimed at under-developed countries. Despite lack of co-operation from certain component suppliers, a 7-ton bonneted prototype was ready by 1959, followed by second and third prototypes incorporating numerous improvements. By 1964 the first production models had been constructed, comprising the bonneted 6-ton 'Master' BN6, bonneted 7-ton 'Senior' BN7 and a forward-control passenger chassis intended for 38/44-seat bodywork.

The BN6 and BN7 goods models were similar to the normal-control Commer 'Superpoise' of the day, having the same Airflow Streamline cab or front-end structure. However, it was an assembled vehicle with specially designed chassis frame supplied by Rubery, Owen & Co Ltd, having an Eaton 2-speed axle, a 120bhp Perkins 6.354 diesel engine, and a 32-cm single dry-plate clutch with hydraulic withdrawal mechanism and 4-point mounting in unit with the gearbox. The 6-tonner had a 4-speed synchromesh box and, with twin rear tyres as standard, produced a maximum speed of 55 mph with a bottom gear gradient capable of 1 in 2.3 in low axle ratio or 1 in 3.2 in high ratio, enabling the vehicle to cope with most gradients. Whilst the chassis frame was of riveted pressed-steel construction, items that might be replaced in service, such as spring hanger brackets, were bolted in place. Semi-elliptic leaf springs were fitted throughout, with helper springs at the rear and shock absorbers standard at the front but optional at the rear. Also optional were single rear tyres, with a front axle rating of 3 tons. The BN6 had a gross weight of 9525kg and was available only with a wheelbase of 420cm. The 7-tonner had a wheelbase of 490cm and a much heavier chassis frame, although suspension, brakes and rear axle were the same as for the 6-tonner. This model had a 5-speed constant-mesh box and optional single tyre equipment. Front axle rating was 4 tons and gross vehicle weight 10,432kg. The passenger model was a forward-control version of the 6-tonner, but it is doubtful if many were sold. Complete vehicle kits were assembled and packed in a factory at Northampton. Although listed for export until 1969, few were actually supplied.

1960 Barreiros 5-ton prototype truck chassis-cab

BARREIROS/*Spain 1958-1979*
Using a small workshop in Orense, Eduardo Barreiros Rodriguez began converting petrol engines to diesel after the Spanish Civil War, moving to Madrid in 1951 where he set up a diesel engine production line under the name of Barreiros Diesel SA. This company's first commercial vehicle was the 6-ton 'Victor', which was quickly joined by the 'Azor' and 'Condor' rigids, and the 16,000kg 'Super Azor Gran Ruta' tractor. Lighter forward-control models comprising the 'Seata' 3000/4500kg range were to follow along with standardized 4 x 4 and 6 x 6 military types such as the bonneted 'Panter III', based on US government designs for a 5-ton 6 x 6. Up-dated in the early 1960s with a new range of cabs, the line soon included trucks from 2500 to 38,000kg GCW and in 1961 a new factory was set up in Madrid to build AEC passenger models under licence, these being marketed as Barreiros-AEC. Involvement with Chrysler of America commenced in December 1963 when the company was re-named Chrysler-Barreiros SA. In 1967 another new passenger vehicle line, built at the former plant of Factoria Napoles SA, Zaragoza, was introduced as the Barreiros-Van Hool, and in July 1970 the company was taken over entirely by the Chrysler Corp, being re-named Chrysler-Espana SA, after which certain US-built Dodge trucks were imported into Spain carrying both the Barreiros and Dodge names.
Up to 1979 the range included trucks, passenger vehicles, agricultural tractors and diesel engines, with vehicle capacities still ranging from 2500 to 38,000kg

GVW and with engines of up to 275bhp. Lighter models were eventually dropped to 13,000kg GCW and the heaviest tractor offered in other European countries as the Dodge K3820P. In 1978 the Barreiros name began to be phased out in favour of Dodge, and by 1979 all models were marketed thus.

BARREIROS-AEC/*Spain 1961-1974*
Barreiros Diesel SA began a long association with AEC Ltd, of Great Britain, when a new factory was built in Madrid to build AEC passenger models under licence. Marketed as Barreiros-AEC, production also included numerous minibuses on the 3000 to 4500kg capacity Barreiros 'Saeta' chassis, but production was gradually decreased, following the British company's takeover by the Leyland Motor Corp Ltd.

BARREIROS-DODGE/*Spain 1970-1979*
Following the partial acquisition of Barreiros Diesel SA by the American Chrysler Corp to form Chrysler-Espana SA, certain US-built Dodge trucks were imported into Spain carrying both the Barreiros and Dodge names. This arrangement ended when only the Dodge name was adopted.

BARREIROS-VAN HOOL/*Spain 1967-?*
When Chrysler-Barreiros SA, Madrid, took over the former Factoria Napoles SA commercial vehicle plant at Zaragoza, the company came to an arrangement with Belgian coachbuilder Van Hool whereby their bodies were mounted on Barreiros chassis and sold as Barreiros-Van Hool.

BARRO/*Spain 1930-1942*
Barro Fabrico de Chavin, Vivero, Lugo, was an agent for De Dion vehicles, introducing commercial truck chassis with petrol engines by 1930 and adding diesel models later. Throughout the Spanish Civil War numerous military derivatives were supplied to the Armed Forces.

BARRON-VIALLE/*France 1912-1920, 1929-1937*
The first commercial to be built by Automobiles Barron-Vialle, Lyons, was a bonneted chain-drive 4-tonner using a variety of 4-cyl Ballot petrol engines. Although commercial vehicle production continued through World War I, it was discontinued in 1920 and resumed in 1929 at Arandon, Isere. New models included a 7-ton truck and 30/55-seat metal-bodied buses.

BARROWS/*USA 1927-1928*
Built by the Barrows Motor Truck Co, Indianapolis, Indiana, the Barrows was a bonneted shaft-drive truck with 4-cyl petrol engine and 4-speed gearbox. It was offered in capacities of 1½, 2½ and 3½ tons.

BARTON/*England 1950-1954, 1959-1961*
Passenger vehicle operator Barton Transport Ltd, Chilwell, Notts, re-conditioned and lengthened pre-war chassis, mainly Leyland 'Lions', and fitted new single-deck bodies. First of these was the Barton BTS/1 Type, which entered service in batches up to 1954 in a variety of body styles. Five years later the BTD/2 double-deck re-build first appeared, continuing to enter service until 1961. These were 70- and 71-seat full-front lowbridge types, many of the chassis being acquired from the Yorkshire Woollen District Transport Co Ltd.

BARTON & RUMBLE/*Canada 1917-1923*
Only about fifty trucks were built by Barton & Rumble, London, Ontario, ranging from 1 to 5 tons capacity. Initially, these were powered by Lycoming engines but later Hinkley units were used.

BAT/*England 1929-1931*
Harris & Hasell Ltd, Bristol, held an agency for various imported American commercials. Later, the company became Harris & Hasell (1929) Ltd, designing a bonneted goods and passenger model, the 'Cruiser', for legal operation at up to 48km/h with an unladen weight of under 2½ tons. Called the BAT (British Associated Transport), it was an assembled job with a 59bhp 6-cyl

1930 BAT 'Cruiser' bus

Continental petrol engine. It was joined by the 'Super Pullman' for 32-seat bodywork with straight-8 petrol engine but the lighter model remained the most popular. Sales were never sufficient and production was transferred to a smaller factory in London, before closing down.

1964 Battronic BTC 30 battery-electric integral van

BATTRONIC/*USA 1964 to date*
The Battronic Truck Corp was founded in Philadelphia, Pennsylvania, to assemble light battery-electric delivery vehicles, the first of which appeared in March 1964. Improved models with ranges of up to 120km per charge were quickly introduced but by 1966 Smith's Delivery Vehicles Ltd, who supplied the chassis, had pulled out of the operation and the company had begun to assemble its own chassis. In 1969 the Electric Storage Battery Co, who supplied batteries and electric traction equipment, also withdrew and from then on the Battronic Truck Corp became a subsidiary of the Boyertown Auto Body Works, production being moved to Boyertown. By 1971 models included both goods and passenger types with one light delivery van and 11-, 15- or 25-seat buses, production of which is continuing, sometimes under the Boyertown name.

BAUER/*Germany c1935*
An old-established manufacturer of manual and horse-drawn municipal equipment, Peter Bauer Fahrzeugfabrik introduced a series of battery-electric refuse collectors.

BAULY/*England c1905*
H C Bauly was an old-established wheelwrights' business in London which also sold a few lorry chassis.

It is not known whether the company actually designed and built these itself or whether they were merely sold on behalf of another manufacturer.

BAY CITY/*USA c1939-c1972*
Bay City Shovels Inc, Bay City, Michigan, developed military truck-mounted cranes during World War II, also marketing these as the CraneMobile. Using 6 x 4 and 6 x 6 carriers of its own design, the company offered Models T40, T50, T60, T61 and T66, developing these into a range of civilian types after the war. Postwar models were mounted on 6- and 8-wheeled chassis, with oneman half-cabs and lattice-section jibs up to 70m high.

BAYLEY/*England 1899-1901*
Bayleys Ltd was founded in North London, E H Bayley teaming up with consulting engineer Sidney Straker to produce the "under-type" Bayley steam wagon, also referred to as the Bayley-Straker. A prototype, with Straker engine and De Dion boiler, was entered in the 1899 Liverpool Trials but the all-gear drive proved too noisy. The chassis, accessories and wheels were built by Bayleys and forwarded to Straker's Bristol works for final assembly. Petrol-engined passenger models were also constructed, including a number of 26-seat double-deck buses with 12hp 4-cyl Daimler engines delivered to the Motor Traction Co Ltd, in 1899. After 1901 all models were known as Straker.

BEACH/*England 1899*
James Beach & Co, Somerset, constructed a functional steam van with liquid-fired vertical boiler at the front supplying 150psi of steam to a 5hp single-cyl engine. Gear-changing was by friction clutch with speeds of 8 and 16 km/h available.

BEAN/*England 1924-1931*
A Harper, Sons & Bean Ltd were component suppliers to the motor industry based at Tipton, Staffs, when they entered the vehicle

manufacturing business in 1919 with patents to continue production of the 11.9hp Perry car and various light commercials. Towards the end of 1924 a 1½-ton commercial based on prototypes built by David Carlaw & Co, Glasgow, was introduced, becoming popular in van, truck, bus and charabanc forms. In 1926 Hadfields Ltd, a Sheffield-based steelmaker, assisted the company financially and re-named it Bean Cars Ltd. One year later a sturdier 1½-tonner was launched, followed by a passenger chassis with 3.8-litre 6-cyl petrol engine. In 1929 eight prototype 2½-ton 'Empire' chassis were constructed for test purposes, each powered by a 22.3hp version of the old 14hp engine and joined the following year by a 4-ton forward-control derivative. Neither these nor a 'New Era' 1¼/1½-tonner with self-starter and 4-wheel brakes could save the company and despite price reductions to boost sales, vehicle manufacture ceased.

BEARDMORE (1)/*Scotland c1920-1929*
Beardmore Motors Ltd, Paisley, Renfrewshire, was a subsidiary of Wm Beardmore & Co Ltd, concentrating on the manufacture of taxicabs. Chassis were also sold and during the 1920s a lengthened chassis with a wheelbase of up to 3.48m was offered for goods operation and a maximum payload of 1½ tons. Only light commercials were built after 1929.

BEARDMORE (2)/*Scotland 1936-1937*
A few years after its involvement in the Beardmore-Multiwheeler operation, Wm Beardmore & Co Ltd, Dalmuir, Dumbartonshire, announced heavy trucks and passenger models with welded steel frames, each powered by a diesel engine of the company's own design. These included a 4-wheeled 8-tonner, a 4-wheeler for drawbar operation at 13 tons GCW and 6- and 8-wheelers for 13 and 15 tons gross respectively. Single- and double-deck passenger types were

BEARDMORE-MULTI-WHEELER/*England 1930-1932*
Another subsidiary of Wm Beardmore & Co Ltd, Dalmuir Dumbartonshire, entered the vehicle-building business in 1930, with the acquisition of manufacturing rights for the Chenard-Walcker road tractor. Beardmore-Multi-

1930 Beardmore-Multiwheeler 'Cobra' tractor

wheelers Ltd was set up in South West London and the range extended from the original 10-tonner, now called the 'Cobra', to include the 'Python' 10/15-tonner and 'Anaconda' 15-tonner. All three models were used in conjunction with specially designed Larkhall swan-neck drawbar trailers capable of transferring 15% of the load to the rear wheels of the tractor, increasing this still more on steep grades. In 1931 Beardmore's own diesel engines were listed for all models but manufacturing rights were sold to a new company, Multiwheelers (Commercial Vehicles) Ltd, South Harrow, Middx, who resumed production under the Multiwheeler brand name.

BEAUFORT/*Germany/England 1902-1906*
The Beaufort Motor Co, London and Baden, Germany, was established to market vehicles built on its behalf by certain German manufacturers. As well as light delivery vans, lorries and buses were also offered. The 3-ton 1904 model was really a 2-cyl Stoewer with a channel-steel frame and a pair of railway-style buffers to protect the radiator. Amongst the last vehicles were some experimental buses for the London General Omnibus Co and the London-District Omnibus Co.

BEAVER (1)/*Canada 1918-1923*
Beaver Truck Builders Ltd, Hamilton, Ontario, started with a 2-ton assembled truck, gradually introducing other models in the 1½- to 3-ton weight range. By 1920 the company had been re-named the

Beaver Truck Corp Ltd, launching a new model, the 'Bullet', in the year 1921.

BEAVER (2)/*USA 1934-1953, 1955-1956*
To answer operators' requirements for a cheap lightweight bus, G M Davis developed the Beaver, the prototype of which was constructed by the Travers Engineering Co, Beaver Falls, Ohio, using a forward-control Ford chassis. Later, the Beaver Transit Equipment Co was founded and an improved model, with increased seating capacity and optional Chevrolet or International Harvester engines, was developed. Re-constituted as Beaver Metropolitan Coaches Inc in 1935, some designs became known as Beaver Metropolitans and three years later the first rear-engined model was built, developing into a complete range for 20 to 35 passengers. In 1953 the plant was closed by flooding and production ceased until Davis re-acquired the business in 1955, re-naming it the National Coach & Mfg Co.

BEAVER STATE/*USA 1914-1915*
The Beaver State Motor Co, Gresham, Oregon, built a few 2.84-m wheelbase trucks powered by 28hp 4-cyl petrol engines. Battery-electric models were rumoured.

BECK (1)/*USA 1911-1921*
The first commercials built by the Cedar Rapids Auto Works, Cedar Rapids, Iowa, were a 2-ton truck and an 18-seat bus, both sold under the Beck name. Three years later the company was re-named Beck & Sons, introducing 2- and 3-tonners with 3-speed transmissions and double-reduction internal-gear drive. In 1916 the firm became the Beck Motor Truck Works and in 1918 the Beck-Hawkeye Motor Truck Works. From then the only trucks listed were 1-, 1½- and 2½-tonners, sometimes referred to as Beck-Hawkeye.

BECK (2)/*USA 1934-1956*
The Beck 'Fleetway' was a stretched 11-seat sedan-type bus launched by C D Beck & Co, Sidney, Ohio, which also introduced chassisless models using proprietary engines and running units. First of these were the composite-bodied 'Airstream' and the all-metal 'Steeliner', both introduced in 1938, joined towards the end of that year by a rear-engined design called the 'Super Steeliner' and an economy job called the 'Scout'. All were superseded in 1940 by the 33-seat rear-engined 'Mainliner' and the luxurious 'Luxury Liner', both 4.69- or 5.58-m wheel-

1930 Bean single-deck bus

1964 Belaz prototype 65-ton artic dump truck

base and normally powered by an International Harvester 'Red Diamond' engine. Although production stopped briefly in 1942, the company continued with a utility version of the 'Mainliner', which was listed until 1948 when all models were up-dated and model names largely discontinued. Much of the company's production was now concentrated upon inter-city models with welded tubular steel-framed bodies, air suspension and Cummins diesel engines. However, home market competition was considerable, and more Beck vehicles went for export. In 1953 the company acquired the Ahrens-Fox Fire Engine Co, transferring production to Sidney before Mack Trucks Inc bought C D Beck & Co in 1956.

BEECH CREEK/*USA 1915-1917*
The Beech Creek Truck & Auto Co, Beech Creek, Pennsylvania, offered a 3-ton 4-wheel drive and 4-wheel steer truck powered by a 29hp 4-cyl petrol engine.

BEERS/*Netherlands 1933-1950*
Adriaan Beers NV, Rijswijk, was a Dutch vehicle distributor, announcing its own model, the 'Floating Tractor', with Kromhout-Gardner 4LW diesel engine at the Amsterdam Motor Show. An articulated passenger version was known as the 'Floating Pullman'. The original engine was replaced by a Dorman-Ricardo unit in 1934 and a new passenger model, the 'Tramcoach', with lightweight cross-braced chassis frame and Hercules petrol engine, went into production. The 'Handyvan' "walk-through" delivery model with front-wheel drive and 4- or 6-cyl petrol engine appeared briefly after the war.

1967 Belaz 540 30-ton dump truck

BELAZ/*Soviet Union 1961 to date*
The first BELAZ dump truck built by the Byelorussian Motor Works, Zhodino, was the 30-ton Model 540. A 4-wheel drive half-

to manufacture production versions of the former Morton steam wagon. Both goods- and passenger-carrying models of 2-, 3- and 5-ton capacity, with water-tube boilers and Morton-Lifu

cab design with modified 375bhp tank engine, this was joined by the 540A, powered by a 360bhp V12 diesel driving through a 3-speed hydro-mechanical gearbox. All models featured scow-end bodies heated by exhaust gases to ease dumping. The 40-ton Model 548 was added later, using a 560bhp V12 diesel, power-steering and air-hydraulic suspension. Tractor versions of the 540 and 548 are known respectively as the 540B and 548B. Since 1972 the Model 7525 40-ton coal truck and the 900bhp Model 549, a 75-tonner, have also been listed, along with a 125-ton articulated model with a gas-turbine engine. Finally, the KRAZ Model 256 6 x 4 bonneted chassis has been converted into a dump truck carrying the BELAZ name under which certain UAZ, URAL and ZIL models are also marketed outside the Soviet Union.

BELHAVEN/*Scotland 1907-1924*
Founded in 1907 as a subsidiary of Robert Morton & Sons Ltd, Belhaven Engineering & Motors Ltd, Wishaw, Lanarks, was established compound "undertype" engines

were listed until 1914. Meanwhile, petrol-engined trucks, using engines supplied by the Aster Engineering Co, were launched in 1908, replaced two years later by heavier chain-driven trucks, buses and charabancs, some of which were marketed, as Goodchild, by F B Goodchild & Co, London. After World War I, production continued with a 30/35hp 4-cyl petrol-engined 3-tonner with chain and spur-gear final-drive, some being used as a basis for the Scottish Co-operative Wholesale Society's Unitas truck.

BELL (1)/*England c1913-1919*
Although 1-, 1½- and 3-ton trucks were planned by Bell Bros, Ravensthorpe, Yorks, World War I prevented their manufacture and the Co-Operative Wholesale Society purchased manufacturing rights in 1919, constructing CWS or CWS Bell trucks by the end of 1920.

BELL (2)/*USA 1913-1915*
Railway engineers Bell & Waring, New York City, developed a 6-ton steam dump truck which had an engine comprising twin double-acting cyls. By 1914 the company was re-registered as the Bell & Waring Steam Vehicle Co, being re-named the American Motor Freight Co Inc in 1915 and the Bell Locomotive Co just a few months later.

BELL (3)/*USA 1918*
A manufacturer of passenger cars and light commercials, the Bell Motor Car Co, York, Pennsylvania, also built a short-lived 1½-tonner.

BELL (4)/*USA 1919-1923*
The Iowa Motor Truck Co was set up at Ottumwa, Iowa, to construct Bell trucks aimed at local agricultural communities. Using 4-cyl Buda petrol engines, Russell internal-gear axles and artillery wheels with solid tyres, the Bell was unusual for a US-built truck in that it had an extended frame

ahead of the radiator, serving also as a bumper. Initially, 1½- and 2½-ton versions were listed, later joined by a 1-tonner.

BELLABEY/*Switzerland 1913-1914*
Soc des Camions Dufour, Nyon, manufacturer of Dufour commercials, was taken over by Etienne Bellabey et Cie in 1913, subsequent models being sold as Bellabey or Dufour-Bellabey. The new company inherited an unusual design with transverse 3-cyl petrol engine located behind the front axle and connected to the gearbox by a belt-drive system. Chain final-drive was employed. The company's last trucks, for payloads of 2½ and 3 tons, were capable of 24km/h flat out, powered by a 3-litre 18/24hp petrol engine.

BELLISS & MORCOM/*England 1907*
Belliss & Morcom Ltd, Birmingham, constructed an open-top double-deck steam bus using a semi-flash boiler located under the bonnet, compound "undertype" engine and chain final-drive. It went into experimental service with the London General Omnibus Co Ltd but was withdrawn towards the end of 1908.

BELLPORT/*England c1918-?*
F B Goodchild & Co, vehicle importers, of Westminster, London, advertised a range of trucks using the Bellport name and believed to be of American origin. Capacities were listed as 1, 2½/3 and 3½/4 tons and the design followed conventional American lines of the period.

BELMONT/*USA 1919-1923*
The 1½-ton Belmont was built by the Belmont Motors Corp, Lewistown, Pennsylvania, using a 26bhp 4-cyl Continental petrol engine and other proprietary components. When truck-building came to an end the factory became a sales and service depot for Kearns trucks.

BEDFORD/*England 1931 to date*
In 1931 General Motors decided to construct a British equivalent of its American Chevrolet range, then assembled at Hendon, North London. New production facilities were set up at the Luton, Beds, factory of Vauxhall Motors Ltd and the Bedford commercial range introduced. The first was a bonneted 2-tonner, almost identical to the imported Chevrolet, inheriting the latter's 4-wheel mechanical brakes and spiral-bevel drive but anglicized by a new 44bhp 3.2-litre 4-bearing 6-cyl petrol engine and 4-speed transmission. Three goods and two passenger models were listed, all on the same chassis, passenger types comprising the 3.27-m wheelbase 14-seat WHB and the 3.92-m wheelbase 20-seat WLB.

By 1932 these had been joined by a new 1½-ton truck running on single tyres. A variety of standardized bodies was offered, from vans to pantechnicons, through flat and dropside trucks to fire appliances. The first 3-tonner – the snub-nosed short-wheelbase WTS or long-wheelbase WTL – was announced in 1934 with a power output of 57bhp and vacuum servo-assisted brakes. In 1936 a 26-seat passenger model appeared, based on the new range and the earlier 1½- and 2-ton models were re-designed to bring them into line.

There were a number of innovations in 1938. The first Bedford-Scammell artics, for gross loads of up to 12 tons, were listed as factory-produced models and a new 72bhp 3.5-litre petrol engine announced. The now legendary "bullnose" Bedfords also appeared, initially with the angular 'W'-Type cab, but by 1940 with a rounded cab incorporating a split windscreen. A new passenger design – the famous 'OB' – was launched in 1939, production being interrupted by the war. The 'OB' was to become the mainstay of virtually every British coach operator up to 1948.

During World War II some 250,000 Bedford trucks were supplied to the Services, comprising mainly the 1½-ton 'OX', 3-ton 'OY' and 4 x 4 3-ton 'QL' – the first factory-built forward-control Bedford. To simplify production and aid repairs, the 'OX' and 'OY' had angular bonnets and heavy-duty bumper bars. In 1941 the 'OY' was offered for limited civilian use and, to aid public transport badly hit by wartime shortages, a utility version of the 'OB', called the 'OWB', was made available, having a 26-seat body with slatted wooden seats.

By 1947 500,000 Bedfords had been built but until 1950 the range was based largely on pre-war

1972 Bedford KMR prototype artic tractor

"bullnose" designs such as the 'K' 1½-tonner, 'MS' and 'ML' 2-tonners, 'OSA' and 'OLA' 5-tonners and the 'OSS' Bedford-Scammell tractor. At the 1950 Commercial Motor Show the 7-ton 'Big Bedford', known as the 'S'-Type, made its debut. This had full forward-control, a 110bhp 4.9-litre 7-bearing 6-cyl petrol engine, a synchromesh gearbox and hypoid rear axle. Brakes were hydro-mechanical but were soon changed to full hydraulic and the 'SB' passenger version quickly introduced. It was followed by a 4-wheel drive load-carrier known as the 'R'-Type which subsequently became the British Services' standard 4 x 4 3-tonner.

The now somewhat dated bonneted range was re-designed in 1953, using synchromesh gearboxes, new cabs and, on heavier models, a hypoid rear axle. Perkins diesel engines were now optional on all models over 4 tons ca-

pacity. In 1954 a truck plant was opened at nearby Dunstable and 1957 saw new 4- and 6-ton 'Big Bedfords' and a bonneted 6½-tonner with single-speed axle. The first Bedford diesel engine, a 97bhp 4.9-litre direct-injection 6-cyl unit, also appeared in 1957, followed by a 3.3-litre 4-cyl model a year later. More powerful diesels came from Perkins and later, Leyland. Five-speed transmissions and 2-speed axles were new options and in May 1958 the millionth Bedford came off the line.

The 1960 Commercial Motor Show was particularly significant as it was here that the much rumoured 'TK' forward-control range made its debut. Prototypes had already been seen on test, mainly on the Continent, carrying the GMC brand name and it was certainly a General Motors inspired design with full forward-control 3-man non-tilt cab and engine behind the seats. On the

passenger front, the short-wheelbase 'VAS', with 3.5-litre 6-cyl petrol or 4.9-litre 6-cyl diesel engine, fitted respectively with hydrovac or air-hydraulic braking, joined the 'SB' and in 1962 the revolutionary 11-m twin-steer 'VAL' for 52-seat bodywork was announced, with a 131bhp 6-cyl Leyland diesel engine, 5-speed gearbox, power-steering and 406-mm wheels.

Two years later the normal-control truck range was re-

1952 Bedford SB coach

vamped as the 'TJ' and heavier 'TK' models for gross weights of up to 12¼ tons appeared the following year, powered by a 6.5-litre Leyland diesel engine. In 1966 1½- and 2-ton low-loading 'TK's were introduced for urban delivery or municipal use and a new medium-capacity passenger chassis, the 'VAM', was added to the passenger line. A new heavy-duty truck, the 'KM', also went into production that year, taking the Bedford range up to the 16 tons GVW mark for the first time and introducing a new 7.6-litre 145bhp 6-cyl Bedford diesel engine.

Another significant year was 1969. The company's first factory-built 6-wheeler with single- or double-drive, began to leave the Dunstable plant where all truck production was now concentrated, and the lightweight 'CA'-Ser-

1933 Bedford WTL truck

ies was replaced by the ¾ to 1¾-ton 'CF' with 1.6- or 2-litre Bedford petrol engines or a new 62bhp 4-cyl diesel option, also inheriting such 'CA' features as independent front suspension, synchromesh transmission and hypoid rear axle. In 1970 the 'R'-Type 4 x 4 was replaced by the 'TK'-derived 'M'-Type while the 'YRT' passenger model introduced a vertical amidships-mounted diesel engine located between the chassis frame side-members.

1931 Bedford WHB single-deck coach

By 1971 operators of Australian Bedfords were being offered a heavy-duty 'KM' tractor powered by a 7-litre 2-stroke Detroit Diesel V6 of 195bhp with 10-speed Fuller 'Roadranger' box and 2-speed axle, and within two years a similar specification was available in limited quantities on the UK market, with Lipe-Rollway twin-plate clutch, Fuller RT0609 constant-mesh 9-speed range-change box, dual-circuit air brakes, an air-assisted handbrake and power steering. The majority joined the company's own works fleet for operation at 32 tons GCW, and a logical improvement on this was the introduction of the 'TM'-Series at the 1974 Commercial Motor Show, with spacious tilt-cabs, Detroit Diesel 2-stroke engines, servo-assisted twin-plate clutches, 9-speed range-change boxes, power steering and full air brakes. The 'TM' embraced numerous drive and axle configurations and various lengths with 6-wheeled rigids for up to 24 tons gross and tractors up to 32 tons.

It was some time before staid British operators accepted the 'TM', perhaps due to the fact that heavyweight Bedfords were an unknown quantity and the thought of a 2-stroke diesel

brought back sour memories of other 2-strokes. To counteract this, an 8.2-litre 6-cyl Bedford diesel engine was offered in 1975 and, gradually, sales picked up.

The official end for the bonneted 'TJ' range came in 1976, although some are still built to special order, and the following year saw a 4 x 4 version of the 'TM' with turbocharged 6-cyl diesel engine. A new 'TM' tractor powered by a 380bhp Detroit Diesel V8 was launched on the Italian market for operation at 44 tons

1977 Bedford TM1700

GCW, while trials were now underway into battery-electric propulsion in association with Lucas Batteries Ltd and a new unitary-construction midibus, called the 'JJL', was developed jointly with Marshall of Cambridge, using a rear-mounted 5.4-litre 6-cyl diesel engine with Allison automatic box and air-hydraulic brakes.

For 1978 the 'TK' range embraced both 4 x 2 and 6 x 2 models, from 5½ to 16 tons GVW, plus tractors; the 'TM' series was offered in a multitude of configurations from 16 tons GVW up to 44 tons GCW; there was the 4 x 4 'M'-Type for 11 tons GVW; and no less than four passenger models, two of which now had underfloor engines. Early in 1980, some twenty years after it first appeared, the 'TK' was at last replaced by the tiltcab 'TL' range.

BEDFORD BLITZ/Germany
1975 to date

In 1975 General Motors announced the demise of the Opel commercial range in favour of British-designed Bedfords marketed under the Bedford Blitz name. A 38-ton GCW tractor was developed for the German market using a V8-engined Bedford 'TM', but this was a short-lived model. The Bedford Blitz range now comprises only badge-engineered British models.

1913 Belsize 3-ton mailvan

BELSIZE/England 1906-1918

Belsize Motors Ltd was established in Manchester in 1906 to develop a series of commercial vehicles. The first was a fire appliance for the London Fire Brigade, fitted out by John Morris & Sons Ltd, Salford, and powered by a 40hp 4-cyl petrol engine. Twin solid tyres were fitted all round. A shaft-drive 3-tonner with 28hp 4-cyl petrol engine was introduced in 1911, also offered as a charabanc, and joined by a series of massive fire appliances with 14.5-litre 50/80hp petrol engines supplied by the Forman Motor Co, Coventry, and incorporating four cyls cast in pairs with valves on both sides. Equipment was again by John Morris with a main turbo pump of 500gpm by Mather & Platt. A 3-cyl exhauster was used to prime the turbine and bodywork was of the "Braidwood" type, often with a 17-m wheeled escape. They remained in production until 1914, by which time new 1½- and 3-ton trucks had been introduced. After World War I production was confined almost entirely to light vans.

BENDER/USA c1961-?

The Bender Co, a division of Bender Oil Operations, Bakersfield, California, developed mobile oil well servicing and exploration rigs mounted on specially designed ultra-long-wheelbase rigid 6-wheeled chassis. Featuring a one-man half-cab and single-section 20-, 25-, 27- or 28-m hinged drilling masts, the Bender system required no securing ropes and was entirely self-contained with all power and winching equipment incorporated.

BENDIX/USA 1908-1909

Offered in wheelbase lengths up to 2.79m, the Bendix was a 4-cyl petrol-engined high-wheeler for 1090kg loads built by the Bendix Co, Chicago, Illinois, using a friction transmission with chain-drive to each rear wheel.

BENZ/Germany 1900-1926

Benz & Co Rheinische Gasmotorfabrik, manufacturer of passenger and light commercial models, was re-registered Benz & Co Rheinische Gasmotorenfabrik AG in 1899 and a year later the first true Benz commercial, a 1¼-ton 6hp job with single-cyl petrol engine located beneath the driver's footboard, was introduced. This had a 4-speed belt-driven gearbox and double chain-drive to the rear wheels, being quickly joined by 2½- and 5-tonners, the first with a 10hp engine and the second with a 14hp unit.

Suddeutsche Automobil Fabrik GmbH, Gaggenau, was acquired in 1910, and the bulk of commercial vehicle production transferred to this plant, the products of which were often referred to as Benz-Gaggenau from 1911, including vans, trucks, buses, municipal types and even fire appliances of up to 6 tons payload. By 1914 a militarized Benz had appeared, with canvas cab roof and tilt body, and after World War I the company, which was now called Benz & Co Rheinische Automobil und Motorenfabrik AG, began developing a pre-combustion chamber diesel engine using principles laid down by Prosper L'Orange. The first examples were fitted in agricultural tractors by 1923 and adapted for truck use soon after, when Benz displayed the world's first diesel-engined lorry at the 1924 Amsterdam Motor Show. This was a 5-tonner with a 50bhp 4-cyl engine driving the rear axle via a cardan shaft.

The 1920s saw a complete line of petrol-engined Benz trucks in 1½-, 2-, 3- and 5-ton capacities with engines of between 25 and 36bhp output. One remarkable development was a "low chassis" model with forward-control offered in truck, bus or special-purpose form in 1924. At about this time, production moved to Ottenau where it finally ceased when the company combined with Daimler-Motoren-Gesellschaft to form Daimler-Benz AG, manufacturer of Mercedes-Benz vehicles.

BERGMANN/Germany 1907-1939

Bergmann Elektrizitäts-Werke AG, Berlin, which had previously built the Bergmann-Gaggenau 1½-tonner, manufactured chain- and cardan-drive battery-electrics carrying the Bergmann or Fulgura brand names, with batteries located under a bonnet, and traction motors beneath the floor. In 1909 Metallurgique-designed commercials were introduced under the Bergmann-Metallurgique name but constructed alongside the battery-electrics which remained the mainstay of production. Heaviest was a two-motor 5-tonner and one of the most popular a 2-ton van.

BERGMANN-GAGGENAU/Germany 1906-1907

The Bergmann-Gaggenau was a 1½-ton chain-drive van built briefly by Bergmann Elektrizitäts-Werke AG, Berlin, using a Benz petrol engine and components supplied by Suddeutsche Automobilfabrik GmbH, Gaggenau. From 1907 this manufacturer concentrated on the construction of Bergmann and Fulgura battery-electrics.

BERGMANN-METALLUR-GIQUE/Germany 1909-1914, 1918-1922

Bergmann Elektrizitäts-Werke AG, Berlin, was already producing Bergmann and Fulgura battery-electric commercials when it acquired manufacturing licences for the French-designed Metallurgique petrol-engined range. With capacities of up to 4 tons, Bergmann-Metallurgique vans, trucks and buses employed components common to the company's bat-

tery-electrics and all were of bonneted layout. Some were merely petrol-engine versions of battery-electric models. Licences were suspended during World War I, but production resumed later.

BERGOMI/Italy ? to date

Using chassis supplied by Lancia and Perlini, Bergomi SpA, Milan, has specialized for many years in the construction of emergency service vehicles, particularly for airfield use. These are usually of 4-wheel drive layout with roof-mounted foam monitoring units and one or two V8 petrol engines located side by side at the rear.

1960 Bergomi fire appliance

BERKSHIRE/USA 1906-1907

The Berkshire Automobile Co, Pittsfield, Massachusetts, constructed several delivery vehicles on modified car chassis, adding a forward-control 3-ton truck with the engine beneath the footboard, a 3-speed transmission and double chain-drive.

BERNARD

France 1923-1966

The first Bernard was a 1½/2-tonner built by SA des Bennes Basculantes E Bernard, Arcueil, Seine. Shown at the 1923 Paris Salon, it had a 2.6-litre 4-cyl side-valve petrol engine driving a double-reduction axle through a 4-speed box. A 2½-tonner was announced in 1926, quickly followed by a bonneted drop-frame high-speed coach along American lines powered by a US-built 6-cyl side-valve petrol engine.

By 1929, when the firm was re-registered Camions Bernard, it was assembling its own 3.6-and 5.2-litre engines. A series of bonneted goods models, developed from the passenger model, was announced, using a straight-frame version of the passenger chassis and obtaining its low-loading qualities from the use of extremely deep and low-slung chassis frame sidemembers.

In 1932 Bernard launched the 6½-ton F8 with 6.8-litre straight-8 side-valve petrol engine, 5-speed overdrive box, hydraulic brakes and automatic chassis lubrication. A licence was acquired to manufacture the British Gardner diesel engine in 70bhp 4- and 100bhp 6-

cyl forms, and by 1934 a 3-cyl version had been developed for use in mediumweight chassis. Air-cooled transmission brakes and 5-speed gear-boxes were standard for all diesel Bernards. Petrol engines were not used after 1935 when a 12/15-ton 6-wheeler with 6-cyl diesel engine and servo brakes was announced. Optional electro-magnetic transmission brakes were listed for 1938 models. At the outbreak of war standard types comprised goods models from 6 to 12 tons capacity, passenger designs with up to 47 seats and an unusual armoured tractor with articulated steering. Pre-war designs continued after the war with passenger models phased out in favour of heavy 4- and 6-wheeled trucks with 8.4-litre 6-cyl diesel engines. Gear-boxes were now mounted in unit with the engine, and other developments included multi-plate clutches and air-hydraulic brakes. A 5-speed box was re-introduced in 1948 in conjunction with a 5.6-litre 4-cyl engine and by 1950 new options included full air brakes and a 12.1-litre engine. Disc-type transmission handbrakes, 2-speed auxiliary boxes and power-steering appeared in 1953, and aluminium chassis frames in 1954/5. Turbocharged engines were at the experimental stage. A 200bhp V8 diesel engine was announced in

1964 Bernard Type 19 D180 tanker

1958, as was the 'Elephant', a weird off-road tractor with track-type steering. In 1960 a bellows-type air suspension system was tried and the goods range now covered capacities of 19 to 35 tons. Wrapround windscreens on bonneted models and a futuristic dual headlamp forward-control cab by Philippe Charbonneaux were brought in to make Bernards more competitive. To improve vehicle performance, engine capacity was increased and 10-speed transmissions standardized. In 1963 the company was acquired by Mack Trucks Inc, who renamed it Automobiles Bernard the following year. Whilst the existing Bernard range continued, some interesting hybrids were developed, usually under the Mack-Bernard name, but the association was unsuccessful and by 1966 the company had been wound up. Despite this, the 1967 Paris Salon included a Bernard display of imported Macks.

BERNA/Switzerland 1905 to date

A 2-tonner, designated Type 'K', with 2-cyl monobloc petrol engine located under the driver's seat, was the first commercial vehicle to be built by J Wyss Schweizerische Automobilfabrik Berna, Olten, but only a few of this chain-drive design were built before it was succeeded by a heavier and even shorter-lived model powered by a massive 2-cyl petrol engine. In 1906 the first of the 5-ton Gl range appeared. It was powered by a 6.3-litre 35/40hp 4-cyl petrol engine driving through a 4-speed box, propeller shaft and differential to a spur hub-reduction system comprising a small pinion meshing with a large-diameter internal-toothed crown wheel.

Both goods and passenger versions were built, one being the second self-propelled post bus to be used by the Swiss Post Office. Later that year the company was reconstituted as Motorwerke Berna AG but sales were far from satisfactory and wasteful development of a new passenger car led the company into a financial crisis. It was saved in 1908 by the British firm of Hudson Consolidated which installed Ernst Marti, a former Berna designer, at the head of the new operation, now anglicized as Berna Commercial Motors Ltd and offering a variety of commercial models based on earlier designs. For 1909 the range included 'C', 'F', 'G', 'H' and 'J' goods models from 1½ to 6 tons capacity with passenger types for between 12 and 36 persons. Engines ranged from a 2-litre 4-cyl monobloc unit through 2-, 3- and 4-cyl 'L'-head units with interchangeable components of 16/20, 26/30 and 35/40hp. A leather cone clutch and 3- or 4-speed transmissions were other features. By 1910 the smallest engine had been superseded by an enlarged version of the 'T'-head 4-cyl design and, with the 'J' range discontinued, a new 'L' model was introduced using a multi-plate clutch and worm final-drive, a new departure for Berna. There was also a new 'V' model, with 3.1-litre 20/22hp 4-cyl monobloc 'L'-head engine and a capacity of 2 tons.

In 1912 the company reverted to Swiss ownership as Motorwagenfabrik Berna AG. Exports were good and from 1914 to 1918 the Swiss-designed Berna was also licence-assembled in Britain as the British Berna by Henry Watson & Sons Ltd, Newcastle-upon-Tyne. Two years later Berna took over the Zurich factory of Franz Brozincevic & Cie where it commenced production of the 2-ton 'E' model with 5.3-litre 20hp 4-cyl monobloc petrol engine. The 3½/4-ton C2 was announced – one of

1959 Berna 'U'-line outside broadcast van

the company's most successful trucks – at this time, utilizing a 5.5-litre 4-cyl 'L'-head petrol engine with cyls cast in pairs. Transmission comprised a leather cone clutch and 4-speed box. It was supplied to Swiss, British and French armies in World War I and was reputed to be virtually indestructible.

A heavier but not dissimilar model for 5-ton loads was the 'G', employing a bored-out C2 engine. More unusual was a short-wheelbase road tractor for hauling Swiss Army howitzers. With an end to hostilities, the C2 was adapted for civilian use and the artillery tractor sold for agricultural applications. To cater for new sales in Austria, Germany and surrounding areas, licence-assembly was introduced by Perl of Vienna and Jakob & Hegedus, Budapest.

After the war the company improved existing models, calling the up-dated 'G' the G3. Meanwhile, 'E' production was closed down and the former Franz factory became purely a maintenance shop. Sales improved somewhat during the early 1920s when the Swiss authorities brought in new duties on imported trucks, and by 1923 the G4 range was in production. This used the old twin-block 4-cyl petrol engine, now increased to 8.5 litres and with a power output of 55bhp. The G4 had a fully-enclosed cab and up-rated payload of 5/6 tons. By 1926 the company's home sales were second only to Soc des Automobiles Industriels Saurer, and by 1928 Berna was licence-building 4- and 6-cyl Deutz diesel engines. Another innovation was a unique braking system controlled by a lever on the steering column which acted upon the engine compression thus retarding the engine and, in turn, the vehicle. We now know this as the exhaust brake.

A complete transformation took place in 1929 when Saurer

1960 Berna 5VU truck

acquired a controlling interest in Berna. It was to be many years before Berna was to lose its own design identity but the move did result in the company adopting Saurer's 8-litre 105bhp 6-cyl overhead-valve diesel engine rather than its own licence-built Deutz units. By 1932 the company was assembling German-designed Adler trucks under licence in the 1½ to 3 tons payload class, designating these the L1, L2 and L3 and fitting a 2.9-litre 50bhp 6-cyl side-valve petrol engine in the smaller and a 3.1-litre 60bhp unit in the larger. Major components were supplied by Adler and later the L2D and L3D types with 4.5-litre 4-cyl diesel engines were added. Heavier L4, L5 and L5A models, as well as the old-style G6A, were all offered with the Saurer BLD diesel engine and later with its successor, the CLD. A few 6-wheeled rigids were assembled briefly but Swiss authorities were not disposed towards this layout and such models were quickly dropped. By the early 1930s the Swiss economy was at a very low ebb, and the company acquired the remains of Soc Nouvelle des Automobiles Martini, in 1933, in whose factory Berna hoped to assemble Renault cars under licence. This was not to be and the factory was resold.

The bonneted 'U' range, equivalent to the 'C' range Saurer, was anounced in 1936 and by 1939 nine goods models were listed. Lightest were the 3.95-m wheelbase L1 and L2 with 1- and 2½-ton payloads, 6-cyl petrol engines, magneto ignition, 4-speed transmission and hydraulic brakes. The mediumweight 'U' range used 4-cyl overhead-valve direct-injection diesel engines and had payloads of between 2 and 4 tons. Other features included a single dry-plate clutch, 5-speed overdrive synchromesh transmission and hydraulic or vacuum-hydraulic braking. Heavy trucks were catered for by the 4-ton 3U-T, with a 6.75-litre 105bhp 6-cyl overhead-valve diesel engine, and the 4U-T1, L5A/1D-L and G6A/1D, with 8-litre 110bhp diesel engine and 5- or 8-speed overdrive box. There were also a number of drawbar tractors for heavy haulage with the Swiss Railways who required a minimum 54-ton load to be hauled up a 10% gradient.

A producer-gas engine based on the old 8.3-litre 4-cyl G5 engine was developed during World War II, followed by producer-gas versions of more modern diesels. Trucks were delivered to the Swiss Army for home defence, most being 3-tonners which, apart from their badges and model designations, were identical to Saurer models. During the war the 8-litre 6-cyl diesel-engined 5U replaced the L5A and G6A and apart from the L1 and L2 all models had air-hydraulic brakes.

After 1945 a forward-control version of the 'U' range was developed, followed in the early 1950s by the forward-control 4UM and 5UM 4 x 4s with 125bhp 6-cyl diesel engines disengageable front-wheel drive and 10-speed transmissions. Both became popular for hauling heavy loads on mountainous roads. City buses, coaches and trolleybuses were developed.

The 'V' range was announced in 1956, and by 1960 the lightest Berna was the forward- or normal-control 4½-ton 2US, with a choice of 4- or 6-cyl diesel engines.

Equipped with an 8-speed transmission incorporating a compressed air overdrive, it had semi-elliptic leaf springs, air-hydraulic brakes and an exhaust brake. For 5½/6-ton loads, the L4U was available. This had an 8.7-litre 125bhp 6-cyl T2 engine but with a similar specification to the 2US, apart from power-steering. The U5 was now offered with the T2 or supercharged T2LM engines, or even the 8-cyl 160bhp H2V or 12.7-litre H5 V8 of 175bhp. Payload was about 9 tons. The heaviest model was the forward-control 6U-H with an 8-cyl engine and a payload of 10/11 tons. New models were headed by the 6-ton forward-control 3VUR with Saurer DCU 10.3-litre 6-cyl 160bhp overhead-valve engine or 210bhp supercharged DCUL beneath the floor. The similar 5VU was designed for 9-ton loads and the 2H was a forward-control bus with rear-mounted R2LM 5.8-litre 115bhp diesel engine. Four-wheel drive models included the 2VM and 5VM powered by a 10.3-litre 160bhp 6-cyl diesel engine.

The 'U' range was replaced by 1965 by forward- and normal-control 2V and 5V models with engines of between 120 and 210bhp output, sometimes located beneath the floor. A tractor range was also offered on these chassis and 4 x 4 models were up-dated. In 1969 the 18-ton double-drive 6-wheeler with 11.6-litre 310bhp engine was announced. The 2V was replaced by the 4V in 1972, powered by an 8.8-litre 200bhp CK 6-cyl diesel coupled to a 12-speed synchromesh transmission. The CK engine was also installed in the 4VF tractor and 4VM 4 x 4 chassis. The heavier 5V range received the 12.5-litre D2K 6-cyl engine by 1974, with the 330bhp turbo-supercharged D2KT optional. The D2KT is also used in the 5VF double-drive rigid-8 for 18-ton payloads.

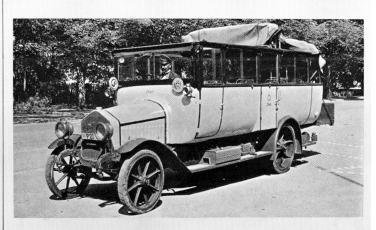

1921 Berna single-deck postbus

BERRY/*England 1902-1903*

A W Berry, Colchester, Essex, constructed a 5-ton "undertype" steam wagon for the Colchester Brewing Co. It incorporated two double-crank compound marine type engines set side by side across the chassis frame. Two 3-speed gearboxes and two chains transmitted drive to the rear wheels, while a shaft clutch between each engine and gearbox enabled either wheel to be freed from that engine to obviate the need for compensating gear. The vertical boiler had a central coke-firing chute, but could not supply the steam that the engines required.

BERTOLINI/*Italy c1964*

Agricultural machinery engineers Bertolini Macchine Agricole SpA, Ferrara, built lightweight load-carriers aimed mainly at agricultural users. These were equipped with 36bhp 2-cyl or 38bhp 3-cyl air-cooled diesel engines and seven forward and three reverse transmissions.

BESSEMER/*USA 1911-1926*

The Bessemer Motor Truck Co, Grove City, Pennsylvania, announced 1- and 2-ton trucks powered by 4-cyl Continental petrol engines. These had a cone clutch, 3-speed transmission and chain-drive. An internal gear-drive 1-tonner appeared in 1916, along with a 1½-ton chain-drive and 2-, 3½- and 5-ton worm-drive models. Chain-drive was discontinued two years later, by which time all models had a dry plate clutch, the 3½-tonner being replaced by a 4-tonner in 1919. In 1923 the company merged with the American Motors Corp, Plainfield, New Jersey, becoming the Bessemer-American Corp, and moved to Plainfield later that year. A 16-seat bus joined the range but the only other new designs were a 3-tonner in 1924 and a 1-ton "speed truck", with 6-cyl Continental petrol engine, in 1926.

BEST/*USA 1913-1914*

The well-known steam traction engine builder, Best Mfg Co, San Leandro, California, introduced a 1-ton petrol-engined truck in 1913. This had a 4-cyl engine located beneath the body, selective transmission and shaft-drive, but few were built.

BEST ON EARTH/*USA 1911-1913*

The Motor Conveyance Co, Milwaukee, Wisconsin, built the Best on Earth truck range, also known as the BOE, as a bare chassis or with flat body. Two-, 3- and 6-tonners were built, the heaviest having a structural steel chassis frame and 11.3-litre 4-cyl petrol engine.

BETHLEHEM/*USA 1917-1926*

The Bethlehem truck was manufactured by the Bethlehem Motors Corp, Allentown, Pennsylvania. Initial production comprised the 1¼-ton Model 'D' with 25hp 4-cyl petrol engine and the 2¼-ton Model 'E' with 30hp 4-cyl petrol engine, quickly joined by a 3½-tonner known as the Model 'F', with a 40hp 4-cyl petrol engine. The company also built some 5-ton Class 'B' "Liberty" trucks for the Armed Forces. In 1919 North American Motors was acquired to provide an in-company engine source and in 1920 the original Bethlehem models were re-designated the 'DG', 'EH' and 'FJ'. Some were assembled briefly in Britain by the Scottish Motor Traction Co Ltd. Bus manufacture also got underway but the American firm went into receivership in 1921. Under new management, a revised range was introduced, comprising the Model 'K' 1-tonner, 'G' 2-tonner, 'H' 3-tonner and 'J' 4-tonner. Production gradually dwindled, however, and despite new 2½- and 3½-tonners, the plant was sold to the Hahn Motor Truck Co.

BETZ/*USA 1919-1929*

The Betz Motor Truck Co, Hammond, Indiana, launched its truck range with a 2½-tonner utilizing a 4-cyl Buda petrol engine, Brown-Lipe 4-speed box and Timken worm-drive axle. A 1-tonner was announced in 1924, and from 1925 both 1- and 1½-ton capacity trucks with 4- and 6-cyl petrol engines were listed.

BEV/*England 1926-1957*

Offering a wide range of battery-electric trucks covering capacities of up to 20 tons, most BEV products were used within the confines of works and factories or for inter-plant journeys. Built by Wingrove & Rogers Ltd, Liverpool, and later by British Electric Vehicles Ltd, Southport, Lancs, production returned to Liverpool before closing completely.

Beyer-Peacock 5-ton steam wagon

BEYER-PEACOCK/*England c1903-c1914*

Also known as the Gorton, the Beyer-Peacock steam wagon was built by Beyer Peacock Ltd, Gorton, Manchester. A 5-tonner, it had Ackermann-style steering designed by H A Hoy of the Lancashire & Yorkshire Railway, who was later to join Beyer Peacock as General Manager. The high-pressure duplex engine was located horizontally beneath the chassis, transmission being effected by a countershaft differential and double chain-drive. The first few had a multi-tube vertical boiler with chimney to one side, but post-1906 models were re-designed, using a top-fired water-jacketed firebox with inclined firetubes carried in a short extension, similar to the angled boiler used in the Wallis 'Simplicity' roller. A prototype was shown at the 1906 Liverpool Motor Show, but subsequently used as works transport, and possibly as a mobile test-bed for a steam railcar the company was developing.

BIAMAX/*Greece 1961 to date*

The first chassisless passenger model to be built by Biamax SA, Athens, was the 'R'-Series, an inter-city bus or coach with rear-mounted 126bhp 6-cyl Mercedes-Benz diesel engine and independent front suspension. In 1962 a prototype single-deck trolleybus, with CGE traction equipment, was also built but it was not until 1968 that the now popular 'F'-Series, particularly for Middle East and African markets, was launched. This has an underfloor 6-cyl Mercedes-Benz diesel.

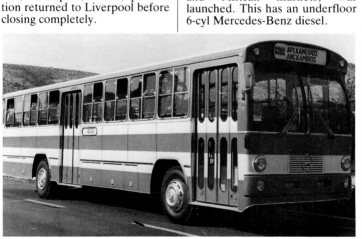

1981 Biamax OF1617 single-deck bus

BERLIET/*France 1906-1980*

The first true commercial built by Automobiles M Berliet SA, Lyons, was an experimental forward-control 2-tonner, with wooden wheels, iron tyres, double chain-drive and petrol engine located beneath the driver. In 1907 the first production models, with 6.3-litre 4-cyl 'T'-head petrol engines and 4-speed transmissions, left the factory, and by 1909 models from 1½ to 4 tons capacity were listed.

Up to 1911 all heavy Berliets were of cab-over-engine layout, the first bonneted model being a 2-tonner popular both for goods and passenger operation. By 1914 the range covered various sizes from a shaft-drive 1-tonner to a chain-drive 6-tonner, all powered by 4-cyl side-valve petrol engines of varying capacities and equipped with magneto ignitions, thermo-syphon cooling and 4-speed transmissions. Nearly 25,000 examples of the bonneted CBA 4/5-tonner were supplied to the Services during World War I, featuring chain-drive and a 5.3-litre petrol engine, and this was the only heavy commercial available from the company after the war. Like so many European manufacturers of the day, the company was badly affected by a glut of war-surplus vehicles and in 1921 went into receivership, just saved by a new 1½-tonner with 3.3-litre 4-cyl monobloc engine. In 1924 the first all-wheel drive Berliets were supplied to the military, later developed to include a 4 x 4 rear-engined command car and various front-engined 6 x 6 types. Experiments with producer-gas, using the Imbert system, also got underway, and the first of a series of battery-electric trucks was introduced. By 1926 the range included models up to 7½ tons capacity with chain-drive on heavier types and worm- or double-reduction bevel-drive for lighter models. Pneumatic tyres were standard for models of less than 4 tons capacity while the only forward-control chassis were the GSB and GSD passenger types. The VKR high-speed coach chassis of 1927 was the first Berliet commercial to use a 6-cyl engine, this being a 4.1-litre side-valve petrol unit. Battery-electric models, all with 2-speed axles, were often indistinguishable from petrol-engined chassis, one forward-control 5-tonner even having a dummy radiator.

In 1930 an 8-litre 6-cyl petrol engine was fitted in a heavy road tractor with solid rear tyres and a new 6 x 6 design with 4-wheel steering and 8 forward speeds. Berliet's first diesel engines – 7.2-litre 4- and 10.9-litre 6-cyl units – were made available from 1932 in

appliance. The company soon constructed complete appliances.

BRADFORD/*England 1913-1922*
Bradford City Tramways constructed 26 trolleybuses for its own use, due mainly to the lack of suitable models available from established builders. Most were small single-deckers but as an experiment in 1920, the world's

1920 Bradford trolley bus

first covered-top, double-deck trolleybus was built. Fitted with Dick Kerr traction equipment, it seated 51 passengers and was demonstrated to many other municipalities. In 1922 a heavy twin-steer 6-wheeler designed to equal the carrying capabilities of existing trams was built, with 59 seats and an unladen weight of 7 tons. It ran on solid tyres and had twin inter-connected steering axles. Metropolitan-Vickers traction equipment was used.

BRADSHAW/*England 1902-1909*
James Bradshaw & Sons, Bolton, Lancs, built five experimental steam wagons. The first had a double compound engine, later re-built as a 4-in-line single-acting unit. A vertical coal– or coke-fired water-tube boiler was fitted and other features included a slip-eccentric reversing mechanism and double chain-drive. The company became the Bolton Motor Wagon Co in 1907, which led to the last of its wagons being referred to incorrectly as Boltons.

BRANT-FORD/*Canada 1917*
The Brant-Ford was a Model 'T' Ford 1-tonner lengthened by the Brantford Motor Truck Co Ltd, Brantford, Ontario. Fitted with chain-drive, this replaced Brantford's earlier truck-building projects.

BRANTFORD/*Canada 1911-1917*
The Brantford Motor Truck Co Ltd, Brantford, Ontario, constructed "coal-scuttle" bonneted trucks of up to 1½ tons capacity, with radiator behind the engine.

These featured a demountable body system, whereby one body could be removed for loading while another was being delivered. The range was discontinued in favour of a lengthened Model 'T' Ford which was known as the Brant-Ford.

BRASIER/*France 1902-1928*
Soc des Ans Ets Georges Richard, Ivry-Port, Seine, replaced its light commercial range by a chain-drive 2-tonner in 1902, being re-named Soc des Automobiles Brasier in 1905. The company's first self-propelled conversion units for horse-drawn buses and vans appeared in 1909, using a 10/12hp vertical twin or 18hp 4-cyl petrol engine. A bonneted 2-tonner, with a 2-litre 12/20hp petrol engine, was built by 1913, joined by forward-control types of up to 4 tons capacity with circular radiators. Vehicles were supplied to the French Air Service during World War I and from 1915 certain military types of Italian Pavesi design were sold as Brasier-Pavesi. In 1919 a standardized normal-control truck range was announced and in 1926 the firm was re-named Soc Chaigneau-Brasier.

BRAUN/*Germany 1898-1918*
Nürnberger Feuerloschgerate und Maschinenfabrik vorm Justus Christian Braun, Nüremberg, manufactured fire-fighting equipment. Self-propelled appliances, with steam, petrol or petrol-electric propulsion, were offered, joined in 1906 by a 10-ton petrol-electric truck. Following the acquisition of Nürnberger Motor Fahrzeug-Fabrik Union GmbH in 1908, certain models were marketed as Kaiser, while 1911 saw the company re-constituted as Justus Christian Braun Premier-Werke AG, re-named two years later Nürnberger Feuerloschgerate Automobillast-Wagen und Fahr-zeug-Fabrik. All Braun trucks were now petrol-engined with conventional transmissions and in 1918 the company merged with Fahrzeugfabrik Ansbach GmbH, Ansbach, to form Fahrzeugfabriken Ansbach und Nürnberg, manufacturer of Faun commercials.

1903 Bretherton 5-ton 'undertype' steam wagon

BRAVIA/*Portugal 1964 to date*
Bravia Sarl, Lisbon, produces 4 x 4 and 6 x 6 military trucks using bought-in components. With payload capacities of up to 6 tons and a choice between petrol and diesel engines, models include the 'Comando', 'Gazella', 'Leopardo' and 'Pantera'.

BREDA/*Italy 1920-1945*
Specializing in the manufacture of military equipment, the most famous truck built by Soc Italiana Ernesto Breda, Milan, was a 4 x 4 heavy artillery tractor. In 1935 a forward-control 6 x 4 load-carrier was announced, later developed into a 7-ton cargo truck, and 1944 saw a large half-track vehicle developed along the lines of the Krauss-Maffei. The only civilian model appears to have been a single-deck trolleybus.

BREMACH/*Italy 1971 to date*
When AMF-Harley-Davidson Varese SpA, Varese, discontinued the Aermacchi 3-wheeler, production was taken over by Fratelli Brenna, using the Bremach name. Production centres upon a 1½-ton model with 1-litre 23bhp 2-cyl petrol engine and 4-speed transmission. This model has a fully-enclosed cab, wheel steering and hydraulic braking.

BRENNABOR/*Germany 1924-1932*
Although the first light Brennabor commercials were introduced in 1905 by Gebr Reichstein Brennabor-Werke, Brandenburg, it was not until 1924 that the company's first true commercial, a 1-tonner with 8/24 bhp petrol engine, made its debut. Trucks of 1½- and 2-tons capacity, plus an 18-seat passenger model, were soon added, all powered by a new 6-cyl petrol engine.

BRETHERTON/*England 1905-1908*
Frank Bretherton and L C Bryan, of Bretherton & Bryan, hauliers and engineers, North London, designed a 5-ton "undertype" steam wagon, which was assembled by traction engine builder Davey, Paxman & Co Ltd, Colchester, Essex, and marketed either as the Betherton or as the Bretherton & Bryan. It had a compound engine driving the rear wheels via 2-speed gearing and all-gear final-drive. The loco-type boiler was fired via the firebox crown. Bretherton later developed a completely stayless firebox for Ransomes and Robey wagons but left the firm in 1906, the company being re-named Bryan & Co, although continuing the Bretherton range.

BRIDGEPORT/*USA 1920-1927*
The Bridgeport Motor Truck Co, Bridgeport, Connecticut, built 4½- and 6-ton Hercules-engined trucks. Both were replaced in 1923 by Buda-engined designs from 1½- to 4-ton capacity, following a change of ownership to the Morrisey Motor Car Co. Vehicles continued as Bridgeport, a 30-seat bus known as the Model '45' being the only design offered in 1924 and 1925.

BRIGHTMORE/*England 1903*
The Brightmore was an ingenious articulated steam tractor assembled in prototype form by T Coulthard & Co Ltd, Preston, Lancs, to designs laid down by a Dr A W Brightmore. It had two wheels, and was carefully balanced with the vertical boiler ahead and engine behind the axle. Connected to the load-carrying trailer by a ball and socket joint, it provided a much larger load area

Brightmore artic steam wagon

than conventional machines and was also far more manoeuvrable. Steering was effected by applying a brake to one or other of the tractor axle half-shafts. Rated at 5 tons capacity, only one Brightmore is believed to have been built, production versions being known as Manchester.

BRILL/*USA 1921, 1930-1942, 1945-1953*
One of America's most well known streetcar builders, the J G Brill Co, Philadelphia, Pennsylvania, developed a prototype trolleybus in 1921. In 1925 the company was absorbed by the American Car & Foundry Motors Co, Detroit, Michigan, manufacturers of railway rolling stock, who wished to enter the passenger vehicle market. In 1930 the Brill name re-appeared on trolleybuses with components common to many ACF buses, production being discontinued during the war. In 1948 a range of small rear-engined city buses with International Harvester petrol engines was also marketed under the Brill name to distinguish them from the Hall-Scott engined ACF-Brill.

BRILLIE/*France 1903-1908*
In 1903 Eugene Brillié founded Soc des Automobiles Eugene Brillié in Paris. Using Schneider petrol engines and circular radiators, he developed various com-

mercials, concentrating particularly upon passenger types. The construction was undertaken at Ets Schneider's Le Havre factory using a driver-over-engine layout and by late 1905 Brillié buses were being tested in Paris. This led to substantial orders, initially of the Brillié P2-Type, which became the Brillié-Schneider P2 in 1908 following Brillié's bankruptcy. Meantime, a 6-wheeled open-top double-deck bus, with steering first and third axles and "knifeboard" seating on the top deck, had seen brief service in Paris.

BRILLIE-SCHNEIDER/*France 1908-1914*
Built by Ets Schneider, Le Havre, early Brillié-Schneider production comprised an order for 150 P2-Type double-deckers for Paris, later joined by the P3 with 4-cyl 35hp petrol engine and Scémia bodywork. Also known as the Schneider, production continued until 1914 when the company merged with Usines Bouhey and Ets Farcot to form Soc d'Outillege Mecanique et d'Usinage Artillerie, Saint Ouen, builder of later Schneider and all Somua commercials.

BRIMPEX-ECCLES/*England 1980 to date*
Brimpex-Eccles Ltd, Camberley, Surrey, builds the 2-ton capacity 'Truckmaster' battery-electric with air suspension and small turning circle. Also offered on the civilian market is the 'Tugmaster', a battery-electric tractor with low-profile cab and independent front suspension originally developed for the Ministry of Defence.

BRINTON/*USA 1913-1924*
Based on a lightweight prototype built by the Chester County Motor Co, Coatesville, Pennsylvania, in 1913, the Brinton truck was a "conventional" 2-tonner with 4-cyl Rutenber petrol engine and worm-drive. The Brinton Motor Truck Co was founded in 1917, production moving to Philadelphia where new 1- and 2½-ton capacity models with Wisconsin and Continental petrol engines were added.

BRISCOE/*USA 1918-1921*
The Briscoe Motor Corp, Jackson, Michigan, offered a double chain-drive 1-tonner from 1918, changing this to internal-gear final-drive in 1920.

BRITISH BERNA/*England 1914-1918*
Based on the products of Motorwagenfabrik Berna AG, Olten, Switzerland, the British Berna was built by Henry Watson & Sons Ltd, Newcastle-upon-Tyne,

and marketed by British Berna Motor Lorries Ltd. Vehicles were offered in 3½- and 5-ton forms with tubular radiators and extra large header tanks. In 1918 this manufacturer began developing its own goods model along similar lines and the British Berna ceased.

BRITISH QUAD/*England 1918-1920*
The success of the US-built FWD 3-tonner during World War I led to the setting up of the British Four Wheel Drive Tractor-Lorry Co in South London, to licence-build it as the British Quad. With the exception of a Dorman petrol engine, this was almost identical to the original and in 1920 the company was re-named the Four Wheel Drive Tractor-Lorry Engineering Co Ltd, after which models were known as FWD.

BRITISH VOLVO/*Scotland 1979 to date*
UK-marketed Volvo and UK-built Ailsa passenger models are now marketed as British Volvo, using predominantly British components. The name is used purely for sales purposes, all vehicles carrying the Volvo name.

BRITON/*England 1915-1918*
The Briton Motor Co Ltd, Wolverhampton, Staffs, was a subsidiary of vehicle manufacturer the Star Engineering Co Ltd, introducing a 2½-ton truck using numerous Star components, such as a 4-cyl side-valve petrol engine and shaft-drive.

BROC/*USA 1909-1916*
A 1-ton battery-electric was sold as Broc or Broc Electric by the Broc Carriage & Wagon Co, Cleveland, Ohio. In 1912 the company became the Broc Electric Car Co until its 1914 merger with the Argo Electric Vehicle Co and the Borland-Grannis Co to form the American Electric Car Co. Later, the American Electric Car Co was itself taken over by the Columbia Motors Co, and Broc ceased.

BROCKWAY/*USA 1912-1977*
The first commercial of the Brockway Carriage Co, Cortland, New York, was a 3-cyl bonneted high-wheeler. The engine was a 2-stroke air-cooled unit, and transmission was by a 2-speed planetary system. Within two years a line of trucks for up to 1587kg capacity was available, the company now registered as the Brockway Motor Truck Co, and all models had 4-cyl Continental petrol engines. By 1917 the company was concentrating on military types, building 587 Class 'B' Liberty

1958 Bristol (2) LS5G single-deck coach

BRISTOL (2)/*England 1908 to date*
From experience gained with proprietary makes, the Bristol Tramways & Carriage Co Ltd, began to build its own vehicles incorporating more power and improved braking, essential for the hilly routes around the city. The first was a 16-seat chain-drive called the C40, followed by others designated C45, C50, C60 and C65. In 1910 production was temporarily halted while it was transferred to a new plant at Brislington, where series production got underway in 1913 with 48hp 'C'-Series 4-tonners. Fifteen C50 lorries were supplied to the War Office early in World War I and in 1915 the improved 'W'-Type made its début before the factory was put over to production of aircraft. All vehicle-building activities were curtailed until 1920 when an up-dated 4-tonner with 40bhp 4-cyl Bristol 'BW' petrol engine and worm-drive was introduced. Most joined the company's own fleet but some were supplied to other passenger and goods operators.

A 2-tonner, with somewhat unconventional and often fully-fronted forward-control bodywork appeared in 1923, again mainly as a 20/25-seat bus in and around Bristol but occasionally supplied to others. By the mid-1920s, goods and passenger chassis were beginning to follow separate design paths and in 1926 the heavy low-loading 'A'-Type was built for single or double-deck body-work but only 23 were actually built, all of forward-control layout with one-man half-cabs. The 4-cyl 'B'-Type or 'Superbus' appeared later that year, this being directed at the single-deck bus and coach market. It was powered by a 4-cyl Bristol 'GW' petrol engine and remained in production until 1934.

Two 3-axle chassis for double-deck bodywork were shown at the

1929 Commercial Motor Show – one, a 'C'-Type, with 6-cyl Bristol petrol engine and the other, an 'E'-Type, equipped for trolleybus operation. Neither was developed further, but a second 'C'-Type chassis was converted to trolley-bus specification. In 1930 an unsuccessful 6-cyl version of the 'B'-Type was announced, in the form of the 'D'-Type with Bristol 'JW' petrol engine.

In March 1931 the company was acquired by the Thomas Tilling organization and all goods models were dropped in favour of passenger types. 'G', 'H' and 'J'-Types were introduced during the early 1930s, the 'G' being a double-decker with 6-cyl 'JW' petrol engine and the 'H' and 'J' single-deckers developed from the 'B' and 'D'-Types with 4- and 6-cyl petrol engines respectively. AEC, Dennis and Gardner diesel engines were offered from 1933, and by 1937 all new vehicles were diesel-powered, with the company developing its own diesel engine in 1938.

The famous 'K'-Type double-decker and 'L'-Type single-decker replaced the 'G' and 'J'-Types in 1937 and although World War II broke out in 1939, chassis production continued until 1942 when searchlight, generating and producer-gas trailers became the staple product. Initially, the 'K'-Type had a 5LW Gardner diesel engine whilst the 'L' could be had with 4-, 5- or 6-cyl units. The 6LW Gardner was made available in the 'K'-Type during the war, with 6-cyl AEC diesels optional for both models and, later, Bristol's own diesel engine – the 6-cyl 'AVW' – as a further option.

From 1944 a small number of "unfrozen" wartime chassis were assembled from spares and others built to utilitarian government specifications to speed replacement of damaged and unserviceable vehicles and by 1954, when the 'L'-Type was finally withdrawn, it

1971 Bristol (2) RELH6G

was also available in long-bodied form as the 'LL' or with a wider 2.4-m body as the 'LWL'. Similarly, the 'K'-Type was also offered as the long-bodied 'KS' and as the 2.4-m wide 'KSW', these increased dimensions being made possible by a change in UK Construction & Use Regulations.

In 1947 the Thomas Tilling organization was nationalized, control of Bristol passing in 1948 to the newly-formed British Transport Commission which restricted the sale of products to other BTC members. Thus, the company became the main supplier of buses and coaches to the country's nationalized bus fleets, usually with bodywork by Eastern Coach Works Ltd, Lowestoft, Suffolk.

The 'M'-Type was developed in 1948, being a 2.4-m wide chassis with Bristol 'AVW' or Gardner diesel engine. Two prototypes, one an 'MS' for single, the other an 'MD' for double-deck bodywork, were shown at that year's Commercial Motor Show but series production was cancelled in favour of the semi-integral 'Lodekka'. Two prototypes, with wide 'M'-Type radiators, appeared in 1949, having a normal seating layout with centre gangway at both levels yet an overall height of only 4m. This was achieved by employing a split drive-line to a dropped-centre rear axle thereby permitting the use of a sunken gangway in the lower saloon and eliminating the usual step between this and the rear platform. Six slightly larger pre-production prototypes followed the original two, incorporating a single offset drive-shaft running to the offside of a re-designed dropped-centre double-reduction rear axle. Designated the 'LD'-Series, these were generally the same as subsequent production types, which did not appear until 1954. The 'LD' was powered by a Bristol or Gardner diesel engine, with bodywork by Eastern Coach Works Ltd. The Bristol 'AVW' diesel engine was later replaced by the larger capacity 'BVW'.

Meanwhile, an integral-bodied horizontal underfloor-engined single-decker conceived in 1950 as the 'LS' (Light Saloon) left the factory in 1952, replaced in 1958 by the slightly heavier 'MW', announced the previous year. The 'MW' (Medium Weight) was not integral but had a horizontal underfloor engine located amidships, as in the 'LS'. It had a 5- or 6-cyl Gardner diesel. Also in 1952, the company re-entered the goods field with a Leyland-engined 22 tons GVW single-drive 'HG' (Heavy Goods) 8-wheeler,

1960 Bristol (2) 'Lodekka' FSF

1950 Bristol (2) L6B

later adding the Leyland- or Gardner-engined 'HA' (Heavy Artic) tractor, many of which were supplied as complete matched artics for 24 tons GCW with Bristol-built semi-trailers. All were supplied to British Road Services Ltd and its constituent companies until 1964, from which date only passenger chassis have been built, although even some of these have received load-carrying bodies such as horse boxes and pantechnicons.

The lightweight semi-integral 'SC' (Small Capacity) single-decker for rural routes was announced in 1954 with vertical front-mounted Gardner 4LK diesel as standard. In 1955 the vehicle production side of the business became Bristol Commercial Vehicles Ltd, and by 1957 six experimental 70-seat 'Lodekka's with 9.1-m bodies, designated the 'LDL', were built, followed in 1958 by two more experimental versions that were the forerunners of 1959's flat-floor 'F'-Series 'Lodekka' with rear air suspension and provision for a front-entrance. The basic 'Lodekka' design was made available to non-nationalized operators through Dennis Bros Ltd of Guildford, Surrey, who licence-built it as the 'Loline'. The last 'Lodekka' was delivered in 1968.

In 1960 the lightweight 'SU' (Small Underfloor) model, with 4-cyl horizontal underfloor Albion EN250 diesel engine appeared, but never attained large-scale

production. Between 1962 and 1975 the company's most famous single-decker, the first British design with a rear underfloor engine and one which can long claim to be the best British-built passenger chassis of the period, was the 'RE' (Rear Engine). This had a Gardner or Leyland horizontal diesel engine located beneath the floor behind the rear axle and was segregated into the 'RELL' and 'RELH' types. From 1966 shorter 'RE' chassis were available and semi-automatic transmissions optional, followed in 1967 by the 11.9-m 'REMH' as a result of another change in UK Construction & Use Regulations.

The only single-decker still listed is the 'LH' (Lightweight Horizontal), now particularly popular as a short-bodied vehicle for rural operation with Leyland or Perkins diesel engines. In August 1965 the Leyland Motor Corp Ltd acquired a 25% share in the business, boosted in 1969 to 50%, allowing the company's products to return to the open market and enabling any bodybuilder to construct bodies on Bristol chassis. In 1966 the prototype of what is currently the company's standard double-decker – the 'VR' (Vertical Rear) – appeared. Fitted with a vertical diesel engine mounted longitudinally on the offside behind the rear axle, this was developed along Bus Grant lines, entering series production in 1968. It also has the 'Lodekka's dropped-centre rear axle and low chassis frame, enabling double-deck bodies of low overall height to be fitted. Semi- or fully-automatic transmissions are available and in 1967 a transverse-engined model was introduced.

From early 1975 the company joined with Eastern Coach Works Ltd and the Leyland National Co Ltd to form Bus Manufacturers Ltd, the Bristol company being known as Bristol Commercial Vehicles – Bus Manufacturers Ltd. Although concentrating on the 'LH' and 'VR' models the company has also been involved in development work on Leyland's B21 single-deck passenger chassis.

1961 Bristol (2) HA611 artic tractor

trucks and a number of fire appliances. Civilian production returned in 1919 with bonneted 1½- and 3½-ton worm-drive trucks, joined by a 5-tonner in 1921. From 1925 lighter 1½- and 2½-tonners were powered by 4- and 6-cyl Wisconsin petrol engines, and from 1928 only 6-cyl engines were used. Also in 1928 the Indiana Truck Corp of Marion, Indiana, was acquired and the Brockway Motor Co Inc expanded its sales operation into the western States and overseas. This, however, was a short-lived arrangement, as the Indiana operation was resold to the White Motor Co in 1932 to help Brockway through the Depression.

Soon after this, the company introduced a series of battery-electric trucks from 1 to 7 tons capacity, often marketed as Brockway Electric, with the massive Model V1200, powered by an American LaFrance V12 petrol engine producing some 240bhp. Load capacity was 27,215kg, but the vehicle was withdrawn in 1937. During the late 1930s, some 16 models were listed, all with Continental petrol engines and capacities of between 1½ and 10 tons.

World War II saw a return to military production, mainly of a 6-ton 6 x 6 which was developed for carrying bridge-building equipment. Series production began in 1942 and later versions were also used as a crane carrier, airfield fire crash tender and general load carrier. Lighter 4-wheelers were also produced for the military.

Soon after the war the '260' Series, powered by an overhead-valve Continental BD engine was announced, and during the early 1950s some 20 models, from 9071 to 29,483kg capacity were listed, all with Continental engines, Fuller transmissions and Timken axles. In 1956 the company became a division of Mack Trucks Inc, introducing the brand new 'Huskie' range in 1958. Despite the connection with Mack, Brockway remained independent, producing its own designs. The first forward-control Brockway arrived in 1963, using a modified Mack 'F'-Series cab, and over the next few years forward-control types took up an increasing proportion of company production. All models now had a choice of Continental petrol or Cummins or Detroit Diesel engines, but only Caterpillar, Cummins or Detroit Diesels were listed from the late 1960s. A new transmission system known as 'Huskiedrive' was announced in 1968, comprising a 5-speed box and 2-speed axle, an 8-speed box being offered later. In 1971 the low-profile forward-control 2-axle

'Huskiteer' was announced, followed soon after by a 6-wheeler.

For 1977 models included normal- and forward-control 4- and 6-wheeled tractors for up to 33,112kg GCW with power outputs of up to 500bhp and rigid types for up to 24,000kg GVW, but in April of that year Mack Trucks Inc announced the plant's closure.

BROCKWAY ELECTRIC/*USA 1933-1938*
As well as normal trucks, the Brockway Motor Truck Co, Cortland, New York State, built battery-electrics from 1 to 7 tons capacity under the Brockway Electric name. Manufacturing rights were later sold.

BRODESSER/*USA 1909-1912*
The Brodesser Motor Truck Co was founded by Peter H Brodesser in Milwaukee, Wisconsin, to construct large chain-drives of "cabover" layout. These comprised the 2-cyl Model 'A' and the 4-cyl Model 'B', both with horizontally-opposed engines and friction transmissions. The range was later re-named Juno.

BROOKS (1)/*USA 1911-1913*
The Brooks Mfg Co, Saginaw, Michigan, built a lightweight high-wheeler known also as the Brooks Motor Wagon. Powered by an air-cooled 2-cyl petrol engine under the body, it had double chain-drive and a friction transmission. Re-named the Brooks Motor Wagon Co in 1912, the firm was taken over by the Duryea Automobile Co in 1913, after which all vehicles were sold as Duryear.

BROOKS (2)/*Canada 1927*
The Brooks Steam Motors Co developed a steam bus using a boiler capable of building up a working pressure of 750psi in just 40 seconds, enabling a laden test chassis to achieve a speed of 96 km/h. Fitted with 4-wheel air brakes, only two were built but in the meantime a new factory opened in Buffalo, New York State, where further developments took place the year.

BROOKS (3)/*USA 1928*
The Brooks Steam Motors Co's, Buffalo, New York State, factory catered for American customers. The only commercial built was a steam conversion of an ACF 'Metropolitan' underfloor-engined bus which was not developed.

BROOM & WADE/*England 1907-1913*
Broom & Wade Ltd, High Wycombe, Bucks, constructed single-

cyl paraffin-engined 3- and 4-ton forward-control lorries, with the engine slung horizontally beneath the chassis. Drive was via a 3-speed gearbox and single roller chain. The company also built some forward-control "colonial"-type paraffin-engined tractors for 6-ton loads. Production was taken over by T C Aveling.

BROSSEL/*Belgium 1922-c1965*
The first commercials offered by Ets Brossel Frères, Brussels, were mediumweight goods and passenger types, mainly of bonneted layout. In 1939 a number of chassis were built for the company by Usines Ragheno, Malines, for use as buses in Brussels, while single-deck trolleybuses were built using ACEC traction equipment. After World War II the company, which was now known as Brossel Frères, Bovy et Pipe SA, built FN 4 x 4 derivatives in association with FN and Miesse. Amongst these was the 'Ardennes' artillery tractor and 1½-ton truck with 4.7-litre overhead-valve petrol engine, 8-speed transmission and air brakes. Eventually the company was bought out by the British Leyland Group, which led to the marketing of Leyland-engined Brossel passenger models in France between 1960 and 1962 by Soc Hotchkiss-Brandt, St Denis, Seine. There were even some 'Vista-Vue' cabbed goods models sold as Brossel before the brand name disappeared.

BROTHERHOOD/*England 1920-1921*
Peter Brotherhood Ltd, Peterborough, Northants, launched a 5-ton "undertype" wagon with bevel-gear transmission and a double-ended return-tube transverse boiler. Fuel feed was by geared pump and automatic injection. Similarities between this and the Yorkshire wagon were to prove the Brotherhood's downfall for, although the Yorkshire boiler patent had expired five years earlier, the Yorkshire Patent Steam Wagon Co complained. In spite of the law being on Brotherhood's side, the directors decided not to continue production, and the company was acquired by Richard Garrett & Co Ltd.

BROWN (1)/*USA 1922-1924*
This Brown was a 2½-ton stake-side or dump truck built initially by the Saint Cloud Truck Co but later by the Brown Truck Co, Duluth, Minnesota. Power came from a 4-cyl Buda petrol engine and both pneumatic tyres and electric lighting were optional.

BROWN (2)/*USA 1936-1938*
The Brown 'Sunset Coach' was a lightweight streamlined passenger model of frameless construction built by Brown Industries, Spokane, Washington. Weighing under 3 tons unladen, the prototype had 24 reclining seats and a rear-mounted Ford V8 petrol engine. When production got underway, this was changed for a Hercules unit and a 28-seat version also introduced.

BROWN (3)/*USA 1939-1953*
Developed by J L Brown, of Horton Motor Lines, Charlotte, North Carolina, the 21-R Brown was a bonneted 4 x 2 tractor with Fuller transmission and Continental petrol engine intended solely for Horton's own use. Manufacture was undertaken by subsidiary the Brown Truck and Trailer Mfg Co. The 513 was introduced in 1946, and by 1948 vehicles were available on the open market, with a Cummins diesel engine offered from 1949. The very last Browns, a series of "cabover" models, were built in 1952 and 1953.

BROWN & MAY/*England 1875 & 1901*
Brown & May, Devizes, Wilts, developed a 4-ton steam van in 1875, with a vertical boiler, rear-mounted vertical engine and a steersman at the front to control the chain-and-bobbin steering gear. Only one such wagon was built, although in 1901 a further model was entered in War Dept Trials.

BRULE/*France 1901*
H Brulé et Cie, Paris, built an experimental 10-seater bus, employing the same unique 3-cyl petrol engine used in the Brulé-Ponsard. Located at the rear of the vehicle, with coil-type radiator beneath, it drove the rear wheels via a chain final-drive system and 4-speed transmission. After this, the company was licenced to build British-designed Thornycroft wagons, marketed as Thornycroft.

BRULE-PONSARD/*France 1900*
H Brulé et Cie's Brulé-Ponsard was an unusual petrol-engined conversion unit for adapting horse-drawn wagons to self-propulsion. It had a 20hp 3-cyl engine built by Rozer et Mazurier, in which explosions took place in the outer cyls whilst the inner was actuated by the exhaust gases from the other two.

BRUNAU/*Switzerland 1907-1908*
One- and 3-ton Brunau trucks, the former with a 12hp 2-cyl petrol

engine and the latter with a 14hp 2-cyl unit, were built by Weidmann & Co Automobilfabrik, Brunau, Zürich. Both were shaft-driven.

1907 Brush 'C'-Type open-top double-deck bus

BRUSH/*England 1904-1968*
The first commercials to be built by the Brush Electrical Engineering Co, Loughborough, Leics, were Daimler-engined passenger models. In 1905 the British Automobile Development Co Ltd, a subsidiary, began building similar models under the BADC name, but it was not unusual for BADC chassis to be converted to forward-control and sold as Brush. Early in 1913 two single-deck trolleybuses were built, each with a single 35hp traction motor. With shaft-drive to an overhead-worm rear axle, these were the first British-built trolleybuses to use a pedal-control system instead of a tram-type controller. During the 1920s and 1930s both passenger bodywork and electric traction equipment were produced, occasionally combining the two to construct both single- and double-deck 4- and 6-wheeled trolleybuses, sometimes using Thornycroft chassis and marketed as Brush-Thornycroft, but in 1946, as the Brush Electrical Engineering Co Ltd, the company launched three battery-electric goods models of which the heaviest was a 1½-tonner. Three-wheelers of more than 1-ton capacity appeared by the end of the 1940s and by 1951 the entire battery-electric range was based on 3-wheeled chassis. Industrial trucks were gradually added during the 1950s and in 1954 the 4-ton 'Cob' towing tractor was announced.

1933 Brush-Thornycroft trolleybus

BRUSH-THORNYCROFT/ *England c1932*
A short-lived series of trolley-buses, marketed as Brush-Thornycroft, had chassis built by John I Thornycroft & Co Ltd, Basingstoke, Hants, with bodies and electrical equipment by the Loughborough-based Brush Electrical Engineering Co Ltd. Using both 4- and 6-wheeled chassis, single- and double-deck bodies, the most popular model was a 32-seat single-decker of which a number were exported.

BTH-WOLSELEY-SIDDELEY/ *England 1907*
This was an experimental 40hp petrol-electric bus constructed by the Wolseley Tool & Motor Car Co Ltd, Birmingham, using a vertical-engined passenger chassis and two BTH traction motors. The system was subsequently adopted only for use in railcars.

BUCEGI/*Rumania 1962 to date*
The bonneted Bucegi truck was introduced by Intreprinderea de Autocamioane Brasov, builder of the SR truck, the design being based on the Soviet ZIL. The Bucegi had a 140bhp V8 petrol engine and a capacity of between 3½ and 5 tons. Apart from 95bhp Torpedo, 112bhp Perkins and 126 bhp Mercedes diesel options, there have been few specification changes over the years, although forward-control models were introduced under the Carpati brand name a little later, and more recently supplemented by DAC and Roman trucks, whilst the company has been re-named Uzina de Autocamioane.

BUCHER/*Switzerland 1976 to date*
Bucher-Guyer AG, Niederweningen, builds 4-wheel drive trucks with payloads of 2½ to 3¼ tons. These include the GET 1200, TR 2200K and TR 2500KK, the first having a centrally-mounted 1.8-litre 70bhp Volkswagen flat-4 petrol engine, automatic transmission and forward-control. The others have a 1·5-litre 40bhp 4-cyl Leyland diesel and 6-speed box.

BUCK/*USA 1925-1927*
The Buck Motor Truck Co, Bellevue, Ohio, built "conventional" trucks from 1½ to 7½ tons capacity. Nine basic models were listed up to 1926, comprising two 4-cyl "speed-wagons", two 6-cyl medium-duty types and five heavy-duty models with sliding cab doors and electric lighting. Ten new models were announced in 1926, five with 4- and five with 6-cyl petrol engines.

BUCKEYE/*USA 1910*
With a reputation for building good light horse-drawn wagons, the Buckeye Mfg Co, Anderson, Indiana, founded the Buckeye Wagon & Motor Car Co, Dayton, Ohio, to build self-propelled delivery vehicles. The only model produced before the company went bankrupt was a 2.5-m wheelbase chain-drive 1½-tonner, powered by a 25hp vertical 4-cyl petrol engine with selective transmission.

BUCKLEN/*USA 1912-1916*
The H E Bucklen Jnr Motor Truck Co, Elkhart, Indiana, listed the 1½-ton Model 'B' and 3-ton Model 'C' with open, stakeside or van bodywork. In 1914 the Model 'C' was de-rated to a capacity of 2½ tons.

BUCKMOBILE/*USA 1905*
The Buckmobile 'Business Wagon' was a product of the Black Diamond Automobile Co, Utica, New York State. A 1-ton open delivery van, it had a 15hp 2-cyl water-cooled petrol engine with planetary transmission and double chain-drive.

BUFFALO (1)/*USA 1908-1910*
The Buffalo Auto-Car Mfg Co was established in Buffalo, New York State, to continue production of vehicles previously sold as Auto-Car. Using a common chassis, the range included 10- and 20-seat buses and a 2-ton goods model, with 4- or 6-cyl petrol engines offered in the latter and double chain-drive throughout. There were also some battery-electrics and later a Model 'F' bus and a 5-ton stakeside truck. In 1910 a bonneted chain-drive 1-tonner with open canopy-type body was announced. The business was re-named the Atterbury Motor Car Co before the end of that year and models re-named Atterbury.

BUFFALO (2)/*USA 1912-1916*
Principally an electric car manufacturer, the Buffalo Electric Vehicle Co, Buffalo, New York State, also built a 1-ton delivery model mounted on a 2.55-m wheelbase chassis, using a General Electric traction motor and shaft-drive.

BUFFALO (3)/*USA 1920-1924*
Trucks built by the Buffalo Truck & Tractor Co, Buffalo, New York State, had 4-cyl Hercules petrol engines, Detroit transmissions and Wisconsin or Sheldon rear axles. First was a 2-tonner, joined by a 1½-tonner in 1921. A year later the 2-tonner was re-rated at 3 tons and the 1½-tonner increased to 2 tons. By 1923 a new and most unusual feature had appeared, comprising three copper balls suspended in a frame ahead of the radiator. These could be switched into the water cooling system to provide additional cooling capacity when needed.

BUFFALO (4)/*USA 1927-1948*
In 1920, fire equipment manufacturer the Buffalo Fire Appliance Corp was founded in Buffalo, New York, to build appliances on ordinary commercial chassis. The first complete Buffalo appliance was built in 1927, developing into a series of bonneted limousine pumpers by 1937. There was little change until production ceased.

BUFFAUD/*France 1905-c1910*
Buffaud et Robatel, Lyons, were general engineers who license-built 5/8 and 8/10-ton payload US-designed Johnson steam wagons under the Buffaud name.

1922 Buick SD4 1-ton truck

BUICK/*USA 1922-1923*
Under the direct control of the General Motors Corp, the Buick Motor Car Co, Detroit, Michigan, built the 1-ton SD4, powered by a 2.8-litre 4-cyl petrol engine in 1922. True commercial production ceased the following year, after which the only Buick commercials were lengthened passenger car chassis bodies by the Flxible Co, Loudonville, Ohio, as midicoaches.

BULKLEY-RIDER/*USA 1914-1917*
One of the more exotic heavy vehicles of the World War I period was the 90hp Bulkley-Rider tractor built by the Bulkley-Rider Tractor Co, Los Angeles, California. Initially, a petrol engine was located beneath the bonnet, driving the rear wheels via a 6-speed double-reduction transmission and double chain-drive. From 1916 the engine was housed beneath the cab floor.

BULL DOG/*USA 1924-1925*
Only a few 2-ton Bull Dog trucks were built by the Bull Dog Motor Truck Co, Galena, Ohio. These were bonneted designs powered by 30bhp 4-cyl Continental petrol engines.

BULLEY/*USA 1915-1917*
The Mercury Mfg Co, manufacturer of Mercury light trucks, Chicago, Illinois, constructed the 3-wheeled Bulley towing tractor. It was one of the earliest "mechanical horses" and was available with

either a single chain-driven rear wheel or single front steering wheel with double chain-drive to the rear axles.

BURFORD (1)/England 1914-1934

H G Burford & Co Ltd, North Kensington, London, began importing the Fremont-Mais truck, under the Burford brand name. To avoid import restrictions, vehicle assembly was soon undertaken in Britain using home-produced components such as Dorman engines, although a US-built Continental was optional. These early Burfords were 2-tonners, joined in 1920 by a 1-tonner and in 1921 by a 4-wheel-braked coach. The first forward-control design appeared two years later and in 1925 the Burford-Kégresse half-track was first shown. However, by 1926 the company had gone into liquidation, assets and manufacturing rights being purchased by D C H Gray, former General Manager, who continued the business on a limited scale, building both forward- and normal-control 4-cyl models of 1½ and 2½ tons capacity. In 1931 the company was re-named the H G Burford Co Ltd and production moved to Teddington, Middx, where apart from the Burford-Kégresse, only bonneted Burfords were built. In 1934 Lacre Lorries Ltd took the business over, after a few Burford designs carrying the Lacre brand name and, of course, the Burford-Kégresse, were built.

BURFORD (2)/USA 1914-1917

Fremont-Mais trucks were built by the Lauth-Juergens Motor Car Co, Fremont, Ohio, and sold in Britain under the Burford brand name by H G Burford & Co Ltd. A year later all Fremont-Mais trucks also acquired the Burford name and manufacture was taken over by the Burford Motor Truck Co. Specifications were identical to the Fremont-Mais, but in September 1917 assets and manufacturing rights were acquired by the Taylor Motor Truck Co, which moved into the old plant to build Taylor trucks.

BURFORD-KEGRESSE/England 1925-1935

Built by H G Burford & Co Ltd, North Kensington, London, using the French-designed Kégresse half-track system and its own forward-control chassis, the 2-ton Burford-Kégresse was powered by a 5.13-litre 4-cyl petrol engine driving through a 4-speed main box and 2-speed auxiliary. Temporary liquidation came in 1926 but under new management production was hardly affected, and a modified tracked bogie, the Ké-

gresse P7, was fitted from 1927. Company development mirrored that of the British-built Burford, but continued a little longer.

BURGLOWE UNIVERSAL/Germany 1963-?

For heavy on/off-road work, Büssing Automobilwerke AG, Braunschweig, developed the 4 x 4 Burglöwe Universal load-carrier, unveiled to the public at the Frankfurt Show. Despite its 4-wheel drive layout, it retained Büssing's traditional horizontal underfloor engine by using a high-mounted chassis frame cranked over the power unit. It was intended for the military, but few were built.

BURRELL/England 1901, 1911-1928

In 1900 plans were drawn up by Charles Burrell & Sons Ltd, Thetford, Norfolk, for a double-crank compound "undertype" steam wagon with vertical boiler. A prototype was constructed the following year but was used only as works transport, no further wagons being built until 1911. The next wagon was a 5-ton compound of "overtype" layout providing greater engine accessibility. Using a short loco-type boiler, this had dual chain-drive and a lockable countershaft differential. One or two early examples incorporated an internal-gear final-drive but this was relatively short-lived, and in 1912 the first single-chain Burrell, with a "live" rear axle, was introduced. The infamous Agricultural & General Engineers combine was founded in 1919, comprising Aveling & Porter Ltd, Charles Burrell & Sons Ltd and Richard Garrett & Co Ltd, steam wagon production being moved to Garrett's Leiston, Suffolk, factory in 1922. Only a few Burrells were built under this arrangement, however, and in 1924 an improved 6-tonner was announced, with Ackermann steering.

BUR-WAIN/Denmark 1938-1940

Using a bonneted truck chassis supplied by the Stewart Motor Corp, Buffalo, New York State, shipbuilders Burmeister & Wain AB, Copenhagen, formed a Truck Divn to assemble Bur-Wain diesel trucks. The engine was also produced by them.

BUSCH/Germany 1898-1912

Specialists in fire appliance construction, Wagenbauanstadt und Waggonfabrik für Elektrische Bahnen vorm W C F Busch, Bautzen, Saxony, sold its first machine in 1898. In 1901 the firm became Waggon und Maschinenfabrik A G vorm Busch, continuing its line

of appliances for some years. Steam, petrol, battery-electric or petrol-electric propulsion was employed and the firm supplied Berlin's first self-propelled appliance in 1906.

1954 BUT 9641T single-deck trolleybus

BUT/England 1946-1958 & 1965

British United Traction Ltd was formed in 1946 to pool trolleybus design and manufacturing interests of arch-rivals AEC Ltd and Leyland Motors Ltd. Initially, BUTs were built at Leyland's Kingston-upon-Thames factory but when this closed in 1948, production was divided between the Middx and Lancs plants of the constituent companies, with some examples built by Crossley Motors Ltd, Stockport, Cheshire. Using mainly Metrovick components, the range was segregated into home market designs at Southall and export models at Leyland, with AEC constructing the 9611T and 9612T 4-wheeled double-decker and the 9641T 6-wheeled single- and double-decker. Leyland built the 4-wheeled 'ETB'-Series single-decker. Between 1947 and 1956 BUT chassis were also supplied to

1950 BUT 9641T double-deck trolleybus

Talleres Carde y Escoriaza, Zaragoza, Spain, for assembly as the BUT-Escoriaza and in 1965 the very last BUTs were constructed at Scammell Lorries Ltd, Watford, Herts, for export to Oporto.

BUT-ESCORIAZA/Spain 1947-1956

British United Traction Ltd supplied a number of BUT trolleybus chassis to Talleres Carde y Escoriaza, Zaragoza, for bodying. These were then sold as the BUT-Escoriaza trolleybus.

BUTLER BROTHERS/Canada ? to date

Originating as a logging company on Southern Vancouver Island, British Columbia, Butler Bros Equipment Ltd builds a rigid 8-wheeled logging truck which, together with its 8-wheeled trailer, can handle up to 200 tons of timber per load. The truck has a low-profile half-cab with power unit alongside.

BVG/Germany 1928-29, 1935-36

In collaboration with front-wheel drive vehicle manufacturer Voran Automobilbau AG, two unusual double-deck buses were assembled by Berlin bus operator Berliner Verkehrs AG. The BVG had a low floor line by using front-wheel drive – most unusual for any heavy vehicle. A huge front overhang of 2.1m was taken up by a 100bhp 6-cyl Maybach engine which drove via a "conventional" clutch and 3-speed gearbox, there being no front axle as such, the wheels being independently suspended on two transverse springs. An overall height of just 3.75 metres was achieved. During 1935 and 1936 a new BVG bus went into production, again for the company's own use, with a Büssing engine.

BUSSING/*Germany 1903-1971*
Founded in 1903, H Büssing AG, Braunschweig, immediately introduced its first motor lorry – a 2-cyl overhead-worm petrol-engined 3-tonner, adding a passenger version early the following year, which was later built under British licence as Straker-Squire. In 1907 manufacturing licences were sold to Maschinenfabrik A Fross, Vienna, re-organized as Maschinenfabrik A Fross-Büssing two years later to produce vehicles of Büssing design under the Fross-Büssing name. Similarly, 1909 saw licence-manufacture of Büssing trucks under the Rathgeber name by Jos Rathgeber AG, Munich, and in 1913 Ganz Waggon es Gepgyar, Budapest, also commenced manufacture of licence-built Büssings, using the Ganz name.

In 1909 the world's first 6-cyl truck engine was built, a 90PS petrol unit, and over the next few years the company's 5-and 11-ton trucks became increasingly popular. By 1914 a 4-wheel drive army truck was available and at the end of the war the range comprised a light 2-tonner, a 2½-ton passenger model and 3- and 5-ton trucks. In 1920 the company was re-named Büssing Automobilwerke KG, only to be re-named again in 1922 Automobilwerke H Büssing AG. By 1923 the first rigid 3-axled chassis in Germany had been launched, powered by a 6-cyl 80PS petrol engine and with tandem-drive. This was suitable for both goods and passenger work.

Interesting experiments at this time included a petrol-electric prototype in 1924, a chassisless forward-control 6-wheeled bus in 1929 and the futuristic 'Trambus' of 1930 with its 6-wheeled chassis, forward-control layout and 6-cyl 110PS petrol engine located amidships.

Mannesmann-Mulag Motoren und Lastwagen AG, Aachen, was taken over in 1928, while yet another acquisition was Automobilfabrik Komnick AG, Elbing, in 1930. A year later, Büssing took over Nacionale Automobil AG, of Berlin and Leipzig, manufacturers of NAG commercials and from then until 1950 all vehicles were referred to as Büssing-NAG.

In 1950 the company became Büssing Nutzkraftwagen GmbH, and a re-designed series of goods and passenger types employing underfloor engines was announced. To cope with increasing demand for both trucks and buses, a plant was opened at Salzgitter, eventually taking over all vehicle assembly, and by 1962 the former factory of Carl F W Borgward GmbH at Osterholz-Scharmbeck had also been ac-

quired, production of that company's 4 x 4 3/4-tonner continuing under the Büssing name until 1968 when these premises were resold to Faun-Werke GmbH. In 1960 the company was re-constituted as Büssing Automobilwerke AG and five years later a revolutionary low-loading goods model known as the Decklaster appeared, comprising a low-line cab cantilevered ahead of the main chassis frame, air suspension, twin-steer front axles, a 150PS underfloor engine and load-carrying deck running the full length of the vehicle right over the cab. Goods models now covered payloads of between 5 and 18 tons, including both 4- and 6-wheeled rigids, 4- and 6-wheeled twin-steer tractors and a new city bus, built entirely by the company, which entered production in 1968. Generally, rigid goods models had underfloor engines while tractors had vertical units. Close co-operation between Büssing and Maschinenfabrik Augsburg-Nürnberg AG the following year ultimately led to the latter's takeover of Büssing in 1971. Underfloor-engined goods and passenger models continued to be built, although now marketed as M A N-Büssing.

BUSSING-NAG/*Germany 1931-1950*
When Automobilwerke H Büssing AG, Braunschweig, acquired the business of Nationale Automobil AG, of Berlin and Leipzig, manufacturer of the NAG commercial range, to form Büssing-NAG Vereinigte Nutzkraftwagen AG, Büssing-NAG normal- and forward-control models were introduced. Various models were inherited from the Büssing and NAG ranges, the first new ones being two petrol-engined military 6-wheelers. The lightest of these was a 1½-tonner with 4-litre 4-cyl engine and the heaviest a 3-tonner with 9.3-litre 6-cyl unit. Two years later a 6½-ton 4 x 4 with 85PS 6.2-litre 6-cyl diesel engine appeared and a 7.9-litre 150PS V8 bus en-

1934 Büssing-NAG 80N twin-engined single-deck bus

gine was introduced about the same time.

Of all Büssing-NAGs, however, the 80N 6-wheeler was not only the most impressive but also the most unique. Known also as the "Langer Sachse", it was a massive bonneted machine with tandem-drive, each rear axle having its own engine and transmission. Introduced at the 1934 Berlin Motor Show, the specification included two 'U'-section sidemembers with

Büssing 5-ton truck c1920

rear bogie suspension utilizing a single leaf spring on each side, each end being mounted on the axle casings and bolted in the middle to the chassis frame. Axle casings were specially lowered with wheels driven by toothed rings mounted on the brake drums. Each driven axle had its own 160bhp diesel engine coupled

side-by-side, with hydraulic clutch, 5-speed gearbox, transmission handbrake and auxiliary 2-speed box in each drive train. The radiator was almost 1.1m wide and served by two 4-bladed fans, while each engine could be shut off independently of the other if required. With a total capacity of 27 litres, both engines running in tandem had a top speed of 60mph

Experimental petrol-electric passenger models appeared briefly in 1935 and a 5-ton half-track, with 3.8-litre 6-cyl Maybach engine, was announced in 1936. The 'Trambus' was now listed with a 6.2-litre 5- or 7.4-litre 6-cyl engine and could be had also as a 6-wheeler with 13.5-litre underfloor engine. Another twin-engined bus, with a 145PS engine at each end, was developed for high speed autobahn running.

By World War II, the goods models included from 2½ to 9-ton capacity vehicles, comprising 4 x 2 and 4 x 4 military types of 4½ tons capacity, 4 x 2 rigids for up to 6 tons and 6 x 4s for 9 tons. The war years saw production of a new 8-ton half-track for hauling heavy artillery and in 1943 the company was re-named Büssing-NAG Vereinigte Nutzkraftwagen GmbH. Civilian models returned in 1945 with a new 5-ton goods/passenger chassis, later up-rated to 7 tons, and in 1949 the first chassisless version of the long-running 'Trambus' made its debut with an underfloor engine.

1930 Büssing Type 6GL 6 x 4 truck

CABI-CATTANEO/*Italy c1946-c1950*

Cabi Cattaneo Sarl, Milan, developed a forward-control medium-weight truck with tubular frame and coil independent front suspension. Models were sold as Cabi-Cattaneo or Cattaneo. The nearby manufacturer of Bianchi commercials, SA Fabbrica Automobili e Velocipedi Edoardo Bianchi, based post-war designs on early prototypes.

CAETANO/*Portugal 1973 to date*

Salvador Caetano IMVT Sarl, Vila Nova de Gaia, was founded in 1946 as a goods and passenger vehicle bodybuilder. The 1970s saw a series of chassisless rear-engined coaches, with 145bhp Detroit Diesel or 230bhp air-cooled Deutz diesel engines introduced. Body framing is of square-section steel tubing and examples are sold throughout Europe.

CALDWELL VALE/*Australia 1910-1912*

The Caldwell Vale Truck & Bus Co, Auburn, NSW, built forty petrol-engined commercials as load-carriers and heavy tractors. Power came from an 11-litre 4-cyl engine with separately cast cylinders via a 3-speed main gearbox and transfer to all four 1.5m diameter steel-shod wheels. It was a bonneted design, employing a unique power steering system, whereby the column engaged with one of two cone clutches connected by chain-driven shaft to the front of the engine crankshaft. When the steering wheel was turned, one of these clutches engaged with a worm connected to the steering drag link, thereby moving the wheels in the appropriate direction.

CALEDON/*Scotland 1914-1926*

When World War I broke out, Scottish Commercial Cars Ltd, Glasgow, the Scottish agent for Commer Cars, found itself without vehicles when these were diverted to war work. To fill the gap, a new 4-tonner was constructed using a 40hp 4-cyl Dor-man petrol engine, Dux 4-speed constant-mesh gear-box and chain-drive. Called the Caledon, it was capable of speeds up to 19km/h but from the start was beset with mechanical problems, not the least of which was severe vibration. In 1919 the company was re-named Caledon Motors Ltd and the range expanded to include vehicles from 1½ to 7-ton capacity and a shaft-drive passenger chassis. An engine production area was organized to combat lack of engines, but the development of a sleeve-valve engine cost so much and took so much time that the company was forced into liquidation in 1922. Assets, premises and name were re-acquired by Scottish Commercial Cars Ltd which proceeded with the new range – again Dorman-powered apart from a Hercules-engined forward-control passenger model. In 1924 a 10-ton rigid 6-wheeler was announced, its Dorman engine being replaced later by a Buda unit. This is believed to have been Britain's first rigid-6 lorry. By the end of 1926 the business had been sold to Richard Garrett & Sons Ltd, who subsequently built three Garrett-Cale-don trucks.

CAMB/*Italy ? to date*

Carelli SpA, Modena, specializes in the manufacture of rigid low-loading machinery carriers under the Camb brand name using mainly Fiat mechanical elements.

Typical is a single-drive forward-control 6-wheeler for 20 tons GVW, with small-diameter wheels at the rear bogie and a loading height of 1m afforded by limited spring travel. All models have right-hand drive as standard. This is a very useful safety aid on narrow mountain roads.

CAMBIER/*France 1897-1901*

Ets Cambier, Lille, built horizontal rear-engined commercials, the first being a 30hp 3-cyl petrol-engined model. In 1898 a 4-cyl fire appliance was constructed with double chain-drive, 500gpm pump and electric starting.

CAMILL/*England c1961-c1976*

The Camill 4/10 was a fully-articulated 4 x 4 dump truck built by E Boydell & Co Ltd, Gloucester, to complement its Muir-Hill range of rigid dump trucks. The 4/10 consisted of a single-axle tractor, with a one-man cab and 4-cyl diesel engine cantilevered out in front. By about 1964 it had been joined by the 6/10, using a 96bhp 6-cyl diesel with torque-converter and powershift box eliminating the need for a clutch and conventional gearbox. Payload capacities of up to 9072kg were possible.

CAMPBELL (1)/*Australia 1968 to date*

Passenger vehicle bodybuilder R M Campbell Vehicle Sales Pty Ltd, Bankstown, NSW, converts Leyland truck chassis into underfloor-engined passenger models, fitting its own bodywork, and marketing these as Campbells. The most popular model is a revamped Leyland 'Comet', with lengthened and reinforced chassis, set-back front axle to take forward-entrance all-steel coach-work and amidships-mounted diesel engine.

CAMPBELL (2)/*Australia 1971- ?*

Inventor Ian H Campbell designed and constructed a prototype Caterpillar-engined bus chassis, his intention being to mount a German-style city bus body on it. By 1979 Ian H Campbell & Co Pty Ltd had been founded in Carlton, Sydney, New South Wales, to build similar vehicles as IBC.

CANADA/*Canada 1956-1958*

Co-operation between Leyland Motors (Canada) Ltd, Montreal, Quebec, and the Canadian Car & Foundry Co Ltd, Fort William, Ontario, resulted in the development of the bonneted Canada truck and tractor range with Leyland diesel engines and International Harvester cabs for weights of between 10,900kg GVW and 45,390kg GCW. They were known in the early stages as the Leyland-Canada range. The last of the line was the 680WT heavy-duty tractor.

CANADIAN/*Canada 1898-1900*

Canada's first commercially-built truck was the battery-electric Canadian delivery tricycle, constructed by the Canadian Motor Syndicate, Toronto, Ontario. Sometimes known as the Canadian Motor Syndicate vehicle, this was followed by a battery-electric adaptation of a horse-drawn wagon. Battery manufacturer W J Still took over the syndicate in 1899 and the Still Motor Co Ltd was formed only to be taken over itself in 1900 and re-named Canadian Motors Ltd. Production of battery-electric goods and passenger models went on for a few months, joined by a 15-seat bus.

CAN-CAR/*Canada 1946-1962*

The first Can-Car was a 44-passenger trolleybus built by the Canadian Car & Foundry Co Ltd, Fort William, Ontario. This also formed the basis of a new Brill machine built in the USA but it was not until 1956 that the Can-Car name was adopted for all Canadian-built models. Air suspension diesel-engined buses for up to 52 passengers were now

1957 Canada 680WT artic tractor

Camill 4/10 4 x 4 dump truck c1961

available and in 1960 the company was re-named the Canadian Car Co Ltd, moving to Montreal, Quebec, where new 43 and 51 passenger buses were built up to 1962.

CANTONO (1)/*Italy 1900-1906*
E Cantono, Rome, developed a 4-wheeled battery-electric conversion unit for horse-drawn wagons using 44 battery cells and two series-wound motors. A French sales office was established in 1902, while the Cantono Electric Tractor Co was formed in New York to licence-build models for the American market. By 1905, the company was also offering rear-wheel drive trolleybuses and 3-ton vans were re-named SA Ligure-Romana Vetture by the end of that year and moved to Genoa in 1906. After this the company was known as Fabbrica Rotabili Avantreni Motori and all subsequent vehicles marketed as FRAM.

CANTONO (2)/*USA 1904-1906*
The Cantono Electric Tractor Co was founded in New York City, New York, to assemble 4-wheeled battery-electric conversion units for horse-drawn wagons along the lines of the Italian Cantono range. In about 1905, the company was re-named the Cantono Electric Fore-Carriage Co but closed when the parent company began building vehicles as FRAM.

CAPACITY/*USA ? to date*
A one-man half-cab terminal tractor for handling maximum-capacity semi-trailers is marketed by Capacity of Texas Inc, Longview, Texas. It has an hydraulically-lifting fifth wheel coupling and an electrically actuated hydraulic tiltcab.

c1969 Capacity terminal tractor

CAPITOL (1)/*USA 1914*
The Capitol battery-electric truck was constructed briefly by the Capitol Truck Mfg Co, Denver, Colorado using 30 cell batteries, ser-

ies-wound General Electric motor. A continuous torque drum provided 4 forward and 1 reverse transmission and speed with shaft-drive and a floating rear axle completing the drive-train. Fitted with an open body and folding buggy type cab,it had semi-elliptic leaf spring suspension with batteries under a bonnet and on each side of the chassis frame. The claimed range was 128km per charge and tiller or wheel steering were used.

CAPITOL (2)/*USA 1920-1921*
The Capitol Motors Corp, Fall River, Massachusetts, built 1½-, 2½- and 3½-ton Capitol trucks, each powered by a 4-cyl Wisconsin petrol engine with 4-speed Cotta transmission and Wisconsin worm-drive rear axle.

CAPITOL CAR/*USA 1910-1912*
The forward-control Capitol Car battery-electric was a product of the Washington Motor Vehicle Co, Washington, DC. Two models were listed, the heaviest being rated initially at 1133kg capacity but later reduced to 680kg. Chain-drive, full-elliptic front springs and also unusual rear platform springs were employed.

CAR/*France 1907-1908*
The Soc des Camions et Autobus à Moteur Rotatif was founded in Lyons to manufacture production versions of petrol-, heavy oil-, or napthalene-powered Burlat commercials called CARs. Only 4 were constructed, each powered by a 20hp 4-cyl rotary engine with 3-speed transmission and chain-drive. The use of napthalene as a fuel proved to be impractical as it had to be carried in block form, liquified by exhaust gases at 60°C and vapourized at 218°C.

CARAVAN/*USA 1920-1921*
Known also as the Karavan, the 1½-ton Caravan truck was a product of the Caravan Motors Corp, Portland, Oregon.

CARDWELL/*USA c1963*
A series of oil well servicing rigs on 8-wheeled rigid low-loading chassis was offered under the Cardwell brand name for operation in American oilfields in the 1960s. Lightest of these was the KM200A with a 26.5m mast for servicing wells up to 2743m deep. A one-man half-cab was fitted. All models had a rear-mounted diesel engine which drove both winch-gear and road wheels.

CARHARRT/*USA 1911-1912*
The Carharrt Automobile Corp, Detroit, Michigan, manufactured passenger cars before turning to a 3-ton flat truck. Called the Model 'T', this had a 38hp 4-cyl petrol engine, 3-speed transmission and double chain-drive.

CARLAW/*Scotland 1920*
Glasgow motor dealer David Carlaw & Co constructed three prototype trucks of bonneted layout and about 1¼-ton capacity. They never reached series production, but manufacturing rights were sold to vehicle and component manufacturer A Harper, Sons & Bean Ltd, who used many of the ideas in the first Bean truck.

CARLSON/*USA 1904-1910*
With a load capacity of 1-ton, Carlsons were built by the Carlson Motor Vehicle Co, Philadelphia, Pennsylvania, favouring a chain-drive "cabover" layout with a 20hp 4-cyl 4-stroke horizontal petrol engine. Unusual features included a one-piece channel-steel chassis frame bent to shape at each corner with internal cross-members hot-riveted to the side-members while suspension was by coil springs and the engine mounted longitudinally with flywheel to the left of the chassis. A leaf spring suspension 3-tonner announced in 1910 had a removable engine for ease of maintenance, detachable crankcase cover (rare at the time), sliding-mesh transmission and shock-proof steering.

CARLTON-HILL/*USA 1915*
Principally a passenger car manufacturer, the Carlton Hill Motor Car Co, East Rutherford, New Jersey, built less than 25 1½-ton Carlton-Hill commercials. Three fire appliances were also constructed.

CARMICHAEL/*England c1960 to date*
During the 1960s Carmichael & Sons (Worcester) Ltd converted the normal-control Land-Rover into the forward-control 'Redwing' for fire-fighting applications. In 1971 the trailing-axle 6-wheeled 'Redwing Sprint', based on the Range-Rover V8A, was in-

troduced. This has a permanently-engaged front-wheel drive, a power-output of some 40bhp per ton and a maximum speed of 257kmh. By 1976 the model had been developed into the Carmichael 'Commando' – currently the company's most popular appliance.

CARMONT/*England 1901-1902*
The Carmont was an unusual rear-steer 4-wheeled steam tractor, designed by H Carmont, Kingston-upon-Thames, Surrey, for converting horse-drawn wagons into self-propelled articulated 6-wheelers. It had a front-mounted vertical firetube boiler, with a 2-cyl high-pressure vertical steam engine driving the large front wheels via a countershaft differential and double chain drive. The belief held that the propulsion system might have been based on that of the French Gardner-Serpollet are unsubstantiated, though some Carmonts were constructed in 1901 under the Latham name in the factory of the British Power Traction and Lighting Co Ltd, which also built Gardner-Serpollet vehicles under the PTL brand name. Manufacturing rights in the Carmont passed to the Centre Steer Tractive Co Ltd, also of Kingston-upon-Thames in 1903.

CARPATI/*Rumania c1967 to date*
Developed from the Bucegi truck and tractor range, the Carpati forward-control series was introduced by Intreprinderea de Autocamioane Brasov, and is now built by Uzina de Autocamioane, Brasov. Powered initially by the same V8 petrol engine adopted for the Bucegi series, the Carpati has a snub-nosed version of the Bucegi cab and is listed as a tractor or 4-or 6-wheeled truck.

CARPENTER/*USA 1923 to date*
The R H Carpenter Body Works, Mitchell, Indiana, entered the vehicle-building field with an oak-bodied school bus which had a canvas-covered roof, mounted on a bought-in truck chassis. By 1935 a line of all-steel school buses had been developed, all on proprietary chassis but marketed as Carpenter. In 1941 the company was re-named the Carpenter Body Works Inc, continuing to offer Carpenter school buses on commercial chassis. By 1969 increasing demand for smaller vehicles had led to the introduction of the 32-seat 'Cadet' CV, mounted on a semi forward-control Chevrolet or GMC 'Step-Van' chassis, with body construction sub-contracted to the A O Smith Co, Milwaukee, Wisconsin. The Oshkosh V-series, with a variety of engines,

formed the basis of a forward-control model, while Carpenter's own rear-engined design, manufactured for them by the Hendrickson Mfg Co, Lyons, Illinois, carried similar bodywork. Current passenger capacities vary from 29 to 72 and automatic transmission is frequently used.

CARR/*England 1900*
Biscuit manufacturer Carr & Co Ltd, Carlisle, Cumbria, assembled a 4/5-ton steam wagon for its own use, using a patented vertical boiler, supplied by wagon builder Toward & Co, Newcastle-upon-Tyne, mounted immediately over the front axle. A 50hp compound "undertype" engine was located midway along the rolled-steel chassis frame, with drive taken by chain from the crankshaft to a countershaft and thence by 2-speed gearing to the rear axle.

CARRIMORE/*England 1926-1928*
Carrimore Six Wheelers Ltd, North London, was famous for its trailers and semi-trailers. In 1926, however, the 'Freighter' 3000 forward-control solid-tyred 2-ton low-loader, running on small-diameter wheels, entered production. Many components were common to the Model 'T' Ford, power coming from a 20bhp 4-cyl petrol engine. Despite a remarkable turning circle, the model was unsuccessful and the project was dropped in 1928. Two years later the Carrimore-Lynx complete matched articulated truck was announced.

1930 Carrimore-Lynx SW15 artic

CARRIMORE-LYNX/*England 1930-1937*
Using Leyland Motors' forward-control 'Lynx' tractor, with a 4.9-litre 6-cyl petrol engine, Carrimore Six Wheelers Ltd, North London, introduced a complete matched articulated truck known as the Carrimore-Lynx. Payloads ranged from 11 to 17 tons, one early model being the 6-wheeled SW15 15-tonner and, a new de-

sign for 1932, the 8-wheeled EW17 17-tonner. The company eventually reverted to trailer and semi-trailer building.

CARTER/*England 1906-c1909*
The Carter steam wagon used an Ellis-Balmforth vertical firetube boiler and compound engine. Built by Carter Bros Ltd, later renamed Carter's Steam Wagon Co, Rochdale, Lancs, it had 3-speed gearing. Despite being more efficient than other machines of this layout, it was commercially unsuccessful.

CASE/*USA 1910-1913*
The Case Motor Car Co, New Bremen, Ohio, offered two commercial types in addition to its passenger cars. The heaviest was the 243-cm wheelbase 1-ton Model 'C' with 24hp 2-cyl 2-stroke engine and open body. Despite the beliefs of some enthusiasts, there was apparently no connection with the Auglaize Motor Car Co, also of New Bremen, Ohio.

CASS/*USA 1910-1915*
The Cass Motor Truck Co, Port Huron, Michigan, built a 2-ton bonneted truck, using a 30hp 4-cyl petrol engine, 3-speed transmission and double chain-drive. Models of 1- and 1½-ton capacity were added in 1912 but, within two years, the company had been re-constituted as the Independent Motors Co.

CATERPILLAR/*USA 1940 to date*
Founded in 1925, following a merger between the Holt-Cater-pillar Co and the C L Best Tractor Co, the Caterpillar Tractor Co was established at Peoria, Illinois, to build earth-moving equipment. The first wheeled model was a 4-wheeled bonneted tractor for operation with single-axle bottom-dump trailers. It had a 90bhp 6-cyl diesel engine, a 5-speed constant-mesh transmission, vacuum-hydraulic braking and a ball-and-socket type drawbar coupling. In

1955, a plant was set up at Decatur, Illinois and, by 1963, production of the company's first heavy-duty on/off highway dump truck, the 4 x 2 35-ton 769 Model, was in full swing. This truck had a 400-bhp turbocharged diesel engine, a 9- forward and 3- reverse transmission and fully-floating rear axle. It developed into the 769B and, by 1979, the 769C had been introduced. Other types included the 50-ton 773B and 85-ton 777, plus tractor derivatives for capacities of up to 150 tons. The company's own turbocharged diesels are used throughout the range and also supplied to other manufacturers.

1977 CBM LMB11 single-deck bus

1979 CBM LMC 12 single-deck coach

CBM/*France 1975 to date*
When bus and coach manufacturer Autocars Verney SAMV, Le Mans, was re-organized as Car et Bus Le Mans following its takeover by the Heuliez Group, the brand name changed from Verney to CBM. Still concentrating on the passenger market, the company builds the LMB and TDU ranges in 4- and 6-wheeled bus or coach form, with full independent suspension, DAF or Mercedes-Benz diesel engines and fully automatic transmissions.

CC/*England 1905-1906*
The CC was a forward-control 4-tonner, built along American lines with chain-drive and a Linley pre-select transmission with steering column control. It was developed by Commercial Cars Ltd, South London, and following extensive

trials a factory was established at Luton, Beds to produce a normal-control version known as the Commer Car.

CCC (1)/*USA 1953 to date*
The Crane Carrier Co was set up by the well-known Zeligson Truck & Equipment Co, Tulsa, Oklahoma, to manufacture crane-carrier chassis under the CCC or Crane Carrier names. These went into production alongside Zeligson models, the first being a small 6-ton carrier. Crane Carrier Canada Ltd was set up the following year and in 1955 the American operation moved to a larger plant. In 1957 the Available Truck Co was taken over and production transferred to Tulsa, where Available trucks also continued to be built for a time. Another acquisition was the Los Angeles-based Maxi Corp in 1959. By the 1960s Crane Carrier offered carriers of 6 x 4, 6 x 6 and 8 x 4 layout and a series of heavy dump trucks. Numerous engines were listed. A plant was established in Sydney, Australia, in 1963. Many machines have been added to the American-designed range since then, including truck-mixer chassis, container carriers, the low-profile tilt-cab 'Centurion' and the bonneted 'Centaur' tractor and load-carrier. In 1973 an agreement was made between the Crane Carriers Co and Soc Automobiles M Berliet, France, whereby carriers were to be licence-built under the Berliet-

1979 Caterpillar 773B 50-ton dump truck

1976 CCC (1) 'Centurion' 6 x 4 refuse collector

1940 Caterpillar DW10 artic dump truck

CCC name, employing Berliet engines and running units.

CCC (2)/*Canada 1954 to date*
One year after the Crane Carrier Co was set up in Tulsa, Oklahoma, a Canadian subsidiary, Crane Carrier Canada Ltd, was established at Rexdale, Ontario. Identical models are assembled at both plants, but the Canadian operation also makes log-haulers for the country's lumber industry. Capacities range from 25 to 75 tons and models include a high-floatation 4 x 4.

CCC (3)/*Australia 1963-1968*
The Crane Carrier Co, Tulsa, Oklahoma, also set up an assembly plant in Sydney, NSW, offering identical models under the same brand names. However, there was also a special bonneted dump truck, unique to the Australian market, which remained in production until the plant closed.

CCF-BRILL/*Canada 1945-1956*
Licence production of the ACF-Brill IC-41 underfloor-engined intercity coach was undertaken by the Canadian Car & Foundry Co Ltd, Fort William, Ontario, under the CCF-Brill and Candian Car brand names. This was joined by the C-36 city transit bus but in 1946 a 44-passenger trolleybus was sold as the Can-Car, a name adopted for all models from 1956.

CEDES/*England 1901-c1916*
Based on the Austrian Lohner-Porsche system, the Cedes battery-electric range was apparently built by Johnson & Phillips, Charlton, London, using hub mo-

tors in the front wheels initially, but changing to rear hub motors in 1908. Like the Lohner-Porsche and its successor, the Mercedes Electrique, the Cedes was specially popular as a fire appliance, but came to an abrupt end when the government outlawed it, and the Cedes-Stoll trolleybus, as an alien product.

1956 CCF-Brill single-deck coach

CEDES-STOLL/*England 1912-1916*
Like the Cedes battery-electric, the Cedes-Stoll trolleybus system was produced by Johnson & Phillips Ltd, Charlton, London, but marketed by Cedes Electric Traction Ltd. Based on the Austrian Lohner-Stoll system, the first demonstration took place at West Ham and the first customer was Keighley Corp, which placed two front-entrance 24-seaters in service. Production models had a 20hp traction motor in each rear wheel hub, current collection being via a 4-wheeled trolley running along twin overhead cables. The marque came to an end when the British government outlawed the Cedes-Stoll.

CEIRANO/*Italy 1925-c1946*
Previously responsible for SCAT truck production, Soc Ceirano Automobili Torino, Turin, introduced a range of bonneted Ceirano trucks to the Italian market. These were 3- and 5-tonners popular with the Italian Army and powered by a 4.7-litre 4-cyl sidevalve petrol engine. Other features included 4-speed transmission and 4-wheel brakes, the 3-

1914 Cedes-Stoll trolleybus

tonner also being marketed in long-wheelbase form for passenger operation. In 1929 Ceirano was merged with Fiat and SPA, but by 1931 all assets and manufacturing rights had been sold to Soc Ligure Piedmontese Automobili, producer of the SPA range.

Ceirano trucks continued under new management until shortly after World War II, most models being sold to the military.

CENTRE STEER/*England 1903*
The Centre Steer Tractive Co Ltd was founded at Kingston-upon-Thames, Surrey, to revive production of the Carmont rear-steer 4-wheeled steam tractor. Few were built although some of the patents for this and for the Carmont machine may have been used in the development of the similar Lomax vehicle.

CHABOCHE/*France 1900-1910*
E Chaboche, Paris, was already building steam cars when he constructed a prototype steam van which was developed into a series of coal-fired goods and passenger models. In 1906 cars were discontinued in favour of commercials, all of which were of under 2½-ton capacity with semi-flash boilers and cardan-shaft drive.

CHALLENGE-COOK/*USA 1958-c1964*
The Cook Bros Equipment Co, Los Angeles, California manufacturer of C-B or Cook Brothers trucks, was acquired by the Challenge Mfg Co, builder of cement- and concrete-mixing machinery and re-named Challenge-Cook Bros Inc. Existing Cook Brothers models, some still with chain-drive, continued Challenge-Cook but production was mainly turned over to truck-mixer equipment for other chassis. The manufacture of complete mixer trucks appears to have ended in 1964.

CHALMERS/*USA 1911-1923*
Formerly known as Chalmers-De-

troit, Chalmers commercials were built by the Chalmers Motor Co, Detroit, Michigan.

CHALMERS-DETROIT/*USA 1907-1911*

A few light- and medium-duty commercials were built by the Chalmers Motor Co, Detroit, Michigan, as Chalmers-Detroit. They were later re-named Chalmers.

CHAMBERLAIN/*Australia c1960*

Concentrating since World War II on the manufacture of agricultural tractors, Chamberlain Holdings Ltd, Welshpool, West Australia, Also designed a vehicle suitable for long-haul work in the Outback. Called the 'Champion', it was of normal tractor configuration, with fully-enclosed cab, regulation lighting and additional fuel-carrying facilities. Eventually the company was acquired by the John Deere organization to form Chamberlain John Deere Pty Ltd and the 'Champion' was gradually phased out.

CHAMBERS/*Northern Ireland 1919-1925*

Two brothers, R and J Chambers, founded Chambers Motors Ltd, Belfast, in 1904. This was one of only a few Irish motor manufacturers. Products were mainly passenger cars and light commercials, one of which was up-rated to 1-ton capacity and fitted with a Meadows gearbox in place of its original 3-speed rear axle-mounted box.

CHAMPION (1)/*USA 1904-1905*

The forward-control Champion 1-ton battery-electric van was built by the Champion Wagon Works, Oswego, New York. This company may have been connected with the later Champion Electric Vehicle Co, New York, or perhaps with the McCrea Motor Truck Co, Chicago, Illinois, who also built a 1-ton Champion battery-electric.

CHAMPION (2)/*USA c1905-1910*

The Champion Electric Vehicle Co, New York, is reputed to have listed both light-and medium-duty Champion battery-electrics. It may have been connected with the earlier products of the Champion Wagon Works, Oswego.

CHAMPION (3)/*USA 1906*

The McCrea Motor Truck Co, Chicago, Illinois, advertised a 1-ton Champion battery-electric. This may have been connected with the similar product of the Champion Wagon Works, Oswego, New York.

CHANG-ZHENG/*China to date*

Based on Tatra designs, Chang-Zheng or Ch'ang-Cheng (Long March) 6 x 6 trucks and tractors are built in the Hopei Ch'ang-Cheng Motor Vehicle Plant, Hopei Province. Models comprise the XD-980 tractor, the 10-ton XD-250 truck, and the 12-ton XD-160.

CHARRON/*France 1908*

Specializing in the manufacture of taxicabs, Automobiles Charron Ltd Puteaux, Seine, also built a fleet of pneumatic-tyred 30hp luxury single-deck buses for the London-based General Motor Co.

CHASE/*USA 1907-1920*

Using a high-wheeler design, the Chase Motor Truck Co, Syracuse, New York, built both light- and mediumweight goods and passenger commercials. The heaviest was a forward-control 3-tonner with 30hp 4-cyl air-cooled 2-stroke engine and 3-speed sliding-mesh transmission. By 1914 only bonneted trucks were listed, with capacities of 1, 2 and 3 tons. These had 4-cyl water-cooled Continental petrol engines, 4-speed sliding-mesh transmissions and worm-drive. The last Chase commercials were probably of up to 3½-tons capacity.

CHASESIDE/*England 1937-1965*

The Chaseside Engineering Co Ltd, Enfield, Middlesex, developed a medium-duty petrol or diesel-engined dump truck. Employing similar mechanical units to the company's front-end loader, this remained in production for many years; by the late 1950s a one-man half-cab, reversible driver's seat and Ford diesel engine were used.

CHATILLON-PANHARD/*France 1911-1914*

The 4-wheel drive, 4-wheel steer Chatillon-Panhard artillery tractor was a product of Soc des Anciens Ets Panhard et Levassor, Paris, powered initially by a 45hp 6.6-litre 6-cyl petrol engine but later by a larger 4-cyl unit. A lighter model entered production in 1914 but was apparently short-lived.

CHAUSSON/*France 1947-1963*

Founded in 1903, SA des Usines Chausson, Asnières, Seine, concentrated on chassisless bus construction from 1947. Powered by a vertical front-mounted Panhard diesel, Hotchkiss petrol engine, early Chaussons had a 5-speed transmission, with braking, servo-steering, door operation and tyre inflation by compressed air. All-steel body pressings were produced at the company's Meudon

CHEVROLET (1)/*USA 1918 to date*

The Chevrolet Motor Car Co was founded by William Crapo Durant in Detroit, Michigan, in 1911 to manufacture automobiles designed by the Swiss racing driver Louis Joseph Chevrolet; in 1918, when the company became the Chevrolet Motor Division of the General Motors Corp, the first Chevrolet commercials appeared. The first of these was a 1-tonner, which had solid tyres at the rear, pneumatics at the front, and was powered by a 3.7 litre 4-cyl overhead-valve petrol engine. Construction of both cab and body was contracted out to other concerns.

In 1923 Chevrolet truck production also began at the former Samson Tractor Co plant, Janesville, Wisconsin and, in the same year, the 1-tonner received a 2.8-litre petrol engine and spiral-bevel drive. The 1½-ton 'R' Series of 1926 was the first closed-cab Chevrolet, while the 'LM' 1-tonner of 1927 had an optional 4-speed transmission. This was later standardized on the 'LP'-Series, which also had 4-wheel brakes. The 'LP' was the last Chevrolet truck to use a 4-cyl splash-lubricated engine, the next model being the 'LQ'-Series 1½-tonner of 1929, with a 3.2-litre overhead-valve 6-cyl unit. A second driving axle had now been added to the 1-tonner for experimental military use.

In 1930 Chevrolet's 'LS'-Series introduced a dual rear wheel option and all-expanding brakes, followed by long- and short-wheel-base versions of most other models. Throughout the 1930s, the company manufactured commercials limited to no more than 1½-ton capacity. These were heavily influenced by Chevrolet's automobile styling, with all heavier models being sold as GMCs. Dur-

1929 Chevrolet (1) 6 x 2 truck

ing this period, too, Chevrolet chassis and running units were supplied both to the Fitzjohn Body Co, Muskegon, Michigan and the Flxible Co, Loudonville, Ohio to form the basis of Fitzjohn and Flxible passenger models.

By mid-1936 a streamlined low-profile cab was standard for the BA series, plus hydraulic brakes; by 1937, General Motors Continental SA had started converting the 1½-ton bonneted model into a "cabover" truck to cater for European requirements. This was 2 years before Chevrolet's own USA-designed "cabovers" were announced. GMC's export-only Oldsmobiles and the Yellow Coach passenger range all used Chevrolet components by 1937.

By 1939 Chevrolet commercials had also moved away from car styling, becoming increasingly like their GMC sisters. A new 1-ton model was added to the range before the end of that year. Hydrovac brakes and 2-speed axles were now optional, with hypoid axles standard from 1940, when the 'KP'-Series 'Dubl-Duti' for-

1964 Chevrolet (1) 6 x 4 tipper

ward-control walk-through urban delivery van was announced. In April of that year an increase in the production of military trucks and equipment took place, centred mainly on a 1½-ton 4 x 4. There was also a 6 x 6 derivative built in the GMC plant.

Between 1941 and 1947, some sixty Chevrolet commercials of all sizes were listed, with full-scale post-war commercial production being resumed in August 1944. School buses, seating up to 54, were included in the range by this time, but engine options were as for pre-war days. A complete restyling took place in 1947 and in

1941 Chevrolet (1) KP 'Dubl-Duti' mobile canteen

1951 another new model – the 'Step-n-Drive' easy-access van, with standee driving position was announced. Chevrolet running units were used in the chassisless Swiss Lauber coach of 1954; a 90bhp 4-cyl 2-stroke Detroit Diesel also became optional in the same year. Twelve-volt electrics, an optional 4-speed hydramatic transmission and low cab-forward or semi forward-control types appeared in 1955, when a short-stroke overhead-valve V8 petrol engine was also fitted to the company's 2-tonners. Heaviest models in 1956 were 2½-tonners, with power steering and 6-speed automatic transmission, as well as the 5-speed manual type. Other developments included an air-hydraulic brake option and more powerful V8s of up to 210bhp. Full air brakes followed later.

Torsion-bar independent front suspension was tried on some trucks in 1960, but abandoned within 3 years. A more successful innovation was the company's first tiltcab truck, offered in gross weights up to 18,144kg. In 1961 the bonneted '60' and '70' ranges were launched, while the option of the 4-cyl Detroit Diesels was reintroduced. The '60'-Series Jobmaster superceded the original '60'-Series in 1962; in 1963 Fuller 'Roadranger' transmissions became optional for heavy-duty models, while some 6 x 4 tractors were offered with 195bhp Detroit Diesel V6s. In 1964 V6 petrol units were introduced for heavy trucks, but soon even more powerful V8s, providing up to 252bhp out of 6.7 litres, were developed. New V6 petrol and V6 or V8 diesel engines were used to power Chevrolet's largest trucks so far, the heavy-duty "conventional" 70000 and 80000 models. These were launched in 1966. The Chevrolet range now catered for GCWs up to 29,483kg.

Experiments into gas-turbines led to the development of the experimental 'Titan III', with automatic transmission, powered tiltcab and windows, retractable headlamps, stereo and radio-telephone. Though the gas-turbine was abandoned as unsuccessful, 1970 saw the debut of the 'Titan' "cabover" range for up to 34,835kg GCW. Offered in 4 x 2 and 6 x 4 form, this was a short tiltcab tractor, with V6, V8 or V12 Detroit Diesel engines of up to 390bhp or Cummins diesels of up to 319bhp. Other features included a twin-disc clutch, 10- or 13-speed transmission, air brakes, power-steering and full air suspension. From 1974, the Chevrolet Motor Division supplied mediumweight truck chassis to the Monarch Mfg Corp for assembly into the Chevalier "cabover" range, available through Chevrolet dealers. Also using the Chevrolet name, the São Paulo plant of General Motors do Brasil SA was now offering a series of medium-duty trucks.

A new 6 x 4 "conventional" truck, christened the Bison, with a GVW of 23,000kg and a GCW of up to 36,300kg appeared in 1977. These were powered by turbocharged Detroit Diesel or Cummins engines, with 5-speed automatic transmission as standard. For 1978 the new '90' Series Bruin "conventional" had a fibreglass tilt bonnet and a choice between Detroit Diesel and Cummins power. The 'Bison' and 'Titan' remained at the top of the range, the latter being available with a roof-mounted wind deflector and even Caterpillar diesel engines. The ur-

1932 Chevrolet (1) 'NB'-Series artic tractor

ban delivery 'Step-Van' continued in production, many being supplied to the Carpenter BodyWorks Inc for conversion into school buses; at the same time, however, Chevrolet's own school bus range for up to 72 passengers was introduced. A further development was a front-wheel drive, forward-control mobile home chassis, with front disc brakes, independent front suspension and a choice of petrol engines.

CHEVROLET (2)/*Belgium 1937-1939, 1952*
General Motors Continental SA, Antwerp, launched a "cabover" conversion of the Chevrolet Motor Co's 1½-ton "conventional" to cater for European requirements. In 1939 it was replaced by the parent company's own "cabover". In 1952 a 391-cm wheelbase forward-control bus, called the GT30, was briefly advertised.

CHEVROLET (3)/*Canada 1940-1945*
Formed by the merger of the McLaughlin Motor Car Co Ltd, Oshawa, Ontario, and the Chevrolet Motor Co of Canada, General Motors of Canada Ltd built commercials along identical lines to its American counterpart until World War II. Then a series of military trucks used components interchangeable with those used by Ford of Canada. Engines and major running units were all by Chevrolet, however, including driven front axles based on the American Marmon-Herrington design.

CHEVROLET (4)/*Brazil to date*
General Motors do Brasil SA was founded in São Paulo in 1925 to assemble and manufacture General Motors products for the South American market. The current range covers a variety of types and weights. One of the lightest is the bonneted C-1504 pick-up truck, similar, apart from its 6 x 6 drive, to its US-built equivalent. Of the larger trucks, only the C-60 is petrol-engined, having a load capacity of between 6½ and 7½ tons. Diesel models have a 5.84-litre 6-cyl unit and include the 14-ton payload D-6803 with Clark 5-speed transmission. The heavy-duty D-60 is available in 4 x 4, 6 x 4 and 6 x 6 forms.

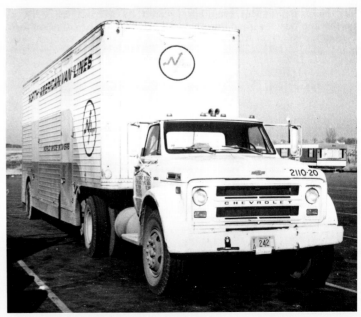

1968 Chevrolet (1) '70'-Series artic tractor

1958 Chasson single-deck bus

plant and transported to the former Chenard-Walcker factory at Gennevilliers for final assembly. In 1951 a luxury single-deck coach was announced, with options of a front-mounted vertical engine or an underfloor Hercules diesel, licence-built by La Hispano-Suiza Fabrica de Automoviles SA. This engine was also made available in the company's city buses, which had Wilson pre-select gearboxes and accommodation for 32 seated and 23 standing passengers. Some engineless body/chassis units were supplied to Soc de Vehicules et Travaux Electriques for conversion into Vetra trolleybuses. Power-assisted steering was standardized in 1956 and in 1958 a new Paris bus was developed, with a 150bhp vertical Hispano/Hercules diesel engine at the front, SCG fully-automatic transmission and enough space for 30 seated and 50 standing passengers. The company also built a number of torsion-bar suspension delivery vans with side-loading doors for SA des Automobiles Peugeot. A year later Chausson merged with SA de Vehicules Industriels et Equipements Mécaniques, manufacturer of the Saviem range, but production of Chausson buses continued, many having 150bhp 6.84-litre fuel-injection Saviem 'Fulgur' diesel engines. But, eventually, the line was absorbed into the Berliet range, when Automobiles

M Berliet also became part of the group in 1977.

CHECKER/USA 1948-1953, 1959-c1965

The Checker Cab Mfg Co, Kalamazoo, Michigan, was already world-famous for its taxicabs when it constructed a series of bus chassis to the requirements of Transit Buses Inc, Dearborn, Michigan, a firm that Checker was to take over two years later. Following this purchase Transit's buses were re-designed and re-launched as the Checker Series 'E', using a Continental 6-cyl petrol engine, with a standard seating capacity of 31. A prototype bus, with rear-mounted LeRoi petrol engine and seating for 28 to 42 passengers, was constructed in 1952 but never reached series production, the old Series 'E' remaining the company's mainstay until 1953. By 1959 the famous 6- or 8-door 'Aerobus' stretched limousine, with seating for 9 or 12 passengers, was being produced using the old side-valve Continental engine, but with an optional overhead-valve unit from 1960. These went to various US Government Depts and the Armed Forces. Chevrolet straight-6 and V8 petrol engines were listed for 1965, a 5.7 litre V8 and automatic transmission being standard for the 'Aerobus'.

CHENARD-WALCKER/France 1919-1951

The Chenard-Walcker road tractor, with its revolutionary coupling system, was built in the Gennevilliers, Seine, factory of SA des Ans Ets Chenard et Walcker. The coupling consisted of a vertical pillar carrying a shouldered collar that could be raised and lowered by a hand crank. A 4-wheeled trailer with drawbar forecarriage ran up a tapered ramp

Chausson single-deck bus c1956

until the towing jaw was clamped securely around the collar. Marketed by a subsidiary, SA des Trains Chenard-Walcker-FAR, the first example had a 3-litre 4-cyl side-valve petrol engine and was rated for a 2/5-ton payload. In 1920 licenced construction had started in the Antwerp factory of SA Auto-Traction as the Auto-Traction but, following a 1925 take-over by Minerva Motors SA, the Belgian version was re-named the 'Minerva'. At Chenard-Walcker itself, a 10-tonner with 8-speed transmission was listed by 1924 and in 1928 a 44bhp overhead-valve petrol engine, disc clutch, 5-speed box and epicyclic final-drive with differential lock were announced for heavy-duty versions. The first British-built Chenard-Walckers were assembled under licence during this period by Hall, Lewis & Co Ltd but production was quickly taken over by Beardmore Multiwheelers Ltd which marketed the range as the Beardmore Multiwheeler. For very heavy work, the French company constructed a chain-drive 6 x 4 for 25 tons GCW; by 1930 the largest versions had 4-cyl sleeve-valve petrol engines. One year later a 250bhp twin-engined 6 x 4 with two 7.5-litre Panhard petrol engines, was added to the series. Diesel propulsion arrived in 1932 and a light commercial range was also launched. By 1933 an 8-speed 5-tonner and a coach chassis had appeared and in 1937 a 6-tonner was announced. Lighter models had 4-cyl Citroën overhead-valve petrol or diesel engines. In 1941 a forward-control 1/1¼-ton petrol or producer-gas front-wheel drive delivery van was introduced. Six years later a 1.3-litre 4-cyl Peugeot overhead-valve petrol engine was offered, continuing until SA des Automobiles Peugeot acquired the business in 1951, dis-

continuing the Chenard-Walcker name. The factory was acquired by SA des Usines Chausson for assembling Chausson passenger models.

CHEVALIER/USA 1974 to date

Offered through Chevrolet dealers, the Chevalier is an assembled medium-duty "cabover" based on a Chevrolet chassis with a V8 petrol engine. Built by former motor-home manufacturer the Monarch Mfg Corp, Napponee, Indiana, and Chatsworth, California, it has an automatic transmission, power brakes and steering and a light-alloy van or stakeside body.

CHICAGO (1)/USA 1899-1905

Sometimes also referred to as the Chicago Motor Vehicle, goods and passenger models were built by the Chicago Motor Vehicle Co, initially in Chicago but later in Harvey, Illinois. Few are believed to have been built, the last examples being constructed by the Monarch Motor Vehicle Co back in Chicago.

CHICAGO (2)/USA 1910-1911

The Chicago Commercial Car Co, Chicago, Illinois, listed a 1-ton open truck known as the S-25. This had double chain-drive, a 20hp petrol engine and selective transmission.

CHICAGO (3)/USA 1919-1932

The Chicago Motor Truck Co, Chicago, Illinois, assembled Hercules petrol-engined goods and passenger models in the 1- to 5-ton weight range from 1919 onwards. In 1923 production was taken over by the Robert M Cutting Co, also of Chicago, which introduced Waukesha petrol engines in 1927 and worm-drive 8- and 12-ton 6-wheelers three years later.

1928 Chenard-Walcker U5 van

1980 Chuting Star 6x6 truck-mixer

CHICAGO-ELECTRIC/USA 1912-1916
A few mediumweight battery-electrics known as Chicago-Electric or simply Chicago, were built by the Chicago Electric Motor Car Co, Chicago, Illinois, in 1912, production being continued until 1916 by the Anderson Electric Car Co.

CHICAGO MOTOR BUS/USA 1916-1920
The Chicago Motor Bus Co, Chicago, Illinois, built 50 open-top double-deck buses for its own use from 1916. Low-loading rear-entrance bodies were supplied by the St Louis Car Co and detachable front-wheel drive units built by the operating company, using Moline-Knight sleeve-valve petrol engines. In 1919 these buses were joined by a fully-enclosed front-wheel drive double-decker (the first in the USA) and a similar rear-wheel drive machine. Company re-organization in 1920 led to the formation of the American Motor Bus Co as the bus-building subsidiary of the operating company and all subsequent vehicles were usually referred to as American.

CHICAGO MOTOR COACH/ USA 1928
In 1923 the Chicago Motor Bus Co, Chicago, Illinois, was taken over by John D Hertz, who established the Yellow Coach Mfg Co to manage the company's bus-building activities, while the Chicago Motor Coach Co ran the fleet. The operating company constructed one experimental 6-wheeled single-decker in 1928.

CHILDS THOROUGHBRED/ USA 1920-1927
The Foamite-Childs Corp, Utica, New York State, marketed fire appliances as Thoroughbred until the company was taken over by the American LaFrance Fire Engine Co, to form the American LaFrance & Foamite Corp. Sometimes known as the Childs or Foamite-Childs, the Childs Thoroughbred was based on a special chassis constructed by the Kearns-Dughie Motors Corp, Danville, Pennsylvania. Later models were sold as American LaFrance.

CHINGHAI-HU/China 1970 to date
The Chinghai Motor Vehicle Plant, Chinghai Province builds the Chinghai-Hu (Chinghai Lake) heavy-duty bonneted 4-tonner, with engine and chassis frame similar to that of the Jay-Fong (Liberation) CA-10B model.

CHIYODA/Japan 1931-1939
Tokyo Gasu Denki KK, Tokyo, was a large engineering concern that had previously built American-style trucks under the TGE brand name. A new range of trucks and buses took the Chiyoda name, after an Imperial residence in Tokyo which had bought one of the earlier TGE models. Most Chiyodas were 2½-ton 6 x 4s, popular with military authorities. In 1937 the company merged with Kyodo Kokusan Jidosha KK, to form Tokyo Motor Industry Ltd, but Chiyoda trucks continued to be made.

CHRISTIE/USA 1911-1918
JW Christie set up the Front Drive Motor Co, Hoboken, New Jersey, to develop a motor tractor for converting horse-drawn fire appliances to self-propulsion. The prototype was a 2-wheeled unit, with a 90hp 4-cyl petrol engine ahead of the axle, drive being via a 2-speed box and roller chain to a countershaft and then by pinions meshing with gear rings on the inside of the road wheels. Production models, with a transverse engine beneath the driver's seat or under a bonnet, were assembled from 1912. New York was to become the company's best customer, the Christie being specially popular as a hook and ladder or water tower truck. Although a leader in its field – the idea being copied by many others – the company failed to progress and, with requirements for such vehicles falling dramatically, went out of business.

CHRISTOPH/Germany 1906
The Christoph was a short-lived front-wheel drive tractor, powered by a single-cyl kerosene engine and constructed by Maschinenfabrik J E Christoph, Niesky. Very few were built.

CHRYSLER/USA 1963
The Chrysler Motor Corp rarely applied the Chrysler name to commercials, with the exception of amphibious 8-wheeled rigids built for the US Army. Known as the XM410, this model had a load capacity of 2½ tons with propulsion on water through rotation of the wheels. It was of integral construction, had a multi-fuel diesel engine and was built entirely of light alloy.

CHUBB/England 1970 to date
Chubb Pyrene Ltd developed a line of fire-fighting vehicles in association with Reynolds Boughton Chassis Ltd, Amersham, Buckinghamshire. Marketed as Chubb, chassis construction was undertaken by Reynolds Boughton, the first being the massive 'Pathfinder'. Later types, with the exception of the road-going 'Pacesetter', have Boughton chassis. Chubb Pyrene Ltd was soon re-organized as the Fire Engineering Division of Chubb Fire Security Ltd after which the 'Pathfinder' became the 'Griffin', and the 'Pacesetter' the 'Scorpio'.

CHUTING STAR/USA 1976 to date
The Chuting Star is a 6 x 6 front-discharge truck-mixer built by Forward Inc, Huron, South Dakota. Powered by a rear-mounted turbocharged Cummins VT555 diesel engine, it has a Sundstrand DMT250 transmission. Although intended as a truck-mixer, the low-mounted cab enables the chassis to be used also as a crane-carrier.

CGA/Spain 1929-1936, 1939-1942
Cia General de Autobuses de Barcelona SA was a Barcelona bus operator which decided to construct vehicles for its own use. First models had 90bhp petrol engines and an electric transmission system, derived from Tilling-Stevens vehicles already in the fleet. Single-deckers carried between 30 and 40 passengers, while double-deckers could take 54 to 60. In 1936, with the outbreak of the Spanish Civil War, the business was taken over by a workers' committee, building vehicles under the CNT-AIT name. After the war, the original name was revived and 5 buses and 33 double-deck trolleybuses were built.

CIEM-STELLA/Switzerland 1904-1913
Cie de l'Industrie Electrique et Mécanique, Secheron, Geneva, built battery-electric and petrol-engined commercials as CIEM-Stella, sometimes known simply as CIEM. The earliest model was a 1½/2-ton battery-electric, with batteries slung amidships beneath the chassis with rear wheels and driven by twin electric motors. In 1905 it was joined by a 16-passenger bonneted petrol-engined model. This design was sold in Britain as the Rolls. An 8-seat design was announced in about 1908 but no other types were developed.

CINCINNATI/USA 1928-1931
When the Versare Corp, Albany, NY was brought by the Cincinnati Car Corp, a streetcar-builder of Cincinnati, Ohio, Versare trolley-coach production was moved to Cincinnati. Re-named the 'Cincinnati', the coach was re-designed as a 2-axle machine.

CIV/France 1953
Constructions Industrielles de Versailles was already well-known for its refuse collection bodies when it announced the rear-engined integral-construction CIV bus. Powered by an 80bhp Hispano/Hercules diesel engine mounted longitudinally at the rear, this single-decker had a capacity of 65 persons, with 26 seated. Although at least one prototype was built, it is doubtful whether production followed.

CLARK/USA 1910-1912
Following earlier experiments with steam-powered delivery vans, Edward S Clark Steam Automobiles, Dorchester, Massachussetts, developed a few 3- and 5-ton petrol-engined vans, both employing the same 4-cyl 2-stroke engine slung beneath the body.

1955 Chrysler T55E3 6 x 6 military truck

CLARKSON/England 1898-1908
The first Clarkson steam lorry built by the Clarkson & Capel Steam Car Syndicate Ltd, Dal-

1965 Citroën T.55 'Sahara' 4 x 4 single-deck bus

CITROËN/*France 1929 to date*
A 1.8-litre 4-cyl petrol-engined 1-tonner built by SA André Citroën, Paris, was joined in 1930 by a 1¾-tonner with 2.4-litre 6-cyl side-valve petrol engine, 4-speed gearbox and vacuum-servo brakes. These were followed a year later by a variety of 6-cyl models, including a 2-tonner, a 22-seat coach, a 3/4-ton single-drive 6-wheeler and a 5½-ton tractor, all of normal-control layout. A re-styled mediumweight range, announced in 1934, incorporated automobile-style front-end treatment; although side-valve engines were retained on some models, the 3½-ton Type '45' received an overhead-valve 6-cyl unit. This foreshadowed the future, for, by 1936 side-valve engines had disappeared, new models including the 1½-ton Type '23' and 2½-ton Type '32'. By 1937 a vast 80-model range included the company's first diesel-powered vehicles, using a new 1.8-litre 4-cyl unit.
Wartime saw producer-gas versions of the Type '45' but otherwise, little development took place until 1946, when hydrovac brakes were standardized. In 1947 the famous 23½-cwt payload 'H'-Series delivery van, with its snubnose, corrugated body panels, torsion-bar rear suspension and a

35bhp version of the 11CV passenger car engine, was announced. Medium-capacity models received new front-ends in 1954. The Type '55' was now available with a 76bhp 6-cyl Citroën diesel engine and, within two years, the petrol unit had been increased to 5.2 litres, with 4 x 4 and tractor derivatives also listed. Another version had a 4-cyl Panhard diesel and, by 1960, the range included the 'H'-Series, the Type '55' 5-tonner and the Type '23' 2-tonner, now listed in semi-forward control form and with a Perkins P4 diesel engine.
For 1961 the 'H'-Series was offered with a 1.6-litre Perkins diesel engine, and a military 4 x 4 with forward-control and 6-cyl petrol engine was developed. New 3- and 6-tonners, with 4- or 5-speed all-synchromesh transmissions and dual-circuit servo brakes, were introduced about this time. By 1966 the heaviest commercials had become forward-control. Within a year, however, the company had acquired Automobiles M Berliet and all Citroën heavies were phased out in favour of Berliet designs, which were occasionally marketed as Citroën-Berliet. Meanwhile, variations on the 'H'-Series van were built under licence in South Vietnam, apparently also carrying the Citroën name.
In 1973 the company was renamed SA Automobiles Citroën but in 1974 became a division of Automobiles Peugeot, the Berliet operation being sold to Saviem-Renault. New front-wheel drive vans in the 1½- to 1¾-ton class, known as the C32 and C35, were based on Fiat's 242 model, with a 2-litre Citroën engine, all-independent suspension, and servo-assisted 4-wheel brakes. By April 1975 only car-based commercials and the C32, C35 and 'H'-Series

Citroën-Kégresse half-track military vehicle c1931

were available. The 'H'-Series is now represented by the 1½-ton HY, while versions of the C32 and C35 are used by Baeten NV.

CITROËN-BERLIET/*France 1967-1974*
When Automobiles M Berliet, Lyons, was acquired by SA André Citroën, the latter's main aim was to add heavy goods and passenger types to its range. Some Berliets subsequently appeared as Citroën-Berliets but, when Citroën became a division of Automobiles Peugeot, control of the Berliet operation was sold to the Saviem-Renault group.

CITROËN-KÉGRESSE/*France 1921-c1940*
Employing a half-track system devised by Adolphe Kégresse, SA Andrē Citroën, Paris, developed the lightweight Citroën-Kégresse. The truck became so popular that the system was adopted by other companies. As Citroën specifications were up-dated, the heavier Kégresse tracked bogie, known as the P7, was developed; the largest Citroën-based types having a 6-cyl petrol engine and payload of 1½-tons. The last Citroën-Kégresse was built under licence by SA des Automobiles Unic during the early days of World War II.

1969 Citroën Model 350 single-deck minibus

1965 Citroën 'H'-Type integral van

1968 Citroën-Berliet 550K truck chassis-cab

1904 Clarkson single-deck steam bus

ston, East London was a 4-tonner of 2-speed chain-drive design with compound vertical engine located at the back of the cab. Built for the 1899 Liverpool Trials, this had a modified oil-fired Merryweather boiler, cab roof condenser and Stephenson's link motion with the engine developing some 14hp and road speeds of 3 and 9km/h. Final-drive was via two chains to the rear wheels, one each side of the chassis frame, and braking was effected by a steam brake acting on the rear wheels and by a foot-operated hand brake on the engine shaft.

This was followed by a single-speed duplex-engined 2-tonner of superior design, with countershaft spur differential and Joy's valve gear, using Clarkson's own paraffin-fired semi-flash boiler. This was eventually developed into a centrally-fired vertical boiler which could be fuelled with coal, coke or paraffin, although the last was by far the most common.

In 1902, the company moved to Chelmsford, Essex and early in 1903 was re-named Thomas Clarkson Ltd. Soon, a bonneted steam bus was constructed on the 2-ton chassis, the design being referred to frequently as the Chelmsford. An oil-fired 12-seat single-decker entered service trials with the London General Omnibus Co in 1904 and this also went to the London Road Car Co.

At Olympia in 1905 Clarkson's first double-decker was shown, still using the original 2-ton chassis. This was subsequently bought by the London Road Car Co, which quickly ordered a further twenty with "flash" boilers and double-acting 2-cyl engines. Two other London operators – Burtwell Bros and John Sharland & Sons – bought similar machines. By the end of 1905 the London General Omnibus Co had bought

a dozen, but maintenance costs proved prohibitive and by 1907 all except the Burtwell and LGOC vehicles had been withdrawn, the exceptions being re-built by Clarkson and returned to service for a further two years. By the end of 1907 just 46 Clarksons had been sold in the capital. The company went into liquidation and a new concern – the National Steam Car Co Ltd – was set up in 1909 to take over the business, premises and rights of Thomas Clarkson Ltd and to design, construct and operate Clarkson's National steam buses; these and a few goods-carrying derivatives continued to be referred to by many as Clarksons.

CLAYTON/*England 1902, 1912-1930*
Clayton & Shuttleworth Ltd, Lincoln, constructed an unsuccessful "undertype" compound-engined steam wagon sold as the Clayton. No further wagons were built until 1912, when the company's first 5-ton "overtype", also with a compound engine, was constructed. Although both reliable and economical, the Clayton 5-tonner was never as popular as its contemporaries. In 1915 and 1916 the company experimented briefly with petrol-engined trucks, using components common to the 5-ton steamer, but series production did not follow, although battery electric models were built between 1919 and 1930, again using steam wagon components. After World War I, the 5-tonner's popularity decreased rapidly, and in 1920 a vertical-boilered "undertype" was constructed. This was a single-speed model of duplex-cylindered layout, but it was another relatively unsuccessful design, even though a heavy-artic version was experimented with briefly in 1926. In the same year an advanced 6-tonner was developed, but only

about forty were built in addition to the thousand or so 5-tonners. In 1926 the company went into liquidation, manufacture being taken over by Clayton Wagons Ltd, which had been set up in 1918 to handle the manufacture of railway stock. When production finally ceased, most of the assets passed to Marshall, Sons & Co Ltd, Gainsborough, Lincolnshire.

CLECO/*England c1950-c1957*
Better known for its industrial works trucks, Cleco Industries Ltd, Leicester, also manufactured a few battery-electric road-going machines of forward-control layout. Apart from the BV3, introduced after World War II in capacities of 1-, 1¼- and 1½-ton, most were lightweight types.

CLEMENT/*France 1903*
Adolphe Clement, an employee of Soc Gladiator, Pré-St Gervais, Seine, formed Clement et Cie, at Levallois-Perret, developing light vans and mediumweight trucks under the Clement name. Because of its close connections with Gladiator, the Clement range was also referred to as Clement-Gladiator but re-named Clement-Bayard when SA des Ets Clement-Bayard was formed late in 1903. Sold in Britain by the British Automobile Syndicate, the 1903 Clements had 1.4-litre L-head vertical-twin petrol engines, 4-speed transmissions, shaft-drive and pneumatic tyres.

CLEMENT-BAYARD/*France 1903-1922*
Clement and Clement-Gladiator commercials, previously manufactured by Clement et Cie, Levallois-Perret, Seine, were re-named Clement-Bayard when the company was re-constituted as SA des Ets Clement-Bayard. Until 1906, these had 2-cyl petrol en-

gines, shaft-drive and a maximum payload of 3 tons. By 1907 forward-control trucks were also being constructed with British sales (as with the Clement and Clement-Gladiator) being handled by the British Automobile Syndicate which formed Clement-Talbot Ltd, to market vehicles under the Clement-Talbot or Talbot brand names. Eventually a totally British-designed and built series was developed. The popular Continental feature of radiator between driver and engine was used on all commercials by 1911 and, by 1913, the range had expanded to include a 3½-ton truck which, with drawbar trailer, could handle payloads of up to 10 tons. Forward-control and chain-drive were standard for the heavier types. By 1914 the company's heaviest model, a 22hp 5-tonner, had been launched but World War I brought about an end to the commercial range and the eventual sale of the factory to SA André Citroën in 1922.

CLEVELAND/*USA 1912-1913*
The Cleveland Motor Truck Mfg Co, Cleveland, Ohio, offered a selection of conventional goods models under the Cleveland brand name. The company was later taken over by C D Paxon.

CLEVELAND-GALION/*USA 1912*
The Cleveland-Galion Motor Truck Co, a subsidiary of the Cleveland Motor Truck Mfg Co, had a factory in Galion, Ohio, where it built a few petrol-electric trucks, marketed either as Cleveland-Galion or simply as Galion. Previously these had been constructed under the Dynamic brand name but only a few months after the Cleveland-Galion had appeared, the Galion-Dynamic Truck Co was set up to continue the operation selling trucks briefly as Galion-Dynamic or Galion.

CLIFT/*England 1905-1910*
Mediumweight Clift goods models were manufactured by Clift's Engineering Co Ltd, initially of London but later of Brighton, Sussex. The company also exhibited a 12/14bhp friction-drive 1-tonner of Frick design at the 1908 Commercial Motor Show, following the bankruptcy of Dougill's Engineering Ltd, but the model did not go into series production.

CLIMBER/*USA 1920-1923*
The 1½-ton Climber was the largest vehicle built by the Climber Motor Corp, Little Rock, Arkansas. This was an assembled model, using a Herschell-Spillman 4-cyl petrol engine, Muncie 3-speed transmission

CLINE/*USA 1953 to date*
The Cline Truck Mfg Co, Kansas City, Missouri, factory was opened in 1953. At first, production was extremely limited, but the company soon established a reputation for fine off-highway machinery particularly suited to construction work or earth moving. The first example was a Waukesha-engined load-carrier for a local construction company, using an assortment of components that the customer already had in stock. By 1968, both 4- and 6-wheeled types, often with all-wheel drive, were being built to special order. For 1970, the largest Cline was a 72-ton 6 x 6 coal-hauler, powered by a turbo-charged Cummins V12 diesel engine. In 1972 Cline became a division of the Isco Mfg Co, from which time numerous trucks have appeared under the Isco brand name, although the Cline name is still used from time to time. An example of this was the Model IC-A20R front-wheel drive articulated 20-ton dump truck, announced in 1973. Powered by a 6-cyl Cummins diesel engine, this has a single-stage torque-convertor transmission and planetary final-drive.

CLINTON (1)/*Canada 1911-1912*
The Clinton Motor Co Ltd, Clinton, Ontario, listed trucks of up to 3-ton capacity, the largest of which had chain-drive and solid tyres.

CLINTON (2)/*USA 1920-1934*
The Clinton Motors Corp assembled trucks on a small scale in New York before acquiring the Schwartz Motor Truck Corp, Reading, Pennsylvania, in 1923. The company concentrated on worm-drive designs, listing some eight models from 1¼-ton to 7-ton capacity by 1925 and adding 30- and 35-seat bus chassis later. Six-cyl Lycoming petrol engines were introduced in 1927; however, regular vehicle production ceased in 1929, subsequent vehicles being built only to special order.

CLUB CAR/*USA 1911-1912*
The Club Car Co of America, New York, was a co-operative formed to sell luxurious passenger cars and a forward-control 3-ton truck to its members. Using the same 4-cyl American and British petrol engine as the car, the truck had a 3-speed transmission and double chain-drive. All vehicles were built by Merchant & Evans, Philadelphia, Pennsylvania, but few commercials were built.

CLYDE (1)/*England 1905-c1914*
George H Wait & Co Ltd, Leicester, added the forward-control Clyde 1-tonner to its range of cy-cles, motorcycles and passenger cars in 1905. This was complemented by a lighter commercial range, but only 15 commercials of any type were actually built.

CLYDE (2)/*Scotland 1913-1938*
The first Clyde trucks from Mackay & Jardine Ltd, Wishaw, Lanarks, resembled the Belhaven, as both Mackay and Jardine were ex-employees of this concern. The first was a chain-drive Aster-engined 3-tonner, joined in 1914 by a shaft- and worm-drive 1½-tonner, which remained in production until the mid-1920s, when 2- and 2½-tonners were launched and Buda petrol engines introduced. An assembled vehicle, Clyde was popular among Scottish operators, particularly as a small bus or charabanc, but production was low. The company managed to survive until 1938 with a series of 2-, 2½- and 3-ton trucks and 20- or 26- seat buses.

CLYDE (3)/*USA 1916-1917*
The Clyde Motor Truck Co, Farmingdale, Long Island, constructed a prototype 1/1½-ton bonneted truck with 40hp 4-cyl 'L'-head monobloc petrol engine, Russel internal-gear rear axle and a 32-litre circular radiator. Few were built and the truck was renamed the Fulton when the business was acquired by the Fulton Motor Truck Co.

CLYDESDALE/*USA 1917-1938*
Clyde Cars Co, Clyde, Ohio, entered the truck market in 1917, setting up the Clydesdale Motor Truck Co soon after. Early Clydesdales had capacities of up to 5/6 tons, using a Continental petrol engine, Brown-Lipe transmission and Sheldon axles, and many were marketed in Britain by Whiting (1915) Ltd as Whitings. From 1925 until 1930, both 4- and 6-cyl petrol engines were used, much of production being for export only, until a new diesel range was launched in 1936. Offered in capacities of between 1 and 10 tons, these had Buda or Hercules engines and were offered as "conventionals" or "cabovers", with 4 x 4 or 6 x 6 drive. Lighter models were added in 1937 and the last Clydesdales had Waukesha-Hesselman diesel engines.

CMV/*Spain 1939-1948*
A manufacturer of trolleybuses since 1939, SA Industrial de Construcciones Moviles de Valencia also exhibited a battery-electric goods/passenger chassis at the 1946 Electric Car Exhibition in Madrid.

CNT-AIT/*Spain 1936-1940*
With the Spanish Civil War in 1936, Compania General de Autobuses de Barcelona SA was taken over by a workers' committee and re-named Colectividad de los Autobuses de Barcelona, vehicles previously built for its own use as CGA being called CNT-AIT. New double-deckers had disc wheels and pneumatic tyres, but production lasted only until 1940, when the company was de-nationalized and the CGA brand name re-introduced.

COACHETTE/*USA 1954-1968*
The Coachette Co, Dallas, Texas, built a 21-seat city bus body on a 436cm wheelbase Ford truck chassis which it marketed as the Coachette. Early production bodies were constructed by the Ward Body Co, Austin, Texas; by 1958 Chevrolet and GMC chassis were also used. By the time production ended specifications included up to 37 seats, full air-conditioning and sliding windows.

COAST/*USA c1958-1974*
Coast Apparatus Inc, Martinez, California, manufactured both forward- and normal-control fire appliances, using Hall-Scott engines and International Harvester cabs. Production ceased when the business was acquired by the Howe Fire Apparatus Co.

COBORN/*England 1908*
The Coborn Motor Co Ltd, Bromley, Kent, constructed an unusual Coborn lorry, featuring an unsprung transverse-engined front-wheel drive power pack which enabled maintenance to be undertaken easily, since a spare unit could be bolted in the original's place. It had a modified 20hp water-cooled 4-cyl Alpha petrol engine which drove the front wheels via a 3-speed gearbox and short drive-shafts. A 4-wheel drive version was also listed where a central drive-shaft drove the rear axle direct or via a counter-shaft and twin side chains.

COCK/*Netherlands 1958-1974*
Cock NV, Assen, built a 1000kg version of its 'Little Tyrant' 3-wheeled commercial, using a single-cyl JLO 2-stroke engine which drove the single front wheel direct, providing a top speed of 14km/h. A battery-electric derivative and 4-wheeled models, such as the 1250kg payload 'Colektro IV', appeared during the 1960s, while larger mobile shops, often with six wheels, were introduced during the early 1970s using mainly Ford components. Following the company's bankruptcy, Cock designs were continued by Assen Transportmiddelen Fabriek, as ATF.

COHENDET/*France 1905-1914*
Trucks built from 1905 by A Cohendet et Cie, Paris, were regularly entered in the various French lorry trials of the period. Of 3 to 5 tons capacity, they were of driver-over-engine layout, with cone clutches, 4-speed transmissions and chain-drive. 'T'-head twin-cyl petrol engines were standard but from 1907 there was also a 3-cyl model and, by 1912, all heavy models had a 35hp 4-cyl petrol engine.

COLEMAN (1)/*USA 1912-1914*
The F Coleman Carriage & Harness Co, Ilion, New York, was re-constituted as the Coleman Motor Truck Co in 1912, adding the 1-ton Model 'B' and 2-ton Model 'C' trucks powered by 4-cyl water-cooled petrol engines to its range of lighter commercials.

COLEMAN (2)/*USA 1925-1943*
Founded in Omaha, Nebraska, in 1923 to build 4-wheel drive vehicles, the Coleman Four Wheel Drive Co constructed no complete vehicles until re-named the Coleman Motors Corp, when it moved to Littleton, Colorado. There Buda-engined 4- and 6-wheel drive trucks and tractors were assembled for civil use, with military 4 x 4 and 6 x 4 types being developed from these. A light fire appliance was also manufactured for a short time. A 7½-ton on/off-highway 6 x 6 was added in 1928. By 1936, models from 2 to 10 tons capacity were listed. Diesel engines arrived in 1938, but by 1941 only a 6-ton 4 x 4 was built. Until 1943 production was concentrated on the 4 x 4 G55A bonneted crane-carrier supplied to the US Corps of Engineers. The firm was re-organized as the American Coleman Co. Although subsequent models have been marketed as American Coleman they are also often referred to as Coleman.

1971 Coles (1) 'Colossus'
170-ton truck crane

1979 Coles (1) 25-ton 'Supertruck'

COLES (1)/*England c1950 to date*
Truck-cranes built by Henry J Coles Ltd, Derby, Derbyshire, and its successor, Coles Cranes Ltd, Sunderland, Co Durham, originally used chassis supplied by other manufacturers, the first complete Coles units being of 6-wheeled rigid design with AEC engines and running units. By 1954 the 8-wheeled Coles 'Colossus', powered by a 250bhp straight-8 diesel engine, was the largest mobile crane in the world, joined five years later by the 60-ton 'Valiant'. In 1962 the Taylor Jumbo hydraulic range with telescopic jibs was absorbed into the range as the Coles 'Hydra', and in 1963 the 8-wheeled 'Centurion' broke the 100-ton lift barrier. The 10-ton 'Hydra' soon developed into 7- and 12-ton versions, and by 1968 even a 30-ton full hydraulic machine had appeared. In 1971 the 'Colossus' 6000 was introduced, with a capacity of 250 tons. In 1973 an hydraulic 100-tonner, the LH1000, was developed, making this the largest telescopic machine in the company's range.

COLES (2)/*Australia c1954 to date*
As well as building mobile cranes from components imported from the UK, Coles Cranes of Australia Pty Ltd also manufactures its own crane-carriers to designs drawn up in Britain. These are built at Revesby, near Sydney, and cater to peculiarities in the Australian Construction & Use Regulations.

COLLIER/*USA 1919-1922*
Already building light commercials, the Collier Co, Cleveland, Ohio, added 1- and 1½-ton trucks in 1919, with Continental petrol engines and worm-drive. At about this time the company was renamed the Collier Motor Truck Co, moving to Bellevue, Ohio, where a new 2-tonner went into production in 1921, followed a year later by a 2½-tonner.

COLLINS/*USA 1900*
The Collins Electric Vehicle Co was formed in Scranton, Pennsylvania, by Patrick J Collins, who had designed a battery-electric vehicle in which both steering and driving was powered by electric current. A 1-ton delviery truck was the only vehicle built.

COLUMBIA (1)/*USA 1904-1907*
The first purpose-built commercials built by the Columbia Electric Vehicle Co, Hartford, Connecticut were battery-electric vans and trucks of up to 5-ton capacity, often referred to as Columbia Electrics. Heavy models had two motors driving the rear wheels via double-reduction gears and chain-drive, some also having electric power-steering. Columbias were the most popular American battery-electrics of their day being of forward-control layout and offered in 4 x 4 as well as 4 x 2 form. They were used as buses, ambulances and police wagons as well as goods-carriers. Battery-electric production ended so that the company could concentrate on petrol-engined passenger cars.

COLUMBIA (2)/*USA 1916-1925*
The Columbia 2-tonner was built by the Columbia Motor Truck & Trailer Co, Pontiac, Michigan, joined a year after its launch by a 1-ton version. Both had 4-cyl Buda petrol engines, 3-speed transmissions and internal-gear axles. Continental petrol engines being fitted from 1918 and a 6-ton tractor announced. From 1919, 1½-, 2½- and 3-tonners were listed.

COMET/*USA 1920-1921*
A bonneted 1½-ton truck was built by the Comet Automobile Co, Decatur, Illinois using a 4-cyl Lycoming petrol engine and worm-drive Wisconsin rear axle.

COMMANDO/*USA c1968-c1972*
Introduced by the Ottawa Steel Divn of the Young Spring & Wire Corp, Ottawa, Kansas, the Commando terminal tractor was available with a multitude of bolt-on accessories, enabling it to be used also as a fork-lift truck or a snowplough. Before production ceased, the company became the Daybrook-Ottawa Divn of the Gulf & Western Metals Forming Co.

1909 Commer Car single-deck bus

COMMER CAR/*England 1907-1926*
Commercial Cars Ltd, manufacturer of the CC goods model, moved from South London to Luton, Beds, in 1906. Although the CC had been a forward-control model, the Commer Car announced the following year, was bonneted. Known as the 'RC'-Type, it was a 3-tonner incorporating a Linley constant-mesh transmission with pre-select lever on the steering column. Power came from a 35hp 4-cyl petrol engine, via a cone clutch and propeller shaft to a 3-speed box – in unit with the differential. Chain final-drive was employed and steering was by worm-and-segment. This model was awarded a Silver Medal in the 3-ton class of the 1907 RAC Commercial Vehicle Trials. By 1911 models from 1 to 7 tons capacity were advertised and a 90hp fire appliance with a drop-frame chassis had been developed normally sold as the Commer-Simonis or Simonis. The 'RC' was particularly popular in the USA, where Wycoff, Clark & Partridge, New York, arranged assembly by the W A Wood Auto Mfg Co, Kingston, New York, until 1913 when Commercial Cars Ltd set up its own short-lived plant in Delaware. Meanwhile, to conform with British War Office "subsidy" requirements, a shaft-drive system was developed and a new model, the 'BC' was launched in 1913. It was accepted as a 3/4-ton general-purpose vehicle and, by the following year, 12 variations were listed. Nearly 3000 of this type were built by the end of World War I. Civilian production resumed after the war but, by 1922 a receiver had been appointed. The range now included 2-, 3-, 4-, 5-, 6- and 10-ton goods models and passenger types for between 16 and 46 persons. The business was finally acquired by Humber Ltd, all subsequent models being known simply as Commer.

COMMER-HARRINGTON/
England 1951-1956
The coachbuilding firm of Thomas Harrington Ltd, Hove, East Sussex, built the chassisless Com-

COMMER/*England 1926-1978*

Commer Cars Ltd resulted from the acquisition of Commercial Cars Ltd, Luton, Beds, by Humber Ltd, the marque name being shortened from Commer Car to Commer. New designs were brought in and by 1928 1½- and 4½-tonners had been introduced. Four drop-frame passenger chassis shown at Olympia could be purchased as 4- or 6-wheelers and in forward- or normal-control guise. By the end of 1928 Humber, and therefore Commer, had been acquired by Rootes Securities Ltd with the intention of introducing a series of cheap mass-produced commercials.

First of the new range was the 2-ton 'Invader' of 1929, employing a 6-cyl Humber 'Snipe' petrol engine. This was followed by the bonneted 6/7-ton G6, with the front axle set under the cab to improve weight distribution. A 100bhp 6-cyl petrol engine powered this and the forward-control 'Avenger' passenger model, which was offered as a 32-seat single- or 50-seat double-decker.

The 'Raider' 1½-tonner appeared in 1931. Within two years, this had a Perkins diesel engine. The goods version of the 'Invader' was called the 'Centaur' and a larger version became the 26-seat 'Corinthian'. The following year saw the first 1-ton forward-control Commer in the form of the N1 and in 1933 an underfloor engined multi-stop forward-control delivery van called the 'Pug'. This joined the Carter Paterson fleet as a 2-tonner while the 'Greyhound' replaced the 'Corinthian'.

In 1934 Rootes acquired Karrier Motors Ltd, transferring production from Huddersfield to Luton, leading to some similarity

1947 Commer 'Superpoise'

between models. The 'N'-range, replacing all medium and heavy goods and passenger models, was launched in 1935. One of the most successful models was the 4/5-ton N5 with an unladen weight of less than 2½-tons. This series introduced streamlined all-steel cabs and pressed-steel radiator surrounds to the Commer line-up, but was replaced in 1939 by the

Commer LN5 5-ton truck c1936

1956 Commer TS3 tipper

bonneted 'Q'-range, also known as the 'Superpoise'. Some of the larger petrol-engined models were powered by 3- or 4-litre Sunbeam-Talbot engines. With capacities of between 1½ and 6 tons, the 'Q'-range was also offered in forward-control form, with a choice between 6-cyl petrol and Perkins diesel engines.

Over 20,000 'Superpoise' Commers were supplied to the Armed Forces during World War II. In 1948 the series was re-styled along Humber passenger car lines, offered in various capacities from 1½ tons and joined by a new forward-control version which was shown at the 1948 Commercial Motor Show. These were powered by underfloor versions of the 6-cyl petrol or Perkins P6 diesel, but from 1954 were fitted with an horizontal 3-cyl 2-stroke diesel developed by Tilling-Stevens, who had joined the group in 1951. Called the TS3, this engine produced 105bhp, each cylinder containing two opposed pistons working a common crankshaft located beneath the combustion area. The fuel mixture was forced through ports, rather than valves, by a blower.

By 1953, commercial vehicle production had moved to Dunstable and two years later a new all-steel cab, common to British Dodge, Baron and certain Leyland models, was fitted to the bonneted 'Superpoise'. As well as the forward-control goods range, a passenger version was listed. This took the old 'Avenger' name while the heaviest forward-control goods chassis was offered with a Perkins diesel. The company's first standard rigid 6-wheeler, the 10-ton Commer-Unipower, also arrived.

In 1959, heavy forward-control

models were again re-vamped, the old TS3 diesel being replaced by the Perkins and a 1-piece windscreen and revised radiator grille fitted. In 1961 the American-style, 'Walk-Thru' multi-stop delivery vehicle for 1½- to 3-ton payloads, was announced, marketed also as Karrier but, later, solely as Dodge. By 1962 the forward-control truck range had received a brand new all-steel cab. Two years later, a larger version of the 2-stroke diesel was fitted in the new 'Maxiloads' 4-wheeler for 16 tons gross. At about the same time, Chrysler acquired a share in the Rootes Group, gradually integrating the British Dodge range with that of Commer and Karrier.

In 1970 the Commer/Karrier Division of Chrysler United Kingdom Ltd was formed. Forward-control 'Commando' trucks arrived in 1974, replacing several former Dodge models. They were also marketed as Karrier for public authority use. The truck was available with a variety of Perkins or Mercedes-Benz diesel engines, or powered by a Chrysler V8 petrol unit for fire-fighting applications. To simplify Chrysler's overall marketing strategy, the name, Commer began to vanish in 1976, however, and by 1978, apart from municipal types which were called Karrier, all British-built Chrysler commercials were marketed as Dodge.

1948 Commer R741 truck

mer-Harrington 'Contender' passenger model employing light-alloy construction and running units taken from the Commer 'Avenger'. Initially, it had a 6-cyl Commer petrol engine, but it later received the 3.26-litre Commer TS3 2-stroke engine. It was in this latter form that most 'Contenders' were supplied. The majority were coaches, but some buses were also built.

1955 Commer-Harrington 'Contender' single-deck bus

COMMER-UNIPOWER/England 1958-c1970
The 10-ton capacity Commer-Unipower was Commer's first 6-wheeled rigid goods model. It was based on a forward-control chassis with extension and third axle conversion by Universal Power Drives Ltd, Perivale, Middx. As Commer Cars Ltd had no intention of building a 6-wheeler themselves, this model was included in their standard lists. Following the Chrysler takeover of the Rootes Group in 1970 – of which Commer was a part – the 6-wheelers were discontinued, as they competed with certain Dodge models.

COMMERCE (1)/USA 1906-1908
The American Machinery Mfg

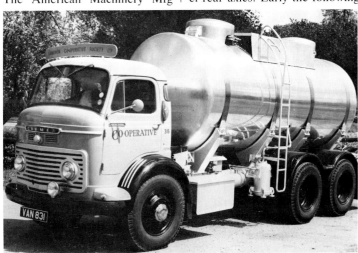

1961 Commer-Unipower TS3 6 x 4 tanker

Co, Detroit, Michigan built a 274cm wheelbase chain-drive forward-control 2½-tonner powered by a 30hp 4-cyl petrol engine. Further types included the Model 'A' 3-tonner and Model 'C' 5-tonner, the former having a 35hp 4-cyl petrol engine.

COMMERCE (2)/USA 1917-1932
Based on earlier light commercials, Commerce Motor Car Co, Detroit, Michigan, intoduced a 1-ton model with internal gear final-drive in 1917. By 1922, Continental petrol engines were standard and models of up to 2½ tons capacity were available. In about 1923 the company was re-constituted as the Commerce Motor Truck Co, moving to Ypsilanti, Michigan, where force-feed lubrication and worm-drive were introduced for all models in 1925. New passenger chassis were announced the following year and other types included a log-hauler, a dump truck, and an oil tanker. Changes in 1926 included 6-cyl Continental petrol engines, 3-speed transmissions and semi-floating spiral-bevel rear axles. Early the following year, the Relay Motors Corp, Wabash, Indiana, acquired the business, moving Commerce production to Service Motors Inc, also of Wabash. Within months, however, both Commerce and Service production, plus that of Relay itself, were transferred to the Lima, Ohio, factory of the Garford Motor Truck Co. Later, the 8-Model Commerce range was re-styled, returning to worm-drive and using 6-cyl Buda petrol engines and 4-wheel hydraulic brakes so that Commerce, Garford, Relay and Service trucks were all nearly identical. By 1928 Commerce production had dropped to 65 trucks and to a low of 16 in 1929, the Relay Motors Corp going into the hands of the receiver and the Commerce range vanishing one year before Relay Motors itself went out of business.

COMMERCIAL (1)/USA 1906, 1910-1912
The Commercial Motor Car Co, New York, experimented with trucks before production began in 1910 with a series of 1-, 2-, 3- and 5-tonners. All had 4-cyl petrol engines and chain final-drive, only 3- and 5-tonners being of forward-control layout.

COMMERCIAL (2)/USA 1911-1912
The Commercial Truck Co of America, built a petrol-engined 1½-tonner at its Newark, New Jersey, plant. Offered with solid or pneumatic tyres, it was of forward-control layout with a 4-cyl 4-stroke engine, 3-speed gearbox and shaft-drive. Later that year the company was re-named the Commercial Motor Truck Construction Co but quickly went out of business.

COMMERCIAL CARRIER/England c1918
Of uncertain origin, the Commercial Carrier was marketed by vehicle importer F B Goodchild & Co, London SW1, which also offered the Bellport and its own Goodchild.

COMMERCIAL-MOTOR-TRUCK/USA 1906-1909
The Commercial Motor Truck Co, Toledo, Ohio, built the Commercial-Motor-Truck for loads of up to 3-tons, all types being of "cabover" layout, with 4-cyl Continental petrol engines and friction transmission. Production was later transferred to Plymouth where, in 1908, a 50hp engine was introduced for the largest models and 12/20-seat sightseeing buses added to the range. In 1909 the company was re-organized as the Plymouth Motor Truck Co, later models being sold as Plymouth.

COMPOUND/USA 1906
The Eisenhuth Horseless Vehicle Co, Middleton, Connecticut, called its delivery van the Model '9' Compound because of its unique 3-cyl petrol engine with a central cylinder larger than the other two. This cylinder had no ignition system itself, as it relied upon the remaining energy of the exhaust gas passed from the other two cylinders. The compound had a 3-speed transmission and double chain-drive.

CONCORD (1)/USA 1917-1933
Based on the Abbott-Downing prototype of 1916, Concord goods and passenger models with capacities of 1- and 2-tons were built by the Abbott-Downing Truck & Body Co, Concord, New Hampshire. A 3-tonner was introduced later. Throughout the production run, all models had 4-cyl Buda petrol engines and worm-drive axles.

CONCORD (2)/Argentina ?
Certain Italian Fiat commercials are assembled under licence in Argentina by an unknown organization and marketed under the Concord brand name.

1933 Condor 'CB'-Series tipper

CONDOR/USA 1932-1941
Condor Motors Inc, was set up in Chicago, Illinois, as a subsidiary of the Gramm Motor Truck Corp to assemble Gramm trucks for export under the Condor brand name. Until 1934 both marques were identical, but then the Condor was given an oil-burning Waukesha-Hesselman engine to cope with the lower-grade fuels found overseas. A petrol engine was optional. Condor sales eventually exceeded the home sales of the parent concern. Like their Gramm equivalents, 1939/40 Condors used a Willys pick-up cab and Buda Lanova diesel engines. Gramm's increasing interest in trailer manufacture led to the company's closure.

CONESTOGA/USA 1917-1920
The Conestoga Motor Truck Co, Lancaster, Pennsylvania, assembled mediumweight goods models, using proprietary components. The range started with a 1½-tonner with worm final-drive and a 4-cyl petrol engine. Continental-

engined 1- and 2-tonners, also with worm final-drive, were announced in 1919.

CONTINENTAL (1)/USA 1912-1918

The Continental Truck Mfg Co, Superior, Wisconsin, built various goods models starting with the forward-control 1½-ton 'AE' with 4-cyl petrol engine, 3-speed transmission and double chain-drive. A 1-tonner was introduced in 1914 and the 1½-tonner re-vamped as a "conventional". A new 1½-tonner, with chain- or worm-drive, appeared the following year, when a 3-tonner was also announced.

CONTINENTAL (2)/USA 1915-1917

Using 4-cyl engines, 3-speed transmission and worm final-drive the Continental Motor Truck Co, of Chicago, Illinois, offered a series of 1-, 1½-, 2- and 3½-ton bonneted trucks.

CONY/Japan c1955-1966

The Aichi Machinery Industry Co Ltd, Nagoya, was launched in 1952 to continue the production of Cony 3-wheelers. By the mid-1950s, the original motorcycle-type steering had given way to wheel steering and mechanical braking on the rear wheels to hydraulic. The heaviest was a 2-tonner, also produced in tractor form with a 5-speed transmission, having a 1½-litre 4-cyl water-cooled horizontally-opposed engine. In 1966 the company was acquired by the Nissan Motor Co Ltd, Yokohoma, and certain Cony designs incorporated in the Nissan light vehicle range.

COOK BROTHERS/USA 1949-1958

The Cook Bros Equipment Co, Los Angeles, California, entered the truck field with giant experimental forward-control 8 x 8 military trucks and tractors. These were followed in 1950 by heavy-duty bonneted trucks aimed at the construction industry. Marketed under the Cook Brothers or C-B brand names, these used numerous Reo components as well as Cummins diesel and Ford V8 petrol engines. Most were designed to conform to West Coast maximum weight restrictions – meaning that they needed long wheelbase dimensions – but there were also a number of artic bottom-dump types with offset cabs for on/off-road operation. Later manufacturing truck-mixer and crane-carrier chassis, often with 1-man half-cabs and Reo or Cummins petrol, diesel or propane gas engines, the company even used chain-drive in some cases. In-

creasing interest in the mixer market led to the firm being acquired by the Challenge Mfg Co, a manufacturer of mixer equipment, subsequent models being sold as Challenge-Cook.

COOKE/USA 1905-1906

The Cooke Locomotive Works, Paterson, New Jersey, built steam wagons under licence from John I Thornycroft & Co Ltd, Basingstoke, England, marketing these under the Cooke name. They are thought to have been identical to the original British design.

COOPER/USA c1955 to date

Fred E Cooper Inc, Tulsa, Oklahoma, built self-propelled oilfield drilling and servicing equipment. Cooper outfits had long wheelbases to accommodate a folding drilling mast, models ranging from the TC-32 6 x 4 up to massive 8-wheeled rigids, all of forward-control layout and with 1-man half-cabs. Diesel, petrol or propane gas engines were employed, driving through a heavy-duty synchromesh transmission, with or without a torque-converter.

COPPOCK/USA 1907-1909

The Coppock Model 'A' 1-tonner was of "cabover" layout, with a twin-cyl 2-stroke petrol engine. Built by the Coppock Motor Car Co, Marion, Indiana, it had a 3-speed progressive transmission

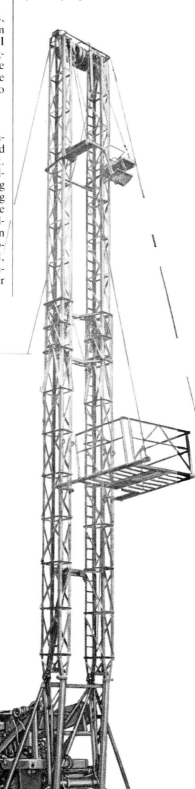

Cooper TC-32

and 220cm wheelbase. In 1908 the company moved to Decatur, Indiana, continuing production until it became the Decatur Motor Car Co, subsequent models being sold as Decatur.

CORBITT/USA 1909-1952, 1957-1958

The first truck to be built by the Corbitt Automobile Co, Henderson, North Carolina, was a 4-cyl Continental petrol-engined "conventional" with a capacity of 1130kg. Various buses were introduced in 1915 and, by the early 1920s, Corbitts were being exported to at least 23 countries by the newly-formed Corbitt Motor Truck Co. Up to 1926 all models had 4-cyl Continental petrol engines for normal use or Budas for heavier applications, but only 6-cyl Continental or Hercules petrol engines were fitted after this date. By 1930 vehicles from 1 to 5 tons capacity were listed. Larger models introduced included a 6-wheeled artic for operation at up to 15 tons GCW. A new medium-weight range, with a Lycoming petrol engine, an Auburn passenger car grille, front wings, and a cab adapted from Auburn body panels was announced in 1934, by which time the company was supplying special types to the US Army. These included a 2½-ton 6 x 6 cargo truck with Lycoming straight-8 petrol engine and 8-ton 6 x 4 and 6 x 6 tractors with 6-cyl Hercules petrol engines. In World War II, production concentrated upon a 6-ton 6 x 6. There were also a few 6 x 4 civilian tractors with 6-cyl Continental engines, an experimental 8 x 8 tractor, and a 2½-ton rear-engined prototype. The company was re-named the Corbitt Co after the war, concentrating from 1946 on 6 x 2 and 6 x 4 "conventional" road tractors, with Continental petrol or Cummins diesel engines. Although the firm closed in 1952, an attempt was made to resurrect the name with the formation of the Corbitt Co Inc, again in Henderson, North Carolina. The only models were bonneted tractors built to special order. The venture quickly collapsed, although a number of re-built ex-military 6 x 6 Macks were sold to various NATO members.

CORNWALL/England 1957-1958

Cornwall Motor Transport Ltd, Helston, Cornwall, constructed a prototype 7/8-tonner of forward-control layout. It had a Meadows 4DC330 diesel engine, Meadows 5-speed transmission and a Moss spiral-bevel or Eaton 2-speed spiral-bevel axle. Other features included a Boalloy plastics cab and

Clayton-Dewandre actuated Girling air-hydraulic brakes.

CORONA/Germany 1905-1909
Corona Fahrradwerke und Metallindustrie AG, Brandenburg, held a licence from the manufacturer of Maurer-Union commercials to build friction-drive vehicles under the Corona name. These originally were powered by a single-cyl 6/8hp Maurer petrol engine, but this was replaced by a 9/11hp twin-cyl Maurer unit.

CORTLAND/USA 1911-1912
Adopting a driver-over-engine layout, the Cortland Motor Wagon Co, Cortland, NY, built a 1½-ton high-wheeler, powered by a 20hp twin-cyl petrol engine. A 2-speed planetary transmission and double chain-drive were used. Production was later undertaken at Pittsfield, Massachusetts.

COTTEREAU/France 1902-1907
Cottereau et Cie, Dijon, launched petrol-engined, chain-drive wagonettes and light buses under the Cottereau name. These had a 1.4-litre twin-cyl petrol engine with automatic inlet valves or a 3.2-litre 'T'-head 4-cyl unit. A new commercial, with 1.8-litre dual-ignition 3-cyl petrol engine, appeared in 1904 and was developed into a 4-tonner with 3.4-litre 4-cyl engine and 4-speed transmission a year later. Only passenger cars were built after 1907.

COTTIN-DESGOUTTES/France 1905-1934
Already producing beautifully constructed passenger cars, Ets Cottin et Desgouttes, Lyon-Monplaisir also introduced shaft-drive commercials with capacities between 1½ and 4 tons. These were of bonneted layout, powered by a 4-cyl petrol engine. Passenger models sold well after 1918 but, by 1931, vehicles were being assembled only from those components still in stock.

COULTHARD/England 1895-1907
The first experimental steam wagon built by T Coulthard & Co Ltd, Preston, Lancs had a compound "unifolw" engine, oil-fired vertical boiler and chain final-drive to a "dead" rear axle. Other prototypes employed either "uniflow" or reversing triple-expansion engines but, by 1898, the compound reversing unit had proved the most popular. A 3-tonner was entered in the 1899 Liverpool Trials, it had a triple-expansion horizontal "undertype" engine with 3-speed and reverse transmission. Within a year the company was using solid fuel boilers, obtaining its first award at the 1901 Liverpool Trials, where an average speed of 9km/h was recorded. The vertical fire-tube boiler on the award-winning machine was mounted behind the front axle to improve driver vision and place

1905 Coulthard Model 'K' 5-ton 'undertype' steam wagon

greater weight on the driving wheels. This drove a vertical 2-cyl compound engine slung beneath the chassis. A contemporary, but unsuccessful, venture was the prototype articulated Brightmore wagon; in the meantime, however, the 1901 award-winner had developed into the Model 'K' 5-tonner. The engine was now a 30hp unit, larger wheels were fitted, and the boiler was also improved. This model was the company's most successful, particularly in America where it was also assembled as the Coulthard or American Coulthard. T Coulthard & Co Ltd was also instrumental in setting up the business of J Sumner Ltd, putting up a half share in the company. This eventually developed into the Lancashire Steam Motor Co Ltd which, ironically, acquired the Coulthard business and brought Coulthard wagon production to an end.

COUPLE-GEAR/USA 1904-1922
The Couple-Gear Electric Truck Co was a subsidiary of the Couple-Gear Freight Wheel Co, Grand Rapids, Michigan, introducing battery-electric commercials for 3- and 5-ton payloads. Petrol-electric models, usually marketed as Gas-Electric, were built simultaneously by the parent organization. Main features were 4-wheel steering with an electric motor in each wheel, and twin tyres all round. Several models were offered, from rigid trucks to artic, as well as conversion sets for horse-drawn fire apparatus. The system was also used by other fire appliance builders. In 1908 lighter 1- and 2-ton models with front-wheel drive were introduced, with a top speed of 14km/h. After World War I, however, decreasing interest in heavyweight battery-electrics, particularly as emergency vehicles, brought about the company's downfall.

CPT/Scotland c 1914
With the start of World War I, the Fraserburgh, Aberdeenshire factory of the Consolidated Pneumatic Tool Co Ltd was turned over to war work and the company began importing the Chicago Pneumatic Tool Co's 1-ton Little Giant commercial under the CPT name. Of forward-control layout, it had double chain-drive but was otherwise similar to the earlier Duntley.

CRAIG-DORWALD/England 1904-1906
The Putney Motor Co, London, was already building passenger cars and marine engines when it constructed the first Craig-Dor-

Cottin-Desgouttes van c1924

121

wald commercial. This was a 3-wheeled "mechanical" horse with a single-powered wheel at the rear and independent coil suspension at the front, a 2-speed gearbox and chain final-drive. A shaft-drive delivery van, a chain-drive truck and a prototype double-deck bus driven from the front of the upper deck where also built.

CRANE TRAVELLERS/England 1971 to date
The 600 Group acquired manufacturing rights for Vickers-AWD crane-carriers, establishing an assembly area for chassis of this type, which were sold as Crane Travel-lers. In 1977 Crane Travellers became a division of crane manufacturer Jones Cranes Ltd, Letchworth, Herts and now constucts 4-, 6- and 8-wheeled carriers with Bedford, Cummins, or Scania diesel engines.

CREMORNE/England 1903-1906
The Cremorne Motor Mfg Co, Chelsea, London built steam vehicles, constructing a 36-seat bus using a kerosene-fuelled vertical Field-tube boiler, 20hp 4-cyl engine and chain-drive. There was also a goods model of about 1 1/4/1 1/2-tons capacity, one example of which was fitted experimentally with an old horse bus body. By the time production came to an end, the company was known as the Cremorne Motor Co Ltd.

CRETORS/USA 1915
Nine special popcorn trucks were built by popcorn machinery manufacturer C Cretors & Co, Chicago, Illinois. Each had a 4-cyl Buda petrol engine and carried a gas-fired boiler and steam engine to drive the popcorn popper and peanut roaster.

CREUSEN/Netherland 1960 to date
Standardizing on 5hp electric motors, Creusen battery-electrics are built by Creusen Electro-Mecanische Industrie NV, Roermond, comprising light delivery types and 6-wheeled mobile shops. The 6-wheelers, for payloads of up to 4 tons, carry electric motors in four of their wheels, all driving through a worm-drive system. Bodies are fibreglass and components are also used in the British-built Techelee range.

CRITCHLEY-NORRIS/England 1906-1908
As soon as the Critchley-Norris Motor Co, Preston, Lancs was founded, a petrol-engined bus was constructed in time for the Royal Agricultural Hall Show. It had a 4-cyl Crossley petrol engine, cone clutch, 4-speed transmission,

chain final-drive and was also available in goods form. A spirit-filled cooling system was particularly unusual. A 40hp model was shown at Olympia in 1907 and in 1908 a 3-ton 3-cyl steam chassis of advanced design took pride of place. Designed for passenger or haulage work, this had an oil-fired semi-flash boiler, 35hp vertical in-line 'T'-head engine and chain final-drive. A condenser was fitted in place of the normal radiator and exhaust gases directed backwards beneath the channel-section chassis frame, resulting in a strong resemblance to bonneted petrol-engined types.

CROCHAT/France 1911-c1925
The first Crochat commercial was a 4-ton chain-drive petrol-electric truck, built by Ets Henri Crochat, Paris. It was especially popular during World War I as an ambulance or mobile workshop. In 1919, it was joined by a Dijon-built, chain-drive road-train, also with petrol-electric transmission. Each of the five trailers carried its own electric motor and batteries to enable it to collect or deposit its own load independently of the main road-train. A petrol-electric 3-tonner was also announced, followed later by a few battery-electric types. Only these were available when the company closed.

CROMPTON/England 1911
Following unsuccessful experiments with an MOC-Crompton battery-electric bus in 1909, the Crompton electrical concern, Chelmsford, Essex, constructed a new double-deck prototype. Batteries were housed beneath a conventional bonnet and were at least half the weight of those fitted in the earlier model, two motors being connected by chains to worm-gearing fitted at each rear wheel.

Production models were never built.

CROMPTON ELECTRICAR/England 1972 to date
When Crompton Leyland Electricars Ltd, a subsidiary of the British Leyland Motor Corp Ltd, was acquired by the Hawker Siddeley Group, all models were re-named Crompton Electricar. By 1975 a sophisticated battery-electric range was offered, and the company was becoming increasingly interested in the use of alternative fuels. In 1976 Crompton Electricars Ltd took over production of Oxford Electrics' Oxcart, a one-man cabbed machine, which had been developed using a 2-ton Crompton Electricar chassis. The latest Crompton-Electricars have a 2-speed control, enabling the vehicle to travel faster when required. The company is now developing a 1 1/2-ton van of all-alloy construction, using lead-acid batteries.

CROMPTON LEYLAND ELECTRICAR/Wales 1968-1972
With the merger of the British Motor Corporation Ltd with the Leyland Motor Corporation Ltd, the British Leyland Motor Corp Ltd was founded. Austin Crompton Parkinson Electric Vehicles Ltd, manufacturer of Austin-Electricar and Morrison-Electricar battery-electric commercials was then re-named Crompton Leyland Electricars Ltd, built at Tredegar, Monmouth, and marketed as Crompton Leyland Electricar. Models continued much as before until 1971, when a series of 1 1/4- to 2-ton 4-wheelers, often sold under the old Morrison-Electricar name, were developed. In 1972 the company was sold to the Hawker Siddeley Group and re-named Crompton Electricars Ltd,

subsequent models being referred to simply as Crompton Electricar.

CROSS/USA 1914-1916
The CJ Cross Front Drive Tractor Co was established at Newark, New Jersey, to manufacture 2-wheeled motorized tractors for adapting horse-drawn fire-fighting apparatus to self-propulsion. Marketed simply as Cross, these had heavy petrol engines carried longitudinally ahead of the front axle, although an underseat-engined model was offered after 1915. Also available were 3-, 5-, 6/7- and 10-ton front-drive trucks.

CROSSLEY-KEGRESSE/England 1925 -?
The Crossley-Kégresse half-track was announced at the 1925 Commercial Motor Show by Crossley Motors Ltd, Gerton, Manchester, Intended for military or colonial use, this was of 1 1/2-ton capacity, using the French-designed Kégresse half-track system and Crossley's own 6 x 4 chassis.

CROWDEN/England 1901-1902
The Crowden Motor Car Co, Leamington Spa, Warwicks, were specialists in constructing self-propelled steam vehicles. Of particular interest was the company's steam fire pump of 1901, which was basically a horse-drawn steam pumper, with rear-mounted vertical boiler and horizontal twin-cylinder "undertype" engine. Towards the end of 1902 a V4 petrol-engined machine was developed.

CROWN (1)/USA 1914-1915
The Crown Commercial Car Co, Milwaukee, Wisconsin, built 1- and 3-ton Crown worm-drive trucks, both powered by a 4-cyl Wisconsin 'T'-head engine.

1979 Crompton Electricar milk floats

1929 Crossley 6 x 4 wireless truck

1931 Crossley 'Condor'

CROSSLEY/*England 1923-1956*
Crossley Motors Ltd, Gorton, Manchester, was well-experienced in the manufacture of passenger cars, light commercials and petrol engines when it announced the legendary Royal Flying Corps tender in 1912, followed by a 1½-ton "subsidy" model with a 5.3-litre 4-cyl petrol engine and worm-drive in 1923, and a series of more austere types for the Indian government. A 1-ton civilian model with 4-wheel brakes was totally unsuccessful but a 1½-ton military 6 x 4 did become popular and became a basis for the Crossley-Kégresse half-track of 1925. The 6-wheeler's bogie axles were mounted on two pairs of inverted semi-elliptic leaf springs, each wheel carrying a brake drum with the footbrake acting on one axle and the handbrake on the other.

Military 2- and 4-tonners, of both normal- and forward-control layout, were also built and in 1928 the company's first passenger model – the 32-seat 'Eagle' single-decker – was announced, using a 4-cyl side-valve petrol engine, vacuum servo-brakes and worm-drive. The bonneted 'Hawk' derivative and the double-decker 'Eagle' arrived a year later. By 1930 the 'Eagle' double-decker had become the 'Condor', which became the first British-built diesel-engined bus when a Gardner unit was fitted in 1931. This was quickly replaced by Crossley's own 87bhp 8.4-litre direct-injection 6-cyl diesel.

By 1933 4- and 6-cyl diesels which featured indirect-injection and pre-select transmissions were available. Meanwhile, military developments included the 3-ton 'IGL' Series. A range of 4- and 6-cyl diesel lorries was announced in 1932, with payloads of between 3

1935 Crossley 'Atlas' 12-ton 6 x 4 truck

and 7 tons. Most were of forward-control layout, although the 1933 'Delta' was bonneted and powered initially by a 3.8-litre version of the 4-cyl petrol engine. In 1936 Freeborn 4-speed semi-automatic transmission was introduced in the passenger range and both 4- and 6-wheeled trolleybuses were launched, with Metrovick electric motors located amidships, air brakes and worm final-drive.

By 1939 Crossley buses consisted of the 'Alpha' single and 'Mancunian' double-decker, both diesel-powered. The previous year had seen the end of the 1932 lorry range; although a new forward-control 5-tonner with petrol engine and hydrovac brakes was announced, it never entered series production. World War II saw a 4 x 4 forward-control model. The 'Q'-Type, entered service with the RAF, this being supplied as a 3-ton load-carrier or as a tractor.

In 1945 production moved to Stockport, Cheshire. There, only passenger vehicles were built, with buses and trolleybuses sharing many components. An 8.6-litre 6-cyl direct-injection diesel engine and three alternative transmission systems were offered in the buses, which now carried model numbers rather than actual names. The company's largest ever civilian order came as soon as it moved, with a request for over 1000 vehicles from the Netherlands State Railways. Amongst vehicles specified were articulated types for up to 80 passengers and high-speed single-deckers, some of which had 5-speed overdrive transmissions and 140bhp supercharged versions of the standard Crossley diesel engine.

In 1948, Crossley Motors Ltd was absorbed into the Associated Commercial Vehicles Group and the last true Crossleys were built in 1951. From then until the company's last appearance at the Commercial Motor Show in 1956, vehicles were merely badge-engineered AECs.

1948 Crossley DD42/3T double-deck bus

1966 Crown Coach single-deck coach

CROWN (2)/*USA 1933 to date*

The first commercial built by the Crown Body & Coach Corp, Los Angeles, California, was a forward-control school bus, with all-steel body and Waukesha petrol engine. By 1937 a series of passenger types, with underfloor Hall-Scott engines and optional Cummins diesels, had been developed. From 1949, fire appliances were constructed as Crown Firecoach and in 1950 inter-city and sightseeing buses were developed from the earlier school bus designs. These were also offered as television transmitters, display and exhibition units, mobile libraries, disaster vehicles and combined passenger- and load-carrying vehicles. In 1952 the company was re-organized as the Crown Coach Corp, the majority of models since then being marketed as Crown Coach.

CROWN COACH/*USA 1952 to date*

Following the Crown Body & Coach Corp's organization as the Crown Coach Corp, Los Angeles, California, Crown passenger models were re-named Crown Coach although fire appliances

1980 Crown Firecoach motor pump line appliance

continued as Crown Firecoach. The first new designs comprised 2- and 3-axle school buses with Cummins or Detroit Diesel engines and seating for up to 97 children. In 1978 agreement was reached with the Hungarian Trading Co, Budapest, Hungary, by which the Ikarus Model 286 107-passenger artic bus was made available in the USA under the Crown Coach name. Initially this would be imported complete but, if demand warranted it, American production was planned. Although a Hungarian-built demonstrator was shipped to the USA, the scheme did not proceed.

CROWN FIRECOACH/*USA 1949 to date*

Using its 4-wheeled school bus chassis, the Los Angeles-based Crown Body & Coach Corp introduced the Crown Firecoach. Fire engines were constructed under this name to suit specific requirements, using Hall-Scott petrol or Cummins diesel underfloor engines and cab-forward layout. The company was re-constituted as the Crown Coach Corp in 1952, but the Crown Firecoach range has continued. Both 4- and 6-wheeled models are built, the latter with tandem-drive. Most are Cummins-powered.

CROWN CLARK/*England 1976*

Crown Cranes Ltd, Alfreton, Derbyshire, was a subsidiary of the American-owned Clark Equipment Group. In 1976, the company constructed a prototype 6-wheeled truck-crane known as the 725CM, featuring a hydraulic

telescopic jib and a turning circle of only 8.4m. The chassis main frame extended from the rear of the vehicle to just behind the front axle, both the front axle and engine being mounted on a lightweight, dropped extension with the cab on an out-rigged sub-

frame. This eliminated cross-movement stresses at the front of the frame. Only a few machines were built.

CRUIKSHANK/*USA 1896-1899*

The Cruikshank Steam Engine Works, Rhode Island, built a

number of steam wagons under the Cruikshank brand name.

CSEPEL/*Hungary 1950 to date*

Based on Austrian-designed commercials by Steyr-Daimler-Puch AG, the Csepel Engineering Works' first truck was a bonneted diesel-engined 3¼-tonner, built at Csepel, near Budapest. Exporting much of its production, the company developed both forward- and normal-control trucks of 4 x 2, 4 x 4, 6 x 6 and 8 x 8 design, plus a number of lightweight chassis for use in Ikarus passenger models. All-wheel drive machines incorporated a transmission system in which one front differential was mounted in the chassis frame in unit with a 2-speed transfer case, two propeller shafts transmitting drive to the front wheels. For years the company used diesel engines of its own make, but the latest heavyweight Csepels have Raba-MAN diesels of up to 215bhp. In recent years, production has moved to Szigethalom and the company has been re-named Csepel Autogyar. Vehicles exported through the Hungarian Trading Co since 1955 have carried the Mogurt name.

CSONKA/*Hungary 1900-1912*

Janos Csonka pioneered the use of the petrol engine in Hungary during the 19th century in association with Donat Banki. His engineering shop in Budapest did not have the capacity to manufacture vehicles on a regular basis, so construction was sub-contracted to other factories. Rock Istran, for example, built ten 11-seat post buses.

CT ELECTRIC/*USA 1908-1928*

Launched by the Commercial Truck Co of America, Philadelphia, Pennsylvania, CT (or CT Electric) battery-electrics included both light- and medium-duty types. By 1912, 6 models of up to 5 tons capacity were on the market, from 1913 worm-drive was used in the 1-tonner. A 5-ton petrol-electric tractor was announced in 1915, but discontinued by 1917. Meanwhile, the company was re-constituted as the Commercial Truck Co, continuing production until it was taken over by a rival manufacturer, the Walker Vehicle Co. The 1921 CT Electric range included models of up to 6 tons capacity.

CUB/*USA 1950-1951*

Howard Munshaw had a long association with the America passenger vehicle industry before he founded Cub Industries Inc, White Pigeon, Michigan, to produce small economical buses. Marketed as Cub, these were

1924 Csepel 706/9 drawbar tractor

mounted on 406cm wheelbase front-engined Ford truck chassis converted to forward-control and fitted with a 19-seat lightweight body. Only 40 examples were delivered.

CUDELL/*Germany 1904-1905*
The Cudell Motor Cie GmbH, Aachen, was already building light commercials when it began to construct trucks and buses of its own design, using 2- and 4-cyl Cudell petrol engines. Production was short-lived.

CUGNOT/*France 1769-1771*
The world's first self-propelled vehicle was a steam-powered 3-wheeler developed by Nicholas Cugnot for hauling field artillery. Assembly started in Paris in 1769 and was completed the following year. A spherical boiler of insufficient capacity was carried ahead of the single driven front wheel, giving a maximum speed of 4km/h. An improved, heavier machine was assembled in 1771 but this, too, was unsuccessful. It now

stands in the Conservatoire National des Arts et Métiers in Paris.

CUMBERLAND/*England 1905-c1908*
Built in Carlisle, Cumbria by Pratchitt Bros, the first Cumberland steam wagon had a vertical cross water-tube boiler set well forward of the front axle, a 30hp fully-enclosed compound "undertype" engine and the rear half of the chassis constructed from two plate frames, with semi-elliptic leaf springs located between them. A hand-operated screw-type tipping body was fitted. An improved design appeared towards the end of 1906 with channel-section chassis and a vertical boiler.

1905 Cumberland 'undertype' steam wagon

CUMMINS/*Brazil to date*
Using Van Hool chassis with rear-mounted Cummins diesel engines, Cummins Nordeste SA Industrial, Salvador, offers a high-floor inter-city coach and a city transit bus with bodies by Marcoplo, also of Salvador. The city bus has perimeter seating for 36 persons and ample standing room.

CUNNINGHAM/*USA 1900-1901*
The Boston-based Cunningham Engineering Co built an unusual 4/5-ton 4-wheel drive steam wagon, using a coal or coke-fired vertical fire-tube boiler at the extreme front of the chassis and a driving position cantilevered ahead to provide maximum body space. The compound "undertype" engine drove both front and rear axles by chain, all wheels being carried on railway-type, outside-mounted semi-elliptic leaf springs. Towards the end of production, the company was renamed the Massachusetts Steam Wagon Co.

CURTIS/*USA 1912-1915*
The Pittsburgh Machine Tool Co, Braddock, Pennsylvania, built 1½- and 2-ton Curtis trucks, using bought-in wheels and electrical equipment, all other items being produced in the company's own factory. Both had a 4-cyl petrol engine, thermo-syphon cooling, cone clutch, 3-speed transmission and chain-drive.

CURTIS-BILL/*USA 1933*
The Bill Motors Co was set up in Oakland, California to develop the 20-seat Curtis-Bill front-drive bus to designs laid down by Harry E Curtis. This, and a 10-ton truck, was powered by a Lycoming straight-8 petrol engine.

CURTIS-NATIONAL/*USA 1934*
Only two Curtis-National vehicles were built by interstate bus operator National Bus Lines, Los Angeles, California. Both had 20-seat streamlined low-loading bodies and were powered by Ford Petrol engines.

CWS BELL/*England 1920-1930*
The CWS Bell, sometimes referred to as CWS or Bell, was built by the Co-operative Wholesale Society Ltd in Manchester following its acquisition of the former Bell Bros concern in 1919. Initially, 1- and 1½-ton bonneted models were constructed but in 1922 a new 1½/2-ton model was introduced as van, truck or 5-row charabanc, remaining in production until 1927. Later, it was joined by the 30bhp 'P'-Type for use with 20-seat passenger bodies.

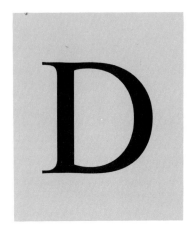

D

DAAG/*Germany 1910-1929*
The first bonneted DAAG trucks built by Deutsche Lastwagenfabrik AG, Ratingern, Düsseldorf, were mainly of the "subsidy" type. Production increased during World War I and by the 1920s, pneumatic-tyred models, from 1½- to 3½-ton capacity, were listed. A normal-control low-loading passenger chassis with 4-wheel brakes and one cardan shaft to each rear wheel was introduced in 1925, and by 1927 Germany's first air-sprung commercial had been built. The factory passed to Fried Krupp, Motoren und Kraftwagenfabriken GmbH.

DAB/*Denmark 1947-c1964*
The first DAB passenger model used Leyland-engined Büssing chassis. Built by Dansk Automobil Byggeri A/S, Silkeborg, various chassis makes were employed until 1964, when a new chassisless range based on Leyland's 'Royal Tiger Worldmaster' running units was launched, the company quickly becoming a wholly-owned subsidiary of the Leyland Motor Corp Ltd, as Leyland DAB A/S. All subsequent models were marketed as Leyland-DAB.

DAC/*France 1905-c1907*
A 2-ton truck known as the D A C or D'Espine was built by D'Espine, Achard et Cie, Paris, using a 16/18hp twin-cyl petrol engine.

DAC/*Rumania 1973 to date*
Intreprinderea de Autocamioane Brasov added DAC commercials to its Bucegi, Carpati, Roman and SR ranges. A medium-duty bonneted chassis with licence-built 135bhp MAN diesel engine and modified SR cab, it was joined by a massive 6-wheeled dump truck with two engines side-by-side, two clutches, and two 5-speed gearboxes. Later on the company was re-named Uzina de Autocamioane, and now also sells forward-control Roman trucks under the DAC brand name.

DAF/*Netherlands c1942 to date*
Previously concentrating on the manufacture of trailers, semi-trailers and military vehicles, Van Doorne's Bedrijfswagenfabriek BV developed front- and rear-wheel drive prototype trucks during the German Occupation, announcing its first civilian model, a 32-seat single-deck trolley bus in 1948, followed by petrol and diesel-powered prototype buses with removable front-mounted engines. Later that year, work started on a new truck factory at Geldropseweg, Eindhoven, and then towards the end of 1949 Van Doorne's Aanhangenwagenfabriek NV, as it had been renamed, built its first trucks, using mainly Leyland mechanical units. Series production got underway in 1950 with a 5-ton forward-control model using a 6-cyl side-valve Hercules petrol engine, 4-speed transmission and hydrovac brakes, a 4.7-litre Perkins P6 diesel being optional. By the end of that year models were listed for payloads of between 3½ and 7 tons and the company was now called Van Doorne's Automobielfabriek NV.

1950 DAF 5-ton truck chassis-cabs

1975 DAF F2800 artic tractor

The 1-ton capacity A10 was powered by a 46bhp 2.2-litre 4-cyl petrol engine, again of Hercules manufacture, and available in forward or normal-control guise with hydraulic brakes and hypoid rear axle. Full-front buses had 5.6-litre Perkins R6 diesel engines and 5-speed constant-mesh transmissions while military vehicles formed an even greater part of production, led by a forward-control Hercules-engined 3-ton 6 x 6.

In 1953, Leyland engines were used in Daf buses for the first time and in 1956 the Leyland 0.350 diesel was licence-built at Eindhoven.

By 1956 the largest military model was the 6-ton 6 x 6 YA616, with double-reduction axles, air-hydraulic brakes, power-steering and a 232bhp 6-cyl Continental petrol engine. This model was also built under licence in Spain by Empresa Nacional de Autocamioanes SA, using the Pegaso brand name. A Leyland-powered 7-tonner was shown at Earls Court, London, that year and by 1957 the Leyland power unit was standard on the 8/9-ton 2000 model, which also had a 6-speed ZF box and power-steering. There was now a line of bonneted models in the 5/6-ton payload category, with 5-speed transmissions and optional air-hydraulic braking. In 1957 an engine factory was opened and by the following year axles were also made, making the Daf range less of an assembled type. Perkins diesels were still standard for passenger models, although a few Verheul-bodied 6-wheelers did have Leyland units.

By 1958, a third of commercial sales on the Dutch market were of Daf manufacture and only Daf-built Leyland engines, from 100 to 165bhp, were used, the company gradually developing a new engine range using Daf-Leyland components. From 1961 the company's commercials were also assembled in Germany by Daf Automobilges für Deutschland Mbh Düsseldorf, and outlets were established in many other countries. In 1962 a military 4 x 4 called the 'Pony' was developed.

Daf trucks were now offered in capacities of between 5 and 14 tons, in forward- or normal-control form and with petrol or diesel engines. New for 1962 was the 19-ton GVW (40 tons GCW) 2600, with forward-control, 11.1-litre 220bhp licence-built Leyland engine, 6-speed overdrive box, double-reduction axle, dual-circuit air brakes and power-steering. For the next two years, passenger models continued to be of front-engine layout, but in 1964 the underfloor-engined MB200 appeared using features already incorporated in the company's trucks. The AZ1900, a 6 x 6 truck with 165bhp turbocharged engine, appeared about the same time, and for 1966 the rear-engined SB200DO passenger chassis was announced, this having a Voith automatic transmission. Cab and axle manufacture was transferred to a new plant at Oevel, Belgium.

The 2600 series was extended towards the end of the 1960s and a new range of Daf diesels up to 11.6-litre capacity announced. In 1970 a new tilt-cab was launched, replacing cabs that still bore signs of 1950s Daf trucks, while bus production was centred upon developments of the old MB200 with midships-mounted horizontal diesel engines. All medium and heavyweight commercials now had air-hydraulic or full air brakes, and an interesting development in 1971 was a coach with

1964 DAF single-deck chassis

an experimental Stirling-Philips hot air engine.

In 1972 one third of the company shares was bought by the American-owned International Harvester Co and all car interests were hived off to AB Volvo, Sweden. International Harvester components became available in certain models and the 2600 range – now known as the F2600 – was offered with a 304bhp, 11.6-litre turbocharged diesel engine with charge-cooling and a 9-speed ZF box. A year later this model was replaced by the F2800 4 x 2 and 6 x 4 series, with engines of up to 320 bhp while American influence produced the short-lived N2500 3-axle "conventional" of International 'Paystar' design with Daf engines and running units. In 1975 one fourth of company shares were acquired by Dutch State Mines, leaving the Van Doorne Holding Co with less than half the company's shares.

By 1978 business was again booming, the lightest models including the mediumweight FA900, for a 8000kg GVW po-

1970 DAF terminal tractor

wered by 4- or 6-cyl diesel engines and with a tiltcab of French Saviem origin. This vehicle was developed by the so-called 'Club of Four', the other three members being Magirus-Deutz, Saviem and Volvo, set up to combine development and financial resources. At the other end of the scale, 6 x 4 heavy haulage tractors for up to 100 tons GCW were also built, based on the F2800 range with a 13-speed crawler transmission.

The lightest commercial is now the F700 for 3835kg GVW, with 5-speed synchromesh transmission and 3.9-litre 4-cyl Perkins diesel engine. A new development is the 8 x 4 rigid, originally intended for tipper operation on the British market but now sold in various countries. On the passenger side, the chassisless 200, with horizontal underfloor diesel engine, and the SB200 chassis with rear-mounted 8.2-litre turbocharged diesel, are still listed. The company's Special Products Divn continues to manufacture trailers and semi-trailers, plus a 1-man cabbed terminal tractor based on normal commercial running gear.

DAIHATSU/*Japan 1956-1977*

By 1956 the Daihatsu Kogyo Co Ltd, Osaka, had added models of up to 2 tons capacity to its range of motorcycle-engined Daihatsu 3-wheelers, the heaviest of which had a 1.5-litre water-cooled 'V'-twin engine and, by 1957, wheel steering. The heaviest model was now the 13T, which had a 2-speed rear axle and was offered as a van, truck, dump-truck, gully-emptier, refuse-collector or fire appliance. Within two years, the 'Best', a 2-ton forward-control 4-wheeler, had become the largest Daihatsu. Other new designs included a series of 1¼- and 1¾-ton pick-ups based on the company's "conventional" car models with petrol or diesel engines. More powerful petrol and diesel engines were listed by 1966 when the Toyota Motor Co Ltd acquired the business and by the end of the decade 3-wheeled commercials had vanished. By 1971 heavier payloads were catered for by the forward-control SV16T, a 1½-ton derivative of the 2-ton 4-wheeler, with Toyota's influence felt in the form of its 4-cyl petrol engines, although Daihatsu diesels continued to be available. The only heavies listed for 1975 were 1½-/2-

1980 Daihatsu 'Delta' V12-H truck

tonners with 80bhp petrol or 70bhp diesel engines and 4- and 5-speed transmissions.

DAIN/*USA 1912-1917*

Joseph Dain, Ottumwa, Iowa, developed 1-, 2-, and 3-ton friction-drive trucks forming the Dain Mfg Co to undertake series production. Powered by a 4-cyl petrol engine with a worm-drive rear axle, the Dain was available only in 1-ton form during its last two years of production.

DAIRY EXPRESS/
USA 1926-1930

Developed from prototypes built in 1925 by Eastern Dairies Inc, Springfield, Massachusetts, the 2- and 2½/3-ton Dairy Express was built in the same plant following the company's takeover in 1926 by the General Ice Cream Corp. The lighter model was powered by a 4-cyl Hercules petrol engine, and the heavier by a 6-cyl Hercules.

DANIELSON/*USA 1912-1914*

The 1-ton Model 'A' Danielson was assembled by the Danielson Engine Works, Chicago, Illinois, using a 4-cyl petrol engine which

drove the rear axle via a 3-speed box and chain final-drive.

DANKS/*England 1914-1918*

During World War I, when the more successful steam wagon builders were occupied with war work, Frederick Danks, Oldbury, Worcestershire, assembled a few "overtype" wagons using loco-type boilers and Foden engines and running units.

DANSK/*Denmark 1904-1906*

Dansk Automobil oy Cyklefabrik H C Christiansen & Co, was founded in Copenhagen in 1901 to manufacture passenger cars and light commercials under the Dansk or Christiansen brand names. It later supplied the first Danish motor bus as Dansk Automobilfabrik. The prototype had an Oldsmobile petrol engine of single- or twin-cyl layout, the last models using a 25hp 4-cyl engine.

DARRACQ/*France 1903-1912*

Although passenger cars and taxicabs were manufactured from 1896, Soc A Darracq, Suresnes, Seine, did not enter the true commercial field until 1903 when it built Renard's first road-train. Within six years the company was building a number of commercial types as A Darracq et Cie (1905) Ltd and had also set up Darracq-Serpollet et Cie to construct steam buses under the Darracq-Serpollet name. Darracq commercials, meanwhile, had conventional transmissions "coal-scuttle" bonnets, radiators behind the engine and thermo-syphon cooling. In 1910 an experimental 50hp single-deck bus with shaft-drive and circular radiator was tested but not produced. A worm-drive 3-ton truck announced in 1912 came to nothing and from then on only light delivery types were offered.

DARRACQ-SERPOLLET/
France 1906-1912

Darracq Serpollet et Cie was formed in Paris in 1906 to construct steam buses and lorries using Serpollet's propulsion system. Most were conventionally-designed bonneted models similar to internal combustion-engined types, but were found to be very under-powered. Some buses were operated by the Metropolitan Steam Omnibus Co Ltd in London from 1907 but these did not last and the company went into liquidation in 1912.

DART/
USA 1907-1961, 1970 to date

After the Dart Truck Co, Anderson, Indiana, was re-named the Dart Mfg Co in 1907 and moved to Waterloo, Iowa, a series of chain-drive 4-cyl engined trucks

was introduced. A new shaft-drive was introduced in 1912, the largest of which was a 1360-kg capacity model, joined in 1914 by the 2-ton Model 'CC' with worm-drive and a 4-cyl Buda petrol engine. The company was re-organized several times, becoming the Dart Truck & Tractor Corp after World War I; the Hawkeye-Dart Truck Co in 1924; and in 1925, the Dart Truck Co when production moved to Kansas City, Missouri.

The early 1930s saw a new range of 1½- to 5-ton models, joined in the late 1930s by a 10-ton rigid and an artic 6-wheeler. In 1937 the first heavy-duty off-highway Darts were aimed at the mining industry, and in 1939 a 6 x 4 diesel-electric tractor was built for hauling two 40-ton coal trailers. Ten- and 40-ton military 6 x 4s and 6 x 6s were supplied during World War II, and in 1947 the business was acquired by the George Ohrstrom Co, New York, passing to the Carlisle Corp of Carlisle, Pennsylvania in 1950. Post-war production comprised both medium- and heavy-duty tractors, but by the early 1950s heavy off-highway dump trucks were the company's speciality. In 1958 the company was acquired by the Pacific Car & Foundry Co, Renton, Washington, and re-named the KW-Dart Truck Co, the product name also changing to KW-Dart by 1961. In 1970 the KW-Dart Truck Co became the Dart Truck Co and products were again called Dart. These included 65-, 75-, and 110-ton 4-wheelers; 100- and 120-ton articulated 3-axle bottom dumps; and 120- and 150-ton 4-wheeled rigids with electric drive. Off-road dump trucks were temporarily withdrawn in 1973, but a new range of rear- and bottom-dump units with capacities of up to 150 tons was launched almost immediately, powered by Caterpillar, Cummins, or Detroit Diesel V12 diesels of up to 1050bhp.

DASSE/*Belgium c1914-1928*

Automobiles Gérard Dasse was established at Verviers, Eastern Belgium, in 1896 to manufacture 3- and 4-wheeled passenger cars. Shaft-drive commercials of up to 24/30hp capacity were soon available, heavier types having cylinders cast in pairs, and in 1924 car production was abandoned in favour of commercials and military types.

DATSUN
Japan 1959-c1966

Jidosha Seizo Kabushiki Kaisha was formed in Yokohama early in 1933 to continue production of Dat light cars and commercial derivatives under the Datsun brand name. Until 1959 these were for

DAIMLER (1)/
Germany 1896-1926

Gottlieb Wilhelm Daimler, pioneered the use of petrol engines in road vehicles in 1885, setting up Daimler-Motoren-Gesellschaft in Berlin. The first Daimler commercials were based on his 'Riemenwagen' passenger car, with a rear-mounted engine driving the back wheels via a system of belts and internally-toothed gears. The engine was a vertical 'V' – twin Phönix, with four gears providing speeds of between 3 and 12 km/h. Suspension was by transverse full-elliptic leaf springs at the front, coil springs at the rear. Payloads of 1500, 2500, 3750, and 5000kg could be handled.

A new model for 1897 had a 2-cyl engine beneath the driver, but to obtain sufficient ground clearance, large-diameter wheels were fitted and the centre of gravity raised. This was rectified in a 3-tonner with front-mounted engine and shaft-drive to internally-toothed gear rings bolted inside the rear wheels. A 1½-tonner was based on a modified 'Victoria' passenger car with a front-mounted twin-cyl Phönix engine and double chain-drive. This model lasted only a few months, being followed by the first true Daimler bus, using a 'V'-twin Phönix engine and a capacity of 16 persons.

In 1900 the internal-gear final-drive became semi-enclosed to keep out dirt and reduce noise and 4-cyl petrol engines were adopted. Also in 1900 the company established Osterreichische Daimler-Motoren-Gesellschaft Bierenz, Fischer & Co, to build Daimler commercials in Austria under the Austro-Daimler brand name. A year later, Motorfahrzeug und Motorenfabrik Berlin AG, Marienfelde – a company that had been set up by Daimler in 1899 to build MMB commercials – was taken over and subsequent Daimler commercials constructed at this factory as Daimler Marienfelde until 1914.

Diesel experiments led to the development of a diesel-powered traction engine during World War I, and when peace returned 3- and 4½-ton trucks were announced, followed in 1922 by a super-charged air-injection bus. Diesel trucks and buses were shown at Berlin in 1923, and the following year saw the debut of a low-loading passenger chassis and a 5-ton pinion-drive truck. From 1924 the company began to collaborate with Benz Werke, finally joining forces in 1926 as Daimler-Benz AG, vehicles being sold as Mercedes-Benz. Undecided as to whether to use the Benz or Daimler diesel systems, diesel development was temporarily dis-

continued and the last Daimlers, 2/3- and 4/5-tonners, were shown at the 1925 Berlin Motor Show. The 6-wheeled dropframe model had 6-wheel braking, a 35.7hp petrol engine and shaft-drive via a tandem-drive bogie, the wheels themselves running on "dead" axles carrying separate differential and half-shaft assemblies. These drove the wheels through pinions and the well-used internal gear ring system.

1921 Daimler (2) 'Y'-Type

DAIMLER (2)/
England 1899-1975

The Daimler Motor Syndicate Ltd was established in Coventry in 1893 to import Gottlieb Daimler's vehicles. In 1896 it was re-constituted as the Daimler Motor Co Ltd. Their early parcels van had a vertical twin petrol engine, tube ignition, 3-speed transmission and chain-drive. In 1899, a much larger 14-seater using 12hp 4-cyl petrol engine was introduced. Designed by Sidney Straker, this was revolutionary in as much as the transmission incorporated a propeller shaft between gear-box and differential instead of the usual chain and sprocket. A 26-seat double-deck version inaugurated the first double-deck motor bus service in London later that year and was followed by one of Britain's first petrol-engined fire appliances.

The company was later renamed the Daimler Motor Co (1904) Ltd but commercial production up to 1907 was very low with the only significant examples being a few 2- and 3-tonners and an 18hp fire appliance. In 1908 the company acquired sole British manufacturing rights for the French-designed Renard road-train system, and later that year

constructed a 34-seat bonneted double-deck bus with 30hp 4-cyl petrol engine, Auto-Mixte petrol-electric transmission and worm-drive rear axle, but this was the only example of its type, serving as a prototype for the later KPL petrol-electric bus. Also in 1908, Charles Knight from Wisconsin, USA, developed the sleeve-valve engine – a power unit far superior to the old poppet-valve type – and Daimler quickly took this experiment a stage further, introducing its famous 'Silent Knight' engine for all 1909 models.

BSA Ltd bought the company in 1910 and it became known as the Daimler Motor Co Ltd. A new programme of commercial vehicle production was instituted the following year – all using the 'Silent Knight' engine – and this led to the company's first major order with the largest single contract ever placed for buses at that time. By 1914 the commercial range covered all types up to 5 tons capacity, all with 'Silent Knight' engines, worm-drive, and radiators different from those used on the company's passenger cars. A 1-tonner announced in 1913 was powered by a 20hp 3.3-litre Daimler car engine in conjunction with a Daimler car transaxle, but this was the exception rather than the rule. Some heavier chassis were delivered with two bodies but it was not until World War I that large numbers of Daimlers were built for load-carrying work.

Before World War I the most popular heavy Daimlers were 2- to 5-tonners with 4- and 5.7-litre petrol engines, cone clutches and flitch-plate frames. Three- and 4-speed transmissions were standard with 4-speed chain-drive transmissions on passenger models and longer chassis used for charabanc bodies. To aid the war effort a 3-ton "subsidy" truck was the main product up to 1918. A period of relative inactivity followed the war, passenger models being similar to their pre-war counterparts with the exception of electric lighting and pneumatic tyres, and it was not until 1926 that any new designs appeared, the first being the lightweight

'CM' which could legally operate at 32km/h on pneumatics. Later that year the company entered into an agreement with the Associated Equipment Co Ltd, builder of AEC vehicles, whereby all future deliveries were to be sold under the name Associated Daimler (or ADC) with components supplied by both companies and much of the assembly work undertaken in southern England. This arrangement lasted until 1928, when long-distance coaching was beginning to take off in Britain and the first of a new line of passenger models, the CF6 was developed. Offered in both forward- and normal-control form, the former having a 1-man half-cab, this had a 5.75-litre sleeve-valve petrol engine, employed much aluminium alloy, and featured servo-assisted 4-wheel braking, dual-coil ignition, underslung worm rear axle and the classically-styled, fluted Daimler radiator previously used only on the company's passenger cars. It was particularly popular in bonneted coach form.

1947 Daimler (2) CVG6

The sleeve-valve engined CG6 passenger chassis with offset normal transmission, and the CH6, with pre-select epicyclic box and fluid coupling, appeared in 1930 and by 1932 conventional transmissions had been dropped and the sleeve-valve engine was being replaced by more conventional poppet-valve units. A new model, the CP6, was announced with an overhead-valve 6.6-litre 6-cyl poppet-valve engine, while diesel engines were fast gaining popularity, the company announcing its first diesel vehicle – the COG5 with 7-litre Gardner 5LW engine – late in 1933. From 1935, the COG6 with 6LW Gardner, was made available and other models included the COA6 with AEC diesel and the COS6 powered by Armstrong-Saurer.

Transport Vehicles (Daimler) Ltd was formed in 1936 to pursue passenger vehicle design still further, and the first Daimler trolley-buses were constructed. These were of 4 x 2, double-drive 6-wheeled layout, with Metrovick motors, Westinghouse air brakes

1927 Daimler (2) ADC424 single-deck coach

1915 Daimler (1) 2-ton truck

and worm final-drive. By 1937 all Daimler buses had hydraulic brakes and the company was developing its own diesel engines, the first being an 8.6-litre unit in the CWD6 model. Bus production ceased in favour of military equipment early in World War II but was resumed in 1942 to replace air raid casualties. With peace, the CWD6 was refined into the CD650 with handbrake servo-assistance and power-assisted gear-changing and rear door actuation. In 1948 the superbly designed Barker-bodied DC27 limousine ambulance with 27bhp 4-litre 6-cyl petrol engine, independent front suspension and hydro-mechanical brakes was developed, some 500 examples being built before production ceased in 1952. Also towards the end of the 1940s, a fleet of specially constructed tandem-drive 6-wheeled double-deckers was supplied to Cape Town, South Africa.

Daimler double-deckers were of much lighter construction by 1952 and soon all front-engined types carried new grilles in place of the familiar fluted radiator. In 1951 an underfloor-engined single-decker, the 37/45-seat 'Free-line' appeared with Daimler or Gardner horizontal diesel engines and 5-speed pre-select transmission as standard, proving successful both at home and abroad, the next major event being the introduction of the electro-pneumatically operated 'Daimatic' epicyclic transmission in 1957 which removed the necessity for a gear-change pedal.

The most famous of modern Daimler passenger models was the rear-engined 'Fleetline' double-decker, sometimes supplied as a single-decker, introduced in 1960 – the same year that the company was absorbed by the Jaguar Group. This was intended for 78-seat bodies and had a quickly removable transverse rear engine, double-reduction bevel-drive, full air brakes and semi-elliptic leaf spring suspension. It was powered by a Gardner 6LX diesel engine. A prototype single-decker, known as the SRD, was constructed in 1962, having a transverse horizontal engine and 'Daimatic' transmission, but this got no further. The next new model was the 50-seat 'Roadliner' powered by a 9.6-litre V6 Cummins diesel mounted vertically at the rear and providing a speed of some 124km/h. No Daimler engines were built after 1963, although traditional half-cab buses were still available up to 1968. By 1967 the company had become the Daimler Co Ltd and Cummins diesel engines, sometimes with optional Allison automatic transmissions, were introduced for the 'Fleetline' passenger models.

In 1968 the Jaguar Group, then part of the British Motor Corp Ltd, merged with the Leyland Motor Corp Ltd to form the British Leyland Motor Corp Ltd and Daimler bus production was hived off to this organization's Truck & Bus Divn by 1972. Meanwhile, new developments continued, including the option of an 8.4-litre V8 Perkins diesel for the 'Road-liner' and a choice between AEC and Cummins units in the 11-m, CR36 with its longitudinal rear engine location. From 1971 only the 'Fleetline' remained in full production under the Daimler brand name; this model was offered with a turbocharged Leyland diesel in 1975. By the mid-1970s 'Fleetline' production had been transferred to Leyland's Lancashire plant and by 1979 the vehicle had become known as the Leyland 'Fleetline'.

1970 Daimler (2) 'Fleetline' SRG6LX-36 single-deck bus

payloads of under 1 ton, but it was then that the company announced the PG222U pick-up for a 1-ton payload. It was powered by a 48bhp 1.2-litre overhead-valve petrol engine, had independent front suspension and steering column gear-change. By 1966 a 67bhp 1.3-litre engine and synchromesh transmission were available.

DAIMLER-MARIENFELDE/
Germany 1901-1914
When Daimler-Motoren-Gesellschaft acquired Motorfahrzeug und Motorenfabrik Berlin AG, builder of the Marienfelde, or MMB truck, all commercial vehicle production was concentrated in this factory. Vehicles were known as Daimler-Marienfelde, having load capacities of up to 5000kg with 'V'-twin or 4-cyl petrol engines. These were bonneted cardan- or chain-drive models with the engine located ahead of the driver and radiator slung beneath. Typical Daimler internally-toothed gear wheel transmissions were used. Daimler-Marienfelde fire appliances, often with engine-driven pumps, appeared in 1907 and a new series of battery-electric commercials with wheel hub motors – sometimes referred to as the Mercedes Electrique – were introduced a year later in collaboration with the Austro-Daimler factory. From 1901 until 1914, Daimler-Marienfelde chassis were sold extensively in Britain as Milnes-Daimler, perpetuating an agreement between the original builder of Marienfelde and MMB trucks and GF Milnes & Co, when these were sold in Britain under the Milnes name. Shortly before World War I a number of 4-wheel drive military vehicles were developed, but in 1914 commercial production was transferred back to Cannstatt and the Marienfelde plant was used for the assembly of Mercedes passenger cars and light commercials.

DAIMLER-RENARD/
England 1908 c1910
The Daimler Motor Co (1904) Ltd, Coventry, secured British manufacturing rights for the French-designed Renard road-train system. For goods or passenger operation, this comprised a petrol-powered tractor and up to six 6-wheeled trucks to the same arrangement as the Renard patents.

DAVEY-PAXMAN/
England 1905-1908
Whilst Davey, Paxman & Co Ltd, Colchester, Essex, had built steam traction engines from 1905, no true commercial types were built under the Davey-Paxman

brand name. However, a number of "undertype" steam wagons were constructed for Bretherton & Bryan Ltd, of North London, and known as Bretherton or Bretherton & Bryan wagons.

1963 David Brown 'Taskmaster' 950 drawbar tractor

DAVID BROWN/*England 1936-c1956*
The first aircraft-towing tractors built by David Brown Tractors Ltd, Meltham, Huddersfield, were developed for the military and used for a multitude of tasks, such as aircraft salvage, snow-clearance, runway and perimeter track sweeping. General towing duties included the handling of service equipment and trailer haulage in bomb and fuel dumps. Immediately after the war, a road haulage version was added with single or twin rear tyres, mudguards and full lighting and braking equipment conforming to regulations current at that time.

DAY-ELDER/*USA 1919-1937*
The Day-Elder or DE was introduced by the Day-Elder Motors Corp Irvington, New Jersey in 1919 and by the early 1920s comprised no less than six models from 1 to 5 ton capacity using Buda or Continental 4-cyl petrol engines. Soon production was being handled by the National Motors Mfg Co, but then the Day-Elder Truck Co was formed and in 1925 the first 6-cyl models appeared and a new 5/6-ton truck and passenger chassis was added to the range. In 1929 the 'Super Service Six' for 1- to 6-ton payloads with 6-cyl Continental petrol engines was introduced. Lighter models had internal hydraulic brakes and the re-designed passenger chassis was available as a high-speed delivery van, using an unusual rear suspension system comprising a single load-carrying semi-elliptic leaf spring above the axle and a smaller auxiliary spring beneath it. There was also a 6-wheeled rigid load-carrier. The range was re-designed in 1930 but the Day-Elder Motor Truck Co, as it was then known, was never to regain its former popularity. Production came to an end in 1937.

DAYTON/USA 1912-1914

The first trucks built by the Dayton Auto Truck Co, Dayton, Ohio were the 2-, 3-, and 5-ton 'H', 'K' and 'M' "cabover" models. These were powered respectively by 35-, 45-, and 60hp 4-cyl 'T'-head petrol engines with 3-speed selective transmissions and chain-drive. In 1914 the company was re-constituted as the Durable Dayton Truck Co and subsequent models sold as Durable Dayton.

DEARBORN/USA 1919-1924

The Dearborn Motor Truck Co, Chicago, Illinois, announced 1½- and 2-ton trucks in 1919. During their production, these were powered by a variety of Buda, Continental and Hercules petrol engines and were joined in 1923 by a 338-cm wheelbase 1-tonner running on pneumatic tyres.

DEARNE/England 1927-1935

Reynolds Bros (Barnsley) Ltd, South Yorkshire, specialized in the conversion of Model 'T' Fords to forward-control, introducing the Dearne brand name to such a conversion before launching its own 20bhp small-wheeled low-loading design in 1928. This featured a single-plate clutch, 3-speed box, overhead-worm rear axle and rear wheel braking, the top of the chassis being just 57.5cm from road level. Later that year the company re-registered as the Dearne Motor Co Ltd offering both 600- and 787.5-cm wheelbase versions with capacities of 2½ and 3 tons.

DECATUR/USA 1909-1915

In 1909 the Decatur or Decatur Hoozier 1½-ton "cabover" truck was introduced by the Decatur Motor Car Co, Decatur, Illinois. It was powered by a 30hp 4-cyl Rutenber petrol engine. In 1912 the business was acquired by the Grand Rapids Motor Truck Co, production moving to Grand Rapids, Michigan, and the following year the company was re-named the Parcel Post Equipment Co, replacing all previous models with the lightweight Decatur parcel wagon.

DECAUVILLE/
France c1905-1911

Already a well-established car manufacturer and light delivery vehicle manufacture, Soc Decauville, Corbeil, Seine-et-Oise, introduced a steam truck chassis in about 1905 which sold as the Petit Bourg for passenger use. This had a flash-type boiler and gilled-tube condenser mounted on the roof, the "undertype" engine being connected to the rear wheels via a countershaft differential and double chain-drive.

DE DIETRICH (1)/
France 1896-1905

Using designs drawn up by Amedée Bollée Fils, De Dietrich et Cie, Luneville, Lorraine, introduced commercials under the De Dietrich brand name. Both goods and passenger models were listed, many being for export, while similar types were built in Alsace for the German market. In 1902 the French factory announced a chain-drive variation and acquired manufacturing rights to Turcat-Méry designs, although these were not adopted until 1907 when the company's products became known as Lorraine-Dietrich. A new model for 1903 was a bonneted type powered by a 4.4- or 5.4-litre 4-cyl petrol engine. The last new French De Dietrich was a double-deck bus with front pneumatic tyres which appeared in 1905.

DE DIETRICH (2)/
Germany 1897-1902

One year after De Dietrich et Cie began building commercials to the Amedée Bollée Fils design in Lorraine, France, a factory was opened at Niederbronn, Alsace, to manufacture similar models for the German market. Powered by 10hp 3-litre twin-cyl petrol engines, these were listed until 1902 when commercials were withdrawn in favour of passenger cars.

DEFIANCE/USA 1917-1930

The Turnbull Motor Truck & Wagon Co, Defiance, Ohio, announced the 1- to 3-ton Defiance truck in 1917, using a variety of Continental, Hercules and Wisconsin petrol engines. Re-organized as the Defiance Motor Truck Co, there was a short-lived 1923, passenger model, but a large part of production was taken up with fire appliances, many of which were used by the Howe Fire Apparatus Co Inc as a basis for its own 'Defender' range. From the mid-1920s there was also a Canadian assembly plant at Digby, Nova Scotia, and during the last few years the company operated as the Century Motor Truck Co, with vehicles occasionally referred to as Century.

DE KALB/USA 1914-1918

Chain-drive "cabover" wagons were produced in capacities from 1360 to 3177kg by the De Kalb Wagon Co, De Kalb, Illinois. Powered by 4-cyl Continental petrol engines, these had optional worm-drive for 1916.

DE DION-BOUTON/
France 1894-1950

De Dion, Bouton et Trépordoux, Paris, entered what was the world's first articulated motor

1922 De Dion-Bouton road-sweeper

vehicle in the 1894 Paris-Rouen Trials, comprising a steam-powered tractor and a horse-drawn carriage with front wheels removed. Unfortunately, it was disqualified as it required a 2-man crew to handle it.

Using the De Dion-Bouton name, frequently abbreviated to De Dion, the company set about producing a range of trucks and buses using a vertical-boilered "undertype" layout with countershaft differential and double chain-drive to the rear wheels. By the end of 1894 the company had been re-organized as De Dion, Bouton et Cie, and steam models continued to appear using a water- and steam-jacketed boiler containing short horizontal fire-tubes within an outer smoke jacket. This design was copied by many others, as was the compound engine with slide valves and Stephenson's link motion.

An articulated bus appeared in 1897 and the following year saw the inauguration of France's first regular motor bus service using De Dions. The company's steam buses were its most popular products at this time, with examples exported all over the world, but experiments with internal combustion engines were also taking place, and by 1896 engines of this type were being fitted to a series of passenger cars and light commercials.

The last De Dion steamers comprised a series of water tankers supplied to Paris in 1904 and, later that year, 4-cyl engines and new 1-, 2-, and 3-ton trucks

with 2-cyl engines, 3-speed transmissions and solid tyres were introduced. By 1905 commercials embraced all types up to the 24/30hp 'AT' Model, with four separately cast cylinders, automatic inlet valves and 3-speed transmission, constructed as a bonneted single-decker or "cabover" double. Ten experimental petrol-electric double-deckers went to the Fifth Avenue Coach Co, New York, in 1908, each with a sliding-gear transmission along Panhard lines, but these were taken out of service due to inferior materials.

De Dion-Bouton bus c1925

Honeycomb radiators arrived in 1906 and in 1907 4-cyl models were fitted with 'L'-head side-valve engines. The heaviest model was now a 5-tonner with 30hp 4-cyl engine, and an 18hp chain-drive fire appliance also appeared about this time. In 1910, circular radiators were fitted to the heavier models which now had hub-reduction drive.

In 1911, a 7.4-litre 6 x 2 version of the company's bus was experimented with, drive being transmitted to the centre wheels with front and rear used for steering. A 3-ton "cabover" called the 'DT' appeared in 1913, again with circular radiator; other features included a 4.4-litre petrol engine, triple-plate clutch, 3-speed transmission and – unusual for De Dion – worm final-drive.

The largest commercials in 1919 comprised the 3½-ton 'FR' and the 5-ton 'FS', both with circular radiators and powered by 4.4-and 5.8-litre petrol engines, respectively. Many were used as street sweepers and sprinklers. New designs appeared in 1921 with monobloc engines, double-reduction drive and pneumatic tyres; some as 2-tonners with 3.6-litre engines and others as 5.7-litre passenger types. For 1923, the 3½-tonner received pneumatics and a new radiator, and within two years a low-loading passenger chassis known as the 'JE' was announced with a 65 bhp 4-litre overhead-valve petrol engine in unit with a 4-speed transmission. The largest model was now a 6-tonner with vacuum-servo braking all round. An unusual departure were a very few single-deck battery-electric buses of full-front rear-entrance design.

Although a comprehensive commercial range, up to 6 tons capacity, was listed in 1927, the factory remained closed for much of that year. Passenger cars were gradually phased out by 1932, but attempts were made to keep the commercial side moving. In 1929, the 'JE' became the 'LC' and for 1930, overhead-valve engines were standardized. A 5-tonner was now the largest model, although 1936 saw the debut of the 6½-ton 'LY', the company's first 6-cyl engined commercial, with a capacity of 6.6 litres. Also new was a 4-tonner with 4.4-litre 4-cyl petrol engine. Production remained much the same up to 1939, with petrol engines as standard, although a diesel unit was briefly offered in 1937 and producer-gas types added in 1939, alongside forward-control 6-cyl models with 8-speed transmissions. Throughout the 1930s the company was known as Soc Nouvelle des Automobiles de Dion-Bouton with only a brief revival between 1947 and 1950, when a 40-seat prototype rear-engined coach was publicly shown. This had a 100bhp turbocharged 6-cyl opposed-piston diesel engine mounted longitudinally, an 8-speed synchromesh transmission with overdrive, and overhead-worm final-drive. Financial problems prevented further development.

DELAHAYE/*France c1903-1956*
Towards the end of 1899 Delahaye production was taken over from Emile Delahaye, Tours, by L Desmarais et Morane. For 1902, models included a variety of 2.2-litre twin-cyl types. The company's first chain-drive commercial was the twin-cyl Type 15 of 1903 and by 1906 a large range was listed.

Another name change, this time to Soc Automobiles Delahaye, came about before the end of 1906, by which time the larger commercials had 4-cyl petrol engines beneath the driver and chain final-drive. In 1907 the company's first fire appliances appeared, these being based on truck chassis with 72hp 8-litre 4-cyl petrol engines and chain-drive. The 1914 Delahaye range covered all types up to 5-ton trucks, the largest models retaining chain-drive and a "subsidy" 3-tonner with 2.8-litre 4-cyl petrol engine perpetuating the driver-over-engine layout. Just prior to World War I, one of the company's most famous trucks, the 4/5-ton bonneted Model 59, was launched. Powered by a 5-litre 4-cyl side-valve monobloc petrol engine, this was still available as late as 1925. For 1920, a new 2-tonner with 4-cyl side-valve petrol engine, 4-speed transmission, bevel-drive, pneumatic tyres and full electrics was announced. Three years later Delahaye's first-serious attack on the passenger vehicle market was led by the '83-59', a front-wheel-braked, pneumatic-tyred model with worm-drive. In 1926 the 59 model was replaced by the shaft-drive 95.

In 1927 the company teamed up with the manufacturers of Chenard-Walcker, Donnet and Unic commercials. Little came of this and the company went its own way in 1932. The first Delahaye diesel was a 7-tonner with 6-speed box and bevel-drive, announced in 1931, the engine being a 10-litre 6-cyl direct-injection design built under licence from Fiat of Italy. The company's first 6-wheeler, with cable-operated front brakes and air-actuated rears also appeared at this time, as did the Type 111 6-litre 6-cyl coach. A limousine fire appliance entered service in Paris in 1931 and the following year a bonneted 3/4-tonner powered by a 3.2-litre coil-ignition 6-cyl engine of 45bhp output was announced. The 95 engine was still listed in 1934, but within two years Delahaye's own overhead-valve engines were standardized. Many commercial types now reflected passenger car lines. In 1935 an experimental half-track fire appliance, and by 1937 the 131 passenger model had introduced the engine-beside-driver layout.

For 1939 the line-up comprised vehicles from the 1500kg capacity 140 up to the Gardner-powered air-braked 149.

During World War II the company joined the GFA Group consortium which included the manufacturers of Bernard, Laffly, Simca and Unic commercials, but once more this proved a wrong move and the company's products never sold well again. In 1950 a luxury coach was introduced, using a de-tuned version of the 4.5-litre Type 175 petrol engine and a new forward-control 4/5-ton truck known as the Type 163. This had a low-loading chassis and a choice between petrol and diesel engines. In 1954, with sales dropping, Soc Automobiles Delahaye merged with Automobiles Hotchkiss to form Soc Hotchkiss-Delahaye, based at St Denis, Seine. Delahaye production staggered on but was finally shelved following internal re-organization.

DELAHUNTY/*USA 1913-1915*
Built by the Delahunty Dyeing Machine Co, Pitton, Pennsylvania, the Delahunty was a 1½-tonner with 30hp 4-cyl Buda petrol engine, cone clutch, 3-speed transmission and double chain-drive.

DELAUGERE-CLAYETTE/
France 1901-1926
SA des Ets Delaugère, Clayette Frères et Cie, was established at Orléans, Loiret, to construct passenger cars and commercials. The marque was virtually unheard of outside France, both buses and trucks having armoured wooden frames, 3- and 4-speed transmissions and chain-drive. Models from 1- to 5-ton capacity were built until the company turned to commercial body building.

DELAUNAY-BELLEVILLE/
France 1910-1939
A light commercial range offered by SA des Automobiles Delaunay-Belleville, St Denis, Seine, was joined by a series of heavier goods and passenger types in 1910 and by 1914 the bonneted Model 'C' had taken the company into an even heavier market. New post-war models included a 3.8-litre 3-tonner of similar design, a 2-ton battery-electric and a heavy chain-drive 6-tonner. By 1928 the only Delaunay-Belleville commercial was a 1-tonner of passenger car design, derivatives of which remained in production until 1939.

DELIVR-ALL/*USA 1945-1952*
The Marmon-Herrington Co Inc, Indianapolis, Indiana, was already building a range of all-wheel drive and similar trucks when it entered the multi-stop delivery van market in 1945 with the Delivr-All, a front-wheel drive forward-control design produced in only small numbers.

DELLING/*USA 1930*
The Supersteam Service Co was established in the former Mercer Auto Co factory, Trenton, New Jersey, in 1930. The company set about constructing a prototype steam bus but the idea developed no further.

DE LOACH/*USA 1911-1912*
Although advertised briefly, it is unlikely that many De Loach trucks were actually built. They were manufactured by the De Loach Mfg Co, initially at Bridgeport, Alabama, and later at Atlanta, Georgia.

DE MARTINI/*USA 1919-1934*
FJ De Martini developed a petrol-engined load-carrier in San Francisco, California, quickly registering the De Martini Motor Truck Co to handle series production.

DENBY/*USA 1914-1930*
The Denby Truck Co, Detroit, Michigan (re-named the Denby Motor Truck Corp in 1923) offered a number of Denby models from 1- to 7-ton capacity. Some were marketed in the UK by Whiting (1915) Ltd using the Whiting brand name. Powered by Continental and later by Hercules petrol engines, the Denby range was joined by a 30-seat passenger model during the last four years of production.

DENMO/*USA 1916-1917*
Built by the Deneen Motor Co, Cleveland, Ohio, and sometimes known as the Deneen, the Denmo was a normal-control 1¼-tonner with a 4-cyl Wisconsin petrol engine, 3-speed transmission and Torbensen rear axle.

DENNING/
Australia c1967 to date
Bus and coach bodybuilder A B Denning & Co (Pty) Ltd, Brisbane, Queensland, began using re-built heavy truck chassis, with rear-mounted Cummins, Detroit Diesel or Scania engines, as a basis for passenger bodies in the mid-1960s, introducing the first Denning 'Monocoach', a chassis-less high-floor model with Detroit Diesel V6 engine, towards the end of 1967. Transmission was via a 5-speed Fuller manual or Allison automatic system.

In 1968 the company was acquired by the British Leyland Motor Corp Ltd, leading to the use of horizontal and V8 Leyland engines. By 1969 a trailing-axle 6-

wheeler had been built and a new production area was set up in Beverley, South Australia. By August 1974 production was again concentrated in the Brisbane factory, only a few 'Monocoaches' being built at Beverley.

Models for 1978 included a 10-m 4-wheeler and a 12-m 6-wheeler, powered by V6 or V8 Detroit Diesel 2-strokes and featuring pressurized cooling, power-steering and air brakes. Production continues on much the same basis.

DENNISON/*Ireland 1977 to date*
Dennison Truck Mfg Ltd, Rathcoole, Dublin, was founded to build trucks offering 4-, 6-, and 8-wheeled types with Gardner or Rolls-Royce diesel engines, Eaton axles, Fuller transmissions and Motor Panels or Sisu cabs.

DENONVILLE/
Belgium 1937-1940
Soc Belge des Automobiles Denonville, Brussels, constructed three commercial models in the medium- to heavyweight class. Powered by Cummins diesel engines of 100 and 150bhp output, the Denonville was offered as a 5- or 8-ton payload load-carrier or as a 10-ton capacity tractor.

DEPENDABLE/*USA 1918-1923*
The Dependable Truck & Tractor Co, East St Louis, Illinois, built 1-, 1½-, 2½-and 3½-ton Dependable trucks, all with Buda petrol engines, Fuller 3-speed transmissions and Wisconsin worm-drive rear axles. Only 1½- and 2½-tonners were built after 1921.

DERBY (1)/*France 1922-1934*
Based on the French cyclecar of the same name, the Derby appeared in 1922, powered by a 900cc Chapuis-Dornier 4-cyl side-valve petrol engine with no differential in the back axle. By 1924 this engine was replaced by a 1.1-litre overhead-valve 4-cyl unit of the same make and by 1925 the vehicle had 4-wheel brakes. In 1927 the company decided to concentrate on car production. To complement its passenger car line, Automobiles Derby, Courbevoie, Seine, as it was now known, developed a forward-control 1-tonner with front-wheel drive, removable engine and transverse leaf spring independent front suspension. Early prototypes were powered by a 1.5-litre overhead-valve Meadows 4ED engine.

DERBY (2)/*England c1938*
The Derby was a 3-wheeled fire appliance constructed by County Commercial Cars Ltd, Fleet, Hants. It was powered by a Ford '8' or '10' engine with an Austin '7' engine operating the pump.

1931 Dennis 'B'-Type 2-ton boxvan

DENNIS/*England 1904 to date*
In 1904 an order was placed with motor manufacturers John and Raymond Dennis, Guildford, Surrey, by Thomas Tilling for a complete bus chassis with shaft-drive and worm rear axle in preference to chain-drive or the noisy internal-gear system favoured by others. The chassis was also novel in that it tapered inwards at the front to provide an improved turning circle. In 1905 production moved to larger premises and in 1908 the company's first fire appliance, with over-drive transmission (a type of vehicle for which Dennis was to become renowned) was supplied to Bradford. This had a single-stage centrifugal pump of 400gpm output and shaft-drive. Early Dennis appliances had White & Poppe engines but these were later replaced by units of the company's own manufacture. Two- and 2½-ton trucks were also listed, powered by a 24hp side-valve 'T'-head petrol engine, with dual ignition, 3-speed transmission and semi-elliptic leaf springs. By 1907 a 5-ton worm-drive truck was also listed.

Before World War I broke out a strange road tractor with rear-mounted engine was supplied to the South African Railways. In 1913 car production ceased and the company went public to raise finance for further expansion. The 'A'-Type 3½/4-ton "subsidy" truck, powered by a 4-cyl 35hp petrol engine driving through a 4-speed crash box, went into production in a new factory on the existing site, and at the end of the war a number of these were used as a basis for the Dennis-Stevens petrol-electric chassis. In 1918 the company acquired White & Poppe Ltd but kept the Coventry

factory as a separate engine plant until 1932, when this facility moved to Guildford. A new 2½-tonner arrived in 1919, and 1921 saw a vacuum-type cesspool emptier heading an expanding range of municipals. In 1922 a new turbine pump was developed from an Italian design, fitted as standard in the company's fire appliances. The 2½-tonner was sold briefly as the Dennis-Portland in 1923 and a 1¼-ton chassis launched the same year led to the development of a 1½-ton model, powered by a 17.9hp 4-cyl side valve petrol engine of 2.7 litres capacity in 1925.

1907 Dennis motor tractor

By the late 1920s, Dennis Bros Ltd had supplied London's first pneumatic-tyred bus, a single-decker, constructed its first 4-wheel braked bus (the first in the country), and produced Britain's first pneumatic-tyred double-decker. The 'E'-Type passenger model of 1925 was very advanced, having a dropped frame and 70bhp 5.7-litre 4-cyl 'L'-head petrol engine, also fitted in new 4- and 5/6-ton goods models announced the following year. By 1927 the 'H'-Type double-decker had appeared, and in 1929 a bonneted 6-ton 6-wheeler was developed from the 4-ton 4-wheeler.

Despite financial problems, the 'Lance' replaced the 'H'-Type in 1930, developed from the 32-seat 'Arrow' single-decker of 1929. The 'Lance', with its 100bhp 6.13-litre 6-cyl Dennis petrol engine, was never a serious contender in the predominantly AEC and Leyland bus market, despite up-dating in 1931 when the multi-plate clutch was replaced by a twin-plate unit, channel section chassis frame crossmembers by tubulars and the suspension system re-designed.

Smaller capacities were catered for by the 20-seat Dart with 60bhp overhead-valve 6-cyl petrol engine. The single-deck 'Lancet', developed from the 'Lance', and also available as a 3½-ton load-carrier, found favour with a number of new clients, being powered by a modified version of the 4-cyl 'E'-Type engine. The company was too slow with new diesel models, none of which appeared until 1936 when competitors had already got a hold on the market, although the company did obtain sole rights to fit Armstrong-Saurer diesels in passenger chassis until its own was ready, and occasionally used Dorman or Gardner diesels as well.

Municipal vehicles were selling far better and the company was the first in Britain to supply fully-enclosed limousine bodies on its fire appliances. In 1933 the 1½-tonner was replaced by a 2/2½-ton design and by the 'Ace' series, for goods and passenger operation respectively. These models were gradually expanded until they covered the entire 2- to 4-ton range. Normally bonneted, the 'Ace' and its derivatives could also be had in forward-control form, with a full-front forward-control version called the 'Mace'. Among heavier variations was a lightweight bonneted 4-tonner for 26-seat passenger bodies, which was sold as the 'Arrow Minor' from 1936. By 1937 it had been joined by the 2/3-ton 'Ajax' and later by a passenger derivative called the 'Pike'. Meanwhile, 1935 saw the launch of the 'Lancet II', which was one of the country's first 40-seat single-deckers. On the heavy side, only the 12-ton 'Max', 10½-ton twin-steer 'Max Major' 6-wheeler, and a lightweight 5-tonner had any sales potential. By 1938 all lightweight passenger models had been replaced by the 20/32-seat 'Falcon', with a choice between a 3.77-litre Dennis petrol engine, Gardner 4LK or Perkins P6 diesel.

Militarized versions of the 'Max' were built for the war and other wartime developments included 6 x 6 and 8 x 8 off-road trucks. With peacetime, the pre-war 5-tonner became the 'Pax'. The 12-ton 'Horla' artic and 'Centaur' rigid were unveiled in 1946 and 1948, with another new 1946 model being the 6 x 4 'Jubilant', with 100bhp 7.6-litre 6-cyl diesel engine, later joined by three 8-wheeled types. In 1948 a new 5-litre diesel engine and a re-vamped 'Lancet' appeared, now called the Mk III for coach operators. A Mk IV was offered for export only from 1949. The first Dennis underfloor engine was introduced in 1950, this being a 7.58-litre 6-cyl diesel fitted initially in the 'Dominant' passenger chassis, and the first Rolls-Royce powered F8 fire appliance. In 1953 and 1954 an underfloor-engined 'Lancet' replaced the 'Dominant', and the AVI ambulance, with De Dion rear axle, Greigoire variable-rate suspension and a 4-cyl Rolls-Royce petrol engine was announced. An underfloor engined goods model called the 'Stork' was also developed, with a 3.14-litre 4 cyl Perkins diesel engine.

which only two examples were built. In 1958 the short-lived 16.9cu m 'Paravan' easy-access delivery vehicle was developed in association with parcels carrier Atlas Express Ltd, employing a Perkins P4 diesel located behind the driver and access via a door angled in the front left-hand corner of the body. An enquiry for a front-entrance version of the 'Loline' led to a prototype appearing at the 1958 Commercial Motor Show. Known as the 'Loline II', this had an air-suspension rear axle and entered production in 1959. In 1960 the most unusual 'Loline' of all was exhibited at Earls Court, London. Constructed to the special order of Barton Transport Ltd, Chilwell, Nottingham, this had an overall height of only 3.78m through the use of a low-height chassis and Northern Counties lowbridge body. Present in the show as well was the first 'Loline III', with a new clutch, constant-mesh transmission and re-vamped front end.

and only the DB15.5, a 15½-ton GVW rigid capable of carrying more than most 16-tonners, a 6-wheeled derivative and its articulated variant, the 'Defiant', were left, these also disappearing before too long.

In an attempt at diversification, the Mercury Truck & Tractor Co was acquired in 1964, with towing tractors re-named Dennis-Mercury. Meanwhile, the requirement that the Bristol 'Lodekka' should be sold only to nationalized operators was rescinded in 1966, which sounded the death knell for the 'Loline'.

Now only municipal and emergency vehicles were left. A revolutionary Jaguar-engined ambulance that had front-wheel drive, independent suspension, ultra-low floor and Borg-Warner automatic transmission was hailed by many as one of the greatest advances in emergency vehicle design when it was announced in 1968, but financial restrictions prevented development and only three were built. The Hestair Group acquired Dennis Motors Ltd in 1972 and, despite a couple of false starts, things are now looking hopeful.

Dennis trucks went into production in the Nicosia, Cyprus, factory of KMC Ltd in 1973 under the KMC brand name. The Dennis front-end was re-styled in 1974 and although commercial models were no longer listed as standard, a number of 16-tonners were supplied to the National Coal Board. Also in 1975, production of a double-drive 6-wheeler got underway following receipt of a £5.5m order from the Middle East. Developed from the 16-tonner, these had USA-built Hendrickson bogies with single-speed Eaton axles and a lockable third differential. Rated at 22 tons GVW, they were constructed to EEC regulations. A totally new range of single- and double-deck passenger models has also been developed, comprising a front-engined 'Jubilant' export model and rear transverse-engined 'Dominators', with Gardner, Perkins or Rolls-Royce 'Eagle' diesel engines. These have now been joined by the 'Falcon' single decker.

Registered since 1977 as Hestair-Dennis Ltd, the company is now experiencing a new life with emergency and municipal vehicle sales booming and a new range of 16 tons gross goods models entering production. Fire appliances now comprise 'D'-, 'F'- and 'R'-Types with Jaguar, Perkins or Rolls-Royce engines and the municipal line has been joined by the narrow-width 'Alleycat' refuse collector.

1963 Dennis 'Delta' aerial platform fire appliance

In 1956 the company signed an agreement with Bristol Commercial Vehicles Ltd to build its own version of the Bristol 'Lodekka', calling this the 'Loline'. The prototype actually had a Bristol chassis and Dennis running units. Series production got underway in 1957, the first deliveries being accomplished early the following year. The 'Loline I', as it was known, was offered with a variety of power units, and a 4- or 5-speed constant-mesh transmission. In 1957 the 'Max' was replaced by the 'Hefty' and the 'Centaur' by the 7-ton 'Condor'. Another short-lived model was the lightweight 'Teal', suitable as a pantechnicon or 40-seat passenger type. An even rarer passenger model was the 5.5-litre underfloor-engined 'Pelican' for between 40 and 44 passengers, of

Another abortive entry into the multi-stop delivery van market was made with the snub-nosed 1½-ton 'Vendor' with front-wheel drive, a 2.26-litre Standard-Triumph diesel or 2.19-litre petrol engine and low-loading body. A year later a heavier low-loading model with low-line cab in the form of the 'Delta' was announced for goods and fire appliance work, with a new fibreglass cab. It was now only the emergency and municipals such as the 'Paxit' refuse collector that were preventing the company from collapsing. A final assault on the heavy vehicle market was made in 1964 with a low-loading single-drive 6-wheeler based on the 'Pax' and the overweight 'Maxim' tractor powered by a 178bhp Cummins or 170bhp Perkins V8. Neither was successful

DENNIS/MANN-EGERTON/
England 1954

The 1954 Commercial Motor Show heralded the appearance of a lightweight lorry of integral aluminium construction capable of carrying an 8½-ton payload at a legal speed of 48km/h. Only one was built, this joining the transport fleet of the British Aluminium Co Ltd who were also responsible for the vehicle's design and development. Construction was undertaken by Mann-Egerton Ltd, Norwich, Norfolk, with horizontal engine and mechanical units supplied by Dennis Bros Ltd, Guildford, Surrey. Weight-saving characteristics were achieved by the use of integral aluminium construction throughout, including the platform body which was rivetted to the mainframe, employing running units common to the Dennis 'Centaur' and a horizontal engine as used in the 'Pelican' passenger model. The 92bhp 5.5-litre diesel engine was slung beneath the chassis, coupled via a 5-speed box and 2-speed Eaton rear axle. A similar vehicle employing Albion mechanical units appeared two years later.

DENNIS-MERCURY/
England 1964-1972

The Mercury Truck & Tractor Co Ltd, Gloucester, built Mercury industrial and aircraft towing tractors until the firm was taken over in 1964 by Dennis Bros Ltd, Guildford, Surrey. All Mercury models were re-named Dennis-Mercury, production moving to Guildford where certain models received modified Dennis truck cabs. A 3-ton load-carrier, known as the 'T3', was also built using a Perkins or Ford diesel engine. When the parent company was taken over in 1972, manufacturing rights for the Dennis-Mercury range were sold to industrial truck builder Reliance of Halifax, Yorks, and the new company called Reliance-Mercury Ltd.

DENNIS-PORTLAND/
England 1923

To commemorate the opening of a new sales office in London, a 2½-tonner introduced by Dennis Bros Ltd, Guildford, Surrey, in 1919 was briefly marketed under the Dennis-Portland brand name.

DENNIS-STEVENS/
England c1918

Using a 3½/4-ton Dennis "subsidy" model as a basis, Stevens' Petrol Electric Vehicles Ltd, London SW1, began marketing a petrol-electric truck and bus chassis at the end of World War I. Although known as the Dennis-Stevens, it carried only the Stevens name on the radiator top tank. Outwardly, the vehicle was a Dennis, with that manufacturer's engine, axles and frame, but with a greater radiator capacity and water pump to prevent over-heating. It employed a 25kw generator with electric motor and controls as for the Tilling-Stevens petrol-electric system although the internal workings were more intricate than for the Tilling-Stevens.

DE SOTO (1)/USA 1937 to date
To provide a greater number of sales outlets overseas for Dodge and Fargo trucks, the Chrysler Motors Corp, Detroit, Michigan, introduced the De Soto brand name, using it first in Europe and then in Australia after World War II. The Australian market was particularly interesting because certain British-built Dodges were also sold under this name, but from 1960 only certain Turkish-built Dodges have carried it.

DE SOTO (2)/Turkey 1964 to date
In 1964 a Turkish-built version of the Chrysler Motor Corp's US designed 'D'-Series bonneted truck

1971 De Soto (2) PD-600 truck

was introduced, fitted with a locally-designed and built angular cab to ease repairs. Marketed under the De Soto, or sometimes the Fargo brand name, this is assembled only in chassis/cab form by Chrysler Sanayi AS, of Cayirova Gebze, Kocaeli, but was built up to 1970 at Kadikoy, Istanbul.

Powered by a 130bhp Perkins 6.354 6-cyl diesel engine, it was later supplemented by a lighter range, some of which are available with 4-wheel drive, these being listed as chassis/cabs, pickups, vans and station wagons, all powered by 140bhp Chrysler petrol engines. In some instances these models were also referred to as Dodge.

DETROIT ELECTRIC/
USA 1909-1927
As well as its battery-electric passenger cars, the Anderson Carriage Co introduced commercial battery-electrics under the Detroit Electric or Anderson Electric brand names. Often referred to simply as the Detroit, the earliest

was a forward-control 1-tonner with Elwell-Parker motor and chain-drive. By 1911 the company had become the Anderson Electric Car Co introducing a 1½-tonner the following year. The company's largest model appears to have been a 2-tonner introduced in 1916, but production dropped after this date until the firm was reconstituted as the Detroit Electric Car Co in 1919. Three years later a prototype forward-control milk float was developed, and although the Detroit Industrial Vehicle Co was founded in 1925 to develop the Divco, a petrol-engined derivative, the battery-electric prototype went no further and within two years the marque had died. Qv Divco.

DEULIWAG/
Germany 1936-1939, 1949-1951
The Deuliwag road tractor was launched by Deutsche Lieferwagen GmbH, Berlin, using a single- or twin-cyl diesel engine located at the rear. By 1937 there was also a front-engined version with Junkers or Guldner diesel, but civilian production ceased with the outbreak of war in 1939. Ten years later, as Deuliwag Traktoren and Maschinenbau GmbH, initially of Hamburg but later of Lübeck, the company constructed another rear-engined model now powered by a 3-cyl MWM diesel engine.

DEUTZ/Germany 1926-1936
Motorenfabrik Deutz AG, Cologne, built its first road tractor in 1926, using a 14bhp single-cyl diesel engine. A 2-cyl unit was fitted the following year, and for the last six years of production the company was known as Humboldt-Deutz Motoren AG. Merging with CD Magirus AG, Ulm, in 1938 led to the formation of Klockner-Humboldt-Deutz AG, builder of Magirus-Deutz trucks and buses.

DEWALD/France 1914-1932
Charles Dewald, Boulogne-sur-Seine, had been building passenger cars since 1900 when, in 1914, a bonneted Dewald truck was entered in military trials. This had a 4-cyl side-valve petrol engine, magneto ignition, cone clutch, 4-speed transmission and chain-drive. Much of the company's subsequent truck production was concentrated on military types with capacities of between 7 and 10 tons. By 1925 producer-gas versions using modified engines and Autogaz generators were also listed.

DIAMOND REO/
USA 1967-1975
In 1957 the White Motor Co,

Cleveland, Ohio, acquired Reo Motors Inc, Lansing, Michigan, followed by the Diamond T Motor Truck Co, Chicago, Illinois in 1960. Both companies continued production under the Reo and Diamond T brand names until 1967, when all models were renamed Diamond Reo and production was carried out by the Diamond Reo Trucks Divn of the White Motor Corp. Both "conventional" and "cabover" models were built.

In 1971 the Diamond Reo Trucks Divn was sold and re-registered by its new owner as Diamond Reo Trucks Inc, bringing in the Royale "cabover" range with straight-6, V8, or V12 engines. "Conventionals" were re-styled as the 'Apollo' range with a choice between 6- or 8-cyl Caterpillar, Cummins or Detroit Diesel engines. The bonneted C119 'Raider' was launched in 1974, mainly as a 6 x 4 tractor but also in 6 x 4 and 8 x 6 rigid form. A new 4 x 2 or

1968 Diamond Reo 6 x 4 tipper

6 x 4 forward-control model, for urban delivery or refuse collection work, was known as the 'Rogue', but financial difficulties led to a receiver being appointed in 1975. The last trucks were the remains of a government contract and in late 1975 the business was sold to Consolidated Industries, Columbus, Ohio. Vehicle production was discontinued but in 1977 Osterlund Inc, Harrisburg, Pennsylvania, acquired certain manufacturing rights and now offers the Diamond Reo Giant.

DIAMOND-REO GIANT/USA 1977 to date
The Diamond Reo name and manufacturing rights for the company's "conventional" models were acquired by former Diamond T distributor Osterlund Inc, Harrisburg, Pennsylvania, and the marque re-launched as Diamond-Reo Giant.

Current designs use all-steel Autocar cabs, tilting fibreglass bonnets and bolted chassis, much of production being centred upon the C11664DB 6x4 model with Cummins or Detroit Diesel engines up to 335bhp output and Fuller, Dana-Spicer or Rockwell-Standard transmissions.

DIAMOND T/USA 1911-1967
Trading as the Diamond T Motor Car Co, Chicago, Illinois, each of C A Tilt's trucks carried the letter 'T' for Tilt in a diamond-shaped emblem. The first was a 1½-tonner with 4-cyl Continental petrol engine and chain-drive. Other early models included 2-, 3½- and 5-tonners. During World War I the company also built some 1500 Model 'B' 3/5-ton 'Liberty' trucks and by 1920 the existing 1½-tonner had been joined by two others, one being known as the 'Farm Special'. This had a 4-cyl Hinkley petrol engine, 3-speed selective transmission and semi-floating worm-drive. Meanwhile, the 5-tonner was replaced by the longer-wheelbase 'S' and 1921 saw 4-speed gear-boxes on all vehicles over 2-ton capacity. A fully-enclosed cab on 3-point rubber mountings was introduced in 1923.

For 1926 the range was re-signed, using 4-cyl Hercules or Hinkley petrol engines, steel spoke wheels and electric lighting. Six-cyl petrol engines with multiple-plate clutches, 4-speed transmissions and spiral-bevel semi-floating rear axles appeared in 1928. Internal-expanding brakes now acted on all wheels and capacities ranged from 1 to 12 tons, the heaviest running on six wheels. An 8-ton 6-wheeler with 6-cyl Waukesha engine appeared in 1932 and in 1933 a chassisless tanker with rear-mounted engine was developed in conjunction with the Heil Co, Milwaukee, Wisconsin. Standard models were

1953 Diamond T Model 520 tipper

re-designed in 1933 using more flamboyant styling, while new developments included variable-rate suspension systems and 'Super Service' engines.

Redesigning again took place in 1936 and lighter pick-ups and vans in the 1½ to 6½-tons weight range were introduced. These had Hercules engines, while two high-speed diesels were developed by the company for use in vehicles in the 2- to 2½-ton class. Diamond T's first "cabovers" appeared in 1937 and the Pak-Age-Kar delivery van range was marketed as Diamond T from 1940 until 1942. Wartime military production included 4-ton 6 x 6 trucks, armoured half-tracks and 12-ton 6 x 4 tractors, armoured half-tracks

1958 Diamond T Model 634 artic tractor

and 12-ton 6 x 4 tractors. With the resumption of civilian production in 1946, fewer models were offered, most being based on earlier designs with Continental, Cummins, or Hercules engines. New models were added in 1947, but in 1951 all small models were discontinued. The model 723C "cabover", announced in 1951, won a National Design Award for its heavy-duty tilt-cab which also appeared on certain Hendrickson and International Harvester trucks, and a second tilt-cab design known as the 923C quickly joined it.

Acquired by the White Motor Co in 1958, the company was renamed the Diamond T Motor Truck Co and production moved to the Lansing, Michigan plant of Reo Motors Inc, where Diamond T's continued to be built alongside existing Reo models, albeit with White 'D'- and 'R'-Type "conventional" cabs.

By 1961 all models used a new tilt-cab also fitted by Reo but not by White. The heaviest model during the 1960s was the 'P'-Series, intended mainly for construction site use, while the last all-new Diamond T was a 10,890-kg gross vehicle introduced early in 1966 and shared with White and, briefly, Reo. This was the HF3000 Trend model. In 1967 Reo and Diamond T production was merged under the Diamond Reo Trucks Div of the White Motor Corp, and all models sold henceforward as Diamond Reo. Qv Diamond Reo, Dina, Pak-Age-Kar, Reo, White (1).

DIATTO/*Italy 1906-1918*
Commencing in 1906, Diatto A Clement Vetture Marca Torino advertised a series of trucks and buses assembled in its Turin factory under licence from SA des Ets Clement-Bayard. Few were built, but during World War I, as Soc Officine Fonderie Frejus Diatto, the company produced a series of 1- to 3½-ton bonneted military trucks with 4-cyl petrol engines.

1934 Diamond T rear-engined integral tanker

DIEHL/*USA 1918-1926*
One- and 1½-ton trucks were built by the Diehl Motor Truck Works, Philadelphia, Pennsylvania from 1918 and 1921, respectively. The 1-tonner was Continental-powered, while the larger model had a Herschell-Spillman petrol engine.

DIESEL/*England c1931*
The Diesel name was adopted by British Mercedes-Benz Ltd, UK distributors of German-built Mercedes-Benz vehicles, when the first diesel-powered models were introduced on the British market in the early 1930s. The use of this name was an attempt to monopolize this new power system in the face of competition.

DIFFERENTIAL/*USA 1931-1936, 1960 to date*
The Differential Steel Car Co, Findlay, Ohio, built tipping bodies for road and rail vehicles when it began to build its own chassis for these bodies. This was a bonneted design powered by an 85bhp 6-cyl Lycoming petrol engine. Capacities ranged from 2½ to 4 tons, but from 1936 the company again built bodies only. In 1960 the firm's descendent, the Differential Co, again entered the truck-building field with a 30-ton capacity, 6 x 4 off-highway dump truck. Power came from an 825bhp Continental V12 diesel with air-cooling and Allison torque-converter transmission. From about 1970 the company has been known as Difco Inc and its products are called Difco as well as Differential.

DINA/*Mexico 1957 to date*
Based on "conventional" Diamond T trucks of the period, Diesel Nacional SA, Ciudad Sahagun, builds DINA trucks and buses. Owned by the Mexican government, the company entered the light pick-up field in 1975 with its 1000 and 3000 models, for 1- and 3-ton payloads, respectively. Later "conventionals" were licence-built International Harvesters in 4 x 2, 6 x 4, and articulated form. In 1975 a factory was opened at Monterrey, Northern Mexico, to assemble the lighter pick-ups, and soon after, a contract to construct Mexico City's new buses was received. More recently, the company acquired a 60% share in Motores Perkins, giving the firm a ready-made engine plant.

DINOS/*Germany 1921-1926*
Dinos light trucks and buses used a heavy 6-cyl engined passenger car chassis. They were built by Dinos Automobilwerke AG, Berlin.

1964 Divco '300'-Series

DIVCO/*USA c1926 to date*
The Detroit Industrial Vehicle Co was founded to construct an internal-combustion engined version of a prototype battery-electric milk float built by the Detroit Electric Car Co. Called the Divco, it had a 4-cyl Continental petrol engine and Warner 4-speed transmission, the first few being forward-control vans with easy-access.

By 1927 the company had been re-named the Divco-Detroit Corp and for 1928 the Model 'G' was introduced. This was the first drop-frame Divco, driven from a seated or standing position with a central aisle through the load-carrying area. By the early 1930s, all Divcos were of semi-bonneted layout and in 1934 the company was re-named the Continental Divco Co, changing again to the Divco-Twin Truck Co in 1936 following the acquisition of the Twin Coach Co, Kent, Ohio. The combined range was marketed under the Divco-Twin name from then until 1944 when the old Divco name returned.

By this time, the company was known as the Divco Corp and the Divco-Twin 'U'-Series formed the nucleus of the new Divco range, the heaviest of which was the

5443-kg GVW 'ULM' with a 6-cyl petrol engine. By 1954 refrigerated versions were listed as an alternative and in 1956 a new forward-control series, called the 'Dividend', made its debut. Four- or 6-cyl petrol engines were now listed and further re-organization led to the operation becoming the Divco Truck Division of the Divco-Wayne Corp. The early 1960s saw a 3-cyl 2-stroke Detroit Diesel offered as an option, joined by optional Ford 6-cyl petrol engines for 1963. The 'Dividend', listed until 1966, was now offered with payload ratings of 2404 to 4173kg. A refrigerated 6½-tonner was built in 1961, offered with a 4.2-, 4.8- or 5.4-m box body.

In 1968 the company was re-organized as the Divco Truck Co of Transairco Inc and by 1972 it was again re-named the Divco Truck Divn, this time of the Hughes-Keenan Mfg Co, Delaware, Ohio. Models now included the '300' and '200'-Series, with capacities of 2720 and 4536kg respectively. Optional engines now included Caterpillar, Deutz air-cooled and Detroit Diesel units. A more recent innovation is a one-man garbage truck with 0.3cu m packer body and sit/stand controls.

DIVCO-TWIN/*USA 1936-1944*
With the acquisition of the Twin Coach Co, Kent, Ohio, by the Continental Divco Co, Detroit, Michigan, in 1936, Twin Coach and Divco urban delivery models were marketed under the Divco-Twin brand name by the newly formed Divco-Twin Truck Co. Completely re-vamped for 1937, the range was based largely on Divco designs using a snub-nosed welded all-steel van body, semi-automatic folding access doors and 4-cyl Continental petrol engine. This was the 'U'-Series, a 1940 example being the first refrigerated Divco. In 1944 the company was re-organized as the Divco Corp and the old Divco brand name re-introduced.

DIXI/*Germany c1910-1920*
An established passenger car builder that had already dabbled in the commercial vehicle market with its Eisenach battery-electric and Wartburg petrol-engined models, Fahrzeugfabrik Eisenach, Eisenach, also introduced Dixi trucks and buses. One of the first was a 5-ton capacity bonneted "subsidy" truck, but with a return to peace a series of shaft-driven trucks and buses powered by a 6.2-litre 4-cyl petrol engine was offered. In 1920 the company was re-named Dixi-Werke AG, production moved to Gotha and only light commercials were built.

DIXON/*USA 1921-1931*

Noted for their hill-climbing capabilities, Dixon trucks were built by the Dixon Motor Truck Co, Altoona, Pennsylvania, originally using 4-cyl Continental petrol engines but later 4-cyl Hercules or 6-cyl Lycoming units. The Lycoming engines were used in conjunction with bevel final-drive.

DJB/*England 1973 to date*

DJB Engineering Ltd was formed in 1973 at Peterlee, Co Durham to build the DJB D250 6-wheeled articulated-chassis dump truck. This was of 6 x 4 configuration with driven first and second axles,

1979 DJB 6 x 4 artic dump truck

could handle a 25-ton payload, and was powered by a Caterpillar diesel engine. In 1975 a larger capacity outfit, the 30-ton payload D300, was launched. Both models were superseded by up-dated versions, the D275 and D330, in 1978, both with a sprung front axle. The D350 for a 32-ton payload and D550 for 50-ton were also launched. New derivatives of existing models include pipe haulers, log-carriers and dumpers.

DKW 1-ton integral van c1970

DKW/*Germany 1927-1948*

DKW and DEW commercials were introduced in 1927, by Zschopauer Motoren-Werke JS Rasmussen AG. The DKW commercials were petrol-engined and although the company merged with Audi, Horch, and Wanderer to form Auto Union GmbH in 1932, these continued to be sold as DKW until 1948 when they were known as IFA.

DMX/*USA 1936-1940*

DMX passenger models were designed by Paul O Dittmar of the South Suburban SafeWay Lines, Chicago, who established the Dittmar Mfg Co, Harvey, Illinois, to handle production. The DMX was a full-front forward-control design.

DOANE/*USA 1916-1946*

The speciality of the Doane Motor Truck Co, San Francisco, California was a low-loading rigid truck for dock and warehouse work. Rated at 6-tons capacity, the first was powered by a 36hp 4-cyl Waukesha petrol engine with chain-drive to a cranked rear axle. The low-loading height was also assisted by locating both front and rear axles above rather than below the semi-elliptic leaf springs, thus providing little ground clearance. In 1918 a new 29bhp Waukesha-engined 2½-tonner was introduced. In 1920 it was joined by a 3-tonner, and in 1924 by a 10¾-ton capacity rigid 6-wheeler. This had chain-drive to the leading rear axle, 7-forward and 3-reverse speeds and a maximum speed of 40km/h. By 1928 some models had 6-cyl Waukesha petrol engines and for 1933, 'Lo-Bed' and 'Hi-Bed' models were listed along with a 10-ton 6-wheeled dump truck chassis. By the late 1930s, models comprised 4/6, 6/9, and 10/12-tonners, all with 6-cyl engines, 4-speed transmissions, and "conventional" Chevrolet cabs. In 1946 the company was re-named the Graham-Doane Truck Co, production was transferred to nearby Oakland, and vehicles were sold as Graham-Doane.

DOBLE/*USA 1918-1930*

Well-known for its steam-powered passenger cars, Doble Laboratories, San Francisco, California, built a 2-ton steam lorry with a paraffin-fired boiler and 2-cyl engine with bore and stroke of 12.5 and 10cm respectively. Using a wheelbase of 360cm, the vehicle ran on pneumatic tyres and was normally supplied with an open body. Few were built from 1919 to 1921, being listed only as 1-tonners. By 1930 the company had moved to Emeryville, where it was known as the Doble Steam Motors Corp. Further experiments with steam-powered commercials took place about this time and Doble principles were used in the Sentinel-Doble lorry.

D'OLT/*USA 1920-1923*

The 1½-ton capacity D'Olt was introduced by the D'Olt Motor Truck Co Inc, Long Island, New York. It was joined briefly by a 2½-tonner in 1923.

DOMINION/*USA 1915-1917*

The Dominion was an articulated truck with a wheelbase of 225cm and a 4-cyl 'T'-head petrol engine located under the double bench seat. It was built by the Dominion Motor Truck Co, Detroit, Michigan using a worm-drive rear axle and 3-speed transmission.

DODGE (1)/*England 1933 to date*

While USA-designed Dodge Brothers and Dodge trucks had been assembled in Britain since 1927, it was some years before Dodge Bros (Britain) Ltd began building models of basically British content at its Kew, Surrey, factory. Only engines and gearboxes were made in the USA but to avoid confusion with USA-built Dodges they were often sold abroad as Kew-Dodge or Kew-Fargo.

Initially, only 1½- and 2-ton bonneted trucks, plus a 20-seat passenger model, were catalogued, all using a 3.3-litre 6-cyl side-valve petrol engine, 4-speed transmission, hydraulic brakes and spiral-bevel final-drive. By 1936 engine capacity had increased to 3.6 litres and forward-control models were also offered, one of the most popular being a short-wheelbase 4-tonner for tipper applications. In 1937 British Dodge design was revised, top of the range being the 4-ton snub-nosed 'Major' with 4-litre petrol engine, 5-speed transmission and a handbrake acting on all four wheels. The Perkins P6 diesel became a regular option the following year and by 1940 some models had hypoid rear axles.

1964 Dodge (1) single-deck coach

After World War II, new 2/3-, 5- and 6-tonners were based on pre-war designs, a re-styling in 1949 introducing a cab similar to that fitted on the bonneted Leyland 'Comet'. Hydrovac brakes were now standard on all heavy models. The next few years saw few radical changes, although new models included an export-only passenger chassis and a 6/7-ton forward-control pantechnicon chassis, the largest diesel engine now being a Perkins R6. After 1957 the smallest British-built Dodge was a 3-tonner and a wider range of 4- and 6-cyl diesel engine options included AEC and Leyland units. Normal-control models now had the Commer 'Superpoise' cab while forward-control types were fitted with a Motor

Panels structure also used by Leyland Motors Ltd.

By 1961 the bonneted range included models for up to 7 tons payload, while forward-control types ranged from 5- to 9-ton capacity, the latter having a 6.2-litre 100bhp diesel engine, 5-speed transmission, 2-speed spiral-bevel axle and air-hydraulic brakes. A single-deck passenger model was now available to UK operators but few were supplied, and in 1963 single- and double-drive 6-wheeled trucks with AEC diesel engines were added to the line. Existing bonneted models were withdrawn about this time, their place being taken briefly by new 5- and 7-tonners with American cabs and front-ends, Perkins diesel engines and 4- or 5-speed transmissions.

Chrysler merged with Rootes in 1964, the Dodge truck range being led by the 'K'-Series tilt-cab design in 4 x 2, 6 x 2 and 6 x 4 guise, using 5-speed transmissions, 2-speed axles, power-steering and air brakes, with automatic transmission available by 1968. Both rigids and tractors were listed for up to 24 tons gross, with 6-cyl Perkins diesels in the smallest and short-lived Chrysler-Cummins V6 or V8 diesels in the largest. In 1967 the Kew plant was closed and assembly transferred to the Commer/Karrier factory at Dunstable, Beds. Three years later Chrysler United Kingdom Ltd was formed, all Dodge trucks being assembled by the Dodge Divn at Dunstable apart from the K3820P tractor, introduced in 1974 for operation at 32 tons GCW, which was produced by the Spanish Barreiros factory, another Chrysler subsidiary.

The Commer name was discontinued in 1976, all existing Commer models being re-named Dodge from the 1¼-ton 'Spacevan' up to the 7/12-ton 'Commando'. Some rationalization was now possible and the old 'K'-Series was restricted to 4-wheeled tractors and 6-wheeled rigids, the former for up to 29 tons GCW.

1940 Dodge (1) Model 84 coach

Top of the range was the Spanish-built tractor, now for 36/37 tons GCW, fitted with an 11.9-litre 6-cyl turbocharged diesel engine, air and exhaust brakes.

The long-running 'Walk-Thru' range, from 1¼ to 3 tons capacity, was replaced by the USA-style '50'-Series in 1979, the experimental battery-electric 'Silent Karrier' becoming the 'Silent Dodge'. In 1980 the 'K'-Series tilt-cab was withdrawn and Barreiros cabs fitted to all heavyweights, including a new 8-wheeled rigid model aimed at the UK tipper market. All municipal vehicles are now sold as Karrier.

1966 Dodge (1) 'K'-Series truck

DODGE (2)/*USA 1936 to date*
In 1936 the Dodge Brothers truck, built in Detroit, Michigan, by the Chrysler Motors Corp, was renamed Dodge, using passenger car front-end styling. The heavier

1967 Dodge (2) C-900 artic tractor

models had hydrovac brakes and by 1937 2-speed axles were a regular option. The first forward-control Dodge was a 1½-ton conversion, also carried out in 1937, but the first true "cabover" did not appear until 1939. By this time many Dodges were being sold abroad as De Soto or Fargo to boost sales.

In 1938 a new Detroit plant opened, and in 1939 the company's first diesel engine appeared, a 7-bearing 95bhp 6-cyl unit fitted in 2- and 3-ton models. A line of military vehicles, headed by a 1½-ton 6 x 6, was also introduced, using a 3.5-litre 92bhp engine, and when civilian production resumed, all models were

based on pre-war designs. The heaviest was now a 3-tonner powered by a 5.4-litre 128bhp petrol engine and fitted with a 5-speed transmission, double-reduction axle and hydrovac brakes, although a series of 6 x 4 rigids with optional air brakes was available by 1949.

Five-speed synchromesh transmissions were introduced on the heaviest models in 1950, and in 1951 the 4/5-ton payload 'T'-, 'V'- and 'Y'-Series were announced, fitted with air brakes and twin-carburettor 145/151bhp petrol engines.

By 1954 power-steering was optional and short-stroke overhead-valve V8 engines were on offer. Twelve-volt electrics and tubeless tyres appeared in 1955, while much re-styling took place in 1957 and 1958.

New 6 x 4s, with V8 petrol engines developing between 201 and 232bhp, were announced in 1957 and in 1960 new bonneted models, with swing-out front wings providing engine access, replaced many of the forward-control models. Smallest of these normal-control types was the 5-ton C600 with various straight-6 and V8 engine options and 5-speed manual or 6-speed automatic transmission. The heaviest types, which had full air brakes, could handle a gross weight of 24,040kg. Diesel requirements were now catered for by Cummins units developing up to 228bhp and coupled to twin-plate clutches and 8- or 10-speed transmissions.

Another innovation was the 6-cyl overhead-valve slant engine range offered in all 1-tonners and in the multi-stop P300 delivery model.

The first Dodge mobile home chassis appeared in 1962 and Perkins diesel engines became a medium-duty option the following year.

In 1964 the 225-cm wheelbase forward-control 'Handyvan' appeared, for payloads of up to 1 ton, while a new heavy was the forward-control tilt-cab 'L'-Line for gross weight ratings of 22,680 kg and more, using a V6 or V8 Cummins diesel. Special vehicles included an 8 x 4 tractor for 80 tons gross and a number of truck-mixers, including a petrol-engined 10 x 6 with 15-speed transmission.

By 1970, turbocharged Cummins diesels producing up to 335bhp, and V8 Detroit Diesels developing up to 318bhp were fitted in the larger models, which also featured air-assisted clutches and 10-, 12- or 16-speed transmissions. For 1972 the 9-ton 6 x 4 'Bighorn' was the largest "conventional" model but the heavy truck range was discontinued in 1975 so

that the company could concentrate on volume production at the bottom end of the market. Bonneted mediumweight trucks continued, however, using 5.2- or 5.9-litre V8 petrol or a 6-cyl Perkins diesel engine, 4- or 5-speed synchromesh transmissions and hydrovac brakes.

DODGE (3)/*India 1946-1972*
Established in 1944, Premier Automobiles Ltd, Bombay, built a variety of Dodge goods and passenger models for payloads of between 1 and 8 tons, using its own cabs or others by Kew-Dodge and American Dodge. Vehicles were powered by 110bhp home-built petrol engines or by 83 or 120 bhp Perkins diesels. To add to the confusion, near identical models were sold as Fargo but eventually the Premier brand name was used.

DODGE (4)/*Australia 1958 to date*
From 1939 Chrysler Australia Ltd assembled mainly USA-designed Dodge trucks in Adelaide, South Australia, introducing its own 8-model range in 1958, employing bonneted USA styling and a 114bhp 6- or 180bhp V8 petrol engine. Later that year a modified Kew-Dodge forward-control design was added for gross weights of up to 11,340kg, again using the V8 petrol engine.

A brand new bonneted range appeared in 1966, covering gross weights from 2721 to 12,246kg, later increased to 16,782kg by the addition of 6 x 4 models. The most powerful petrol engines were now 212bhp V8s but 131bhp Perkins 6- and 185bhp Cummins V8 diesels were also available. A new forward-control model, with modified Commer cab and 185bhp Cummins V8 diesel or 202bhp Chrysler V8 petrol engine was announced in 1971, while the Japanese-designed Mitsubishi 'Canter' range for gross weights of up to 6½ tons was marketed as Dodge Canter. All Australian-built Dodges were also available as De Soto.

DODGE (5)/*Turkey 1964 to date*
The first Turkish-built Dodge trucks were derivatives of the USA-designed 'D'-Series, using locally-designed angular cabs to aid maintenance.

Built initially at Kadikoy, Istanbul, by Chrysler Sanayi AS, these were also supplied under the De Soto and Fargo names, heavy types being delivered in chassis/cab form only. Engines include a 140bhp Chrysler petrol unit and a 130bhp Perkins 6.354 diesel. Since 1970 production has taken place at Cayirova Gebze.

DODGE BROTHERS/*USA 1929-1935*
Although light commercials had been built by Dodge Bros, Detroit, Michigan, since 1916 under the Dodge Brothers name, it was not until 1929 that the first mediumweight models appeared. These were previously marketed as Graham Brothers, one of the heaviest being a 2½-tonner with 7-bearing 6-cyl Dodge side-valve petrol engine, 4-speed transmission, spiral-bevel rear axle and 4-wheel hydraulic brakes. The company was now part of the Chrysler Motors Corp and by 1931 a new 4-tonner was powered by a 96bhp 6-cyl petrol engine. Four-cyl engines were used in lighter types but the 4/7½-ton G80, announced in 1933, had a 6.3-litre Chrysler straight-8 and 5-speed transmission until it was withdrawn in 1935. Also in 1933, Dodge Bros (Britain) Ltd, which had assembled Dodge Brothers trucks for the UK market since 1927, adopted its own specifications.

The USA-built range now covered various capacities up to 4 tons, and in 1935 a new 3-tonner was launched, using a 5.1-litre 6-cyl petrol engine and 5-speed transmission. At the end of 1935 the Dodge Brothers name was shortened to Dodge.

DOMINO/*Australia 1976 to date*
Domino Industries Brisbane, Queensland, manufactures two passenger models one, the 'S'-Type, with a straight frame and vertical centrally- or rear-mounted Detroit Diesel engine, the other, the 'DC'-Type, with a twin-tier frame and the same power unit initially mounted centrally under the floor. Both have considerable ground clearance, a choice between 6-speed Spicer manual and Allison automatic transmission, full air braking with a Jacobs exhaust brake, Rockwell axles and power-steering. Production 'DC'-Types are understood to have a rear-mounted engine.

DONAR/*Germany 1921-1926*
Frankforter Maschinenbau AG vorm Pokorney und Wittekind, Frankfurt-am-Main, built the 5-ton Donar using the company's own 9-litre 4-cyl petrol engine. Both goods and passenger models were available.

DONNET/*France 1925-1934*
SA des Automobiles Donnet was established in the former factory of Vinot et Deguingand, Nanterre, Seine, also acquiring this company's Neuilly plant and the Pontarlier, Doubs, factory of Soc Française des Automobiles Zédel. As well as passenger cars, the new company built commercial

types using the Donnet and Donnet-Zédel brand names. Most common was the C16 1/1¼-ton delivery van, powered by a 2.1-litre 4-cyl side-valve petrol engine. In 1934 the firm went bankrupt and the factory was acquired by Soc Industrielle de Mécanique et de Carrosserie Automobiles who built Simca commercials.

DORRIS/*USA c1906-1925*
The Dorris Motor Car Co, St Louis, Missouri, was set up as a passenger car manufacturer in 1906, introducing 2- and 3-ton trucks soon after, both using Dorris engines. Between 1916 and the end of production there were seven basic commercial models, two of which a 2½- and a 3½-tonner were introduced in 1918 and 1919 respectively. From 1922 there were also two passenger types, one with a 4-cyl and the other with a 6-cyl engine, plus a petrol-electric bus with General Electric traction equipment which appeared briefly in 1925.

DOUBLE DRIVE/*USA 1919-1930*
The Double Drive Truck Co was established in Chicago Illinois, to build Double Drive trucks up to 3½-tons capacity. Until 1922, when production moved to Benton Harbor, Michigan, Rutenber petrol engines were used, the one exception being a Hercules Model 'K' in the 3½-tonner. After this date, Buda engines and worm-drive became common until production ended. A 1½-tonner was marketed briefly as the Front Drive.

DOUGLAS (1)/*USA 1917-c1931*
Starting with the 1½-ton 'TA' Model, the Douglas Truck Mfg Co, Omaha, Nebraska, instituted truck production in 1917, and by 1920 two other models, the 1-ton 'C' and 2½-ton 'E' were also listed with 2- and 3-tonners added the following year. All had 4-cyl Buda or Weidely petrol engines but 6-cyl units were available in 2- and 3-ton designs in 1927. In 1929 the company's first 6-wheeler, a 6-tonner known as the F66, was launched. Popular as a livestock transporter, this had a double-deck body, also built by the company, and incorporated two worm-drive Wisconsin axles at the rear. Although production ceased about 1931, models were listed until 1935, the company being known by then as the Douglas Motors Corp.

DOUGLAS (2)/*England 1947 to date*
F L Douglas Equipment Ltd, Cheltenham, Glos, entered the truck-building field with a timber

Douglas (2) 'Prospector' 4 x 4 oilwell servicing unit c1964

tractor employing AEC 'Matador' running units and chassis, shortened for forestry work. This had 4-wheel drive, AEC cab, power winch, land anchors, and folding jib. A wide range of cross-country vehicles was introduced, the smallest being the 'Pathfinder' pick-up with 6-cyl Commer petrol or Perkins diesel engine and full independent suspension. Oilfield trucks, fire appliances, snow ploughs and 4- and 6-wheeled 'Automaster' dump trucks were also built. In 1952 the 'Tugmaster' aircraft towing tractor was introduced, later joined by the 'Ro-Ro' terminal tractor with one-man half-cab and various specifications. In 1959 a prototype 6 x 6 gritter/snowplough with 8-cyl Rolls-Royce petrol engine and automatic transmission were built, and a 4 x 4 forward-control chassis developed for use with rotary snowplough equipment. By 1966 many of these machines had been withdrawn, although a bonneted 4 x 4 5-tonner using Commer components was still listed. The 'Tugmaster' towing tractor was developed further and is now the mainstay of the Douglas range, along with its 'Ro-Ro' terminal tractor derivative.

DOUGLAS-ACM/*England 1946-1952*
Following earlier attempts at producing a successful petrol-engined milk float, Douglas (Kingswood) Ltd, Kingswood, Bristol, launched the battery-electric Douglas-ACM using designs drawn up by electric vehicle manufacturer AE Morrison & Sons. Heaviest of the early models was a 1/1¼-ton design with two motors located inside the rear axles. One-

and-a-half and 2-tonners were announced at the end of the 1940s but never built and battery-electric production ceased in 1952.

DRAKE/*USA 1921-1922*
The first Drake truck was powered by a 6-cyl Herschell-Spillman petrol engine. Built by the Drake Motor & Tire Mfg Co, Knoxville, Tennessee, it was of about 2 tons capacity but was not particularly successful.

DREDNOT/*Canada 1913-1915*
Drednot Motor Trucks Ltd, Montreal, Quebec, built Drednot trucks, offering a range of models from 1- to 3-tons capacity powered by 2- and 4-cyl petrol engines.

DSO/*USA/England 1915*
Vulcan trucks built by the Driggs-Seabury Ordnance Corp, Sharon, Pennsylvania, were sold briefly in Great Britain as DSO to avoid confusion with Vulcans built by the Vulcan Motor & Engineering Co Ltd.

DUCOMMUN/*Germany 1903-1905*
Werkstatte für Maschinenbau vorm Ducommun, Mulhausen, Alsace, built a number of shaft-drive commercial vehicles in the 2½- to 6-tons capacity range. One or two were supplied as open-top double-deckers to a London-operator.

DUFOUR/*Switzerland 1897-1913*
One of the first petrol-engined trucks built in Switzerland was the Dufour, built by Dufour et Tissot, Nyon. Powered by a single-cyl engine, this was replaced in 1903 by a 16hp truck with flat-twin engine

driving the rear wheels via a leather belt, 3-speed transmission and chain final-drive. In 1905 the company was re-constituted as Soc des Camions, Automobiles et Moteurs Dufour and by 1908 another new model, with 3-cyl transverse engine behind the front axle was in production. This design continued, with improvements, until the company was re-named Etienne Ballabey et Cie and vehicles became known as Dufour-Ballabey or Ballabey.

DUFOUR-BALLABEY/*Switzerland 1913-1914*
Soc des Camions Dufour, Nyon, manufacturer of Dufour trucks, was re-named Etienne Ballabey et Cie in 1913, all subsequent models being marketed as Dufour-Ballabey or just as Ballabey. The initial model was a re-named 3-cyl Dufour which continued to be built until early 1914 when new 2½- and 3-tonners with 18/24hp 3-litre petrol engines were announced. Few were built.

DUPLEX (1)/*England 1907*
The London-based Duplex Motor Engine Co was a passenger car manufacturer who also advertised two commercial chassis. One was a 1-ton shaft-drive design powered by a 20hp 2-cyl petrol engine while the other was a 1½-ton chain-drive with 30hp 3-cyl engine.

DUPLEX (2)/*USA 1908 to date*
Established at Charlotte, Michigan to undertake series production of the Dolson Automobile Co's light 4 x 4, the Duplex Power Car Co developed a larger 4-wheel drive model of "conventional" layout and 3½-ton capacity and a 1½-ton "conventional" of 4 x 2 configuration soon after. In 1916 the company was re-named the Duplex Truck Co, moving to Lansing and by the following year 2-, 3-, and 3½-ton 4 x 4s were listed, these being known as the 'A', the 'SAC' and the 'AC', respectively, with Buda or Hercules petrol engines. By the 1920s 2-wheel drive trucks were again built using Hinkley engines and certain models became known as Duplex Four Wheel Drive and Duplex Ltd. The old internal-gear final-drive was still used and the largest models often hauled road-trains of up to five trailers before curtailed by legislation. For 1929 the Model 'EF' 3½-tonner was the only 4-wheel drive Duplex still available, but there were a number of other types in the 1½ to 7-ton category, at least one having a 7-speed transmission. By 1938 the lightest model had gone and by 1940 a 9/10-tonner was also listed. Some 6 x 4

Duplex (2) pumper fire appliance c1966

1929 Durkopp L2 single-deck bus

searchlight trucks were supplied during World War II.

Civilian production resumed after the war with "conventionals" powered by 6-cyl Hercules diesel engines with 5-speed Fuller transmissions and fully-floating Timken axles incorporating bevel-or double-reduction gearing. Four-by-four types remained in production and crane-carriers were introduced during the 1950s mainly of 6 x 4 layout, although an 8 x 4 25-tonner powered by an International petrol or Detroit Diesel engine was introduced in the late 1960s. In 1955 the firm was acquired by the Warner & Swasey Co, becoming the Duplex Divn of that organization which was already using Duplex crane-carriers for its Gradall and Hoptoe excavation equipment.

In 1975 the Duplex Divn became the Badger & Crane Divn, moving to Winona, Minnesota, where a line of specialist trucks is now built. Among these are road/rail maintenance units, tunnel maintenance trucks, 4-wheel drive airfield snowploughs with rear-wheel steering, forward-control 4 x 2 and 6 x 4 fire appliance chassis and on/off-highway dump trucks. "Conventional" cabs are also used by the Oshkosh Truck Corp and 225 to 318bhp engines are by Caterpillar or Detroit Diesel.

DURABLE DAYTON/*USA 1914-1917*
Previously marketed as the 'Dayton' by the Dayton Auto Truck Co, Dayton, Ohio, the Durable Dayton "cabover" range appeared after the company was reconstituted as the Durable Dayton Truck Co. Specifications were similar to the earlier models but were now listed in 2-, 3½- and 7½-ton capacities as Models 'U', 'A' and 'E'.

DURHAM-CHURCHILL/*England 1905-1914, 1918-1925*
Durham, Churchill & Co, Attercliffe, Sheffield, South Yorks, constructed a bonneted chain-drive 3-tonner for goods or passenger operation, marketing this as the Durham-Churchill or Churchill. Shown at the Royal Agricultural Hall Show, it was powered by a 24hp 4-cyl Aster petrol engine with friction clutch and 3-speed transmission. At Olympia in 1908 a 26-seat charabanc was shown, using a 30hp Aster 4-cyl petrol engine. By 1909 a range of chain-drive models from 1½- to 5-tons capacity was listed, with 4-cyl petrol engines of 20, 30, 35 and 45hp output. Production was discontinued at the outbreak of World War I but later a 3-ton chain-drive design with 40bhp 4-cyl petrol engine was built until 1925.

1911 Durkopp 4-ton truck

DURKOPP/*Germany 1901-1930*
Bielefelder Maschinenfabrik vorm Dürkopp & Co AG, Bielefeld, introduced a series of commercial vehicles powered by an 8hp 2-cyl petrol engine, joined in 1902 by a 15hp bus. These evolved into a wide range of commercial types, the largest being a 5-ton truck, all with cardan-driven and 4-cyl petrol engines. The company bought out Berliner Motorwagenfabrik GmbH, Tempelhof, Berlin in 1908, continuing this firm's Eryx van range, later basing these on Dürkopp passenger cars. Meanwhile, some Dürkopp buses were purchased by the London Road Car Co, and during World War I a 4-ton military truck was built, followed, after the war, by 2- and 3-tonners and later, by a low-loading passenger type. By 1927, only the L2, with 4.1-litre 4-cyl petrol engine, was offered, this having a capacity of some 2½ tons. Three years later a new low-loading passenger chassis, with a 100bhp 6-cyl petrol engine was launched but few were built.

DUTRA/*Hungary 1950-1973*
The first true Dutra commercial built by the Dutra Works, Budapest, was a half-cab dump truck of 6-ton capacity with dual controls and reversible seat based on Csepel truck components and powered by a 60bhp diesel engine. This design was sold under the Mogurt brand name in other countries from 1955. Towards the end of production, a self-loading version appeared, joined in 1968 by a 10-ton 4-wheel drive model with 125bhp Csepel diesel engine.

DUTY/*USA 1913-1922*
The Duty Motor Co, Greenville, Illinois, advertised a bonneted 2-tonner, with unusual channel frame incorporating outward-turned flanges. Powered by a 35bhp 4-cyl Gray-Bell petrol engine, it had a 3-speed covert transmission, Russel internal-gear final-drive and solid or pneumatic tyres.

DUX/*Germany c1915-1926*
Three- and 4-ton Dux trucks were introduced by Dux Automobilwerke AG early in World War I, but by 1916 the company was concentrating on lighter types. In 1926 it was taken over by Presto-Werke AG of Chemnitz, who continued the 22/80 PS Dux goods and passenger model with a 3.1-litre 4-cyl petrol engine under the Presto brand name.

DYNAMOBIL/*Germany 1904-?*
EH Geist Elektricitats AG, Zollstock, Cologne, concentrated on petrol-electric developments, constructing a number of truck and bus types employing this form of propulsion. These were sold as Dynamobil, frequently using a 24hp petrol engine and two 12hp electric motors.

DYNAMIC/*USA 1911-1912*
Four-wheel drive and 4-wheel steering were features of the Dynamic petrol-electric truck manufactured by the Cleveland Motor Truck Mfg Co, Cleveland, Ohio. Horizontal 4- or 6-cyl engines were spring-mounted, with power transmitted via a herring-bone gear and drive-shaft system, with air or mechanical brakes acting on all wheels. Early in 1912 the company began marketing a new range of commercials as Cleveland, continuing production of the Dynamic range as the Cleveland-Galion or sometimes simply as the Galion.

E

EADON/*England 1927-?*
The South Lincolnshire Engineering Co Ltd, Spalding, Lincs, developed the bonneted 2½-ton Eadon lorry. Assembled from bought-in components, this had a 3.8-litre 6-cyl petrol engine and a maximum speed of 80km/h, but only one vehicle was built, with a multi-plate clutch and 4-speed crash box.

EAGLE (1)/*USA 1920-1928*
The Eagle Motor Truck Corp, St Louis, Missouri, constructed a number of Buda-engined trucks with capacities of up to 5 tons.

Eagle (2) single-deck coach c1971

EAGLE (2)/*USA/Belgium 1956 to date*
The Transcontinental Bus System, Dallas, Texas, arranged for Karl Kassbohrer AG, West Germany, to construct a prototype high-floor intercity bus, known as the Eagle or Golden Eagle, for its own use, followed by another fifty in 1957 and 49, plus four artics, in 1958. All had MAN diesel engines. A 1960 batch, known as Silver Eagles, from the same manufacturer had an increased seating capacity, while by 1961 a European plant had been set up in St Mihiel, Belgium, as Bus & Car SA, introducing alternative designs marketed simply as the Eagle, for the European tourist trade. Belgian-built vehicles were based on Kassbohrer designs, but employed rear-mounted 8V-71 Detroit Diesels or Caterpillar units. There was also a city transit bus design, believed marketed as the Bus & Car. Most popular,

however, were the company's 6 x 2 models with nonpowered second axles and capacity for fifty passengers. Towards the end of 1974, Eagle International Inc was established in Brownsville, Texas, to continue production for the American market while European production was transferred to Mol NV, another Belgian specialist vehicle builder.

EASTERN DAIRIES/*USA 1925*
The first prototypes for a series of 2- and 2½/3-ton trucks were built by Eastern Dairies Inc, Springfield, Massachusetts in 1925. Production models, which were called Dairy Express, appeared in 1926 after the company had been taken over by the General Ice Cream Corp.

1931 Easyloader refuse collector

EASYLOADER/*England 1928-1931*
With a frame height of 60cm the solid-tyred 3/4-ton Easyloader built by Easyloader Motors Ltd, London, was aimed at the rigid low-loader market when introduced in 1928. A 2.18-litre 4-cyl petrol engine located ahead of the front axle drove the rear axle via a 3-speed transmission, providing a maximum speed of 48km/h. The Easyloader lasted a few years and the Company was wound up in 1931. In 1932 it was re-introduced as the New Easyloader by New Easyloader Motors Ltd, London.

EBRO/*Spain 1956 to date*
Motor Iberica SA, Barcelona, was set up to build bonneted British-designed Ford trucks under licence as well as special snub-nosed versions for the local market. These followed the Ford Motor Co Ltd's practice of naming its truck range after the local river and were sold as Ebro, or in Syria later, as Frat (after the River Euphrates). During the early 1960s the range was based on the Ford Thames 'Trader', with load capacities of up to 5000kg. In 1966

the company merged with engine builder Perkins and agricultural manufacturer Massey-Ferguson, introducing tilt-cab Ford 'D'-Series derived trucks for loads of between 1½ and 7 tons and gradually adding new models until the range covered 2- and 3-axle rigids and articulated types from 3 to 27 tons capacity. In 1970 Aeronautica Industrial SA, Madrid, was partially taken over and their trucks sold under the Avia Ebro name. By 1975 Motor Iberica SA had taken over the business completely, although trucks were still called Avia Ebro. Further diversification came in 1974 when Motor Iberica SA became responsible for the distribution of licence-built Jeeps under the Willys-Viasa brand name. The most recent

Ebro is the 'E'-Series, again based on the British 'D'-Series Ford, comprising some six models from 3500 to 11,200kg gross, and the 'P'-Series for gross weights of 13,000 to 27,000kg.

ECLIPSE/*USA 1911-1913*
The Eclipse Motor Truck Co, Franklin, Pennsylvania, listed four versions of the Eclipse truck, with capacities ranging from 1 to 4 tons. All were powered by a 4-cyl petrol engine with compressed air starter and double chain-drive.

ECONOM/*Germany 1950-1953*
Econom-Werk Hellmuth Butenuth, Haselhorst, Berlin, previously fitted steam engines in Ford trucks, introducing the 5-ton Econom lorry powered by a 2.3-litre 2-cyl 2-stroke MWM diesel engine in 1950. An articulated version was also listed and a 3-wheeled road-sweeper powered by a single-cyl diesel engine quickly joined it. Later models included a 6-tonner and a 9-ton articulated tractor, another design being a 6-wheeled twin-steer rigid. These were powered by 3 or 4-cyl diesels.

ECONOMIST/*England 1913-1914*
Stag & Robson Ltd, Selby, Yorks, offered both goods and passenger types under the Economist brand name, but little is known about them.

EDISON/*USA 1920-1928*
The Detroit-based Edison Electric Vehicle Co offered a variety of battery-electric commercials, usually of about 1-ton capacity. These were mainly forward-control types, marketed as Edison.

EFAG/*Switzerland 1919-1937*
A Tribelhorn AG, Alstetten, Zurich, manufacturer of Tribelhorn battery-electric trucks and buses, was re-formed as Elektrische Fahrzeuge AG in Oerlikon in 1919, its products being sold as EFAG. Concentrating upon battery-electric municipal equipment, aircraft re-fuelling tankers and heavy-duty electro-tractors, the company was re-organized again in 1937 as Neue Elektrische Fahrzeuge AG, after which the company's products were sold as NEFAG.

EHRHARDT/*Germany 1906-1922*
Heinrich Ehrhardt AG had premises at Düsseldorf and Zella-St Blasii, Thuringia, where a substantial number of Ehrhardt passenger cars were built. On the commercial side, much of production was given over to military types, although there were also rigid load-carriers for payloads of up to 6 tons.

EICHER/*Germany 1963-1967*
Gebruder Eicher Traktorenfabrik, Forstern, Upper Bavaria, expanded its agricultural range in 1963 to include road tractors, light trucks and a ubiquitous 4 x 4 on/off-highway vehicle, with 70bhp, 4-litre 4-cyl Deutz air-cooled diesel engine. The 'Express' had a Tempo cab and a payload of 15 tons, a gross weight capability of 65 tons being claimed. The 'Farm Express' was similar but with cross-country tyres, while the 'Transexpress' was a 5800-kg GVW truck. After 1967 Eicher trucks were marketed by Klockner-Humboldt-Deutz AG as Magirus-Deutz while the tractor model appears to have been discontinued.

EIGHT WHEEL/*USA 1918-1923*
The Eight Wheel Motor Vehicle Co, San Francisco, California, was founded to manufacture multi-wheel drive vehicles. Early designs included a petrol-engined tractor driving an electric generator which provided current for

electric motors mounted in the wheels of the tractor and of the road-train behind. Several passenger-carrying designs were also perfected including a 56-seat double-deck bus, as well as an 8-ton, 8-wheeled truck. The company acquired numerous patents relating to multi-wheel designs, and perfected systems to cushion the effect of drive and brake torques on tandem suspension.

EISENHAUER/USA 1945-1946, 1957
The first Eisenhauer was a prototype 5-axle "conventional" built by the Eisenhauer Manufacturing Co, Van Wert, Ohio, using Chevrolet running units and front-end. Featuring twin front steering axles, a tracking rearmost axle, and twin-engines-in-tandem layout, this 20-ton payload machine was unsuccessful. In 1957 five similar vehicles were constructed for evaluation with the US Army but no further development took place.

ELBIL/Norway 1971-1972
Constructed by Elbil A/S, Oslo, the Elbil battery-electric commercial was designed to cope with a payload of 1500kg or 18 passengers, and was powered by two 13kw motors, one driving each rear wheel. It formed part of a government-sponsored experiment into electric vehicle propulsion, the prototype going to the Oslo Electricity Board and others to the Norwegian Post Office and State Railways.

EL DORADO/USA 1925-1930
The Motor Transit Co was a bus operator based in Los Angeles, California. Dissatisfied with commercially-built buses, it began fitting 6-cyl Buda petrol engines in 4-cyl White buses, calling these El Dorados, and the company was soon constructing a variety of commercial types under this name, ranging from combined goods- and passenger-carrying types to 33-seat city transit models, all of "conventional" layout. Production ended when the company was acquired by the Pacific Electric Railway.

ELDRIDGE/USA 1913-1914
The Eldridge Mfg Co, Boston, Massachusetts, built a few petro-electric tractors using a modified front-wheel drive Couple-Gear propulsion unit.

ELECTRIC KARRIER/England 1959-?
A battery-electric version of the Karrier 'Bantam' tractor, known as the Electric Karrier, was introduced by Smith's Delivery Vehicles Ltd, Gateshead, Co Durham,

1959 Electric Karrier 'Bantam' battery-electric artic tractor

for operation at up to 9 tons GCW in conjunction with refuse collection semi-trailers on door-to-door collections. Normal internal combustion-engined 'Bantams' hauled these to the tip.

ELECTRICAR/England 1920-1939
Electricars Ltd, Birmingham, took over the manufacturing rights for the lightweight Edison Accumulator Electric battery-electric commercial in 1920, introducing 1-, 2- and 5-ton Electricar models. The 1-tonner, known as the 'W'-Type, was actually a product of the Walker Vehicle Co, Chicago, Illinois, using this company's motor and differential within the rear axle. By the mid-1920s the range included 1-, 2½-, 4- and 5-ton models, the two middleweight designs employing two motors each while the lightest and heaviest types featured the old Walker system, but this was replaced in 1928 by worm-drive in a new 1½-tonner and the bevel-gear method in 2½-, 3½- and 5-ton designs. In 1929 a single-motor worm-drive layout was adopted throughout the range, which quickly expanded to include vehicles up to a 14-ton road tractor, and a 7-ton 6-wheeler, joined later by an articulated municipal type produced in association with Scammell Lorries Ltd. In 1933 the company took over Electromobile Ltd, Otley, West Yorks, but merged two years later with Hants Electric Chassis, A E Morrison & Sons and Young Accumulators to form Associated Electric Vehicle Manufacturers, lighter models being discontinued in favour of the Morrison-Electric range of AE Morrison & Sons. In 1939 the Electricar brand name was last used, Electricar designs being incorporated in the Morrison-Electric range which, from 1941, was known as the Morrison-Electricar.

ELECTRICAR-SCAMMELL/England 1936-1939
The Electricar-Scammell was a 3-wheeled battery-electric "mechanical horse" designed by Electricars Ltd, Birmingham. The

special 302.5-cm wheelbase tractor had Scammell steering gear, automatic coupling and cab. Rated as a 6-tonner, it actually grossed over 11 tons when in service with an Eagle 'Compressmore' refuse trailer.

ELECTRIX/France 1900-c1923
For a short time battery-electric commercials are alleged to have been built by SA des Vehicules Automobiles Electrix, using the Electrix brand name. Both light- and mediumweight types were offered but production was not very high.

ELECTROBUS (1)/England 1907-1910
The London Electrobus Co Ltd ran 12 battery-electric double-deckers between Liverpool Street and Victoria. Called Electrobuses, these were constructed by the Electric Vehicle Co, West Norwood, London, using imported French chassis and 14hp Thomson Houston electric motors. Although smooth and quiet, their batteries at 1½ tons were far too heavy and in 1910 all 12 were re-sold.

ELECTROBUS (2)/Belgium 1963-1964
As an experiment, in 1963 Ateliers de Constructions Electriques de Charleroi SA, which had previously built ACEC passenger models and supplied traction equipment for use in trolley-buses, introduced the Electrobus. Only a few of these diesel-electric vehicles were built, each powered by a 150bhp Fiat engine driving an electric motor in each of the rear wheel hubs and with a Van Hool body for up to 90 passengers.

ELECTROBUS (3)/USA 1974-1975
Electrobus Inc was founded in Van Nuys, California, to construct a 20-passenger low-loading battery-electric bus, the first three going to Long Beach. Carrying a 72-volt battery at the rear, the Electrobus used a 50hp DC motor and was equipped with full air-conditioning and air-assisted hydraulic braking. Towards the end

of 1974, the business was acquired by the Otis Elevator Co, becoming the Electrobus Divn, and moving to the Otis plant at Stockton.

ELECTROJAN/England 1951-1956
In an attempt to counter customer resistance to the peculiar 2-stroke petrol engine fitted in early versions of the post-war Trojan 1-tonner, Trojan Ltd, Croydon, Surrey, introduced a battery-electric version known as the Electrojan. It was short-lived, as the introduction of a 2.4-litre Perkins P3 diesel engine eradicated animosity against the petrol unit.

ELECTROMOBILE/USA/England 1914-1933
Based on imported American chassis, mainly the Commercial Truck Co of America's battery-electric types, Electromobile Ltd, Otley, West Yorks, constructed a series of light- and mediumweight battery-electric commercials. Including models of up to 5-ton capacity, the series was especially popular with municipal customers, having a range per charge of up to 64km. Two of the lighter models had 243-cm wheelbases. The 260-cm wheelbase 1-tonner and 290-cm wheelbase 2-tonners each had two electric motors driving the rear wheels via a double-reduction epicyclic gear system. The two heavier types had an electric motor bolted to the back of each wheel with batteries slung either side of the chassis frame. Of forward-control layout, these had conventional semi-elliptic leaf spring suspension, worm-and-sector Ackermann-type steering, and contracting wood-lined brakes all round. Towards the end of the 1920s, a new 1½-ton single motor model was announced, followed in 1930 by a 2/2½-ton version. In 1933 the company was bought out by Electricars Ltd, Birmingham.

ELECTROVIA/Spain 1905-1909
SA Azarola, Madrid, introduced Electrovia trolleybuses, built under licence from Gesellschaft für Gleislose Bahnen Max Schiemann & Co, Wurzen, Saxony.

ELECTRUK/England 1949-1961
Dairy vehicle specialist T H Lewis Ltd, London, NW1, announced a 1-ton pedestrian-controlled battery-electric milk float called the 'EB' in 1949. The company's first non-pedestrian model came in 1954 when the 'Rider' EC, another 4-wheeler, was launched. Practically all Electruk production went to the Express Dairy Co Ltd, of which T H Lewis Ltd was a subsidiary.

ELEKTRIC/*Germany 1922-1924*
Previously sold as the AAA, 2-ton battery-electrics built by AG für Akkumulatoren und Automobilbau, Berlin and Driesen-Vordamm, were sold as Elektric from 1922. A series of petrol-engined commercials was listed under the Alfi brand name.

ELITE (1)/*England c1921*
About 1921 Elite Electricars Ltd listed a snub-nosed battery-electric 5-tonner.

ELITE (2)/*Germany 1930*
Elite-Werke AG was founded in 1922 to manufacture car-derived petrol-engined commercial vehicles. Most had 4-cyl engines but a later model, for capacities of 1, 2, or 3 tons had a 6-cyl petrol unit.

ELITEWAGEN/*Germany 1923-1928*
Built by Elitewagen AG, Berlin and Ronneburg, the first Elitewagen was a battery-electric 3-wheeler, joined later by a series of battery-electric and petrol-engined trucks from 1 to 5 tons capacity.

ELIZALDE/*Spain c1916-1928*
Biada, Elizalde & Cia, Barcelona, introduced the 2-ton Elizalde commercial capable of carrying 24 passengers, adding the 5-ton 30c for up to 45 passengers in 1922. This had a 55bhp petrol engine, 4-speed gearbox, 2-speed axle and, like all heavy Elizalde commercials, a fully-floating rear axle. Vehicle production came to an end when the company, as Fabrica Espanola de Automoviles A Elizalde, began to manufacture aircraft engines.

ELK/*USA 1912-1914*
The Elk Motor Trucks Co, Charleston, West Virginia, built forward-control 2-, 3- and 5-tonners, each powered by a 4-cyl petrol engine.

ELKHART/*USA 1929-1931*
With capacities of between 2½ and 4 tons, Elkhart trucks were built by the Elkhart Motor Truck Co, Elkhart, Indiana. They were previously sold as Valley or Valley Dispatch.

ELLIOTT & GAROOD/*England 1890*
Built at Beccles, Suffolk, the Elliott & Garood steam wagon could be easily dismantled so that the engine and boiler could be used for powering a saw bench or other equipment.

ELWELL-PARKER/*USA 1906-1908, 1920*
With capacities ranging from 5 to 7½ tons, Elwell-Parker battery-electric trucks were built by the Elwell-Parker Electric Co, Cleveland, Ohio. Transmission was via double roller chains and it is recorded that the marque was revived briefly in 1920.

EMA/*Czechoslovakia 1971 to date*
Based on the Barkas B1000 1-tonner, a battery-electric van was developed called the EMA by Výzkumný Ustav Elektrických Stroju Točivých, Brno. Small-scale production followed, power coming from batteries carried under the chassis with front-wheel drive via a 2-speed clutchless gearbox.

ENFIELD (1)/*England 1907-1908*
A 3-ton forward-control chain-drive truck, powered by a 25hp 4-cyl 'T'-head petrol engine and called an Enfield was built by Royal Enfield a subsidiary of the Enfield Autocar Co Ltd, Redditch, Worcs. In 1908 the business was acquired by the Alldays & Onion's Pneumatic Engineering Co Ltd, builder of Alldays commercials, and Enfield production was transferred to Birmingham. Few other Enfields were built, however, and later commercials were known as Enfield-Allday.

ENFIELD-ALLDAY/*England 1920-1923*
Following the acquisition of the Enfield Autocar Co Ltd by the Alldays & Onions Pneumatic Engineering Co Ltd, Enfield-Allday Motors Ltd was formed in Birmingham. This company concentrated on the manufacture of passenger cars but also built one commercial type, a 2-tonner, known as the Enfield-Allday, announced in 1920. This had a 25bhp 4.4-litre 4-cyl petrol engine, 3-speed transmission and chain-drive.

ENGESA/*Brazil 1969 to date*
Specializing in the conversion of proprietary truck chassis to 4 x 4, 6 x 4 and 6 x 6 layout, Engenheiros Especializados SA, Sao Paulo, also constructs military-style, all-wheel drive vehicles using the Engesa brand name. The first was a 1½-ton payload 4-wheel drive bonneted cargo truck with locally built 140bhp Perkins diesel or 149bhp Chevrolet petrol engine. Later, a forward-control version was also listed and by the 1970s a series of twin-engined 8 x 8 amphibious trucks for payloads of up to 10 tons had joined the range.

ENGLISH/*England 1903-1907*
The English Steam Waggon Co was established at Hebden Bridge, Yorks, to construct 2/3-and 5-ton wagons, sold under the English brand name. These employed American Herschmann patents, incorporating a vertical fire-tube boiler and compound undertype engine. Final-drive was via internally toothed gear rings bolted to the rear wheel rims.

ENSER/*Germany 1963 to date*
Hanomag-Enser Fahrzeugbau, Bavaria, converts Hanomag road tractors by shortening the chassis and fitting diesel engines. Both normal- and forward-control 'Kurier' models have been developed in this way.

ENSIGN/*England 1914, 1919-1923*
In 1914 British Ensign Motors Ltd, London, announced the bonneted 3-ton Ensign or British Ensign truck. This had a 35hp 4-cyl petrol engine, 4-speed transmission and bevel- or worm-drive. A break in production during World War I came to an end in July 1919 when two new models were introduced.

ENTWISLE & GASS/*England 1902-1910*
The Bolton engineering concern of Entwisle & Gass developed an unusual "undertype" steam wagon using a vertical boiler behind the driver, a double chassis frame and all-gear drive. Few were actually built, although examples appear to have been available as late as 1910.

EPPING/*England 1955-?*
The Epping 'Auto-Shunter', based on a Fordson 'Major' tractor engine/transmission unit, was intended for operation as a railway wagon shunter for a gross load of 175 tons, or as a road-going haulage tractor. It had a 6 forward and 2 reverse gear transmission and was built by F E Weatherill Ltd.

EREWASH/*England 1936-1940*
In 1936 the first Erewash battery-electric trucks were launched, the heaviest being a 1/1¼-ton model with a wheelbase of 195cm. Built by the Erewash Electric Traction Co, Heanor Derbyshire, this had three forward speeds, a single electric motor and worm final-drive to the rear axle.

ERIE/*USA 1914-1922*
The Erie Motor Truck Mfg Co, Erie, Pennsylvania, listed a series of trucks in the 1½-, 2- 2½- and 3½-ton categories, each powered by a 4-cyl Continental petrol engine and 4-speed transmission. By 1921 only the 2½-tonner was available.

ERYX/*Germany 1907-1914*
After 1907 BMF commercials were sold under the Eryx brand name. However, they were still built by Berliner Motorwagenfabrik GmbH, Tempelhof, Berlin, until the business was acquired by Bielefelder Maschinenfabrik vorm Dürkopp & Co AG and renamed Eryx Motorenwerke, Zweigniederlassung der Dürkoppwerke AG. Unlike the BMF, the Eryx was built only in shaft-drive form and was later based on Dürkopp passenger cars.

ES/*Bulgaria c1960-?*
The Electric Truck Works Shesti Septemvri, Sofia, built ES tipping lorries from about 1960.

ESCO/*USA 1933-1937, 1945-1946*
A subsidiary of truck operator the Exhibitors Service Co, the Esco Motor Co, Pittsburgh, Pennsylvania built 2- and 3-ton bonneted trucks under the Esco brand name. These were similar to the Sterling Motor Truck Co's designs, with a 6-cyl Continental petrol engine and 5-speed transmission.

ESPANA/*Spain c1920-1927*
A light car-based delivery model known as the España and built by Fabrica Nacional de Automoviles F Batllo S en C, Barcelona, was joined about 1920 by several heavier models with capacities of up to 4 tons, each powered by a 40hp 4-cyl petrol engine.

ESSLINGEN/*Germany 1927-1939, 1948-1956*
Esslingen battery-electric goods vehicles were built by Maschinenfabrik Esslingen, Esslingen. Available in various capacities up to 2½ tons, the Esslingen was fitted with wheel steering and a 2-man cab. World War II brought production to a halt but in 1948 it was resumed with capacities of between 1½ and 5 tons, augmented by a 30-ton battery electric road tractor.

ET/*Austria 1913-1918*
The ET was a bonneted commercial chassis intended for passenger operation with the Austrian Postal Authorities. Assembled in the postal workshops at Stadlau, Vienna, from 1913, it employed components specially manufactured by other Austrian vehicle manufacturers. Power came from a 40hp 4-cyl Austro-Daimler petrol engine. These components included chassis and radiator from Laurin & Klement, front axle from Saurer, rear axle from Graf & Stift, clutch and gearbox from Austro-Fiat and other items from Fross Büssing and Puch. Production during World War I was confined to military truck versions.

ERF/*England 1932 to date*

Having broken away from E Foden, Sons & Co Ltd following a dispute over company policy, ER Foden & Son began work on a new diesel truck at Sandbach, Cheshire in 1932. The first ERF used the best bought-in components and, although weighing under 4 tons unladen, was the first British diesel lorry of this weight to carry a 7½-ton payload. Called the CI4, it was a four-wheeler with Gardner 4LW diesel engine, David Brown 4-speed box, Kirkstall axles and Jennings cab. In 1934 the first 5-cyl model, the CI5, appeared, for drawbar operation, plus the first rigid 6- and 8-wheelers, both powered by Gardner's 6LW diesel engine. These were known, respectively, as the CI6-6 and CI6-8, later offered in single and double-drive form. There was also the lightweight 'OE' range, which had a Gardner 3LW engine and a chassis weight of under 2 tons.

Production space was severely limited but E Foden, Sons & Co Ltd were happy to sell their Sun Works to the Breakaway operation which was then known as E R Foden Ltd. By 1937 the world's first 'Chinese six' twin-steer, 6-wheeled lorry had been built, and unlike many other British manufacturers, the company was sanctioned to build some 400 diesel vehicles a year, even during World War II. To maintain production, 7.7-litre AEC diesel engines began to appear in ERF chassis and quantities of CI4 and CI5 models were supplied to the War Office for use with the Royal Army Service Corps.

In 1948, a continuous-flow Lockheed braking system and new 'Streamline' front scuttle with curved dummy grille was intro-

ERF C16-6 brewer's dray c1937

duced, many vehicles having complete Jennings cabs fitted before leaving the factory. Some ERF-supplied cabs even incorporated pressings such as front wings common to the Morris-Commercial Series III forward-control range. By 1954 full hydraulic air-assisted braking was offered and in 1956 the wrap-around 2-piece screen 'KV' cab was launched following brief production of an intermediate type based on the 'Streamline' design, but again with the oval grille. A semi-bonneted version for applications where a 3-man crew was required was also made avalable, and, within two years, both Rolls-Royce and Cummins diesels were offered in certain models and power-steering introduced with dual headlamps fitted on most models for 1960.

In 1961 the 'LV' cab was developed, the majority being built by Jennings which was later absorbed into ERF to improve manufacturing facilities. Announced at the 1962 Commercial Motor Show, this was followed two years later by the company's first 32-ton GCW tractor which was also the first British commercial to have spring braking and a Fuller 'Roadranger' transmission. A heavy 6 x 6 bonneted tractor with 212bhp Cummins diesel engine was also

developed at this time for operation under desert conditions at 50 tons GCW. Fire appliances were added to the range in 1967, powered by Rolls-Royce, or Perkins engines with cabs and bodies again by Jennings. The first was a 235bhp Rolls-Royce petrol-engined outfit with 'Snorkel' hydraulic lifting boom. There was also a short-lived and totally unsuccessful attempt to infiltrate the mediumweight goods vehicle market by fitting a low-line fire appliance cab on a load-carrying chassis. For a while, manufacture of this type of equipment was undertaken at a separate factory but in 1977 the company halted fire chassis development and the former Jennings plant took over production of fire-fighting bodies as Cheshire Fire Engineering Ltd.

1952 ERF 6.8 8 x 4 tanker

The 1970 Commercial Motor Show saw the debut of the 'A'-Series. This saw a complete rationalization of chassis design incorporating numerous mechanical changes although the 'LV' cab continued in re-styled form. In 1973 the company constructed a new tractor model using every possible Continental feature while taking into account all legislation concerning the international operation of articulated vehicles at up to 42 tons GCW. Shown for the

1967 ERF pump water tender

first time at that year's Brussels Show, this used the then-current Motor Panels sleeper cab, and in turn led to the announcement of the famous 'B'-Series range in 1974. Chassis were similar to the earlier 'A'-Series but the cab was totally new, being the first tiltcab offered by the company. Known as the 'SP' cab, this was the first British-designed and -built truck cab to meet standards laid down by the European Economic Commission. Listed initially only as a rigid 8-wheeler, 'B'-Series tractors did not enter production until 1975. A sleeper version of the 'SP' cab made its debut in 1977 replacing the earlier Continental design.

The 1978 Birmingham Motor Show marked the first public showing of ERF's 'M'-Series, lowloading 16-ton, 4- and 26-ton 6-wheelers. The 'SP' cab is mounted lower than the 'B'-Series range to provide easier, and therefore faster, access for multi-stop delivery work. Similarly, low-profile tyres enable the body to be kept as low as possible to promote rapid loading and unloading.

1975 ERF 'B'-Series 8 x 4 truck

EUCLID/*USA 1934-1968, c1977 to date*

The first Euclid dump truck was the 10/11-ton 'Trak-Truck', a 4 x 2 petrol-engined bonneted machine, built by the Euclid Crane Hoist Co, Euclid, Ohio. In 1936 the company was re-organized as the Euclid Road Machinery Co and a new model, the 15-ton 1FB, was announced. Gradually, other types of earthmoving plants were introduced but it was the dump truck that was to become the company's most famous product. In 1950 the 15-tonner was first assembled in Britain by Euclid (Great Britain) Ltd, and one year later a 3-axle machine, the 45-ton 1LLD, was introduced, powered by two 300bhp Cummins diesel engines located side-by-side.

In 1953 the company was taken over by the General Motors Corp,

who set up the Euclid Division in Cleveland, Ohio, but was forced to re-sell in 1968 to the White Motor Corp following an anti-trust investigation. Numerous new models appeared during this period including what was then (1958) the world's largest truck, a 6-wheeled twin-engined tractor powered by two 375bhp Cummins diesels for a payload of 120 tons.

With the sale of the business to White, Euclid production was apparently discontinued for a while although vehicles continued to be built at the British plant under the Terex brand name, as this factory was still owned by General Motors. Gradually, Euclids went into production under the White Motor Corp's ownership and new assembly plants were set up in Australia, Belgium, and Canada to cope with increas-

1961 Euclid R-22 BITD 22-ton dump truck

ing overseas demand. Early in 1977 the Euclid Division was sold to Daimler-Benz AG and renamed Euclid Inc. By this time the business was concentrating entirely upon the manufacture of heavy dump trucks, comprising the 4-wheeled 'R'-Series for loads of 22 to 170 tons, 'B'-Series artic bottom dumps for up to 110 tons, and the 'CH'-Series artic for up to 150 tons.

EVO/*USA 1968 to date*

Specialists in the design and manufacture of refuse-handling equipment since 1953, Lodal Inc, Kingsford, Michigan, announced its EVO refuse truck as part of a complete refuse collection system. A forward-control front-wheel drive house-to-house collection vehicle with demountable skip body and both left- and right-hand drive, it is called the EVO 1650, having a Chrysler V8 petrol engine and Allison automatic transmission.

EXSHAW/*France 1913-1929*

Previously marketed as the Purrey, the Exshaw steam wagon appeared when Purrey et Exshaw, Bordeaux, was renamed H Exshaw et Cie. Production gradually declined despite a brief attempt at revival.

FABCO/*USA 1938-1939, 1957 to date*
In 1938 and 1939 the Californian Fire Dept took delivery of a few Fabco appliances built by the FAB Mfg Co, Oakland. After the war this company concentrated on the conversion of standard truck chassis to all-wheel drive but in 1957, as the Fabco Mfg Co, it resumed production of complete vehicles. The 'FT'-Series is a flat-bodied 4 x 2 or 6 x 4 design with 1-man half-cab and Ford V8 petrol engine under the floor. It has automatic transmission and often carries a hydraulic self-loading crane for loading pipes, transmission poles or lengths of steel. Similar is the 'WT'-Series with Ford petrol or Detroit Diesel engine located alongside the 1-man half-cab. This is aimed at agricultural

1972 Fabco UV 64 6 x 4 truck chassis-cab

users, having 6-wheel drive and a wide track. The transmission system comprises a 5-speed Clark main box, 3-speed Spicer auxiliary, and 2-speed Fabco transfer case providing thirty forward and six reverse speeds. As the Fabco Division of the Kelsey-Hayes Co, the firm launched its 4 x 2, 4 x 4, 6 x 4 and 6 x 6 'UV'-Series in 1972. This is a full "cabover" model with tiltcab and Ford petrol, Caterpillar or Detroit Diesel engines.

Models are available with gross weights of up to 25,400kg. In addition, the company also offers a terminal tractor, the 'Fab' 151.

FACCIOLI/*Italy 1905*
Soc Ing Aristide Faccioli was founded in Turin by the former Chief Engineer of Fiat who wished to build his own commercials. Among the few that were built was a chain-drive single-deck bus shown at that year's Italian Motor Show.

FACTO/*USA 1920-1926*
A 4-cyl Buda petrol-engined 2½-tonner appears to have been the sole offering of Facto Motor Trucks Inc, Springfield, Massachusetts.

FADA/*Spain 1955-1958*
Catering for the Spanish 3-wheeler market, Fada, Vallodolid, introduced the 1500kg capacity Fada, which used a tubular steel frame, 5-speed transmission and shaft-drive to the rear axle. It was powered by a 20bhp 673cc single-cyl petrol engine.

FAFNIR/*Germany 1922-1926*
Fafnirwerke AG, Aachen, constructed 1- and 1½-ton trucks with 2.5-litre petrol engines.

FAGEOL/*USA 1916-1938*
Founded by F R Fageol, W B Fageol and L H Bill, the Fageol Motors Co was found at Oakland, California, in order to build passenger cars and agricultural tractors. In 1916 these were replaced by bonneted trucks with capacities of 2½, 3½, and 5 tons, with 4-cyl Waukesha petrol engines. A characteristic peculiar to these and many subsequent Fageols was a row of ventilation louvres along the bonnet top. The first 'Safety Coach' appeared in 1921, this having a 4-cyl Hall-Scott petrol engine, 22-seat body and low centre

'Safety Coach' production was transferred to the former Kent, Ohio, factory of the Thomart Motor Co. Later that year the company was acquired by the American Car & Foundry Co, the Fageol brothers became vice-presidents of ACF, and in 1926 bus production was moved to Detroit, Michigan. Trucks were still built at Oakland under the Fageol brand name, features now including aluminium cabs, electric lighting and starting, full-pressure lubrication and 4-wheel hydraulic brakes. A 10-ton 6-wheeler was also announced, but 1932 saw the business in receivership. It was re-organized as the Fageol Truck & Coach Co, but financial problems continued and in 1938 all assets were acquired by the Sterling Motors Corp, Milwaukee, Wisconsin, who suspended Fageol production by the end of that year and sold manufacturing rights to T A Peterman, who developed the Peterbilt truck range. Although the Fageol name had come to an end, it was revived in the 1950s by the Twin Coach Co, Kent, Ohio, which the Fageol brothers had founded in 1927. These later Fageols were marketed as Fageol Pony Express and Fageol Super Freighter.

FAGEOL PONY EXPRESS/
USA 1954
The Fageol Pony Express was a short-lived multi-stop delivery vehicle manufactured by the Twin Coach Co, Kent, Ohio, who also built the Fageol Super Freighter.

FAGEOL SUPER FREIGHTER/
USA 1950-1954
Using old stainless-steel bodied Fruehauf van semi-trailers, the Twin Coach Co, Kent, Ohio, introduced the Fageol Super Freighter removal van. Initially, a 6-cyl petrol or lpg engine was fitted and the driving compartment located in the bowed front of each trailer. By 1951 these vehicles were scratch-built, using new Fruehauf semi-trailer components and International Harvester engines and mechanical units. Of integral construction, the range was available in eight wheelbase lengths from 270 to 555cm, with both 4- and 6-wheeled versions offered.

FAIRBANKS-MORSE/*USA 1908-?*
Better known for its agricultural tractors, Fairbanks, Morse & Co, Chicago, Illinois launched a 1587kg capacity delivery vehicle and a forward-control 3-ton truck in 1908. Few were built, the 3-tonner having a 25hp 4-cyl Sheffield petrol engine, 4-speed constant-mesh transmission and double chain-drive.

FAMO/*Germany 1937-c1957*
Heavy-duty military half-tracks were constructed by Fahrzeug und Motorenwerke GmbH vorm Maschinenbau Linke-Hoffmann, Krefeld, using a 9.8-litre Maybach engine and later, a 250bhp 10.8-litre Maybach. Production continued throughout World War II and with a return to peace the company was re-named Famo Vertriebsgesellschaft GmbH, introducing a 45bhp diesel tractor and, later, a heavier road tractor powered by a 125bhp 2-stroke Junkers diesel engine.

FAMOUS/*USA 1923*
Although Famous Trucks Inc was originally registered in Chicago, Illinois, no vehicles were built until the business moved to St Joseph, Michigan. Only a 1-tonner appears to have been listed, having a 4-cyl Continental petrol engine, 3-speed transmission and shaft-drive.

FAP 4 x 4 riot control vehicle c1975

FAP/*Yugoslavia 1951 to date*
Mediumweight Austrian Saurer trucks were built under licence by Fabrika Automobilova Priboj, Priboj na Limu, under the FAP brand name. These developed into a line of trucks and buses powered by Leyland or Perkins diesel engines, with normal-control Saurer-type cabs and forward-control cabs common to the Italian OM. All passenger models were front-engined and a series of trolleybuses was added in the mid-1960s. Chassisless passenger models were sold as FAP Sanos and by the end of the 1960s FAP trucks comprised both normal- and forward-control models, some with 4-wheel drive, for payloads of between 6½ and 13½ tons. In 1972 the licence-building agreement with Oesterreichische Saurer Werke AG was replaced by an agreement with Daimler-Benz AG, which led to the use of both forward- and normal-control Mercedes-Benz truck cabs and the licence-building of certain Mercedes-Benz passenger models.

FAP SANOS/*Yugoslavia c1965 to date*
During the mid-1960s Fabrika Automobilova Priboj collaborated with 11 Octomvri Autokaro-

serija to design and construct FAP Sanos chassisless passenger vehicles, sometimes known simply as Sanos. These are mainly rear-engined, powered by Famos diesels of up to 210bhp output, comprising an articulated city bus for up to 160 passengers, various types of coaches and a 12m city bus.

1965 FAR 6-ton artic tractor

FAR/*France 1919 to date*
Road tractors, based on Chenard-Walcker designs with Legache & Glaszman semi-trailers, were marketed as FAR by SA des Trains Chenard-Walcker-FAR, Gennevilliers, Seine. From 1937, as Tracteurs FAR, the company licence-produced the 6-ton Scammell "mechanical horse" and its successors – the 'Scarab' and the 'Townsman' – using Chenard Walcker or Citroën petrol and diesel engines. After World War II, a smaller 3-wheeled tractor with air-cooled flat-twin Dyna-Panhard petrol engine was introduced for loads of up to 2¾ tons and often used as a basis for street sprinklers and sweepers. This was listed until 1970, by which time it was joined by a bonneted 4-wheeled version called the 'S'-Type. Later, a forward-control design with Berliet cab and 60bhp 4-cyl Perkins diesel engine was introduced for loads of up to 6 tons.

FARGO (1)/*USA ?-1921*
The heaviest commercials built by the Fargo Motor Car Co, Chicago, Illinois, were 2-tonners on 360cm wheelbase chassis using 4-cyl Continental petrol engines. Other models were for capacities of less than 1 ton.

FARGO (2)/*USA 1928 to date*
The Fargo Motor Corp was established in Detroit, Michigan, in 1928 as the fleet sales operation for the Chrysler Motors Corp, the

Fargo name being applied to certain USA-built Dodge commercials after 1931 to provide increased sales outlets other than established Dodge dealers. Despite this, some Fargos were completely different models, such as the 1-ton 'Freighter' listed from 1928. From 1935 the name was carried by various trucks sold in Canada, while the British-built Dodge was sold as Fargo or Kew-Fargo in certain countries, as were Australian, Indian and Turkish-built Dodges. Canadian Fargos were discontinued in 1972 but the marque still prevails in Scandinavia, Africa and the Middle East.

FARM-O-ROAD/*USA 1951-1952*
With rapidly falling sales of its passenger cars, delivery vans and utility models, Crosley Motors Inc, Marion, Indiana, announced the multi-purpose 'Farm-O-Road'. With 6 forward and 2 reverse speeds, this was a road-going machine for the agricultural industry, which was able to undertake numerous tasks and retailing at US$800. Like the Crosley, it was unsuccessful.

FARRIMOND/*England 1931*
The Farrimond Diesel Motor Co Ltd, Thornton Heath, Surrey, developed a diesel road tractor using a single-cyl horizontal 2-stroke engine capable of running on petrol, diesel or a 50/50 mixture of both. Capable of handling a gross weight of 15 tons, the Farrimond had an unusual starting system effected by removing the steering wheel and applying it to the flywheel hub.

FAUN/*Germany 1918 to date*
A merger between Fahrzeugfabrik Ansbach and Nürnberger

Feuerloschgerate Automobillastwagen und Fahrzeugfabrik Karl Schmidt, builders of Ansbach and Braun commercials, respectively, led to the founding of Farzeugfabriken Ansbach und Nürnberg and the introduction of the Faun brand name. Various trucks from 2 to 5 tons capacity, with petrol or battery-electric propulsion, and a petrol-electric bus were announced in and in 1920 the company was re-organized as Faun-Werke AG Karl Schmidt, continuing the Faun range until 1926 when Fahrzeugfabrik Ansbach withdrew to market Faun-designed vehicles under the old Ansbach name, the Faun marque continuing with a series of petrol-electric goods and passenger types.

In 1930 the two firms were united once more, concentrating on municipal types, some with petrol-electric transmissions and all powered by 55bhp 6-cyl Rasmussens or a 100bhp 6-cyl Maybach engine. There was also a 90bhp Maybach-engined passenger model, a number of prototype trolleybuses with motors mounted in the wheel hubs and a diesel-electric refuse collector. New goods models, ranging from a 4-cyl petrol-engined 2-tonner to a 9-ton model with 8-cyl diesel engine were announced in the 1930s, joined by a 6-wheeler in 1934, and an 8-wheeler four years later, this being the first rigid 8-wheeler to be built in Germany.

After World War II the company introduced the M6, again for refuse collection work, powered by a 6-cyl Maybach petrol engine, and built in a new factory at Neunkirchen. This was joined by a forward-control 7-tonner called the L7. By 1956 a 2/2¾-ton forward-control truck was announced but by 1969, normal goods models had been discontinued. The company was now concentrating on

1962 Faun F284D/370 integral van

special vehicles such as crane-carriers up to 16 x 8 configuration, airfield fire crash tenders, heavy dump trucks and special on- and off-road heavy tractors. The largest crane-carriers now have engines of up to 530bhp while the largest crash tender is an 8 x 8 machine powered by two 500bhp diesel units. Heavy tractors include single-axle artic units for hauling steel slag or molten steel and drawbar or articulated types up to 8 x 8 configuration with maximum engine outputs of 730bhp. Another plant at Butzbach concentrates on heavy dump trucks for payloads of up to 80 tons. There was also a brief marketing agreement with Fodens Ltd of Britain in 1974, when certain Faun dump trucks were offered through Foden distributors as Foden-Faun. Municipal vehicles, municipal equipment mounted on other chassis and military trucks of 4 x 4, 6 x 6 and 8 x 8 configuration are built at the former Borgward plant at Osterholz-Scharmbeck.

1978 Faun LF16.30/42 4 x 4 airfield fire crash tender

1977 Faun HZ40.45/45 W 6 x 6 drawbar tractor

FAWCETT-FOWLER/England 1907

Only two Fawcett-Fowlers were built, comprising one light goods and one passenger model. Both had a liquid-fired flash boiler at the rear and a 4-cyl single-acting horizontally-opposed engine at the front. Built by Fawcett, Preston & Co Ltd, Liverpool, this 20/25hp machine employed shaft-drive from engine to countershaft with double chain-drive to the rear wheels.

FBW/Switzerland 1918 to date

The bankrupt firm of Motorenfabrik Wetzikon AG was acquired by Franz Brozincevic, designer and manufacturer of the Franz shaft-drive lorry, in 1916 and renamed Franz Brozincevic et Cie Motorwagenfabrik FBW, the brand name FBW being derived from the inventor's initials and the name of the town, Wetzikon, in which the factory stood. Production of goods and passenger models eventually got underway after World War I, with a shaft-driven range built to the special requirements of each customer.

By 1922 the company was manufacturing 4-cyl overhead-valve petrol engines, introducing a 3-tonner powered by a 35bhp 5.3-litre unit and a 5-tonner with 2-speed rear axle. Henschel und Sohn GmbH, Kassel, Germany, was granted a licence to build and sell FBW vehicles abroad in 1924, leading to the establishment of the Henschel range. FBWs of the period now had 4-cyl petrol engines of between 20- and 60bhp output with 4-wheel brakes and a tight turning circle. All were of bonneted layout. Numerous FBWs went to the Swiss Army and in 1928 the company began building standard Swiss Post Office 17- and 25-seat post buses, introducing a low-loading passenger chassis, and 6-cyl engined double-drive 6-wheeled buses and lorries in 1929. These had double-drive, with two extra-long semi-elliptic leaf springs cushioning both rear axles and mechanical brakes acting on all six wheels.

The company was re-formed in 1930 as Franz Brozincevic et Cie Automobiles Industrielles FBW, with staff and production drastically reduced because of the Depression. Trolleybuses were built by the early 1930s and in 1934 the company's first 6-cyl diesel engine was built. During the war, vehicles were built for the Swiss Army and an engine developed for running on substitute fuels. Trolleybus development continued, and in 1949 the first Swiss-built horizontal diesel engine was constructed. This was an overhead-valve unit of 11-litre capacity with an

1963 FBW 1½-deck coach

output of 145bhp. FBW goods models were now available in bonneted and forward-control form, and by 1950 the first long-distance coach with underfloor diesel engine and semi-automatic transmission was shown at Geneva. Another new model was a 4-wheel drive truck aimed at both civilian and military customers.

At the 1959 Geneva Motor Show was a low-loading trolleybus with double-reduction axle, Ramseier & Jenzer body and Ateliers de Sécheron traction equipment. It was the largest bus on show – a Type 100 with 160bhp horizontal diesel engine, auxiliary rubber suspension, electro-pneumatically operated transmission, servo steering and an air starter. By 1960, the lightest goods models were the L40 and L50, with payloads of between 5 and 8 tons. Passenger models included the L70U, CA40U and B51U, all with 11-litre 6-cyl horizontal underfloor diesel engines.

To increase the appeal of the FBW range, new models were introduced. The lightest was the L35U, a forward-control lorry with 7-litre 6-cyl overhead-valve horizontal underfloor diesel engine. Other features included a hydraulic single dry-plate clutch and a choice between a 4- or 5-speed transmission. The slightly larger L40UA was able to carry some 7.1 tons, having a turbo supercharged version of the same engine; for 8.5 tons payload there was the L45UA. The L7OU3 had a payload of between 8 and 10 tons and was fitted with 6-speed main box and electro-pneumatically controlled auxiliary. Another new model was an articulated single-deck bus called the 91UA52/64L, powered by a 260bhp supercharged underfloor diesel engine with pre-select automatic transmission and air suspension.

1911 FBW 5-ton boxvan

The 1970s saw the 320bhp E6A diesel engine introduced, and in 1975 a new diesel with low pollution characteristics, particularly suited to town use, entered service with various Swiss transport authorities. Goods vehicle sales began to decline at this time, so a completely new range of diesel and trolleybus chassis was developed, incorporating interchangeable components whilst enabling vehicles to be constructed to virtually any requirement. Changes in Swiss traffic regulations permitting the use of larger rigid goods models led to the development of the 75U 6 x 2 and 85V 8 x 4 for 26 and 30 tons gross, respectively. Other new types include a bonneted 6 x 6 for tipper applications called the 80X. To cater for the lighter vehicle market, the company markets the Japanese Mitsubishi 'Canter' 2-tonner and Mitsubishi Fuso 6½-tonner under the MMC-FBW brand name.

FCS/USA 1909-1910

The Schmidt Bros Co, South Chicago, Illinois, constructed a 1-ton truck called the FCS, possibly marketed as the Schmidt towards the end of its life. It had a 2-cyl air-cooled petrol engine located under the body connected by a planetary transmission and double chain-drive to the rear wheels.

FEDERAL/USA 1910-1959

The Federal commercial range was developed from a prototype of the Bailey Motor Truck Co, soon embracing bonneted chain-drives with capacities of 1- and 2-

tons, each powered by a 4-cyl Continental petrol engine with 3-speed selective transmission. By 1913 the Federal Motor Truck Co, Detroit, Michigan, had built its thousandth truck, and 1916 saw chain-drive replaced by Timken worm-drive. A 5-tonner was announced in 1917, followed by a 7-tonner in 1918, by which time both light and heavy artic tractors were also available. Some models were sold in Britain as Whiting.

By the early 1920s, some seven models were offered, and by 1923 18- and 25-seat passenger vehicles with all-steel bodies and 6-cyl petrol engines were also listed. Apart from the Federal-Knight, all vehicles had Continental engines until 1927, when the Waukesha-engined 'Scout' 4-cyl model made its debut. Models from 1- to 7½-tons capacity with a choice between bevel- and worm-drive were now available, and by 1929 the company was offering sleeper cabs on its largest tractors and all models had brakes on their front wheels.

In 1930, 50bhp 4- and 72bhp 6-cyl petrol engines were offered in the company's 4- and 6-wheelers for 1/8-ton capacity, and in 1931 a bevel-gear tandem-axle drive system was announced for both 4- and 6-cyl 3-tonners. Considerable re-styling took place in 1935 when Continental, Hercules, or Waukesha 4- and 6-cyl petrol engines were offered. Streamlining took place in 1935, 1½- to 4-tonners having bevel-drive, and 4- to 6-tonners double-reduction gearing with optional worm-drive on the largest model. In 1937 numerous "cabovers", from 1½ to 3 tons capacity, were introduced.

More styling changes came

1938 Federal Model 75 bottle float

1950 Federal 'Style Liner' artic tractor

about in 1938 with increased use of chromium-plating, and during World War II the company received four citations for its military production figures, models including a 7½-ton 6 x 6 wrecker with 180bhp 6-cyl Hercules engine, front-mounted Cleveland Pneumatic air suspension, and a 20-ton 6 x 4 tractor powered by a 130bhp 6-cyl Cummins 2-stroke diesel. Post-war production continued much as before until 1951, when the bonneted "Styleliner" with 145bhp Federal engine was announced. This also had hypoid-gear single-speed or double-reduction drive axles. First in this range was the 1800 for 1133kg GVW and 20,410kg GCW. Ten smaller models were also introduced plus a good selection of other vehicle types with petrol or diesel engines.

Among special vehicles built at this time was an aircraft-towing tractor with high-mounted cab assembled from two GMC cabs welded back to back. Another, which appeared in 1954, was the 'Octo-Quad', an unusual "cabover" built as a special project for the Timken-Detroit Axle Co and using tandem Timken axles at front and rear, with a cab formed

from the front of a bus body.

In 1952 the company became the Federal Motor Truck Division of the Federal Fawick Corp, but this lasted only until 1955 when the business was acquired by Napco Industries Inc and production transferred to Minneapolis, Minnesota. The company was now relying upon special orders to keep going. One was for 100 4 x 4 "conventionals" with Continental and Hercules engines, Allison 'Torqmatic' transmissions and tipping bodies for the US Air Force. A new contract for the supply of military truck axles brought about the end of vehicle production, the last complete Federals being a number of passenger chassis. Numerous Mexican Bus mechanical kits have since been shipped to Argentina and the chassisless Masa Motor Coach assembled overseas from other Federal components.

FEDERAL-KNIGHT/USA 1924-1928
The Federal Motor Truck Co, Detroit, Michigan, introduced a light commercial chassis powered by a 4-cyl Willys-Knight sleeve-valve petrol engine. Called the 'Federal-Knight', this was claimed to be the only Knight-engined truck on the market at the time, remaining in production until the Willys-Overland Co announced its own Knight-engined truck.

FEG/Germany 1904-1908
Friedrich Erdmann, Gera, developed a friction-drive system for use when starting or for tackling steep grades. FEG trucks and buses had shaft-drive for normal running and were powered by 2- or 4-cyl Kopting, Fafnir or Horch petrol engines.

FEROLDI/Italy 1914
Car builder Enrico Feroldi moved to Saluzzo where he constructed a few bonneted trucks powered by a 3.3-litre 4-cyl side-valve petrol engine.

FERRARI/Italy ? to date
Officine Meccaniche Ferrari, Reggio Emilia, is in no way connected with the famous car firm of the same name. Concentrating on

the agricultural market, this company constructs general-purpose load-carriers with outputs of up to 45bhp.

FIREFLY/England 1902-1904
The Firefly was a 1¼-ton delivery van built by the Firefly Motor & Engineering Co Ltd, Croydon, Surrey. It was based on the company's largest passenger car chassis and powered by a 4.6-litre 4-cyl petrol engine.

FISCHER/USA 1901-1904
Using a 20hp 4-cyl petrol engine to charge a number of batteries which, in turn, supplied power to two 10hp electric motors mounted in the vehicle's rear wheels, the Fischer Motor Vehicle Co, Hoboken, New Jersey, built both goods and passenger types. In 1903 a double-deck bus entered trial service with the London General Omnibus Co Ltd but proved unsuitable. It was the first motor bus to be used by the LGOC. The company ceased trading in 1904, but the Fischer system was redesigned in Belgium by Henri Pieper, adopted by SA Auto-Mixte, Liège, and later developed into the Daimler Motor Co Ltd's unique KPL system.

FISHER/USA c1925-1930
The Standard Motor Truck Co, Detroit, Michigan, introduced a light "speed" truck called the Fisher Fast Freight to supplement existing Standard models. By 1928 all the company's lighter models were sold as Fisher, comprising the 1-ton Fisher Junior Express, 1½-ton Fisher Fast Freight, 2-ton Fisher Mercantile Express and 2½- to 3½-ton Fisher Heavy Duty Six, which had a 6-cyl petrol engine. From 1930 all the company's models were marketed as Fisher-Standard.

FISHER-STANDARD/USA 1930-1933
All commercial models built by the Standard Motor Truck Co, Detroit, Michigan, were marketed as Fisher-Standard from 1930. Models appear to have been largely the same as those marketed previously as Fisher, Fisher Fast Freight, Fisher Heavy Duty Six, Fisher Junior Express, Fisher Mercantile Express and Standard.

FLADER/Germay 1904-1910
E C Flader, Jöhnstadt, Saxony, was a manufacturer of fire-fighting equipment that began building its own fire appliances in 1904. These were battery-electric models until 1906 when petrol versions appeared.

FLAG/Italy 1905-1908
Fabbrica Ligure di Automobili di

Genoa, La Spezia, Genoa, licence-built Thornycroft commercials under the FLAG brand name. In 1906 both trucks and buses of the company's own design were advertised but it is doubtful whether any were actually built.

FLEET ARROW/USA 1927-c1931
The Fleet Arrow range of light trucks was manufactured by the Pierce-Arrow Motor Car Co, Buffalo, New York, using a 70bhp 6-cyl Pierce-Arrow petrol engine and based on the company's Series '80' passenger car. Enclosed cabs were supplied by the Highland Body Mfg Co, Cincinnati,

FLEXI-TRUC/USA 1970 to date
The Flexi-Truc is a one-man-cabbed terminal tractor with hydraulically lifting fifth wheel coupling constructed by the Ibex Divn of Jelco Inc and marketed by Flexi-Truc Inc, Los Angeles, California. Two models, one with a high cab, the other with a low cab, are listed.

FLEXTRUCK/Canada c1980 to date
Manufacturing rights for the Rubber Railway or RRC articulated-frame 8-wheeler were acquired by Flextruck Ltd, Breslau, Ontario, and a completely new design for use as a forward-discharge truck-mixer introduced as the Flextruck. This again has an articulated frame but the 305bhp V8 Detroit Diesel engine is now mounted longitudinally at the rear while a centrally-positioned 1-man cab containing both drive and mixer controls is located at the front.

It is of 10 x 6 layout, with the front three axles driven via a 6-speed transmission and the rearmost axle having a lifting mechanism for use when unladen.

FLINT ROAD KING/USA 1926
The 1½-ton Mason Road King, built by the Mason Motor Truck Co, Flint, Michigan, was renamed the Flint Road King in 1926. Specification was similar to that of its predecessor, including a 4-cyl Herschell-Spillman petrol engine, 3-speed transmission, double-reduction final-drive and choice of two wheelbase lengths.

FLORENTIA/Italy 1901, c1906
At the 1901 Milan Show, Fabbrica Toscana di Automobili, Florence, exhibited a 6hp Florentia charabanc with Buchet petrol engine, but there appear to be no records of other commercials built by this car manufacturer until, as Fabbrica d'Automobili Florentia, commercials are again mentioned in about 1906.

FIAT/Italy 1903 to date

Fabbrica Italiana Automobili Torino, Turin, built its first "heavy" commercial under the Fiat brand name in 1903, this being a 3½-tonner of "cabover" layout. This featured one of the longest load-carrying areas of any goods vehicle of the day and had a 6.3-litre 24hp 4-cyl 'T'-head petrol engine. The gearbox was located amidships, shaft-driven from the engine and driving the rear wheels by double roller chains. By 1906 a 5-tonner powered by a 7.4-litre 40hp 4-cyl 'T'-head petrol engine had also been developed. This engine also powered the first Fiat passenger models, with 36-seat double-deck bodies and twin water-cooled transmission brakes. By 1907, a bonneted layout had been adopted and vehicles were marketed simply as Fiat. Certain Fiat trucks were built under licence in Austria under the AF, AFA, AFN and Austro-Fiat names. The first new commercials were of 1–3-ton capacity, the lighter type using a passenger car engine and running units. The 1/1¼-tonner had a 4.4-litre 40hp 4-cyl petrol engine, multi-plate clutch, 4-speed gearbox and shaft final-drive.

The onset of World War I boosted production of load-carrying vehicles which were joined by the 5/7-ton Type 30 forward-control model. A new model used extensively during the war was the Type 20B, available as a load-carrier and artillery tractor, in both normal- and forward-control form. The load-carrier had a 3½-ton payload while the tractor could haul 40 tons. Production fell dramatically after the war due to the vast numbers of war surplus vehicles on the market, but new models continued to be built. By 1920 semi-enclosed cabs and optional self-starters were new Fiat features.

A worm-drive 2-tonner with 4-litre 4-cyl overhead-valve petrol

1914 Fiat 18B1 single-deck bus

engine and full-front cab announced in 1923 failed to sell in sufficient numbers, and was followed in 1925 by new 2/2½-ton models using 4- and 6-cyl side-valve car engines and including a 50-seat bus. Light commercials modelled on the Fiat range were now being manufactured by Automobilnoe Moskovskoe Obshchestvo as the Amo and the Mitsubishi Shipbuilding & Engineering Co Ltd as the Mitsubishi. Also in 1925, Soc Ligure Piemontese Automobili, manufacturer of SPA commercials, was acquired, enabling the company to concentrate on the development of lighter models while offering 3- to 5-ton SPA trucks for heavier use. The 3-axle Type 621, powered by a 6-cyl petrol engine, was announced in 1929, this being designed for loads of between 3½ and 4½ tons. Features included a fully-enclosed cab, wind-up windows, windscreen wipers and optional heater.

In 1931 Soc Ceirano Automobili Torino, manufacturer of Ceirano commercials, was also ac-

quired and at about the same time the 640 double-deck bus of 6 x 4 worm-drive layout was announced, having a 7-litre 6-cyl side-valve petrol engine, dual ignition, and Westinghouse servo brakes all round. In 1931 the company's first diesel lorries were announced, in the form of the 4-ton 632 and 6-ton 634. Both were bonneted with servo brakes all round, transmission handbrakes and double-reduction worm final-drive. The first diesel passenger model was the 40-seat 635, also available with a petrol engine, and trolleybuses were also built. In 1933 the company acquired yet another rival in the form of OM Fabbrica Bresciana di Automobili.

Vehicles running on producer-gas began to appear in 1934, and petrol-engined types were gradually phased out. Catering for payloads of up to 6½ tons, a goods range introduced in 1939 had forward-control and was powered by 6-cyl diesel engines of 70 and 105bhp output. Other features included 5-speed transmissions and air-hydraulic braking. The Type 626 'Coloniale' was designed for a 3-ton payload plus trailer and was also listed as a 26-seat passenger model. Just before World War II a new heavy model, the 9/10-ton 6 x 4 A1000, was announced, powered by a 10-litre diesel engine, with 10-speed transmission and full air brakes.

During the war, production was diverted entirely to the military, but with a return to peace, models continued as before, with the addition of a 100-passenger trolleybus and the heaviest Fiat so far, the Type 666 double-drive 6-wheeler which, with a drawbar trailer, grossed 32 tons. This had a 9.4-litre 113bhp 6-cyl diesel engine driving through a 10-speed transmission. A medium-duty range, with capacities of 4 to 8

tons, was introduced in 1949 with engines of up to 10.2-litre capacity. A coil spring independent front suspension system was used on a new 1½/1¾-ton snub-nose truck called the 615 introduced in 1951. This had a 1.4-litre 4-cyl overhead-valve petrol engine but was soon fitted with a 1.9-litre diesel unit. In 1954 the company's first horizontal underfloor-engined passenger model appeared – the 401UM 80-passenger city bus with separate entrance and exit – the components of which formed the basis for a new generation of large-capacity buses and coaches developed by other firms. Two years later a bonneted 6 x 6 called the CP56 was developed for military use, having 16 forward speeds and a payload rating of 13½ tons.

By 1958, turbocharging was listed for some heavy diesels and a new bonneted range for 4/5-ton payloads was introduced with 4.7-litre 6-cyl diesel engines, hydrovac brakes, and a front-end design that later found its way into the French Unic range. Passenger models were now principally horizontal underfloor-engined designs, with clutchless electro-pneumatic transmissions, power-steering and air suspension. Trolleybuses were built along similar lines. The Type 314 underfloor-engined coach chassis appeared in 1959, designed to carry 33 persons. The 6 x 4 690 range was pow-

1975 Fiat 619 T1 artic tractor

ered by a 210bhp 12.9-litre 6-cyl diesel by 1960 and at the end of 1964, the company announced the 3-ton forward-control 625N powered by a 2.7-litre diesel engine and the 693T1 6 x 4 tractor for 38 tons GCW.

The 1966 truck range covered models from 1½- to 12-ton capacity, the heaviest featuring multi-range transmissions with up to 16 forward speeds, air brakes and double-reduction drive. Also in 1966 the French firm of SA Unic was bought out but continued to build vehicles in its own right as Fiat France SA, as well as offering Fiat heavies under the Unic name. By 1968 both Autobianchi SpA and OM SpA were absorbed completely and a year later Fabbrica Automobili Lancia & Cia, Turin, was taken over, Lancia produc-

1960 Fiat 309 single-deck coach

1960 Fiat 690N 6 x 2 truck

tion continuing for another year before concentrating on specialist military models bearing the Fiat brand name. By the early 1970s light commercials were built by the company's passenger car division, as they used the same components. Vehicles of between 3 and 10 tons gross were the responsibility of the former OM factory, Unic dealt with those in the 10- to 16-ton GVW range and the former SPA plant produced the heaviest Fiats. One of the first tilt-cab models was the 619. Passenger models now covered vehicles with capacities of up to 117 passengers, the largest being the 421A with 250bhp horizontal front engine, automatic transmission and pneumatic suspension. A new 1¾-ton forward-control van, called the 242, was developed jointly in 1973 by Fiat and Citroën. Featuring disc brakes and independent suspension all round, this was marketed both as a Citroën and a Fiat, the latter having a 2-litre twin overhead-cam 4-cyl petrol engine.

In 1975 Fiat Veicoli Industriali SpA, as it was then known, signed an agreement with Klockner-Humboldt-Deutz AG whereby both would co-ordinate production and marketing activities under the name Iveco. New in 1976 were the 170 and '190'-Series for up to 17 tons payload and a range of cross-country 4 x 4s in the form

of the '65'-, '75'- and '90'-Series. The '170' was powered by the company's first 'V'-engine, a 17.2-litre 330bhp V8. Four-by-fours were built in the old Lancia factory at Bolzano, having 3.5-litre, 4- or 5.2-litre 6-cyl engines, a tiltcab and air-hydraulic braking. In 1977 the first real effects of the Iveco consortium were felt when the 38-ton GCW 320M19 tractor with 320bhp Magirus V10 air-cooled diesel engine, plus a range of bonneted 4 x 4, 6 x 4 and 6 x 6 dump trucks of Magirus design but with Fiat engines, were announced.

The 3/4-ton 'Daily', powered by a 2.4-litre 4-cyl diesel taken from the Alfa-Romeo marque with which Fiat is also closely associated, arrived in 1978, also incorporating torsion-bar independent front suspension. The heaviest Fiats could now handle gross weights in excess of 40 tons, and passenger models ranged from the 20-seat 50A1 through various chassisless models for up to 52 passengers, to the massive 421 model for up to 120 persons. This has a 13.8-litre horizontal front engine, automatic transmission and a dropped rear axle to provide the lowest possible loading height. Fiat commercials are currently built under licence by Concord in Argentina and Zavodi Crvena Zastava in Yugoslavia, sold respectively under the Concord and Zastava brand names.

1976 Fiat OM75 refrigerated boxvan

FLXIBLE/USA 1924 to date

Using modified Buick and Studebaker passenger car chassis, the Flxible Co, of North Water Street, Loudonville, Ohio, introduced the Flxible passenger model in 1924, catering for small bus operators. By 1936 Chevrolet truck chassis were used in conjunction with the company's streamlined 'Airway' body and a longitudinal rear engine of Buick or Chevrolet origin was used in the 1939 'Clipper' which quickly became the company's standard model. In 1941 the Flxible Co pioneered the use of parallelogrammed windows since adopted by numerous other American passenger body and vehicle manufacturers and in 1946 a 2 + 1 seating arrangement was introduced

1964 Flxible integral van

1974 Flxible single-deck coach

in the 'Airporter', popular on American airport services for many years. A new model for 1950 was the 'Visicoach' and during the early Fifties the company collaborated with the Twin Coach Co, of nearby Kent, Ohio, to supply hundreds of buses to the US Army that could be quickly converted into ambulances or load-carriers and in 1953 the Kent-based firm sold its manufacturing rights for underfloor-engined city transit buses to Flxible. For some time most of these vehicles had lpg engines for use in Chicago, the only large American city to use this type of fuel at the time, and to help with overseas sales arrangements were made with bus builder Ansair Pty Ltd, of North Essendon, Victoria, Australia, in 1960 to build the 'Clipper' model under licence using the Ansair-Flxible brand name.

In 1961 a new series of city transit buses, with longitudinal

rear-mounted Detroit Diesel engines and Spicer torque-converter transmissions was announced and in an attempt at diversification the company acquired the Southern Coach Co, of Evergreen, Alabama, about 1963 to establish production facilities for a series of small passenger models using the Flxette brand name. Seven years later the company became a subsidiary of the Rohr Corp, having discontinued its line of inter-city vehicles the previous year, and in 1974 moved to new premises in Delaware.

Models are now restricted to a line of city transit buses available in three lengths and powered by V6 or V8 Detroit Diesels with Allison fully-automatic transmission. Since September 1977 Grumman Corp have owned the company.

FMC/USA 1974 to date

The Motor Coach Divn of the FMC Corp, Santa Clara, California, was previously known as the Recreational Vehicle Divn, concentrating on the design and construction of self-propelled motor homes. A line of transit buses, based on the motor home, was introduced, and many examples have hydraulic wheelchair lifts, space for wheelchairs and internal locking devices to secure them to the floor. Generally, models are designed for semi-rural operation.

FN/Belgium 1932-c1939, 1946-1965

Fabrique Nationale d'Armes de Guerre, Herstal, Coronmeuse, Liège, was a small arms firm whose first FN commercial was a bonneted 2½-tonner with a 3.3-litre side-valve straight-8 petrol engine and 4-speed transmission. In 1934 a 1-tonner was based on the new 'Prince Albert' passenger car with 2.25-litre side-valve petrol engine. Even trolleybuses were built by this time, the first entering service in Liège in 1933. There was also a Kégresse-type half-track with 6-cyl Minerva or FN petrol engine. A forward-control 5-tonner called the 63C replaced the 3½-tonner in 1937, using a 3.9-litre 75bhp 6- or 8-cyl petrol engine. Also available were various passenger derivatives and a 4-wheel drive military truck with an 8-speed transmission and three lockable differentials. Arms production took precedence during World War II, but truck production resumed in 1946 with 5- and 6½-ton versions of the 63C with a 4.3-litre petrol engine and 5-speed synchromesh or overdrive transmission. Four-by-four derivatives were built in association with the manufacturers of Brossel and Miesse commercials. One was an artillery tractor called the 'Ardennes' also listed as a 1½-ton load-carrier, with 4.7-litre overhead-valve petrol engine, 8-speed transmission and air brakes. Between 1953 and 1955 the company built 25 100-passenger trolleybuses for Liège and in 1960 constructed the AB11 prototype diesel city bus with two Perkins P6 engines mounted horizontally over the rear axle, a semi-automatic transmission and air suspension. By 1963 the 'Ardennes' artillery tractor was also available commercially but within two years regular vehicle production had been abandoned.

1937 FN 63C 3½-ton truck

FNM/*Brazil 1949 to date*
In 1942 Fabrica Nacional de Motores SA was founded in Rio de Janeiro to assemble aircraft and machinery imported from the USA. Late in 1949 the first FNM truck, the R-80, was built. Based on Isotta Fraschini designs, this was replaced in 1950 by an Alfa-Romeo based model using 31% home-produced components within two years. Brazilian content gradually increased and when the heavy diesel-engined D-1 100 was announced in 1957, it had nearly all home-produced components. A new range announced in 1975 is of Fiat design, comprising the 4½-ton payload FNM-70, 9-ton payload FNM-130 and 12½-ton payload FNM-210/S. The lightest has a 5-litre 4-cyl diesel engine and 5-speed transmission, the intermediate model a 7.4-litre 6-cyl diesel engine and 5-speed transmission and the heaviest a 13.8-litre 6-cyl diesel engine and 12-speed transmission.

FOAMITE-CHILDS/*USA 1924*
The Foamite-Childs Corp was formed in Utica, New York State, in 1922 after the merger of fire equipment manufacturers the Foamite Firefoam Co and the O J Childs Co. Producing all types of fire prevention and extinguishing equipment, the company also built a series of pumpers and aerial ladder units based on other manufacturers' chassis, but in 1924 constructed a few of their own design, sometimes known simply as Childs. In 1927 the company was absorbed into the American LaFrance Fire Engine Co Inc to form the American LaFrance & Foamite Corp.

FODEN/*England 1899 to date*
The Sandbach, Cheshire, firm of Hancock & Foden started experimenting with steam wagons, the first having a vertical boiler, front wheel drive and rear wheel steering, and the second a loco-type boiler and "overtype" engine layout. In 1901 a third wagon was successfully entered in War Office Trials. With rear wheels inside the chassis frame in locomotive style, this had a 2-speed gear train with final-drive by tandem roller chains. A year later the business was registered as E Foden, Sons & Co Ltd, and series production got underway. The first new development was a 5-tonner with smaller rear wheels outside the frame, a larger boiler operating at higher pressures and increased load space, joined briefly by a 2-ton derivative in 1905. The company became one of the best known manufacturers of "overtype" wagons, gradually improving on the design until, in 1925, the 6-ton 'C'-Type was launched. Driving position was much higher than before, cam-operated brakes and Ackermann steering were fitted, and a speed of 29km/h was possible. The same 2-cyl compound engine was modified to produce 23bhp. This model also formed the basis of an articulated 6-wheeler built in small numbers up to 1928, and a 12-ton payload double-drive model, with chains linking the rear axles, was also launched.

A 6-ton "undertype", with vertical front-mounted water-tube boiler and 2-cyl double-acting engine beneath the chassis frame, was built in 1925. Called the 'E'-Type, this had cardan shaft, worm-drive to the rear axle, and was also offered in 6-wheeled and tractor form. Few were built and the 4- or 6-wheeled '0'-Type or 'Speed Six' appeared in its place having a vertical front-mounted boiler which was replaced by a horizontal boiler and, finally, by a reversed unit with cross watertubes. This was one of the first steam wagons to be designed for pneumatic tyres. It had a 2-cyl high-speed 90bhp engine, shaft-drive, 4-wheel steam brakes and was said to be capable of up to 96km/h. It was withdrawn in 1932 in favour of diesel lorries, but a few more "overtypes" were built up to 1934 using existing stock. An interesting intermediate model, also using some wagon components, was a timber tractor fitted with a transverse 5LW Gardner diesel engine behind the cab, 3-point suspension, and chain-drive to a gearbox in the cab and thence

by chains to the rear axle.
Although the first Foden diesel lorry was delivered in 1931, some members of the Foden family broke away to form E R Foden Ltd and built ERF diesel lorries. The first Foden diesel was the 6-ton 'R'-Type, with Gardner 6L2 engine and a 4-speed transmission. In 1934 a new range for between 2- and 7-ton capacities was launched, using Austin, Dorman, Meadows or Perkins engines, but few were sold; although single- and double-deck buses were offered for 1934, these never did well. By 1935 the company was building maximum-capacity Gardner-engined lorries, including 10- and 12-ton 6-wheelers, and towards the end of that year a new 4-tonner, with a Gardner 4LK diesel engine, was introduced which was unsuccessful. One successful model was a 15-ton rigid 8-wheeler announced about the same time. In 1937 this was joined by a 10-ton twin-steer 6-wheeler, and by the end of the 1930s the diesel series was marketed as the 'DG' and many were supplied for military use. Another wartime product was a 'DG'-based timber tractor with rigidly-mounted pivoting front axle and Gardner 5LW diesel engine.

Single- and double-deck passenger types were announced in 1945, and the 'DG' range developed into the 'FG' soon after. In 1947 the company's first dump truck was built for the Steel Co of Wales. Based on a suitably modified 12-ton 6-wheeler, this had a full-width 'FG' cab, single cross-

1900 Foden 3-ton "overtype" steam wagon

country tyres and scow-end body. The following year saw the development of the first Foden diesel engine, a 4.09-litre supercharged 2-stroke producing 126bhp, listed from 1948 as an option for both goods and passenger models. In 1949 the first all-steel cabs appeared and in 1950 a rear-engined single-deck coach chassis was announced, with transverse 2-stroke or Gardner 6LW diesel engine.

By the early 1950s all dump trucks had all-steel half-cabs and a series of heavy road tractors for handling loads of up to 80 tons – usually powered by a Gardner 8LW diesel engine – were added to the line. A 1.5 cu m 4-wheeled dump truck was announced in 1954, and by 1956 air brakes and power-steering were available throughout the range. In 1958, all-steel, alloy and fibreglass cabs were listed and disc brakes and air suspension introduced. A further excursion into the special vehicle field included the FR6/45 4-wheeled bonneted dump truck powered by a 300bhp Rolls-Royce diesel engine, and a 6-wheeled crane-carrier. In 1962 the first tilt-cab Fodens appeared at the Earls Court Show. In 1964 a change in Construction & Use Regulations brought about the unique 'Twin-Load', an 8-wheeled rigid load-carrier with fifth wheel coupling at the rear and single-axle semi-trailer which

1954 Foden FED4 dump truck

1978 Foden 'Super Haulmaster' 6 x 4 tipper

1946 Foden DG6/10 6 x 4 tipper

could legally operate at 32 tons GCW within the UK.

By the mid-1960s the Rolls-Royce powered dump truck had gone, but 4- and 6-wheeled half-cab models remained, increased to 15 and 39 tons gross respectively by 1967. In 1968 half-cabs were available on most models, a few being fitted to artic tractor units, but most on 6 x 4 and 8 x 4 tipper and mixer chassis. Now called Fodens Ltd, the company rationalized its models for 1971, offering a choice of cabs. Plants were now operating in Australia, New Zealand, and South Africa, building vehicles suited to local conditions. In 1973 the company was awarded a £10m NATO contract to construct 4-, 6- and 8-wheeled military trucks, including some of 4 x 4 and 6 x 6 configuration. The all-steel S90 cab arrived the following year, replacing a Motor Panels cab on the Continental-style heavy artic tractor, and an agreement was signed with Faun-Werke GmbH, Germany, whereby certain Faun dump trucks would be marketed by Fodens' distributors as the Foden-Faun. A lightweight 6-wheeler for use as a truck mixer was announced in 1976, having the dated S39 cab, and in 1977 the company attempted to enter the UK bus market with the Foden-NC double-decker.

Fodens Ltd was now in a poor financial state, due mainly to problems encountered with the NATO contract, and only just avoided a Rolls-Royce takeover. New models were badly needed and at the 1977 Scottish Motor Show, the 'Haulmaster' and 'Fleetmaster' tractor units were announced. The 32-ton GCW 'Haulmaster' was for UK operation, with Cummins, Gardner, or Rolls-Royce diesel engines, while the 'Fleetmaster' was for export at 38 tons GCW, with Cummins or

Rolls-Royce diesels. Finances did not improve, however, and early in 1980 the company went into receivership and all production was halted. Orders were few, but later that year Paccar Inc, builder of Kenworth and Pacific trucks, acquired the business and re-named it the Sandbach Engineering Co. Until the end of that year the only vehicles completed were those that were partly built when the receiver was called in, but from January 1981 new vehicles again rolled off the line; a new range having yet to be announced.

FODEN-FAUN/*Germany/England 1974-1976*
Fodens Ltd, Sandbach, Cheshire, came to an agreement with Faun-Werke GmbH, West Germany, whereby certain Faun dump trucks would be marketed through the Foden dealer network as Foden-Faun. This arrangement lasted only until 1976, when increasing disparity between respective currencies led to its conclusion.

1976 Foden-NC double-deck bus underframe

FODEN-NC/*England 1977-1978*
The late Seventies saw much development work in the double-deck bus field in the UK and certain manufacturers who had long since left the passenger vehicle market showed an interest in it again. One of these was Fodens Ltd, of Elworth Works, Sand-

bach, Cheshire, who developed the transverse rear-engined Foden-NC in association with Northern Counties, coachbuilders, of Wigan. Although of chassisless construction, it was intended that the Foden underframe could be supplied to various independent body-builders once production got under way, but the Sandbach company's financial problems appear to have curtailed the scheme after only a few prototypes had been built. The specification included a Gardner 6LXB diesel engine, Allison automatic transmission and Ferodo friction retarder.

FOIDART/*Belgium 1914*
M Foidart announced a new "undertype" steam wagon to be built in Brussels by his own company, Camions à Vapeur Foidart. Only prototypes appear to have been constructed, with a kerosene-fired flash boiler and a pair of horizontal 2-cyl compound engines and chain-drive to the rear wheels. The project was aborted following the German invasion.

1961 Ford Thames 'Trader 1' 5-ton caravan transporter

FORD THAMES/*England 1957-1965*
With the announcement of the semi forward-control 'trader' truck range, the Ford Motor Co Ltd's British-built commercial models became known as Ford Thames. 'Traders' had synchromesh transmissions and hypoid rear axles, all engines being Ford-

built petrol or diesel units. Models were initially grouped in the 1½/7-ton payload range, later extended to include two low-loading types, 6 x 2 and 6 x 4 derivatives by County Commercial Cars Ltd and a 41-seat passenger model. By 1962 5-speed transmissions and 2-speed rear axles were optional

and a new variation was the bonneted 'Trader', aimed primarily at overseas markets, but the debut soon after of the famous 'Transit' and 'D'-Series models once again heralded a return to the Ford brand name.

1935 Fordson Model 'BBE' 2-ton integral van

FORDSON/*Ireland/England 1929-1939*
During the 1920s a common sight on British roads was the light road tractor, usually derived from agricultural models. The Fordson was one of these, built until 1929 at the Ford Motor Co Ltd's County Cork, Ireland, factory before being transferred to Dagenham, Essex, in 1931. The road tractor version had an enclosed cab, downswept exhaust and solid rubber tyres. In 1933 all British-built Ford trucks were re-named Fordson, carrying this name until 1939 when they became known as Fordson Thames.

The first new Fordson truck was the forward-control 'BBE' 2-tonner, built between 1934 and 1938. It was also the first to employ conventional fore-and-aft semi-elliptic leaf springs instead of transverse springing. Heavier requirements were catered for by 6 x 2 'Surrey' and 6 x 4 'Sussex' derivatives. In 1935 a new 2/3-tonner, known as the Model '51', and the 3-wheeled 'Tug' "mechanical horse" were launched, and by 1938 over 30,000 of the 2/3-ton Model '79' had been sold, the Model 81/81T 2/3-tonner being just as successful with over 28,000 sold by 1939. All 1936 models had V8 petrol engines, while for 1937 a new 1¼-tonner was of forward-control layout with a USA-designed normal-control cab. The forward-control range was enlarged in 1938 and for 1939 another 2/3-tonner – the 91/98T, with 24 or 30bhp engine – was announced, along with a new 4/5-tonner. Early in 1939 all vehicles became known as Fordson Thames.

FORDSON THAMES/*England 1939-1957*
In honour of the Ford Motor Co Ltd's successful Dagenham factory on the banks of the River Thames, the company re-named its trucks Fordson Thames, often abbreviated to Thames. Wartime

FORD (1)/*USA c1908 to date*
Prior to the introduction of the Model 'T' in 1908, the Ford Motor Co, Dearborn, Michigan, had built only light passenger cars and commercial derivatives for under 1-ton payload, but soon after the 'T''s launch, various commercial conversions were offered including a lengthened chassis with chain-drive and chain- or shaft-drive artics. All had a 2.9-litre 4-cyl 'L'-head petrol engine and also a 2-speed and reverse planetary transmission.

The first purpose-built Ford commercial was the 'TT' 1-tonner announced in 1917. This was a lengthened Model 'T' with worm-drive, and over one million examples were sold within ten years. The 'TT' was offered ex-factory in many guises, including fire appliances, ambulances, light buses and even railcars. Agricultural tractors were also built from 1917 but these were marketed as Fordson from 1919, the Fordson name being used later for a 3-ton forward-control prototype and for various British-built Ford trucks. A new screen-sided 'TT' 1-tonner appeared about 1925, the same year that a polished aluminium-bodied air transport luggage carrier was built to special order.

The heavier all-commercial version of the Model 'T''s successor was the 'AA' for 1/1½-ton payloads. This worm-drive design arrived in 1928 but was replaced the following year by a spiral-bevel model with 4-speed transmission and a dual rear wheel option. Various factory-built bodies were listed. For 1930 the 'AA' could be had with a 396-cm wheelbase if required, and now had longitudinal cantilever-type rear springs and a revised front-end style. Passenger versions were also offered.

In 1931 the first Russian GAZ trucks were based on 'AA' designs but Ford itself announced the 'BB' for 1932, initially using the 4-cyl petrol engine also fitted in the 'AA' but introducing a 65bhp 3.6-litre V8 as an option later that year, this becoming standard for 1933. A slightly raked radiator distinguished 1933 and 1934 'BB's and again a 1½-tonner was the heaviest, also available as an artic unit. For 1935 the 'BB' was re-styled along passenger car lines and "cabover" conversions were offered by custom-builders, the first factory-produced "cabovers" not appearing until 1938. The first 4-wheel drive Fords were Marmon-Herrington conversions announced in 1933.

On the passenger vehicle front, the long-wheelbase 'BB' with V8 petrol engine was fast becoming popular, and numerous body-builders were sub-contracted to

construct distinctive styles. Detroit was quick to realize the Ford's potential as a passenger model and, following an experiment with 35 such vehicles in 1934, acquired three hundred Model '51' 1½-tonners. In 1936 five hundred more, with bodies by the Union City Body Co, were pressed into service and by the end of that year the Ford Motor Co was offering its own complete transit bus, called the Model '70', with 25 seats and air brakes. One year later this was re-designated the 70A and the longer 70B was introduced.

The three millionth Ford truck was delivered during 1936 by which time the range included numerous light models, the 1½-ton 'BB' and various passenger types. For 1937 60- or 85bhp V8 petrol engines and various wheelbase lengths were listed for the truck range and in 1938 a new 1-tonner and a forward-control 1½-tonner, both with new rounded grilles, were announced. Hydraulic braking arrived in 1939. A new 95bhp 3.9-litre Mercury V8 petrol engine was listed for both goods and passenger models from 1939, while some export models had Hercules diesels. The new V8 was even mounted in a transverse rear posi-

1972 Ford (1) 'Louisville' 6 x 4

the war effort but the post-war range was much the same as that for 1942. The company lost passenger vehicle orders when Transit Buses Inc went its own way, determined to up-date its range. In an attempt at a passenger vehicle revival, Ford set up Metropolitan Motor Coaches Inc to market 27- and 31-seat Wayne-bodied vehicles, but even this failed and the new company closed in 1950.

Things were much brighter on the goods vehicle side. All trucks were completely re-styled for 1948 and F6, F7 and F8 models introduced for 2/3-ton payloads. The heaviest had a 5-speed transmission, hydrovac brakes and a 135 bhp V8 engine. The F8 was also available in 6 x 4 form. In 1949 a 6-cyl forward-control parcels de-

1975 Ford (1) F950 6 x 4 tipper

tion in a new 27-seat bus supplied to Detroit. Bodied by Union City, this had a wheelbase of 377cm, an overall length of 772cm and, apart from the roof which was of canvas, was constructed entirely of steel. Early in 1941 the company set up Transit Buses Inc to market these and other passenger types. By this time, Ford trucks had again been re-styled, the "heavies" now having a hydrovac brake option, while some American components were used in certain British military Fords of the period. Also in 1941 a 3.7-litre 6-cyl in-line petrol engine, the first Ford engine of this type since 1908, became an option. The company was heavily involved in

livery model appeared, and in 1950 a large 110bhp 6-cyl petrol engine was announced, some 2-tonners now having synchromesh transmissions. In 1952 the company's first overhead-valve engines appeared, comprising a 3.6-litre in-line 6-cyl unit and V8s of 145 and 155bhp output.

For 1954 the goods vehicle range was extended upwards to include models of up to 24,947kg GCW, the largest being the F-900. Power-steering was now optional for some models, while the 1956 range had tubeless tyres and 12-volt electrics as standard. Six-cyl in-line and V8 engines now had outputs of up to 200bhp. In 1957 the now well known forward-control tilt-cab 'C'-Series for payloads of between 5 and 9 tons was announced. This had a 4- or 5-speed synchromesh transmission as standard, with Ford's new 'Transmatic' automatic system as an option. Other features included hypoid driving axles; hydraulic, hydrovac, air/hydraulic or full air brakes; and various V8 petrol engines from a 178bhp 4.5-litre unit up to a 190bhp 5.5-litre lump.

By 1958 a series of extra heavy-duty bonneted trucks had been announced and the most powerful V8 was 8.7 litres producing 277bhp. Six-cyl Perkins diesels were now fitted in certain medium-duty trucks. In 1960 a prototype gas-turbine engine was installed in a Ford truck and at the top end of the range the forward-control tilt-cab 'H'-Series tractor, in 4 x 2 and 6 x 4 guise, was available with a choice of various Ford V8 petrol engines or Cummins diesels. These had twin-plate clutches, air brakes, and numerous transmission arrangements containing up to 12 forward speeds.

A prototype 6 x 4 gas-turbine tractor known as 'Big Red' was unveiled in 1963, using a 600bhp power unit, 5-speed automatic transmission and air suspension.

1963 Ford (1) 6 x 4 prototype gas-turbine artic tractor

1978 Ford (1) CL-9000 6 x 4 artic tractor

Soon after this, Cummins V6 diesels were listed for the snub-nosed 'NS'-Series. By 1965 independent front suspension, previously fitted only to car-based commercials, was offered on light Ford trucks. The 1966 truck and bus line included no less than one thousand different models, and was now using increasing quantities of proprietary components, even introducing 6-cyl Caterpillar diesels as options for some heavy-duty models. Medium-duty trucks were offered with power-actuated front disc brakes for 1968 and for 1970 the 'L'-Series of heavy-duty bonneted trucks went into production at a new plant in Louisville, Kentucky. These were soon referred to as the 'Louisville' range, taking the company's maximum GCW up to 29,000kg. Available in 4 x 2 or 6 x 4 form, these could be had with a variety of specifications including V6 or V8 Detroit Diesel engines, air brakes and a tilting fibreglass bonnet. A variation on this theme was a set-back front axle model called the 'LN'-Series which was announced soon after.

A new heavy-duty "cabover" line was the 'W'-Series, which appeared in 1971, also in 4 x 2 and 6 x 4 form, with Hendrickson bogie on the latter. This was the company's first maximum-capacity model, employing numerous aluminium components to keep unladen weights to a minimum. By 1978 the CL-9000, with light-alloy tilt-cab, Caterpillar, Cummins or Detroit Diesel engines of up to 600bhp output, and a standard gross weight of up to 37,200kg, had replaced the 'W'-Series. Special versions for gross combination weights of up to 62,600kg were also built.

Both the bonneted 'F'- and the forward-control 'C'-Series are still offered, with gross weights of between 10,890 and 25,400kg, while options on these models include a 6 x 4 layout, choice of 6- or 8-cyl petrol engines or Caterpillar diesels producing up to 210bhp and various transmissions. There are numerous lighter types, as well as bonneted 'B'-Series school buses

and the forward-control 'P'-Series parcels van with 4.9-litre 6-cyl in-line engine and 4-speed transmission.

FORD (2)/England 1932-1933, 1965 to date

The British Ford commercial range was much the same as the American line-up until 1932 when, after a move from Trafford Park, Manchester, to premises by the River Thames at Dagenham, Essex, the Ford Motor Co Ltd announced a 3-speed 1-tonner with 3.3-litre 4-cyl side-valve petrol en-

1967 Ford (2) D550 pantechnicon

gine. To avoid confusion with USA-built Fords, a new model designation scheme was introduced whereby all Dagenham-built vehicles incorporated a letter 'E' in their model numbers. By 1933, however, a new 2-tonner was being marketed as the Fordson, the same name that had been used for many years on the company's agricultural and road tractors, and this name was quickly adopted for all but the lightest commercials.

The Ford name was not used again to describe commercials over 1-ton capacity until October 1965, when it was used on an extensive new range of semi forward-control trucks and vans for payloads of up to 1¾ tons. Developed from the German subsidiary's 'Taunus Transit', this was called the 'Transit' and was built initially in the company's Belgian plant at Genk. It had semi-elliptic leaf springs all round, a choice of 265- or 295-cm wheelbase and twin rear wheels on the heaviest models. A Perkins 4.99 4-cyl diesel or 1.7- or 2-litre Ford V4 petrol

engine was used. The 'Transit' was assembled in the company's Langley, Berks, factory with a new forward-control truck called the 'D'-Series. With capacities of between 2 and 9 tons, the tilt-cab 'D'-Series used inclined engines developed from the old 4D and 6D diesels, originally launched in 1947. These comprised an 83bhp 4-litre 4- and 128bhp 6-litre 6-cyl unit, petrol options being two American-built Fords developing 129 and 149bhp. The heaviest models in the series had standard air-hydraulic brakes and an optional 'Custom Cab' package. Passenger equivalents were the R192 and R226, of 480- and 565-cm wheelbase respectively, for up to 53 passengers. Petrol or diesel engines were also available and a 5-speed transmission could be had in the most powerful model.

By 1967 a 'Transit' with Borg-Warner automatic transmission was listed and by 1968 turbo-charged V8 diesels were offered in the heaviest 'D'-Series models, such as the 28 tons GCW D1000 tractor unit. By the following year the heaviest rigid load-carrier was a 24-ton GVW 6 x 4 with 8.3-litre Cummins or 8.4-litre Ford V8 diesel engine. In 1971 'Transit' production was moved to a new plant

1968 Ford (2) R192 coach

at Swaythling, Southampton, and the Langley-based Special Vehicle Order Dept was by then capable of assembling vehicles to virtually any specification, starting with a standard chassis. Among these special types were "baby" artics and low-loading 6-wheeled bottle floats. Also in 1971 the company's own 61bhp 2.4-litre 4-cyl diesel engine with cogged belt drive from the camshaft was of-

fered for the 'Transit' in place of the Perkins unit. A new series of heavy-duty synchromesh transmissions with 4, 6 and 8 speeds was announced, followed a year later by a 2.5-litre V6 petrol unit. Throughout this period, the old Ford Thames 'K'-Series bonneted range had remained on the books as the Ford 'K'-Series, still aimed principally at the export market, but this was withdrawn in 1972, by which time the heaviest 'D'-Series

1972 Ford (2) 'Transit' minibus

models could be had with a 6-speed Allison automatic transmission and rear air suspension.

The early 1970s saw a massive increase in Ford passenger sales, while 1973 saw the gap between the 'Transit' and the 'D'-Series filled by a 'Transit' look-alike called the 'A'-Series. With a gross weight of between 3½ and 5½ tons, this was never as popular as the company had hoped, having dual-circuit servo brakes as standard, 4- or 5-speed transmissions and a variety of engines. The company joined the "heavy" league in 1975 with its 'Transcontinental' 4 x 2 and 6 x 4 truck and tractor range for gross weights of up to 44 tons built in the company's Amsterdam plant. Features include a 3-man tilt-cab common to the heaviest forward-control Berliets of the day, 9- or 13-speed Fuller constant-mesh transmissions, and a 14-litre 6-cyl Cummins diesel engine, now turbocharged and aftercooled to provide outputs of up to 355bhp.

Ford Motor Co Ltd became number one in 1977, not only in

1979 Ford (2) D2418 6 x 4 refuse collector

the British commercial vehicle and agricultural tractor fields, but also in the passenger car market, making this the first company to take all three honours simultaneously. For 1978 a re-vamped 'Transit' range had servo disc brakes as standard at the front, with 4-cyl in-line petrol engines replacing V4 units. The 'D'-Series was also up-dated, now using 4- and 6-cyl in-line and V8 diesels of the company's own make or Cummins V8s, with full air brakes on heavier models and optional exhaust brakes with 6-cyl in-line and V8 engines. In 1981 the 'D'-Series was replaced by the revolutionary 'Cargo' range. The company also announced that in future the 'Transcontinental' would be built in Britain.

FORD (3)/_Spain 1920-1936, 1940-1954_
Apart from the Civil War years, British-designed Ford trucks and agricultural tractors were built under licence by Ford Motor Iberica, Barcelona, until an entirely new British-based range was developed from 1954 and launched as the Ebro two years later.

FORD (4)/_Germany 1935-c1971_
The Cologne plant of Ford-Werke AG based its first truck on the parent company's Model 'BB', using a 3.2-litre 4-cyl petrol engine and adding a 95bhp 3.6-litre V8-engined 3-ton van, truck or bus in 1936. Military versions were also built. In 1948 this model was joined by a 4-cyl petrol-engined 3-tonner called the 'Ruhr' and one year later the V8 version was re-designated the 'Rhein'. Also in 1949 a V8-engined forward-control bus was developed, and by 1951 the 4-cyl engined 3-tonner was known as the FK3000 and the V8-engined model, now up-rated to 3½ tons capacity, as the FK3500. A new version was the

Ford (3) Model 'BB' truck c1936

FK3500D, using a 94bhp 4.08-litre diesel engine and also available with 4-wheel drive. The 1-ton FK1000 appeared in 1953, and by 1956 the FK2500 was also listed, power units comprising a 100bhp 3.9-litre 8-cyl in-line petrol engine or 80bhp 2.8-litre 2-stroke V4 diesel. In 1961 the FK1000 was re-named the 'Taunus Transit' and by 1965 the forward-control version had been succeeded by the snub-nosed British design, the largest of which, on the German market, was the FT1750 for 1750kg payload. All Ford commercials sold in Germany are now of British or Dutch manufacture.

FORD (5)/_Australia c1940-c1945, 1975 to date_
While Ford commercials had been assembled in Australia for many years, it was not until the outbreak of World War II that distinctly Australian derivatives began to appear. Built by the Ford Motor Co of Australia Pty Ltd, Geelong, Victoria, these included military all-wheel drive vehicles and 6 x 6 conversions of standard chassis, as well as some armoured types. With a return to peace, Australian production centred up-

on light commercials, heavier requirements being catered for by the British and American Ford truck ranges, although in 1975 a 4 x 4 1-tonner was developed for the Australian Army.

FORD (6)/_France 1947-1954_
Ford SAF, Poissy, Seine-et-Oise, took over production of the forward-control Matford 5-tonner, re-naming this Ford. It now had a 3.9-litre V8 petrol engine; by 1949 a new all-steel cab; and by 1950 a 4.1-litre 6-cyl Hercules diesel engine. Military versions were also built and 4-speed synchromesh transmissions, 2-speed back axles and hydrovac brakes were soon listed. The company was acquired by Simca in 1954, production of

the 5-tonner continuing as the Simca 'Cargo'.

FORD (7)/_Netherlands 1975 to date_
By the mid-1970s, the Ford Motor Co had begun to centre some of its European manufacturing facilities in a new plant near Amsterdam, and on the truck front introduced the 'Transcontinental' 4 x 2 and 6 x 4 truck and tractor range which was to be marketed throughout Europe.

FORD (8)/_Philippines 1978 to date_
In common with other major vehicle producers, Ford Philippine Inc, Makati Rizal, has offered an easily-maintained light pick-up truck for use throughout Asia for some years. A little more recently, however, a 1¾-ton version has been developed with a choice between a 1.6-litre petrol and a 2.4-litre diesel engine.

1959 Ford (4) Model 55 chassis-cab

1973 Ford (4) 'N'-Series tipper

1979 Ford (7) 'Transcontinental' 4427 artic tractor

1947 Fordson Thames 7V mobile cinema

models included 1½-ton light trucks and personnel carriers, 1½- and 3-ton 4 x 4s and 3-ton 6 x 4s, all powered by the 7V range of V8 petrol engines, the 3.6-litre version of which was used in various military vehicles, including the unique twin-engined Garner-Straussler 4 x 4.

Civilian production resumed immediately after the war with a series of forward-control V8s in the 2/5-ton class, replaced before 1950 by new ET6 petrol and ET7 bonneted diesel trucks. Payloads of up to 8 tons were now catered

1940 Fordson Thames Model '61' mobile canteen

for, with new features including semi-elliptic front leaf springs and hydraulic brakes with vacuum-servo assistance on the heavier models. A Perkins P6 diesel was now optional.

In 1953 a new 70bhp 3.6-litre overhead-valve 4-cyl unit appeared, this developing into the company's first diesel truck engine the following year. Meanwhile, in 1952, a new 3-ton 4 x 4 had been introduced for the military, with forward-control Commer cab and Canadian V8 petrol engine. The first semi forward-control 'Trader' civilian model appeared in 1957, signalling the adoption of the Ford Thames brand name.

FOREMOST/*Canada c1965 to date*
Canadian Foremost Ltd, Calgary, Alberta, specializes in the con-struction of high-floatation off-highway vehicles from 4 to 70 tons capacity. Wheeled models, such as the Delta Three, Magnum Four and Marauder CFR, are of all-wheel drive configuration, the latter being a 6 x 6 airfield fire crash tender with articulated frame steering. Detroit 'V' engines are used throughout with Clark power-shift transmissions, the 8 x 8 Magnum Four being the first high-mobility all-terrain vehicle designed to carry loads of up to 70 tons.

FORSCHLER/*USA 1914-1922*
The Philip Forschler Wagon & Mfg Co, New Orleans, Louisiana, built 1½- and 3-tonners with 4-cyl water-cooled petrol engines, 3-speed gearboxes and double chain-drive. By 1917 a worm-gear differential was used, and by 1919 the company had been re-named the Forschler Motor Truck Mfg Co. Other models included 1- and 2-tonners but Forschlers were on-ly sold locally.

FORT GARRY/*Canada 1937-1942*
The Fort Garry Motor Body Co, of Winnipeg, Manitoba, was al-ready a well-established truck and bus bodybuilder when, in 1937, it began to build complete pass-enger vehicles under the Fort Garry brand name. Generally, Fort Garry buses were similar to the American Yellow Coach, with an International Harvester engine located at the front. At first, prod-uction was very low indeed but with the Greyhound Corp's ex-pansion across the border in 1940 production increased and by 1942, when the company was re-named Motor Coach Industries and its products MCI, approximately one vehicle was being delivered every week.

FORT WAYNE/*USA 1911-1913*
Using a 4-cyl petrol engine, 3-speed transmission and double chain-drive, the Fort Wayne Au-tomobile Mfg Co, Fort Wayne, Indiana, listed 1- and 3-tonners. Known as Models 'A' and 'B', the former had a maximum speed of 28km/h and the latter 24km/h.

FOSTER/*England 1905, 1919-1934*
Wm Foster & Co Ltd, Lincoln, was a traction engine manufac-turer experimenting with an "overtype" steam wagon in 1905.

1952 Fordson Thames ET6 truck

This idea was shelved but in 1919 the first production "overtype" wagon was built. Rated at 5-ton capacity, this was a 2-speed design with a flat-topped Belpaire boiler, Ramsbottom safety valves and a continuous-action water pump. It had a cross-compound engine with single-piece cast-iron cylind-er block mounted over the boiler. Stephenson-Howe valve gear with 'D'-shaped slide valves was also fitted. As an option, an unusual power tipping gear was available. Driven off the flywheel by a fric-tion disc, drive was transmitted via a roller chain to cross-shafts carrying bevel wheels. It was then taken vertically to a pair of gear wheels, one of which formed the nut to wind up the screw. A pulley at the top of this screw carried rope attached to the forward end of the body and a friction clutch was fitted to avoid over-winding. The Foster wagon was never as popular as its competitors, being somewhat dated even when it first appeared.

FOUILLARON/*France 1906-1907*
G Fouillaron, Levallois-Perret, Seine, built a light commercial version of his passenger car in 1901. Heavier types did not ap-pear until 1906 when a 32-seat passenger model was constructed. No further records can be found although Jesse Ellis & Co Ltd, Maidstone, England, offered a ¾/1-ton van briefly in 1907, perhaps in an attempt to remain solvent, and possibly built by Fouillaron. This had a typical Fouillaron infi-nitely variable transmission sys-tem and a 2.8-litre 4-cyl petrol engine.

FOUR WHEEL DRIVE/*USA 1904-1907*
Powered initially by a 30hp 4-cyl Rutenber petrol engine, the Four Wheel Drive was a 4 x 4 truck built by the Four Wheel Drive Wagon Co, Milwaukee, Wiscon-sin. It also had 4-wheel steering with drive transmitted from gear-box to each wheel by a separate chain. A 40hp engine was used by 1906, and the earlier chain-drive replaced by shafts transmitting drive from the central gearbox to a differential within each axle.

FOWLER/*England 1924-1935*
John Fowler & Co Ltd, Leeds, West Yorks, developed the unsuc-cessful Fowler "undertype" steam wagon, with shaft- rather than chain-drive, a vertical fire-tube boiler, vertical 'V'-twin com-pound engine and a 3-speed trans-mission. The 1931 Commercial Motor Show saw the debut of a new diesel-engined Fowler called the 'Marathon', a 6/7-ton rigid of semi forward-control appearance intended for drawbar operation and powered by a 90bhp 6-cyl di-rect-injection Fowler diesel en-gine with drive via a multi-plate clutch, 4-speed main and 2-speed auxiliary boxes to a worm-drive back axle. There was also a short-wheelbase tipper known as the 'Crusader', a 10/12-ton 6-wheeled 'Marathon' and a heavy haulage tractor called the 'Warrior'. All were unsuccessful due to their weight and price, and surplus trac-tor chassis were sold to the Union Cartage Co Ltd, London, E3, where they became the basis for some of this operator's Union drawbar tractors. By 1934 the lightest model had a Gardner die-sel engine and in 1935 a diesel showman's engine was announced in an attempt to revolutionize the travelling fair business. Powered by an 80bhp Fowler-Sanders 6-cyl engine, this was a bonneted ma-chine with traction engine rear wheels and two gearboxes provid-ing 6 forward and 2 reverse speeds. Only one appears to have been delivered.

1935 Fowler diesel tractor

FRAM (1)/*Italy 1906-1913*
When SA Ligure-Romana Vet-ture, manufacturer of Cantono commercials, moved to Genoa in 1906 it was re-organized as Fab-brica Rotabili Avontreni Motori and vehicles marketed as FRAM.

1908 Frayer-Miller 1¹/₂-ton chemical engine fire appliance

Models continued much as before until the plant closed, but until 1915 other FRAM models continued to be built at the premises of De Dion, Bouton et Cie in France.

FRAM (2)/*France 1913-1915*
E Cantono, Rome, had established a French sales office in 1902 to market its battery-electric commercials. When the Italian business closed in 1913, the French operation continued for another two years with vehicles built under the FRAM brand name in the De Dion-Bouton factory at Puteaux, Seine. The largest was a 5-tonner, with two 7hp electric motors and twin front wheels. Another model was a cranked-frame 3-tonner popular for refuse collection work.

FRAM (3)/*Czechoslovakia 1927-1939*
Vozovka A.S, Kolin, began building the Austrian Perl bus under licence, using the FRAM brand name. The majority of these were operated in the city of Kolin for some years and although this manufacturer did not close down until 1939, it is doubtful whether any other complete vehicles were built.

FRAMO/*Germany/c1930-1939, 1949-1954*
Production of DKW vans, originally developed by JS Rasmussen in 1926, got underway in the Hainichen, Saxony, factory of Framo-Werke GmbH the following year, vehicles being re-named Framo. The first model of over 1-ton capacity was a 4-wheeler powered by a 600cc DKW engine, and by 1937 a 1.1-litre Ford petrol engine was listed as an option. The V501 1-tonner was introduced in 1939 but was halted due to the war. In 1949 this model re-appeared, following the company's absorption into the East German motor industry as VEB IFA Kraftfahrzeugwerk Framo. Initially, the specification included a 500cc 2-stroke petrol engine, but in 1952 this was replaced by a 3-cyl 2-stroke unit. From 1954 this F9 model was sold as the Barkas.

FRANKLIN/*USA 1905-1920*
Using a passenger car chassis, H H Franklin Co, Syracuse, New York State, introduced a bonneted truck in 1905. This had an air-cooled 4-cyl petrol engine, wooden chassis frame and full-elliptic leaf spring suspension. A forward-control 1-tonner, with 1.8-litre overhead-valve petrol engine, 2-speed transmission and shaft-drive, was announced in 1906 and within two years a 2-tonner had also been introduced. A 3-speed model appeared in 1912 but, apart from a 1-ton prototype constructed in 1920, the company then concentrated on passenger cars.

FRANZ/*Switzerland 1910-1918*
The disinterest shown by the management of Zurcher Automobilfabrik Orion, Zürich, in Franz Brozincevic's design for a 4-cyl petrol engine led to the young Croatian designer opening a car and lorry repair shop in the same city. Business expanded so rapidly that he was forced to move to larger premises where, as Franz Brozincevic et Cie, he developed his engine further, moving again in 1909 before constructing a chain-drive lorry for the Swiss Post Office. This had Brozincevic's own 15/20hp engine and was followed by a series of shaft-drive mailvans.

Early in 1911, Franz commercials were on the open market and within a few months the company claimed to have built the first 5-ton shaft-drive lorry in Europe, a distinction usually attributed to Berna. The 5-ton Franz had a 30/35hp 5.4-litre 4-cyl petrol engine, multi-plate clutch and 4-speed transmission to the rear axle. Models soon included 2¹/₂-, 3¹/₂- and 5-tonners, all of which were so well regarded that others got interested in the Franz operation and, early in 1914, the company became part of Motorwagenfabrik Berna AG, Olten, Franz Brozincevic remaining as General Manager.

The arrival of World War I boosted production considerably, models being based on pre-war designs. One particularly popular type was a 4-ton military design announced in 1916, but at about this time Franz Brozincevic left the company and founded Franz Brozincevic et Cie Motorwagenfabrik FBW, where he began building agricultural tractors and factory machinery, and a decreasing Franz production.

FRASER/*Scotland 1920*
Fitted with a liquid-fired boiler, 3-cyl vertical engine, countershaft differential and chain final-drive, the Fraser steam wagon was constructed by Douglas S Fraser & Sons Ltd, Arbroath.

FRAYER-MILLER/*USA 1906-1910*
Introduced by the Oscar Lear Automobile Co, Springfield, Ohio, the Frayer-Miller was a 1½-tonner with air-cooled 4-cyl petrol engine, 4-speed transmission and chain final-drive, available only as an open stakeside truck. Production continued latterly as the Kelly Motor Truck Co, Columbus, Ohio, and was sold as Kelly or Kelly-Springfield.

FREAKLEY/*England 1898-?*
William Freakley, Stoke-on-Trent, Staffs, developed a 2-ton steam wagon for use as a refuse collector, tanker or bus. A vertical boiler powered a 2-cyl vertical engine, with connecting rods transmitting drive to the rear axle. Full-elliptic laminated springs were used at the front and semi-elliptics at the rear while steering was effected by a chain-and-bobbin system.

FREEMAN/*USA 1928-1934*
The first Freeman 4-wheel drive lorry quickly developed into a 3-model range with outputs of 65, 75 and 110bhp. Built by the Freeman Motor Co, Detroit, Michigan, the design called for an 8-forward and 2-reverse speed transmission with rear-wheel drive via internal gearing and that to the front wheels through a "live" axle located above the fixed axle. Later renamed the Freeman Quadrive Corp, the company's largest model had a load capacity of 20 tons using two 4-wheeled drawbar trailers and could achieve laden speeds of up to 40km/h.

FREIGHTLINER/*USA 1940-1942, 1947-1951, 1977 to date*
Dissatisfied with many of the trucks on the American market towards the end of the 1930s, Consolidated Freightways Inc, Spokane, Washington, formed the Freightways Mfg Corp, Salt Lake City, Utah, in 1939 to develop lightweight heavy-duty trucks to its own requirements. The first Freightliner, as it was called, was the CF-100 "cabover" using proprietary components, production of which ceased in 1942 due to wartime shortages.

Production resumed in 1947 at Portland, Oregon, now as the Freightliner Corp. Generally, Freightliners were 1-ton lighter than comparable makes and by 1949 the first example had been sold to an outside operator. The first sleeper-cab Freightliner was also built that year.

Sales and service were taken over by the White Motor Co in 1951 so that the Freightliner Corp could concentrate on production and vehicles began to carry the White-Freightliner name. From 1977 vehicles were again known simply as Freightliner, the line continuing with established White-Freightliner models plus 'Powerliner' "cabovers" with extra-large grilles and radiators to accommodate larger engines.

FREMONT-MAIS/*USA 1914-1915*
With a capacity of 1360kg, the Fremont-Mais was built by the Lauth-Juergens Motor Co, Fremont, Ohio. It had a 4-cyl Buda petrol engine, Warner transmission and shaft-drive and was offered in wheelbase lengths of 330 and 360cm. Numerous examples were exported to Britain through H G Burford Ltd, West London, and sold as Burford, although these were eventually assembled in Britain using mainly British components.

FRICK/*England 1903-1908*
Having previously marketed the Hagen steam wagon, Alfred Dougill & Co Ltd, Leeds, West Yorks, built Frick commercials from 1903, incorporating friction-and-chain transmissions made under Maurer licence. Early types, such as a 1½-ton forward-control machine of 1905, had single-cyl underfloor engines, but later models of up to 3 tons capacity had vertical front-mounted units, the largest being a 4.6-litre twin-cyl design. In 1906 the company became Dougill's Engineering Ltd, a new departure being a 22-seat bus with 20/30hp 7.2-litre 3-cyl petrol engine. This was exhibited at the 1906 Cordingley Exhibition. Towards the end of 1907, the business went into liquidation but at the 1908 Commercial Show Clift's Engineering Co Ltd, Brighton,

1977 Freightliner Model FLT-7564T 6 x 4 artic tractor

Sussex, exhibited a 12/16hp Alpha-engined Frick 1-tonner possibly assembled from spares.

FRISBEE/*USA 1922-1923*
The 2½-ton Frisbee was built by the Frisbee Truck Co, Webberville, Michigan, using a 4-cyl Continental petrol engine.

FRONT DRIVE/*USA 1925-1928*
Companion to Double Drive trucks built by the Double Drive Truck Co, Benton Harbour, Michigan, was the 1½-ton Front Drive. It was powered by a 4-cyl Buda petrol engine.

FRONTENAC/*USA 1906-1912*
The Frontenac goods vehicle range was built by the Abendroth & Root Mfg Co, Newburgh, New York, alongside passenger cars of the same name. In 1912, the Abendroth & Root name was applied to all commercial models. The first design was a bonneted chain-drive 5-tonner, joined by a bonneted 7-tonner with 50hp 4-cyl petrol engine in 1910, a forward-control version in 1911 and a 2-ton model by 1912.

FROSS-BUSSING/*Austria/Czechoslovakia 1909-1945*
Various German-designed Büssings were licence-built in the Vienna factory of Maschinenfabrik A Fross-Büssing using the Fross-Büssing brand name. During World War I, 3-ton "subsidy" types were supplied to the Austrian Army and in 1920 an assembly plant was set up in Prague, Czechoslovakia. This was operated by Tavarna na Stroje A Fross-Büssinga Liberta, vehicles sometimes being sold as Liberta. Both factories built similar models with capacities of up to 5 tons or 55 passengers. In 1930 VL truck and FB passenger ranges were announced, using 75- or 100bhp 6-cyl Maybach engines or an 8-litre V12, but by 1931 the Prague factory had closed, leaving the Vienna plant to struggle on.

FS/*USA 1912-1913*
Built by the Filer & Stowell Motors Co, Milwaukee, Wisconsin, the FS commercial range comprised mainly lightweight models, although there was also a 3½-tonner with a 4-cyl petrol engine and a wheelbase of 300cm. Production ended soon after the company was re-named the FS Motors Co in 1913.

FTF/*Netherlands 1966 to date*
Floor's Handel en Industrie NV, Hilversum, had been the concessionaires for American Mack trucks in the Benelux countries since 1952 when it began to construct its own heavy commercials under the FTF brand name. The first used numerous Mack components but later types employed Detroit Diesel engines, Allison or Fuller transmissions, Timken-Rockwell or Kirkstall axles, and Motor Panels cabs. The earliest FTFs were 2-axle tractors for artic or drawbar

1978 Freightliner 6x4 artic tractors

operation, quickly joined by double-drive 3-axle designs for gross loads of up to 100 tons. In 1972 the Dutch military authorities placed an order for 39 articulated tank transporters and further orders have been placed since, the latest vehicles of this type being capable of handling up to 200 tons. Late in 1975 a new assembly plant was opened at Nijkerk and latest heavy designs include 4- and 5-axle heavy haulage outfits.

FTH/Australia 1915-c1918
Fred T Hack Ltd, Adelaide, fitted a 20hp 4-cyl MAB petrol engine in the first FTH truck. With a 1½-ton payload, it was quickly joined by 14.4 and 22.5hp models, although only a few were built.

FUCHS/Germany 1926-1932
The articulated Fuchs truck was built by H Fuchs Wagenbaufabrik AG, Heidelberg. It was powered initially by the company's own 6.7-litre petrol engine or by a Deutz diesel, but later fitted with a 100bhp Maybach unit. From 1930 until production ceased this model was built by Fuchs Lastzug und Schlepperbau GmbH in new premises in Munich.

FUKIEN/China 1970 to date
The Fukien Motor Vehicle Plant, Foochow, Fukien, builds a 2½-ton bonneted truck called the 130.

FULTON/USA 1916-1925
Although the Clyde Motor Truck Co, Farmingdale, Long Island, was already building commercials under the Clyde brand name, it also developed the Fulton truck. Easily identified by its characteristic round radiator and bonnet, the first Fulton was a 1½-tonner called the 'FX', powered by a 30bhp 4-cyl petrol engine and fitted with a Russel internal-gear rear axle. Thermo-syphon cooling was employed and up to 1924, all engines were of Herschell-Spillman origin. The Fulton Motor Truck Co was formed in 1917 to continue production, which now included a 1-ton Model 'A', also marketed as the Full-Ton. The 2-ton Model 'C' arrived in 1919, having a 40bhp 4-cyl petrol engine, this being developed into the Model 'D' truck-tractor in 1920 with an increased rating of 4½ tons. Exports were handled by the Fulton Motors Export Co, New York, and in the final year of production, both the Model 'A' and Model 'C' were powered by a 4-cyl Buda petrol engine.

FUSO/Japan 1930-1950
The Mitsubishi Shipbuilding & Engineering Co Ltd, Kobe, which had built some Mitsubishi trucks in 1920, introduced bonneted Fu-

1979 FTF 6 x 4 artic tractor

so passenger types ten years later. By 1935 Japan's first diesel-engined bus had been built, and a year later a number of 2½- and 3-ton trucks, powered by 45bhp 4- and 50bhp 6-cyl engines respectively, became available. In 1941 production moved to Tokyo and Kawasaki, but civilian models did not re-appear until 1946, when a bonneted 6/7-tonner was announced. The Fuso range came to an end when the American occupational forces dissected the company into Mitsubishi Heavy Industries Reorganized Ltd and Mitsubishi Nippon Heavy Industries Ltd, vehicles built by the former being sold as Mitsubishi and by the latter as Mitsubishi Fuso.

FWD (1)/USA 1912 to date
A unique double 'Y' universal joint encased within a ball-and-socket was applied to a 2-ton truck to provide a 4-wheel drive configuration in 1910, a similarly treated passenger car passing to the US Army for evaluation. As a result, the Four Wheel Drive Auto Co was founded at Clintonville, Wisconsin in 1912 and, with the outbreak of World War I, orders for 3- and 5-ton FWDs poured in to such an extent that other manufacturers had to be brought in to licence-build the range.

Designated the Model 'B', the most famous of these had a 4-cyl Wisconsin petrol engine, 3-speed constant-mesh transmission and external-contracting brakes all round. A speed of 25km/h was possible, and a track gauge of 143cm enabled the vehicle to be readily adapted as a light railway locomotive by replacing road wheels by railway wheels. Some 15,000 trucks of this type were supplied for military use and at the end of hostilities, many were

re-sold on the civilian market. The company was forced to cut back on vehicle production and instead set about supplying spares and service back-up for these ex-military FWD's, establishing the British Four Wheel Drive Tractor Lorry Co to handle the European end of the business. To aid these activities a factory was opened at Kitchener, Ontario, in 1919 and in 1921 the Menominee Motor Truck Co was acquired.

The Model 'B' remained in production until the 1930s, but was joined in the 1920s by a bonneted model, again supplied both to civilian and military users. By the late 1930s multi-speed axles were offered with 5-speed transmissions and extremely low gearing. Meantime, a new 2-tonner was joined in 1937 by a streamlined "cabover" and what is believed to have been the first 4-door crew-cabbed truck was constructed. A 6 x 4 rigid "cabover" also appeared and Cummins diesel engines were introduced by 1938.

The arrival of World War II saw the company supplying military versions of its heavy-duty civilian range, particularly the 'SU' "cabovers". New bonneted 4 x 4s appeared after the war, in-

1948 FWD (1) Model MU 6 x 6 artic tractor

cluding some light-duty types with high ground clearance and a heavy-duty 'U'-Series for gross weights of up to 20,000kg. During the early 1950s the company adopted the same basic cab structure for its bonneted models as that used by other manufacturers and widened versions were sometimes used on FWD "cabovers".

Among new models was a special short-wheelbase design for use as an earth-borer. Called the 'BXU', it was perhaps better known as the 'Blue Ox'. As well as the standard 4 x 4 types, there were 6 x 6, 10 x 8 and even a 12 x 10 design. One of the company's most spectacular vehicles was the 8 x 8 'Teracruzer' for operation in areas where heavy loads such as oil well exploration equipment had to be taken but where normal road-going machines could not gain access. Weighing 9978kg unladen, it had massive high-floatation tyres providing an extremely low ground pressure and could actually haul a train of such tyres, all connected to the vehicle's braking system, carrying 22,730 litres of fuel distributed between the tyres.

The company became the FWD Corp in 1960, acquiring fire equipment manufacturer the Seagrave Corp in 1963. In the mid-1960s a new 6 x 4 "cabover" called the 'Forward Mover' was introduced and towards the end of the decade the 8 x 8 'CFR' fire crash

truck was developed for airports.

The company offers a vast range of specifications using Cummins, International Harvester or Detroit Diesel engines of between 195 and 350bhp output. Current listings include the 4 x 4 "conventional", the multi-axle 6 x 6, 8 x 6, 8 x 8 and 10 x 8 'CB' "conventional", and the 4 x 4 'DF' "cabover".

FWD (2)/England 1918-1929

A British FWD production line was set up in South London by the British Four Wheel Drive Tractor Lorry Co in 1918. Two years later it became the Four Wheel Drive Tractor Lorry Engineering Co, moving to West London where it remained until 1927, becoming Four Wheel Drive Motors Ltd. It then moved to Slough, Berks, where it collaborated with Hardy Rail Motors Ltd, a company that had been set up to service and recondition World War I FWDs for the civilian market and to manufacture rail vehicles employing FWD components. Throughout this period the 'B'-Series FWD was built, one version of which was an articulated 6-wheeler called the Harford Haulier in 1922. In 1927 a 6-ton 6 x 6, powered by a 78bhp 6.6-litre 6-cyl Dorman petrol engine was introduced. The prototype R6T, as it

was known, underwent military evaluation in 1929 but if this vehicle was to be acceptable it would have to include a greater proportion of British components. In accordance with this, arrangements were made with the Associated Equipment Co Ltd to fit numerous AEC dealerships. Henceforward, all vehicles were sold as FWD-England.

FWD (3)/England 1929-1936

In 1929, Four Wheel Drive Motors Ltd agreed to use AEC components in all future British-built FWDs which would be known as FWD-England and offered through AEC's existing sales network. One of the first models to carry this name was a 2½-ton payload 3-wheeler with body mounted over the drive axle, 4-cyl petrol engine over the single steering wheel and body ahead of the driv-

er. Capable of turning within a 5m circle, this design was intended for works transport. A civilian 8-tonner, based on the company's earlier R6T model, was shown at the Commercial Motor Show, having a longer chassis frame than the original. For a while assembly continued at Four Wheel Drive Motors Ltd's Slough factory, but in 1930 a new company, Hardy

1972 FWD (1) 6 x 4 artic tractor

Motors Ltd, was formed and links with AEC became even closer. Production moved to AEC's Southall plant in 1932 and, although Hardy Motors launched a number of new designs under the Hardy and Hardy-Roadless names, the FWD-England series was continued. The old R6T was now powered by a 6-cyl AEC engine and transmission was also by AEC, comprising a 4-speed main and 2-speed transfer box.

1941 FWD (1) Model SU-COE 4 x 4 drawbar tractor

1914 FWD (1) Model 'B' 3-ton 4 x 4 military chassis-cab

FWD (1) aerial platform fire appliance c1970

GABRIEL/*USA 1913-1920*

The Cleveland, Ohio, based W H Gabriel Carriage & Wagon Co built its first 1-ton truck in 1913 – the same year that the company became the Gabriel Auto Co. A 2-tonner appeared in 1914 and was later joined by 1½-, 3½- and 4-ton types, all with petrol engines, 4-speed transmission, and worm-drive. In its last year of production the company was renamed the Gabriel Motor Truck Company.

GAETH/*USA 1908-1910*

Founded in 1902 by Paul Gaeth, the Gaeth Automobile Works, Cleveland, Ohio, launched a bonneted 1-tonner, with 4-cyl petrol engine and chain-drive in 1908. By 1911 the company had been acquired by the Stuyvesant Motor Car Co, Sandusky, Ohio.

GALLINARI/*Italy 1906-1908*

One of the lesser-known Italian truck-builders of the pre-World War I period was SA Cantieri Gallinari, Livorno, who concentrated on a 40hp 5-tonner which was powered by a 10.6-litre 4-cyl overhead-valve. A pressed-steel chassis frame was used.

GANGLOFF/*France c1960-1962*

Using a longitudinal rear-mounted Perkins diesel engine, Carrosserie Gangloff, Colmar, Alsace, constructed a chassisless 32-seat coach with jack-knife doors ahead

c1962 Gangloff chassisless single-deck coach

of the front axle or a single hinged door amidships.

GANZ/*Hungary 1913-1920*

Following the development of a diesel engine in 1912, Gyorgy Jendrasik, who worked for the railway engineering firm of Ganz Waggon es Gepgyar, Budapest, launched a series of medium-weight trucks using the Ganz and Ganz-Danubius brand names.

GARDNER-PAGEFIELD/*England 1930*

The Gardner-Pagefield 5/6-ton diesel lorry was built by Pagefield Commercial Vehicles Ltd, Wigan, Lancs. It is believed to have been the first new truck to be fitted with a Gardner diesel engine, which was a rather heavy 4L2 unit intended mainly for marine applications.

GARFORD/*USA 1909-1933*

In 1909 the Garford Co, Elyria, Ohio, began building forward-control trucks of various capacities and, as the Garford Motor Truck Co, Lima, offered 1-, 1½-, 2-, 3½- and 5-tonners by 1916. The three lightest were bonneted types whereas the others were "cabovers" designed for operation with 2-wheeled artic or 4-wheeled drawbar trailers, the 3½-tonner having worm final-drive and the 5-tonner dual chain-drive. As well as one thousand of the USA Army's 5-ton 'B'-Class 'Liberty' trucks and a number of Holt-Caterpillar half-track conversions of certain "conventional" models, the company introduced three new artic tractors in 1917 with capacities of 4½-, 7-, and 10-tons.

After the war, only "conventionals" were offered, the company being known as the Garford Truck Co. For 1920 models comprised capacities from 1¼ to 5 tons, each powered by a 4-cyl Buda petrol engine. As the 1920s progressed, passenger models were added, initially in the form of 25/29-seat dropframe bus chassis but later as a 17-seat luxury coach with 6-cyl petrol engine.

British petrol engine sales were handled by E B Horne & Co, London, who soon found that new import restrictions were hitting sales, so began to build near-identical vehicles under the Gilford name, and in 1925 R M Kincaid, former vice-president of the Garford Motor Truck Co, set up Gramm & Kincaid Motors Inc, with B A and W J Gramm to manufacture Gramm-Kincaid trucks.

The Garford business was acquired by the Relay Motors Corp which also bought out the Commerce Motor Truck Co, Ypsilanti, Michigan and Service Motors Inc, Wabash, Indiana in 1927. The new organization introduced a brand new series of Garfords similar to the Relay in the 1- to 4-ton range. Sales diminished rapidly as the Depression grew, and the Relay Motors Corp went into receivership. Despite an attempt by the Consolidated Motors Corp to save the operation in 1932, only a few more Garfords were built.

1920 Garner Model '15' 1½/2-ton truck

GARNER/*England 1914-1939*

In 1914, Henry Garner Ltd, Moseley, Birmingham, imported some 200 Continental-engined truck chassis manufactured specially for it by the Gramm-Bernstein Co, Lima, Ohio, and sold as Garners. Soon the range covered capacities from 2 to 6 tons, the latter being a rare heavyweight for those days, and was joined by the end of World War I by a new 1½-ton design. One particularly interesting Garner was the 'Busvan', announced in 1921, which could carry goods or passengers through the use of fold-away seating, and was intended for operation in country areas. A dropframe passenger chassis appeared in 1925, when the first completely British-built Garner appeared – a 2-tonner with 24.8hp Dorman petrol engine.

In 1927 the company became Garner Motors Ltd, moving to Tyseley, Birmingham, where a new 1½-/1¾-ton model was announced. This had a 4-cyl monobloc engine of 2.61-litre capacity fitted with a single detachable head, and driven through a cone clutch and 4-speed crash box. New forward-control models featured ingenious hinged wings and

cab floor to provide good engine access, a popular model for 1929 being a 3½-ton design available in both bonneted and forward-control form. Also in 1929, a forward-control 2½-ton 6-wheeled rigid with WD-type rear bogie and single transverse leaf spring suspension at the front went into production.

New for 1931 was a 3-ton low-loader running on small-diameter wheels, produced for the War Office but derived from an earlier municipal model. This also had a hand winch at the front of the load platform, with ramps and hinged jacks at the rear. By 1933 the 'Progressor' and 'Precursor' passenger models were powered by Austin '20' engines, while other models were offered with Meadows or Coventry Climax units. In 1933 the company began to concentrate on heavier models but was taken over by the Sentinel Waggon Works (1920) Ltd, Shrewsbury, and production transferred there the following year. In 1935 a new range of Sentinel-Garners was introduced, but the Garner operation was re-sold to a group of former Dodge employees who established a factory in Willesden, London, using the

GARRETT/*England 1904, 1909-1939*

Founded in 1778, Richard Garrett & Sons Ltd, Leiston, Suffolk, introduced its first steam wagon in 1904, this being an experimental "undertype" with vertical firetube boiler. Two examples were exported, but further wagon building did not occur until 1909 when a 5-tonner was announced, followed by a 3-tonner in 1911. By 1912 these wagons were available in superheated form and a 4-ton-

1933 Garner 3-ton transporter

old name of Garner Motors Ltd.

A new Garner range was similar to the old Sentinel-Garner but in 1937 was up-dated as a new 2- to 5-ton series with British-built Austin, Meadows or Perkins engines or American-built Buda or Waukesha units. The little 2-tonner frequently appeared with a streamlined body, and tipping bodies were often fitted to heavier models. The company was spending an increasing amount of time and money on the development of military prototypes, but by the outbreak of war Garner production had ceased. Although the company planned a comeback in 1946 using a twin-engined truck as a basis for an articulated tractor, nothing came of this and instead it turned its attention to body-building and to producing light agricultural tractors in a new factory at Sunbury-on-Thames, Middx.

GARNER-STRAUSSLER/*England 1938-1941*

Designed by Nicholas Straussler,

1939 Garner-Straussler 3-ton 4 x 4 military truck

ner was also built in small quantities.

A 3½-ton battery-electric truck was built to special order in 1916 but it was not until 1918 that battery-electrics entered series production. In 1917, however, the Garrett "overtype" wagon made its entrance but only one was built, having a reversed boiler with driving accommodation in front. Meanwhile, the "undertypes" had been temporarily discontinued, re-appearing in 1922

the first Garner-Strausslers were 1- and 2-ton 4 x 4 prototypes using Ford components. Built by Garner Motors Ltd, Willesden, London, these were known as Types G1 and G2, differing only with respect to wheelbase, suspension, wheels and tyres. They never passed prototype stage.

Meanwhile, a prototype twin-engined 3-tonner known as the G3 had been built by H Manfred Weiss RT, Csepel, near Budapest, to Straussler's designs. It was decided to build this at the Garner factory following receipt of an order from the Turkish government. The G3 was intended to pull a 25pdr field gun and was powered by two Ford V8 petrol engines mounted side by side, each with its own clutch and gearbox, drive being directed to a common transfer box and thence to front and rear axles. Either of the two engines could be run independently if required, the appropriate gearbox being disconnected. Two radiators and fans were fitted, header tanks being interconnected. Suspension comprised semi-elliptic leaf springs at the rear with a single pivoting transverse leaf spring and Ford diagonal radius rods, forming a 3-point suspension system at the front. The Turkish order was eventually cancelled and the vehicles were then diverted to the British War Office.

1921 Garrett 5-ton steam tipper

with a vertical cross water-tube boiler and double-cyl engine. A modified boiler was used in all subsequent "undertypes", comprising 6- and 8-tonners and a rigid 6-wheeler announced in 1926. This was mechanically similar to the 8-ton model with a double-drive bogie and roller chain final drive.

Meanwhile, the company had combined with Aveling & Porter Ltd and Charles Burrell & Sons Ltd to form the ill-fated Agricultural & General Engineers combine, whereby all steam wagon production was to take place at Leiston although retaining the original brand names. Later, Peter Brotherhood Ltd also joined the combine. Soon after this, a range of 1½-, 2½- and 3½-ton battery-electric trucks went into production, joined by 1- and 1½/2-ton delivery models and a 5/6-tonner.

Garrett 5-ton battery-electric refuse collectors c1929

By 1925 a 32-seat centre-entrance single-deck trolleybus was under construction. This had solid rubber tyres but most production models were fitted with pneumatics. Prototypes were known as 'S'-Types and were first demonstrated on the Leeds system. Few orders resulted but a few went to Ipswich in 1926. Production versions were called 'O'-Types and one demonstration of a left-hand drive example led to some overseas orders. Four-wheeled trolleybuses had single or dual traction motors of 50 or 35hp output respectively, while later 6-wheelers had one 60 or two 40hp motors, all supplied by another AGE member, Bull Motors Ltd, Stowmarket. Caledon Motors Ltd was also acquired and Garretts set about building the Garrett-Caledon petrol-engined lorry in 1926. A cam-operated poppet valve engine and better cab and driving position were introduced on the company's steam wagon in 1927.

"Overtypes" gave way to "undertypes" in 1927 and three 60-seat double-deck trolleybuses were constructed for Doncaster Corp early in 1928. Later that year two of the company's "undertype" wagons – one a 4-wheeler with drawbar trailer, the other a rigid 6-wheeler – were fitted with heavy oil engines for operation with Garrett subsidiary, Barford & Perkins, Peterborough. Claimed to be the first all-British oil-engined trucks, both had McLaren diesel engines. The only external difference between these and normal steam wagons was their external radiators. By the

Garrett road tractor 1933

end of 1929 trolleybus production had ceased and the additional space was made available for further development of internal-combustion engined vehicles using Meadows petrol and Blackstone diesel engines. The only result appears to have been a 6-ton lorry with Blackstone 6-cyl diesel engine shown at Olympia in 1931.

The company collapsed with other members of the Agricultural & General Engineers combine in 1932, but was quickly re-registered Richard Garrett & Co Ltd to concentrate on battery-electric production. In 1936 the business was re-named the Richard Garrett Engineering Co Ltd and commercial production tailed off.

1930 Garrett GB6 6-ton diesel lorry

GARRETT-CALEDON/*England 1926-1927*
Following the acquisition of Caledon Motors Ltd, Glasgow, by Richard Garrett & Sons Ltd, Leiston, Suffolk, Garretts decided to launch a range of petrol-engined lorries known as the Garrett-Caledon. Three vehicles were constructed using spares purchased in the Caledon deal. There was an impressive listing of eight goods and passenger models, none of which materialized.

GAR WOOD/*USA 1936-1939, 1957-?*
Wm B Stout, an aircraft designer, drew up plans for a lightweight streamlined bus, using a framework of welded tubing and aluminium alloy panelling. A prototype was constructed by Gar Wood Industries Inc, Detroit, Michigan, using a rear-mounted Ford V8 petrol engine. The vehicle entered series production in the Gar Wood plant, using Ford, Chevrolet or Dodge mechanical units but in 1939 the bus-building operation was sold to the General American Transportation Corp, Chicago, Illinois. In 1957 Gar Wood Industries Inc began development work on a military trenching machine based on a bonneted 4 x 2 chassis. By c1960 an improved version, known as the Model '832', had appeared, this being air-droppable from military transport planes.

1960 Gar Wood Model 832 4 x 4 trencher

GARY/*USA 1916-1927*
Using 4-cyl Continental petrol engines, the Gary Motor Truck Co, Gary, Indiana, offered four goods models of up to 2 tons capacity. In 1922 the company became the Gary Motor Corp, offering 1 to 5 Buda-engined trucks.

GAS-ELECTRIC/*USA 1905-1920*
The Couple-Gear Freight Wheel Co, Grand Rapids, Michigan, built petrol-electric trucks under the Gas-Electric brand name, battery-electric versions being sold as Couple-Gear by the Couple-Gear Electric Truck Co. Initially, the Gas-Electric was of 4-wheel drive, 4-wheel steer layout with capacities of 3 and 5 tons, but from 1908 1- and 2-tonners with front-wheel drive only were also introduced. Both rigid and articulated types were available. A new range arrived in 1914, again of all-wheel drive layout, but with a tram-type controller and 5-speed transmission. For added traction, heavy models were fitted with twin tyres all round.

GAUBSCHAT/*Germany 1951-1955*
Gaubschat Elektrowagen GmbH, Berlin, manufactured Gaubschat battery-electric commercials mainly of 1- or 2-ton capacity. These were especially popular with the German postal authorities for parcel work.

GAULT/*France 1923*
Using premises at Montreuil, Seine, an anonymous manufacturer offered a 6-wheel rigid truck called the Gault, assembled from components supplied by the White Motor Co, Cleveland, Ohio. Few were built.

GAUTIER-WEHRLE/*France 1896-1900*
In 1896 Rossel, Gautier et Wehrlé, Levallois-Perret, Seine, introduced petrol- and steam-powered commercials which it sold as Gautier-Wehrlé. Petrol-engined models had an amidships-mount-ed 2-cyl horizontal engine initially, with engines moved to the front for 1897.

GAY/*USA 1913-1915*
The S G Gay Co, Ottawa, Illinois, launched the Gay truck in 1913. Offered as a 1-tonner, this was of bonneted layout with a 4-cyl petrol engine, 3-speed transmission and double chain-drive.

GAZ/*Soviet Union 1932 to date*
Gorkovska Automobilova Zavod, Gorky, was founded in 1932 with assistance from the Ford Motor Co, USA. The first GAZ commercial for a payload of 1 ton or more was the GAZ-AAA 6 x 4 based on Ford designs which had a 50bhp 4-cyl petrol engine and a 4-speed transmission. By the end of the 1930s derivatives included a light bus, a dump truck, the GAZ-60 half-track and the GAZ-42 producer-gas lorry. A 4 x 4 called the GAZ-64 developed into the GAZ-67 of 1942; and by 1953 the GAZ-69, with 55bhp 4-cyl petrol engine 3-speed main box with transfer and semi-elliptic leaf springs all round, was the leading commercial model. When some production moved to the new Ulyanovsk Automobile plant, this was usurped by the UAZ-469.

1971 GAZ-66 4 x 4 military truck

Ford designs began to disappear after World War II, replaced by new models such as the 1½-ton GAZ-63 4 x 4, the 2½- and 5-ton GAZ-51 and the GAZ-93. The GAZ-51 was also built under licence in Poland as the Lublin-51 and is still produced in North Korea as the Sungri-58. About 1964 the bonneted GAZ-53 was introduced with various body types powered by a 130bhp V8 petrol engine and with a 4-speed transmission. There is also a forward control model, the 2½-ton GAZ-66.

GEIST/*Germany 1907-1908*
A brief entry into commercial vehicle production was made by Ernst Heinrich Geist Electrizitats AG, Cologne, which built a few Geist petrol-electric lorries powered by Argus engines.

GEM/*USA 1921-1922*
For a brief period, the Gem Auto Truck Co, Watervliet, New York, listed some light commercial types but it is unlikely that more than a few were actually built.

GENERAL/*England 1919-1926, 1929-1931*
The General name was cast into the top radiator tank of the LGOCs 'K'-, 'S'- and 'NS'-Type buses built by the Associated Equipment Co Ltd. The name was also applied to a series of prototype passenger models built at the LGOCs Chiswick Works between 1929 and 1931, and to agricultural and road tractors built unofficially by AEC Works Manager George Rushton.

GENERAL-DETROIT/*USA 1937-1955*
The General Fire Truck Corp, Detroit, Michigan, constructed a 600gpm fire pumper using the General-Detroit name. The company used its own chassis, an 8-cyl Packard engine and Ford cab, but in 1938 constructed several more appliances using Federal, Ford, GMC or V12 Packard chassis. By

c1940 General-Detroit pumper

1948 the General Pacific Corp, a subsidiary, was also building appliances under the General-Pacific name and the parent company was using Available and Duplex chassis.

GENERAL-MONARCH/*USA 1932-1935*
The General Fire Truck Corp, St Louis, Missouri, apparently had

no connection with the Detroit-based company of the same name. The St Louis company marketed its appliances under the General-Monarch name using massive 200bhp petrol engines.

GENERAL-PACIFIC/*USA 1948-1955*
The General Pacific Corp, Los Angeles, California, was a subsidiary of the Detroit-based General Fire Truck Corp, manufacturer of the General-Detroit range of appliances. Marketed under the General-Pacific name, Los Angeles-built machines were generally custom pumpers.

GER/*England 1905-c1907*
To provide feeder bus services for its railway stations, the Great Eastern Railway Co Ltd built about a dozen open-top double-deck buses at its Stratford Works. Called GERs, these had 30hp Panhard petrol engines hidden beneath a long bonnet, with chain-drive to the rear wheels. Unfortunately, they were not satisfactory, and almost as soon as they entered service suspension modifciations had to be made. Some had replacement charabanc bodies for summer use and a few ended their days as trucks.

1904 Germain open-top double-deck bus

GERMAIN/*Belgium 1902-c1907, 1937-1939*
SA des Ateliers Germain had built railway equipment at Monceau-sur-Sambre for some years, introducing a series of commercials in 1902. The heaviest was a 5-ton truck of forward-control layout with the driver seated on top of the bonnet. A number of 32-seat open-top double-deck buses were operated by the London Road Car Co Ltd but proved too delicate for London operation. By 1907 a normal-control

passenger model with 28hp 4-cyl petrol engine and multi-plate clutch was shown at Olympia. For many years the company concentrated once more on the manufacture of railway equipment, but later announced a 5-ton truck powered by a 3-cyl opposed-piston CLM 2-stroke diesel engine which the company licence-built.

GERSIX/*USA 1916-1923*
Louis and Edgar Gerlinger founded the Gerlinger Motor Car Co at Portland, Oregon, in 1916 and late that year began constructing their first truck, sometimes known as a Gerlinger but more usually referred to as a Gersix. The prototype was a worm-drive "conventional", powered by a 6-cyl Continental petrol engine. In 1917 production slowly got underway, using Wisconsin engines, and the company re-organized as the Gersix Mfg Co, Seattle, Washington. It was eventually decided to market vehicles under a different name and in 1923 the company was re-registered as the Kenworth Motor Truck Co with vehicles sold as Kenworth.

GFV/*Germany 1900-1901*
The GFV was an unusual battery-electric bus built by Gesellschaft

GIDEON/*Denmark 1913-1920*
Rudolf Kramper & Jørgensen, Horsens, was a manufacturer of stationary engines, but also developed a range of passenger cars, trucks and fire appliances. Only a handful of vehicles was built until production ceased, commercials being powered by a 3.9-litre side-valve or 5.5-litre overhead-valve 4-cyl petrol engine.

GIFFORD-PETTIT/*USA 1907-1908*
The Gifford-Pettit was a solitary 3-tonner built by the Gifford-Pettit Mfg Co, Chicago, Illinois. Called the Model 'A', it was powered by a 35hp 4-cyl petrol engine and had a wheelbase of 300cm. Of forward control layout, it was equipped with a 3-speed transmission and double chain-drive.

GIHO/*Netherlands c1975 to date*
Following the construction of two prototype trucks in 1975 under the Hobri name, American truck spares specialist GIHO BV, De Klomp, set up production facilities for GIHO heavy tippers. It is uncertain whether any have yet been built.

GILBERT/*England 1899*
Ralph Gilbert & Son, Birmingham, built the 12-seat Gilbert charabanc. Powered by a 10hp horizontal twin-cyl petrol engine with a separate coil and battery for each cylinder, it had a 2-speed belt-and-pulley transmission and chain final-drive.

GILDA/*Argentina 1957*
Designed by Giovanni Rossi, the Gilda or Rycsa pick-up truck was available briefly in 1957, assembled mainly from proprietary components. It was powered by a 57bhp V4 petrol engine.

GILERA/*Italy 1939, 1945-1960*
Built by motorcycle manufacturer Moto Gilera SpA, Arcone, Milan, the Gilera 3-wheeler had a motorcycle front-end, two driven rear wheels and a single-cyl air-cooled petrol engine. Earliest types had a foot-operated gear-change, chain-drive and disc wheels, the largest being a 1½-tonner with a 500 or 600cc overhead-valve engine. During World War II the company concentrated on lighter models, re-introducing a 1½-tonner with spiral-bevel rear axle in 1945. The company has concentrated on motorcycle production since 1960.

GILFORD/*England 1925-1935*
E B Horne & Co, London N7, was a vehicle importer specializing in the products of the Garford Truck Co, Lima, Ohio, during the

1929 Gilford 1680T coach

early 1920s. New import restrictions quickly affected sales so the company produced its own 'C', 'D' and 'F' 1½-, 2- and 2½-ton models bearing a strong similarity to the bonneted Garfords. Powered by 4-cyl Buda petrol engines, these had Goodyear pneumatic tyres, detachable rim wheels and characteristic ribbed radiators. The company became the Gilford Motor Co Ltd in 1926, introducing a passenger version of the 'F' known as the 'Swift' and a low-loading coach chassis with 6-cyl Buda engine and optional 4-wheel brakes. Proprietary components included Buda or Lycoming engines, Rubery Owen chassis frames, ENV transmissions and Kirkstall axles. Production was moved to a new factory at High Wycombe, Bucks, towards the end of 1927 and Gilford's own bodybuilding business, Wycombe Motor Bodies Ltd, was founded.

1931 Gilford DF6 2½-ton boxvan

The 150T and 1660T forward-control models appeared in 1928, intended for passenger operation but also available in goods form. The 2½-ton CP6 was introduced in goods and passenger form the following year. Hundreds of Gilford passenger models were sold in 1929 and 1930 when a moving assembly track had to be intalled to keep pace with demand. The forward-control 1680T, with Gruss air springs at the front, was announced in 1929 as was a normal-control version. In 1930 the 20-seat AS6 was introduced, and its 2½-ton load-carrying sister, the DF6, while the 1680T was offered for the first time with a British power unit, a Meadows 6-cyl engine, in 1931. Other models continued to use Lycoming engines. Poor finances and the announcement of single and double-deck front-wheel drive buses were to be the company's downfall. These were of chassisless construction, with independent suspension, no rear axle and 6-cyl Tangye opposed-piston 2-stroke diesel engine.

Despite the financial situation, the 'Zeus' double-decker appeared in 1932, followed in 1933 by the 'Hera', its single-deck counterpart, which was offered with Vulcan or Leyland petrol engines or a Tangye diesel. Later that year the company moved to smaller premises in London while Gilford exhibits at that year's Commercial Motor Show included a 3-ton goods model called the OS4. The only Gilfords built after 1935 were Gilford HSGs with producer-gas engines.

GILFORD HSG/*England 1937-1938*
Gilford (HSG) Ltd was founded at Park Royal, London, early in 1937 to develop producer-gas vehicles using patents taken out by High Speed Gas (Great Britain) Ltd. Some prototype goods carriers known as HSGs were developed, but only one passenger model, the Gilford HSG, was built. Based on a modified Gilford CF176 chassis, this had an AEC 'Regal' diesel engine bored out to 8.1 litres. A large fuel hopper was mounted at the rear offside of the chassis. This vehicle went on extensive trials before it received a body and entered service with Cardiff Corp who converted it to diesel. The company was absorbed by the Sentinel Waggon Works (1936) Ltd which was based in Shrewsbury.

GILLETT/*England 1898, 1903*
It is recorded that a steam-powered open-top double-deck bus was supplied to Lawson's Motor Omnibus Syndicate Ltd, London, by the Gillett Motor Co, Hounslow, Middx, in 1898. Gillett steamers are not mentioned again until 1903 when a vertical-boilered steam van was sold. Designed by E H Gillett, this had a paraffin-fired vertical water-tube boiler, a single-speed compound piston-valve engine and was fitted with a Joy's valve gear.

GILLET-FOREST/*France 1902-1907*
Soc Gillet-Forest commercials were easily identified by their large curved gilled-tube radiators acting as condensers for the steam emanating from the water jacket around the single-cyl engine. Based at St Cloud, Seine, the range comprised six models with capacities of up to 3000kg. All had chain final-drive but by 1905 shaft-drive had been adopted and the range reduced to two models – a 12hp single-cyl type and a 24hp 4-cyl design.

GILLIG/*USA 1932 to date*
Founded as a commercial body-building business in 1914, Gillig Bros, San Francisco, California, later introduced the Gillig school bus which had become the sole product by 1937. A transit bus sold in small numbers, but the following year saw the company in a new factory at Hayward where an underfloor-engined design with Hall-Scott engine and Fabco chassis was in production by 1941. The first rear-engined Gilligs appeared in 1945 but were again used only as school buses. During the early part of the 1970s the company designed and constructed the front-engined 'Microcoach' but built only 75 examples before selling the manufacturing rights to Sportscoach. Production currently includes school buses and German-designed Neoplans built under licence as the Gillig-Neoplan.

GILLIG-NEOPLAN/*Germany/USA 1977 to date*
Passenger vehicle manufacturer Gillig Bros, Hayward, California, has taken out a licence to construct certain German-designed Neoplan passenger models for sale in the USA. Known as Gillig-Neoplans, the first comprised a small lpg-powered fleet fitted with Ford truck engines for Santa Clara County, California. Some Gillig-Neoplans contain American air-conditioning systems and wheelchair loading equipment.

1976 Ginaf KFS16 8 x 8 tipper

GINAF/*Netherlands c1967 to date*
Gebr Van Ginkel NV, Ederveen, began re-conditioning ex-USA Army military vehicles during the 1950s for sale to civilian users and by 1967 was offering a series of bonneted 6 x 6 trucks under the Ginaf name, using Diamond T or Reo chassis, new engines and a new cab. Soon complete new vehicles were constructed using bought-in components or ex-USA Army spares. Now called Ginaf Automobielbedrijven BV, the company offers a complete range of 6 x 6, 8 x 6, and 8 x 8 vehicles of both forward- and normal-control layout. Many now use DAF cabs and are specially popular as on/off-highway tippers.

GIRON/*Cuba c1974 to date*
The only Cuban-built commercial, the Giron, appeared mainly as a single-deck bus, although a few trucks are also recorded. Based on a Hino chassis with front-mounted diesel engine, these have British SCG transmissions that may well have come from the famous Leyland buses which had been operating in Cuba since the late 1950s

GLADIATOR/*France 1902-c1906*
Soc Gladiator, Pré St Gervais, Seine, was already well-known for its passenger cars when a car-derived commercial with 12hp vertical-twin petrol engine and chain-drive was announced. In 1904 this was joined by a forward-control 2-tonner powered by the same engine but with a 3-speed transmission.

GLASGOW/*Scotland 1901-?*
George Halley began experimenting with steam propulsion for road vehicles in 1900, forming the Glasgow Motor Lorry Co Ltd in Glasgow in 1901. Two prototypes were constructed under the Glasgow name but most of the wagons were sold as Halley and a new company, Halley's Industrial Motors Ltd, set up in 1906 to handle the manufacturing side of the business. The Glasgow Motor Lorry Co on the other hand became

a hire company for Halley wagons and petrol-engined lorries.

GLOBE/*USA 1916-1919*
The Globe Furniture Co, Northville, Michigan, set up the Globe Truck Dept to build vehicles for its own use. These had capacities of up to 2 tons and a maximum wheelbase of 385cm. Re-organized in 1917 as the Globe Motor Truck Co, 4-cyl Continental petrol engines replaced 6-cyl side-valve units by 1918.

GLOSTER-GARDNER/*England 1933-1935*
Powered by a Gardner 6LW diesel engine, with both chassis and body built by the Gloucester Railway Carriage & Wagon Co Ltd, the Gloster-Gardner (or 'Gloucester') was a forward-control half-cab coach supplied initially to local operator Red & White Services Ltd. Featuring an overdrive transmission, this was joined in 1934 by an experimental short-wheelbase double-deck trolleybus with set-back front axle and centre door, shown at the 1935 Olympia Show. The model which was exhibited was purchased by Southend-on-Sea Corp.

GLOVER (1)/*England 1904*
A brief entry into the vehicle manufacturing world was made by Glover Bros Ltd, West London. Previously concentrating upon body-building, the company constructed several mediumweight commercials, listing both petrol and paraffin engined models. The lightest types were known as Gloverly.

GLOVER (2)/*England 1904-c1907*
Glover & Co, Bury St Edmunds, Suffolk, was a manufacturer of horse-drawn vans that turned to petrol-engined commercials. The first was a 2½-tonner powered by a 12/14hp 2-cyl Aster engine located under the driver's seat. For 1905 all models featured a sliding body to provide access to engine and gearbox and various types, with capacities of up to 3 tons, were listed. Up to 1906 all were of forward-control layout but from then until production ceased there were also a few bonneted models being made.

GLOVER (3)/*USA 1911-1912*
George T S Glover, Chicago, Illinois, listed a 5-ton Glover truck with a single driven wheel in the middle of the rear axle and double drive-chains on each side. It was powered by a 6-cyl petrol engine mounted in the middle of the chassis, and this was level with the body floor. Drive was transmitted via a 3-speed gearbox.

1925 GMC open-top bus

GMC/*USA 1912 to date*
The General Motors Truck Co was founded at Pontiac, Michigan, in 1911 from various truck-builders acquired by W C Durant, but it was not until 1912 that the first GMC trucks appeared, the earliest being built in the former Rapid plant at Owosso. These were normal-control 1- and 2-tonners with 4-cyl petrol engines and 4-speed transmissions. Heavier was the former Reliance range, a forward-control design for payloads of 3½ and 5 tons, using a 6.4-litre petrol engine and 3-speed transmission. All had chain-drive until 1915 when shaft-drive was adopted and GMC Electric trucks discontinued.

One year later a 1½-ton GMC was driven successfully from Seattle to New York to Seattle, and by the end of World War I some 16,000 2-tonners and many lighter models had been supplied to the Armed Forces. Post-war production centred upon the 'K'-Range, the lightest being a 1-tonner with 3.6-litre 4-cyl petrol engine, 3-speed transmission and bevel-drive, and the heaviest, the 5-ton K101 and its 15 tons GCW tractor derivative, both with worm-drive. Canadian production got underway in 1922 and from 1925 the largest USA-built GMC was the K102 'Big Brute' for 9978kg GVW. Up to this time GMC buses had been based on the 1½-ton K16 and 2/3-ton K41, but only truck-derived school buses were built after this date, all others were assembled by the Yellow Truck & Coach Manufacturing Company.

Apart from the 'Big Brute' which was listed until 1929, all models were replaced in 1927 by the 'T'-Series, covering various payloads up to 5/6 tons and featuring 6-cyl petrol engines, full electrics and pneumatic tyres. Four-wheel brakes were standard by 1928. By 1931 payloads of up to 15 tons were catered for, rigid 6-wheelers and a trailer range had been introduced. Heavy-duty models now used numerous proprietary components and a fall in demand for lighter types led to the introduction of the T18 1½/2-tonner at under US$600. Bodies for the T18 were also offered on equivalent Chevrolets.

In 1933 a sleeper-cab option for heavy models appeared, while a new 8/15-ton range was announced using 10- and 11.7-litre 7-bearing 6-cyl petrol engines, twin-plate clutches, 5-speed transmissions and air brakes. For 1934 the largest engine was a 7.3-litre 120bhp unit. Medium-duty models now had vacuum-servo brakes. A new forward-control range for payloads of between 3 and 9 tons had slide-out engines to ease maintenance. After 1935 GMCs were regularly re-styled and from that year hydraulic brakes were also available. Some lighter models, previously fitted with Pontiac engines, now used Oldsmobile units, and for certain overseas markets carried the Oldsmobile name. Synchromesh transmissions arrived in 1939 and diesel-engined models from 2- to 6-ton capacities were added, these used 3- and 4-cyl 2-stroke Detroit Diesels.

By the start of World War II the company had become the GMC Truck & Coach Divn of the General Motors Corp, and the largest manufacturer of military vehicles, supplying some 560,000 examples of the legendary 2½-ton 6 x 6, known as the "jimmy". Post-war heavies covered gross weights of up to 40,820kg, the heaviest employing a 5-speed transmission, air-operated 2-speed back axle, worm-drive and

1979 GMC 'General' 6 x 4 artic tractor

a 200bhp 6-71 Detroit Diesel engine which had only 6.9 litres capacity.

Like other USA manufacturers, the company built some vehicles specifically for West coast operation, using much aluminium to save weight and no front wheel brakes. By 1951 the 6 x 6 "jimmy" had developed into a new military 6 x 6 with 'Hydramatic' transmission. Within two years this system was also available on civilian models, initially on lightweights only but on medium-duty types by 1954. The lightest models were now almost identical to equivalent Chevrolets and, in 1955, new overhead-valve V8 petrol engines with outputs of up to 232bhp became available. In 1960 independent front suspension appeared on some medium-duty models and air suspension on some heavies, as well as the launch of a new forward-control tilt-cab on models with gross weights in excess of 8845kg. New V6 petrol engines were also announced, but the largest new engine was an 11.2-litre V12 producing 275bhp, fitted only in conjunction with a twin-plate clutch, 10-speed transmission and air brakes. This was of-

fered until 1964 when new 4-stroke diesels supplemented the 2-stroke range. Most powerful was a 220bhp V8. Numerous cab designs were offered, including both "conventional" and "cabover" types, and by the mid-1960s 8-, 10- and 16-speed transmissions were listed.

For 1970 the GMC range was identical to that of Chevrolet, apart from vehicle badges, model names and designations. Heaviest for 1978 were the "cabover" 'Astro' and "conventional" 'General' for gross combination weights of up to 36,290kg, with engines producing up to 412bhp. The current range comprises updated versions of these as well as numerous light- and medium-duty types.

GMC ELECTRIC/*USA 1912-1916*
Introduced one year after the founding of the General Motors Truck Co, Pontiac, Michigan, GMC Electrics were battery-electric goods models in various capacities up to 6 tons. Short "coal-scuttle" bonnets were fitted.

1963 GMC Model 'D' 6 x 4 artic tractor

1964 GMC 'Bison' prototype artic tractor

1961 GM Coach TDH-4517 single-deck bus

GM COACH/*USA 1944 to date*
The Yellow Truck & Coach Manufacturing Co, Pontiac, Michigan, was absorbed into the GMC Truck & Coach Divn of the General Motors Corp in 1943 and when post-war production resumed the following year, vehicles were known as GM Coach instead of Yellow Coach. Models were based on pre-war designs, particularly with respect to the Model 719 'Super Coach', a 41-seat air-conditioned design with transverse rear-mounted 6-71 Detroit Diesel engine and silver-sided body.

By 1953 full air suspension had replaced the old semi-elliptic system and the company's competitors gradually dropped out. Another 1953 innovation was the 43-seat high-floor 'Scenicruiser', developed with Greyhound to provide increased luggage space and a rear toilet compartment. This had two 4-71 Detroit Diesels, a fluid coupling connecting both and a common propeller shaft, but was plagued by unreliability

1961 GM Coach PD-4106 single-deck high-floor coach

until the arrival of the 8V-71 Detroit in 1961. Meanwhile, the 6V-71 was used in a series of transit buses announced in 1959, while later engine-driven air-conditioned transit buses used the 8V-71 for improved performance.

During the 1960s and early 1970s, models included 10- and 12-m high-floor intercity vehicles with 8V-71 engines and Spicer mechanical transmissions; 10.5-m city transit buses with 6V-71 engines and Allison torque-converter transmissions; and 12-m city

buses with 243- or 255-m wide bodies, 6V-71 or 8V-71 engines and Allison transmissions.

A new rapid transit series known as the 'RTS-Type', was delayed by the government but finally appeared in 1977, using a stainless-steel body frame and fibreglass panels. Apart from the running gear, many features were common to a government-backed low-floor 12-m city bus catering for elderly travellers which is now the standard model.

1966 GM Coach PD-4107 single-deck high-floor coach

GNR/*Ireland 1937-1938, 1941-1942, 1947-1952*
Ireland's Great Northern Railway Co Ltd, Dundalk, Co Louth, built single-deck buses in its railway works. Known as GNRs, these used many of the company's own components such as chassis frames, radiators and springs, as well as a Gardner 5LW diesel engine mounted on an ingenious flexible suspension. GNRs were built in three batches between 1937 and 1952, using bodies for between 27 and 35 passengers.

GOBRON-BRILLIE/*France 1899-1903*
Founded by Eugene Brillié in 1898, Soc Gobron-Brillié, Boulogne-sur-Seine, introduced its first commercials, based on its 8hp 2-cyl passenger car chassis, the following year. The opposed piston engines were by Gobron and capable of running on petrol, alcohol or spirits. The earliest types had vertical-twin engines located either amidships or at the rear of the vehicle's tubular frame with chain-drive to the rear wheels,

1907 Gobron-Brillié steam pump

while later models had front-mounted engines with side chain-drive. From 1900 Soc Nancéienne d'Automobiles, Nancy, offered heavier commercials based on Gobron-Brillié designs, but these and Gobron-Brillié's own commercials ceased when Eugene Brillié left to form Soc des Automobiles Eugene Brillié.

GODOLLO/*Hungary 1974 to date*
When production of the Dutra 4 x 4 10-ton dump truck was transferred to the Voros Csillag Traktorgyar factory at Gödöllö, the model was re-named Gödöllö, although still sold as Mogurt for export. The specification is as for the earlier Dutra.

GOLDEN WEST/*USA 1913-1914*
The Golden West Motors Co, Sacramento, California, offered a 4-wheel drive 4-wheel steer 2-tonner under the Golden West brand name. This had a 4-cyl Continental petrol engine and underslung springs to provide the lowest possible loading height. Later it was marketed as the Robinson.

GOLDONI/*Italy 1960 to date*
Goldoni SpA, Modena, is a manufacturer of agricultural equipment which also developed a 4-wheel drive truck capable of tackling the steepest grades. Current model is the 1760kg capacity 3500 RTS powered by a 38bhp 3-cyl air-cooled Slanzi diesel engine.

GOLDSCHMIDT/*Belgium c1906-c1913*
Designed by Robert Goldschmidt, Liége, the Goldschmidt steam lorry was built by Soc de Construction Mécaniques et d'Automobiles, Brussels. Built along petrol vehicle lines, it had a flash boiler under the bonnet, "undertype" engine and countershaft differential with double chain final-drive to the rear wheels. Of 1/1½ tons capacity, it was a wood-burner.

GOLIATH/*Germany 1931-1961*
At the end of 1931, Goliath-Werk Borgward & Co GmbH merged with Hansa-Lloyd-Werke AG to form Hansa-Lloyd und Goliath-Werke Borgward und Tecklenburg which up-dated the earlier Goliath 3-wheeler with increased engine and load capacities. The new layout incorporated a single front wheel, 2-seater cab ahead of the body and shaft-drive to the rear wheels. In 1937 the company was re-named Hansa-Lloyd Goliath-Werke Carl F W Borgward but changed yet again in 1938 to Carl F W Borgward Automobil und Motorenwerke. The re-de-

signed 3-wheelers were listed throughout this period. After World War II, 3-wheeler production continued from 1949 when the company was re-formed as Goliath-Werke GmbH and in 1950 the 4-wheeled 'Express' model, with full forward-control, 2-cyl 465cc underseat petrol engine and various body styles, was announced. Later, this was powered by a 586cc engine and by 1953 a 2-cyl 700cc unit with fuel-injection was used. The last 3-wheeler was the 'Goli' of 1955, which had a 500cc 2-cyl air-cooled petrol engine. In 1957 a front-wheel drive 'Express' with 1.09-litre 4-cyl 4-stroke petrol engine, was offered in van, truck, kombi and minibus styles, continuing until the end of production.

GOODCHILD/England 1912-1914
A highly confusing entry into the British commercial vehicle market was made by F B Goodchild & Co, London SW1. This company was a sales organization and body-building concern holding agencies for Autocarrier, Belhaven and Oryx commercials prior to 1912. After this a number of models were offered under the Goodchild name. Among the models listed was a 4-tonner built by W S Laycock Ltd, Sheffield, and marketed as the Laycock-Goodchild. There were also believed to be 1½-, 2-, 3- and 5-ton capacity goods models and charabancs, possibly also sold as Laycock-Goodchild.

GOODWIN/USA 1922-1924
The Goodwin Car & Mfg Co, New York, introduced a series of heavy trucks with massive cast-aluminium radiators, marketing these under the Goodwin name. They were replaced by the Guilder, although some were

supplied up to 1924 as Goodwin-Guilders.

GOODWIN-GUILDER/USA 1922-1924
The Goodwin-Guilder was a dropframe bus chassis built alongside Goodwin trucks by the Goodwin Car & Mfg Co, New York, to the design of the company's Chief Engineer, a Mr Guilder. The chassis frame side members were expensive single-piece pressings making the vehicle somewhat uncompetitive for the American market despite its proprietary Buda petrol engine. Other models are believed to have been built under the Goodwin-Guilder name but after 1924 all types were renamed Guilder.

GOODYEAR/USA 1918-1926
To prove the practicality of pneumatic tyres for heavy vehicles, the Goodyear Tire & Rubber Co, Akron, Ohio, built America's first multi-wheeled commercials to the design of E W Templin. First came a number of 6-wheeled double-drive trucks with roller chain final-drive and a walking beam bogie arrangement employing a single semi-elliptic leaf spring on each side. Apart from this, these vehicles were assembled largely from proprietary components and rated at 5-ton capacities. Three passenger models were also built, the first being of bonneted layout, with a dropped frame to facilitate ease of entry. The second was a straight-frame forward-control design carrying an old tram body with the engine mounted low at the front and a set-back front axle. The third was similar to the second, with tandem bogies at front and rear. All three had a re-designed bogie comprising two worm-drive Timken axles suspended on inverted semi-elliptic leaf springs, again on walking

beams but pivoted at their centres on trunnions with the axles at their ends. The USA Army Motor Transport Corps conferred with Goodyear and Templin in 1920 to develop a militarized version of the multi-wheeler, leading to the conversion of a Class 'B' 3½-ton World War I 'Liberty' truck into a Class 'C' 5-ton 6 x 4 and ultimately into the QMC 6 x 6 1½-tonner.

GOOSENS-LOCHNER/Germany 1924-1928
The 4/5-ton Goosens-Lochner was built by J P Goosens, Lochner & Co, Brand-bei-Aachen. It is believed to have been a bonneted model with an 8.1-litre BMW petrol engine and Soden pre-select transmission.

GOPHER/USA 1909-1912
The Gopher was a forward-control 1-tonner developed by Thomas F Robinson, Minneapolis, Minnesota. By 1910 he had teamed up with Freeman L Loomis to form the Robinson-Loomis Truck Co which completed 57 Gophers before Robinson left the partnership and set up his own business, the Robinson Motor Truck Co, in October 1912. All subsequent models were marketed as Robinson.

GORHAM-SEAGRAVE/USA 1912-1920
Centrifugal pumpers built by the Seagrave Co and its successor, the Seagrave Corp, Columbus, Ohio, between 1912 and 1920 had Gorham pumping equipment and were thus marketed as Gorham-Seagrave. Most had 6-cyl petrol engines, a very long bonnet and chain-drive.

GRAAFF/Germany 1952-1954
Niedersachsische Waggonfabrik Joseph Graaff GmbH was a coachbuilding business based in

the town of Elze which introduced a forward-control integral bus called the Graaff. Powered by a rear-mounted Henschel diesel engine, only a few were built.

GRABOWSKY/USA 1908-1913
In 1908 Max Grabowsky left the Rapid Motor Vehicle Co, Pontiac, Michigan, to set up the Grabowsky Power Wagon Co in Detroit. New trucks comprised 1- and 1½-tonners and passenger models, powered by 22hp horizontally-opposed twin engines, easily removable for maintenance purposes. Transmission was via a planetary system and double chain-drive. A larger model, powered by a 4-cyl petrol engine, was introduced in 1910.

GRADALL/USA 1955 to date
Following the acquisition of the Duplex Truck Co, Lansing, Michigan, by the Warner & Swasey Co in 1955, Duplex crane-carriers began to carry Gradall and Hoptoe crane and excavator equipment, also marketed by the Warner & Swasey Co. Most of these carriers were thus sold under the Gradall name, being listed in 4 x 2 and 6 x 4 form until the late 1960s, when a new 8 x 4 model with a gross weight of 34,926kg, and International Harvester petrol or Detroit Diesel engine, was announced. This policy was continued after 1975 by the Badger & Crane Divn of the Warner & Swasey Co, based at Winona, Minnesota.

GOTFREDSON (1)/Canada 1920-1932
Founded in 1920, the Gotfredson & Joyce Corp Ltd was established at Walkerville, Ontario, to build commercials for the Canadian market, initially under the G & J brand name but within a few months using the Gotfredson

1959 Goliath 'Express' 1100 1-ton integral van

c1968 Gradall 8x4 excavator

1932 Gotfredson (1) truck

name. For 1923 the company was re-named the Gotfredson Truck Corp Ltd and an assembly plant set up by the newly-founded Gotfredson Corp in Detroit, Michigan, where near identical models were constructed for the American market. Gotfredsons included trucks of up to 7 tons capacity, 4- and 6-wheeled bonneted passenger types and fire appliances, using Buda petrol engines, Brown-Lipe or Fuller transmissions and Timken axles. Production continued until the plant was bought by the Ford Motor Co.

GOTFREDSON (2)/*USA 1923-1948*
The Gotfredson Corp was founded in Detroit, Michigan, in 1923 to build Canadian-designed Gotfredsons to customers' particular requirements. In 1929 the company was re-formed as the Robert Gotfredson Truck Co and by the early 1930s both Buda petrol and Cummins diesel engines were used, often in conjunction with GMC cabs and front-ends. The firm also became the sales and service agency for Cummins in the state of Michigan. By the 1940s all USA Gotfredsons had Cummins engines, including some for gross combination weights of up to 45,359kg. Only custom-built Gotfredsons were available as late as 1948.

GOTTSCHALK/*Germany 1900-1901*
Berliner Motorwagenfabrik Gottschalk & Co KG was established in Berlin to build petrol-engined passenger cars and commercials from 1900. The first Gottschalk commercials were lightweights, followed by friction- and shaft-drive trucks and passenger models, the latter for up to 10 passengers, powered by Aster, Daimler, De Dion or Hille engines. The company was re-organized in 1901 and all subsequent types sold as BMF.

GOVA/*Netherlands c1973 to date*
GOVA Trucks BV was founded at Wormerveer to build light 3-wheeled delivery vehicles. Marketed under the GOVA name, these had a single powered front wheel and were joined about 1973 by a series of mobile shops.

1965 Gräf & Stift mobile canteen

GRAF & STIFT/*Austria 1909 to date*
Founded by three brothers in 1895, Gräf and Stift was a passenger car builder whose first commercial was a 45hp 2½-tonner. This was followed by 3- and 5-ton models and by the start of World War I many had been adopted by the Austrian Army as "subsidy" vehicles. The company was now called Wiener Automobil Fabrik vorm Gräf and Stift, the 3- and 5-tonners continuing until 1926 when they were replaced by a 2½-tonner with pneumatic tyres and a top speed of 48km/h fully laden. During the 1930s new 3- and 3½-ton load-carriers and buses were announced and diesel engines fitted for the first time but after World War II, as Gräf und Stift Automobilfabrik AG, the company concentrated on its Type 120 6-tonner powered by a 125bhp 6-cyl diesel engine. By 1953 a front-engined 37-seat bus, with 125bhp 2-stroke V4 diesel engine, and a chassisless rear-engined coach were also listed. In 1957 new forward-control trucks, including a 10-ton capacity twin-steer 6-wheeled rigid with 200bhp V6 diesel engine and 6-speed transmission were introduced and 4 x 4 and 6 x 6 dump trucks using 145bhp 6-cyl diesel engines built under Mercedes-Benz licence were also announced. By the early 1960s sleeper cabs began to appear. Increasing numbers of passenger vehicles were now being built, one of the largest being a 103-passenger 6-wheeled double-decker with underfloor Büssing diesel engine. In 1970 the company combined with Oesterreichische Automobilfabrik AG to form Oster-reichische Automobilfabrik OAF Gräf und Stift AG. All goods models are now marketed as OAF, while passenger types continue to be known as Gräf und Stift. MAN diesel engines are used and the largest model cur-

rently available is a 141-passenger artic single-decker with 230bhp 6-cyl engine and Voith-Diwa bus automatic transmission.

GRAHAM BROTHERS/*USA 1920-1928*
Graham Bros, Evansville, Indiana, assembled Truck-Builder commercial conversions until part of the operation was purchased by Dodge Bros. At this time, the company began to assemble complete vehicles bearing the Graham Brothers name and using 4-cyl Dodge petrol engines and transmissions. The range was almost identical to that of Dodge Bros, using pneumatic tyres and, from 1924, spiral-bevel rear axles. In 1922 production also got underway at Dodge Bros in Detroit, Michigan, and by 1928 a 6-cyl petrol-engined 2½-tonner and many lighter types were offered. Towards the end of 1927 the business was taken over completely by Dodge Bros, becoming the Graham Bros Divn from early 1928. In 1929 Graham Brothers trucks were re-named Dodge Brothers.

1948 Graham-Doane truck

GRAHAM-DOANE/*USA 1946-1948*
In 1946 the Doane Motor Truck Co, San Francisco, California, was re-named the Graham-Doane Truck Co and manufacture transferred to Oakland. Models were now known as Graham-Doane and a forward-control low-loading rigid, with 6-cyl Continental engine and 5-speed Clark transmission was built until the company went into liquidation.

GRANT/*USA 1918-1923*
One-and-one-half and 2-ton Grant trucks were introduced by the Grant Motor Car Corp, Findlay, Ohio, both using 4-cyl Continental petrol engines, Grant-Lees 3-speed transmissions and Torbensen rear axles. Production quickly moved to Cleveland where it continued until 1923.

GRANTON/*Scotland 1905-1907*
The Scottish Motor Engineering Co, Edinburgh, offered both goods and passenger commercials. Granton load-carriers had a 2-cyl petrol engine while the passenger model was powered by a 40hp 4-cyl petrol unit with dual ignition and double chain-drive.

GRAMM (1)/*USA 1910-1913*
The Gramm-Logan Motor Car Co, Bowling Green, Ohio, moved to Lima in 1910, changing its name to the Gramm Motor Car Co and its trucks to Gramm, the original Gramm-Logan 3-tonner being up-rated to 5 tons. Other models included 1-, 2- and 3-tonners and the company soon became the Gramm Motor Truck Co. In 1912 B A Gramm formed the Gramm-Bernstein Co in conjunction with Max Bernstein, but Gramm production continued until 1913.

GRAMM (2)/*USA 1926-1942*
When R M Kincaid left the board of Gramm & Kincaid Motors Inc, Delphos, Ohio, B A Gramm and his son W J Gramm re-registered the business as Gramm Motors Inc, offering commercials under the Gramm brand name, although a few Gramm-Kincaids were still available. Vehicles had capacities of between 1 and 5 tons using 4- or 6-cyl Continental, Hercules, or Lycoming petrol engines. From 1929 only 6-cyl engines were used and up to 1930, 1-, 1½-, 2- and 2½-ton trucks and a series of bus chassis powered by Willys-Knight petrol engines were built for Willys-Overland's export market. The Condor truck appeared in 1932, identical to certain Gramm until 1934, when a new Gramm range appeared. By 1936 larger Gramms of up to 7½-ton capacity were available. In 1938 Bickle Fire Engines Ltd, Woodstock, Ontario offered Gramms built un-

der licence but only one such vehicle was built. In 1939 a new Gramm range appeared, the company now being called the Gramm Truck & Trailer Corp.

GRAMM-BERNSTEIN/*USA 1912-1930*
In 1912 B A Gramm of the Gramm Motor Truck Co, Lima, Ohio, left to form the Gramm-Bernstein Co with Max Bernstein, also in Lima. The first Gramm-Bernsteins, sometimes referred to simply as Gramms, were 2- and 3½-tonners, joined by a 6-tonner in 1915. Early British Garner trucks were specially built Gramm-Bernsteins, and for 1916 the company

'B'-Class "Liberty" truck of which Gramm-Bernstein built 1,000 examples, carrying the letters USA on the radiator top tank. This model became the 'Liberty' truck and was also built by some 14 other manufacturers. By 1917 civilian Gramm-Bernsteins were offered in seven sizes from 1½ to 6 tons, with worm-drive and usually Continental petrol engines. From 1918 until 1925, Gramm-Bernsteins were also known as Gramm-Pioneers and in 1923 the company was re-organized as the Gramm-Bernstein Corp. Two years later, was re-named the Gramm-Bernstein Motor Truck Co, developing the USA Army's famous 5-ton

1911 Gramm (1) motor pump fire appliance

B A Gramm joined with his son W J Gramm and R M Kincaid, former vice-president of the Garford Motor Truck Co, to form Gramm & Kincaid Motors Inc.

GRAMM-KINCAID/*USA 1925-1926*
Gramm & Kincaid Motors Inc was formed by B A Gramm of the Gramm-Bernstein Corp, Lima, Ohio, in association with his son, W J Gramm, and R M Kincaid, former vice-president of the Garford Motor Truck Co. Production got underway with a series of assembled trucks in the 1- to 4-ton range powered by 4- or 6-cyl Continental, Hercules or Lycoming petrol engines. Production later moved to a new plant at Delphos where an unusually low double-dropframe passenger chassis was introduced in 1926. This was listed as a 20-seat inter-city coach or 21-seat city transit bus, but later R M Kincaid left and the company became Gramm Motors Inc.

GRAMM-LOGAN/*USA 1908-1910*
Designed by B A Gramm, the Gramm-Logan was a 3-model series of commercials built by the Gramm-Logan Motor Car Co, Bowling Green, Ohio. The intermediate type was the 25hp Model 'V' 1½-tonner and the heaviest the 45hp Model 'X' "cabover" 3-tonner with chain-drive to the rear wheels. In 1910, when the company moved to Lima, Ohio, it was re-named the Gramm Motor Car Company.

GRASS-PREMIER/*USA 1923-1937*
The Grass-Premier Truck Co was formed in Sauk City, near Madison, Wisconsin, in 1923 when two 1½- and a ¾-ton Grass-Premier were offered, powered by Continental or Lycoming petrol engines and with Clark or Timken axles. Only ten were built that year but by 1926 the range included 2-, 2½- and 3½-tonners with 4- or 6-cyl Continental or Lycoming engines. By 1930 5-, 7-, 10- and 15-tonners were also being built, including massive 6 x 4 "conventionals" with Lycoming straight-8 engines and other heavy-duty types with Waukesha engines and Wisconsin axles. Models from 1 to 12 tons capacity were available from 1932, and in 1935 a short-lived "cabover" rigid powered by a Ford V8 petrol engine was developed. This never became a standard model.

GRAY/*USA 1923-1925*
The Gray Motors Corp, Detroit, Michigan, offered two commercials based on modified car chassis. The heaviest was a 1-tonner

with an extended wheelbase of 300cm. Suspension was by ¼-elliptic leaf springs all round.

GRAY'S/*USA 1911*
Gray's Motor Co, Newark, New Jersey, built the Gray's 1-tonner briefly in 1911. With a wheelbase of 257.5cm, it was powered by a 24hp 2-cyl petrol engine and had a planetary transmission and pneumatic tyres.

GREAT SOUTHERN/*USA 1915-1917*
Although the Great Southern Automobile Co, Birmingham, Alabama, announced the Great Southern commercial in 1912, it did not construct the first, a 25-seat bus, until 1915. This was followed by 2- and 4-ton trucks with underslung worm-drive to provide a low frame height.

GREAT WESTERN/*USA 1911-1912*
Transport operator the Great Western Transportation Co, Chicago, Illinois, introduced a 10-ton capacity petrol-electric truck

called the Great Western. It had a wheelbase of 437cm and was probably used only by the manufacturer.

GREBESTEIN/*Germany 1929-1931*
Mitteldeutsche Schlepperwerke Johann Grebestein, Eschwege, offered a diesel road tractor called the Grebestein. It was powered by a 30bhp 2- or 4-stroke petrol engine.

GREENBAT/*England 1907-1908*
Greenwood & Batley Ltd, Leeds, West Yorks, built a prototype petrol-electric bus powered by a 35hp 4-cyl Mutel engine. Marketed as the Greenbat, but sometimes referred to as the Greenwood & Batley, it had two traction motors.

GRETHER/*Germany 1902*
The Grether fire appliance was built by Grether und Co, Freiburg, Baden. This was a 165gpm triple-action pumper powered by a 15hp 2-cyl Deutz engine with 2-speed transmission and chain final-drive. It could be driven

from front or rear and had two clutches, one for road travel, the other for pumping.

GROS/*France 1903-1905*
F Gros, Suresnes, Seine, designed an unusual 6-wheeled commercial with central driving and front and rear steering axles. A number of prototypes were built when production got underway in the Denain, Nord, plant of Soc Cail, using the Borderel-Cail brand name.

GROUT
USA 1901-1904
The Grout was an ungainly looking steam lorry built in various capacities by Grout Bros, Orange, Massachusetts. Of forward-control design, it had a one-man cab mounted centrally just ahead of the front axle. Most popular was the 2½-ton version with a fire-tube boiler located under the driving seat and 12hp slide-valve engine in an "undertype" position. Drive was transmitted by chain to a countershaft and then by further chains to the rear wheels. At the

end of 1903, the company was reorganized as Grout Bros Automobile Co, continuing production only until the following year.

GRUBE/*East Germany 1952-1967*
Also marketed under the IFA brand name, the Grube commercial range was developed from the earlier Lowa. Built at Werdau, Saxony, by VEB Kraftfahrzeugwerke Ernst Grube, the first model was the bonneted H6 6-tonner with 4-cyl engine. It was also offered in passenger form but was replaced in 1960 by the S4000-1, previously built by VEB Sachsenring Automobilwerke, Zwickau, under the IFA or Sachsenring name. A special road tractor for up to 14,000kg was available and all East Berlin's double-deck buses were built by the Grube company.

GRUMMAN/*USA 1963 to date*
After Grumman Allied Industries Inc acquired the J B Olson Corp, Garden City, New York, a series of alloy-bodied delivery vans known as the 'Kurbmaster' was introduced. Based on Chevrolet, Ford and GMC chassis, they were joined in 1970 by a 19-seat midibus of similar design.

GTS/*Netherlands 1973*
The GTS was an unsuccessful attempt by the American truck spares specialist GIMO BV, De Klomp, to develop a heavy-duty truck for the Dutch market. Using a Hanomag-Henschel chassis, this 6 x 6 machine was of normal-control layout but appeared only in prototype form. Following a lull, they developed the Hobri truck.

GUILDER/*USA 1924-1936*
Guilder goods and passenger commercials were developed from the earlier Goodwin and Goodwin-Guilder ranges. Announced by the Guilder Engineering Co, Poughkeepsie, New York, the range included models powered by Buda, Continental or Hercules engines, with Shuler or Timken axles. By 1927 vehicles from 1¼ to 7 tons capacity were listed and by the early 1930s, 8/10- and 12/16-ton 6-wheeled rigids were also available. Twenty-one, 25- and 30-seat passenger models were also listed. By 1930 the company was concentrating on the manufacture of trailing third axles, truck and bus production slackening.

GUILLIERME/*France 1906-1908*
Automobiles Guillierme, Paris, was a passenger car manufacturer

that attempted to build some commercials, introducing a short-lived 1200kg payload delivery van which was powered by a 15/17hp petrol engine.

GULDNER/*Germany 1969-1971*
The Güldner 'Hydrocar' was a small vehicle with hydraulic transmission used mainly as a snow-plough, farm truck, works tractor or other municipal applications. It was built by Güldner Motorenwerke, Zweigniederl der Gesellschaft für Linde's Eismaschinen, Aschaffenburg. Originally offered only as a 2½-tonner, it was joined by a 3-ton version for operation at speeds of up to 16kmh, with open driver's seat and 2-lever control. Finally, a 4-ton model, with normal dashboard, steering wheel and pedals, was announced. All three had a single-cyl diesel engine.

GURGEL/*Brazil 1976 to date*
Originally a manufacturer of beach buggies, Gurgel Veiculos, São Paulo, introduced a light commercial range using space-frame construction, Volkswagen petrol engines and coil spring suspension. Fire appliances were a speciality, and in 1978 an articulated van was shown at the São Paulo Motor Show.

GURNEY/*England 1827-1832*
Goldsworthy Gurney conducted numerous experiments with steam power before constructing a massive 19-seat prototype steam carriage in his London NW1 premises in 1827. With an unladen weight of 3½ tons, this had a coke-fired double-drum watertube boiler of welded wrought iron and a 2-cyl "undertype" engine. Drive was transmitted via a system of connecting rods and cranks to the rear axle, one of the wheels being fixed rigidly to it. The other free-wheeled, but could be used in a variety of situations such as a steep grade or uneven surface.

In 1830 Gurney constructed an improved machine weighing just 2 tons unladen. This was the 'Royal Patent' steam carriage, joined later that year by a second version powered by a 28hp engine. Neither vehicle had brakes, so reverse gear had to be used when stopping. A series of steam tractors for use with 16-seat trailers was developed from these for use on Sir Charles Dance's Cheltenham to Gloucester route. A series of catastrophes brought an end to Gurney's activities, production ending the following year, although an improved version of his steam tractor was constructed by Messrs Maudslay & Field in 1833.

Gurney steam carriage 1827

all GV models had adopted the shaft-drive system. A decimated range was offered for 1934, all with worm- or spiral-bevel axles. As demand waned, so the company moved to smaller premises at Tyseley, Birmingham.

GV ELECTRIC/*USA 1906-1920*
Previously known as the Vehicle Equipment Co, builder of VEC battery-electrics, the General Vehicle Co was founded in Long Island City, New York, in 1906 to continue battery-electric vehicle production under the GV, GV Electric and General Vehicle brand names. For 1907 a 9-model range of trucks and buses for up to 5 tons capacity was listed, all with General Electric motors mounted amidships driving the rear wheels by roller chain. In 1913 the company took over licence-production of the German-designed Daimler, initially under the American Daimler name but later sold as the GV Mercedes, and in 1916 the GV range was offered in Britain by the General Vehicle Co, Haymills, Birmingham. Also in 1916 the parent company built a few petrol-electric tractors for the New York Sanitation Dept while battery-electric types continued until 1920.

GV MERCEDES/*USA 1913-1918*
Battery-electric vehicle manufacturer, the General Vehicle Co Inc, Long Island City, New York, introduced a petrol-engined 6-tonner which was a licence-built Daimler, known initially as the American Daimler but marketed for much of its life as the GV Mercedes. It was powered by a 5.4-litre 4-cyl engine which drove the rear wheels via a 4-speed transmission and shaft-drive.

GWW/*USA 1919-1925*
Powered by a Weidley petrol engine, the 1½-ton GWW was available in goods or passenger form. It was built by the Wilson Truck Mfg Co, Henderson, Iowa, and was joined in 1924 by a short-lived 2-tonner with Wisconsin SU engine.

GWYNNE/*England 1922-1928*
Famous for its centrifugal fire pumps, Gwynne's Engineering Co Ltd, Chiswick, London, also built a series of light passenger cars, quickly adding a fire appliance on the same chassis. Powered by a 950cc overhead-valve petrol engine, this carried a Gwynne pump with its own clutch and separate drive-shaft. In 1925 the company was re-registered Gwynne Cars Ltd, fire appliance production continuing for three more years.

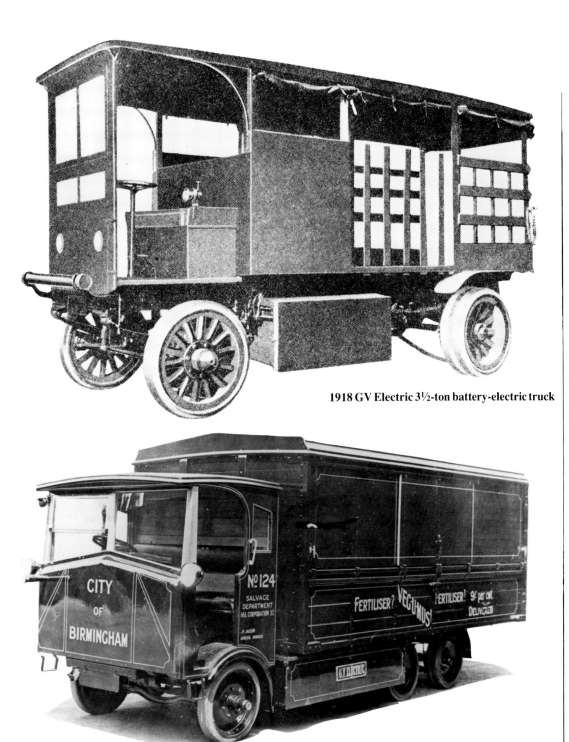

1918 GV Electric 3½-ton battery-electric truck

1933 GV 6 x 4 battery-electric refuse collector

GUTBROD/*Germany c1950-1954, 1976 to date*
Previously known as Standard Fahrzeugfabrik GmbH, manufacturer of Standard and Moto Standard vans before the war, Gutbrod Motorenbau GmbH, Plochingen, Wurtemburg and Calw, introduced the lightweight Gutbrod range in 1946 adding the 1-ton payload 'Atlas 1000' with rear-mounted 662cc air-cooled 2-cyl petrol engine. In 1953 a 3-cyl 990cc engined pick-up, van and microbus range called the 'Type 1000/3' was announced, but discontinued a year later. As Gutbord-Werke GmbH, Bubingen, the company introduced a new all-purpose vehicle called the 'Kom-

mutrac 34' in 1976. This is particularly popular for agricultural and municipal applications.

GV/*England 1916-1935*
The General Vehicle Co Inc, Long Island City, New York, introduced its battery-electric commercials to the British market through the General Vehicle Co Ltd, Haymills, Birmingham, in 1916, marketing these under the GV brand name. Initially, the British range comprised models with capacities of 1, 2, 3½ and 5 tons, all of forward-control layout with Ironclad or Edison batteries slung beneath the chassis frame. Each was powered by a single motor located just ahead of the rear

axle which was driven via chain and countershaft and then side chains. All except the lightest were popular with breweries and local authorities, the 5-tonner being adopted by many as a refuse collector. In 1924 the GV Giant 10-ton payload artic was announced, using a 22.5cm wheelbase tractor with 500amp/hr battery located behind the cab. In 1927 a new 2/2½-tonner was added and in 1930 a rigid 6-wheeler with tipping refuse-collection body was constructed to the order of Birmingham Corp. Still employing a single motor, shaft-drive was now employed but by 1928 the GV Giant had been withdrawn through lack of orders and

1929 Guy OND single-deck bus

GUY/*England 1914,1918-1979*
At the end of 1913 Sydney Slater Guy resigned as Works Manager at the Sunbeam Motor Co Ltd to develop his own 1½-ton commercial. Unconventional features included a direct third gear and overdrive fourth, with a governor to restrict the road speed to 48km/h. The 4-cyl White & Poppe side-valve petrol engine was mounted on a subframe in unit with a cone clutch and separate gearbox, suspended from the chassis frame at three points.

Guy Motors Ltd was registered in Wolverhampton, Staffs in 1914, the first Guy passenger model appearing later that year; few commercials were built before production halted in favour of armaments and aircraft engines. Vehicular production resumed at the end of World War I and in 1920 a 2½-ton model was announced and experiments took place with a pneumatic suspension system for buses, rendered unnecessary by the use of the pneumatic tyre. There was also a farmers' lorry fitted with "spud" wheels offered on a 3-tonner and in 1922 a display at the Royal Agricultural Show, Sydney, Australia, brought a rush of orders for both 2½- and 3-ton vehicles, particularly in passenger form. A new 30-seater, similar mechanically to the original 1½-tonner was added to the range and an artic 6-wheeler was also built.

In 1923 a unique twin-engined narrow-gauge road/rail tractor appeared, based on earlier Stronach-Dutton designs. Another 1923 innovation was a one-man-operated front-entrance bus with patented emergency exit door at the rear, long before this became a legal requirement. A new passenger model of the period was the 'Promenade Runabout', a modified 1¼-tonner with 4-cyl petrol engine, 4-speed gearbox and small-diameter solid-tyred wheels, carrying a "toastrack" body for up to 16 passengers.

In 1924 a series of half-track lorries was supplied to the War Office, Admiralty and Crown Agents. A 1924 landmark was a new low-loading passenger model, the first low-loading type to enter series production in Britain. Of bonneted layout, this had running units similar to those used in the 3-tonner, with a chassis frame which dropped 17.5cm behind the engine and was upswept over the rear axle to provide a loading height of just 55cm. The 'Premier Six' passenger model was launched at the 1925 Olympia Show. Available in two wheelbase lengths, a dropped frame was again employed but a 6-cyl 45bhp Knight sleeve-valve engine fitted for the first time in a bus chassis. The company's first forward-control single-decker was launched in 1926, employing 'Premier Six' chassis units and allowing for up to 35 passengers. There was a choice between an underslung worm axle and a double-reduction unit.

Experiments with a double-drive 6-wheeled military lorry were successfully concluded at this time, and the company's findings were also applied to a low-loading passenger chassis. Featuring normal-control, this was offered as the double-deck BX or BKX 56-seater. This, the company's first double-decker, used the old engine subframe system and with the 6-wheeled military lorry, earned the company the distinction of being one of the first to adopt a 6-wheeled rigid layout for both goods and passenger models. The prototype 6-wheeled bus joined the Wolverhampton Corp fleet in 1926 and, in the same year the company built the world's first pneumatic-tyred double-deck trolleybus which also went to Wolverhampton Corp. By 1927 a forward control 6-wheeler had also appeared, which was the first complete 6-wheeled bus to operate on London streets. Later that year a producer-gas lorry went into production, aimed mainly at the export market, and before the end of 1927 a new 6-cyl Guy petrol engine was announced.

By 1928 there were also new 28- and 32-seat 4-wheeled single-deckers. Meanwhile, the Star Engineering Co Ltd, Wolverhampton, manufacturer of passenger cars and commercials, was taken over and re-named the Star Motor Co Ltd. It was at this stage that the famous Red Indian symbol and accompanying slogan 'Feathers in our cap', appeared to mark the company's achievements in the automotive world. Another passenger innovation of 1928 was the 'OND'-Type, a semi-bonneted 20-seater with 38bhp 4-cyl overhead-valve petrol engine and 4-wheel brakes actuated by a Dewandre servo – the first time this system had been applied to either a goods or a passenger chassis.

1931 Guy 'Goliath' 11-ton truck

The 'Invincible' double-decker had a dropped frame either side of the rear axle and an offset transmission line to provide a single-step rear entrance and uncluttered lower saloon floor. Renowned for its silent running, both the 'Invincible' and its single-deck counterpart, the 'Conquest', were the first Guy passenger models to be subsequently offered with Gardner oil engines. By 1930 the normal-control 6-wheeled bus had been discontinued and on the military front a new 6 x 6 chassis had been developed followed, in 1931, by an 8 x 8 version. Two new heavies announced that year were the 'Warrior' 4-wheeler and the 'Goliath' 6-, for 7- and 10/12-ton payloads respectively. Based on the

1929 Guy BTX single-deck trolleybus

'Invincible', these were available only until 1934 and were the first lorries to be fitted as standard with Gardner 5 or 6LW diesel engines. Power was transmitted via a 4-speed main and 2-speed auxiliary box and braking was by means of a triple-servo vacuum system.

Trolleybuses now ranged from the BT32 2-axle model for single-deck bodies to the BT48 54-seater, the BTX60 60-seater and the BTX66 for single- or double-deck bodies. These had Rees-Stephens low-shunt compound-wound motors and regenerative controls, the world's first double-deck 6-wheeled trolleybus being built at the Guy factory in 1932. A change in regulations created the need for a 6-wheeled bus or coach in 1933, although trolleybuses of this configuration were still available as late as 1959. The 20-seat 'OND'-Type had now been joined by a competitively priced bonneted model, also of 20-seat layout, called the 'Victory'. The old 4-cyl engine was replaced by a 55bhp 6-cyl unit, the wheelbase increased and larger tyres fitted.

The 2-ton 'Wolf' was another new model available in forward- or normal-control form and quickly followed by the 3/4-ton 'Vixen' with Dorman 4-cyl diesel engine, 6-ton 'Otter' with a Meadows 4-cyl unit and 10-ton trailing-axle 6-wheeled 'Fox', also powered by the 4-cyl Meadows. A lightweight passenger model, based on the 'Wolf' chassis, was also announced.

The most famous of all Guy passenger models was undeniably the 'Arab', which also arrived in 1933. For single- or double-deck

bodies, this was the first passenger model designed specifically to take the new Gardner oil engine and whether one had a single- or a double-deck model, all mechanical components were interchangeable. Both 5 and 6LW Gardners could be fitted, both engine and gearbox being offset to provide better stability when running on heavily-cambered surfaces and to counteract the effect of an offside gangway in the upper saloon.

Civilian production was curtailed in 1936 in favour of military vehicles, one of the first being a 4-wheeled lorry using standard commercial components but with a high ground clearance, short wheelbase, small turning circle and low-pressure tyres. This was the 'Ant', which entered production almost immediately and in 1937 led to a 4 x 4 derivative called the 'Quad-Ant'. Series production of this was undertaken by Humber Ltd, Coventry. A heavier 4 x 4 was the Gardner-engined 'Lizard' which was used for a variety of military duties. A few single-deck 'Arabs' were delivered to Burton Corp in 1940 and by 1941 there was a considerable shortage of civilian lorries in the UK. Limited sales of a civilianized 'Ant' called the 'Vix-Ant' were authorized for essential users, continuing in production until 1946 when new post-war models were introduced. An austerity version of the 'Arab' double-decker, with cast-iron replacing aluminium, went into production during the war.

Trolleybus production resumed in 1947 with several BT 4- and BTX 6-wheelers and a year later the company acquired the Sunbeam Trolleybus Co, al-

though this continued as a separate operation until 1963. In 1948 Guy and Meadows jointly developed a new 10.35-litre diesel engine for the 'Arab', bus range and Wilson pre-select transmissions were offered in the same model. Two years later a Gardner 4LK-engined 'Otter' 6-tonner, also available with a Perkins P6, was introduced, an underfloor Gardner-engined version of the 'Arab' single-decker appeared and the 'Arab' double-decker now had a fully-enclosed radiator and streamlining. In 1953 a special bonneted 'Vixen' passenger model was constructed for London Transport and Douglas Corp (Isle of Man), using a bonnet along the style of the contemporary Ford Thames while, on customer's resistance, the 'Arab' double-decker again became available with exposed radiator. Mediumweight goods models acquired all-steel cabs in 1952 and in 1954 were joined by new 4-, 6- and 8-wheeled heavies using AEC chassis and axles, Gardner and later Meadow engines. Initially, these all carried the 'Goliath' name but, following representations from the German manufacturer using the same name, became the 'Invincible' in 1955. Bridging the gap between the 6-ton 'Otter' and the 10-ton 'Goliath' was the new 'Big Otter,' re-named the 'Warrior' by the time it entered series production in 1955.

Ten of the largest double-deck buses of the decade were built for Johannesburg, South Africa, in 1957. Each seated 105 passengers, had three axles and was powered by a 12.17-litre Rolls-Royce diesel engine. Other export models in-

cluded the Perkins-engined 'Seal' lightweight, the heavier 'Victory' single-decker and special versions of the 'Arab'. Another new model for 1957 was the 'Formidable' tractor, powered by an 8-litre Meadows diesel engine.

In 1958 the revolutionary 'Wulfrunian' double-decker appeared. Intended as an 'Arab' replacement, it proved expensive to develop, was far more reliable and brought about the demise of the Guy passenger range. It was the first British commercial to feature disc brakes and air suspension, and was originally powered by a 150bhp mid-mounted Leyland diesel engine, later replaced by a Gardner unit. The goods range was now completely re-vamped, with new fibreglass cabs and a distinctive sun visor on all models but the expense of this led the company into financial difficulties. By 1960 a lightweight 8-wheeler called the 'Warrior Light-8', powered by an AEC diesel, had been introduced and 6 x 4 bonneted and forward-control heavy haulage tractors, the former for export, were being produced with Cummins or Rolls-Royce engines.

The business was acquired by Jaguar Cars Ltd in 1961 and re-named Guy Motors (Europe) Ltd, absorbing the nearby Meadows engine combine soon after. A less complicated version of the 'Wulfrunian' soon appeared, as did a MKV version of the old 'Arab'. A real advance was the introduction in 1964 of the 'Big J' heavyweight range with all-steel tilt-cabs and Cummins diesel engines, although there was also a fixed-cab Gardner-engined version. At the end of 1964 the Jaguar Group merged with the ailing British Motor Holdings organization (BMC) and the Guy operation was again re-named Guy Motors Ltd. British Motor Holdings itself merged with the Leyland Motor Corp in 1968 to form the British Leyland Motor Corp Ltd, Guy becoming part of the new company's Truck and Bus Divn but no changes were made to the Guy goods vehicle range, which was now available with AEC, Cummins, Gardner, Leyland, Perkins or Rolls-Royce diesel engines. The only really new model was a special 350bhp export 8-wheeler shown at the 1970 Commercial Motor Show for gross train weight of 56 tons.

In 1975 it was announced that the 'Big J' range would be phased out as demand fell, but in fact these were still built until 1979. Even now, the Wolverhampton factory continues to supply components for other constituents of Leyland Vehicles Ltd, as well as ckd chassis for export.

1948 Guy 'Vixen' 4-ton boxvan

H

HAGEN (1)/*England 1898-1900*
Alfred Dougill & Co Ltd, Leeds, West Yorks, marketed a vertical-boilered "undertype" steam wagon called the Hagen, referred to in some contemporary reports as the Dougill. Little is known of this machine and by late 1900 it was no longer listed. After a gap of three years the company introduced Frick commercials.

HAGEN (2)/*Germany 1902-1903*
Using a single-cyl petrol engine and lever transmission, Rudolf Hagen & Co GmbH, Mungersdorf, Cologne, listed Hagen trucks and buses for less than two years. Manufacturing rights were sold to Helios Elektrizitäts AG, Ehrenfeldt, Cologne, who built identical models under the Helios name.

HAGEN (3)/*Germany 1903-1908*
Battery manufacturer Kolner Accumulatorenwerke Gottfried Hagen, Kalk, Cologne, introduced a 1- to 3-ton range of battery-electrics, marketing these under the Hagen, KAW or Urbanus brand names. Vans, trucks, fire appliances, street sweepers and small buses were listed.

HAGGLUNDS/*Sweden to date*
As the largest engineering company in Northern Sweden, AB Hagglund & Soner manufactures equipment for ships, railways and mining. Some buses have also been built but the company is better known for its range of armoured fighting vehicles such as personnel, recovery and bridge-laying types.

HAHN/*USA 1907 to date*
W G Hahn established a carriage and wagon business in Pennsylvania in 1898, building his first self-propelled commercials in 1907, by which time the business was known as W G Hahn & Brother, Hamburg. The first Hahn fire truck was built in 1913, by which time a range of bonneted chain-drive commercials had been built up. Later that year the company became the Hahn Motor Truck & Wagon Co, and within two years worm-drive Hahns covered capacities of up to 3½ tons, although a 5-tonner announced in 1918 was chain-driven.

Models from 1 to 6 tons capacity were available by 1922 and by 1923 the firm was called the Hahn Motor Truck Co, using both 4- and 6-cyl Continental and Hercules engines by 1926. New models included a Hercules-engined 20-seat passenger chassis and 27- and 35-seat Continental-powered types. In 1927 the company was re-named the Hahn Motor Truck Corp, moving administration into the former Bethlehem plant at Allentown, Pennsylvania, and in 1929 seven new models, with capacities of up to 5 tons were announced. Later that year the Rochester, New York based Selden Truck Corp was acquired and a new company, the Selden-Hahn Motor Truck Corp, was formed. Lasting 16 months, this liaison saw both Hahn and Selden trucks assembled at Allentown, where production now centred, although these often bore the Selden-Hahn brand name.

All reference to Selden vanished in 1931 when Hahn Motors Inc, as it was now known, returned to the Hamburg factory. A 4.5-litre 6-cyl Franklin engine was used for some models, and from 1933 the company concentrated more on fire appliances. Goods models were still listed, however. During the war a few mobile shops and some recovery vehicles were built and with a return to peace, Ford-chassised delivery vans were built to special order. In 1946 D H Spangler, the company's president, designed the Spangler Dual multi-wheeler which was assembled in the Hamburg plant. However, in 1948 it was decided to concentrate on fire appliance construction. Since the early 1950s, both chassis and bodies have been of Hahn manufacture, many being cab-forward pumpers powered by Detroit Diesel or Waukesha petrol engines.

HAL-FUR/*USA 1919-1931*
Goods models from 1 to 6 tons capacity, including an articulated tractor, were offered by the Hal-Fur Motor Truck Co, Cleveland, Ohio. The majority were assembled "conventionals" with 4-cyl Hinkley petrol engines, Brown-Lipe transmissions and Timken worm- or bevel-drive axles. Production later moved to Canton, where the Model 6YB, introduced in 1928, was claimed to be the world's largest removal van. This was a rigid 6-wheeler with 6-cyl Hinkley engine, air brakes, single balloon tyres and a payload rating of 6 tons.

HALL/*USA 1915-1922*
Three and one-half and 5-ton trucks were introduced by the Lewis Hall Iron Works, Detroit, Michigan, the lighter model being available with worm- or double chain-drive.

In 1917 the range was expanded to include 2- and 7-tonners and by the following year only the latter had chain-drive. About this time the company became the Lewis Hall Motors Corp, all models having 4-cyl Continental petrol engines and 3-speed transmission.

HALLEY/*Scotland 1901-1935*
The Glasgow Motor Lorry Co Ltd, Glasgow, was founded by George Halley in 1901 to construct steam wagons, and although two prototypes were assembled under the Glasgow name the design was soon known as the Halley, featuring a vertical boiler, compound "undertype" engine, chain final-drive and Ackermann steering. Petrol-engined commercials were also introduced. Steamers were soon abandoned and in 1906 the company was re-constituted as Halley's Industrial Motors Ltd, moving to premises at Yoker, Glasgow. The following year the company was awarded Gold and Silver Medals in the 1½- and 2-ton classes of the RAC Trials and a complete range of models, from 1 to 6 tons capacity, was introduced. Fire appliances were especially important, the lightest of which had a 2-cyl Crossley engine and shaft-drive while the heaviest had a Tylor engine and chain-drive.

Some 400 3-ton "subsidy" models were supplied during World War I, but at the end of the war the company concentrated on one model – a 3½-ton or 25/35-seat 6-cyl worm-drive chassis. By 1922 a new range was offered, examples of which could be had in forward-control as well as bonneted form. The 31-seat 'Kenilworth' coach chassis and 'Ivanhoe' charabanc chassis were announced in 1925, both using Halley's 35bhp 6-cyl petrol engine, smaller capacities being catered for by the 4-cyl 20-seat 'Talisman'. A new 1½-ton "subsidy" model was also introduced.

At the end of 1927 the company was re-formed as Halley Motors Ltd and in 1928 an 85bhp 4-cyl petrol engine was announced for the new 'Conqueror' passenger model. A rigid 6-wheeled single-deck bus chassis introduced later that year was called the 'Challenger' from 1929, when it was joined by an 8-ton 6-wheeled rigid goods model known as the BS3. A new radiator design incorporating a Scottish lion on the badge was introduced in 1931, appearing first on the 'Clansman' and 'Neptune' passenger types for single- and double-deck bodies.

The company was now losing ground in the diesel race and when a new goods model from 4 to 13 tons capacity, and a new passenger series for between 26 and 51 passengers, were introduced they were still only available with petrol engines. At the 1934 Scottish Show the company attempted to catch up by fitting a Perkins 'Leopard' engine in a 4-tonner but in 1935 the business went into liquidation, the remains were bought by Albion Motors Ltd.

1907 Hallford open-top bus

HALLFORD/*England 1907-1925*
J & E Hall Ltd, Dartford, Kent, entered the commercial vehicle business with the 3-ton chain-drive Hallford, using a licence-built 4-cyl petrol engine of Swiss Saurer design. This model had a fish-bellied chassis frame. That same year one of the prototypes was awarded a Gold Medal and Special Diploma in the RAC's Commercial Motor Trials, the company also becoming involved with W A Stevens Ltd, Maidstone, in the manufacture of the Hallford-Stevens petrol-electric bus. By 1911 J & E Hall was building engines of its own design, offering vehicles from 1¾ to 5 tons load capacity. Lightest models were a 325-cm wheelbase 1¾- and a 370-cm or 400-cm wheelbase 2½-tonner. Both had Hall's Type 'CC' 25hp 4-cyl petrol engine with cylinders cast in pairs. A foot pedal acted upon a band-type transmission brake between gearbox and differential counter shaft. A 3-tonner was perhaps the most popular, with wheelbase of 360-

Hallford 10-ton artic tractor c1923

cm or 450-cm, while a 4-tonner had 405-cm or 450-cm in wheelbase. Both were powered by the Type 'EA' 32hp 4-cyl petrol en-

1909 Hallford charabanc

gine. A 450-cm wheelbase 5-tonner used the Type 'EE' engine. Three, 4- and 5-tonners all had 4-speed gearboxes and the 3-tonner was easily accepted as a "subsidy" vehicle. Sales dragged considerably after the war, not helped by the vintage design which was virtually the same as for the 1911 range with a 'CC'-engined 2½-tonner and 'EA' and 'EE'-engined 4- and 5-tonners. The only new model was a 10-ton 6-wheeled rigid, announced in 1923.

HALLFORD-STEVENS/*England 1907-1911*
J & E Hall Ltd, Dartford, Kent, collaborated with W A Stevens Ltd, Maidstone, to produce a number of prototype petrol-electric buses known as Hallford-Stevens. Based on the Hallford 3-tonner, these had a 30/38hp 4-cyl petrol engine driving two electric motors, one on each side of the chassis which, in turn, drove each rear wheel via a worm-and-wheel final-drive. Other features included air-compression brakes and a "dead" rear axle. The first of these, a double-deck open-topper called 'Queenie', was demonstrated in Coventry in 1908. By 1911 development work had been taken over by Thomas Tilling Ltd, and some vehicles were even referred to as the Frost-Smith Petrol-Electric. Towards the end of that year the first Tilling-Stevens TTA1 petrol-electric bus was introduced.

HALSEY/*USA 1901-1907*
In 1901 James T Halsey, New York, designed a steam lorry with vertical water-tube boiler, front-wheel drive and steering and no less than two single-acting 4-cyl steam engines, each driving a front wheel through a spur-gear system. A 12hp prototype appeared later that year, followed by another in 1902. In 1904 the Halsey Motor Co was founded in Philadelphia, Pennsylvania, and production of a 30hp model, with two 8-cyl engines, got underway. In 1905 the business was re-named the Halsey Motor Vehicle Co,

production of the 8-ton payload 30hp model continuing until the business was closed.

HANCOCK/*England 1830-1840*
Walter Hancock was the most successful of all early steam carriage manufacturers. In 1824 he patented a steam engine using a bellows system in place of the usual cylinder and piston, and in 1827 took out a further patent on a coke-fired boiler. This system was fitted in a 4-wheeled 10-seat carriage called 'Infant' in 1830, this having a rear-mounted oscillating engine driving the rear axle via chain wheels and link. This concept proved unsatisfactory and the carriage was re-built with a vertical twin-cyl engine, mounted ahead of the chain-drive rear wheels. Transverse seating was retained, but now increased to 14 passengers.

The second wagon was 'Era', built to the order of the London & Brighton Steam Carriage Co. It was mechanically similar to its predecessor but had a double coach body carrying eight persons in each compartment, with two additional seats on either side of the driver. Meanwhile, a Parliamentary Select Committee recommended the commercial exploitation of Hancock's ideas, which led to the formation of the London & Paddington Steam Carriage Co in 1832.

Three new carriages were ordered, the first being the 'Enterprise' with two longitudinal seats each carrying seven passengers, which was withdrawn after 16 days following a disagreement between Hancock (who operated the vehicles) and David Redmund (Engineer of the L & PSCC), who cancelled the remaining order and began constructing his own carriages.

Next came the 12-seat 'Autopsy' which Hancock himself operated. Another 'Era' was now under construction, this time with only eight passengers inside but with a further five up front with the driver. Both 'Era' and 'Autopsy' entered experimental service in 1835 but 'Era' later became 'Er-

in' and was shipped to Dublin for further trials. In 1836 a carriage was constructed called 'Automaton'. Seating 22 passengers, it could haul a trailer carrying another 18, but by now the railways were capturing the public's imagination and no further Hancock steamers were built.

HANLEY/*USA 1940-1941*
Previously Chief Engineer at the Prospect Fire Engine Co, Keenan Hanley formed the Hanley Engineering Service, Prospect, Ohio, after the former company closed down in 1934. The new company began to construct complete fire appliances, one of the first being a quad pump combination powered by a V16 petrol engine, making this the world's first appliance with a 16-cyl engine. Using GMC sheet metal, it was joined a year later by a triple combination and a ladder truck, also with V16 engines but resembling later Ahrens-Fox appliances.

HANNIBAL/*USA 1915-1917*
The 1-ton Hannibal was introduced by the Hannibal Wagon Works, Hannibal, Missouri, in 1915. This company was re-named the Hannibal Motor Wagon & Body Co later that year and in 1916 became the Hannibal Motor Car Co.

HANNO/*Germany 1936-1950*
Marketed as Hanno or Hoffman, a series of road tractors was built by Hannoversche Fahrzeug-Fabrikation F K Hoffman, Laatzen, Hanover. Throughout World War II normal-control road tractors were supplied to the German Armed Forces with rear-mounted opposed-piston vertical single-cyl Junkers diesel engines. A Deutz-engined type was introduced in 1949 but was withdrawn the following year.

HANSA/*Germany 1906-1914*
Hansa Automobil GmbH, Varel, Oldenburg, offered commercial derivatives of some of its passenger cars. The first was a delivery van built until 1910. In 1913 the company was re-named Hansa Automobil AG, production continuing for one more year before a merger with Norddeutsche Automobil und Motoren AG, Bremen, manufacturer of Lloyd commercials, to form Hansa-Lloyd Werke GmbH.

HANSA-LLOYD/*Germany 1914-1938*
In 1914 the first Hansa-Lloyd commercials, a series of petrol-engined and battery-electric light goods models, left the Varel, Oldenburg, and Bremen factories of Hansa-Lloyd Werke GmbH,

formed by the merger of Hansa Automobil AG and Norddeutsche Automobil und Motoren AG. All were based on earlier Lloyd designs. A new 2-ton truck, with worm final-drive appeared in 1921, as well as some battery-electrics employing an unusual bogie steering system and front-wheel drive. There was also a 10-ton battery-electric tractor of 4 x 2 or 4 x 4 configuration. In 1925 a low-loading bus was announced and by 1929 a rigid 6-wheeler with petrol or petrol-electric drive had been added to the range.

1938 Hansa-Lloyd turntable ladder fire appliance

In 1928 the company was taken over by Kühlenfabrik Borgward & Co, but the Hansa-Lloyd name continued, the company being re-organized as Hansa-Lloyd und Goliath-Werke Borgward und Tecklenburg in 1931. By this time the range comprised the 1½-ton 'Columbus', 2-ton 'Bremen', 3½-ton 'Europa', 4-ton 'Merkur' and 5-ton 'Roland'. The company was also responsible for marketing the Goliath range. In 1935 a 6 x 6 2½-tonner was developed for the military, later appearing in 4 x 2 and 4 x 4 form and for an increased payload of 3 tons.

In 1937 the company was re-named Hansa-Lloyd Goliath-Werke Carl F W Borgward and gradually the model range became indistinguishable from that of Borgward.

HARBILT/*England 1947 to date*
Harbilt battery-electrics were built by the Harborough Construction Co Ltd, Market Harborough, Leics, these being pedestrian-controlled 4-wheelers of 1-ton capacity carrying batteries on each side of the chassis. Even a tipping model was available and, during the 1950s the rider-type Model 750 was introduced, followed by a 1¼-tonner of similar layout. New 3- and 4-wheelers were added during the 1960s and a 1½-tonner also introduced, while 1974 saw the Post Office Telephones Divn place one of these in experimental London service. The company has concentrated on heavier models since 1973 and now builds 3- and 4-wheeled battery-electric personnel-carriers under the Harbilt-Melex brand name.

Hanomag truck c1938

HANOMAG/*Germany 1905-1908, 1925-1969*
The first Hanomags comprised a series of steam trucks and buses built by Hannoversche Maschinenbau AG vorm Georg Egestorff, Linden, Hanover, up to 1908. Designed by Peter Stoltz and sometimes referred to as the Stoltz, these were also licence-built by Suddeutsche Automobilfabrik GmbH, Gaggenau, Baden, and Friedrich Krupp, Essen. After a gap of some years, the company introduced a 3/4-ton payload forward-control lorry, followed by a road-going version of its agricultural tractor powered by Hanomag's own diesel engine from 1928.

In 1932 the firm was re-named Hanomag Automobil und Schlepperbau GmbH, introducing a new forward-control truck with 60bhp 5.2-litre 4-cyl diesel engine located amidships. This was a 3/4-tonner listed also as a passenger chassis, the same engine being fitted in an express road tractor and a heavy-duty 15-ton tractor. A 20-ton road tractor, powered by a 100bhp 8.5-litre 5-cyl diesel, appeared in 1935 but other commercials were based on Hanomag passenger car chassis. Before the end of that year the company had become Hannoversche Maschinenbau AG, but existing models continued largely unchanged until 1950, when a new 1½-tonner, with 45bhp 4-cyl diesel engine was announced, joined by 2-, 2½- and 3-tonners. The lighter model was soon available in 4-wheel drive form while the 2½-tonner became popular for passenger work.

In 1952 the company became Rheinstahl-Hanomag AG but no significant changes were made to the range until 1958 when the 'Garant', 'Kurier' and 'Markant' trucks, with capacities of between 1¾ and 2½ tons, were announced. Meanwhile, the company had acquired an interest in Vical and Sohn Tempo-Werk GmbH, manufacturer of lightweight Tempo commercials, taking this company over completely in 1963 but retaining the Tempo brand name until 1966. In 1967 Hanomags comprised the F45, F55, F65 and F75, types with 65- or 80bhp 4-cyl diesel engines. A heavier series comprised the F55, F76, F85 6-cyl types powered by a 100bhp 4.25-litre diesel. The old Tempo models became the Hanomag F20, F25, F30 and F35, using a 54bhp 1.62-litre 4-cyl petrol unit or 50bhp diesel equivalent. These new ranges had payload capacities of between 1¾ and 5½ tons.

1967 Hanomag F45 fire appliance

In 1968 the company merged with Rheinstall-Henschel AG, Kassel, manufacturer of Henschel heavy commercials, enabling it to offer a complete range of commercials. One year later Daimler-Benz AG took 51% share in the business and later that year all models became known as Hanomag-Henschels.

HANOMAG-HENSCHEL/*Germany 1969-1973*
A year after the merger of Rheinstahl-Hanomag AG, Linden, Hanover, and Rheinstahl-Henschel AG, Kassel, Daimler-Benz AG acquired a 51% share in the business and all models were re-named Hanomag-Henschel. Models ranged from the former Tempo 1-tonner, now designated the F20, up to a 22-tonner previously marketed under the Henschel name, the heaviest types being bonneted or forward-control tractors of 6 x 4 layout. In 1970 Daimler-Benz AG took the business over completely, introducing

1971 Hanomag-Henschel F45

Mercedes engines in various models. The Hanomag-Henschel range came to an end when, as Hanomag-Henschel Fahrzeugwerke GmbH, it was absorbed totally into the Daimler-Benz operation, certain light Mercedes commercials being built along Hanomag-Henschel lines.

1973 Hanomag-Henschel truck

Harder chemical fire appliance

HARDER/*USA 1909-1914*
The Harder Fire Proof Storage & Van Co, Chicago, Illinois, was a removal and storage company which began building vehicles for its own use. These were forward-control models with 4-cyl petrol engines, chain final-drive and capacities of between 1½ and 5 tons. The company soon found its commercials popular with other operators and a few were even fitted out as fire appliances. Accordingly, Harder's Auto Truck Co was founded in 1913.

HARDY/*England 1932-1938*
Hardy Motors Ltd was formed in 1931 to take over production of former FWD-England trucks at the Associated Equipment Co's Southall, Middx, factory, and from 1932 these were sold as Hardy or Hardy-Roadless. Most significant was the 4/4 4-tonner, first built as an FWD-England in 1930 and later used as a basis for the AEC 'Matador' medium artillery tractor of World War II. In appearance, the 4/4 resembled other AECs with the familiar AEC radiator at the front. Another important model was the R68 6 x 6, later developed into the AEC (0)854 6 x 6 of World War II.

HARDY-ROADLESS/*England c1935*
In association with Roadless Traction Ltd, Hardy Motors Ltd, Southall, Middx, produced a few rugged half-track vehicles for civilian and military use about the mid-1930s. These were adaptations of "standard" Hardy models, featuring special tracks in place of the driving wheels.

HARFORD HAULIER/*England 1922*
A 6-wheeled articulated version of the FWD built by the Four Wheel Drive Tractor Lorry Engineering Co Ltd, West Ealing, London, was available briefly as the Harford Haulier.

HARMENING/*Germany 1954-1957*
Hermann Harmening, a coachbuilding firm, of Buckeburg, offered an integral bus with rear-mounted 85bhp Henschel diesel engine known as the 'Club-Bus'.

HARMER-KNOWLES/*Canada 1923*
The Harmer-Knowles heavy goods range was built briefly in Toronto by the Harmer-Knowles Motor Truck Co Ltd, Ontario, using a building previously occupied by the Russell Motor Car Co Ltd. It employed numerous US-built components but production was low and sales restricted mainly to the Toronto area.

HARPER/*Scotland 1898-1900, 1908*
John Harper, his sons and Thomas Mowat, trading as the Harper Motor Co, Holburn Junction, Aberdeen, built a few Benz- and Daimler-engined road tractors at the end of the 19th century. After a break from commercial vehicle production, the company introduced a short-lived steam lorry in 1908.

HARRINGTON/*England c1952-1954*
A Rolls-Royce-engined version of the Commer-Harrington 'Contender', marketed simply as the Harrington, was built in small numbers by Thomas Harrington Ltd, Hove, East Sussex, to the order of the British Overseas Airways Corp in the early 1950s. Later, the company also built a small fleet of 12-seat chassisless crew cars employing Ford running units and 'Cost-Cutter' 4-cyl petrol engines. These were also supplied as 19-seat buses, ambulances and general cargo vehicles.

HARRISON/*USA 1911-1917*
Harrison trucks comprised three models of which the largest was probably also the largest US-built

truck of the period, weighing 5900kg in chassis form. Built by the Robert Harrison Co, South Boston, Massachusetts, these were forward-control 3½-, 5- and 12-tonners of which only the lightest was built until the end of production. With a wheelbase of 355cm, this had a 4-cyl petrol engine, 3-speed transmission and double chain-drive.

HARRODS/England 1937-1939
Already a firm believer in the battery-electric delivery van, Harrods Ltd, London SW1, built almost 60 1-ton capacity battery-electrics for its own use at its Engineering & Coachbuilding Works, Barnes, London. Traction equipment was supplied by Bruce Peebles & Co Ltd; each vehicle followed closely the design of Harrods' American-built Walker battery-electric.

HART-DURTNALL/England 1907
The Hart-Durtnall petrol-electric system was developed by Hart & Durtnall, Luton, Beds. A petrol engine drove a 1½ hp DC dynamo and multi-polar AC generator which supplied current to a single electric motor. Drive was transmitted to a "live" back axle with differential gear. A few goods and passenger models were built using this system.

HART-KRAFT/USA 1911-1913
The lightweight Hart-Kraft highwheeler was a product of the Hart-Kraft Motor Co, York, Pennsylvania, but it was not until 1911 that the company introduced a heavier design using the company's own water-cooled 4-cyl petrol engine, an armoured timber chassis frame, cone clutch and double chain-drive. Although the company went into receivership before the end of that year Hart-Kraft production continued using 4-cyl Continental petrol engines for two more years.

HARVEY/USA 1911-1932
The Harvey Motor Truck Works, Harvey, Illinois, introduced Harvey goods models in the 1½ to 3 tons class, adding a 5-tonner in 1916. All were Buda-engined, joined in 1927 by the 'Road Builders' Special', a dump truck with 7 forward and 2 reverse speeds. All had 6-cyl engines from 1929, when 6- and 10-ton articulated types were announced.

HASBROUCK/USA 1899-1901
The Hasbrouck Motor Co, Newark, New Jersey, developed both goods and passenger models based on its passenger car. These were powered by a large centrally-mounted single-cyl petrol engine

with 2-speed epicyclic transmission and chain final-drive. By the time production ended, the company was known as the Hasbrouck Motor Works, having moved to Piermont, New York.

HATFIELD (1)/USA 1910-1914
The Hatfield Motor Vehicle Co, Highland Falls, Elmira, New York, launched the 1-ton Hatfield truck in 1910. This had a 3-cyl air-cooled petrol engine, friction transmission and double chain-drive, some being of normal- and others of forward-control layout. For 1911 the company moved to Cornwall-on-Hudson and was reconstituted later that year as the Hatfield Automobile Truck Co.

HATFIELD (2)/USA 1916-c1924
The Cortland Cart & Carriage Co, Sidney, New York, was yet another manufacturer offering commercial derivatives of its passenger cars. The first had a 4-cyl petrol engine but little else is known about it. Production of passenger cars ceased in 1924 although commercials may have ended earlier.

HATHI/England 1923
As an experiment, the Royal Army Service Corps constructed a 4-wheel drive gun tractor, using components taken from captured German 4 x 4s. This was one of the earliest British-designed 4 x 4s, fitted with pneumatic tyres and a power winch, but only one prototype was built, series production being put out to tender. The production model, known as the Mk II, was built by John I Thornycroft & Co Ltd, Basingstoke, and carried the Thornycroft name. The first British-built 6 x 6 comprised a Thornycroft version fitted with WD-type double-drive bogie by the RASC at Aldershot in September 1927.

HAULAMATIC/England 1968 to date
Haulamatic Ltd, Ilkeston, Derbys, fitted a fully-automatic 6-speed Allison transmission and its own design of tipping gear and scow-end dump body to a modified Commer chassis/cab in 1968. Tests were successful and a number of Commer-chassised vehicles were sold, some with half-cabs. Mid-1969 saw the introduction of the 6-15 dump truck, the first machine constructed entirely by the company. This was a 6-wheeled half-cab for 22/26 tons GVW powered by a 180bhp Perkins V8-540 diesel with 5-speed fully-automatic Allison transmission. In 1970 the 10-ton capacity 4-10 replaced the Commer-based machine, using a 146bhp Detroit Diesel engine, 4-speed fully-auto-

1979 Haulamatic 4-10 dump truck

matic Allison transmission and 2-speed rear axle. Largest in the current range, now built at Heanor, Derbys, is the 6 x 4 620, with a 215bhp Perkins V8-640 or 210bhp Caterpillar V8 diesel engine and Allison transmission.

HAULPAK/USA 1957-1968
In addition to other types of earth-moving machinery and experimental land-trains for the US Army, the Le Tourneau-Westinghouse Co, Peoria, Illinois, introduced the Haulpak dump truck in 1957. The first were 27- and 30-ton 4-wheelers for on/off-highway operation but heavier models were soon added, all of the same basic layout with one-man half-cab and engine mounted ahead of the front axle. In 1968 the company was re-organized as the Construction Equipment Divn of the Westinghouse Air Brake Co, the Wabco marque name was adopted and the Haulpak name relegated to model designation.

HAWKEYE/USA 1915-1933
The first Hawkeye truck was a 1½-tonner built by the Hawkeye Mfg Co, Sioux City, Iowa, employing a 4-cyl Buda petrol engine and 3-speed Fuller transmission. In 1916 the company was renamed the Hawkeye Truck Co and by 1919 a 2-tonner, also with 4-cyl Buda petrol engine, had been introduced. A 4-cyl Buda engined 3½-tonner was added in 1921, changed to a 6-cyl Buda in 1927. From 1931 engine options also included Hercules and Wisconsin units.

HAY/England 1905-1906
What is believed to have been the only single-cyl steam wagon ever built, the Hay 6-tonner was a product of the Hay Motor Co Ltd, Liverpool, Lancs. It employed a vertical cross water-tube boiler

mounted ahead of the front axle, and an "undertype" engine located amidships. The rear wheels were driven via an unusual ratchet-and-pawl drive system. Later the company moved to new premises in Birkenhead, Cheshire, showing a compound wagon at the 1906 Cordingley Show.

HAYES/Canada 1934-1975
Previously sold as Hayes-Anderson, Hayes trucks were built by the Hayes Mfg Co Ltd, Vancouver, British Columbia, certain models being sold as Hayes-Lawrence. Popular products included logging trucks, low-loading rigids for dockside work, buses and coaches and even tandem-axle kits for converting 4-wheelers into double-drive rigid 6-wheelers.

Appointed a Leyland dealer during the late 1930s, the company used an increasing percentage of Leyland components, and soon after World War II launched a new range of highway tractors. In 1947 three company executives left to set up the rival Pacific Truck & Trailer Ltd, but by the 1960s Hayes logging tractors and heavy haulage outfits were being assembled in some numbers, using Caterpillar, Cummins, Rolls-Royce and Detroit Diesel engines. In 1969 Mack Trucks Inc acquired a major interest in the business which was re-named Hayes Trucks Ltd, introducing the all-new 'Clipper 100' "cabover" the following year. This could be had in rigid or articulated form, as could the 'Clipper 200' "conventional", the 'HS'-Series off-road range and the HDX logging tractor. The latter was a bonneted 6 x 4, capable of handling a 130-ton load of round timber at a time. Specification included a 430bhp V12 Detroit Diesel, 6-speed Allison 'Power-Shift' transmission and braking systems comprising water-cooled brake drums and hydraulic transmission retarders. Despite its apparently rosy future in the logging and heavy haulage fields, Mack's Hayes interests were sold to a subsidiary of the Pacific Car & Foundry Co, Renton, Washington, USA, in 1974 and closed down the following year.

HAYES-ANDERSON/Canada 1928-1934

The Hayes Mfg Co Ltd was established in Vancouver, British Columbia, to build light-, medium- and heavyweight goods models with capacities of between 1½ and 15 tons as well as buses and coaches, the first trucks appearing under the Hayes-Anderson brand name. Using Continental, Hercules or Leyland engines, the company developed a series of bonneted logging tractors aimed at the local lumber industry and a patented coupling system enabling trailers to track closely behind the tractor. After 1934 models were referred to simply as Hayes or, occasionally, as Hayes-Lawrence.

1970 Heathfield DE50 25-ton dump truck

HEATHFIELD/England 1966 to date

Axle manufacturer Centrax Ltd founded Heathfield Engineering Ltd, Newton Abbot, Devon, in 1966 to build on/off-highway 4-wheeled dump trucks. The first was a 2cu m design with Perkins 6.354 diesel engine and a 5-speed David Brown transmission. A longer wheelbase called the DF20 and its derivatives were quickly added and the series re-vamped in 1972. The 19-ton H19 and 28-ton H28 4-wheelers appeared two years later powered, respectively, by a 200bhp 11.1-litre Leyland and 310bhp 14-litre Cummins diesel engine. The H19 had a 5-speed manual transmission while the H28 had either a 9-speed Fuller manual or an Alliton automatic system. These models were re-vamped for 1978, being re-designated the H20 and H30 for 18,140 and 27,215kg payloads, respectively. The lighter model has a Leyland UE680 or Rolls-Royce CE220 engine, while the H30 has a Cummins NT310 or NTA855C. Both have independent front suspension.

HELECS/England c1951-1957

Hindle, Smart & Co Ltd, Ardwick, Manchester, was responsible for manufacturing and marketing all post-war Wilson battery-electric trucks designed by Partridge, Wilson & Co Ltd, Leics as well as being involved in the manufacture of the Jen-Helecs battery-electric artic in collaboration with Jensen Motors Ltd since 1946. About 1951 a 1¼-ton 287-cm wheelbase battery-electric delivery vehicle was announced, named the 'Intruder' from 1953 and joined by the 1½-ton 'Endeavour'. A year later the narrow 165-cm wheelbase 'Help-Mate' was introduced for operation in congested areas, and in 1955 the company was re-constituted as Helecs Vehicles (Mfgs) Ltd, moving to new premises in Rusholme, Manchester.

HELIOS/Germany 1903-1906

After Helios Elektrizitäts AG, Ehrenfeldt, Cologne acquired the manufacturing rights for Hagen commercials from Rudolph Hagen & Co GmbH, these were continued as Helios, still using lever transmission until chain final-drive was announced. In 1906 the company diverted its attention to general engineering.

HENDRICKSON/USA 1900, 1913 to date

Having built his first truck in Chicago, Illinois in 1900, Magnus Hendrickson went on to build Lauth and Lauth-Juergens trucks until 1913, when he and sons George and Carl set up the Hendrickson Motor Truck Co, its first model being a chain-drive "cab-over". By 1920 the company was offering three basic worm-drive models from 2½- to 5-ton capacity with multi-plate clutches and Timken worm-drive axles.

The company's first rigid 6-wheeler, using double-drive worm axles and balance beam suspension appeared in 1926 and, to cater for increasing business, a new plant was established at Lyons, Illinois, the following year. By 1933 tandem bogies were being supplied to International Harvester and later this company's fire trucks were also being built by Hendrickson. Models of up to 12 tons capacity were available by 1939, with 6-cyl Waukesha petrol or Cummins diesel engines, although the 1940/1 range covered capacities only up to 10 tons.

During World War II the company supplied 600 tandem suspension units a week to International Harvester exclusively, although in 1948 these were made available to other manufacturers and, with the business now called the Hendrickson Mfg Co, a separate division

1964 Hendrickson 12 x 6 crane-carrier

was set up to handle this aspect. Vehicle building continued as the Mobile Equipment Divn, "conventional" Hendricksons now using the 'K'-Series International cabs with set-back front axle and long bonnet, and in 1950 Hendrickson's new 'B' – Series "conventionals" also had International cabs in long bonneted, standard or snub-nosed versions.

1960 Hendrickson refuse collector

The early 1950s also saw a new "cabover" with the company's own rear-tilting cab and bonnet, and another forward-control design fitted with International's Co-405 cab. Some models carried other makes of cab and gradually custom-building took precedence over other activities. Crane-carrier production increased dramatically using "cabover" and cab-forward layouts, often with low-profile cabs and tandem- or tri-axles front and rear for capacities of up to 200 tons.

Another specialist field is the construction of low-profile fuel tankers, snow clearance vehicles and scissor-lift cargo-handling trucks for airfield use, while some specialist manufacturers now use Hendrickson chassis carrying their own badges. Amongst these are Manitowoc crane-carriers and the experimental Ryder tractor while the Cline Truck Mfg Co regularly uses Hendrickson sheet metal. The "conventional" 'H'-Series, using International Harvester's 'Fleetstar' cab and a long reinforced fibreglass bonnet was announced in 1970. This is still current, as is the Switchmaster road/rail shunt tractor built by an associate company – the White Machinery Corp. Hendrickson now use Cummins, Deutz, Harnischfeger, International Harvester and Waukesha engines.

HENRIOD/Switzerland 1896-1898

C E Henriod, of Henriod Frères, Bienne, constructed a number of 6/8-seat buses with front-mounted air-cooled flat-twin petrol engines. These had chain-drive to the rear wheels with access to the fully-enclosed body via a central rear door. In 1903 brother Fritz set up a vehicle-building operation at Boudry where he constructed Henriod-Schweizer and SNA commercials.

HENSCHEL-COMMER/England/Germany 1963-1965

An arrangement was made between Great Britain's Rootes Group and Henschel-Werke AG, Kassel, West Germany, whereby the latter was to market medium-weight forward-control Commers in mainland Europe. These carried the Henschel-Commer or simply the Henschel name above their radiator grilles, but it was a short-lived agreement which was concluded following the takeover of Henschel-Werke AG by the Rheinstahl organization.

HERCULES(1)/Switzerland 1900-1913

The first Hercules truck built by Carl Weber-Landolt, Menziken, comprised a range of chain-drive vehicles from 1- to 7½-ton capacity within two years. These had front-mounted twin-cyl petrol engines of 6, 10, 14 and 30hp. An 8-seat bus, with 6hp twin- or 12hp 4-cyl engine, was also offered and in 1906 the company was re-named Hercules AG. Heavy models were soon powered by a new 50hp 4-cyl petrol unit, vehicles with this engine having a 4-speed transmission. Although the company scored considerable successes in the Swiss Commercial Vehicle Contest of 1907, it was unable to compete against other manufacturers and eventually ceased production in 1913.

HERCULES (2)/England 1903-c1909

The first Hercules steam wagon was built by the Hercules Motor Wagon Co, Levenshulme, Manchester, in 1903, having a totally-

1961 Henschel (2) HS 34 TAK

HENSCHEL (2)/*Germany 1924-1969*

Henschel und Sohn GmbH, Kassel, was a railway locomotive builder when it took out a licence to manufacture a Swiss-designed FBW commercial under the Henschel name in 1924. This was a 5-tonner, powered originally by a 50bhp 4-cyl engine with chain-drive and replaced in 1925 by a 60bhp version with shaft-drive. A low-loading passenger model was also listed and in 1928, as Henschel und Sohn AG, the company began building its own diesel engines. One of the most powerful European trucks of the 1930s was a 6-wheeled rigid using a 12-cyl petrol engine of 250bhp output. Payloads now ranged from 2½ to 10 tons in rigid form and up to 16 tons for artic models.

In 1932 the company experimented with steam power, leading to the production of 18 such goods- and passenger-carrying machines between 1933 and 1936, mainly for the German State Railways, while 1933 saw the introduction of a 6 x 4 on/off-highway truck for 3-ton payloads. By the late 1930s the company was again called Henschel und Sohn GmbH, trolleybuses had been introduced and a 12-cyl opposed-piston diesel engine of 300bhp output was available. By World War II chassisless buses were also being built. Production resumed after the war with the twin-engined 'Bimot-Bus', powered by two 6-cyl diesel engines located in a transverse frontal position, and a 6-wheeled artic tractor was built along similar lines. Other post-war models included a full range of normal buses and trolleybuses with bonneted trucks of 4½, 6½ and 8 tons capacity. A 4½-ton payload 4 x 4 appeared in 1952 and one year later a 200bhp 6-cyl horizontal diesel engine was fitted in the HS 200 UN forward-control goods and passenger chassis. Both normal- and forward-control trucks were now offered and in 1957 the company was re-named Henschel-Werke GmbH.

In 1961 an agreement was signed with the French manufacturer of Saviem commercials,

1969 Henschel (2) 6 x 4 military truck

whereby development and distribution of both marques was to be undertaken on a mutual basis. This lasted for two years, during which certain models were sold as Saviem-Henschel and some heavy Saviems received Henschel diesel engines. This was followed by a brief liaison with Britain's Rootes Group which ended with the acquisition of Henschel-Werke AG, as it was now known, by the Rheinstahl organization, forming Rheinstahl-Henschel AG. Now Henschel, Hanomag and Tempo commercials were all part of the same organization. Further consolidation occurred in 1968 when Henschel and Hanomag activities were merged as Hanomag-Henschel Fahrzeugwerke GmbH and a year later Dailmer-Benz AG took a 51% share in the business and all models became known as Hanomag-Henschels.

submerged type vertical fire-tube boiler located just behind the driver. This powered a compound "undertype" engine. The wagon was coke-fired via a central chute and was designed as a 5-tonner. Early models had a countershaft differential and chain final-drive to the rear axle. About 1907 the first loco-boilered Hercules was constructed, this arrangement being used repeatedly until the end of Hercules production.

A more unusual design employed a double-ended transverse boiler with exhaust gases directed to offside and nearside smoke-boxes and out via two chimneys. Using a larger compound engine, this developed 50hp and incorporated a power take-off on the end of the crankshaft which enabled one wagon to be fitted out and used as a self-contained threshing machine.

Before Hercules production ended a few double chain-drive trucks with 36bhp 4-cyl petrol engines were also built at the Manchester works.

HERCULES (3)/*Germany 1909-1926*

With capacities of up to 4 tons, Nürnberger Hercules-Werke AG, Nüremburg, listed a series of cardan-drive trucks. All were powered by the company's own petrol engines.

HERCULES (4)/*USA 1913-1915*

The Hercules Motor Truck Co, Boston, Massachusetts, listed a 1-ton truck with open express or stakeside bodies.

HERSCHMANN/*USA 1902-c1903*

Also known as the American Ordnance, the Herschmann steam truck was a 3-tonner introduced by the American Ordnance Co, Bridgeport, Connecticut. It had a vertical fire-tube boiler behind the driver, a compound "undertype" engine and all-gear drive. Production was taken over by the Columbia Engineering Works, Brooklyn, New York, in 1903, one of this company's agents being the American Steam Truck Co, Elgin, Illinois, which later built its own steam lorry. Herschmann patents were used in the English steam wagon built by the English Steam Wagon Co, Hebden Bridge, Yorks, England.

HEWITT/*USA 1906-1914*

In 1906 Edward Ringwood Hewitt's Hewitt Motor Co, New York, announced a 4-cyl 4-ton truck which was quickly up-rated to a 5-tonner of forward-control layout with 36hp engine, 2-speed planetary transmission and chain final-drive.

Two- and 3-tonners, both with flat-twin engines, arrived in 1907, followed by a monster 10-tonner in 1909.

They had little room for producing such machines, so later that year assembly of the 10-tonner was sub-contracted to the Machine Sales Co, Peabody, Massachusetts, and the Hewitt Motor Co merged with the Metzger Motor Car Co, Detroit, Michigan, introducing a 1-ton delivery van the following year. This had a 17hp 4-cyl Everitt petrol engine and 3-speed transmission but when the two companies split in 1911 this became the Metzger Motor Car Co's Everitt van. Meanwhile, the 10-tonner was also being built by Philip H Gill & Sons, Brooklyn, New York, this company's examples sometimes being referred to as Gill.

In 1912 the Hewitt Motor Co became part of the International Motor Co along with Mack Trucks Inc and the Saurer Motor Co, Plainfield, New Jersey, with only the 5- and 10-tonners remaining.

HEWITT-LINDSTROM/*USA 1900-1901*

A battery-electric truck and 14-seat bus were constructed by the Hewitt-Lindstrom Electric Co, Chicago, Illinois, a company that had originally been founded by John Hewitt and Charles A Lindstrom.

HEWITT-LUDLOW/*USA 1912-1921*

The Hewitt-Ludlow Auto Co, San Francisco, California, announced commercial models in 1912, using the Hewitt-Ludlow and Hewitt-Talbot brand names. Little is known about either marque apart from the fact that Hewitt-Ludlow production later passed to the Ralston Iron Works and then back to the original company.

HEXTER/*USA 1913-c1914*

A comparatively short-lived petrol-electric commercial which may have been only a prototype was the Hexter, built by P K Hexter, New York. After 1914 it was marketed as the Roland.

1976 HHT 8 x 4 artic tractor

HHT/*England 1976 to date*

Based at Heanor, Derbyshire, Heanor Haulage Ltd are specialist in the movement of abnormal and indivisible loads, now building their own heavy haulage tractors under the HHT brand name. They first employed a Scammell

'Contractor' chassis frame, 380bhp 8V-92 Detroit Diesel engine, Lipe-Rollway clutch and 15-speed Fuller 'Roadranger' transmission. The rear bogie comprised three 11-ton capacity Leyland hub-reduction axles of which the leading one ran "dead", with hydraulic rams to raise it clear of the ground when running light or requiring difficult manoeuvring. A Volvo F89 sleeper cab provided crew quarters.

Another HHT, running on three axles, entered service early in 1977 for lighter work, the principle feature here being a 52-speed transmission obtained via another 15-speed Fuller gearbox coupled to a 4-speed Spicer auxiliary. Another machine was assembled during 1977, and two more have joined the fleet since. Despite enquiries, Heanor Haulage have no plans to sell similar machines to any other operators.

HIGHWAY (1)/*USA 1918-1919*
A 3-wheeled 3-ton tractor with Martin fifth-wheel coupling and Weidely petrol engine was marketed as the Highway by the Highway Tractor Co, Indianapolis, Indiana. This had a single steering front wheel to which both engine and driver's seat were attached.

HIGHWAY (2)/*USA 1918-1930*
The United Motors Co, Grand Rapids, Michigan, is said to have introduced a series of commercials bearing the Highway brand name. Later, the company was renamed the United Motor Products Co, continuing production until 1930.

HIGHWAY (3)/*USA 1960-1968*
Founded in 1960 in the former Twin Coach plant at Kent, Ohio, Highway Products Inc acquired important Post Office contracts for the supply of specialist vehicles. Referred to as 'Highways', the first comprised a series of 12-m rigid 6-wheeled mobile post offices, powered by underfloor Cummins or Fageol-Leyland diesel engines. In addition to this, the forward-control 'Compac-Van', for gross weights of between 8164 and 11793kg was assembled on behalf of the White Motor Co, Cleveland, Ohio, with a one-man half-cab and both front and rear loading. From 1965 this was marketed as the Highway. Three years later passenger vehicle production was resumed under the Twin Coach and Twin Coach Highway names, and no further commercials appear to have been built under the Highway banner.

HIGHWAY-KNIGHT/*USA 1919-1922*
Using a 4-cyl sleeve-valve Knight petrol engine built under licence by the Root & Vandervoort Engine Co, the Highway-Knight was a 4- or 5-ton bonneted truck with a wheelbase of 397cm. Built by the Highway Motors Co, Chicago, Illinois, it had a Brown-Lipe 4-speed transmission and worm final-drive.

HIGRADE/*USA 1917-1921*
The Higrade 1-tonner was built by the Higrade Motors Co, Grand Rapids, Michigan. Features included a 4-cyl Wisconsin petrol engine, 3-speed Cotta transmission and wheelbase of 288cm. By 1918 the plant had moved to Harbor Springs and for the last year of production both 1- and 1½-tonner were listed.

HIJIRI/*Japan 1935-1943*
The Hijiri Motor Vehicle Mfg Co Ltd was set up to supply components to the Ford Motor Co's Japanese assembly plant but also introduced 1½- and 2-ton Hijiri trucks mainly for military applications. Early examples were similar to the 1933 Model 'BB' Ford while later types resembled Ford trucks of the 1935/6 period.

HILLE/*Germany 1924-1926*
Hille-Werke AG had premises in Dresden, where it built 3- and 5-ton Hille trucks with shaft- and chain-drive. The lighter vehicle was powered by a 45bhp petrol engine and the heavier by a 50bhp unit.

1905 Hindley "undertype" steam wagon

HINDLEY/*England 1904-1908*
E S Hindley & Sons, Bourton, Dorset, designed and constructed an experimental 2-ton vertical-boilered "undertype" steam wagon in which the driver sat behind a vertical fire-tube boiler. The compound engine used a roller chain between crankshaft and countershaft and spur-gear drive transmitted the motion to the rear axle. The design led to the development of a refined model with all-gear drive and by 1906 new 3- and 5-ton designs, both with a short loco-type boiler and circular firebox, were developed. Despite the model's potential, the company lost interest against enthusiastic competition and wagon production ceased.

HINDUSTHAN/*India 1968 to date*
From 1942 Hindusthan Motors Ltd, Calcutta, built Bedford, Chevrolet and Studebaker truck chassis under licence, but in 1968 introduced the first true Hindusthan trucks comprising a series of bonneted and forward-control types based on Bedford designs. Normal-control models featured Bedford's J4/J6 model cab while forward-control types had cabs of Hindusthan design. All versions are powered by a licence-built 112bhp 6-cyl diesel engine which is also used in a specially constructed passenger chassis.

HISPANO-ARGENTINA/*Argentina 1929-1942*
Carlos Ballester Molina set up Ballester Molina in Buenos Aires to act as Argentinian distributor for Hispano-Suiza cars and commercials. In 1929 a small factory was established to assemble Hispano-Suizas under licence and both passenger cars and heavy trucks were built under the Hispano-Argentina brand name. Imported components were mainly used and the majority of models were similar to their Spanish counterparts.

Hispano-Suiza bus c1934

HISPANO-SUIZA/*Spain 1908-1946*
SA Hispano-Suiza, Barcelona, began building commercial vehicles in 1908, the first being a 1000kg truck or 10-seat bus with 12/15hp petrol engine and the second a 2000kg truck or 18-seat bus with 24/30hp petrol unit. A larger chain-drive model introduced in 1911 was popular with the military. From 1912, a 15/20hp 4-cyl petrol-engined chassis was produced in large numbers, initially with a 3- but later a 4-speed box, and this was soon joined by a 30/40hp model for 22 passengers or a 3-ton payload. A larger 40/50hp design was adopted as standard for the Spanish Army and also formed the basis of Argentinian-built Hispano-Argentina trucks.

A 5-model range with capacities of between 2500 and 7000kg

or 18 and 50 seats replaced all types in 1930 using the company's own petrol engines, but in 1934 an experimental 6-tonner was fitted with a Ganz-Jendrassik diesel engine and from the mid-1930s the company built its own diesels. Trolleybuses and fire appliances were built during the Spanish Civil War and in 1944 a 7-ton diesel-engined goods or passenger chassis known as the '66'-Series made its debut. A year later a 55-seat 120bhp petrol-engined coach chassis appeared, but in 1946 vehicle-building came to an end when Empresa Nacional de Autocamiones SA was formed, introducing Pegaso commercials three years later.

HITACHI/*Japan 1935-1937*
Hitachi Ltd, Tokyo, briefly manufactured a bonneted truck powered by a 5.8-litre 4-cyl diesel engine.

HMW/*Belgium 1937-1940*
Previously involved in the manufacture of the Willems truck, a member of the family left SA des Ets Willems in 1937 to form HM Willems NV, also in Antwerp. The HMW truck appeared almost immediately, being an assembled model with a high percentage of foreign components, and a Gardner-Miesse diesel engine.

HOBRI/*Netherlands 1975*
American truck spares specialist GIHO BV, De Klomp, had already made one unsuccessful attempt at producing a heavy truck later constructing two prototypes under the Hobri brand name. Using a Diamond Reo chassis, DAF engine and cab, Fuller automatic transmission and super single Michelin tyres, these served as prototypes for the GIHO range which the company planned for 1976.

HOEK/*Netherlands 1907-1908, 1913*
A 5-ton steam wagon delivered to a Rotterdam haulage contractor in 1907 was designed by Willem Adriaan Hoek. It was an "undertype" machine with vertical coke-fired cross water-tube boiler at the front and a 20hp high-speed compound engine located beneath the chassis in unit with the differential and countershaft. Fitted with special long laminated springs, this model had chain final-drive. The boiler incorporated a special heating device to burn off exhaust steam and smoke. Further wagons were ordered and Machinefabriek W A Hoek founded at Schiedam to continue production which ceased the following year.

In 1912 the company became NV W A Hoek's Machinen Zuurstoffabriek after which it concen-

HINO (1)/*Japan 1942 to date*

A subsidiary of Tokyo Gasu Denki KK, manufacturer of TGE trucks, Hino Heavy Industries Ltd was founded at Ohmuri, Tokyo, to build heavy diesel trucks, the first of which was a bonneted 7-tonner with 4-speed transmission, spiral-bevel axle and air brakes. This was also listed as a 15-ton artic and by 1947 could even be had as a 150-passenger articulated bus.

In 1946, meanwhile, the company became the Hino Industry Co Ltd and by 1949 trolleybuses had been added to the model line.

In 1948 the business was re-organized as the Hino Diesel Industry Co Ltd and by 1951 a special 6 x 6 truck with 5-speed overdrive transmission called the 'ZC', had appeared, becoming popular with military customers. Two years later the 'ZG' heavy-duty half-cab dump truck made its debut and by 1956 the truck range covered payloads of between 5 and 8 tons. Passenger types were also built initially on stretched bonneted truck chassis but by 1952 on a specially designed horizontal underfloor-engined chassis with 5-speed constant-mesh transmission and air brakes.

By the mid-1950s almost half the company's production comprised passenger models, with automatic transmissions offered on some coach types and air suspension available from 1958. The truck range, meanwhile, now had 2-speed axles as an option, and in

1970 Hino (1) BT61 single-deck bus

1958 the first heavy forward-control model, a twin-steer 6 x 2 rigid, was announced. In 1959 the company was re-registered as Hino Motors Ltd and by 1961 the heavy truck range comprised the bonneted 'TE' and 'TH'-Series and the forward-control tiltcab 'KC', joined in 1964 by the 'KM' 4-tonner with 4.3-litre 6-cyl diesel engine, 4-speed synchromesh transmission and hydrovac braking. For 1966 the light weight 'Briska' pick-up was up-rated to 1-ton capacity, with 1.25-litre engine, while both forward- and normal-control "heavies" were offered for payloads of up to 15 tons, while a series of buses and coaches had underfloor engines, all mounted amidships, in conjunction with 5-speed transmissions. The most advanced passenger type was a high-speed chassisless motorway coach called the RA100, powered by a 320bhp 16-litre flat-12 diesel engine and fitted with air suspension. Later that year the company merged with the Toyota Motor Co Ltd, divesting itself of all lighter models to concentrate on heavier types.

The 'KM' medium-duty rigid was now at the bottom of the range, with the 6 x 4 'ZM' at the top, this equipped with a 20-speed transmission and auxiliary exhaust brake. A 4 x 4 version of the 'KM', known as the 'WB', was quickly added, as was a 29-seat bus based on the same chassis and called the 'BM'. The slightly heavier 'KL' truck, with 5-litre 6-cyl engine, was also launched, while both forward- and normal-control "heavies" in a variety of configurations were also available.

Rear-engined buses and

1965 Hino (1) 'KM'-Series truck

coaches were now appearing, and in 1972 the 40-ton GCW 'HE' tractor unit was introduced as was a 270bhp 13.8-litre V8 diesel and 10-speed splitter box. Most Hinos had air brakes as standard by 1975 and the passenger range had expanded still further with the front-engined 'BM' at the bottom of the ladder and the rear-engined 'RV', with V8 engine and air suspension at the top. In between was the 76-seat 'BT' with amidships-mounted

8-litre underfloor engine, the chassised 'RF', with 9.8-litre rear engine, and the 'RC' and 'RE' integral models. The rear-engined 'RV' vanished in 1976. Specialist commercials now include crane-carriers and truck-mixer chassis while the 'ZG' dump truck has a 210bhp 6-cyl turbocharged engine and 10-speed overdrive box. Hinos are also assembled in other countries with specifications similar to Japanese models. One exception is a heavy 8 x 4 rigid tipper built in Dublin, Ireland, by Harris (Assemblers) Ltd.

1966 Hino (1) 'KC'-Series

HINO (2)/*Ireland 1967 to date*

Harris (Assemblers) Ltd, Dublin, began assembling Japanese-designed Hino trucks under licence in 1967. These were much the same as Japanese-built Hinos, but during the 1970s an 8 x 4 rigid chassis was developed for the Irish tipper market from the existing forward-control 6 x 4 tipper chassis. By 1981 various Irish-built models were offered on the British mainland.

---

trated on the supply of gases to Dutch industry. One year later, however, there was a further brief excursion into steam propulsion when two self-propelled fire appliances were constructed. Both were forward-control oil-burners with a rear-mounted vertical boiler and 400gpm pump located amidships.

HOFFMAN/*USA 1913-1914*

The Hoffman Motor Truck Co, Minneapolis, Minnesota, built a bonneted 3-tonner in 1913. Powered by a 4-cyl Waukesha petrol engine with single chain final-drive, it was not very reliable.

HOGRA/*Netherlands 1955-1960*

For five years Van Hoek's Automobielfabriek NV, Rovenstein, built a few bonneted 4 x 2 and 4 x 4 trucks under the Hogra brand name. Mechanical components came mainly from the Austrian Steyr-Daimler-Puch AG stable.

HOLDEN/*Australia 1972 to date*

Previously concentrating on the manufacture of passenger cars and light commercials, General

Motors Holdens Ltd, Fisherman's Bend, Victoria, introduced a 1-ton chassis/cab in 1972 for utility use. More recently, as Holdens Pty Ltd, Melbourne, Victoria, the company has marketed certain Japanese-built Isuzu trucks under the Bedford name.

HOLLMANN & JERABEK/*Austria 1907-1913*

Founded in 1861 to construct fire-fighting equipment, Hollmann und Jerabek, Plzen, introduced a 2-cyl petrol-engined 3-ton bonneted truck designed by František Kec, who was later responsible for Praga production. This was a chain-drive design, which was followed by other models of up to 10-ton capacity. Sales were never very good, and in 1913 the company returned to the manufacture of fire-fighting equipment.

HOLMES/*USA 1921-1923*

The Holmes Motors Mfg Co, Littleton, Colorado, produced a few goods models between 1921 and 1923 but these were never signifi-

cant. Following the comany's closure, the plant was acquired by the Coleman Motors Corp.

HOLVERTA-VULCAN/*England 1926*

Employing engine, gearbox and bonnet assembly from the Vulcan Mfg & Eng Co Ltd, Crossens, Lancs, the Holverta-Vulcan had both 4-wheel drive and 4-wheel steering, with independent suspension all round. Behind the 4-speed gearbox was a worm-driven countershaft with diff lock, carrying a brake drum at each end and transmitting the drive via four propeller shafts located outside the chassis frame to each of the four wheels. This vehicle was seen only in prototype form.

HONG-HE/*China c1970 to date*

The Hong-He or Hung-Ho (Red River) truck is a 2½-tonner which is built by the Kochiu Truck Works, Kochiu, Yunnan Province.

HONG-WEI/*China 1966, 1968 to date*

A prototype Hong-Wei or Hung-

Wei (Red Guard) truck was constructed in 1966 but it was two years later that the GZ-140 3½-tonner actually went into production at the Kuangehou Motor Vehicle Plant, Kuangehou, Canton Province. A forward-control model powered by a 120bhp engine, it is also built as a 2½-tonner in Shansi.

HONG-YAN/*China 1965 to date*

The Chichiang Gear Plant, Chungking, Szechuan Province, builds the 25-ton 4-wheeled bonneted Hong-Yan or Hung-Yan (Red Crag or Red Rock) dump truck. Fitted with twin underbody hydraulic rams, it is similar to certain USSR designs.

HOOVER/*USA 1917-1920*

The Hoover Wagon Co, York, Pennsylvania, specialized in the construction of car and truck bodies and light battery-electric trucks until 1917 when a 1-ton truck powered by a 20hp 4-cyl Continental petrol engine entered production. Supplied mainly to the US government as a mail van, it had bevel final-drive.

HORA/*England 1905*

Originally a horse-drawn carriage, wagon and van builder, E & H Hora Ltd, Peckham, London, attempted to market both steam- and petrol-powered commercials. The steamer was a vertical water-tube boilered "undertype" with boiler located ahead of the front axle and a twin-crank compound engine slung beneath the chassis with chain-drive to the rear axle. Both lorry and bus bodies were fitted to the petrol chassis which may actually have been an imported vehicle of French origin. Power came from a 24hp 4-cyl engine located under the driver's seat.

HORCH/*Germany 1913-1945*

In 1913 A Horch & Co, Reichenbach, Vogtland, added heavier trucks and buses to its car-based commercial range. After World War I, the company became A Horch & Co Motorenwagenwerke AG, moving to Zwickau where it offered a 1½- and 3½-tonner, the former powered by a 10/20hp 4-cyl engine and the latter by a 25/42hp unit. Heavy truck and bus production ended in 1925, but in 1926 a new on/off-highway rigid 6-wheeler, powered by a 3.5-litre 8-cyl petrol engine, was constructed. Light commercials now included various emergency vehicles, also used by the military, and in 1932 the company was re-named Horch Werke AG.

Before the end of the 1930s a new 4 x 4 vehicle, powered by a 3.8-litre V8 engine, was developed for military use but in 1945 the product name changed briefly to Sachsenring and then to IFA.

HORN-LITTLEWOOD/*England 1905-1906*

Horn, Littlewood & Co Ltd, Gainsborough, Lincs, built the 1½ ton Horn-Littlewood van. Powered by a 15hp 2-cyl petrol engine under the driver's seat, this had chain final-drive and was joined by a short-lived series of 3- and 5-ton commercials. In 1906 models were re-named Hornwood.

HOTCHKISS/*France 1936-c1970*

Prior to 1914 certain heavy Hotchkiss passenger car chassis were used as fire appliances but it was not until 1936 that Hotchkiss et Cie, St Denis, Seine, introduced a model specifically for goods-carrying. This was a bonneted 2-tonner with a 2.3-litre 4-cyl overhead-valve petrol engine, 4-speed transmission and double-reduction final-drive. By the late 1940s this had developed into the 2½-ton PL20 with hydraulic brakes and, by 1954, servo-assisted hydraulic braking.

1961 Hotchkiss 5½-ton truck

A forward-control 22-seat coach chassis appeared early in 1954 and a few months later the company merged with Automobiles Delahaye, to form Soc Hotchkiss-Delahaye, models continuing as Hotchkiss. By 1956 the company had been re-named Soc Hotchkiss-Brandt and in 1958 a Perkins P4-engined version of the earlier 22-seat passenger chassis was announced.

About 1960 the company began selling Leyland products and Leyland-engined Brossel buses in France but this did not last long and by 1962 a diesel-engined chassisless coach was developed in association with a French coach-builder. The bonneted PL range was still available as late as 1967 but the last new model, a 3/4-ton tiltcab truck with 3.5-litre 4-cyl Hotchkiss petrol or diesel engine and 4- or 5-speed synchromesh box, was launched in 1964. Derivatives of this included a passenger model and various 4 x 4s. In 1968 more powerful Hotchkiss engines appeared and the company was again re-organized, this time as Cie Française Thomson-Houston-Hotchkiss-Brandt, but gradually production ceased in favour of armaments, the vehicle-building side being acquired by SA André Citroën.

HOWARD (1)/*USA 1903*

The Howard Automobile Co, Yonkers, New York, built a few commercials designed by W S Howard, previously of the Grant-Ferris Co. These comprised a few light models, and a 4-ton petrol-electric fitted with a 25/30hp 4-cyl petrol engine mounted vertically under the floor. This drove a dynamo which, in turn, powered two General Electric traction motors, one for each rear wheel. Coil radiators were fitted at front and rear.

HOWARD (2)/*England 1903-1904*

J & F Howard Ltd built a 5-ton "undertype" steam wagon in its Britannia Works, Bedford, using a vertical water-tube boiler with coiled steel water tubes and a central coke firing chute. The horizontal compound engine had Stephenson's link motion and superheat facilities. Exhibited at the 1903 Smithfield Show, the design also had a lockable countershaft differential and double chain-drive to the rear wheels.

Unfortunately, the 2-speed transmission could only be altered from ground level when the vehicle was not in motion, so production was brief.

HOWE/*USA 1930 to date*

Founded in 1872, the Howe Fire Engine Co, Indianapolis, Indiana, built various appliances on proprietary chassis until 1930 when it began constructing its own chassis for its 'Defender' range which also used Chevrolet, Ford and International chassis. In 1953 the 'New Defender', based on a Waukesha-engined Duplex chassis, was announced, with 750, 1000 or 1250gpm pumps and open or closed cabs.

A new 'Defender', of open or closed cab-forward design, appeared in 1967, joined by the cab-forward 'Centurion' during the early 1970s. The company was now known as the Howe Fire Apparatus Co Inc and in 1974 acquired both Coast Apparatus Inc, Martinez, California, and the Oren-Roanoke Corp, of Roanoke and Vinton, Virginia.

HSG/*England 1936-1937*

High Speed Gas (Great Britain) Ltd was founded to develop producer-gas plants for use in road vehicles and other machinery. The prototype was a Fordson truck with a producer-gas plant incorporating a tuyere forming the only air intake into the producer.

In 1936 Gilford (HSG) Ltd was established to take over the plant and all remaining stock of the Park Royal, London, factory of the Gilford Motor Co Ltd. The first complete HSG – a 4/5-ton lorry – appeared soon after, having a "coal-scuttle" bonnet under which the producer unit was located with a flap for fuel in the bonnet top. The 5.3-litre 4-cyl side-valve Coventry Climax engine lay beneath the cab floor.

A second HSG lorry soon appeared, with a modified front-end and revised cab structure. This was heavier than its predecessor but mechanically similar. The future production programme was announced, comprising the G2/1 and G2/2 lorries of 300 and 295cm respectively, for gross loads of up to 3½tons. The G2/1 was to have a 5-speed box and the G2/2 a 4-speed, both being powered by a 5.25-litre 6-cyl side-valve engine with a power output of 60bhp. Other features included a single-plate clutch, Lockheed hydraulic footbrake acting on all four wheels, cam-and-lever steering and fully-floating bevel-gear

rear axle. None of these vehicles was built but a new 3-tonner, with 60bhp 6-cyl engine appeared early the following year. The only HSG bus, called the Gilford HSG, appeared about the same time, based on a redundant Gilford CF176 chassis. Two military prototypes were also assembled comprising the G4 2-tonner and G6 3-tonner. The G4 was a 61bhp semi-forward-control model and the G6 an 80bhp vehicle with full-width bonnet. No further production appears to have taken place, and in 1938 the business was acquired by the Sentinel Waggon Works (1936) Ltd, Shrewsbury.

HUANG-HE/*China 1959, 1964 to date*

Although prototypes appeared some five years earlier, the Huang-He or Huang-Ho (Yellow River) 8-ton diesel truck did not go into production as the JN-150 at the Tsinan General Motor Vehicle Plant, Tsinan, Shantung Province, until 1964. Powered by a 160bhp 6-cyl engine, it has a 5-speed transmission, and has since been joined by the smaller JN-151, a series of passenger models and a 7-ton dump truck powered by an identical engine and fitted with a one-man half-cab and 5-speed power-assisted transmission. This is built in the nearby Tsingtao Motor Vehicle Mfg & Parts Plant, being similar to the Nanying dump truck built in Honan Province.

HUBER/*USA 1903*

The Huber Automobile Co, Detroit, Michigan, designed a 2-ton truck and a 30/40-passenger bus. Only the goods model appears to have been built and only in very limited numbers.

1963 Hudson 'Frontomatic' mixer

HUDSON/*England 1963-1964*

First shown at the International Construction Equipment Exhibition in 1963, the Hudson 'Frontomatic' was a front-discharge truckmixer constructed by Robert Hudson (Raletrux) Ltd, Leeds, West Yorks. The chassis was basically a Leyland's 'Super Comet', using a 125bhp Leyland diesel engine and 5-speed transmission. The 1.14cu m mixer drum was hydraulically driven by a pump running off the engine crankshaft and a centrally-located one-man fibreglass cab gave the driver superb visibility when discharging via a chute over the cab. Although full-scale production was planned, this model never left prototype stage.

HUFFMAN/*USA 1916-1927*
The 1½-ton Huffman went into production at the Huffman Bros Motor Co, Elkhart, Indiana, using a Continental petrol engine, 3-speed transmission and either a worm or bevel-gear final-drive. By 1923 the bevel-drive version had a Buda petrol engine and within two years various other models up to 3½ tons capacity were available. Buda, Continental, Hercules or Wisconsin engines were featured in the 1927 range which had capacities of between 1½ and 4 tons but later that year the marque was re-named the Valley or Valley-Dispatch.

1935 Hug 43LD-6 artic tractor

HUG/*USA 1921-1942*
C J Hug was an Illinois civil engineer who designed and constructed his own prototype which entered series production at the Hug Co's Highland, Illinois, premises. Called the Hug Model 'T', it was the world's first dump truck powered by a 34bhp 4-cyl Buda petrol engine driving through a Warner 3-speed box and Clark spiral-bevel rear axle. Although a 2-tonner, it had a high speed of 72km/h, pneumatic tyres, open cab and either a normal tipping body for dry loads or a scow-end design for water-bound materials.

It was tremendously popular, even amongst rival civil engineering concerns, and in 1925 was joined by the 3½-ton Model 'CH' and in 1927 by the 4/6-ton Model '88', which had a 43bhp Buda engine, 7-speed Brown-Lipe transmission and Wisconsin back axle. Known generally as Hug 'Roadbuilders', these had grown into 6½-, 18- and 20-ton machines by 1937 with 6-cyl Buda petrol or 4-cyl Caterpillar diesel engines,

adopting 4 x 2 or 6 x 4 shaft-drive and 6 x 2 or 6 x 4 chain-drive, bogies being supplied by the Six Wheel Co.

Many Hug dump bodies incorporated a protective shield over the driver, which quickly became standard for dump trucks built all over the world, and a special option for Hug 6-wheelers was a detachable half-track system supplied by J Walter Christie. During the 1930s the company also became well-known for its Hug Speed Trucks and particularly for its 'Xpress' 2-, 3- and 3½-tonners with 6-cyl Buda petrol engines. Long-distance sleeper cab tractors were also built and a few "cabovers" listed with Buda petrol or Cummins diesel engines.

Rear-engined passenger types appeared about 1938 and complete buses were built for a short time along similar lines to Wayne buses built later by the Wayne Works, Richmond, Indiana, where one of Hug's offices was situated. Models for 1939 generally had Waukesha petrol engines while diesel models were still powered by Caterpillar. Soon after World War II broke out, the company constructed eight Model '50-6' 6 x 6 7½-ton cargo trucks that were sent overseas under the lend-lease scheme plus a number of civilian on-highway models using Reo front ends.

HUMBER/*England 1951-1954*
Humber Ltd of Coventry, West Midlands, built a 1-ton military 4 x 4 powered by a 4-litre 6-cyl Rolls-Royce B60 petrol engine and equipped with a 5-speed transmission, hydraulic brakes and independent suspension. All mechanical components were manufactured at the Rootes Group's Maidstone factory and transported to Humber's Ryton-on-Dunsmore factories.

HURLBURT/*USA 1912-1927*
The Hurlburt Motor Truck Co, New York, introduced 1-, 2- and 3-ton petrol-engined trucks before moving to the Bronx in 1915 and offering 6-cyl engined 5- and 7-tonners for 1918. These had Buda engines, Brown-Lipe transmissions and worm-drive axles but until 1919 most sales were only in the New York area. That year production was transferred to the Harrisburg Mfg & Boiler Co, Harrisburg, Pennsylvania, vehicles built there being referred to also as Harrisburgs. Sales were now made throughout the eastern seaboard but in 1920 the 7-tonner was discontinued until 1924. When production ended completely, the company offered five Buda-engined models from a 3-ton rigid up to a 10-ton articulated 6-wheeler.

HURLIMANN/*Switzerland 1957, 1964, 1974-1975*
Theodor Hürlimann Transporte was a truck operator from Wetzikon, near Zurich that built a 4-wheel drive tipper for its own use. It was an unusual design with an articulated chassis frame and twin tyres all round. Power was provided by a 90bhp 6-cyl Mercedes-Benz diesel engine.

In 1964 five 7-tonners of similar layout were constructed under contract by Jules Egli, also of Wetzikon, but were still known as Hürlimanns. Another prototype appeared in 1974, this being an even more unusual design of 8 x 4 configuration, still with an articulated chassis frame but with steering first and third axles and driven second and fourth axles, providing a turning circle of just 11.2m. Power was provided by a 320bhp Mercedes-Benz V10 diesel and a Mercedes-Benz cab was fitted.

HURRYTON/*USA 1923-c1928*
The smallest commercial built by the Menominee Motor Truck Co, Clintonville, Wisconsin, was the Hurryton 1-tonner. Built alongside normal Menominee trucks, Hurryton production is believed to have continued through 1928 when the Four Wheel Drive Auto Co acquired the business and then re-named it the Utility Supply Co.

HURST & LLOYD/*England 1898-1900*
George Hurst and Lewis A Lloyd built light goods models and fire appliances under the Hurst & Lloyd brand name, using a 2-cyl underfloor-engined passenger car chassis with belt-drive, in Wood Green, London. Later, Lloyd dissolved the partnership to form Lloyd & Plaister Ltd in the same premises.

1963 Hydrocon 'Hebridean' 10/12-ton truck-crane

HYDROCON/*Scotland/England c1958-c1969*
Using its own purpose-built chassis or others supplied by Albion, Foden, Leyland or Thornycroft, the Lambert Engineering Co (Glasgow) Ltd began building Hydrocon truck-cranes towards the end of the 1950s at plants in Coatbridge, Lanarks; Rochdale, Lancs; and Feltham, Middx. Models comprised the 6-ton 4 x 2 or 4 x 4 'Highlander', 10-ton 4 x 2, 4 x 4 or 6 x 4 'Hamilton' and an 8 x 4 50-tonner. Engines were normally by Leyland, with a Cummins option for the 50-tonner. Crane movements were powered by the vehicle's own road engine and although popular, the manufacturer hit financial problems towards the end of the 1960s. Assembly was resumed briefly in the Coatbridge factory by J N Connell Construction (1969) Ltd.

HYDROTECHNIEK/*England 1979-1980*
Using mechanical units and control gear supplied by Creusen Electro-Mecanische Industrie NV, Netherlands, the first battery-electric built by Hydrotechniek (UK) Ltd, Toft, Cambs, was a 6-wheeled 6½ tons GVW mobile library. This had 24 lead-acid batteries providing a normal range per charge of up to 80km and a top speed of 20km/h. In 1980 it was joined by an improved model with a maximum speed of between 32 and 40km/h. Other examples were ordered but in 1980 the company is believed to have been re-formed as Techelec Ltd, all subsequent models being sold as Techelecs.

HYUNDAI/*Korea 1978 to date*
The Hyundai Motor Co was established in Seoul by former British Leyland executive George Turnbull in 1974, quickly introducing a light pick-up version of the 'Pony' passenger car. Heavier models were designed by Trevor Lacey of Bedford Commercial Vehicles Ltd in 1978, using locally-built Perkins diesel engines such as the 4.108 in a 1-tonner and turbocharged 6.354 in a 7-tonner.

I

IBC/*Australia c1979 to date*
Originally appearing in prototype form as the Campbell, a Caterpillar-engined city bus is believed to have entered series production during 1979 as the IBC. It is a product of Ian H Campbell & Co Pty Ltd, Carlton, Sydney, NSW.

IBEX/*USA 1963 to date*
The Ibex was introduced as a custom-built 4 x 4, 6 x 4 or 6 x 6 "conventional" truck or tractor by the Hafer-Ibex Corp, Salt Lake City, Utah. Power was supplied by a 195bhp 6-cyl Detroit Diesel, 270bhp 6-cyl Caterpillar or 340bhp V8 Caterpillar engine. The company was later re-named the Ibex Motor Truck Corp and, finally, Jelco Inc, of which it be-

1970 Ibex 6 x 6 artic tractor

came the Ibex Divn. During the latter period a new 6 x 4 rigid known as the '900'-Series, of low cab-forward or high "cabover" layout, was added to the range using Ford petrol or Caterpillar, Cummins or Detroit Diesel engines. Another design was the Flexi-Truc terminal tractor manufactured by subsidiary Flexi-Truc Inc, Los Angeles, California.

IDEAL/*USA 1910-1915*
In 1910 the Ideal Auto Co, Fort Wayne, Indiana, introduced a 1-ton truck of bonneted layout with planetary transmission, double chain-drive and solid tyres. It was powered by a 4-cyl water-cooled petrol engine, and by 1912 had become a forward-control design. For 1915, 1½- and 2½-ton versions were also offered, these were all fitted with chain-drive and selective transmissions.

IDECO/*USA to date*
Ideco manufactures oil well servicing equipment and in particular offers mobile well-servicing derricks of which the largest is the 8 x 4 'Rambler' with one-man half-cab and folding derrick mast. When operating, the mast is erected at the forward end of the vehicle with all winding gear located amidships.

IDEN/*England 1905-1907*
The Iden Motor Car Co Ltd was set up at Parkside, Coventry, by the former Works Manager of the Motor Mfg Co Ltd, builder of MMC commercials, in 1904. The following year a 2-ton lorry with 25hp 4-cyl petrol engine, and load carried direct on the chassis frame, was shown at Olympia, later joined by a 25-seat passenger version, but both were short-lived.

IFA/*East Germany 1948-1956, 1965 to date*
Following the formation of the German Democratic Republic, the East German motor industry combined its marketing resources to form the Industrieverband Fahrzeugbau Association (IFA). Until 1956 the products of the various constituent factories were sold either under their original

IFA W50L truck c1970

names or as IFA, but after this date only original or new names were used. The only exceptions were the Phänomen and Granit ranges, marketed as IFA-Granit, and the W 50 5-ton truck built at the VEB IFA Automobilwerke factory, Ludwigsfelde, from 1965.

The W 50 is a forward-control model, powered initially by a 100bhp 6.5-litre 4-cyl diesel engine but fitted with a 125bhp unit after 1967. This design can be had also in 4 x 4 rigid form, as a 10-ton artic tractor or as a 16-ton drawbar.

IHC/*USA 1907-1913*
Although the International Harvester Co of America's Auto-Buggy and Auto-Wagon models were also sold as IHC, it is not until 1912 that the first true IHC appeared in the form of the Model 'MW' with a 2-cyl water-cooled petrol engine located behind a conventional radiator. From the beginning of 1914 all types were sold as International.

IKARUS (1)/*Hungary 1948 to date*
Founded in 1948, Ikarus Karosszeria es Jarmugyar was established in Budapest to build passenger vehicles based on Csepel chassis. Powered by 85bhp Csepel diesel engines, these were marketed as Ikarus and were joined by a chassisless range powered by Csepel, Perkins or Henschel diesel engines. In 1960 the company announced the '180'-Series of underfloor-engined chassisless buses and coaches, using Leyland, Saurer and Raba diesels of up to 200bhp output. Soon an articulated city bus had been developed and in 1967 the '200'-Series arrived. The company built numerous integral buses on Scania underframes at this time and in 1977 the 107-passenger Model 286 articulated transit bus replaced the earlier artic. Nearly 80% of all Ikarus models were now being exported and this type was no exception, being sold to European, South American and African operators. Although agreement was reached with the Crown Coach Corp, Los Angeles, California, whereby they would market and ultimately build this model in the USA employing some 50% of US-

built components, this scheme did not proceed although a demonstrator was shipped over to get the idea underway.

IKARUS (2)/*Yugoslavia 1970 to date*
Although also a bus-builder, the Yugoslavian Ikarus should not be confused with the previous entry. Built by Karoserija Ikarus, Zemun, the first Yugoslavian Ikarus is a 100-passenger design announced in 1970. Power comes from a 192bhp Hungarian-built Raba underfloor diesel engine with running units also by Raba.

IKEGAI/*Japan 1934-1940*
The Ikegai Automobile Mfg Co Ltd, Kawasaki, had already developed a diesel engine when it introduced 2- and 3-ton diesel trucks. Powered respectively by 4- and 6-cyl petrol engines, they were joined by a series of passenger models but production was never very great.

IML/*England 1925-?*
Metropolitan Motors, London SW3, is said to have built a number of goods models using what is believed to have been an imported American chassis. These were marketed under the IML brand name but were built only in small numbers.

IMV/*Yugoslavia 1960 to date*
Industrija Motornih Vozil, Novo Mesto, which assembled DKW commercials under licence from 1955, later introduced the IMV range with a 44bhp 3-cyl 2-stroke DKW petrol engine and front-wheel drive. Called the IMV 1000, it was offered in van, pick-up, minibus and ambulance form and in 1958 received a 62bhp 1.6-litre BMC petrol engine. During the 1960s a 1½-ton 6-wheeled version with driven front axle and trailing rear axles was also built and the early 1970s saw a Renault petrol engine fitted. At the 1975 Belgrade Show a 1¾-ton payload model, a 6-wheeler, was introduced, with optional Mercedes-Benz diesel engine.

INBUS/*Italy 1975 to date*
Industrie Autobus, Milan, is a

Ikarus (1) 6ZO mobile home

consortium of manufacturers set up to construct chassisless passenger models under the Inbus brand name. The consortium comprises Breda of Pistoia, De Simon of Udine, Sicca of Treviso and Sofer of Naples. Ladder-type frames and air suspension units are manufactured at Treviso, other components including Fiat diesel engines, power steering and Allison automatic transmissions. The smallest model is the 8.5-m '150'-Series with side-mounted engine and air-hydraulic braking. Larger models have rear engines and full air braking, the largest being a V8-engined coach with hydraulic retarder.

INDEPENDENT (1)/*USA 1917-1921*

The Independent Motor Truck Co assembled 1- and 2-ton Independent trucks in Davenport, Iowa. These had respective wheelbase lengths of 342cm and 370cm, Continental petrol engines, Fuller 3-speed transmissions and Russel bevel-drive axles.

INDEPENDENT (2)/*USA 1918-1923*

The Independent Motors Co originated out of the Cass Motor Truck Co, Port Huron, Michigan. It was based in Youngstown, Ohio, building 1- and 2-tonners initially, 1½- and 3½-tonners appearing the following year. All had 4-cyl Continental petrol engines, 3-speed Fuller transmissions and worm-drive axles.

INDEPENDENT (3)/*England 1980 to date*

Coach operator Independent Coachways (Leeds) Ltd, Horsforth, Leeds, West Yorks, has developed a vertical rear-engined turbocharged coach chassis for fast motorway running. The prototype started life as a 10-m underfloor-engined Leyland 'Leopard' but was stretched both amidships and at the rear to 11m overall. A specially turbocharged Leyland 0.680 diesel engine was mounted at the rear, coupled to a 10-speed splitter transmission, with cooling provided by an AEC radiator and by air intakes on each side of the integral Plaxton body which was originally developed for rear-engined DAF passenger chassis.

If trials are successful it is intended to construct further vehicles of this type for the company's own use.

INDIANA/*USA 1911-1939*

The Indiana was an assembled truck built by the Harwood-Barley Mfg Co, Marion, Indiana. Originally, it was available only as a 1½-tonner, using a 3.3-litre 4-cyl Rutenber petrol engine, 4-speed

1933 Indiana Model 95 2-ton boxvan

transmission and chain-drive. By 1920 the range covered capacities of between 1½ and 5 tons, powered by Rutenber or Waukesha petrol engines, with worm-drive and mainly 4-speed transmissions. As the Indiana Truck Corp, the company introduced a 7-tonner about this time, re-designing earlier models in 1924. New for 1925 was a 7-speed 4/5-tonner with a 6.5-litre Waukesha petrol engine. A new Hercules-engined 3-tonner was added the following year and in 1927 the business was acquired by the Brockway Motor Truck Co, although remaining fairly independent. A new 3-tonner, with overhead-valve 6-cyl Wisconsin unit, spiral-bevel drive, and full electrics, was quickly introduced and spiral-bevel axles were soon standard for all light models.

Indiana 2½-ton truck chassis c1935

Late in 1927 a new 4/5-tonner, with 78bhp Wisconsin petrol engine and 7-speed transmission, replaced the 1925 model, and in 1928 the 1-ton 'Ranger', with a 3.7-litre 6-cyl Wisconsin engine and front-wheel brakes, was announced. By 1929 the largest Indianas had 5-speed transmissions, with 6-cyl Wisconsin engines as standard, but by 1930 a heavy tractor and a 5½- ton payload 6-wheeler had a 10-litre 6-cyl Continental petrol engine.

In 1932 Brockway sold the business to the White Motor Co, which re-named it the Indiana Motors Corp, moving production to Cleveland, Ohio. Six-cyl Hercules engines were soon standard, while the heaviest trucks had double-reduction axles. The company was the first American manufacturer to list a series-produced diesel truck, this being a bonneted 5-tonner with 125bhp 6-cyl Cummins engine announced in 1932. By 1936 the largest standard Indiana was a 2½-tonner, heavier vehicles being constructed only to special order, small forward-control city buses had been added to the range which expanded in 1937 and 1938 to include various types, from 1 to 5 tons capacity. Sales were falling, however, and closure became unavoidable.

INTERBORO/*USA 1913-1914*

The Interboro Motor Truck Co, of Philadelphia, Pennsylvania, listed a single 1-tonner with 23hp 4-cyl petrol engine in 1913 and 1914.

IRAT/*France 1949*

When Automobiles Georges Irat SA became Irat et Cie and moved to Begles-Tartifumes, Gironde in 1948, it concentrated on the manufacture of 2-, 4- and 6-cyl DOG diesel engines. One year later,

however, a single Irat commercial was built for display at the Paris Salon. Powered by a 4.3-litre 4-cyl DOG engine driving the front wheels via a Cotal gearbox, this was a road tanker of chassisless construction with independent coil spring suspension at the rear.

IRGENS/*Norway 1899*

Using a British-built Toward boiler, 3-cyl single-acting engine and all-gear drive to the front steering axle, the 18-seat Irgens steam bus was built by Jacob Irgens, Bergen. It is reputed to have featured a steam-heated interior to combat the severe Scandinavian winters.

IRIS/*England 1905-1910, 1919*

Introduced by Legros & Knowles Ltd, London NW10, the Iris commercial range was based on the earlier Legros & Knowles passenger car, incorporating a 20hp 4-cyl petrol engine and double chain-drive. Models included trucks, buses, tractors and express delivery vans but few of any type were built. An Iris tower wagon was supplied to Halifax Corp in 1906. Later, the company was re-named Iris Cars Ltd, moving to Aylesbury, Bucks, following its takeover by the Bifurcated & Metal Rivet Co. With the exception of a crane-carrier built in 1919, no commercials were built after 1910.

IROQUOIS/*USA 1906*

The Iroquois Iron Works, Buffalo, New York State, built roadrollers, light commercials and a 4-ton truck, this had a 60hp engine under the seat and chain-drive.

ISCO/*USA 1972 to date*

The Isco Mfg Co Inc was founded in Kansas City, Missouri, following the acquisition of WT Cox, the Cline Truck Mfg Co, the Hardwick Mfg Co and the Shuttle Wagon Corp by the Interstate Securities Co. The new firm introduced a series of heavy trucks comprising seven bonneted 4-wheelers from 13 to 50 tons capacity, a 15-ton "cabover", a 22-ton articulated rock-hauler with front-wheel drive, a 60/75-ton articulated slag-hauler, 70- and 90-ton coal-haulers and a heavy logging tractor. Other types include underground personnel carriers, a terminal tractor for shunting railway wagons and semi-trailers, a locomotive re-railer and a series of road/rail conversion units for capacities of up to 36,287kg GVW. Most are similar to the earlier Cline range and for some time these continued to carry the Cline brand name. Engines include 6-cyl Cummins diesels of between 250 and 420bhp and 4-, 6-cyl, V6, V8 and V12 Detroit Diesels of up to 434bhp out-

1921 International (2) 'Speed' 1-ton truck

INTERNATIONAL (1)/USA
1908
The International Motor Co, Philadelphia, Pennsylvania, offered unusual 3- and 5-ton trucks, both using 4-cyl water-cooled petrol engines mounted direct on the pivoting front axle, friction transmissions and front wheel chain-drive.

INTERNATIONAL (2)/USA
1914 to date
Built in Chicago, Illinois, by the International Harvester Co of America, IHC trucks were soon re-named International and a new design with "coal-scuttle" bonnet using a 4-cyl 'L'-head petrol engine with radiator behind, 3-speed selective transmission, shaft-drive, internal-gear rear axle and semi-elliptic leaf springs was introduced. Various capacities up to 2 tons were available, the heaviest being of "cabover" layout.

By 1921 trucks from 1 to 5 tons capacity were offered, a range of "speed trucks" being built in a new Springfield, Ohio plant, and within three years the "coal-scuttle" bonnet characteristic had been replaced by a more conventional design with front-mounted radiator. Shaft-drive, with double-reduction bevel-gearing, was now standard on all 2-, 3-, 4½- and 5-tonners, although some chain-drive vehicles were built to special order. In about 1925 a special passenger chassis was developed for up to 33 persons, using a 6-cyl petrol engine, spiral-bevel final-

drive,.fully-floating rear axle and 4-wheel brakes. A new feature for 1926 goods models was an enclosed cab.

The company quickly realized the potential of the agricultural tractor in an industrial environment, and by 1927 was offering pneumatic-tyred road-going versions, while the International 1-tonner had become known as the "6-speed special" with the addition of a 2-speed axle in 1928. One and one-half and 2½-ton "speed trucks", plus a standee driver milk delivery model, were also introduced.

New models for 1930 included spiral-bevel drive 'A'-Series 2- and 3-ton "speed trucks" and a number of larger 'A'-Series models, as well as the revolutionary double-reduction herringbone-drive 'W'-Series, with overhead-valve engines incorporating removable cylinders. The first International diesel engines arrived in 1933, just as the 'A'-Series was re-designated the 'B'-Series, and one year later the 'C'-Series was announced. There were now 18 models for payloads of up to 7 tons and by 1935 a 10-ton 6-wheeler was also available, using a Hendrickson bogie. In 1936 the "cabover" C-300 was introduced but for 1937 the 'C'-Series was ousted by the 'D'-Series. Modified versions of the old 'A'-Series were to continue until 1942, being specially popular in the construction industry. The first sleeper cabs appeared in 1938, at almost the same time that the Metro delivery model was introduced with International running units and bodies by the Metropolitan Body Co, Bridgeport, Connecticut.

The 'K'-Series, for payloads of up to 8-tons, was announced in 1940, while wartime production included 2½- and 5-ton 4 x 2, 4 x 4 and 6 x 6 trucks for civilian and military use, many H-542-11 open "cabover" models being built also by Marmon-Herrington and Kenworth. Production of the 'K'-Ser-

ies, now known as the 'KB', was resumed in 1946 and in 1947 a new factory at Emeryville, California, began to construct West Coast types for operation at up to 40,823kg gross. A re-designed 'W'-Series also appeared and both the Chinese Jay-Fong and the Soviet ZIS-150 were based on the 'KB' model, itself replaced in 1950 by 'L'-Series light- and medium-duty types, known later as the 'S'- and 'A'-Series and, by 1962, as the 'B'-Series.

1970 International (3) C-1800 6 x 4 tipper

A new all-steel "conventional" cab designed by the company was manufactured by the Chicago Manufacturing Co and shared with a number of other marques, becoming familiar on the heavy-duty International 'R'-Series. Most familiar of all US "cabover" designs was that developed by Diamond T and used also on International's 'CO' cab-forward model. This was a medium-duty type, available also as the 'VCO' with V8 petrol engine. Heavier "cabovers", such as the CO-405 and 'Transtar', used variations on this theme.

In 1962 the "conventional" 'M'-Series and F-230 models for operation at up to 35,380kg GVW were introduced, mainly in the construction business, while the bonneted 'Loadstar' replaced the 'B'-Series in 1963 and heavier 'Fleetstar' "conventionals" eventually replaced the 'R'-Series four years later.

In about 1964 heavy single- and 4-wheel drive dump trucks for up to 69,852kg GVW was introduced and by the early 1970s a line of seven models from 36,718 to 76,404kg GVW was available, us-

ing 12- or 16-cyl diesel engines up to a maximum output of 560bhp and 9- or 12-speed Allison or Twin Disc transmissions. New 'Transtar' 4200 and 4300 models were announced in 1971, while current models include 'Loadstar' and 'Fleetstar' "conventionals"; 'Cargostar' "cabovers"; 'Transtar' "cabovers" and "conventionals"; 'Paystar' 4 x 4, 6 x 4 and 6 x 6 construction industry "conventionals"; school buses; fire appliances; and dump trucks.

1964 International (2) 'Loadstar'

INTERNATIONAL (3)/
Australia 1959 to date
Whilst US-designed International trucks have been built in Australia for many years, it was not until 1959 that the International Harvester Co of Australia Pty Ltd, Melbourne, Victoria, introduced its first specifically Australian model in the form of a 2½-ton 4 x 4 for the Australian army. Of forward-control layout, this had a 148bhp 6-cyl petrol engine. By 1961 this had been joined by the ACCO civilian series comprising 4- and 6-wheeled rigids and tractors using 6-cyl or V8 petrol or Perkins 6.354 diesel engines.

1965 International (4) 'Loadstar'

A 6 x 6 military model arrived in 1966, and by 1972 the ACCO had developed into the ACCO-A for up to 31,000kg GCW with V8 petrol or diesel engines. Meanwhile, a bonneted range based on American designs had developed into the 'C'-Series 4 x 2 and 4 x 4 types with Australian cabs and, in turn, into the 'D'-Series. To celebrate the company's 25th year, ACCO 510A/410A 4 x 2 and 4 x 4 trucks were announced, using a new forward-control cab and a 177bhp International Harvester V8 petrol engine. Finally, as International Harvester Australia Ltd, the company constructed a handful of 4 x 4 military 1-tonners in 1975 that are still undergoing evaluation. For 1981 a new forward-control truck and bus range has been announced comprising the ACCO 630A 4/7-ton truck and the 1830TC passenger model.

1941 International (2) 'K'-Series

1937 International (2)1½-ton truck

INTERNATIONAL (4)/
England 1965-1969
For four years the International Harvester Co of Great Britain Ltd ran a truck production facility at Doncaster, South Yorks, basing its models on the bonneted American 'Paystar' range, re-named 'Loadstar' and suitably modified to conform to British Construction & Use Regulations. Only a few 4 x 2 rigids and tractors were built.

1978 International (2) 'Paystar' 5000 6 x 6 truck-mixer

put. Transmissions are normally 6-speed Allisons which are of power-assisted manual or automatic type.

ISHIKAWAJIMA/*Japan 1918-1923*
The Ishikawajima Shipbuilding & Engineering Co Ltd, Tokyo, acquired a manufacturing licence for the British-designed Wolseley commercial range, quickly introducing a pneumatic-tyred version of the 1½-ton Wolseley 'CP' Model, powered by a 3-litre 4-cyl side-valve petrol engine, under the Ishikawajima brand name. In 1919 production also got underway in the subsidiary factory of Ishikawajima Jidosha Works Ltd but from 1923 the range was sold as Sumida.

ISOBLOC/*France 1937-1956*
Carrosseries Besset SA, Annonay, acquired a licence to build the American Gar Wood integral coach in France, under the Isobloc brand name. It was powered by a V8 Matford petrol engine or a Georges Irat diesel, both located at the rear. After World War II the company became known as Soc d'Automobiles et Carrosseries d'Annonay, continuing Isobloc production using a Panhard diesel engine. The company was now associated with SA Sylvain Floirat, St Denis, Seine, and in 1956 both were merged into the Saviem group.

ISOTTA-FRASCHINI/*Italy 1906-1918, 1934-1949, 1958-1959*
Car manufacturer Fabb Automobili Isotta Fraschini, Milan, entered the commercial vehicle field with a series of hotel buses, using 3.2- or 4.4-litre 4-cyl petrol engines, joined in 1911 by chain-drive trucks from 1½ to 6 tons capacity, the heaviest having a 7.2-litre 4-cyl petrol engine and 4-speed transmission.

The company concentrated on passenger cars after World War I, but in 1934 resumed commercial production with bonneted 4- and 7-tonners with 6-cyl diesel engines. A new range announced three years later was headed by the 8-ton D120, featuring a 120bhp 9.5-litre diesel engine and 4-speed transmission, although later models had a 5- or 8-speed transmission. A forward-control 3½-tonner, using an 8-speed transmission and air-hydraulic brakes, was built during World War II, military versions having a 5.8-litre 4-cyl petrol engine. By 1946 this had developed into a diesel-engined 4½-tonner and trolleybuses were also being built. In 1949 the company was forced to close, the name being acquired by Breda who formed Fabb Automo-

bili Isotta Fraschini e Motori Breda, re-introducing the Isotta-Fraschini name in 1958 in the form of the D160 truck powered by a 155bhp 10.2-litre 6-cyl diesel engine. This also had an 8-speed synchromesh transmission, air brakes and double-reduction drive but was short-lived.

ISUZU/*Japan 1933 to date*
Kyodo Kokusan Jidosha KK was formed in Kawasaki to continue production of DAT and Ishikawajima trucks, and to build standard models for the Imperial Japanese Army under the Isuzu name, TGE trucks being absorbed in 1937. One of the first was the Type 94 1½/2-tonner, with 4.4-litre 6-cyl side-valve petrol engine and 4-speed transmission. A 6 x 4 derivative, with bevel- or worm-drive, and a half-track were also built.

Re-named Tokyo Motor Industry Ltd in 1937, a series of diesel-engined 4 x 2 and 4 x 4 bonneted models were under development by 1942, by which time there was also a normal-control 7-tonner, using an 8.6-litre 6-cyl diesel engine and 5-speed transmission. After World War II this was developed into the 5-ton 'TX'-Series, using petrol or diesel engines, 4-speed transmissions and hydrovac brakes.

The company became the Isuzu Motor Co Ltd in 1949 and by the mid-1950s the 'TX' had been up-rated to 6 tons, using a 5-speed overdrive transmission. A 6 x 6 military derivative and a bonneted bus were also built. The first Isuzu light commercial was the 1-ton forward-control 'Elf', announced in 1959. This had a 1.5-litre 4-cyl overhead-valve petrol engine with 52bhp diesel option, 4-speed synchromesh transmission and was Hillman-inspired, joined in 1960 by the 1¾-ton bonneted 'Elfin' with independent front suspension. Meanwhile, new 7- and 8-tonners, with 10.2-litre diesel engines and air-servo brakes, were introduced along with new rear-engined buses with optional turbocharged engines, air suspension, power-steering and exhaust brakes. The 'Elf' was later up-rated to 2 tons capacity and forward-control tilt-cab 8-tonners added to the heavy range. The largest passenger model that they made was the 200bhp transverse rear-engined 'BU'.

The General Motors Corp acquired a 35% interest in Isuzu Motors Ltd, as it was then known, in 1971, by which time the 'Elf' was aimed at the 1/2-ton market, using 1.5- or 2-litre petrol or 3.3-litre diesel engines. Heavy-duty trucks were now listed for up to 20 tons GVW and 30 tons GCW,

most using 6-cyl direct-injection diesel engines, 5-speed transmissions and air brakes. Heaviest was the TV402 6-wheeled artic tractor, using a 330bhp 16.5-litre V8 diesel engine.

The 8½-ton GVW 'Forward' arrived in 1973 which, as the name implies, was a forward-control tilt-cab model, with 5.4-litre 6-cyl diesel engine, 5-speed synchromesh transmission and hydrovac brakes. The largest models were now 'SP' and 'VP' 6-wheelers, listed in 6 x 4 and twin-steer 6 x 2 form. Another new model was the KC20 powered by a 100bhp 3.6-litre 4-cyl diesel engine, while 'TX' and 'TD' types were available in forward- or normal-control form. By 1978 there was also a low-loading derivative of the 'Elf', while certain Isuzu trucks were assembled in Australia by General Motors subsidiary Holdens Pty Ltd and these were marketed as Bedford.

ITALA/*Italy 1908-1918*
Using improved 4-cyl shaft-drive passenger car chassis, Fabbrica Automobili Itala SA, Turin, launched a 1½-ton truck and light bus derivative using the Itala brand name. A 16/20hp chain-drive road-sweeper was built in 1910 and by 1913 a full range of commercials of up to 6 tons capacity, was listed, all with 4-cyl petrol engines, magneto ignition and 4-speed transmissions. Most had 'T'-head engines and solid tyres while the largest had a water-cooled transmission brake and chain-drive. Fire appliances were also built and in 1914 an unusual cranked-frame 1½-tonner, which was designed for military applications, was added to the range.

IVECO/*France/Italy/West Germany 1974 to date*
Set up in 1974 to co-ordinate the ideas and technical advances of Fiat, Magirus-Deutz, Unic and Lancia, the Industrial Vehicles Corp is also known as Iveco. Although not a marque in its own right, the Iveco name is carried by all new models. Apart form this each vehicle carries the name of the old manufacturing plant.

Typical is the 16-ton GVW Fiat 159 introduced in 1976. Built in Turin, this carries the Fiat name but is principally of Unic design, developed at the Trappes plant near Paris. Power comes from Unic's CP3 6-cyl diesel engine bored out to provide 160 instead of the original 140bhp. Similarly, Fiat's OM range of medium-duty commercials are now powered by Magirus-Deutz air-cooled diesel engines.

JACKSON/*USA 1920-1923*
Previously concentrating on light commercials, the Jackson Motors Corp, Jackson, Michigan, also built a 3½-ton 4 x 4 truck, with 4-cyl Continental petrol engine, and 4-speed transmission.

JACKSON-HOLROYD/*England 1919*
James Whitely Ltd, Halifax, Yorks, briefly offered a 1½-ton shaft-drive truck called the Jackson-Holroyd, powered by a 25-6hp 4-cyl petrol engine.

JACQUEMONT
France 1947-?
Built in Lyons, the single-deck Jacquemont trolleybus is understood to have been short-lived.

JAMES & BROWNE/*England 1905-1909*
Built by James & Browne Ltd, Hammersmith, West London, the first heavy James & Browne or J & B was a chain-drive 5-tonner powered by a 20hp 4-cyl horizontal petrol engine located beneath the floor. Later, a 24/30hp engine was listed. For 1907 only vertical engines were fitted, new 2- and 3-tonners being supplied to the Lacre Motor Car Co Ltd, London W1, for sale as the J & B Lacre. In 1908 the first petrol-engined vehicle in the fleet of Pickfords Ltd was a James & Browne with a 2-cyl petrol engine, but this proved unsatisfactory and was returned to the maker. In 1909 the company built a new 5-tonner, now powered by a 45hp 4-cyl vertical petrol engine but this was also fairly insignificant and the company's last project was the construction of an experimental Railless trolleybus chassis.

JAMES & MEYER/*USA 1909-1911*
Known also as the James, the James & Meyer was a high-wheeler built by the James & Meyer Motor Car Co, Lawrenceburg, Indiana. It had an opposed-piston 2-cyl air-cooled petrol engine but few were built.

JANNEY-STEINMETZ/*USA 1901-?*
In 1901 Janney Steinmetz & Co, Philadelphia, Pennsylvania, listed a variety of coal-burning goods- and passenger-carrying steam vehicles from 1 to 10 tons capacity, which were marketed as the Janney-Steinmetz.

JANSON/*Netherlands 1934-1940*
Built by W A Janssens & Zoon, Rotterdam, the first Janson 3-wheelers were mainly light-duty models, the heaviest in 1935 being the 1000kg 5G model with a 2-cyl JLO 2-stroke engine, single steering front wheel and driven rear wheels. By 1938 the largest model was the 1250kg Model 52 powered by a 400cc 2-cyl air-cooled JLO 2-stroke engine.

JANVIER/*France 1905-1907*
Victor Janvier, Paris, constructed a 7-ton 6-wheeled truck with twin steering axles and double chain-drive at the rear. The driver was seated above a 30hp 4-cyl petrol engine and braking was effected not only by shoes acting on the rear wheel rims but also by wooden blocks acting on the axle shaft.

JARRETT/*USA 1921-1934*
Dissatisfied with the poor hill-climbing ability of trucks then on the market, James C Jarrett Jnr designed 2½- and 5-ton trucks aimed specifically at those operators working in the mountainous regions of Colorado. Built by the J C Jarrett Motor & Finance Co, Colorado Springs, some 300 were produced, each carrying the letters JCJ on the finned cast-aluminium radiator. Power came from a 6-cyl Waukesha petrol engine connected via a 7-speed transmission to a double-reduction rear axle.

JARVIS-HUNTINGTON/*USA 1911-1914*
Jarvis-Huntington trucks were all forward-control models ranging in capacity from 1½ to 5 tons. Built by the Jarvis-Huntington Auto Co, Huntington, West Virginia, these had 4-cyl petrol engines, with 3-speed transmissions in the lighter types and 4-speed in the heavier. Double chain final-drive was standard. Later, the company was known as the Jarvis Machinery & Supply Co.

JAY-FONG/*China 1956 to date*
Based on the Soviet ZIS-150 truck, the first Jay-Fong, also known as the Chieh-Fang or Jie-Fong (Liberation), was a bonneted 4-tonner built in the No 1 Automobile Plant, Changchun, Kirin Province. Powered by a 95bhp 6-cyl side-valve petrol engine with 5-speed transmission and double-reduction rear axle, it was also offered as a bus or trolleybus chassis or as a 6-wheeler. Using a short version of this chassis, the nearby Szuping Municipal Machinery Plant offers the DD-340 dump truck and DD-400Y tanker, while it is also used as a crane-carrier and as a fire appliance. A more modern design is the CA-30A, a 2½-ton 6 x 6 powered by a 110bhp 6-cyl engine. There are also 3-, 5- and 7-tonners.

JEANTAUD/*France 1900-1906*
Charles Jeantaud, Paris, developed a series of battery-electric taxi-cabs towards the end of the 19th century, later adding a charabanc of similar design. With a range per charge of approximately 61km this was equipped with five forward speeds and by 1903 a series of Jeantaud commercials had been introduced, including a prototype trolleybus. For 1905 front-wheel drive was standard.

JEFFERY/*USA 1914*
The Thomas B Jeffery Co, Kenosha, Wisconsin, added trucks to its light commercial range shortly before World War I. However, an earlier visit to the plant by the US Army Quartermaster Corps resulted in the development of the 4-wheel drive 4-wheel steer and 4-wheel braked Jeffery Quad 1½/2-tonner which quickly overtook all other vehicle production.

JEFFERY QUAD/*USA 1914-1917*
Following a visit by the US Army Quartermaster Corps to the Thomas B Jeffery Co's Kenosha, Wisconsin, vehicle plant in 1913, the 4-wheel drive 4-wheel steer and 4-wheel braked Jeffery Quad 1½/2-tonner was developed for military use. It quickly replaced existing Jeffery models and wartime demand became so great that production was also farmed out to other manufacturers, although it was still known as the Jeffery Quad. Powered by a 36hp 4-cyl Buda petrol engine, it had a 4-speed box with central differential transmitting power to both axles. The engine was offset to one side to provide sufficient room for the driver and 4-wheel steering provided a turning circle of just 13.7m. The Thomas B Jeffery Co was acquired by Charles W Nash in 1916 and re-named the Nash Motor Co in 1917 when the Jeffery Quad became the Nash Quad.

JELCZ/*Poland 1968 to date*
Previously marketed as the Zubr, the Jelcz truck and bus range was introduced by Jelczanskie Zaklady Samochodow, Jelcz Kholawy, using licence-built Wola-Leyland diesel engines. The first goods model was a rigid forward-control 8-tonner powered by a 200bhp engine, while the passenger field was catered for by versions of the Skoda RT0706. In 1972 the goods range was re-designed and joined by various tractor versions and by a new 3-axle rigid, all using up-rated Wola-Leyland diesels. For operation at up to 32 tons GCW, tractor versions now include a 6 x 4 model powered by a 320bhp Steyr diesel. Fire-fighting vehicles are also available, some being constructed on Star 4 x 2 and 6 x 6 chassis renamed Jelcz. Towards the end of the 1970s an agreement was signed with Berliet of France, whereby Skoda-based passenger models would be phased out in favour of the PR100 city bus, powered by a 170bhp Berliet diesel or by a 185bhp Wola-Leyland unit, both located under the floor.

JEN-HELECS/*England 1949*
The Jen-Helecs was a 2-ton payload battery-electric version of the Jen-Tug built by Jensen Motors Ltd, West Bromwich, Staffs, in

1977 Jelcz PR110 single-deck bus

association with Hindle, Smart & Co Ltd, Ardwick, Manchester. Outwardly identical to its petrol-engined companion, the Jen-Helecs carried 192 or 240amp/hr batteries slung pannier-fashion on either side of the chassis.

JEN-TUG/*England 1946-1959*
Jensen Motors Ltd, West Bromwich, Staffs, built a small petrol-engined artic with an unladen weight (including trailer) of 1½ tons and a gross combination weight of 3 tons. Designed by George Reikie and called the Jen-Tug, it had a narrow rear track, a 1.17-litre 4-cyl side-valve Ford petrol engine located behind the driver, a 3-speed transmission and hydraulic brakes. In 1949 it was joined by a short-lived battery-electric version known as the Jen-Helecs and by 1952 a 1.2-litre Austin engine and 4-speed transmission were used, increasing the payload to 3 tons. Later, there was a choice between a 1.5-litre Austin petrol or 2.2-litre BMC diesel engine, enabling the Jen-Tug to operate at up to 4 tons payload rating until production of this vehicle was discontinued in the year 1959

JENATZY/*Belgium/France 1899-1901*
Camille Jenatzy developed battery-electric passenger cars, using a small workshop in Brussels. Commercial derivatives were actually built by Cie Internationale des Transports Automobiles, Paris, although sold under the Jenatzy name. All of these were somewhat overweight and uncompetitive.

JENKINS/*USA 1901-1902*
The Jenkins was a 22-passenger steam bus with revolving seats aimed at the tourist trade in Washington, DC. It was constructed by the Jenkins Automobile Co, also of Washington, using a marine type water-tube boiler, horizontal 4-cyl compound engine and a differential shaft engaging with ring gears bolted to the inside of each rear wheel. At the time, it was claimed to be the largest self-propelled bus in America.

JENNINGS/*Canada 1911-1914*
Jennings & Co, Montreal, Quebec, was founded by Arthur Jennings to build horse-drawn wagons and bodies for self-propelled chassis but also built light trucks and fire appliances of "conventional" layout and about 1½ tons capacity.

JENSEN/*England 1938-1962*
In collaboration with the Reynolds Tube Co Ltd, Jensen Motors Ltd, West Bromwich, Staffs,

1939 Jensen chassisless prototype truck

developed a goods model of light-alloy integral construction. Classed as a 5/6-tonner, the prototype had a Ford V8 petrol engine and light-alloy body components supplied by the operator. The vehicle weighed 2½ tons unladen. A 6 x 2 prototype of steel-panelled wood frame construction, weighing under 2½ tons unladen was completed two years later. It had a 24bhp 4-cyl Fordson petrol engine and 5-speed transmission. Full-scale production got underway in 1946 as a 4.9m wheelbase dropside or pantechnicon. This was powered by a Perkins P6 diesel with Moss 5-speed transmission. A 38/40-seat passenger model was also available but few were built. This range went out of production in 1956 but a small petrol-engined artic called the Jen-Tug continued until 1959, along with an electric version called the Jen-Helecs. From 1958 to 1962 the company also built the German-designed Tempo 1500 under licence. A wide variety of body types were available for this independently-sprung front-wheel drive 1¼-ton payload machine and at the 1958 Commercial Motor Show no less than five Jensen-built vehicles were displayed, ranging from a fixed-side pick-up in normal and crew-cab form and 14-seat minibus to a hydraulic tower wagon and a variable-height "self-loader". Between 1974 and 1978 the company was involved in the development of the Stonefield light cross-country range.

JESSE ELLIS/*England 1897-1907*
Jesse Ellis & Co Ltd, Maidstone, Kent, built its first steam wagon in 1897, this having a vertical field-tube boiler and 3-cyl radial "undertype" engine. A 2-ton vertical-boilered chain-drive "undertype" was shown at Maidstone in 1898, while a 4-tonner, with De Dion type boiler, compound "undertype" engine and chain-drive went

to a local brewer in 1899. Subsequent Jesse Ellis wagons had all-gear drive trains. The company's last few wagons, built in 1907, had short loco-type boilers and compound engines developing some 35hp. The Jesse Ellis 6-tonner had Stephenson's link motion, 2-speed gearing and chain final-drive with differential mounted on the rear axle. The last wagon was a loco-type 2-tonner with Fairfax 3-speed epicyclic transmission.

JIAN-SHE/*China 1958 to date*
The Antung Automobile Plant, Antung, Liaoning Province, has built the 2-ton Jian-She or Chien-She (Construction) lorry powered by a 50bhp engine for over 20 years.

JIANG-HUAI/*China 1969 to date*
The Chianghuai Motor Vehicle Plant, Chianghuai, Anhwei Province, has built the Jiang-Huai or Chiang-Huai (River Huai) forward-control 3-tonner since 1969. Designated the HF-140, this has a 120bhp 6-cyl engine which, in conjunction with a 4-speed transmission, provides a maximum speed of 136km/h.

JINGGANGSHAN/*China 1968 to date*
The 2½-ton Jinggangshan or Chingkanshan truck was developed in the Chingkan Mountains Motor Vehicle Plant at Kiansi. Similar to the Tiao-Jin NJ-130, this did not enter full series production until 1969 when it was powered by a 79bhp 6-cyl engine driving the rear wheels via a 4-speed transmission.

JOHNSON/*USA 1901-1912*
The Johnson Service Co, Milwaukee, Wisconsin, introduced a 1-ton steam van with underfloor boiler and chain final-drive. Similar models were listed until 1907, a fleet of four being the first self-propelled mail vans in America. Petrol-engined Johnsons were pow-

ered by 30, 40 or 50hp engines built under Renault licence and available in capacities ranging from 1 to 4 tons. The smaller models utilized shaft-drive while heavier types had double chains, the range including both forward- and normal-control trucks, buses, fire appliances, police wagons and ambulances.

JONES/*USA 1918-1920*
The Jones Motor Car Co, Wichita, Kansas, was a passenger car manufacturer. They were also responsible for building trucks of up to 2½ tons capacity.

JUMBO (1)/*USA 1918-1924*
Introduced by the Saginaw Motor Car Co, Saginaw, Michigan, the Jumbo truck was a 2½-tonner with 4-cyl Buda petrol engine, 4-speed Fuller transmission and Clark bevel-gear axle until 1920, when the company was re-organized as the Nelson Motor Truck Co, building 1½-, 2-, 3-, 3½- and 4-tonners of similar specification.

JUMBO (2)/*Netherlands c1926-1930*
The Jumbo Motor Co was founded in Helmond as a trailer-building subsidiary of the Ford vehicle agents in Eindhoven. It also constructed a number of trucks using Ford engines and radiators to cater for those customers requiring greater payload capacity than that available on Ford's standard range. These were marketed as Jumbos and were of bonneted layout with proprietary axles and chassis frames.

JUNGBLUTH/*West Germany 1950-1951*
Powered by a rear-mounted 95bhp Henschel diesel engine, the Jungbluth chassisless bus was constructed by Karosserie und Fahrzeugbau Jungbluth & Co Kg, Bad Lauterberg, but few were sold. The company was only operational for a year.

JUNO/*USA 1912-1915*
In 1912 the Brodesser Motor Truck Co, Milwaukee, Wisconsin, adopted the Juno brand name for its trucks, later forming the Juno Motor Truck Co and moving to nearby Juneau. Initially, the Juno was a 2- or 3-ton chain-drive "cab-over" powered by a 4-cyl Wisconsin 'T'-head engine with a 3-speed selective transmission. In 1913 the company acquired manufacturing rights to the Brockway Motor Truck Co's short-lived battery-electric series. Previously sold as the Brockway Electric, these were also re-named Juno but the project was brief and production gradually petered out and finally ceased in 1915.

K

KADIX/*USA 1912-1913*
The Kadix-Newark Motor Truck Co, Newark, New Jersey, listed 3-, 4-, 5-, 6- and 7-ton trucks with 4-cyl petrol engines, 3-speed transmissions, countershafts and double chain-drive.

1978 Kaelble 8 x 4 crane-carrier

KAELBLE/*Germany/West Germany c1905 to date*
Building the world's first fast-running petrol engine in 1903, Gottfried Kaelble, Backnang, was soon producing self-propelled stone-crushing equipment and in 1925, as Carl Kaelble GmbH, built its first road tractor, called the 'Suevia', powered by a 2-cyl diesel engine. An improved chassisless model, powered by a 2- or 3-cyl diesel engine and with a rear swing-axle, was built soon after. By 1933 a bonneted 6-wheeled tractor known as the GR/1 was being supplied to the German Railways for hauling railway wagons on low-loading trailers and in 1937 the company built what was then the largest diesel road tractor on the market, powered by a 180bhp engine. A year later this record was broken by a 6 x 6 model with twin steering axles and an amidships-mounted 200bhp diesel engine. There was also a forward-control road tractor. Post-war production began in 1949 with heavy road tractors, articulated versions and a 7-ton rigid truck powered by a 130bhp 6-cyl diesel engine. A 200bhp V8 diesel was developed in 1951 and installed in Europe's first large-capacity on/off-highway dump trucks launched the following year. In 1953, a new forward-control truck range was announced with capacities of 6½, 8 and 11 tons powered

1978 Kaelble fire crash tender

by 6-cyl diesel engines of up to 150bhp output, although a 13-tonner used a V8 diesel. During the 1960s the company's standard rigid truck was a front-wheel drive 9-tonner, with road tractors comprising both 4- and 6-wheeled units and an ever-expanding series of heavy dump trucks. Standard truck production ceased in 1933 in favour of new special equipment carriers for cranes, fire-fighting equipment and similar applications, while the German Railways continued to use Kaelble heavy tractors, now with outputs of up to 425bhp. By the end of the 1970s, the carrier range comprised 6 x 4, 8 x 4, 10 x 6, 12 x 8 and 14 x 8 models with engines of up to 1100bhp. Dump trucks now had 6- or 10-cyl diesels of between 265 and 475bhp and payload ratings of up to 35 tons, while a new line of articulated liquid slag haulers could cope with loads of up to 150 tons. A range of hydrostatically-driven road tractors for loads of between 100 and 300 tons with engines of up to 880bhp output completed the on/off-highway range. Underground requirements were catered for by low-profile dumpers, often with articulated chassis.

KAISER (1)/*Germany 1908-1913*
After Nürnberger Motor Fahrzeug-Fabrik Union GmbH, Nüremberg, was acquired by Nürnberger Feuerlöschgeräte und Maschinenfabrik vorm Justus Christian Braun AG, also of Nüremberg, former Maurer-Union models were re-named Kaiser. Braun production continued as before.

KAISER (2)/*USA 1946*
The American-built Kaiser was an 18-m articulated high-floor coach built by the Permanente Metals Corp, Permanente, California. Used by the Santa Fe Trail Transportation Co, it had a 6-cyl Cummins diesel engine, 10.7cu m of luggage space under the floor, and accommodation for 63 passengers. A 'Torsilastic' suspension system, originally developed by the Twin Coach Co, was used.

KAISER JEEP/*USA 1963-1971*
When the Willys-Overland Co, Toledo, Ohio, manufacturer of the famous Jeep, was re-organized as the Kaiser Jeep Corp, it began assembling rugged 2½- and

5-ton 6 x 6 military trucks, initially with Continental petrol and Cummins diesel engines, but later with a multi-fuel Continental unit. These were bonneted models following US Government guidelines but a year after the Jeep Corp was formed in 1970, production moved to the AM General Corp's factory at South Bend, Indiana. Thereafter, the series was known as the AM or AM General range.

KALAMAZOO/*USA 1913-924*
The Kalamazoo Motor Vehicle Co was set up in Kalamazoo, Michigan, introducing a 1½-tonner with 4-cyl side-valve Buda petrol engine, 3-speed transmission and double chain-drive. In 1914 the company acquired the manufacturing rights for the designs of the Clark Power Wagon Co, Lansing, and incorporated some Clark features in new 2½- and 3½-tonners, the original Kalamazoo being offered on the British market as the Shakespeare. From 1916 the Columbia Motor Truck & Trailer Co, Pontiac, constructed certain Kalamazoos under its own name and in 1919 the Kalamazoo Motor Vehicle Co became the Kalamazoo Motors Corp, offering 1½-, 2½- and 3½-ton trucks with Wisconsin petrol engines in the two heaviest models, a Continental unit in the lightest and a 4-speed transmission and worm final-drive in all three. By 1922 seven models, from 1 to 5 tons capacity, were listed.

KALAMAZOO CRUISER/ *USA 1948-1951*
A 25- or 29-seat forward-control passenger model called the Kalamazoo Cruiser was built by Kalamazoo Coaches Inc, Kalamazoo, Michigan. This joined the existing Pony Cruiser range and is believed to have been based on Chevrolet, Ford or International Harvester chassis.

KALMAR/*Sweden 1970-1974*
As well as light delivery vans for the Swedish Post Office, Kalmar Verkstads AB, Kalmar, built a few heavy-duty terminal tractors, with Cummins V8-210 diesel engines, Allison automatic transmission, rear-facing folding fork-lift equipment and cab access was via a single door in the front panel.

KAMAZ/*Soviet Union 1976 to date*
Following assembly of prototypes at the Zavod Imeny Likhachev factory, Kamaz production got underway in a brand new plant at Naberezhyne, Chelny, on the River Kama. The world's largest truck factory, this has a planned

1978 Kamaz Model 54112 6 x 4 artic tractor

annual output of some 150,000 vehicles, including 4 x 2 tractors, 6 x 4 tippers, a 6-wheeled rigid drawbar outfit and dump trucks, all of forward-control layout. Three direct-injection diesel engines are also built and supplied to other Soviet truck plants.

KANAWHA/*USA 1911-1912*
The 2-ton Kanawha had a 4-cyl petrol engine, 3-speed transmission, countershaft and double chain-drive. Built by the Kanawha Auto Truck Co, Charleston, West Virginia, its wheelbase was 330cm.

KANSAS CITY/*USA 1905-1917*
Using the Kansas City or Kansas City Car brand name, the Kansas City Motor Car Co, Kansas City, Missouri, offered chain-drive models, light delivery buses and trucks, the largest of which had a payload rating of 2 tons.

KARBACH/*USA 1906-1908*
Few, if any, examples of the Karbach 1½-tonner were built. A product of the Karbach Automobile & Vehicle Co, Omaha, Nebraska, this had a 20hp 2-cyl petrol engine, 3-speed transmission and double chain-drive.

KAROSA/*Czechoslovakia 1965 to date*
While Karosa np, Vysoké Mýto, had been engaged in coachbuilding for many years, it was not until 1965 that the company's first complete passenger models appeared. These were of chassisless construction with 180bhp 6-cyl horizontal diesel engines, offered as the SM city bus, the SL sight-seeing coach and the SD long-distance tourer. Now available with power outputs of up to 210bhp, the SD can be supplied with a special dormitory trailer.

KARPETAN/*Spain 1963-1968*
Lerma Autobastidores Industriales SA, Zaragoza, offered medium- and heavy-duty Karpetan trucks, passenger models being marketed under the Layetan brand name. Trucks were powered by licence-built Perkins diesels or imported MAN diesels, drive axles being by Timken or Eaton. Capacities ranged from 7 to 12 tons.

1948 Karrier 'Bantam' artic tractor

KARRIER/*England 1907 to date*
Clayton & Co (Huddersfield) Ltd
built its first petrol-engined Karrier for operation in hilly areas such
as are found around Huddersfield, known as 'A'-Types and powered by Tylor petrol engines. All
were fitted with large platform bodies with the driver located over
the engine. The first bonneted
Karriers, known as 'B'-Types, appeared in 1911 and in October
1913 a 3/4-ton "subsidy" model
was accepted by the War Office.
'A'- and 'B'-Types were used for
both goods and passenger applications with load capacities of between 1 and 5 tons. Karrier Motors Ltd was formed in 1920 and
by the end of that year the bonneted 3-, 4- and 5-ton 'K'-Type,
developed from the "subsidy"
model, had been announced, powered by a 50bhp petrol engine.
Forward-control versions were
announced in 1922 and the 1½-ton
'C'-Type and 2-ton 'H'-Type introduced in 1923.

New 2- and 3-tonners arrived
in 1924, the 'H'-Type being uprated to 2½ tons payload. In 1924
the development of a military-style rigid 6-wheeler got underway. Powered by a 2.9-litre 4-cyl
petrol engine, this had a gross
weight of 4½/5 tons and a payload
capacity of 2 tons, one special feature being the use of overhead-worm rear axles with a pivoting
tube enclosing the inter-axle universal joints and propeller shafts.
Launched in 1927 as the WO6,
two of these were the first
wheeled vehicles to travel right
round Australia. Early types had
Dorman petrol engines and air
brakes while later deliveries had
Tylor engines and servo-assisted
braking.

Meanwhile, 1926 had seen the
company's first purpose-built
passenger models in the form of
the 4-wheeled 'CL'- and 'KL'-Types and rigid 6-wheeler WL6
and CY6. All except the 'KL'
were of the low-loading type. For
goods and passenger applications,
the 1½-ton 'ZX'-Type was introduced and municipal requirements were satisfied by a new
'RSC'-Type road sweeper/collector adapted from the earlier 'K'-Type. Further 6-wheeled developments included the WL6 for passenger work and, late in 1927, the
sleeve-valve engined DD6 with
72-seat double-deck body.

The company's first trolleybuses appeared in 1928 but early
examples were sold as Karrier-Clough. In 1929 an improved 'Z'-Type, the 30-seat ZA, was announced, the 2½-ton CYR was introduced for municipal work and
the 6-wheeled heavy-duty KW6
added for 7- and 8-ton payloads,
and the company was now offering short-wheelbase forward-control versions of its bonneted
models.

It was at about this time that
the company first became involved with the LMS Railway on
new road vehicle developments.
One was a matched articulated
outfit based on French Chenard-Walcker designs.

1939 Karrier E6 trolleybus

By 1930 the K5 had been uprated to 6 tons payload, the WO6
had been re-designated the 5-ton
FM6 and RM6 and the KW6 had
become the 8-ton KWR6 and 9-ton KWF6. Encouraged by the
LMS Railway, the company
experimented with a quickly detachable "mechanical horse"
known as the 'Rorailer'. Prototypes were built in 1930, the main
requirements being that the vehicle could carry a 3- or 6-ton payload and could reverse and turn
between railway tracks. Trailers
also had to be quickly detachable.
This led to the first 'Colt' 3-wheeler, with 7bhp flat-twin Jowett petrol engine, in 1930 and to its 4-cyl
Humber-engined companion, the
'Cob', in 1931. Other new models
included the 4-wheeled double-deck 'Monitor' for 50 passengers.
By this time the company's trolleybuses were being marketed
simply as Karrier and for 1932 the
'Cob' and 'Colt' models had been
re-rated at 4 and 2 tons payload
respectively as the 'Cob Major'
and 'Colt Major'. Other goods
models included the 6-ton capacity 'Consul' and 12-ton rigid 6-wheeled 'Colossus'. New passenger types ranged from the 28-seat 'Coaster' to the 68-seat 6-wheeled 'Consort', while a particularly significant new goods model was the 243-cm wheelbase
'Bantam' rigid with 4-cyl petrol
engine and 4-speed transmission
for a 2½-ton payload.

In 1934 a receiver was appointed and a new company, Karrier
Motors Successors Ltd, registered, following a takeover by
Humber Ltd which was itself a
subsidiary of Rootes Securities
Ltd. By the summer of 1935 production had moved to Commer
Cars Ltd's Luton plant, with the
exception of trolleybuses which
remained at Huddersfield, and
the company became Karrier Motors Ltd. On the trolleybus front,
a new 6-wheeler with conventional chassis and an extended wheelbase of 541cm was announced as
the E6A in 1935, designed to take
a 9-m 70-seat double-deck body.
A new E4 double-deck chassis appeared the following year with a
wheelbase of 472cm.

The Luton-built Karrier range
was now restricted to lighter applications than the companion
Commer line-up and incorporated
a number of Commer components. Models comprised the
'Colt', 'Cob Junior', 'Cob Senior'
and 'Bantam' types, plus the new
CK3 3-tonner and CK6 6-wheeler. The 4-wheeled forward-control 'Bantam' tractor appeared in
1936, gradually replacing the
'Cob', and 'Colt' models, and
many of the company's municipal
models were now built jointly by
Karrier and by the Yorkshire Patent Steam Wagon Co. Wartime
production included the 3-ton
CK6 rigid 6-wheeler, the K6 4 x 4
3-tonner, numerous versions of
the 'Bantam' and the KT4 4-wheel
drive gun tractor. Meanwhile,
Karrier trolleybus production had
merged with that of Sunbeam,
another Rootes subsidiary, and
certain Sunbeam models were even sold as Karrier.

Rigid and articulated versions
of the 2-ton 'Bantam' re-appeared
after the war as did the CK3 3/4-tonner and, later, a half-cab bonneted road sweeper based on a
279-cm wheelbase left-hand drive
version of the Commer 'Super-poise'. The 'Bantam' received a
new all-steel cab in 1948 and in
1950 the CK3 became the 'Game-cock', also with a new all-steel cab
and 6-cyl underfloor engine. In
1951 a 4-cyl forward-control ambulance chassis was introduced
and by 1954 the 3-cyl 6-piston
Commer TS3 2-stroke diesel engine was an option for the 'Gamecock', a Perkins P4 being offered
in the 'Bantam'.

New cabs with single-piece
windscreens were introduced for
both the 'Bantam' and 'Gamecock' in 1958, the latter receiving
a Perkins 6.305 6-cyl diesel engine, and a battery-electric version of the 'Bantam' tractor built
in association with Smith's Delivery Vehicles Ltd in 1959. By 1962
a new ambulance designed in collaboration with Dennis Bros Ltd
was offered as a Karrier on Commer's 'Walk-Thru' chassis. The
'Bantam' was again up-dated in
1963 and with an increasing requirement for heavier refuse collection vehicles with still greater
capacities, the Commer CC8 and
VB7 chassis were made available
under the Karrier brand name in
1965, followed in 1968 by the 16
tons gross Commer CE16 with a
4cu m capacity body. Meanwhile,
the American-based Chrysler
combine took over control of the
business in 1966, setting up
Chrysler United Kingdom Ltd in
1970. The Karrier operation became part of the Commer/Karrier
Divn which was based at Dunstable, Beds.

Later the Commer 'Commando' range was developed and marketed as the Karrier for municipal
applications with models ranging
from 7½ to 16 tons gross, often
with crew-cabs, and with diesel
engines by Perkins or Mercedes-Benz. The Commer name was replaced by that of Dodge in 1976
but Karrier versions continue for
municipal applications. From early 1981 the Karrier Motor Company have managed all Karrier
products; this company is owned
by Renault and Peugeot.

KARRIER-CLOUGH/*England
1928-c1931*
When Karrier Motors Ltd, Huddersfield, Yorks, introduced its
first trolleybus this was marketed
as the Karrier-Clough. Based on a
modified WL6/2 motor bus chassis, the first was the E6 6-wheeler
for use with a 64-seat double-deck
body. Early examples had
Clough-BTH traction equipment
with the motor mounted amidships and drive via twin worm-drive axles. Westinghouse or Peters air brakes were used. In 1930
the first 4-wheeled Karrier-Cloughs were delivered to York
with 32-seat Roe single-deck bodies. These were apparently based
on the Karrier 'Chaser' motorbus
chassis and were designated the
E4. Soon after this, Clough traction equipment was phased out
and models marketed simply as
Karrier.

191

KARRYALL/*USA 1900-c1965*
Main features of the Karryall were its 77-cm frame height on 38-cm tyres, 101-cm wide chassis frame, swing-out cab and ability to unload in any direction. Built by the Koehring Co, it had a Ford V8 petrol engine with drive via torque-converter and automatic transmission.

KATO/*USA 1909-1913*
The 4 x 4 1½-ton payload Kato was designed by sweet manufacturer Ernest Rosenberger and assembled by the Four Traction Auto Co, Monkato, Minnesota. Powered by a 4-cyl petrol engine found under the driver's seat, drive was transmitted via propeller shaft to a transfer box located halfway along the chassis and thence forward and aft via other drive-shafts. A 3-ton version was announced in 1913 but manufacturing rights were sold to the Nevada Mfg Co, Nevada, Iowa.

KAYSER/*Germany c1905-c1910*
Both light- and medium weight goods models were built by Pfalzische Nahmaschinen und Fahrrader-Fabrik vorm Gebr Kayser, Kaiserslautern, under the Kayser brand name.

KAZ/*Soviet Union c1951 to date*
Koutaissi Automobilova Zavod, Koutaissi, Georgia, concentrated on the production of trucks using ZIL chassis and components. Marketed as the KAZ, these were near identical to ZIL models until 1961 when the KAZ-606A 'Kolhida' forward-control tractor was introduced on a ZIL-164A chassis. This had a 6-cyl engine that could be easily removed for maintenance via the front of the vehicle. A new "cabover" model called the KAZ-608 'Kolhida' entered production a year later. This had a tilt-cab and 150bhp ZIL V8 engine and was re-styled in 1973.

KEARNS/*USA 1908-1920*
The Kearns Motor Buggy Co, Beavertown, Pennsylvania, introduced a commercial version of its high-wheeler, using a 3-cyl 2-stroke Speedwell air-cooled petrol engine, friction transmission and dual chain-drive. In 1909 the company was re-named the Kearns Motor Car Co, production of the high-wheeler continuing. By 1913 the business was known as the Kearns Motor Truck Co and for 1914 a more conventional model was introduced. Powered by a 20hp 4-cyl petrol engine, this had a cone clutch, 3-speed transmission and Hotchkiss final-drive. After World War I a Herschell-Spillman-powered 1½-tonner with dry-plate clutch and internal-gear final-drive was announced,

receiving a Continental engine by 1920, when the company moved to Danville and was re-named the Kearns-Dughie Motors Corp. Models were now sold as Kearns-Dughie.

KEARNS-DUGHIE/*USA 1920-1928*
The Kearns-Dughie Motors Corp took over the activities of the Kearns Motor Truck Co in 1920, moving production to Danville, Pennsylvania. Previously sold as the Kearns, the Kearns-Dughie was listed in capacities from 1 to 5 tons, with worm final-drive, including a range of fire appliance chassis assembled for the Foamite-Childs Corp and marketed as the Childs Thoroughbred.

KELLAND/*USA 1922-1925*
Available in three sizes, the Kelland was a battery-electric model listed by the Kelland Motor Car Co, Newark, New Jersey. Using the same 259-cm wheelbase chassis with solid rubber tyres and General Electric traction equipment, the heaviest was the 1-ton Model 'C'.

KELLER/*Germany c1900-1903*
Originally built by Motorfahrzeug und Motorenfabrik Berlin AG, Marienfelde, Berlin, the Keller was a heavy road tractor with track-ring drive capable of hauling 13 trailers with a total capacity of over 40 tons. In 1902 Keller set up its own production line at Hoerschel, Westphalia.

KELLY/*USA 1910-1912*
The Kelly Motor Truck Co was formed to take over production of air-cooled Frayer-Miller commercials at Columbus, Ohio. These were later re-named Kelly, continuing to use air-cooled engines until 1912 when, as the Kelly-Springfield Motor Truck Co, Springfield, Ohio, 4-cyl water-cooled units were introduced, the trucks being sold as Kelly-Springfield.

KELLY-SPRINGFIELD/*USA 1912-1929*
Re-organized as the Kelly-Springfield Motor Truck Co, Springfield, Ohio, the air-cooled models of the Kelly Motor Truck Co received 4-cyl water-cooled engines and became known as Kelly-Springfields in 1912. All had "coal-scuttle" bonnets with radiators between driver and engine, 3-speed transmission and double chain-drive, and 1-, 2- and 3-tonners were listed. By 1918 the range included eight models, from 1½ to 6 tons capacity, with worm-drive on the lightest, internal-gear drive on others and chain-drive on the 6-tonner. From 1924 the

Kelly-Springfield chemical engine and hose car fire appliance c1918

smaller models had conventionally-mounted radiators. In 1926 the business was acquired by the American Bus & Truck Co, being re-named the Kelly-Springfield Bus & Truck Corp later that year.

KENWORTH (1)/*USA 1922 to date*
Previously sold as the Gersix, the Kenworth truck range appeared after the formation of the Kenworth Motor Truck Corp, Seattle, Washington, which acquired numerous components from the HRL Motor Co and the Vulcan truck operation, both of which had recently ceased production. Early models were all "conventionals" with capacities of 1½, 2½ and 4 tons, each powered by a 4-cyl Buda petrol engine. Five models were listed by 1925 with capacities of between 1 and 5 tons.

Some Kenworths were even bodied as passenger vehicles, of normal- or forward-control layout and with single- or 1½-deck coachwork. While custom-built models took up much of production, a range of standard trucks, from 2 to 10 tons capacity, was listed during the late 1930s using Buda, Hercules or Herschell-Spillman petrol or Cummins diesel engines. By 1937 the first 4 x 4 Kenworth had been built and the first true "cabovers" appeared about the same time. Sleeper boxes were another new feature.

During World War II 6 x 6 wreckers were built, as well as prototypes of a new 8-ton 6 x 6. In 1941 the world's first all-aluminium diesel engine was built by Cummins for installation in a Kenworth, and by 1944 the company had developed an extruded

1934 Kenworth (1) artic tractor

In 1927 a new 78bhp 6-cyl petrol engine was fitted in certain models while more rugged specifications included 7-speed transmissions, stronger axles and extra front springs. By 1929 an assembly plant had been set up in Vancouver, British Columbia, to handle Canadian sales and in 1932 the parent company became the first in America to list an optional diesel engine. Other developments included hydraulic brake vacuum boosters, torsion-bar suspension, trailing axle and tandem-drive 6-wheelers and fire appliances.

aluminium chassis frame, also introducing aluminium cabs, bonnets and transmission casings. In 1944 the business was acquired by the Pacific Car & Foundry Co and transferred to the former Fisher body plant, also in Seattle. Later, a heavy-duty Kenworth truck plant was established in Kansas City, Missouri.

Civilian production was built up again during the late 1940s, and a new line of desert trucks developed for Middle East use in 1947. Three years later a Boeing gas-turbine engine was fitted in a

Kenworth (1) 'K'-Series artic tractor c1971

Kenworth to make this the first gas-turbine truck in regular service and the company's first full-width "cabovers" – the 'K'-Series made their debut. One military project was the US Army's T10 heavy equipment transporter comprising two 4 x 4 units, one for the front and one for the rear, each powered by a 375bhp Continental engine and with a total weight of 85 tons. In 1953 the Kenworth Motor Truck Divn announced a novel "cab-beside-engine" layout for use in mountainous areas where maximum visibility was essential. This was available in 4 x 2 and 6 x 4 form with a low-profile one-man half-cab but was never particularly popular. Another special model was the 4-axle 'Dromedary' built in association with Pacific Intermountain Express in 1956. This had two steering axles and a short van body between cab and fifth-wheel coupling and was sometimes known as the PIE. In 1958 the Model 953 oilfield truck powered by a Cummins NTC350 diesel engine was developed.

The 'PD'-Series appeared in 1971, this being of cab-forward layout for urban delivery work and later re-named 'Hustler', while 1973 saw the 6 x 4 'Brute' "conventional" launched. Both types were still listed for 1980, as were 'W'-Series "conventional" tractors and 'K'-Series "cabover" tractors. Kenworths are also assembled in Victoria, Australia, some being specially constructed for local requirements.

KENWORTH (2)/*Australia ? to date*
Based on the American Kenworth truck range, Australian Kenworths are built by the Kenworth Truck Co at Bayswater, Victoria, often incorporating special features to conform with Australian Construction & Use Regulations. Some "conventional" models even have twin steering axles.

KERR-STUART/*England 1929-1930*
Kerr, Stuart & Co Ltd, Stoke-on-Trent, Staffs, designed an oil-engined lorry in 1928, building a 6-ton semi forward-control prototype the following year. Constructed from proprietary components, it was powered by a 6-cyl Helios engine, replaced six months later by a 4-cyl McLaren-Benz unit providing 60bhp, with an air-cooled single-cyl JAP petrol engine for starting. The specification for a lighter model, to be known as the KS4, was also drawn up, calling for an inverted cone clutch and a gearbox located amidships on a 3-point mounting.

Chain-drive was employed, with conventional semi-elliptic leaf springs at the front and a Kerr-Stuart "enharmonic" system at the rear. Servo-assisted brakes were optional. Although announced as the first "all-British diesel truck", the Kerr-Stuart was actually beaten by a couple of prototype Garretts which, admittedly, were converted steam wagons. In 1930 the company announced that it was ready to take orders, appointing Bonallack & Sons as London area agents. Although a second prototype, based on the KS4 specification, was constructed, series production never got underway.

KEYSTONE/*USA 1919-1923*
The Commercial Car Unit Co, Philadelphia, Pennsylvania, manufactured Truxton conversion units for the Ford Motor Co when it introduced the Keystone 2-tonner. This had a 26bhp 4-cyl petrol engine and from early 1920 the business was known as the Keystone Motor Truck Corp, assembly being transferred to Oaks, Montgomery County. A 1-tonner was advertised from 1921 when Buda engines were standardized but H W Schofield, the vehicle's designer, left to form the Penn Motors Corp which subsequently acquired the Keystone operation, closing it down.

KFT/*USA ? to date*
Manufactured by Klein Products, the KFT is an articulated tanker for airfield fire-fighting duties. Similar to some articulated earth scrapers, a 2-wheeled tractor carries both power unit and cab forward of its single axle with the tank semi-trailer also single-axled and supported at its front by a swan-neck attached to the tractor.

KIDDER/*USA 1900-1901, 1920*
Based in New Haven, Connecticut, the Kidder Motor Vehicle Co built steam-powered goods and passenger models, each using two separate 3hp cylinders located horizontally on each side of the boiler. All-gear drive was used on goods models while passenger types had direct-drive to the rear axle. Nearly twenty years later, Kidder commercials were offered once again, apparently assembled in a plant at Hartford, Connecticut.

KIMBALL/*USA 1917-1926*
The E S Kimball Co, New Haven, Connecticut, introduced 1½-, 2-, 2½-, 4- and 5-ton trucks using 4-cyl Wisconsin petrol engines and worm-drive axles. In 1920 the company was re-named the Kimball Motor Truck Co and production transferred to Los Angeles,

California, where the range was reduced to 2½-, 3½- and 5-tonners by 1922. Long-wheelbase 1½- and 4-tonners were re-introduced two years later but by 1926 only one type, a Wisconsin-engined 2½-ton worm drive model was available.

KING/*USA 1912-1918*
A forward-control 3½-ton truck was constructed by the AR King Mfg Co, Kingston, New York State. Based on a 304-cm wheelbase chassis, it was powered by a 4-cyl petrol engine with 3-speed transmission and double chain-drive.

KING-SEAGRAVE/*Canada 1965 to date*
When the remains of Bickle Fire Engines Ltd, Woodstock, Ontario, were acquired by the King body and trailer organization, fire appliances were re-named King-Seagrave, and re-registered as King Seagrave Ltd, continuing to use chassis and special assemblies, such as ladders, which were supplied by the American Seagrave company.

KING-ZEITLER/*USA 1919-c1929*
The King-Zeitler or KZ goods range covered capacities of up to 5 tons. Built by the King-Zeitler Co, Chicago, Illinois, these were similar to the earlier Zeitler & Lamson range and were joined by a short-lived passenger model in 1923.

KISSEL/*USA 1908-1931*
Based on a 4-cyl shaft-drive passenger car chassis, the first Kissel truck was built by the Kissel Motor Car Co, Hartford, Wisconsin, and by 1910 a range of models up to 5 tons capacity was available, with chain-drive on larger types. Powered by Waukesha or Wisconsin petrol engines, some incorporated a differential lock to improve traction. During World War I the company was engaged in design work on 'A'- and 'B'-Class military trucks and in 1918 the factory was turned over entirely to the production of 4-wheel drive FWD trucks. A "conventional" range of Kissels, from 1 to 5 tons capacity, was re-introduced in the early 1920s and in 1923 a stretched passenger car chassis was used as a basis for the 18-seat 'Coach Limited', developed still further in 1925 into the 'Heavy Duty Safety Speed Truck' with double dropframe and Kissel 6-cyl petrol engine. From 1926 the bulk of production was given over to ambulances and hearses, although trucks, buses and taxicabs were marketed by Bradfield Motors Inc, Chicago, Illinois.

KLATTE/*Germany 1952-1954*
The Klatte was a chassisless forward-control bus powered by a rear-mounted air-cooled Deutz diesel engine. Built by Omnibuswerke Theodor Klatte, Huchting, Bremen, it was of all-metal construction with independent suspension throughout, later versions having all-wheel hydrostatic drive.

KLEIBER/*USA 1914-1937*
Built by the Kleiber Motor Co, San Francisco, California, the earliest Kleibers were offered in capacities of 1½ to 5 tons, all with Continental petrol engines. Six-cyl Buda engines were listed from 1927 and by the end of the 1920s the largest model was a 10-ton rigid. The company's first 6-wheeler appeared in 1930 and from 1934 Cummins diesel engines were available as an option. In the mid-1930s the company was re-named Kleiber & Co Inc, changing to the Kleiber Motor Truck Co in 1937.

KLEMM/*USA c1915-c1920*
Little is known about the short-lived Klemm truck range other than it was built in about 1915 by E R Klemm, of Chicago, Illinois. Few are believed to have been built.

KLINE/*USA 1909-1914*
The first Kline truck built by the York Carriage Works, York, Pennsylvania, had a 12hp 2-cyl petrol engine and chain-drive. Production continued under the BCK Motor Car Co until it passed to the Kline Motor Car Corp in 1911, after which a modified version was built, latterly at the company's new Richmond, Virginia, plant.

KLUNZINGER/*Germany 1902-1910*
A somewhat obscure marque was the Klunzinger, built in light- and mediumweight form between 1902 and 1910. It was constructed by J Klunzinger & Co at its works in the Carmeliterstrasse, Heilbronn.

KMC/*Cyprus 1973 to date*
KMC commercials were introduced by KMC Ltd, Nicosia, based on Dennis models, using components shipped from Britain and powered by Perkins 6.354 diesel engines. Both 16-ton rigids and tractor units were built, some carrying both KMC and Dennis badges, but when Dennis Motors Ltd decided to concentrate on fire appliances and municipal vehicles, supplies dried up and KMC began to use Chrysler's Commer/Dodge range. These appeared in 1974, the lightest being the PB2000 'Spacevan'. The 'Walk-

Thru' range is also available and the 'Maxiload' was offered for a short time but quickly replaced by Cypriot versions of the 'Commando' series. One non-standard model is a military 6 x 6 type.

KNICKERBOCKER/*USA 1911-1916*
Knickerbocker battery-electrics were introduced by the Knickerbocker Motor Truck Co, New York, in 3½-, 4 and 5-ton capacities. By 1915 a 2-tonner was also listed and all types had become petrol-engined with double chain-drive and forward-control. In 1916, as Knickerbocker Motors Inc, the company offered only 2½ and 3½- ton models of bonneted layout with worm final-drive.

KNOX (1)/*USA 1904-1905*
An offshoot of the Knox Automobile Co, Springfield, Massachusetts, the Knox Motor Truck Co built delivery vehicles under the Knox name, using a 20hp 2-cyl 2-stroke petrol engine. This caused

much confusion with the parent Knox range, and in 1905 all the Knox Motor Truck Co's products were re-named Atlas.

KNOX (2)/*USA 1908-c1913*
Previously sold as the Knox Waterless, commercials built by the Knox Automobile Co, Springfield, Massachusetts, became known simply as Knox when water-cooled engines were fitted. In 1909 employee Charles Hay Martin invented the Martin Rocking 5th Wheel, developing this into the Knox-Martin artic system. As well as the Knox-Martin, the Knox Motors Co, as the Knox Automobile Co was now called, offered 2-, 3-, 4- and 5-ton forward-control trucks by 1911, plus a bonneted fire appliance.

KNOX-MARTIN/*USA 1909-1924*
Charles Hay Martin was an employee of the Knox Automobile Co when he invented a coupling for attaching single-axle trailers to a self-propelled motive unit. The

first Knox-Martin tractors were 3-wheelers produced in the Springfield, Massachusetts, plant of the Knox Automobile Co's successor, the Knox Motors Co. Both 7- and 10-ton capacity models were listed, both powered by a 40hp 4-cyl overhead-valve petrol engine located between the driver and a single steering front wheel. The 3-wheeled layout was certainly unusual but had its advantages in that a lock of 90⁰ was possible, enabling the unit to turn almost within its own length.

In 1915 a 4-wheeled version was developed. Mechanical specification was as before, apart from a slightly re-designed engine, and in 1916 the business was re-organized as the Martin Rocking 5th Wheel Co, moving to Chicopee Falls and then on to Longmeadow, Massachusetts, in 1918. The Martin idea was also taken up by the Associated Equipment Co Ltd, Walthamstow, London, and G Scammell & Nephew Ltd for its first articulated models.

1910 Knox (2) R-5 fire patrol truck

KNOX WATERLESS/*USA 1904-1908*
The Knox Automobile Co, Springfield, Massachusetts, offered a number of light air-cooled commercials under the Knox Waterless name, adding a 244-cm wheelbase forward-control 1¼-ton truck in 1904, a 3-ton chain-drive in 1905 and a 1½-tonner in 1906. Later that year the company's first fire appliance, a 4-cyl bonneted Model 'G', went to the local fire department and by 1908 water-cooled engines were beginning to be used in such vehicles which were marketed merely as Knox.

KNUCKEY/*USA 1943-c1955*
Specializing in the construction of heavy dump trucks, the Knuckey Truck Co, San Francisco, California, offered 2- and 3-axle models for loads of up to 56,700kg, with petrol, butane or Cummins diesel engines. Most had chain final-drive, with tandem-drive types employing a centre-pivot double chain system.

KOBE/*Japan 1935-c1939*
Built by the Kobe Steel Works Ltd, Kobe, a series of diesel trucks was offered, using 4-cyl, 3.6-litre or 5.3-litre 6-cyl engines.

KOCKUMS/*Sweden 1960 to date*
AB Kockum-Landsverk, Lands Krona, specializes in the construction of on/off-highway dump trucks, the first of which were the 36,302-kg KL-420 and 54,000-kg KL-440. Current production comprises three 4-wheelers, all with one-man half-cabs and forward-control, including the 25-ton 425 and the 45-ton 445, all with Scania or Detroit Diesel engines and 6-speed Allison 'Powershift' transmissions. There is also an articulated frame 4-wheeler called the 412. With a payload of 18 tons, this is for cross-country operation, powered by a 7.8-litre Scania diesel.

KOEHLER/*USA 1913-1923*
The H J Koehler Sporting Goods Co, Newark, New Jersey, introduced a bonneted 1-ton truck, examples of which were also built by the L E Schlotterbuck Mfg Co, East Orange. It was powered by the company's own 4-cyl overhead-valve petrol engine and joined by a 1¼-ton model in 1918. By then known as the H J Koehler Motor Corp, the company offered a series of 1½- to 5-ton trucks, built latterly at its Bloomfield, New Jersey, factory.

KOEHRING/*USA 1907-1912, c1960-c1969*
The Koehring Co's first trucks may have been sold under the Dumptor brand name, which was also used for a series of dump trucks marketed by the company's Koehring Divn, Milwaukee, Wisconsin, during the 1960s. A particularly interesting vehicle was the Roadrunner, an 18-ton 6-wheeled truck-crane announced in about 1963. Unusual features included hydraulically-actuated flanged railway wheels enabling the vehicle to operate on railway tracks, and a full reversing transmission permitting the vehicle to travel in either direction at the same speed.

KOMAREK/*Austria 1901-c1912*
F X Komarek, Vienna, constructed a vertical-boilered "under-type" steam wagon. This had a vertical boiler at the front and a compound engine beneath, with countershaft differential and double chain-drive. Various versions were built, including steam buses.

KOMATSU/*Japan 1953 to date*
The earth-moving and mining machinery business of the Komatsu Mfg Co Ltd, Tokyo, offered medium- and heavy-duty on/off-

1978 Kockums Model 425B 25-ton dump truck

highway dump trucks for many years. Now known as Komatsu Ltd, models cover payload ratings of between 20 and 68 tons, the largest being a one-man half-cab 4 x 2 powered by a 775bhp 28-litre V12 Cummins and fitted with a 6-speed torque- converter transmission and air-hydraulic brakes.

KOMNICK/*Germany 1907-1930*
F Komnick Autofabrik, Elbing, West Prussia, offered a variety of commercial types on its passenger car chassis, featuring "coal-scuttle" bonnets and radiators located between engine and driver. In 1913 these were joined by a specially-built 5-tonner and after World War I the range was expanded to include a new 3-tonner and passenger versions of both, the company re-registering as Automobilfabrik F Komnick AG in 1922. The 5-ton model and a new road tractor announced in 1926 were powered by a 75bhp 6-cyl petrol engine but in 1930 the business was taken over by Automobilwerke Heinrich Büssing AG. With the exception of the road tractor all models were immediately discontinued.

KOPP/*USA 1911-1916*
The Kopp Motor Truck Co, Buffalo, New York State, offered trucks with payloads of 1, 1½, 2, 3 and 5 tons. The largest was of forward-control layout on a 320cm wheelbase chassis and powered by a 4-cyl petrol engine.

KPL/*England 1909-1911*
From 1906 the Daimler Motor Co (1904) Ltd, Coventry, experimented with various petrol-electric transmissions, eventually announcing the KPL bus. This was a steel-framed double-decker with body and chassis constructed as one unit. Two 12hp Knight sleeve-valve engines were slung beneath the vehicle and the transmission operated via two universally-jointed shafts and worm gearing

to two short "live" axles carrying the rear wheels. The type entered brief production alongside more conventional Daimler passenger models but was withdrawn due to infringements of rival Stevens petrol-electric patents.

KRAMER/*West Germany 1956-1974*
Kramer-Werke GmbH, Uberlingen, Badensee, built a series of 4 x 4 and 6 x 6 prime movers and a special front-drive conversion unit for non-powered construction and agricultural equipment. All had 100bhp Deutz 6-cyl air-cooled diesel engines.

KRAUSS *Germany 1926-1931*
Lokomotivfabrik Krauss & Co, Munich, built Saurer-engined passenger models, merging in 1931 with J A Maffei AG to form Krauss-Maffei AG. All subsequent types were sold as Krauss-Maffei or KM.

KRAUSS-MAFFEI/*Germany/West Germany 1931-1965*
Following the merger of Lokomotivfabrik Krauss & Co and J A Maffei AG to form Krauss-Maffei AG, Allach, both Krauss buses and Maffei road tractors were marketed as Krauss-Maffei or simply KM. A light road tractor, already in production, was joined by a new heavy model in 1933, the lighter having a 60bhp 4.7-litre 4-cyl Deutz petrol engine or diesel option, and the heavier a 95bhp 7-litre 6-cyl Maybach unit. Mainly buses were built after World War II. The first was the KMO 130, a forward-control model with rear-mounted 6.2-litre Maybach 6-cyl diesel engine. A goods version was offered briefly but in 1954 the first chassisless passenger model was built. From 1959 to 1963 only MAN engines and other components were used in Krauss-Maffei buses and soon after this a few passenger models were built for Büssing Automobilwerke AG,

carrying both Büssing and KM insignias.

KRAZ/*Soviet Union 1959 to date*
When YAAZ truck production was transferred to the Krementschug Automobilova Zavod factory at Krementschug, all models were re-named KRAZ. Models continued as before until 1966 when a new series based on a 6 x 4 bonneted chassis truck introduced. These were listed as a 14-ton rigid (Model 257), heavy dump truck (Model 256) and 5th wheel tractor (Model 258). Others included the 255B 8-ton 6 x 6 and 255L logging truck. All vehicles are powered by 265bhp YAMZ V8 diesel engines, driving through a 5-speed transmission in the case of 6 x 4 models. The KRAZ range is normally sold outside the Soviet Union as the Belaz.

1967 KRAZ-256 6 x 4 dump truck

KREBS (1)/*USA 1912-1916*
Built by the Krebs Commercial Car Co, Clyde, Ohio, the Krebs range was available in capacities of up to 3 tons. Models had a "coal-scuttle" bonnet and a radiator behind the engine which was normally a 2-cyl 2-stroke unit. The business was acquired by the Clyde Cars Co, who launched the Clydesdale truck range.

KREBS (2)/*USA 1922-1925*
The Krebs Motor Truck Co was founded in Bellevue, Ohio, introducing a range of Continental-engined goods models with capacities of up to 6 tons. The business was re-named the Buck Motor Truck Co in 1925 and all subse-

quent models sold as Buck.

KRICKWELL/*USA 1912-1917*
A lesser – known American truck manufacturer was the Krickwell Motor Truck Co, address unknown, which advertised the Krickwell range from 1912 to 1917.

KRIEGER/*France 1898-1909, c1923*
Cie Parisienne des Voitures Electriques, Paris, sold commercials under the Kriéger name. A large truck appeared in 1898 with front-wheel drive using two hub-mounted electric motors, while numerous Kriéger components were also used in ABAM battery-electrics. Petrol-electric systems were introduced in 1903 and by 1905 various petrol-electrics were in production, one being a 4-ton forward-control truck with 4.1-litre 4-cyl engine and chain-drive to the rear wheels. A double-deck bus had direct drive, however, with engine mounted beneath the driver. By 1906 Kriégers were mainly petrol-electric types and in 1907 production moved to Colombes, Seine, where a petrol-turbine-electric propulsion system was patented the following year. The last Kriéger trucks were of bonneted layout, of 2 or 3 tons capacity and with rear-wheel drive. During these years Kriégers were licence-built in various countries and their propulsion systems utilized in many others. About 1923 an experimental Kriéger van was developed by a successor of the original com-

pany, Automobiles Kriéger, in the Colombes, Seine, factory. This employed a centrally-mounted traction motor driving the rear wheels and all-independent suspension.

KROMHOUT/Netherlands 1926-1961

The first commercials built by Kromhout Motoren Fabriek D Goedkoop Jnr NV, Ketelstraat, Amsterdam, comprised a series of bonneted trucks but it was not until 1935, when the company acquired a manufacturing licence for British Gardner diesel engines, that production really got underway with medium- and heavy-duty bonneted trucks, and a few passenger models, occasionally with forward-control. By 1939 trucks and tractors for gross loads

1955 Kromhout 6 x 6 oilfield truck

1954 Kromhout 6 x 4 tanker

of up to 30 tons and passenger types for up to 60 persons were built. The bonneted goods range was re-introduced after World War II, while passenger types were resumed with a forward-control 6-cyl engined single-decker. In 1948, however, a chassisless 48-seater was developed in association with NV Auto-Industrie Verheul, using a supercharged 6-cyl diesel, 5-speed overdrive transmission, power-steering and air-operated doors. A year later the company began assembling Leyland vehicles for the Dutch market and a new bus announced by Verheul in 1950 utilized a Kromhout chassis frame. By 1953 a 10-ton payload forward-control rigid goods model, with supercharged 8.4-litre 6-cyl diesel en-

gine located vertically beneath the floor, was added to the range and passenger requirements were now catered for by a series of horizontal-engined types. Two years later forward- and normal-control double-drive 6-wheeled trucks were announced, using Kirkstall worm-drive axles, while a bonneted 6 x 6 for gross weights of up to 28 tons was developed for oilfield work. A 97-seat one-man-operated passenger model also appeared in 1955, this having a Leyland diesel engine and pneumocyclic transmission instead of a 6-cyl ardner and 2-pedal ZF transmission. By 1957 some 6 x 4 trucks were available with optional Rolls-Royce engines, but in 1959 Kromhout merged with Verheul, and the Kromhout name disappeared.

c1958 Kromhout 'TC' artic tractor

KUANG KUNG/China 1970 to date
A 4½-ton forward-control truck and an 8-ton dump truck are built under the Kuang Kung brand name in the Chaohu Truck Parts Plant at Hafei, Anhwei Province.

KUHLSTEIN/Germany 1898-1902
Battery-electric and petrol-engined commercials were built by Kuhlstein Wagenbau Gesellschaft, Charlottenburg, Berlin. The company also built both battery-electric and petrol-engined fore-carriages for converting horse-drawn vehicles to self-propulsion. In 1902 the business was acquired by Neue Automobil GmbH.

KUMMER/Germany ?-1899
Built by AG Elektrizitatswerke vorm O L Kummer & Co, Dresden, Kummer battery-electric buses were re-named Kummer & Stoll when the company was reconstituted as Niedersedlitz und Wagenfabrik C Stoll.

KUMMER & STOLL/Germany 1899-1900
Previously known as Kummer, the Kummer & Stoll battery-electric range was built by Niedersedlitz und Wagenfabrik C Stoll, Dresden. Most were passenger models.

KUNMING/China 1970 to date
The 4½-ton payload Kunming truck is built in the Kunming Motor Vehicle Plant, Kunming, Yannan Province. It is intended for use in mountain regions.

KUROGANE/Japan c1956-1962
By 1956 various Kurogane commercials, with capacities of up to 2 tons, were built by the Japan Internal Combustion Engine Mfg Co Ltd, Tokyo, with engines of up to 1.4-litre capacity, the largest models having overhead-valves and water-cooling. Rival manufacturer Ohta Jidosha Kogyo Co Ltd was acquired in 1957 and the business re-organized as Nippon Motor Industries Co Ltd. Heavier models were then added, with overhead-valve 4-cyl petrol engines and wheel steering, and by 1959, when the company was re-named Tokyu Kurogane Co Ltd, the 3-wheelers were powered by 1- and 1.5-litre 4-cyl petrol engines. New normal- and forward-control 1-tonners with 4-speed synchromesh transmissions were also announced.

KW-DART
USA 1961-1970
When the heavy vehicle specialist the Dart Truck Co, Kansas City, Missouri, was re-named the KW-Dart Truck Co, its products became KW-Dart and by 1962 included a number of off-road dump trucks for payloads of up to 100 tons. By 1965 models ranged from 15 to 120 tons capacity, the heaviest being artic bottom dump designs, known after 1970 as Dart.

KRUPP/*Germany/West Germany*
1905-1908, 1914-1968
Friedrich Krupp AG, Kiel, entered the vehicle-building business in 1905 with a series of steam lorries manufactured under Stoltz licence. No further advances were made until 1914 when a military gun tractor was developed by a successor of the original company – Friedrich Krupp Motoren und Kraftwagenfabriken GmbH, Essen. Only a few were built but in 1919 series production of a 5-ton chain-drive truck got underway. Powered by a 28/45 P5 4-cyl petrol engine, this was joined in 1921 by a 10-ton articulated tractor and later by a 3-wheeled road-sweeper. In 1924, 1½- and 2-tonners were built, both powered by a 50bhp petrol engine with shaft-drive, and by the following year the 5-tonner also had shaft-drive. Six- and 8-ton 4- and 6-wheelers also appeared, while Krupp passenger models now had low-loading chassis. The first forward-control trucks arrived in 1930, being of 4 x 2 and 6 x 4 layout with 100 or 110bhp engines, later up-rated to 150bhp, and a cross-country 6 x 4 appeared, powered initially by a 55bhp 4-cyl air-cooled engine, later up-rated to 110bhp. The Krupp-Flettner artic was developed and numerous Krupp components were supplied to Waggonfabrik Uerdingen AG for use in its trolleybuses. Junkers diesel

1960 Krupp 0124 single-deck bus

'Buffel'. A bonneted version of the 'Mustang' was used as a 1½-deck coach, another new model being 1952s 'Cyklop' – a heavy dump truck powered by a 210bhp 6-cyl diesel. A 4 x 4 6/8-tonner called the 'Drache' appeared in 1953. This had a 145bhp 4-cyl diesel engine, the next most significant design being a series of forward-control trucks announced in 1956. These had 3-, 4- or 5-cyl 2-stroke diesels with power outputs

1965 Krupp K-960

ing stock of forward-control truck cabs being sold off to NV Atkinson Vehicles (Europe) SA.

KRUPP-ARDELT/*West Germany 1969 to date*
Krupp-Ardelt truck-cranes appeared following the demise of

the Krupp truck and bus range. Built by Friedrich Krupp GmbH Kranbau, Wilhelmshaven, these are hydraulic designs powered by Deutz diesel engines. By the end of the 1970s models ranged from mediumweight 4-wheelers up to a heavy 12 x 6 powered by a 450bhp engine.

KRUPP-FLETTNER/*Germany c1930-c1931*
A unique articulated vehicle was developed by Friedrich Krupp Motoren und Kraftwagenfabriken GmbH, Essen. Called the Krupp-Flettner, it was a 5-axle bonneted machine with non-driven single-axle tractor coupled to a 4-axle trailer with two front axles tracking after the motive unit's wheels and two rear axles driven. In goods form this had a load capacity of 13½ tons but was also available in passenger guise.

Krupp artic tractor c1955

engines were built under licence from 1932, these being available as 2-, 3- and 4-cyl double-piston 2-strokes with outputs of up to 125bhp. Following the collapse of the Krupp empire the company was re-named Sudwerke GmbH in 1944 and production transferred to Kulmbach. Between then and 1954 models were also known as Sudwerke, the first new post-war type being a 4½-tonner powered by a 110bhp engine. Production returned to Essen in 1951 and a new 6-tonner and the 8-ton 'Titan' were launched, quickly joined by the 5/5½-ton

ranging from 100 to 200bhp and were soon joined by normal-control versions and passenger derivatives. Cummins 4-stroke diesels were made available from 1963, one of the first to have this as standard being a 30-ton capacity dump truck fitted with a 430bhp 15.5-litre unit. New rigid road-going models powered by 200bhp 4-cyl Cummins units appeared soon after. A V8 4 x 4 road tractor with an output of 265bhp appeared briefly in 1967 but the following year saw the end of standard truck production in favour of Krupp-Ardelt truck-cranes, the remain-

1971 Krupp-Ardelt 75 GMT 75-ton truck crane

LA BUIRE/*France 1907-1929*

Built by Soc des Automobiles de la Buire, Lyons, early La Buire commercials comprised a number of forward-control types with 15hp 4-cyl petrol engines, especially popular as 10/15-seat buses. Shaft- and chain-drive trucks and buses of up to 3 tons payload were added in 1908. Later known as Soc Nouvelle de la Buire Automobiles, the company announced a series of long-stroke 4-cyl engined commercials in 1910 with capacities of up to 4 tons, 2- and 3-tonners being "subsidy" models but from 1925 the only commercial model was a 1½-ton car-based design.

LA CUADRA/*Spain 1899*

The La Cuadra was a 15-seat battery-electric bus built in the Barcelona factory of Cia General Espanola de Coches Automoviles E de la Cuadra S en C. It proved impractical due to its 6-ton unladen weight.

LA HISPANO/*Spain 1917-1932*

La Hispano Fabrica Nacional de Automoviles Aeroplanes y Material de Guerra, Guadalajara, built trucks under the La Hispano or La Hispano-Guadalajara brand names. Models were based on 15/20, 30/40 and 50hp chassis for loads of between 1500 and 6000kg. In 1932 the business was acquired by the Italian Fiat combine.

LA LICORNE/*France 1912-1950*

Previously marketed as the Corre, commercials built by Soc Française des Automobiles La Licorne, Courbevoie, Seine, were called La Licorne from 1912, the heaviest being a 4-cyl Ballot-engined 1¼-tonner with shaft-drive. After World War I, a 3½-tonner with a 3.8-litre petrol engine was listed briefly but by 1925 the heaviest model was again a 1¼-tonner using a 1.7-litre petrol unit. The 1930s saw a new 30-seat coach chassis called the D6H, with a 3.2-litre 6-cyl Delahaye petrol engine, joined between 1933 and 1935 by a series of 1- and 3-ton payload diesel lorries with single- or 4-cyl CLM 2-strokes. Four-cyl petrol engines were used across the board by 1938, a short-stroke overhead-valve unit powering a 1½-tonner by this time. But only a few post-war commercials were built.

LA SALLE-NIAGARA/*USA 1906*

The La Salle-Niagara was a 225-cm wheelbase 1-tonner with 2-cyl petrol engine located horizontally under the driver's seat. A chain-drive design, it was built by the La Salle-Niagara Auto Co, Niagara Falls, New York.

1960 Labourier TL3 truck

LABOURIER/*France c1947-c1970*

Labourier et Cie, Mouchard, Jura, began building a 7-ton payload low-loading truck after World War II, using a Unic engine and offset drive. A front-drive version was offered from 1948 as well as 4-wheel drive and 4-wheel steer bonneted logging tractors using 6-cyl Perkins diesel engines.

The largest model was a 10-ton 4 x 4 oilfield tractor, with air-cooled Deutz or water-cooled Berliet engine, of which a number were exported. In 1960 a 5½-tons GVW 4 x 2 forward-control lorry appeared, with a fibreglass cab and 50bhp 1.8-litre Peugeot diesel engine. The last new model was the HUD of 1967, which was a semi forward-control 4-wheel drive and optional 4-wheel steered design for use as tractor, tipper, and snowplough.

LACOSTE & BATTMANN/*France 1906-1908*

Lacoste et Battmann, Levallois-Perret, Seine, offered a variety of models including a 4-ton truck or bus with 3.6 or 3.9-litre petrol engine, 3-speed transmission and chain-drive.

LACRE/*England 1904-1952*

The first commercial to be built by the Lacre Motor Car Co Ltd, London was a 25hp 2-cyl Albion chassis with Lacre body quickly followed by a 1¼-ton van with 16hp petrol engine. Between 1907 and 1909 2- and 3-ton trucks were built on the company's behalf by James & Browne Ltd and sold as J & B Lacre, but by 1909 the company was offering one of the most comprehensive commercial ranges then available in Britain, with models of up to 5 tons capacity, the heaviest being the chain-drive 'O'-Type powered by a 4.82- or 7.12-litre 4-cyl petrol engine.

Completed in 1910, a factory at Letchworth, Herts was the first in Britain to be designed specifically for the manufacture of commercial vehicles, and by 1914 the company was building 19 different models there, the company's entire production during the first two years of World War I going to the Belgian Army. A number of specially built 'O'-Type tractors were supplied to the War Dept for handling aircraft fuselages up to 15m long.

For tropical use some 'O'-Types had special radiators and paraffin vaporizers, while the company also developed a tractor/trailer combination in which the trailer had a set of wheels at the front which ran up a ramp at the rear of the tractor when this was backed under the trailer. The two were then locked in position with the trailer swivelling on the tractor's turntable.

The company's first road-sweeper, a 2-cyl petrol-engined 4-wheeler, was built in 1917, but it was two more years before the 'L'-Type sweeper/collector made its debut. This was a 3-wheeler with two steerable wheels at the front, a chain-driven rear wheel and a channel-section steel chassis frame. The driver sat in a central position at the rear of the frame, providing a clear view of the brush which was slung amidships. Early versions were powered by a 12hp 4-cyl petrol engine, with a 6-cyl unit optional later.

Despite the post-war vehicle slump, Lacre developed its municipal activities still further and continued with 'O'-Type production, adding new models such as the 'N'-Type 4-tonner of 1922. Powered by a 38/45bhp engine, this was aimed at overseas markets, joining 1½- and 1¾-ton and 2- and 2½-ton chain-drive models and 3- and 5-ton gear-driven machines. The 'E'-Type was introduced in 1926 being a forward-control 2½-tonner with electric starting, worm back axle and a wheel-out subframe carrying engine, gearbox, radiator and petrol tank, which could be removed through the front of the vehicle for maintenance in only eight minutes and replaced in ten.

Despite an announcement in 1927 that it was to merge with Walker Bros (Wigan) Ltd, the company continued on its own until it was wound up and a new company, Lacre Lorries Ltd, established early in 1928. The Letchworth plant was closed and production transferred to the London Sales & Service Depot at Kings Cross, London, where from 1929 to 1935, the company also marketed small-wheeled goods models manufactured by Low Loaders Ltd. The basic range now comprised the chain-drive 'O'-Type, worm-drive 'E'-Type 2½-tonner and 'L'-Type sweeper. There was little demand for 4-wheelers, however, and by 1936 production was centred almost entirely upon the 'L'-Type. This was streamlined in 1935 and soon had an Austin engine. The company was now selling more road-sweepers than any other British firm, with 4-wheelers built only to special order.

In 1934 H G Burford & Co Ltd was acquired. Apart from the Burford-Kégresse half-track, built using numerous Lacre components until the following year, this line was not perpetuated and the Teddington premises were quickly disposed of. In 1936 Lacre moved to Welwyn Garden City, Herts, this factory later being requisitioned by the Ministry of Aircraft Production, and it was not until 1946 that the company was able to resume civilian production, concentrating upon its 'M'-Type sweeper/collector. The Institute of Public Cleansing's Conference and Exhibition in Edinburgh in 1949 saw a new Lacre sweeper/collector called the 'T'-Type, mounted on a 3-wheeled Opperman Motocart chassis. This was to bring about the end of the totally Lacre-built vehicle in 1952 when agreement was reached between Lacre Lorries Ltd and Vauxhall Motors Ltd. The most significant point in the agreement was that Lacre municipal equipment was to be supplied only on Bedford chassis.

1934 Laffly turntable-ladder fire appliance

LADOG/*West Germany 1971 to date*

The Ladog was announced by Ladog Fahrzeugbau, Nordrach, in 1971, but has been built by Albrecht Bertsche, Braunlingen, since 1975. Available with 4-wheel drive and 4-wheel steering, it originally had a Volkswagen petrol engine but now uses a 4-cyl horizontal air-cooled Citroën unit.

LAFFLY/France 1925-1953

Vehicles previously sold as Laffly-Schneider by Ets Laffly, Asnières, Seine, were later marketed as Laffly, the first being 1¼- 2-, 3-, 4-, 5- and 8-tonners. These remained in production, alongside passenger models, until 1930 when an opposed-piston Junkers diesel engine was introduced.

The 1930s saw a multiplicity of petrol- and diesel-engined models offered by the company, particularly in the municipal and fire-fighting fields, and in 1934 an unusual 6-wheel drive chassis was introduced. This had a fully independent rear bogie and a Hotchkiss or Laffly engine. In 1936 the ADRHS 6 x 4 with 100bhp CLM diesel engine was announced and by 1938 various petrol- and diesel-engined models from 2¾ to 10 tons payload were offered. CLM diesels had vanished by 1940 and when peace returned production resumed with two 3½-tonners. By 1948 the range included various capacities from 2½ to 6½ tons.

LAFFLY-SCHNEIDER/France 1922-1925

The first Laffly-Schneiders built by Ets Laffly Asnières, Seine, were 3- and 7-tonners of forward-control layout and similar to the Brillié-Schneider passenger range. The lighter model had a 22.5hp petrol engine and the latter a 30hp unit, both of Schneider origin. This arrangement continued until Schneider engines were replaced and the series sold simply as Laffly.

LAFRANCE/USA 1910-1914, 1920-1929

The American LaFrance Fire Engine Co, Elmira, New York, built a 5-ton commercial truck between 1910 and 1914, marketing this as American LaFrance, or simply LaFrance, until production was discontinued in favour of the company's increasingly popular fire appliances. LaFrance trucks were re-introduced later and a new company, the American La-France Truck Co, set up at Bloomfield, New Jersey in 1923, offering models from 2 to 7½-tons capacity. These were never competitive on price and in 1929 the operation was merged with the Republic Motor Truck Co Inc to form the LaFrance-Republic Corp.

LAFRANCE-REPUBLIC/USA 1929-1942

The merger of the American La-France Truck Co, Bloomfield, New Jersey, and the Republic Motor Truck Co Inc, Alma, Michigan, led to the formation of the LaFrance-Republic Corp, based at Alma, and the introduction of LaFrance-Republic commercials. Many were based on a fairly new Republic design with a couple of badge-engineered LaFrance models at the top of the range.

In 1931 the 6-wheeled 'Mogul', powered by an American La-France V12 petrol engine was introduced but few were interested in such a novelty and it quickly vanished. In 1932 the business was taken over by the Sterling Motor Truck Co, West Allis, Wisconsin, and production moved there. Subsequent LaFrance-Republics were no more than badge-engineered Sterlings.

LAMBOURN/England 1937-1939

Lambourn Garages, Lambourn, Berks, and Universal Power Drives Ltd, Perivale, Middx, constructed an unusual horsebox called the Lambourn, using a rear-mounted Ford V8 petrol engine but front-wheel drive. A dummy Ford radiator was fitted at the front. It was re-designed in 1938 and a passenger version was even offered. For 1939, a front-mounted Ford V8 was used.

LAMSON/USA 1911-1920

Lamsons were listed in five capacities from 1 to 5 tons by the Lamson Truck & Trailer Co, Chicago, Illinois, all being of bonneted design with 4-cyl petrol engines, 3-speed transmissions and worm-drive. There was probably a connection between these and the products of the Zeitler & Lamson Motor Truck Co, also of Chicago, but Lamson production appears to have passed to the United Four Wheel Drive Truck Co, Chicago, about 1919.

LANCASHIRE & YORKSHIRE RAILWAY/England 1901

H A Hoy of the Lancashire & Yorkshire Railway Co developed a 4-ton vertical-boilered steam wagon. It was a coke-fired design with inclined water-tubes and vertical compound engine located under the driver's seat. Drive was transmitted from engine to countershaft by single roller chain and thence by two other chains to the rear wheels. Only prototypes were built.

LANCASHIRE STEAM MOTORS/England 1896-1907

Following James Sumner's experiments with steam propulsion, the Lancashire Steam Motor Co was formed at Leyland, near Preston, Lancs. The first Lancashire Steam Motors wagon appeared in the form of a 1½/2-tonner with vertical firetube paraffin-fuelled boiler, 2-cyl vertical compound engine and three forward speeds, each worked by a separate control lever and friction clutch. This machine was successful at a number of commercial vehicle trials and a similar 4-tonner was developed.

For 1901 a coal- or coke-fired vertical firetube boiler and horizontal compound "undertype" engine with Stephenson's link motion were adopted, although a 5-tonner of 1905 introduced Joy's valve gear. Meanwhile, the business had become a limited liability company in 1903, and by 1904 experiments with internal combustion-engined vehicles had got underway, engines being built to Sumner's 'L'-head design by the Crossley brothers, resulting in vehicles being marketed as Leyland-Crossley.

1896 Lancashire Steam Motors 5-ton "undertype" steam wagon

In 1907 the old Coulthard steam wagon business was acquired to consolidate activities in this field and the firm was renamed Leyland Motors Ltd, all subsequent models being sold as Leyland.

LANCIA/Italy 1911-1970

Based in the former Fides plant in Turin, Fabbrica Automobili Lancia & Co SpA built a hundred 1½-ton bonneted trucks for the Italian Army in 1911, using a 4.9-litre side-valve 4-cyl petrol engine, 4-speed transmission and shaft-drive. By 1914 the 'Iota' and 'Diota' models had been developed

1959 Lancia mobile crane

followed by the 2½-ton 'Triota' and 'Tetraiota', often used as 20-seat buses, coaches or charabancs.

By the 1920s the company was deeply involved in the passenger vehicle market, the 1925 'Pentaiota' being the first Lancia with front-wheel brakes, while the following year's 'Esaiota', with low-loading chassis, was tried unsuccessfully as a double-decker. A significant new model was the 1928 'Omicran' with a 7.1-litre 8-cyl petrol engine, vacuum-servo assisted front brakes and 4-speed transmission.

In 1931 the company acquired a licence to build the opposed-piston 2-stroke Junkers diesel engine, the first was a 3.2-litre 2-cyl job fitted in the 6½-ton bonneted RO truck, while the immediate post-war 'Esatau' 8½-tonner had a 150bhp 8.4-litre 6-cyl diesel, 8-speed transmission and air brakes.

The first forward-control Lancia truck was the 2½-ton 'Beta' of 1950, joined one year later by a light petrol-engined 4 x 4 for military applications. In 1953 a turbocharged 2-litre 2-cyl 2-stroke diesel was listed as an option for the 'Beta' and introduced as standard a little later. On the passenger front, the forward-control 'Esatau' with front-mounted horizontal engine was announced in 1950, while forward-control versions of the 'Esatau' truck chassis did not appear until 1955. By 1957 the passenger version had an amidships-mounted engine, both versions now having an 8.9-litre unit and air-assisted gear-change. New models in the 'Esatau' goods range included sleeper cab versions and a 10½-ton single-drive 6-wheeler.

The 1-ton forward-control 'Jolly' delivery model arrived in 1958, heavier payloads being catered for by the 5/7-ton forward-control 'Esadelta' range with 8.2-litre diesel engine. Military customers were offered the 506, powered by a 195bhp 6-cyl petrol engine located under the floor. New for 1962 was the 'Esagamma' for gross weights of up to 19 tons. Initially, this had a 187bhp 10.5-litre 6-cyl diesel engine but by 1964 a turbocharged version had been fitted. This range included 6 x 2 and 6 x 4 rigids, the former having its undriven axle ahead of the driven one. By 1964 the 'Jolly' had been ousted by the 1½-ton 'Superjolly', using numerous components common to the 'Flavia' passenger car. In 1965 an arrangement was made between the manufacturers of Büssing, Hotchkiss and Lancia vehicles, whereby they would combine resources to develop all-wheel drive military vehicles for NATO members, but little seems to have come of this and by the

Lancia single-deck bus c1931

end of 1969 Lancia & Co SpA, as it was then known, was bought out by the Fiat combine. Lancias continued to be built but since 1970 only military Fiats have been assembled in the Turin factory.

LANDMASTER/*England 1978 to date*
The Landmaster was designed by Stan Metherell of S Metherell Ltd, St Denis, Cornwall. It is a long-wheelbase bonneted vehicle with Ford V6 petrol engine and permanently engaged 4-wheel drive, although the prototype had a Perkins 4.203 diesel engine.

1971 Land-Rover 1¹/₂-ton truck

LAND-ROVER/*England 1962 to date*
Although the first Land-Rover utility vehicle left the Solihull, West Midlands, factory of the Rover Co Ltd in 1948, it was not until 1962 that the first model of more than 1-ton capacity appeared. This was a relatively short-lived forward-control 1-tonner, later up-rated to 1¹/₂ tons, powered by a 2.3-litre petrol engine. Since then, a more austere militarized forward-control type, using Rover's 3.5-litre V8 petrol engine, has been built.

LANDSCHAFT/*USA 1911-1920*
William Landschaft & Sons, Chicago, Illinois, built a forward-control 1-ton truck with a 2-cyl petrol engine, planetary transmission and chain-drive. A 1¹/₂-tonner was introduced in 1913 but from 1916 only 1- and 2-tonners were listed, with 3-speed transmissions and shaft-drive.

LANE (1)/*USA 1902*
The Lane, Daley Co, Barre, Vermont, planned to launch a number of steam-powered vehicles but only one was built. This was a 6-seat passenger model, too heavy and slow to be of interest.

LANE (2)/*USA 1916-1919*
The Lane Motor Truck Co, Kalamazoo, Michigan, built 1¹/₂-, 2¹/₂-, 3¹/₂- and ³/₄-ton trucks, all with 6-cyl Continental petrol engines and worm final-drive.

LANGE/*USA 1911-1931*
The H Lange Wagon Works, Pittsburgh, Pennsylvania, assembled- 1- and 2-ton Lange trucks from 1911, re-organizing as the Lange Motor Truck Co in 1912. All were bonneted with Continental petrol engines and in 1923 a 3-tonner was added to the line.

LANPHER/*USA 1909-1912*
The Lanpher high-wheeler was manufactured by the Lanpher Motor Buggy Co, Carthage, Missouri. With a wheelbase of 190cm and 14hp 2-cyl petrol engine located under the body, it had a planetary transmission system, chain-drive and transverse leaf spring suspension.

LANSDEN/*USA c1907-1928*
The Lansden battery-electric commercial was introduced by the Lansden Co, Newark, New Jersey, in 1904 but it was not until about 1907 that a 1¹/₂-tonner became available. Five double chain-drive models were offered in 1910, the heaviest being a forward-control 8-tonner with batteries carried amidships inside the chassis frame and at the rear with the electric motor mounted transversely just ahead of the chain driven rear axle. A 5-tonner, with a claimed range per charge of up to 80km was announced in 1912, the same year that production moved to the Allentown, Pennsylvania, plant of the Mac-Carr Co, which now owned the Lansden business, but this operation collapsed at the end of 1913 and from 1914 the Lansden Co was using premises in Brooklyn, New York.

Models of up to 6 tons capacity were now available and in 1921 the company became the Lansden Co Inc, moving to Danbury, Connecticut.

LANZ/*Germany/West Germany 1928-1953*
Heinrich Lanz AG, Mannheim, developed a road haulage version of its 'Bulldog' farm tractor, using a 35bhp 10.3-litre single-cyl hot-bulb 2-stroke engine. Other models were developed but production, discontinued during World War II, was resumed soon after, continuing until the company began to concentrate entirely upon agricultural types.

LAPEER/*USA 1919-1920*
A 5-ton articulated truck was built by the Lapeer Tractor Truck Co,

Lapeer, Michigan. It was powered by a 4-cyl Wisconsin petrol engine with a 3-speed transmission and Torbensen internal-gear final-drive.

LAPORTE/*France 1922-c1925*
The Laporte 5-tonner was a battery-electric model introduced by SA des Automobiles Electriques Laporte, Toulouse. Propelled by two 7¹/₂hp traction motors located behind the rear axle, final-drive was by internal gearing and the range per battery charge was said to be 96km.

LARRABEE-DEYO/*USA 1915-1933*
Building Larrabee-Deyo and Larrabee trucks in the 1 to 5 ton payload category, the Larrabee-Deyo Motor Truck Co Inc, Binghampton, New York, used 4-cyl monobloc Continental petrol engines, Brown-Lipe transmissions and Sheldon worm-drive axles. A 1-ton "speed" truck with 6-cyl Continental engine was announced in 1922. By the late 1920s, 6-cyl engines, 4-speed transmissions, spiral-bevel axles, 4-wheel hydraulic brakes and electric lighting and starting were standard features but the Depression led to the company's downfall.

LATIL (1)/*France 1914-1955*
George Latil was well known for Blum-Latil front-wheel drive trucks, establishing his own factory at Suresnes, Seine, where he constructed vehicles under his own name. Called Cie des Automobiles Industrielles Latil, his own company began building 4-wheel drive and 4-wheel steer LL tractors, developing the heavy-duty TAR from these. Using a 50hp 4-cyl petrol engine, it had a towing capacity of 12 tons and was fitted with the familiar "coal-scuttle" front. Post-war versions had a radiator mounted at the front of a conventional bonnet. A more conventional model was the low-loading 'B'-Series of 1923. A loading height of 45cm was aided by a "dead" and cranked back axle, drive being transmitted via a differential bolted to a frame cross-member. This was the smallest vehicle in the range and, apart from the 4 x 4 4-wheel steering

1964 Lancia truck

tractors, one of the most popular. By 1925 models from 1¹/₂ to 10 tons capacity were available, one an artic six-wheeler having front-wheel drive. Seating was provided for 29 passengers with room for a further 10 standees.

The 6-ton lorry of 1929 was the first of a new generation of pneumatic-tyred Latils, having a 70bhp 4-cyl detachable-head petrol engine, 4-speed transmission with pto and/or a tyre inflator. The rear axle was "dead", these wheels receiving power via two short shafts from a chassis-mounted differential unit. Four-wheel servo brakes comprised hand operation at the rear and a servo-assisted pedal up front which also applied a transmission brake.

1955 Latil (1) oilfield fire tender

Early in the 1930s the company took up licence production of Gardner diesel engines and introduced its first rigid 6-wheeler, the H2Y10. This developed into a heavy 6 x 6 road tractor for operation at gross weights of up to 45 tons, and there was even a 6 x 6 off-road tractor powered by a 100bhp V8 petrol engine.

Four-by-four models were also developing well, the earlier TAR model giving way to the 61bhp TARS and eventually to the TARH, with a larger engine, 6-speed transmission and pneumatic tyres, and finally to the TARH2. Less rugged requirements were catered for by the TL and KTL ranges, built in the company's Brussels plant for the Belgian and Dutch markets but licence-built by Shelvoke & Drewry Ltd who sold them as Trauliers in Great Britain. The company also experimented with substitute fuels such as coal or gas and fitted a Latil bus with a Gazomalle producer-gas unit in the rear luggage compartment.

Latil (1) drawbar tractor c1952

One year before war broke out, a Latil tractor was converted into a dual-purpose road/rail vehicle, carrying railway wheels at

Latil (2) 4 x 4 drawbar tractors c1932

front and rear, enabling it to haul up to 10 tons on the road and 250 on the track. Post-war models were nearly all diesel-powered, ranging from the light H14A1B3 to a massive 6 x 6 chassis used as an airfield fire crash tenders.

Four- and 6-cyl diesel engines with outputs of 85, 112 and 150bhp were now available but by 1955 plans were afoot to merge with Régie Nationale des Usines Renault and Soc d'Outillage Mécanique et d'Usinage Artillerie to form SA de Véhicules Industriels et d'Equipements Mécaniques. The combined range sold initially as LRS.

LATIL (2)/*England 1932-1939, 1948-1955*
Developed in France by George Latil, the 4-wheel drive and 4-wheel steer Latil road tractor was introduced to Great Britain in 1927 by Latil Industrial Vehicles Ltd but in 1932 licence production commenced at the Letchworth, Herts, factory of Shelvoke & Drewry Ltd, this version being sold as the Traulier or Loco Traulier.

With the outbreak of war, Shelvoke & Drewry Ltd began building tank transporter trailers, but in 1948 assembly re-commenced, this time by US Concessionaires Ltd, Ascot, Berks, and the vehicle was once again marketed as the Latil. Now with a Meadows diesel engine as standard, the majority went to timber merchants.

LAURIN & KLEMENT/*Czechoslovakia c1907-1925*
Laurin und Klement AG, Prague, was already building light commercials when it introduced a 4-cyl petrol-engined chain-drive 22-seat bus and 4-ton load-carrier, followed by the Type 'F' 1½-tonner.

By 1914 models with capacities of 2, 3, 4 and 6 tons were listed, with 18-, 22- or 35hp 4-cyl petrol engines. Some were built only to special order. Production later moved to Mlada-Boleslav where the bonneted 'M'-Series was developed early in World War I. Powered by a 22/40hp 5.9-litre 4-cyl petrol engine, this had a capacity of between 2 and 4 tons. After the war it was joined by a 2.4-litre

1-tonner, 4.7-litre 1¼-tonner and by the 4-ton 540.

Production moved to Pilsen by 1924 when a 6-wheeled articulated bus for between 24 and 30 passengers was offered on the 540 model, but the last new Laurin & Klement was the 1¼-ton Type 115 introduced in 1925, just as the company was absorbed into the Skoda organization.

LAUTH/*USA 1907-1908*
Magnus Hendrickson built light bonneted petrol-engined trucks for Jacob Lauth & Co, Chicago, Illinois, using the Lauth brand name. In 1908 Theodore Juergens joined the company and all models became known as Lauth-Juergens.

LAUTH-JUERGENS/*USA 1908-1915*
After Theodore Juergens joined the staff of Jacob Lauth & Co, Chicago, Illinois, all commercials built for them by Magnus Hendrickson were known as Lauth-Juergens. In 1910 vehicle-building moved to Fremont, Ohio, and the Lauth-Juergens Motor Car Co was formed with Magnus Hendrickson as Chief Engineer. Models were assembled with chain-drive forward-control types which had 1-, 2-, 3- and 5-ton chassis. In 1913 Hendrickson left the company to form the Hendrickson Motor Truck Co back in Chicago, and two years later the brand name was changed to Fremont-Mais.

LAVIGNE/*France 1933-1937*
Previously sold as the AS, Ets Paul Lavigne's goods vehicle range was known as the Lavigne following a move to Courbevoie, Seine.

LAW/*USA 1912-1913*
One-, 1½- and 2-ton LAW trucks were listed by the LAW Motor Truck Co, Findlay, Ohio. These had "coal-scuttle" bonnets, 4-cyl petrol engines, shaft-drive and double-reduction drive axles.

LAYCOCK/*England 1913-1915*
The Millhouses, Sheffield, engineering concern of W S Laycock Ltd introduced a 4-ton lorry powered by a 35hp 4-cyl petrol engine. One-, 2-, 3-, 5- and 6-ton versions

were also offered, normally marketed by FB Goodchild & Co, London SW1, sometimes as the Laycock-Goodchild. In 1915 a 3-ton "subsidy" type was built, using a 4-cyl Dorman petrol engine.

LAZ/*Soviet Union c1957 to date*
L'vov Automobilova Zavod, of L'vov, specializes in bus and coach production under the LAZ brand name. For many years the LAZ-695 and -697 have been the most popular, the former being a single-deck bus powered by a rear-mounted 170bhp V8. The LAZ-697 uses the same chassis but is an inter-city vehicle with extra luggage space, night lights and a sliding roof. Towards the end of the 1970s, these were joined by the LAZ-699 'Karpatia'.

1961 LAZ-697 single-deck coach

LEA/*USA 1908*
The Lea was a little known front-wheel drive truck with steering accomplished by turning the whole front axle. Built by the International Motor Co, Philadelphia, Pennsylvania, it was short-lived and built only in prototype form.

LEADER/*Australia 1972 to date*
H W Crouch Pty Ltd, Sydney, New South Wales, was a road transport undertaking which registered Leader Trucks Australia Pty Ltd to undertake series production of its own heavy trucks. Called Leader, the range now includes 4-, 6- and 8-wheeled rigids and a number of tractors assembled mainly from US components such as 6-cyl or V8 Caterpillar engines, Fuller or Allison transmissions, Hendrickson suspensions and Rockwell axles.

LEBLANT/*France 1892-c1907*
Maurice LeBlant's first steam van used a rear-mounted Serpollet-type flash boiler and 3-cyl single-acting high-pressure engine. Passenger wagons were also built and in 1894 one of each type was entered in the Paris-Rouen Trial, the world's first recognized motor competition. Soc des Trains Routiers LeBlant was formed to continue production in 1895 but later models were of little significance.

LECTRA HAUL/*USA 1963 to date*
The Unit Rig & Equipment Co, Tulsa, Oklahoma, has built heavy Lectra Haul dump trucks for some

years ranging from the 85-ton M-85 up to the 200-ton M-200. Engines include a 700bhp Cummins in the M-85, M-100 and M-120-15 up to a huge 2475bhp EMD V12, built by the Electro-Motive Divn of General Motors, in the M-200. All models use electric drive, their engines driving General Electric generators which power planetary-geared General Electric wheel motors. Suspension is by Dynaflow rubber-cushioned column units and engines can be easily removed for maintenance.

LEHIGH/*USA 1925-1927*
The Lehigh was a 2-tonner with Buda or Hercules petrol engine built by the Lehigh Co, Allentown, Pennsylvania, a subsidiary of the Bethlehem Motors Corp. Production ceased completely when the parent company was purchased in 1927 by the Hahn Motor Truck Co.

LEMOON/*USA 1906, 1910-1913, 1927-1939*
Nelson & LeMoon, Chicago, Illinois, built a prototype LeMoon truck four years before series production got underway with a bonneted 1-tonner. A new 1½-tonner was announced in 1912, followed by 2- and 3-tonners in 1913, but from then until 1927 all models were sold as Nelson-Le-Moon.

In 1927 the Nelson-LeMoon Truck Co was registered and the LeMoon brand name re-appeared. By 1928 the company offered an 8-model range from 1 to 5 tons capacity. Eleven models were available by 1930, using Waukesha 6-cyl units in the heavier types. For 1931 a 12-ton capacity bonneted 6-wheeler with double worm-drive was announced, and about the same time Lycoming straight-8 petrol engines offered briefly, the first Cummins diesel appearing in 1932.

By 1936 both "conventional" and "cabover" models, with capacities from 2 to 12 tons in both rigid and tractor form, were listed, a more streamlined design appearing in 1938. Caterpillar diesels and Continental, Cummins or Waukesha petrol engines were available. LeMoon production ceased when the company was renamed the Federal-LeMoon Truck Co and became vehicle dealers.

LENZ & BUTENUTH/*West Germany 1948*
The Lenz & Butenuth was not a marque in its own right but a steam conversion kit for internal combustion-engined lorries which were then sold as such. The idea was short-lived and only prototypes may have been built.

LEON BOLLEE/*France c1931-1933*

Following the acquisition of Automobiles Léon Bollée by A D Mackenzie and H Smith, the company became Soc Nouvelle Léon Bollée, Morris-Léon Bollée, earlier designs being retained and a new lightweight truck, the bevel-drive ELB, introduced. Three- and 4-tonners were also announced, the former powered by a 3.7-litre 4-cyl petrol engine and the latter by a 4.1-litre 6-cyl unit, both with coil ignition. Only three load-carrying commercials plus a 22-seat low-loading Hotchkiss-engined passenger chassis were listed when the business closed.

LESSNER/*Russia 1905-1910*

The G Lessner Works, St Petersburg, built a variety of commercials, the heaviest of which were fire appliances and buses up to 1496kg capacity and a 2½-ton truck.

Le Tourneau Westinghouse 'Overland Train' land train c1961

LETOURNEAU-WESTING-HOUSE/*USA 1953-c1962*

Construction equipment manufacturer R G LeTourneau Co, Peoria, Illinois, was acquired by the Westinghouse Air Brake Co in 1953 to form the LeTourneau-Westinghouse Co. As well as earthmoving equipment, the company constructed a number of military prototypes, some of which went into production. All were based on earthmoving technology, greatest production figures being achieved by the M2 guided missile carrier, developed in the mid-1950s in association with the Firestone Tire & Rubber Co. This was a diesel-electric machine with Continental engine, DC generator and hub-mounted electric traction motors in each of the four wheels.

In 1957 the Haulpak dump truck range appeared, but most spectacular of all the company's vehicles, built in the Longview, Texas, factory, was the 'Overland Train' or 'Tourneau Train', comprising a 6-wheeled "control car", ten 15-ton load-carrying cars, and two power generating cars. Intended for off-road operation, this had four 1170shp Solar gas-turbine engines driving electric motors in each of the vehicle's 54 wheels, the total length being 171m.

1958 Lewin 'Mechanical Orderly'

LEWIN/*England c1930-c1963*

Lewin Road Sweepers, Leeds, West Yorks specialized in the manufacture of motor-driven road-sweepers. Later re-named Lewin Road Sweepers Ltd, the company moved to West Bromwich, Staffs, where it became best

1962 Lewin road sweeper

known for its 'Mechanical Orderly', a small bonneted design powered by a Perkins diesel engine. Later types were based on lightweight forward-control Seddon chassis.

LEWIS/*USA 1912-1915*

Using a 360-cm wheelbase chassis with semi-elliptic leaf springs at the front and platform springs at the rear, the Lewis Motor Truck Co, San Francisco, California, built 2½-, 3- and 5-ton Lewis trucks. Each had a 4-cyl side-valve petrol engine, 3-speed transmission, countershaft and double chain-drive. The company was later known by a slightly different name, it was the Lewis Motor Truck Co Inc.

LEY/*Germany 1925-1931*

Although Rudolf Ley Maschinenfabrik AG, Arnstadt, Thuringia, introduced Loreley passenger cars and commercial derivatives as early as 1906, heavier commercial types did not appear until 1925 when a 2-ton capacity "express" truck was launched. Initially, this had a 3.1-litre 4-cyl petrol engine but it was replaced by a 3.6-litre 6-cyl unit. Later on a passenger version was introduced before the company ceased trading in the year 1931.

1919 Leyland (1) 5-ton "undertype" steam wagon chassis

LEYLAND (1)/*England 1907 to date*

With the setting up of Leyland Motors Ltd at Leyland, near Preston, Lancs, steam and petrol-engined vehicles previously sold as Lancashire Steam Motors and Leyland-Crossley were re-named Leyland and a 5-ton chain-drive wagon with fully-enclosed 2-speed transmission was introduced as the 'H'-Type, an up-rated version called the 'T'-Type appearing in 1909. This same year saw the debut of shaft-drive steamers using chassis and running gear common to the company's petrol-engined commercials, but fitted with a vertical firetube boiler, 3-cyl poppet-valve single-acting engine, and condenser in place of the radiator. Simultaneously, the company's first fire appliance was built, this having an 85bhp 6-cyl petrol engine capable of producing a top speed of 96km/h. By 1910 'T'-head petrol engines were standardized and new 5- and 6-ton steam wagons had been announced.

A bonneted 3-ton lorry was approved for the War Office "subsidy" scheme in 1912. This was better known as the 'RAF'-Type which originally had a 32hp 4-cyl petrol engine and worm-drive but, in final form, had a 36hp engine, cone clutch, 4-speed crash box and double-reduction spur and bevel rear axle. Steam wagon production was transferred to Chorley in 1913 to make way for the new 3-tonner, but was discontinued the following year because of wartime requirements.

With thousands of secondhand trucks flooding the market at the end of the war, the company took over a former munitions factory at Kingston-upon-Thames, Surrey, and bought up half its entire production of 'RAF'-Types and reconditioned them. Despite this, the company still suffered from a post-war slump in sales, although the Leyland plant was now producing petrol-engined goods and passenger types from 1½ to 6 tons capacity, while the Chorley plant was concentrating on fire appliances and, from 1920, new 5- and 6-ton steam wagons employing vertical cross watertube boilers, 2-cyl high-pressure engines, 2-speed transmissions, countershaft differentials and double chaindrive.

In 1925 a completely new passenger range, comprising the bonneted 'Lioness' for coach and charabanc work, the dropframe forward-control 'Lion' single-decker, and the aptly-named 'Leviathan' forward-control dropframe double-decker for 52 passengers, were announced. The 40bhp petrol engine fitted in the double-decker was also used in the 6-ton QH2 goods model, successor to the 'RAF'-Type, which was joined in 1927 by the 10-ton 6-wheeled SWQ2 and the world-famous lowbridge 'Titan' double-decker.

The end of steam wagon production came about in 1926, all spares being sold to Atkinson-Walker Waggons Ltd, and in 1928 the bonneted 6 x 4 'Terrier' 3-tonner was added to the range, mainly for military duties. The 6-cyl 'Titan' was joined by a single-deck counterpart, the 'Tiger', in 1929, and a new 4-cyl 'Lion' was announced. Animal names prevailed on the goods front with the 'Beaver', 'Bison', 'Buffalo', 'Bull' and 'Hippo', with capacities of between 2½ and 12 tons, often using components interchangeable with passenger types. In 1929 a prototype Leyland diesel engine of the spark-ignition Hessleman type was fitted in a vehicle for the first time, and by 1930 a full direct-injection unit was on the road, offered from 1931 in a new bonneted 6-wheeler which was called the 'Rhino'.

The 1931 2-ton 'Cub', was a US- influenced goods/passenger design with a 6-cyl petrol engine aimed at the popular end of the market as were fully-enclosed limousine-bodied fire appliances produced at Chorley. The company's diesel engines were specially designed to be interchangeable with existing petrol units, as so much conversion work was undertaken by operators. By the end of 1934 nearly two-thirds of all British bus-operating local authorities had Leylands on their fleets.

The development of the passenger chassis-based 'Llama' 6½-tonner, the short-lived 'Titanic' 6-wheeled double-decker and a 4-cyl version of the 'Cub' were all seen in 1932, while in 1933 the application of the Lysholm-Smith torque-converter transmission to the 'Tiger' single-decker, created a "gearless" bus. A year later the first rigid-8 Leyland goods model,

1924 (1) 'S'-Type

the 'Octopus', appeared, and in 1935 one of the largest fire appliances then in Britain was built – the 45-m Leyland Metz turntable ladder. Another new model was the lightweight 'Cheetah' bus, bearing some similarity to the 'Cub' range which was now built at Kingston-upon-Thames and included rigid models of up to 4 tons capacity and artics for 5 and 6 tons. But the 'Cub' was soon replaced by the semi forward-control 'Lynx', which weighed less than 2½ tons unladen and could carry 6 tons. Experiments with a twin-steer 6-wheeled 'Beaver' led to the development of the 'Panda' and 'Gnu' passenger models (a twin-steer 6-wheeled trolleybus was also built) and the 10½-ton 'Steer' goods chassis.

1930 Leyland (1) 'Hippo' 12-ton

With the war fast approaching, military vehicles were not ignored, the bonneted 'Terrier' now being replaced by the 6 x 4 forward-control 'Retriever', while a militarized 'Lynx' was also built. Some 10,000 wheeled military vehicles were manufactured up to

1945, including over 1000 6 x 4 'Hippo' Mk IIs from 1943. In 1946 Leyland trolleybus interests were combined with those of the Associated Equipment Co Ltd to form British United Traction Ltd, all subsequent models, whether Leyland or AEC-built, being sold as BUT. A year later the normal-control 5/7-ton 'Comet' goods model was announced, and in 1948 a 35-seat export passenger model.

The 8-wheeled 'Octopus' reappeared in 1948, sharing a new all-steel cab with the forward-control 'Beaver', 'Comet', 'Hippo' and 'Steer' models, and export-only bonneted trucks were introduced in the form of the 'Super Beaver' and 'Super Hippo'. The company was also developing chassisless passenger models in association with Metropolitan-Cammell-Weymann Motor Bodies Ltd to be known as Leyland-MCW, and in 1951 acquired Albion Motors Ltd, Glasgow. Underfloor-engined passenger types were gaining in popularity, Leyland's first contribution being the mid-engined 'Royal Tiger', followed in 1952 by the lighter 'Tiger Cub' with horizontal 'Comet' engine, and in 1954 by the export-only 'Royal Tiger Worldmaster'. Another new development was the 'Pneumo-Cyclic' transmission for passenger vehicles. Meanwhile a revolutionary transverse rear-engined double-decker was undergoing development.

Scammell Lorries Ltd, Watford, Herts, was acquired in 1955 although left, like Albion Motors, to fend for itself. Not only did 1958 see the arrival of the bonneted 6 x 6 'Martian' for military duties, but also a brand new wraparound screen cab on the 9-ton 'Super Comet' which, along with other components, was quickly absorbed into the Albion range. This was also a significant year in the fire-fighting field with the announcement of the unique 'Firemaster', based on the 'Royal Tiger Worldmaster'. Features included a horizontal 0.600 diesel engine located amidships, semi-automatic 4-speed transmission, and a front-mounted pump. Even more interesting was the announcement of the transverse rear-engined 'Atlantean' double-decker, shown in prototype form at the 1956 Commercial Motor Show, with 125bhp vertical diesel engine, fully- or semi-automatic transmission and a diagonal propeller shaft. The underfloor-engined 'Leopard' single-decker was added in 1959 and an export-only single-decker of similar layout to the 'Atlantean' was the 'Lion', announced in 1960. The vertical front-engined 'Titan' was still

1933 Leyland (1) 'Titan' TD2 double-deck bus

available, and 'Power-Plus' diesels were introduced in 1960.

The Coventry-based Standard-Triumph organization was bought in 1961, and some Standard commercials re-named Leyland. The first new model from this factory was the none too popular Leyland 2-tonner announced in 1962, using a 2.26-litre Standard-Triumph diesel engine. The largest takeover to date was in 1962 by the competitor Associated Commercial Vehicles Ltd, comprising AEC, Crossley, Maudslay and Thornycroft. This merger created the Leyland Motor Corp Ltd, the first new models being the 1964 Leyland 'Freightline' range with 'Ergomatic' tiltcabs later introduced on some AEC and Albion trucks. Underfloor-engined 'Panther' and 'Panther Cub' passenger models also appeared, as did an unusual export-only 'Comet' with Airflow Streamline cab, used by Baron, Commer, Dodge and Douglas trucks.

In 1965 Bristol Commercial Vehicles Ltd and its bodybuilding subsidiary Eastern Coachworks Ltd were also acquired, although vehicles continued to be called Bristol; while 1966 saw the takeover of the Rover Co Ltd and Alvis Ltd, and in 1967 Aveling-Barford Ltd was also acquired. Semi-automatic transmissions made their debut on the home market in 1966 on 'Beaver' and 'Steer' tractors, the latter being a twin-steer 6-wheeler discontinued in favour of the AEC 'Mammoth Minor'.

At the 1968 Commercial Motor Show, a prototype 6 x 4 gas-turbine tractor for 38 tons GCW was the centre of attraction. Another new idea was the '500'-Series diesel engine with fixed cylinder heads to eliminate gasket problems, fitted initially to 'Lynx' and 'Bison' models sporting a restyled 'Ergomatic' cab. The greatest landmark in Leyland history, however, was the merger of the

Leyland Motor Corp Ltd with British Motor Holdings Ltd, bringing Austin, Daimler, BMC, Guy and Morris commercial vehicles into the Leyland fold, the new organization being called the British Leyland Motor Corp Ltd. Scottish-built BMC's were re-named Leyland Redline, although sometimes known as Leyland Scotland. Lighter types from Austin and Morris were marketed jointly as Austin-Morris, while Daimler and Guy continued much as before.

Another significant year was 1970. Pride of place at the Commercial Motor Show went to the first chassisless Leyland National single-deck bus. As well, the first mass-produced Leyland Redline trucks appeared, sharing cabs inherited from BMC days with premium models built in the former Albion factory as Leyland Scotstoun or Leyland Clydeside.

Following extensive trials with US-style prototypes at the former AEC factory in West London, the Leyland 'Marathon' 32-ton GCW tractor unit was announced in 1973, using a 280bhp 6-cyl TL12 turbocharged diesel engine and a heavily modified 'Ergomatic' tiltcab mounted high on the chassis to give maximum visibility. Series production was undertaken at Southall, while the 32-ton GCW 'Buffalo' tractor, with a 212bhp turbocharged '500'-Series engine, was Lancs-built, as was a new 'Bison' rigid 6-wheeler. To confuse matters further, vehicles for export frequently carried the Leyland name.

By 1975 financial problems were increasing and, in an attempt to keep going, the government acquired 95% control. The heavy vehicle activity was re-named Leyland Vehicles Ltd, and led to the demise of the AEC, Daimler and Guy marques, the only Wolverhampton-built model being the export-only 'Victory J' passenger

1980 Leyland (1) 'Constructor' 8 x 4 tipper

chassis. The Daimler 'Fleet-line' became the Leyland 'Fleet-line' when production moved to Lancs where the last 'Atlanteans' were being built.

A new generation double-decker was the B15, eventually called the 'Titan', which made its debut shortly before the end of 1975. Like the Leyland National, this was chassisless, with a choice of transverse rear engines, fully-automatic transmission and air suspension. Unlike the National, its bodywork was constructed at the North London factory of Park Royal Vehicles Ltd which had also been taken over with Associated Commercial Vehicles Ltd. However, the closure of this plant in 1980 led to the model's transfer to the Leyland National plant where it is now built as the Leyland National 'Titan'.

In 1976 a new rigid 8-wheeled 'Octopus' was announced, claimed to be the cheapest and lightest 8-wheeler in Britain, while the 'Buffalo' tractor received the normally-aspirated L12 version of the 'Marathon' engine. The 'Marathon' itself was offered with Cummins or Rolls-Royce engines to entice customers who had previously bought the Guy 'Big J'. By 1979 'Marathon' production moved to Wolverhampton but in the background, work was forging ahead in the Lancs experimental department with two brand new ranges of heavy commercials, designated T43 and T45.

The T43 is a bonneted export model, now called 'Landtrain', developed at the Watford and Wolverhampton plants to replace the ageing 'Super Beaver' and 'Super Hippo'. Cab and front-end are of angular design to aid repairs with the minimum of facilities and the range of models has been developed for easy shipping in ckd form, particularly to Third World countries.

The T45, however, is an artic tractor unit for operation at up to 40 tons GCW. Now called 'Road-train', it has been designed as a complete concept in modular construction, enabling a multitude of specifications to be produced using the same or similar components. The first 'Roadtrain', announced in 1980, was the narrow-cabbed 16.28 with 280bhp version of the TL12 engine and a 10-speed Spicer transmission. Later versions included a sleeper-cab model with cab mounted higher on the chassis frame, and Cummins and Rolls-Royce powered derivatives for operation at only 36 tons GCW. Shortly before the end of 1980, the first T100 models began to appear, these having a TL11 engine and a narrower, lower version of the Ogle-designed Motor Panels cab. Early in 1981 the first European versions of the 'Road-train' were shown in Brussels and, simultaneously, this model was voted Truck of the Year, ensuring its future. Back in Britain the old Scammell 'Routeman' was replaced by yet another version, an 8-wheeled rigid called the Leyland 'Constructor'.

One of the most significant passenger vehicle developments was the B45, a perimeter-chassised version of the 'Titan' intended to replace the Leyland 'Fleetline' and 'Atlantean' and the Bristol VRT. Called the 'Olympian', this has a transverse rear-mounted TL11 or Gardner 6LXB diesel engine and 5-speed hydra-cyclic transmission. Also announced in 1980 was the B43, now called the 'Tiger', which entered production in 1981. The B43 has a horizontal version of the TL11 and a 5-speed semi-automatic 'Pneumo-Cyclic' box which is close-coupled to the engine.

Early in 1981 saw a complete re-shuffle of Leyland's commercial vehicle interests in preparation for these and other models. The new Leyland Group comprises Leyland Vehicles, Self-Changing Gears and BL's Indian and African truck interests, with Leyland Vehicles sub-divided into Leyland Trucks & Tractors, Leyland Bus and Leyland Parts.

LEYLAND (2)/Canada 1920-1939, 1948-1956

Branches of Leyland Motors Ltd were set up in Toronto, Montreal, Vancouver and Winnipeg to assemble British models for the Canadian market, one of the first being the 'RAF'-Type fitted with a distinctively Canadian cab. The 'Lioness' passenger model was introduced as the 'Canadian Lioness' in 1925, quickly catching on with long-distance operators and through its success many other Leylands, mainly bonneted, were offered in Canada. Amongst these were special versions of the 'Badger', 'Cub', 'Hippo', 'Lynx' and 'Terrier'.

In 1936 the Hayes Manufacturing Co Ltd became a Leyland distributor, developing the Hayes-Leyland truck using Leyland engines and mechanical units. This was short-lived and nothing appears to have happened between 1939 and 1948, when Leyland Motors (Canada) Ltd attempted to launch the under-powered 'Comet'. This was a failure and a new range of specifically Canadian models announced in 1951 was also short-lived. These comprised the 'Beaver', 'Bison' and 'Bull Moose', with gross weights of between 10,886 and 16,329kg, all with Leyland 0.600 diesel engines and modified 'Comet' cabs. In 1952 another new series appeared, using a 155bhp diesel engine, but sales were poor and remained so until the introduction of the Canada or Leyland-Canada range in 1956.

LEYLAND (3)/Israel 1960-1973

After Leyland Motors Ltd had set up an Israeli factory at Ashdod under the auspices of the Leyland Ashdod Motor Corp, two goods models were offered, both under the Leyland name. The lightest was the 12-ton GVW 'Super Chieftain', a development of the Albion of that name, with a locally-built 'Ashdod Vin' fibreglass cab and 106bhp 6-cyl diesel engine. The heavier model was the 20-ton gross 'Super Beaver' with 200bhp 6-cyl diesel engine. This could be had with optional 2-pedal 'Pneumo-Cyclic' transmission and was joined by various passenger chassis virtually identical to their British counterparts. Production ceased when the factory was given over to the assembly of American Mack trucks under a different company name.

1974 Leyland (4) 'Super Comet'

LEYLAND (4)/Iran 1970 to date

The British Leyland Motor Corp Ltd transferred production of its export-only bonneted Leyland 'Comet' 4-wheeled rigid to the Tehran factory of Haml Va Naghle Dakheli Iran Co, where production began in 1970. Both cab and front-end were re-designed later and the model was eventually joined by other more recognizable Leylands built in the same plant.

LEYLAND-CROSSLEY/England 1905-1907

The earliest motor buses to be built by the Lancashire Steam Motor Co Ltd, manufacturer of Lancashire Steam Motor vehicles, were powered by an 'L'-head petrol engine built by the Manchester-based Crossley brothers, resulting in the Leyland-Crossleys. These were among the most successful of early British buses, one of the largest fleets being that of the New London & Suburban Omnibus Co Ltd re-constituted as the London Central Motor Omnibus Co Ltd in 1906 with both financial and vehicle maintenance support supplied by the Lancashire manufacturer. By 1907, when the old Lancashire Steam Motor Co Ltd was re-organized as Leyland Motors Ltd, goods vehicles were also using the Crossley engines for up to 5 tons payload, but from 1907 the marque was known simply as 'Leylands'.

LEYLAND-DAB/Denmark 1964-1973

When bus-builder Dansk Automobil Byggeri A/S, Silkeborg, was taken over by the Leyland Motor Corp Ltd, it was re-named Leyland DAB A/S and all models sold as Leyland-DAB. These were chassisless models employing Leyland 'Royal Tiger World-master' engines and running units. This arrangement continued until 1973 when British Leyland (UK) Ltd, as it was then known, announced the signing of a new agreement between Leyland DAB A/S and Adolph Saurer AG, Arbon, Switzerland, which led to the development of the Leyland-DAB/Saurer.

1977 Leyland-DAB-Saurer artic single-deck bus

LEYLAND-DAB/SAURER/
England/Denmark/Switzerland 1973 to date
New city and inter-city passenger models were announced by British Leyland (UK) Ltd following the signing of an agreement between bus-builder Leyland DAB A/S, Silkeborg, Denmark, and Adolph Saurer AG, Arbon, Switzerland. Marketed as the Leyland-DAB/Saurer, models would be built in Denmark with marketing and back-up service provided by Saurer who will also supply engines for the range. Two types were to be launched – one, a 12-m city bus for 102 passengers and the other a 3-axle 18-m artic for 155 passengers, both of single-deck layout. Both are for one-man operation on rapid transit services, powered by mid-mounted turbocharged Saurer diesel engines. Other features include 5-speed Leyland 'Pneumo-Cyclic' transmissions, Leyland and Saurer axles and Leyland air suspension. By 1978 there were three rigid types, but the artic had appeared only in prototype form, a chassis version being exhibited at that year's Birmingham Motor Show.

LEYLAND-GEC/*England 1935*
Leyland Motors Ltd, Leyland, near Preston, Lancs, and GEC Ltd teamed up to exhibit an unusual 6-wheeled double-deck trolleybus at the 1935 Commercial Motor Show. Loading height was a mere 27cm, with unobstructed floors in both saloons and full head-room throughout. To obtain such a low floor height the entire drive train was located outside the chassis frame sidemembers, the

frame being of narrower construction than usual and completely inverted to permit the lowest floor possible.

The drive train was divided, with a 40hp traction motor on each side of the chassis frame immediately behind the front wheels, driving the leading rear wheels through underslung differential units and then the rear-most wheels by differentially-coupled shafts. Both drive axles were of the "dead" type with dropped centres to provide a flat-floored central gangway.

LEYLAND-MCW/*England 1948-1968*
The first prototypes of a new chassisless single-deck passenger model, using Leyland engines and running gear, were constructed in the Birmingham factory of Metropolitan-Cammell-Weymann Motor Bodies Ltd. This led to series production of the Leyland-MCW 'Olympic' in 1950, both in Birmingham and in an associated plant at Addlestone, Surrey, the majority being sold abroad.

A lightweight aluminium, rather than steel, construction was announced as the 'Olympian' in 1953, but was nowhere near as popular. Up-dated versions of the 'Olympic' were built until 1968 when Leyland National plans brought the project to an end. A particularly unusual version was a rear-engined design for Montreal in 1966, and among the last was a three hundred-vehicle order for Istanbul, sold as the 'Levend'.

1964 Leyland-MCW 'Olympic'

LEYLAND NATIONAL/*England 1969 to date*
The first Leyland National was shown at the 1970 Commercial Motor Show, being a prototype

chassisless single-decker constructed in the experimental department at the British Leyland Motor Corp Ltd's Leyland, Lancs, factory. Developed jointly with bus operator the National Bus Co Ltd, it had a horizontal turbocharged version of the company's fixed-head '500'-Series diesel engine mounted at right-angles behind the rear axle, with its propeller shaft driving through the axle casing and back via reduction gears to a conventional differential housing. Other features included air suspension and a forced air ventilation system via a distinctive pod at the rear of the body.

As the Leyland National Co Ltd, production got underway in a purpose-built plant at Lillyhall, Workington, Cumbria, in 1972, assembly being of the modular type permitting various lengths and numerous alternative specifications. From 1973 certain specialist types were produced, including a mobile disaster unit or casualty station, two mobile banks and the 'Business Commuter' – a low-capacity mobile office. There was even a double-ended mock-up, which came about following an enquiry from a tunnelling contractor who required a large-capacity vehicle to deliver his tunnellers to the workface and return to the tunnel entrance without turning round.

Since then, numerous modifications have been made to the basic concept, and although the majority of production has inevitably gone to the National Bus Co Ltd subsidiaries, a number have also been delivered to independents both at home and abroad.

In 1980 a huge extension was made to the existing plant so that the Leyland National 'Titan', previously built at Leyland and Park Royal, can be built there. Entire 'Titan' production for 1981 will go to London Transport to complete outstanding orders.

LEYLAND REDLINE/*Scotland 1970 to date*
While carrying only the Leyland name, all trucks built at Leyland Motors (Scotland) Ltd's Bathgate, West Lothian, plant are marketed as Leyland Redline to differentiate them from premium-built Leylands assembled in the Leyland and Glasgow factories. The first Leyland Redlines were the 'Terrier', 'Laird', 'Boxer' and 'Mastiff' for 6½ to 28 tons gross, the odd one out being the 'FG' urban delivery model inherited from British Motor Holdings Ltd.

Leyland Redline cabs are modified versions of the old BMC 'FJ' cab, also available on certain former Albion models from 1972 and sold as Leyland Scotstoun or

c1979 Leyland Scotstonn

Leyland Clydeside. Apart from the introduction of a 'Terrier' passenger chassis now called 'The Cub' and the 6-wheeled 'Super Mastiff' for tipper duties, plus various specification changes and other modifications such as a complete cab re-styling towards the end of 1980, the range has changed little, although the 'FG' is no longer listed. For a short while, however, some models were also marketed under a different name as Leyland Scotland.

LEYLAND SCOTSTOUN/*Scotland 1972-c1979*
In accordance with the British Leyland Motor Corp Ltd's rationalization policy, the famous Albion brand name disappeared from the premium products, leaving the company's Glasgow factory in favour of the Leyland name. Although these were marketed either as Leyland Scotstoun or Leyland Clydeside, they shared a cab structure with the mass-produced Leyland Redline from nearby Bathgate. 'Chieftain' and 'Clydesdale' 4-wheelers and the 'Reiver' 6 x 4 formed the backbone of the operation, although some export-only 'Viking' passenger chassis were also assembled.

LEYLAND-VERHEUL/*Netherlands c1948-1960, 1962-1973*
Soon after World War II NV Autoindustrie Verheul, Waddinxveen, introduced chassisless single-deck buses employing Leyland engines and running units. Known as Leyland-Verheul, these were very successful, production continuing alongside less popular goods models until the business was acquired by Associated Commercial Vehicles Ltd in 1960. The Leyland-Verheul range re-appeared with the Leyland takeover of ACV in 1962 when the Dutch company was re-named Leyland Verheul Nederland NV, later becoming British Leyland Nederland BV.

The last model was the LVB, production coming to a premature end in 1971 as a result of a factory fire. Although a prototype is said to have appeared in 1973, it did not enter production.

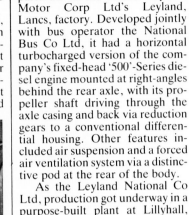

LGO/*England 1924*
Some fifty 1½- and 2-ton trucks were built by the London General Omnibus Co Ltd, West London. Called the LGO, these Dorman-engined vehicles were for the company's own use.

LGOC/*England 1909-1912, 1929*
July 1908 saw the merger of London bus operators the Vanguard Motor Omnibus Co, London General Omnibus Co and London Road Car Co to form the London General Omnibus Co Ltd, with repair facilities in Walthamstow, London, where the earlier MOC bus had been built. By 1909 this factory was building the LGOC 'X'-Type, incorporating the best features of other makes.

Up to 1910, sixty 34-seat double-deck buses and one lorry were constructed on this chassis, which had a cone clutch, shaft-drive and a 28hp engine. An improved model, the 'B'-Type entered service late that year. This was also a 34-seater, powered by a 29.8hp 4-cyl engine, with a cone clutch, 3-speed chain transmission, shaft-drive to a 'live' worm rear axle and a wheelbase of about 385cm. In 1912 the Underground Group of Companies acquired a majority shareholding in the London General Omnibus Co Ltd, separating the vehicle manufacturing facility from the operating division and registering the Associated Equipment Co Ltd to continue vehicle production under the AEC name.

In 1929 the LGOC's Chiswick Works designed new 2- and 3-axle passenger models as prototypes for a range which it was hoped would replace the many solid-tyred AEC 'S'- and 'K'-Types still on the fleet. Known as the 'CB', the 2-axle model was a single-decker of 29-seat front-entrance layout, while the 'CC' was a 3-axle double-decker with 56-seat LGOC body. It was another two years before three 'CB' and four 'CC' models actually took to the road, and in the meantime the AEC 'Regal' and 'Renown' had cornered the market.

LIAZ (1)/*Czechoslovakia 1951 to date*
When Avia np, Prague, discontinued licensed production of Skoda trucks and buses, Liberecké Automobilové Zavody, Jablonec na Nisou, took up production of the 7-ton 706 model under the Liaz brand name. This could be had in both goods and passenger form but was replaced in 1957 by the up-dated 706RT forward-control type.

In 1968 the 706MT range appeared, using a 200bhp 11.94-litre 6-cyl diesel engine. This series was still available at the end of the

1914 LGOC 'B'-Type single-deck bus

1970s, comprising 10- and 12-ton capacity 4 x 2, 4 x 4 and 6 x 4 rigids and articulated types for up to 32 tons gross. The '100'-Type appeared towards the end of 1974 but did not replace the earlier design. Listed as the 100.05 4 x 2 rigid, 100.45 4 x 2 tractor (for up to 38 tons GCW) and 090.22 6 x 4 tipper, these have a 270 or 304bhp 6-cyl turbocharged diesel engine. A more unusual model is the 6-wheeled 'Ferona' 22.22.21D powered by a horizontal underfloor diesel engine located amidships and specially constructed at a subsidiary plant at Zvolen to carry long steel bars.

1976 Liaz (1) 'MT'-Series tipper

LIAZ (2)/*Soviet Union c1959 to date*
The Soviet Liaz is a passenger range introduced by the Likino Bus Plant, Likino. One of the earliest was the Liaz 158 with a capacity of between 32 and 60 passengers and a 109bhp 6-cyl Liaz diesel engine. Later came the Liaz 677, a pneumatic suspension city bus powered by a 200bhp V8 diesel with seating for up to 41 passengers. It was awarded a Gold Medal at the Leipzig Fair.

LIBERTY (1)/*USA 1917-1918*
The Liberty was a standardized design based on US Army specifications for a Class 'B' 5-tonner. Developed by the Gramm-Bernstein Co, Lima, Ohio, and the Selden Motor Vehicle Co, Rochester, New York, it was quickly nicknamed the 'Liberty' truck, despite 'USA' carried on the radiator, and the 'Liberty' name stuck. It was powered by a 4-cyl petrol engine with drive via a 4-speed transmission to a fully-floating worm-drive rear axle.

By the end of World War I both companies had built about one thousand trucks. It became

the basis of the French Willème truck, marketed as the Liberty-Willème, and was also used in multi-wheeled experiments and half-track developments by the US Quartermaster Corps.

LIBERTY (2)/*Belgium 1920-1940*
Soc Franco-Belge des Camions Liberty was established in Brussels to salvage and re-build American Liberty trucks but in 1920 began to construct vehicles of this

type using original components. During the 1930s, however, a lighter range was introduced, using 6-cyl petrol engines, and by about 1936 Deutz and Hercules diesels were often used.

LIBERTY-WILLEME/*France c1919-1939*
Ets Willème, Neuilly, Seine, began operations by salvaging and re-building 5-ton Class 'B' Liberty trucks abandoned in France at the end of World War I. These were re-sold as Liberty-Willème. Initially it was identical to the original model, but gradually pneumatic tyres were listed as an option, a more powerful 7.7-litre petrol engine introduced, and a producer-gas version made available.

By 1930 the Liberty-Willème could be had as a 7½-ton dump truck, 12-ton 6 x 2 rigid or in standard load-carrying form. The 6-wheeler retained the original overhead-worm axle, but had 8 forward speeds and brakes on all but the trailing wheels. In 1931 the company began fitting CLM-built Junkers opposed-piston 2-stroke diesel engines, later offering its own version, but Liberty-Willème production gradually dropped during the 1930s to make way for new Willème models.

LIFU/*England 1897-1905*
The first Lifu was a 1-ton steam van built by the Liquid Fuel Engineering Co Ltd, East Cowes, Isle of Wight. It had a twin-drum water-tube boiler and two compound engines each driving a rear wheel via a countershaft and internal gearing.

In 1898 a 2-ton steam lorry was entered in the Liverpool Trials. The boiler was mounted at the front of a channel-steel frame powering a 25/30hp horizontal compound engine. All-gear drive and a countershaft differential were employed. The Lifu's high price precluded its popularity and few were sold. Lifu designs were used for the slightly later Belhaven range, and Lifu wagons were also built under licence by Melevez Frères, of St Servon-lez-Namur, Belgium.

LIGIER/*France 1978 to date*
Racing car manufacturer Automobiles Ligier, Vichy, also builds a forward-control Fiat-engined 1½-ton truck.

LILLOISE/*France 1929*
Cie Lilloise de Moteurs, Lille, which specialized in the manufacture of automotive engines, exhibited a miniature 1-ton forward-control diesel lorry, also known as the CLM, at the 1929 Paris Salon. It had a single-cyl CLM petrol engine, solid tyres and a transaxle.

LINDSLEY/*USA 1909*
Based on an earlier high-wheeler, a 1089kg capacity truck was built briefly by J V Lindsley & Co, Dowagiac, Michigan, before the company was absorbed into the Dowagiac Motor Car Co.

LINK-BELT/*USA 1949 to date*
The Link-Belt Speeder Corp, Cedar Rapids, Iowa, was formed following the merger of the Speeder Machinery Co with the Link-Belt Machinery Co. Six- and 8-wheeled truck-mounted cranes were among the products offered, often using carriers supplied by other manufacturers but carrying the Link-Belt name. By the 1960s all-hydraulic yard cranes, some with 4-wheel drive, were also in production and the all-hydraulic 'HydraXcavator' appeared on a 4-wheeled commercial chassis.

LINN/*USA 1916-1950*
The Linn was a half-track built by the Linn Mfg Co, Morris, New York, as a bonneted load-carrier or tractor, in which form it was known as the Linn Tractor. It had a gear-driven rear axle transmitting drive to tracks located outside the main chassis frame but inside two dummy sidemembers. Initially, the Linn had a 4-cyl Continental petrol engine, but later 4- or 6-cyl Waukesha petrol units or 6-cyl Cummins or Hercules diesels.

H H Linn left the company in 1927 to form the Linn Trailer Corp and in 1928 the Linn Mfg Co was acquired by the Republic Motor Truck Co Inc, Alma, Michigan. It continued independently, despite the merger of Republic and American LaFrance. The 8-ton T3 half-track arrived in 1933. This had a 246bhp American LaFrance V12 petrol engine.

In 1940 a 5-tonner with front-wheel drive arrived, which had two wheels behind the tracks which could be lowered for operation on ordinary roads. For cross-country work the tracks were also driven, the engine being a 105bhp 6-cyl Hercules. One of the last new models was a heavy front-wheel drive truck with twin front wheels.

LION/*USA 1907-1912*
The Lion Motor Co, Adrian, Michigan, built commercial versions of its passenger cars, using a 40hp 4-cyl petrol engine. A factory fire brought operations to an end in 1912.

LIPPARD-STEWART/*USA ?-1919*
Light commercials with "coal-scuttle" bonnets were a speciality of the Lippard-Stewart Motor Car Co, Buffalo, New York. Later, models of up to 2 tons capacity

were listed using 4-cyl Continental petrol engines, 3-speed transmissions and worm final-drive, production moving to Syracuse, New York, before the marque was discontinued.

LITTLE GIANT/*USA 1912-1918*
The 1-ton forward-control Little Giant was built by the Chicago Pneumatic Tool Co, Chicago, Illinois, using a 2-cyl petrol engine, planetary transmission and double chain-drive. Models for up to 3½ tons were available later, having 4-cyl Continental engines, 3-speed transmissions and worm-drive. All were sometimes marketed as Chicago Pneumatic or CPT, but the latter should not be confused with the CPT brand name, used on exported models sold in Great Britain by the Consolidated Pneumatic Tool Co Ltd.

LIUCHIANG/*China 1969 to date*
The Liuchiang (Liu River) LZ-130 is a heavy-duty truck built by the Liuchou Farm Machinery Plant and the Liuchou Machinery Plant, both in Liuchou, Kwangsi.

LLOYD/*Germany/West Germany 1908-1914, 1948-c1958*
A 40hp 5-ton chain-drive truck was the first true Lloyd commercial built by Norddeutsche Automobil- und Motoren AG, Bremen, followed by a variety of delivery vans, trucks and buses with capacities of 1½, 3 and 5 tons as well as battery-electrics. From 1910 trolleybuses were also offered, using a single traction motor, cardan shaft and differential. These were also built under licence for the British market by the Brush Electrical Engineering Co. Following a merger with Hansa Automobil AG, all vehicles were marketed as Hansa-Lloyd.

The Lloyd brand name was revived after World War II by Lloyd Motoren-Werke GmbH, set up to construct commercials for the Borgward empire. Most were lighter models, the one exception being a 3-ton bonneted truck.

LLOYD & PLAISTER/*England 1905-1911*
Lewis A Lloyd teamed up with W E Plaister to found Lloyd & Plaister Ltd, taking over the Hurst & Lloyd premises in London N22. This company built commercials to special order. Fire appliances were a speciality, 1909 models being among the first to have front-wheel brakes. There was also a tractor for converting horse-drawn steam fire appliances to self-propulsion.

LMC/*USA 1919-1920*
The 2½-ton LMC was a product of the Louisiana Motor Car Co,

Shreveport, Louisiana. It had a 4-cyl Continental petrol engine, 4-speed transmission and bevel-drive.

LOCO TRAULIER/*England 1932-1939*
As well as the Traulier, Shelvoke & Drewry Ltd, Letchworth, Herts, also offered a road/rail derivative called the Loco Traulier. This had flanged wheels both in front and behind each pneumatic-tyred road wheel.

LOCOMO/*England 1910-1914*
The Lowcock Commercial Motor Co, Manchester, sold a 4-ton commercial under the Locomo or Lowcock brand names. These were built by Sir W G Armstrong, Whitworth & Co Ltd, Newcastle-upon-Tyne, who also sold them as Armstrong-Whitworths.

LOCOMOBILE/*USA 1912-1916*
Previously building only light commercials, the Locomobile Co of America Inc, Bridgeport, Connecticut, eventually introduced a 5-ton "cabover" using a 4-cyl petrol engine, 5-speed transmission, countershaft and double chain-drive. By 1915 this was joined by 3-, 4-, and 6-ton versions, but only the 3- and 6-tonners were listed for 1916, after which models were sold as Locomobile-Riker until they became Riker in 1917.

LOCOMOTORS/*England 1949*
Locomotors Ltd was a vehicle bodybuilding concern in Birkenhead, Cheshire, that built a 1¼-ton delivery van. This was a forward-control model with sliding cab doors and Ford 'Ten' petrol engine, which was based on a chassis that had been supplied by the Mercury Truck & Tractor Co, Gloucester.

LODEMOR/*England 1930-1937*
The Laycock Eng Co Ltd, Mill-

houses, Sheffield, formerly WS Laycock Ltd, returned to vehicle production with Lodemor industrial and road-going trucks.

LOHNER-PORSCHE/*Austria c1900-1908*
Heavy battery-electric commercials built by Jacob Lohner & Co, Vienna, were usually marketed as Lohner-Porsche, after Ferdinand Porsche, the engineer who had designed the system of front hub-mounted traction motors for which these vehicles were famous. All were of bonneted design, with batteries in place of the engine, and particularly popular as fire brigade escape carriers. Trolleybuses were sold as Lohner-Stoll.

LOHNER-STOLL/*Austria 1902-1908*

1913 Locomobile 5-ton tipper

Ludwig Stoll of Oesterreichische Daimler Motoren Gesellschaft, Vienna, developed a trolleybus current collection system using a 4-wheeled trolley hauled along twin overhead lines by a flexible cable. The idea was adopted by Jacob Lohner & Co, Vienna, called the Lohner-Stoll system and first demonstrated on an experimental 1¼-mile line at Johannisthal. The vehicle used had four 15hp hub motors, although subsequent production types had two 20hp motors, one in each rear wheel. A distinctive feature of the system was a drum hanging from the collector trolley, which carried sufficient flexible cable to allow the vehicle to swing away from the overhead lines to negotiate an obstruction.

Licence production also took place in Britain under the Cedes-Stoll name, production here outliving the original marque, and rival designs were produced as Mercedes-Electrique-Stoll by Ludwig Stoll's original employer.

LOKKERI/*Finland 1967 to date*
The Lokomo Works, Rauma Repola Oy, Tampere, builds logging vehicles under the Lokkeri brand name. These include an articulated 4 x 4 tractor and a 6 x 6 log-hauler, both powered by a 130bhp Perkins diesel engine and with automatic transmission.

LOMAX/*England 1906*
In the City of London, John Goode built the Lomax steam tractor for converting horse-drawn wagons to self-propulsion. A prototype, with front-mounted vertical boiler, a twin-cyl compound engine, countershaft differential and twin chains to the front wheels, was the only example.

LOMBARD/*USA 1916-1921*
The Lombard Auto Tractor-Truck Corp, Waterville, Maine, built a petrol-engined half-track tractor-truck powered by a 75hp 4-cyl engine. A fleet of these was used by the Russian Armed Forces but many went to civilian logging contractors.

LOMOUNT/*England 1961-1962*
Lomount Vehicles & Engineering Ltd, Colnbrook, Bucks, was established to continue production of heavy diesel road tractors previously manufactured by Rotinoff Motors Ltd. Some received AEC engines and synchromesh transmissions and some were also marketed as Atlantic.

LONDONDERRY/*England 1903-c1908*
For the colliery's own use, the Marquis of Londonderry's colliery maintenance shops at Seaham Harbour, Co Durham, began constructing steam wagons. Early types had a vertical water-tube boiler and double high-pressure steam engine. Later, the Seaham Harbour Engineering Works was formed and this design replaced by a 5-tonner with vertical fire-tube boiler. A special feature was that both chimney and smokebox were removable, enabling the vertical tubes to be swept with steam up. The engine was a totally enclosed compound "undertype" and a 3-point suspension system was employed.

LONGEST/*USA 1913-1915*
The Longest was a bonneted 3/4- or 5/6- tonner with 40hp 4-cyl petrol engine, 4-speed transmission and double chain-drive. It was built by the Longest Bros Co, Louisville, Kentucky.

LORD BALTIMORE/*USA 1911-1916*
Built by the Lord Baltimore Motor Car Co, Baltimore, Maryland, the first Lord Baltimore was a 3-tonner known as the Model 'A'. This had a 4-cyl petrol engine, 3-speed transmission and chain-drive. By 1912 production was handled by the Lord Baltimore Truck Co. By 1913 there were five models with capacities ranging from 1- to 5-tons but in the last two years of production only 1- and 2-tonners were listed.

LORRAINE/*France 1930-1950*
The Lorraine was built by Soc des Moteurs et Automobiles Lorraine, Argenteuil, Seine-et-Oise, using Tatra designs. Among these was a light 6 x 4 with a 2-litre air-cooled flat-4 engine and an 8-tonner with an 11.2-litre 6-cyl water-cooled petrol engine. Only a few road/rail terminal tractors were built up to 1950.

LORRAINE-DIETRICH/*France 1905-c1918*
When De Dietrich et Cie, Luneville, Lorraine, became Soc Lorraine des Ans Ets de Dietrich et Cie, the product name changed to Lorraine-Dietrich. The first new commercial was a Turcat-Méry design of 6 x 2 configuration, with chain-drive to a centre pair of wheels, those at front and rear being steered and all three axles equidistant. It had a 40hp 4-cyl petrol engine and was listed as a bus, truck or passenger car.

This was supplemented by a series of bonneted trucks and buses, with 4-cyl petrol engines, 4-speed transmissions and chain final-drive, and by 1909 commercial types included various designs up to 5 tons capacity. The largest load-carriers had engines of 5.5-litre capacity although some passenger models used 8.8-litre units. By 1911 the first forward-control Lorraine-Dietrich, the 3-ton C3T, had appeared and within three years shaft-drive 1-tonners were also offered. After World War I the company concentrated entirely upon passenger car manufacture until a new commercial line, called Lorraine, appeared in 1930.

LOTHIAN/*Scotland 1913-1924*
Locating the driver alongside the engine was one novel idea incorporated in the Lothian bus built by the Scottish Motor Traction Co Ltd, Edinburgh. Thus, a 6.9-m single-deck body could hold 32 seated passengers. The prototype had a rear entry platform, smoking and non-smoking compartments. It had a 38hp Minerva 'Silent-Knight' sleeve-valve petrol engine, 4-speed chain-driven gearbox and worm-drive rear axle. From 1914 35hp Tylor engines were fitted and chassis sold to other operators as buses, 3-ton lorries, or charabancs. One Lothian received a 31-seat charabanc body but towards the end of World War I petrol supplies began to dry up so the company began using coal gas. New and existing Lothians were fitted with roof-mounted gas bags. The company also assembled some Bethlehem trucks imported from the US but this was a short-lived arrangement.

LOTIS/*England 1908-1912*
Sturmey Motors Ltd, Coventry, replaced its lightweight Sturmey commercial by the heavier Lotis, powered by an underseat 18hp 'V'-twin Riley petrol engine coupled to a 2-speed epicyclic box. By 1911 2- and 4-cyl bonneted models up to a 30hp 3-tonner were listed, with 'colonial' types available for kerosene fuel.

LOTZ/*France 1865-?*
Using R W Thomson patents, Lotz Fils, Nantes, constructed a vertical-boilered steam tractor with engine located amidships. This was teamed up with a passenger trailer.

LOUET & BADIN/*France 1906*
Passenger car manufacturer E Louet et Badin, Auxerre, Yonne, built chain-drive forward-control 2-tonners with 15hp 4-cyl petrol engines.

LOUGHEAD/*Canada 1919-1923*
The remains of the W E Seagrave Co were acquired by a Sarnia munitions manufacturer to form the Seagrave-Loughead Co Ltd in 1918. Loughead trucks, with capacities of up to 7 tons, appeared the following year, joined later by lighter pneumatic-tyred models.

LOW-DECK/*England 1926-1927*
Corber & Heath Ltd, Dartford, Kent, built the 2½-ton Low-Deck ultra low-loading goods model. With a platform height of 67cm, this had a perimeter chassis frame, 2.18-litre 4-cyl petrol engine located transversely under the driver's seat, and 4-speed constant-mesh transmission

LOW LOADER/*England 1929-1934*
Low Loaders Ltd, London W12, built a small-wheeled low-loading truck following the ideas of J M Roberts & Son Ltd. The earliest model was a 2-tonner with 1.5/2.5cu m all-steel refuse body. It had a 4-cyl Coventry-Climax petrol engine located transversely alongside the driver and front-wheel drive. The front wheels were so close together that it was almost a 3-wheeler and the axle could rotate through 360°, enabling the vehicle to turn within its own length. Available in wheelbase lengths of 240, 270 and 300cm, the Low Loader was marketed by Lacre Lorries Ltd.

LOWA/*East Germany 1949-1952*
The first commercial to be built by VEB Lokomotiv- und Waggonbau, Werdau, Saxony, was the Lowa SD 65 steam tractor pow-

1905 Londonderry "undertype" steam wagon

1913 Lothian single-deck bus

ered by a 65bhp 3-cyl engine. Of forward-control layout, this was of modern streamlined appearance and was soon joined by a number of trolleybuses, including an artic double-decker. A 120bhp Maybach diesel engine powered the W 500 bus, announced in 1951, while the company's last model was a passenger version of the Horch H3 model. The business was re-organized in 1952 and all subsequent models sold as Grube.

LOWDALL/*England 1935-1936*
The Lowdall 1¼-ton delivery van developed by Trojan Ltd, Croydon, Surrey, was based on the company's 'Mastra' passenger car. It had a rear-mounted 2.2-litre 6-cyl 2-stroke petrol engine and synchromesh transmission but got no further than mock-up stage.

LOYAL/*USA 1920*
The heaviest commercial offered by the Loyal Motor Truck Co, Lancaster, Ohio, was a short-lived 1-tonner with 4-cyl petrol engine.

LOZIER/*USA 1910-1912*
The Lozier Motor Co, Detroit, Michigan, built a 5-ton forward-control truck known as the Model 25. It had a 4-cyl water-cooled petrol engine. 4-speed transmission, countershaft and chain-drive to the rear wheels.

LUAZ/*Soviet Union 1966 to date*
Lutsk Automobilova Zavod, Lutsk, introduced a 2-wheel drive version of the ZAZ-969 utility vehicle called the Luaz. A 4-wheel drive model was added in 1970. Known as the 969M, the latest model has a 40bhp engine and headlamp wipers.

LUBLIN/*Poland 1951-1959*
Fabryka Samochodow Ciezaro-

wych, Lublin, introduced licence-built versions of the bonneted GAZ-51 truck under the Lublin brand name. With a capacity of 2½ tons, this was a somewhat dated design and production ended when new Polish vehicles had become well established.

LUC/*Germany 1913-1920*
Knight-engined LUC light delivery vans built by Loeb & Co GmbH, Hohenschönhausen, Berlin, were joined by a series of commercial chassis which remained in production until after World War I. The company was later re-named Loeb-Werke AG, moving to Charlottenburg, but in 1920 all products were re-named Dinos.

LUC COURT/*France 1900-1950*
Luc Court commercials were built by SA des Ans Ets Luc Court et Cie, Lyons. This company's most significant development was a 4-cyl overhead-valve petrol engine announced in 1909 which had a capacity of 2.15 litres and was used for both cars and commercials, the latter employing oil-bath chain-drive. Later, shaft-drive was adopted and in 1936 passenger cars were discontinued in favour of petrol- and diesel-engined trucks and buses.

LUDEWIG/*West Germany 1968 to date*
Gebr Ludewig GmbH, Altenessen, Essen, was an established coachbuilding firm that developed a chassisless 6-wheeled single-deck trolleybus to the requirements of the city of Solingen. Of double-drive layout, this is still manufactured solely for this client.

LUEDINGHAUS/*USA 1919-1931*
In order to remain in business, the Luedinghaus-Espenschied Wagon

Co, St Louis, Missouri, turned to trucks. The first Luedinghaus models ranged from 1 to 2½ tons capacity, using Waukesha petrol engines and Shuler or Wisconsin axles. By 1925 the heaviest model was a 5-tonner and in 1928 a 6-wheeler, with set-back front axle, Hendrickson rear bogie and balloon tyres, was supplied to a local operator. In 1931, the final production year, only 1½- to 2½-ton models were built.

LUMB/*USA 1918*
The Lumb truck had a capacity of 2041kg. Built by the Lumb Motor Truck & Tractor Co, Aurora, Illinois, it had a 4-cyl Buda petrol engine and 3-speed transmission.

LUTZMANN/*Germany 1893-1898*
F Lutzmann, Dessau, Anhalt, built both van and bus versions of his passenger car range. Little is known about them apart from the fact that some Benz influence was apparent in the engine design.

LUVERNE/*USA 1912-1917*
Founded by the Leicher brothers in 1903, the first commercial built by the Luverne Automobile Co, Luverne, Minnesota, was a fire appliance, using a 6-cyl Rutenber petrol engine. Truck production soon got underway, the company's name changing to the Luverne Motor Truck Co, and by 1917 all passenger cars had been withdrawn. The company's last model was a bonneted 3-tonner powered by a 4-cyl Continental petrol engine.

LUX/*Germany 1898-1902*
Lux'sche Industriewerke AG, Ludwigshafen, offered both petrol and battery-electric commercials under the Lux brand name. The first petrol-engined design was a 2/3-tonner powered by a 6hp

opposed-piston twin-cyl petrol engine. A later type used a 10/12hp 2-cyl unit.

LVL/*England 1923-1926*
Available as a 1¼/1½-ton load-carrier or 14/16-seat passenger model, the LVL was built in the Wolverhampton works of Light Vehicles Ltd. It had a 20hp 4-cyl Dorman petrol engine, 4-speed transmission and overhead-worm final-drive.

LWD/*Germany 1923-1925*
Lippische Werke AG, Detmold, Lippe, marketed a mediumweight forward-control truck called the LWD. This had a 30bhp 2.5-litre petrol engine driving the front axle via an hydraulic transmission.

LYNCOACH/*USA 1938-1952, 1960-c1972*
Founded in 1929 as a specialist commercial bodybuilder, the Lyncoach & Truck Mfg Co, Oneonta, New York used the same factory as that purchased by H H Linn in 1927 when he founded the Linn Trailer Corp. The first complete Lyncoach was an outside broadcast van, subsequent models comprising a series of mobile showrooms with low floors and front-wheel drive. During the war, a number of ambulances powered by 6-cyl Dodge or Ford V8 petrol engines were built.

Civilian production resumed in 1945 with front-drive delivery vans fitted with Waukesha petrol engines, but from 1952 until 1960 production appears to have centred upon bodybuilding. In that year a plant was opened at Troy, Alabama, and the 'Lyn Air-van', with capacities of up to 3 tons on Ford or other commercial chassis, was built. Later, this was re-named the 'Lyn Arrow,' but by the early 1970s only commercial bodies and trailers were built.

M

MACCAR/*USA 1914-1935*

When Mac-Carr Co, Allentown, Pennsylvania, ceased trading, the Maccar Truck Co was incorporated at Scranton, Pennsylvania. The first Maccar trucks were Wisconsin-engined models of up to 2 tons capacity but by 1917 had expanded to include 3½- and 5½-tonners.

By the 1920s vehicles from 1 to 6 tons capacity were available, having 4-cyl Continental petrol engines, Brown-Lipe transmissions and Timken axles. Buda and Wisconsin 6-cyl engines were added in 1926.

At the end of the 1920s a 6-wheeled rigid was introduced and 1931 saw 4- and 5-ton high-speed trucks with 6-cyl engines, 4-piece cast-aluminium radiators and air brakes. The company had now teamed up with the Hahn Motor Truck Corp and the Selden Truck Corp to form the Maccar-Selden-Hahn Truck Corp. From 1930 only 6-cyl engines were used and one unusual development was a 10/15-ton capacity rigid 6-wheeler with a 6-cyl Sterling petrol engine and the company's own double-drive springless walking-beam bogie. Unfortunately, the Depression was now biting hard and by 1933 the Maccar Truck line had been discontinued.

MACCARR/*USA 1912-1913*

Jack Mack who, with his brothers, had formed the Mack Bros Co, teamed up with Roland Carr to form the Mac-Carr Co, also in Allentown, Pennsylvania. Early Maccarr trucks had capacities of up to 1360kg, and for a brief period Lansden battery-electrics and Webb fire appliances were all built in the same plant. Production passed to the Maccar Truck Co at the beginning of 1914.

MACDONALD/*USA 1920-c1952*

The MacDonald was a low-loading rigid introduced by the MacDonald Truck & Tractor Co, San Francisco, California. Five- and 7½-ton models were offered, the

1939 Mack (1) EX-BX 18-ton 6 x 4 tank transporter

1952 Mack (1) LRVSW 34-ton 6 x 6 oilfield truck

MACK (1)/*USA 1902 to date*

Gus, Jack and Willie Mack set up the Mack Bros Co in Brooklyn, New York, introducing a chain-drive 18/20-passenger charabanc with 24hp horizontally-opposed 4-cyl 'F'-head petrol engine. A second vehicle was built in 1903 but when series production got underway in 1904 vehicles were sold as Manhattan.

A move to Allentown, Pennsylvania, in 1905 resulted in the formation of the Mack Bros Motor Car Co but while Manhattan production continued the first Mack trucks also appeared, comprising a bonneted 1½/2-tonner and 3-, 4- and 5-ton "cabovers" with 4-cyl 'T'-head petrol engines and constant-mesh selective transmissions. By 1908 bonneted models were available for up to 5 tons capacity and in 1909 new 1-, 1½- and 2-tonners, with pressed-steel rather than rolled-channel frames, were announced and the company's first fire appliance constructed. The new models were later known as 'Juniors' while vehicles from 3 to 7½ tons capacity became 'Seniors'.

An attempt to gain more capital led in 1911 to the formation of the International Motor Co which also built Saurers under licence and which absorbed the Hewitt Motor Co the following year. Even lighter Macks were now on the way as well as the mediumweight 'AB' and the company's most famous product, the 'AC'.

Announced in 1914, the 'AB' was to replace the 'Junior' series

and was similarly offered in 1-, 1½- and 2-ton form. Power came from a 30hp 4-cyl petrol engine, worm-drive was introduced and various proprietary components used until Mack equivalents were employed in 1915, when chain-drive options were also listed. 'Senior' Macks were replaced in 1916 by 3½-, 5½- and 7½-ton 'AC' models, quickly nicknamed 'Bulldogs' by army engineers, using a 75hp 4-cyl petrol engine, pressed-steel chassis frame and chain-drive, the 'AC''s most distinctive features being its unusual bonnet and radiator between driver and engine.

In 1920 double-reduction drive was adopted for the 'AB' and a passenger version offered the following year. In 1922 Mack Trucks Inc was formed and a dropframe version of the 'AB' passenger model was introduced two years later, sometimes with petrol-electric transmission and occasionally sold in truck form as a 'Bus Commercial'. The first 6-cyl engined Mack was the 'AL' bus, built between 1926 and 1929, with a 4-speed transmission and vacuum brakes, and in 1927 a shaft-drive version of the 'AC', designated the 'AK', was added to the model line. The 'BJ' ¾-tonner, with 126bhp 6-cyl petrol engine, was another new model.

Six-wheeled 'AC's and 'AK's were also listed and inevitably a 6-cyl version appeared as the 'AP' for 7½ tons as a 4-wheeler, 10 tons as a rigid-6 and 15 tons in tractor form. The 'BJ' was up-rated to 5/8

tons capacity in 1931, other models in this series including the 1-ton 'BL' and the 8-ton 6-wheeled 'BQ'. A new "cabover" range was produced in 1933, comprising 3/5-ton 'CH' 4 x 2s and 3½/6-ton 'CJ' 6-wheelers, and in 1934 a transverse rear-engined bus line was introduced, starting with the 30-seat 'CT', trolleybuses being added in 1935.

Light "cabovers" in the 1½ to 6 tons range were the 'EC' and 'EB' types of 1936, later 'E' models including the 6-ton shaft-drive 'EM', 6-ton chain-drive 'ER' and 10/12-ton 'EQ' tractor. Another new goods model was the 1-ton payload 'MR' multi-stop delivery vehicle. Between 1936 and 1938

1960 Mack (1) C95FD-135 pumper

agreement was reached to sell 1½-, 2- and 3-ton bonneted Reos through Mack distributors as Mack Jr but at the opposite end of the scale the Mack 'F'-Series of 1937 added chain-drive 4 x 2 and 6 x 4 on/off-highway trucks to the line, one of the largest being a 10cu m 30-ton 6-wheeler with 175bhp diesel engine sold to the Sunlight Coal Co, Indiana. Mack-built diesel engines were now offered in the company's buses and at long last the 'Bulldog' range was withdrawn.

The early stages of World War II saw rigid tank transporters and cargo trucks in the respective forms of the 6 x 4 EX/BU and NR4 supplied to the Allies in Europe, while full wartime production included thousands of 6-ton 'NM' and 7½-ton 'NO' 6 x 6s. There was even an experimental twin-engined and double-ended tank transporter.

Post-war production was restricted to models of over 3 tons capacity, based on the 'E'-, 'F'- and 'L'-Series and including the company's first 'West Coast' tractor – the long-wheelbase LTSW with engines of up to 306bhp and a 10-speed transmission. The only passenger model was the 41-seat rear-engined C41 with air-operated clutch and 3-speed transmission, replaced by a Spicer torque-converter transmission in 1947 when the 45-seat C45 arrived. From 1948, 33- and 37-seaters were also offered, but in 1950 a 50-passenger design called the C50 was delivered to New York. One C50 was exported to Scandinavia where it acted as prototype for a new range of Scania-Vabis city buses. On the heavy truck side, meanwhile, Mack was developing a good reputation in the off-road field, one of the largest machines of this type being the

LRVSW 34-ton 6-wheeler powered by a 400bhp Cummins V12.

'A'-Series trucks, from 7711 to 18,143kg GVW, were also announced in 1950 but replaced three years later by the bonneted 'B'-Series, while a considerably lightened bus line introduced a year later employed a diesel engine based on Scania-Vabis designs. Other new trucks included the 'West Coast' W71 "cabover" rigid and 'H'-Series "cabover" tractors, both powered as standard by a Mack END673 'Thermodyne' diesel with petrol option. The 1955 'D'-Series was a short-wheelbase "cabover" for city delivery work.

Bus sales were not going well so in 1956 the C D Beck Co was acquired, bringing its passenger vehicle and fire appliance expertise into the Mack fold. Sales continued to decline, however, and

eventually stopped altogether, although fire appliance sales increased considerably, particularly after the introduction of 'C'-Series cab-forward appliances with pumps of 500 to 1250gpm capacity available as rigid or artic machines with open or closed cabs. Another acquisition was the Brockway Motor Co Inc, although this was allowed to continue largely as a separate entity until its closure in 1977.

The 'West Coast' 'G'-Series "cabover" tractor arrived in 1959, with normally-aspirated or turbocharged Mack or Cummins diesel engines of up to 335bhp output. A short-wheelbase city "cabover" was the 'N'-Series and from 1962 the 'F'-Series, with similar specification to the 'G'-Series, was also listed. Assembly plants were set up in various countries from about 1963, constructing vehicles mainly along US lines, one exception being the Australian factory where 8- and 10-wheeled rigids are now built for stock-train haulage. Also in 1963, Camions Bernard of France was taken over, some US Macks being sold in Europe as Mack-Bernard.

Bonneted tractors were now represented by the 'C'-Series, although these were replaced in

1965 by the offset-cabbed 'U'-Series, bonneted 'B'-Series rigids being replaced the following year by the 'R'-Series, also offered in fire appliance form. The 'DM' was a new heavy-duty model for the construction industry, also announced in 1966, the same year that a plant was opened at Haywood, California, to construct 'RL' "conventional" and 'FL' "cabover" models.

In 1969 the company purchased a two-thirds interest in the Canadian Hayes Manufacturing Co Ltd but again permitted Hayes production to continue as before. In 1973 a revolutionary off-highway bottom-dump truck was marketed as the 'Mack-Pack'. Powered by a 475bhp rear-mounted V12 Detroit Diesel or Cummins engine, this has a capacity of 35 tons and is a 4-wheel drive artic design.

The 'W'-Series 'Cruiseliner' "cabover" tractor was added in 1975 with no less than 31 engine options up to a 430bhp V8 Detroit Diesel. Other relatively new models are the 8 x 6 HMM front-discharge truck-mixer and 'M'-Series off-highway dump trucks from 15 to 120 tons capacity. These are produced in both rigid and articulated form.

1972 Mack (1) 'DM'-Series 10 x 4 truck mixer

1977 Mack (1) R685RT artic tractor

1975 Mack (1) F-700 6 x 4 artic tractor

1959 Mack (2) H9T 9-ton truck

smaller being the front-wheel drive Model 'O' and the latter the Model 'AB'. Both had 4-cyl Buda petrol engines ahead of the driver, internal-gear final-drive and hydraulic power steering. The Model 'O' had a loading height of 41cm, with neither springs nor brakes at the rear.

Production was eventually taken over by the Union Construction Co, and later by the MacDonald Truck & Mfg Co, which was to become part of the Peterbilt Motors Co, moving to Oakland, California. Few MacDonalds were built after this.

MACK (2)/*England 1954-1964*
Mack Trucks (Great Britain) Ltd was established at Barking, Essex, to re-condition and service World War II American Macks. An attempt was made to import new American-built Macks, but this was unsuccessful and the first British-built Mack appeared. This was a 7-tonner with Perkins R6 diesel engine, 5-speed David Brown transmission and an American bonnet and cab. Long- and short-wheelbase models were shown at the 1954 Commercial Motor Show, both with British-built bonnets and cabs. One year later, a production 7-tonner, with full forward-control, 6-cyl Leyland diesel engine, 5-speed Albion transmission and all-steel Bonallack cab, was announced. A bonneted 9-tonner was built in 1956, again with Leyland engine and Albion transmission but with a modified Bedford cab.

In 1961 a 4-wheel drive forward-control 8-tonner with Commer TS3 engine and cab was introduced, joined two years later by a 6-wheeled crane-carrier, with Leyland 0.680 engine. This, and

an AEC-engined seismographic truck built in 1964, were special orders and the latter was probably the last British Mack to be built.

MACK-BERNARD/*France 1963-1966*
After the acquisition of Camions Bernard, Arcueil, Seine, by Mack Trucks Inc, vehicles built at the former Bernard plant were turned out with both Mack and Bernard badges, while some imported trucks were sold as Mack-Bernard.

MACK JR/*USA 1936-1938*
The signing of an agreement with the Reo Motor Car Co in 1934 whereby Mack Trucks Inc was to sell certain Reo models through its regular sales outlets, led to the introduction of the Mack Jr series of trucks and buses, all built in Reo's Lansing, Michigan, plant using a combination of Mack and Reo styling. These comprised four models up to 3 tons capacity, all of lighter construction than regular Macks, and including a forward-control design with engine between the seats.

MADARA/*Bulgaria c1962-?*
Soviet- and Czechoslovakian-built trucks imported into Bulgaria were sold under the Madara name for many years.

The Jay Madsen Equipment Co Inc, Bath, New York, specialized in custom-building buses, fire appliances and refuse collectors. Passenger types were of 4- or 6-wheeled layout with front, mid or rear engines.

All were available with a vast choice of components. Ford, Hall-Scott, International Harvester and White petrol engines were available, with diesels supplied by

1960 Mack (2) 6 x 6 tractor chassis-cab

Cummins, Detroit and Waukesha.

A particularly striking refuse truck was the Model FC-180-C of 1968, which had an automatic transmission, 2-man half-cab, stand-up or sit-down driving position and a payload of up to 11,698kg. In 1971 the company was absorbed into Air Springs Inc, becoming the Jay Madsen Divn, based at Allentown, New York. One of the last Madsens was a twin-cabbed refuse truck powered by a Ford V8 engine.

MAFFEI/*Germany 1928-1931*
Former traction engine builder J A Maffei AG, Munich, introduced a road tractor following Chenard-Walcker design. It had a 60bhp 4.7-litre 4-cyl Deutz engine but was re-named the Krauss-Maffei in 1931 when production was taken over.

MAFSA/*Spain ? to date*
The Mafsa is a 4-wheel drive truck built by IPV for the mining, logging and agricultural industries. It has a Perkins 4.203 4- or 6.305 6-cyl diesel engine and can operate at gross weights of 2000, 4500 and 6000kg.

MAG/*Hungary c1914-c1939*
Magyar Altanos Gepgyar, Matyasfold, Budapest, built MAG

trucks and aircraft. Some commercials were battery-electrics, while others had 4-cyl petrol engines of 25 and 35hp output. From 1920 a new range comprising the 1.8-litre 4-cyl engined Magomobil and 3.4-litre 6-cyl engined Magosix or Magosupersix, with hydraulic 4-wheel brakes, was introduced in light commercial form. Production included a number of fire trucks built in collaboration with Teudhoff-Dittrich.

MAGIRUS/*Germany 1903-1938*
Specializing in the manufacture of fire-fighting equipment, C D Magirus, Ulm, was soon building steam-powered appliances before introducing its first petrol-engined model in 1906. Re-constituted as C D Magirus AG in 1911, the company is believed to have built the world's first powered turntable ladder in 1914, expanding its activities two years later with the introduction of a 40hp 3-ton truck. Shaft-driven passenger types arrived in 1919 and by the mid-1920s the standard Magirus truck was a 2/3-tonner with 4.7-litre 4-cyl petrol engine.

A low-loading passenger chassis, with 7-litre 6-cyl Maybach petrol engine, arrived in 1927, using a 100bhp V12 Maybach by 1930. Fire appliances were still much in evidence and by the early 1930s 2-, 2½- and 4-ton trucks, all with 6-cyl petrol engines, were readily available. In 1933 a forward-control 1-tonner was introduced, powered by a 670cc 2-cyl 2-stroke JLO engine with air-cooling. Later that year the first Magirus diesel engine, of 7.5-litre capacity, was developed and fitted in new 4 x 2, 4 x 4 and 6 x 4 military trucks.

The company's first forward-control trucks appeared in 1936, using a 150bhp 12-cyl opposed-piston diesel engine under the

1919 Magirus 2CV11D single deck post bus

1920 Magirus 4-ton tipper

Magirus 2-ton truck c1928

1934 Magirus 6 x 4 military truck

driver, and were quickly joined by passenger derivatives. Klockner-Deutz Motoren AG was now taking an interest in the business, taking it over completely in 1938 after which all models were sold as Magirus-Deutz, Klockner or Klockner-Humboldt-Deutz. Despite this, some models are often referred to simply as Magirus.

MAGIRUS-DEUTZ (1)/*Germany/West Germany 1938 to date*
The acquisition of C D Magirus AG, Ulm, by Humboldt-Deutz Motoren AG led to the introduction of Magirus-Deutz commercials. At first, these were identical to the earlier Magirus series but from 1943 comprised a complete range of Deutz air-cooled diesel-engined types, sometimes also referred to as Klockner or Klockner-Deutz. A new 3-tonner appeared in 1946, a passenger derivative followed and by the early 1950s, apart from 4 x 4 models, all types had a distinctive rounded bonnet. Air-cooled diesel engines were now available as 4- or 6-cyl in-line units or in V6 or V8 form.

A rear-engined forward-control bus, with 130bhp 8-litre 6-cyl air-cooled diesel power unit, was introduced in 1951 and by 1956 bus production was being undertaken at Mainz. The 1957 'Saturn II' passenger model was the first built by the company with full air suspension, and from then on all trucks were listed both in forward- and normal-control form, model names such as 'Jupiter', 'Mercur', 'Pluto' and 'Sirius' being used.

Numerical designations were employed after 1964.

By 1967 lighter Eicher trucks made up the bottom end of the range while heavier requirements were catered for by 4 x 2, 4 x 4, 6 x 4 and 6 x 6 types in forward- or normal-control form, using 6-, 8- or 10-cyl air-cooled diesel engines of up to 250bhp output. The passenger market, meanwhile, was covered by a rear- or amidships-engined single-deck city bus.

Gas-turbine experiments were given the go-ahead in 1968 but were short-lived. More significant was the 'Club of Four' (DAF, Magirus-Deutz, Saviem and Volvo), established in 1971 to develop standard trucks in the 3½ to 8½ tons payload range. Using numerous common components, particularly cabs, these have been built

Magirus refuse collector c1936

Magirus-Deutz (1) truck c1939

1951 Magirus-Deutz (1) O3500

1975 Magirus-Deutz (1) 232D artic tractor

1972 Magirus-Deutz (1) MD230L117 single-deck bus

by each of the four since 1975, Magirus-Deutz versions being the only ones with air-cooled diesel engines. At the same time, heavier trucks were listed for up to 22 tons payload. using engines up to a 340bhp 14.7-litre 10-cyl unit.

Re-organized as Magirus-Deutz AG, the company also joined with Fiat, Lancia, OM and Unic in 1975 to form the Industrial Vehicles Corp (IVECO), again reaping the benefit of combined resources and producing a series of trucks in the 2¼ to 4½ tons range with 4.1-litre 4-cyl air-cooled diesel engines.

MAGIRUS-DEUTZ (2)/*Greece 1973*
Velo SA, Athens, imported German-built Magirus-Deutz commercials and for a short while converted a rear-engined passenger model to front-engined layout, using the original air-cooled V8 diesel engine. With a capacity of 100 passengers, the 12-m city bus body was also built by Velo SA, and all examples supplied to the same Thessalonika operator.

MAGIRUS-DEUTZ (3)/*England 1974 to date*
Magirus-Deutz (Great Britain) had been importing German-built Magirus-Deutz commercials for some time when it developed the 232D30FK double-drive 8-wheeled rigid for the British tipper market. This sold extremely well and was soon listed for other European countries as well, being progressively up-dated in line with

1978 Magirus-Deutz (3) 232D30FK

other Magirus-Deutz trucks.

MAGIRUS-VOMAG/*USA 1924-1926*
The Magirus-Vomag Machine Co, Wehawken, New Jersey, sold imported Magirus and Vomag commercials under the Magirus-Vomag name.

MAGISTRAL/*Belgium 1938-1940*
A few Magistral trucks and buses, with capacities of between 3½ and 5½ tons, were constructed somewhere in Belgium. Of lightweight construction, they had Hercules petrol or diesel engines.

MAHINDRA/*India 1949 to date*
Mahindra & Mahindra Ltd, Bombay, constructs its own version of the forward-control Jeep FC150/160 range under the Mahindra

1980 Magirus-Deutz (1) 232D24K 6 x 4 dump truck

brand name. Marketed as a pick-up, minibus, van or ambulance, it has a 75bhp Hurricaine petrol engine and 4 x 2 or 4 x 4 drive.

MAIS/*USA 1911-1914*
The bonneted Mais truck was designed for payloads of between 1360 and 1814kg. It was built by the Mais Motor Truck Co, Peru, Indiana, and had a 24hp 4-cyl petrol engine, 3-speed transmission and internal-gear final-drive. By 1912 it had been joined by 1½-, 2½- and 5-ton versions, production being transferred to a plant at Indianapolis. The concern was bought by the Premier Motor Mfg Co.

MAKO/*Germany 1926*
Norddeutsche Waggonfabrik AG, Bremen, had built horse-drawn carriages before announcing the 1-ton Mako truck. This had a 4-cyl petrol engine and shaft-drive.

MALEVEZ/*Belgium 1898-c1905*
Malevez Frères, St Servais-lez-Namur, assembled goods- and passenger-carrying steam wagons under Lifu patents.

MALTBY/*England 1905-1922*
Starting as an agency for MMC commercials, Maltby's Motor Works, Sandgate, Kent, began building charabancs using Coronet petrol engines and transmissions supplied by the Iden Motor Car Co Ltd. By 1911 most Maltby charabancs were of the "toast-rack" type, with 40hp White & Poppe petrol engines and worm final-drive but in 1922 the business was acquired by local garage operator Caffyns Ltd.

MAN (1)/*Germany/West Germany 1920 to date*
Two years after the last MAN-Saurer trucks were built at Lindau, Maschinenfabrik Augsburg-Nürnberg AG introduced the first MAN in its Nuremburg factory along similar lines. The company's first diesel truck was exhibit-

ed at the 1924 Berlin Show, the engine being a 45bhp 4-cyl direct-injection type, but public opinion was against it, forcing the company to fit sparking plugs and a petrol fuel system for urban use.

A 150bhp 6-cyl petrol-engined rigid 6-wheeler with a capacity of 10 tons appeared in 1926 but by the end of the 1920s diesel engines were optional and a low-loading passenger chassis was offered with an 80bhp 6-cyl diesel unit as standard.

For 1931 a 5-tonner could be had with 80, 100 or 120bhp petrol engines or a 120bhp diesel unit, while a new 6-wheeled chassis used the 120bhp petrol engine and could also be supplied in trolley-bus form. By 1933 a 140bhp 16.6-litre diesel was available for this model and with the exception of a 3-tonner, which was powered by a 4-cyl version, all other rigids had diesel engines of between 6.7 and 13.3 litres capacity. A distinctive feature of most MANs at this time was a dropped-centre rear axle incorporating a special drive arrangement to the rear wheels and providing both a low loading height and a low centre of gravity. A number of vehicles were supplied to military authorities also, including both 4 x 4 and 6 x 6 adaptations of the company's 2½- and 4½-tonners.

1979 MAN (1) 4,0,400 tractor

Financial interest in Oesterreichische Fiat Werke AG, Vienna, builder of Austro-Fiat trucks, provided MAN with increased production capacity which was used for manufacturing axles before turning to its own OAF commercials. Severe bomb damage brought MAN production to a premature end but it was resumed immediately after World War II with the 'MK' 5-tonner, using a 110bhp 6-cyl diesel engine, which quickly developed into the MK25 truck and MKN bus, both using a 120bhp 6-cyl diesel. A heavier version was the MK26 which was also listed as an artic tractor unit.

A rear-engined chassisless for-

1961 MAN (1) Model 415 4 x 4 tipper

1969 MAN (1) Model 750 HO-U11 single-deck coach

1974 MAN (1) Model 13.304 artic tractor

1980 MAN (1) Model SR280 single-deck coach

1979 MAN (2) Model 30.240 8 x 4 tipper

ward-control bus, the MKH2, was announced in 1951 as were the company's first turbocharged diesel engines. The world's first V8 diesel arrived soon after, being featured in the 10-ton F8 truck, and by 1955 Germany's first multi-fuel engine had been developed. In 1957 commercial production moved to a new plant in Munich and existing passenger models were joined by an underfloor-engined design, while by 1960 the goods series covered various forward- and normal-control 4 x 2 and 4 x 4 models from 5 to 10 tons capacity, passenger types being built in association with Krauss-Maffei, thus carrying the KM or Krauss-Maffei names also.

Two 17-ton 6-wheeled rigids were introduced in 1961 and co-operation with Saviem of France led to the introduction of 1¾- and 3½-ton Saviems under the MAN name in 1967, the same year that passenger vehicle production commenced in a new factory at Penzberg. The passenger range included city service and touring types with 160bhp rear-mounted diesel engines and new articulated models using 192bhp underfloor diesels. A new 15-litre V8 diesel was fitted in the latest long-distance and heavy-duty trucks and gas-turbine development work got underway in 1969, a 350bhp experimental unit being subsequently fitted in a 4 x 2 rigid chassis.

The company became associated with Büssing Automobilwerke AG in 1969, taking it over completely in 1971 and withdrawing all models. An outcry amongst Büssing operators quickly reinstated a number of underfloor-engined goods models which were marketed for some time as MAN-Büssing. Büssing's former plant at Salzgitter-Watenstedt now builds MAN buses and all MAN vehicles now carry the Büssing lion motif on their grilles.

Experiments with alternative fuels has led to the development of the MAN Elektro and MAN Erdgas prototypes, while specialist 8-wheeled rigids developed in the UK are now offered to other European clients. During 1975 negotiations got underway between the company and Volkswagen AG to co-operate in the manufacture of spares and of light- and mediumweight commercials, now marketed as MAN-Volkswagen or MAN-VW, but the company is now also a subsidiary of Daimler-Benz AG.

The current standard range covers capacities of between 1 and 24½ tons, with engine outputs of up to 320bhp, although there is also a 'Jumbo' 6 x 4 heavy haulage machine and various 4 x 4, 6 x 6 and 8 x 8 military models. Certain MANs are also built under licence in Rumania as Roman and in the bus market, the company offers the only standard double-deck model in Germany.

MAN (2)/*England 1975 to date*
MAN Concessionaires (GB) Ltd are importers of ready-assembled German MAN trucks for the UK market but at the 1975 Harrogate Tipper Show launched a new rigid 8-wheeler aimed specifically at British tipper operators. This is for operation at 30 tons GVW and is powered by a 232bhp MAN diesel of 11.045-litre capacity.

MAN-BUSSING/*West Germany 1971 to date*
With the takeover of Büssing Automobilwerke AG by Maschinenfabrik Augsburg-Nürnberg AG, all Büssing models were withdrawn. Public opinion, however, persuaded MAN to introduce a new series of underfloor-engined commercials using MAN cabs and sold as MAN-Büssing.

MAN ELEKTRO/*Germany ? to date*
Maschinenfabrik Augsburg-Nürnberg AG undertook much development work on alternative propulsion systems during the

1970s, one being a battery-electric system for passenger vehicles. A fleet of electrically-propelled MAN Elektro single-deckers, each hauling its own battery trailer, entered experimental service, backed by the German Government's Department of New Technology and the Westphalian Land Department. Each vehicle changes battery trailers at the end of its trip, range being about 90km per charge.

MAN ERDGAS/*Germany 1972 to date*
Maschinenfabrik Augsburg-Nürnberg AG has also been researching into the use of natural gas as a vehicle fuel. This has been applied experimentally to certain passenger models, carrying the MAN Erdgas name. Normal engines take their liquid gas supplies from cryogenic storage tanks mounted on the chassis.

MAN-MECCANICA/*Italy ? to date*
MAN-Meccanica SpA builds mediumweight all-wheel drive vehicles for cross-country and other special purposes using Fiat engines and other proprietary components.

MAN-SAURER/*Germany 1915-1918*
The first commercials built by KG Lastwagen-Werke MAN-Saurer in a former Saurer factory at Lindau were licence-built Saurers maketed as MAN-Saurer. One was a chain-drive 4-tonner with 36hp petrol engine, while others had 30 or 45hp engines and cardan- or chain-drive. In 1916 the company was re-named Kraftwagenwerke MAN-Saurer GmbH, production continuing until 1918 when there was a break to develop the first true MANs, announced in 1920 by the company's successor, Maschinenfabrik Augsburg-Nürnberg AG.

MAN-VOLKSWAGEN/*West Germany 1979 to date*
During 1975 negotiations took

place between Maschinenfabrik Augsburg-Nürnberg AG and Volkswagen AG, whereby the two would co-operate in the manufacture of vehicle spares and light- and medium-duty commercials. At the time, MAN had full order books and a total lack of light- and medium-duty models, while production at Volkswagen was dropping due to lack of exports. The new range, marketed as MAN-Volkswagen or MAN-VW, was to be built in the former Audi car plant at Neckersul and the first model, in the 6 to 9 tons GVW weight range, known as the 'MT', was shown at Frankfurt in 1979. Development and production is shared, with Volkswagen supplying cabs, rear axles and transmissions and MAN the engines, chassis frames, front axles and specialist bodies. The tiltcab is based on Volkswagen's lighter 'LT' range and transmission choices include synchromesh 4-speed and 5-speed overdrive systems.

MANCHESTER (1)/*England 1905*
Known in prototype form as the Brightmore, the articulated Manchester wagon was built by Turner, Atherton & Co Ltd, Denton, Manchester.

MANCHESTER (2)/*England c1928-1933*
Willys-Overland-Crossley Ltd, Heaton Chapel, Stockport, Cheshire, was established to assemble Willys-Overland vehicles for the British market. Its own 1¼-tonner, previously marketed as the Overland or Willys-Overland, was later called the Manchester or Willys-Manchester, having a 2.5-litre 4-cyl side-valve petrol engine, 3-speed box and pneumatic tyres. Typically American features included coil ignition and spiral-bevel rear axle. It was soon joined by a 1¾-ton version with 43bhp 3.6-litre petrol engine. The larger model was also offered as a 14-seat coach or 6-wheeler and 1930 saw the launch of a 2½-tonner with 4-wheel servo brakes. All

1980 MAN-Volkswagen 'MT' Model 8.136 vehicle transporter

1930 Manchester (2) B1 1½-ton tipper

but the lightest model had 4-speed transmissions by 1931 and for 1932 a short-chassis 2½-tonner with forward-control was announced but never entered series production.

MANCHESTER GNU/*England 1973-1975*
The Manchester Gnu was built by the Nigel Engineering Co Ltd, Swinton,Greater Manchester. It was a 1-ton capacity 3-wheeler which could also handle a single-axle trailer. Intended mainly for export, it had a 1.3- or 1.6-litre Ford petrol engine, gearbox, propeller shaft and rear axle. Wide-section tyres aided traction on soft ground.

MANDERBACH/*West Germany c1946-1954*
Previously offering light 3-wheelers, the Wissenbach factory of Louis Manderbach & Co introduced a 1-ton 4-wheeler after World War II. This had a 34bhp 1.2-litre Ford petrol engine.

MANFRED WEISS/*Hungary 1935-c1940*
After Manfred Weiss Loszer Acel es Femarugyar RT, Csepel, Budapest was re-named Dunai Repulogepgyar, a programme of military vehicle development was embarked upon leading to various 4 x 4 designs. Nikolas Straussler started his career with the company and was quick to use its facilities to develop his own vehicles. The first was a 15-ton rigid 8-wheeled petrol tanker, which was sold under Straussler's own name, but most famous was his twin-engined G3 4 x 4 military truck, further development of which was curtailed by hostilities. A proto-type was smuggled out of the country and subsequently formed the basis of the Garner-Straussler twin-engined 4 x 4. After World War II the company's premises formed the basis of the Csepel truck factory.

MANHATTAN/*USA 1904-1910*
When series production got underway at the Mack Bros Co, Brooklyn, New York, models were headed by the Manhattan sight-seeing vehicle, powered by a 4-cyl 'F'-head petrol engine of the company's own design. In 1905 production moved to Allentown, Pennsylvania, and the company was re-named the Mack Bros Motor Car Co, but production of the Manhattan passenger model continued until it was ousted by new Macks.

MANLY/*USA 1917-1920*
The Manly Motor Corp, Waukegon, Illinois, introduced 1½-, 2- and 2½-ton trucks. All had 4-cyl Waukesha petrol engines and worm-drive rear axles, the two lighter models having a 3-speed transmission and the 2½-tonner a 4-speed. For 1918 production was handled by the O'Connell Manly Motor Corp, and then by the O'Connell Motor Truck Corp until the marque was discontinued in favour of the Super Truck which this company had built since 1919.

MANN (1)/*England 1897-1926*
The first self-propelled steam wagon built by Mann & Charlesworth Ltd, Hunslet, Leeds, West Yorks, was a small compound "overtype" steam tractor based on P J Parmiter patents, with side-fired loco-type boiler, detachable load-carrying box pivoting directly on the gear-driven rear axle and single full-width rear wheel. In 1898 it was joined by a larger model with an "undertype" engine, and one machine entered in the 1901 Liverpool Trials had the engine re-positioned over the boiler, making this Britain's first true "overtype" wagon.

Mann (1) 3-ton "overtype" steam wagon c1913

The company was now known as Mann's Patent Steam Cart & Wagon Co Ltd and a series of plate-frame "undertypes" from 4 to 7 tons load capacity was introduced. A new "undertype" with channel-steel mainframe, and engine and gearing mounted on a plate subframe, replaced the earlier series and soon included 2- and 3-tonners.

A 5-ton "overtype" arrived in 1909, using a shorter boiler than most other makes and with side-firing. It was not superheated and carried fuel in a container in front of the driver who was seated on the right, thereby requiring no second man.

Initially, it was a 2-speed model, with gearing carried between the hornplates and behind the boiler. Final-drive was by roller chain to a rear axle differential. A year later a new 3-tonner appeared and this led to a 4-ton model about 1915. Soon after World War I the 5-tonner was replaced by a new 6-ton model. A vertical-boilered 'Express' "un-

1917 Mann (1) 5-ton "overtype" steam wagon

dertype" was launched in 1924. This had a cross water-tube boiler with superheater, a double-cyl engine, 2-speed enclosed gearbox and cardan shaft-drive. The last year of "overtype" production was 1926, and the firm went into liquidation two years later, the remains being purchased by Atkinson-Walker Waggons Ltd.

MANN (2)/*England 1907-1908*
G H Mann constructed a steam wagonette in his workshop at Holbeck, Leeds, West Yorks, using a vertical fire-tube boiler and compound "undertype" engine. This served as a prototype for the Brotherhood wagon which G H Mann also designed.

MANNESMANN-MULAG/
Germany 1913-1928
Previously sold as Mulag, Mannesmann-Mulag commercials were mainly in the 3½ to 5 tons payload range. Both trucks and buses were available from the Aachen factory of Mannesmann-Mulag Motoren und Lastwagen AG, with cardan-drive listed from 1921. In 1928 a 2-ton on/off-highway 6 x 4 truck was developed but not proceeded with. The company closed soon after, and two years later was acquired by Automobilwerke Heinrich Büssing AG.

MANTON/*England 1946-1951*
Manton Motors Ltd was a lorry repair shop established in Croydon, Surrey, which introduced a 12-ton GVW Perkins P6-engined truck for the export market. The first few went to various Spanish operators, and by 1951 between fifty and sixty vehicles had been built, the largest being a rigid 6-wheeler. Orders from Spain and Portugal were increasing rapidly when the company was re-named Motor Traction Ltd in 1951. Simultaneously, the Manton name disappeared and a new marque, MTN, was introduced.

MANULECTRIC/*England 1953-c1963*
Sidney Hole's Electric Vehicles was established at Brighton, Sussex, in 1948 to build battery-electrics. Sold as Manulectric, the first 4-wheeler was a 1-ton capacity 122-cm wheelbase pedestrian-controlled design. In 1954 the first rider-controlled model, also known as the Standon, appeared, also a 1-tonner. Both pedestrian- and rider-controlled types were offered throughout the 1950s, joined towards the end of the period by the 1¼-ton 'Mobile', another rider-controlled unit, this time on a 175-cm wheelbase with bevel-drive. In 1961 the 1½-ton Model 7 arrived, and by 1962 the Model 4 was the only pedestrian-con-

1961 Manulectric Model 730 1½-ton battery-electric milk float

trolled vehicle listed. The company was later re-constituted as the Stanley Engineering Co Ltd and production transferred to Egham, Surrey.

MAPLE LEAF/*Canada 1930-c1948*
Built by General Motors of Canada Ltd in its Oshawa, Ontario, plant, the Maple Leaf truck was based on a heavy-duty American Chevrolet design, powered latterly by a GMC engine.

MAPLELEAF/*Canada 1919-1922*
Not to be confused with General Motors' Maple Leaf truck, the Mapleleaf was an assembled vehicle of between 1½ and 5 tons capacity. It was built by the Mapleleaf Mfg Co Ltd, Montreal, who had acquired assets and manufacturing rights of the Menard Motor Truck Co, Windsor, Ontario.

MARATHON (1)/*USA 1912-1913*
The Marathon Motor Works, Nashville, Tennessee, augmented its passenger car range with a series of light commercials and heavier trucks with capacities of 1½, 3 and 5 tons. Heavy models were of forward-control layout with 4-cyl petrol engines and worm-drive rear axles.

MARATHON (2)/*England 1920-1925*
This Marathon was a 1¾-ton goods model built by James Walmsley & Co Ltd, Preston, Lancs. Of bonneted design, it had a 25hp 4-cyl Dorman petrol engine, 4-speed transmission and David Brown worm-drive rear axle. In 1921 the wheelbase was extended.

MARATHON (3)/*Canada 1970 to date*
Marathon Electric Vehicles Inc, Montreal, Quebec, constructs battery-electric delivery vehicles, much development work being centred upon the 6-wheeled Marathon C-360 which hauls its 16-battery power pack on a small trailer. Optional equipment includes an 18bhp 2-cyl petrol engine which can be combined with the batteries to provide a maximum range per charge of 482km and speeds of up to 80km/h.

MARATON/*Spain 1936-1939*
With the onset of Civil War in 1936 the General Motors Corp's Barcelona plant was taken over by a workers' collective and re-named General Motors Peninsular Empresa Collectivizada. Trucks were sold as Maraton for loads of up to 4 tons and buses were also built, all models using an 86bhp 6-cyl petrol engine. Most Maratons, however, were used as troop-carriers by anti-Franco factions.

MARCHAND/*Italy c1900-1907*
It was not until about 1900 that Fratelli Marchand, Piacenza, introduced light delivery models with 'T'-head engines and double chain-drive, adding a few light buses also. When the company became Marchand & Dufaux commercial types were withdrawn.

MARIENFELDE/*Germany 1899-1902*
Motorfahrzeug und Motorenfabrik AG, Marienfelde, Berlin, assembled commercial vehicles under the Marienfelde name, using components common to the Daimler range. In 1902 the com-

pany was taken over by Daimler-Motoren-Gesellschaft and subsequent models sold as Daimler-Marienfelde. Marienfeldes employed shaft-drive from a front-mounted engine with gearbox located beneath the driver's seat and final-drive by internally-toothed gear rings. In the summer of 1901 agreement was reached with G F Milnes & Co Ltd for vehicles to be sold in the British Isles as Milnes.

MARION/*USA 1904-1914*
The Marion Motor Car Co, Indianapolis, Indiana, also offered some commercial types. Early models featured transverse 16hp air-cooled petrol engines with double chain-drive but from 1906 4-cyl petrol engines were used, a 48hp model was introduced later.

MARMON/*USA 1963 to date*
Production of a new highway tractor developed by the Marmon-Herrington Co Inc was taken up by one Marmon Motor Co, Denton, Texas, when the original company went out of business. The new Marmon was a heavy-duty "cabover" of lightweight construction, using fibreglass and aluminium components. "Conventionals" were also offered, with a single-piece full-width fibreglass bonnet. By 1964 production got underway at Dallas and Garland, models continuing along similar lines until the present day. Chassis frames are of all-bolted construction with Cummins or Caterpillar diesel engines coupled to a twin-plate clutch, 13-speed overdrive Fuller 'Roadranger' transmission and tandem-drive Rockwell Standard single-reduction bogie. In 1973 the company was purchased by the Interstate Corp, Chattanooga, Tennessee, boosting production from 100 to 700 units a year.

MARMON-BOCQUET/*France 1963 to date*
When the American Marmon-Herrington concern was sold, the French subsidiary - Marmon-Herrington SAF, Villiers-le-Bel - became SA Marmon Bocquet, developing a new version of the Marmon-Herrington MS600B. A 1½-ton 4 x 4 intended for military applications, it is actually manufactured by the Unic Divn of Simca Industries and forms the basis of numerous other military machines. It is also known as the SUMB or Simca-Marmon.

MARMON-HERRINGTON (1)/*USA 1931-1963, 1973*
The Marmon-Herrington Co Inc was founded at Indianapolis, Indiana, to construct all-wheel drive trucks, mainly for the military.

1964 Marmon-Bocquet MH600BS 1¹/₂-ton 4 x 4 military truck

The first was a 4 x 4 refuelling truck with a 6-cyl Hercules engine, followed by various other 4 x 4 and 6 x 6 types. The first civilian models were truck-trailer combinations for airfield construction, but perhaps the most famous of all Marmon-Herringtons was a 36/40-seat articulated desert coach hauled by a THD-315-6 6 x 6 bonneted tractor with 90bhp 6-cyl diesel engine and sleeper cab, which ran between Damascus, Syria, and Baghdad, Iraq.

As it specialized in the construction of all-wheel drive vehicles, it was perhaps inevitable that all-wheel drive conversions of standard trucks would also be offered. Most were on Ford chassis although Chevrolet, Dodge, GMC and International models were also used, all carrying the Marmon-Herrington name. There was also a Ford-based half-track with powered front axle – possibly the first use of such a layout.

Genuine Marmon-Herringtons now comprised various models from 1¹/₂ to 20 tons capacity with Ford or Hercules engines, but during World War II a 4 x 4 "cabover" of Autocar design and a 4 x 2 snub-nosed tractor of International design were supplied to military customers. In 1945 the company diversified and began to build the forward-control front-wheel drive Delivr-All multi-stop delivery van and a series of lightweight trolleybuses. Buses with 27 and 31 seats previously offered by Ford, were manufactured and marketed by the company from 1950 but during 1952 the Delivr-All range was discontinued. By the mid-1950s, both buses and trolleybuses had also been withdrawn in favour of other engineering products, although a few all-wheel drive trucks continued to be built and there was even a further batch of trolleybuses in 1959.

1932 Marmon-Herrington (1) DSD-800-6 6 x 6 artic tractor

1938 Marmon-Herrington (1) C30-6 8-ton 6 x 6 tipper

Three school bus models, all with Ford V8 engines, were listed in 1961 but in 1963 the company was sold and a new "cabover" tractor already on the drawing board passed to a Marmon-Herrington distributor, who later introduced it as the Marmon. Nearly ten years later a Ford-engined 4 x 4 Marmon-Herrington with 1-man half-cab was launched by the Marmon Group's Transmotive Divn, Knoxville, Tennessee, a descendant of the original company.

MARMON-HERRINGTON (2)/
France 1957-1963
Marmon-Herrington Inc, Indianapolis, Indiana, set up Marmon-Herrington SAF at Villiers-le-Bel to convert Ford trucks to 4-wheel drive and construct special vehicles for the French Army. These were 1¹/₂-ton forward-control 4 x 4 trucks using Simca V8 or Panhard

4-cyl engines. There was also a bonneted 6 x 6 called the FF6, which had a Simca V8 or Perkins P6 diesel engine. When the parent company was sold, production continued as Marmon-Bocquet, Simca-Marmon or SUMB.

MARQUETTE/USA 1910-1912*
The 243-cm wheelbase Marquette was built by the Penninsular Motor Co, Saginaw, Michigan, using an opposed-piston 2-cyl petrol engine, planetary transmission and double chain-drive. The Marquette Motor Vehicle Co was formed towards the end of 1910 and production transferred to Chicago, Illinois, where no less than seven body types were offered, ranging from an open stakeside to a 12-seat bus.

MARTA/Hungary 1909-1918*
Magyar Automobil RT, Arad, was set up by the French Westinghouse company to build light trucks and buses of German Daimler design under the Marta brand name. These were bonneted models with 4-cyl petrol engines but in 1918 a change of country boundaries placed the works in Rumania and the company was re-named the Rumanian Wagon & Motor Factory Ltd, introducing Astra commercials.

MARTIN (1)/USA 1911-1915*
Light commercials built by the Martin Carriage Works, York, Pennsylvania, were joined by a series of 4-cyl forward-control trucks with capacities of between 1¹/₂ and 6 tons. These had 29 or 36hp Wisconsin petrol engines, disc clutches and 3-speed transmissions, but were discontinued in preparation for the Atlas range.

MARTIN (2)/England 1925-1926*
Martins Cultivators Ltd, Stamford, Lincs, constructed a number of complete fire appliances, using 4-cyl Dorman petrol engines, 4-speed Martin transmissions and a 250/300gpm pump. Other appliances were built on Tilling-Stevens chassis.

MARTINI/Switzerland 1901-1933*
F Martini et Cie, Frauenfeld, was one of the first Swiss manufacturers to construct a true commercial, this being a 10hp 4-cyl engined 4-tonner with chain-drive. By 1903 production had moved to St Blaise, Neuchatel, where increased production was possible. One of Switzerland's first regular bus services was provided by 14-seat Martinis with exhaust heating from 1904 and by 1905 trucks from 3 to 10 tons capacity were offered.

In 1906 the business was acquired by a British consortium and re-named the Martini Automobiles Co Ltd but this came to an end in 1908 when it became Soc Nouvelle des Automobiles Martini. Shortly before World War I a shaft-drive 2¹/₂/3-tonner was developed, becoming popular with both Dutch and Swiss Armies.

The post-war slump hit business badly. However, a new 1¹/₂-tonner, powered by a 3.8-litre 4-cyl car engine, appeared in 1920, finding popularity as touring coach, hotel bus or fire appliance. Towards the end of the 1920s the business was bought by German car manufacturer Walter Steiger and from 1928 a new 4.4-litre petrol engine was fitted in a revised 1¹/₂/2-tonner, later up-rated to 2¹/₂ tons capacity. For 1930 a 3-litre petrol engine was available in this chassis and by 1931 Lockheed vacuum servo brakes were offered.

MARTYN/England 1898*
David Martyn & Co Ltd, Hebburn-on-Tyne, Co Durham, developed an unusual steam bus with boiler and engine located beneath the floor. The former was a horizontal diagonal multi-tube type running on coke while the latter had two cylinders, link motion reversing gear and numerous aluminium components. It was a single-speed design with chain final-drive.

MASERATI/Italy 1940-1944, 1948-1952*
More famous for its high-powered racing and sportscars, Officine Alfieri Maserati SpA, Modena, also built battery-electric trucks, heaviest of which was a forward-control 1-tonner, with truck, hearse or tank body, 6¹/₂hp motor, single-plate clutch, 4-speed transmission and hydraulic brakes.

The next commercial Maserati

appeared eight years later, this being a light forward-control 1-tonner with a 2-cyl 2-stroke water-cooled diesel engine developing 15.5hp. Front wheels were independently sprung.

MASON ROAD KING/USA 1922-1925/

The first Mason Road King truck was a 1-tonner with a 25.6hp 4-cyl Herschell-Spillman petrol engine, 3-speed transmission and double-reduction final-drive. It was introduced by the Durant Motor Co to supplement its Star range and after a few months was being assembled by the Mason Motor Truck Co, Flint, Michigan. In 1923 the model was up-rated to 1½ tons capacity and before production came to an end assembly was undertaken by the Road King Divn of the Flint Motor Co.

MASS/France 1912-1914

Sponsored by M Masser-Horniman, Automobiles Mass, Courbevoie, Seine, built an unusual forward-control front-wheel drive truck. This had a circular radiator, cone clutch, 4-speed transmission and chain final-drive, with either a 2.8- or 3.6-litre 4-cyl Brasier petrol engine mounted in a subframe forward of the front axle. Capacity varied from 3 to 6 tons.

MASTER/USA 1917-1929

Master Trucks Inc was founded in Chicago, Illinois, to build Buda-engined trucks from 1¼ to 6 tons capacity. Over the years the company was re-named the Master Motor Corp, the Master Motor Truck Mfg Co and finally the Master Motor Truck Co, while between 1921 and 1924 21- and 29-seat passenger models were also listed and from 1925 certain vehicles had Jackson petrol engines.

MASTER TRUCK/USA 1972 to date

Aimed at the refuse-collection market, the Master Truck was developed by the Engineered Fibreglass Co, Fountain Valley, California. It is a low cab-forward design of 4 x 2, 6 x 2 or 6 x 4 configuration, powered by Caterpillar,

Cummins, Detroit or Perkins diesel engines. Particular attention has been paid to sound insulation as this type of truck frequently operates at night and often in residential areas. Much fibreglass insulation is used around engine and exhaust, keeping external noise levels down. The company is now a division of Hallamore Inc.

MATFORD/France 1935-1946

SA Matford was founded at Poissy, Seine-et-Oise, following a Ford Motor Co takeover of the SA Mathis factories and almost immediately introduced the 3-ton Matford truck assembled from numerous Ford components. This was joined by a 5-ton forward-control model and wartime production went mainly to the German authorities. With a return to peace and the re-organization of Ford's European activities, former Matfords became French Fords.

MATHIAN/France 1903-1904

The Mathian was a load-carrying commercial with a 2-cyl petrol engine, double chain-drive and steel tyres.

MATHIS/France c1928-1936

SA Mathis, Strasbourg, added 1½/2½-ton trucks to its light commercial range, these having 4-cyl petrol engines. Later, even larger models, such as a 3-ton 6 x 4 with 6-cyl side-valve petrol engine and 4-speed transmission, were introduced. In 1935 the factory was acquired by the American-owned Ford Motor Co, the company re-named SA Française Matford and production moved to Poissy, Seine-et-Oise, after which models were sold as Matford.

MATTES/Germany 1932

The Mattes was a short-lived 3-wheeled tractor built by A Mattes & Co, Ulm. It was intended for hauling light trailers and had a single driven front wheel.

MAUDSLAY/England 1903-1960

Founded at Parkside, Coventry, in 1901, the Maudslay Motor Co

Ltd built its first commercial in 1903, based on the company's 20hp 3-cyl passenger car chassis. It was unusual for an early commercial in having overhead valves and an overhead camshaft – very advanced for the day. The first bus was a six-seater built on this chassis in 1904 but other commercials had 2- or 4-cyl engines. Shaft-drive was standard.

The first large fleet of Maudslays comprised a number of 40hp chain-drive buses delivered to the Great Western Railway Co, these being unusual in that railway-type brakes, with a handwheel acting upon the steel rear tyre rims, were fitted. In 1907 a chain-drive 3-tonner won a Gold Medal at the RAC Trials and an Army Diploma for engine accessibility. Maudslay passenger cars were selling far better than commercials and

Maudslay 7-ton truck c1924

production of the latter was virtually abandoned, apart from buses and charabancs, until 1912 when new 1½- and 3-ton types were announced. The smallest had a 17hp 4-cyl petrol engine and worm-drive, while the 3-tonner had a 32hp 4-cyl unit and was quickly joined by a 40hp "subsidy" model. During World War I examples of the latter were built by Maudslay and under licence by the Rover Co Ltd, while variations of the 32 and 40hp models continued until 1923 when a forward-control 7-tonner, powered by a 50hp petrol unit, and new 1½- and 2-ton models, both with 25hp petrol engines, were introduced.

Using AEC's 'NS'-Type chassis as a model, the company developed a dropframe passenger chassis in 1924, launching versions of this the following year. These were of bonneted and forward-control layout, all powered by 4-cyl petrol engines driving through a cone clutch and 4-speed box. Instead of concentrating on this range, the company attempted a 54-seat double-deck model and

transferred much of their interest to trucks which were some way behind their closest competitors.

In 1925 an 8-ton version of the forward-control 7-tonner was announced and in 1927 a 120bhp overhead-valve 6-cyl petrol engine became available in passenger models. Lighter goods models were phased out and heavier types introduced, such as a 40bhp 4-cyl 10-ton 6-wheeler in 1929. A 6-wheeled passenger model was also announced but found few customers.

Producing only fifty trucks a year by the 1930s, Maudslay's most popular model in this field was the 'Six-Four', introduced in 1933. A 6-tonner weighing less than 4 tons, it had a 4-cyl over-head-valve petrol engine but could have a 4LW Gardner diesel if required.

Later the following year the company introduced the ultra-modern SF40 passenger chassis with a front overhang permitting the use of a forward entrance. This was one of the earliest British single-deckers to fit forty seats within an 8.3-m maximum length.

From 1932 certain passenger models carried model names, such as 'Majestic', 'Masta', 'Meteor' and 'Montrose', and in 1937 this idea was extended into the goods range, the 'Six-Four' being up-rated to 7½tons and re-named the 'Mogul'. Joining it were the 6-wheeled 'Maharajah' and the 8-wheeled 'Mikado'. Meanwhile, the SF40 was also offered as a goods model, becoming specially popular as a brewer's dray. As World War II got underway, the company set up a factory at Alcester, Warwicks, where production was gradually transferred as the Coventry plant was damaged by enemy action. The 'Mogul' remained in production for essential civilian users and a militarized version, called the 'Militant', was developed.

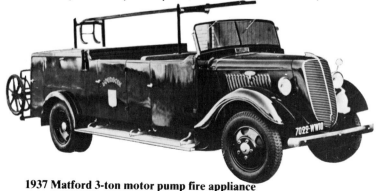

1937 Matford 3-ton motor pump fire appliance

1914 Maudslay 35hp charabanc

With a return to peace the 'Mikado' was re-named the 'Meritor', and the 'Maharanee' tractor, the twin-steer 6-wheeled 'Mustang' and the 'Marathon' coach were introduced. In 1948 the company combined with Crossley and AEC to form Associated Commercial Vehicles Ltd, that year's Maudslay range including four 4 x 2 rigids, one 4 x 2 tractor, two 6-wheelers, one 8-wheeler and a passenger model. The Gardner 4LW-engined 'Militant II' was the least powerful of the 4 x 2 rigids. Grossing 12 tons, it had a 5-speed transmission and overhead-worm rear axle. Tipper, Mk II and Mk III versions of the 'Mogul' were available. Gross vehicle weight, transmission and final-drive were as for the 'Militant II' but power came from a 7.7-litre AEC diesel engine.

The 'Maharanee' tractor was designed for 22 tons GCW and was mechanically similar to the 'Mogul'. One 6-wheeler was the twin-steer 'Mustang' for 16 tons GVW whilst the other was the 6 x 4 'Maharajah'. The 'Mustang' was really a long-wheelbase 'Mogul' with second steering axle, a choice of 7.7- or 9.6-litre AEC engines and 6-wheel vacuum-hydraulic braking. The 'Maharajah' was a 19 tons GVW machine similar to the 'Meritor' 8-wheeler, a 22 tons GVW vehicle of double-drive layout, powered by a 9.6-litre AEC diesel with 5-speed constant-mesh transmission and an overhead-worm rear bogie. The passenger model was the 'Marathon', intended for 32/39-seat bodies and with a choice between petrol and diesel engines. The petrol engine was a 6-cyl overhead-valve unit of Maudslay design, while the diesel was a 7.7-litre AEC.

Models competing with those of AEC manufacture were quickly

1947 Maudslay 'Marathon' single-deck coach

1956 Maudslay 'Mammoth Major 111' 6 x 2 truck

1949 Maudslay 'Mogul' boxvan

dropped and the company's factories switched to the manufacture of components. By 1951 all true Maudslays had been withdrawn and in 1953 the Coventry plant was closed, the company concentrating on axle production at the Castle Maudslay factory. Despite this, vehicles could still be bought with the Maudslay badge fitted up to 1960 but these were strictly Southall-built AECs in disguise. The very last Maudslay (which actually carried the AEC badge) was the 1100 'Dumptruk', 4.5cu m machine for off-road operations. By 1968 the company had become yet another subsidiary of the Brit-

ish Leyland Motor Corp Ltd, finally being sold to the American-owned Rockwell company in the mid 1970s.

MAUDSLAY & FIELD/*England 1833-1835*
At premises in South London, Messrs Maudslay & Field made considerable improvements to a Gurney steam carriage on behalf of steam bus proprietor Sir Charles Dance, building similar machines as Maudslay & Field. The prototype was used by Sir Charles to haul a 15-seat trailer on a regular service between London and Greenwich, but the steam bus boom was soon over and in 1840 the business moved to Parkside, Coventry, where tools and factory machinery were produced. It was not until 1903, as the Maudslay Motor Co Ltd, that the company re-entered the commercial vehicle field.

MAURER-UNION/*Germany 1902-1908*
In 1900 Ludwig Maurer developed a friction-drive system which was used in Maurer-Union commercials from 1902, and in Braun, Corona and Kaiser commercials. The first Maurer-Union was a 2-cyl van or truck. Later, a 4-cyl truck or bus with twin-disc drive was announced and in 1904 one of these was the first to be used for passengers and mail in Bavaria.

MAVAG/*Hungary 1924-1940*
The first Mavag trucks built by Magyar Allami Vas-Acel es Gepgyar, Budapest, were joined three years later by a passenger model and in 1928 the company introduced new 2½- and 3½-ton petrol-engined trucks under German Daimler licence, followed by 4½-ton petrol- and 6-ton diesel-engined models, also of Daimler design, in 1934. Meanwhile, the Hungarian fire appliance manufacturer Teudloff-Dittrich was acquired but World War II put a stop to further production.

Maudslay 'Mercury' truck c1960

MAXFER/*USA 1917-1919*

The Maxfer Truck & Tractor Co, Chicago, Illinois, originally built rear-end units for converting the Model 'T' Ford into a 1-tonner but later introduced the Maxfer 1-tonner. It was a bonneted model with a 31hp 4-cyl petrol engine, semi-floating worm-drive rear axle with Bailey non-stalling differential and electric lighting and starting.

MAXI/*USA 1940-1942*

Six Wheels Inc, Los Angeles, California, built one of the largest trucks of its day. Called the Maxi, it was a bonneted 6 x 4 with a drawbar pull of 14,514kg and maximum payload of 99,789kg. It was intended for heavy-duty on/off-highway work and had a 225bhp Waukesha-Hesselman engine, Fuller clutch and transmission and the company's own walking-beam bogie, incorporating a set of reduction gears and roller chains transmitting drive to all four wheels. Production ended two years later but the company was also responsible for fitting some of the larger Hug trucks with Maxi bogies.

MAXIM/*USA 1914 to date*

The first Maxim was a light assembled truck built by the Maxim Motor Co, Middelboro, Massachusetts. Soon, the company turned to fire appliances, the first being based on a 2-ton Thomas chassis. In 1916 the first Maxim-chassised model appeared, using a triple-ignition 6-cyl petrol engine and worm final-drive. A complete range of motor pumpers, combinations and hook-and-ladder trucks was available by 1918, continuing with little change throughout the 1920s and 1930s.

One special model was a 6 x 4 pumper/tanker built for Falmouth, Massachusetts, in 1938, the same year that the company attempted to re-enter the commercial truck market using a 2-ton Ford chassis with a strengthened chassis frame, heavy-duty Timken axles and oversize tyres to carry loads of between 3 and 5 tons.

New bonneted pumpers, ladder trucks and quad combinations were announced in 1946, and in 1952 a licence agreement was signed with the manufacturer of the German Magirus rear-mounted turntable ladder, enabling this to be offered on Maxim and other chassis, both in rigid and articulated form. Four years later the business became a division of the Seagrave Corp but it continued to operate independently.

Maxim's first cab-forward model was the 'F'-Series, announced in 1959, but bonneted types were still listed, and a short-wheelbase "conventional", known as the 'S'-Series, appeared in 1960 and is still available. Engines currently employed include Waukesha petrol and Cummins or Detroit diesels, while transmissions are mainly Spicer synchromesh or Allison automatic.

MAXWELL/*USA 1917-1923*

Jonathan Maxwell formed the Maxwell Motor Corp in Detroit, Michigan. In 1917 a bonneted 1-tonner was developed, using a 21hp 4-cyl petrol engine. In 1920 it was up-rated to 1½ tons capacity and became popular as a truck, fire appliance or bus.

MAXWERKE/*Germany 1900-1901*

Built by Maxwerke Elektrizitats und Automobil Gesellschaft Harff und Schwarz AG, Cologne, the Maxwerke was a battery-electric model with each rear wheel driven by its own traction motor. Van and bus bodies were made.

MAYOR/*Switzerland 1960-1966*

The first Mayor commercial was

1960 MAZ-500 7-ton truck crane

1961 MAZ-530 40-ton 6 x 4 dump truck

1922 Maxwell 1½-ton charabanc

1972 MAZ-516 10-ton 6 x 4 truck

1970 Mazda E3800 truck

the 'Monotrac' with rear-wheel drive and a 12bhp twin-cyl MAG engine. Built by Arnold Mayor Constructions Mécaniques, Bramois, it was of forward-control layout with engine and transmission under the floor. The heavier 'Chassis-Trac' had 4-wheel drive and a 34bhp 4-cyl Volkswagen petrol or Mercedes diesel engine, while a 1½-tonner with Ford 'Transit' front-end had six cross-country speeds, three road speeds, hydraulic brakes and a three-way tipping body.

The 'Chassis-Trac MB2' was the last Mayor. This was a 4-wheel drive, 4-wheel steer multi-purpose utility model which could turn on the spot and had an automatic differential lock.

MAZ/*Soviet Union 1947 to date*
Minskevska Automobilova Zavod was set up in Minsk to assemble various petrol- and diesel-engined trucks, including 4-wheeled rigids and tractors and a 6-wheeler. The first was the MAZ-200, a 7-tonner with an output of 110bhp, followed by a tractor version and by the MAZ-205, a 6-ton dump truck. All were bonneted types, but since 1965 production has centred upon a forward-control model known as the '500'-Series.

The first was the 9-ton MAZ-500A with 200bhp V6 diesel engine, 5-speed transmission, power steering and sleeper cab. The MAZ-503A is a 9-ton dump truck, while the MAZ-504A and 504B are both tractors, the latter having a 265bhp 8-cyl diesel engine. A further derivative is the MAZ-509 for timber haulage. Two 8 x 8 models appeared during the 1970s, the first being the 10-ton capacity MAZ-537, a tractor with dolly for handling long loads, and the second the 15-ton payload military and civilian MAZ-543 with twin half-cabs and space between for crane jib, water cannon or even rockets. This has a 525bhp V12 tank engine. MAZ products are sometimes exported as Belaz.

MAZDA/*Japan c1961 to date*
While the Toyo Kogyo Co Ltd, Hiroshima, had commenced commercial production in 1931 with a

made but this is still a prototype.

McBRIGHT/*USA 1953-1955*
Designed by McBright Inc, Lehighton, Pennsylvania, the McBright truck was unusual in that its White engine, radiator and transmission were all located behind the rear wheels and below floor level. Four-, 6- and 8-wheeled rigid prototypes were built but series production never got underway.

MCI 'Courier' 95 single-deck coach c1959

series of 3-wheeled Mazdas, it was not until the early 1960s that models of any size were built, the largest being a 2-ton 3-wheeler. The ultimate in this configuration was the T2000, announced in 1965, with an 81bhp 4-cyl diesel engine producing 104km/h.

Later that year work started on a series of forward-control petrol- and diesel-engined trucks in the 2/3-ton bracket. These were also available as midi-coaches, with hydraulic or hydrovac brakes, power units comprising an 86bhp 2-litre petrol engine and a 2.5-litre Perkins diesel. By 1969 the largest model was the 4-ton E3800 using a 6-cyl diesel engine but by 1978 the range had been slimmed down to include 2/3½-tonners at the heaviest end and also the 26-seat 'Parkway' bus.

MBB/*West Germany 1970 to date*
Developed from an experimental battery-electric passenger car, the MBB appeared as a 1-ton minibus. Built by Messerschmitt-Bolkow-Blohm GmbH, Ottobrunn, it had a sandwich-construction self-supporting plastic chassis and an operational range per charge of between 60 and 100km. Although it never attained series production, some were used at the 1972 Munich Olympic Games. More recently, an experimental petrol-engined amphibian has been

With a return to peace, these models were re-introduced but production ceased in 1921 and was not revived until 1925 when, as McCurd Motors Ltd, operations were re-established at Slough, Berks. A new 2/2½-tonner went straight into production, using a 25bhp 4-cyl monobloc engine, 4-speed transmission and overhead-worm drive. Few were sold and a low-frame passenger chassis for 26/30-seat bodies announced in 1927 was abandoned.

MCI/*Canada 1942 to date*
The Fort Garry Motor Body Co, Winnipeg, Manitoba, became Motor Coach Industries during World War II, all Fort Garry models being re-named MCI. The rear-engined Courier arrived in 1946 and four years later the company's biggest customer, Greyhound, took it over, setting up Greyhound Lines of Canada to run the business.

There were no significant changes until 1959, when the MC-1 Challenger introduced slanted windows to the range and in 1963 a plant was established at Pembina, North Dakota, to handle US requirements, finishing Canadian-built shells for US and overseas clients. Current at that time

1969 MCI MC-7 6 x 2 high-floor single-deck coach

McCORMICK-DEERING/*USA ?-c1928*
Although the McCormick-Deering name is better associated with agricultural equipment, many of the McCormick-Deering Co's early tractors, built at Rock Island, Illinois, were constructed for road haulage use. Later, they were sold as International.

McCURD/*England 1912-1921, 1925-1927*
W A McCurd announced a bonneted 3½-ton truck chassis, with a 42hp 4-cyl petrol engine, 4-speed transmission and worm-drive. Two- and 5-tonners were built up to World War I, by which time the business had become the McCurd Lorry Mfg Co Ltd, Hayes, Middx.

was the 39-passenger MC-5 with Detroit Diesel 8V-71 engine and Spicer transmission but in 1968 this was joined by the high-floor 6-wheeled 47-passenger MC-7, the MC-6 being an experimental over-width model, again for Greyhound, powered by a 12-cyl Detroit Diesel engine.

In 1973, the MC-8 appeared, while the MC-9, generally similar to its predecessors, remains current. Unfortunately, labour problems in the Winnipeg plant led to the organization of a new Greyhound bus assembly facility at Rosewell, New Mexico, in 1975.

McINTYRE/*USA 1909-1914*
Initially, the W H McIntyre Co, Auburn, Indiana, advertised a

1940 McLaren diesel drawbar tractor

series of eight trucks. These were chain-drive high-wheelers powered by a 2-cyl petrol engine. For 1910, the front axle was set back under the dashboard and a 24hp water-cooled petrol engine employed in conjunction with a 2-speed transmission. By 1913 the range had received front wings and cab and the front axle was now under the engine.

McLAREN/*England 1940*
J & H McLaren Ltd, Leeds, West Yorks, designed and constructed steam traction engines, rollers and agricultural machinery. Later, a unique heavy diesel tractor was built to the order of Pickfords Ltd, using traction engine type driving wheels at the rear and normal pneumatics at the front. Power came from a 125hp 5-cyl McLaren-Ricardo 5MR diesel engine located amidships. Of forward-control layout, it weighed 17 tons in full working order and could handle loads of up to 109 tons.

M & D/*England 1925-1927*
The Rhode Motor Co Ltd, Tyseley, Birmingham, added the M & D or Mead & Deakin 1½-ton lorry to its light commercials range. This had an enlarged Rhode engine of 2.41-litre capacity. Of 4-cyl overhead-cam layout, it had an output of 15.9hp. Other features included electric lighting and starting, 4-wheel brakes and overhead-worm final-drive. Only six were built.

M & E/*USA 1913-1915*
Having previously built Club Car commercials, the Merchant & Evans Co, Philadelphia, Pennsylvania, built the M & E or Merchant. Models listed for 1915 were of 3½- and 5-ton capacity.

MEBEA/*Greece 1970-c1978*
Mebea SA, Athens, built the Reliant TW9 1-ton 3-wheeler under

licence, marketing it as the Mebea. It is believed that when British production of the TW9 passed to BTB Engineering Ltd, the Mebea was discontinued.

MEILI/*Switzerland 1958 to date*
E Meili Traktoren und Greiferderfabrik, Schaffhausen, introduced the unconventional 'Flex-Trac' 6 x 6 for negotiating water or swamp up to 75cm deep. Various prototypes were constructed with Ford V8 and Willys 4-cyl petrol engines or MWM 4- and Ford 6-cyl diesels. Payloads varied between 1½ and 3 tons but although licence agreements were signed with manufacturers in Great Britain, Germany and the United States, series production did not begin.

The similar 'Metrac' was exhibited at the 1959 Geneva Show. This was also a 6-wheeler, with a universal coupling between the 4-wheel drive forward section and 2-wheel drive load-carrying section. Both were controlled hydraulically in a vertical plane so that the vehicle could negotiate virtually any obstacle.

Later, the company launched the 'Agromobil' multi-purpose light truck fitted originally with a 700cc flat-twin BMW petrol engine and with rear-wheel drive. This was quickly replaced by a 4 x 4 version with 4-cyl Volkswagen or MWM air-cooled diesel and a payload of up to 2 tons. These were for agricultural use, while an underfloor-engined 6-wheeled industrial artic – the 'Multimobil' – could handle payloads of up to 3½ tons.

In 1964 the company was reconstituted as Meili Fahrzeugbau AG, by which time one of the lightest models was the MA-1500 powered by a 45bhp Perkins diesel engine. By the end of the 1970s three basic types were listed, comprising the 2-ton MA-2000, 3-ton

MERCEDES-BENZ/*Germany/*
West Germany 1926 to date
The merger of Benz & Cie Rheinische Automobil- und Motorenfabrik AG and Daimler Motoren Gesellschaft brought about the introduction of Mercedes-Benz commercials, frequently using pre-combustion chamber Benz diesel engines. The first new model was a 1½-tonner announced in 1927, with a 6-cyl petrol engine, plate clutch and 3-speed transmission as one unit, ¾-floating spiral-bevel rear axle and footbrake acting on all four wheels. The first diesel-powered truck was a bonneted 5-tonner of 1928, using a 75bhp 8.5-litre 6-cyl engine employing many aluminium components and Bosch fuel-injection. By 1931 similar vehicles were being sold in Britain under the Diesel brand name.

Also in 1931 a new model designation system was adopted, using the letter 'L' for "lastwagen" and 'LO' for "omnibus". Numbers after these designated the vehicle's payload in kilograms. Thus, there were the L1000, L2000 and L3000, also known as the 'Miracle', plus the LO2500, LO3000,

LO4000, LO5000 and 6-wheeled LO8500. Petrol engines were still available in certain models and the company's first trolleybuses were built, but by 1935 only diesel engines were fitted.

New models introduced about 1936 included the L1500, LO2600 and L3000 with 4-cyl engines of 2.6- and 4.8-litre capacity; and the L3750, L4500, L5000, L6500, L10000 and LO10000 with various sizes of 6-cyl unit, the LO10000 being for double-deck operation. Another interesting development was the construction of various forward-control passenger models in association with specialist coachbuilders. Much of this range continued until World War II, with the addition of the L3000A and L4500A 4 x 4 models, a 1937 half-track for civilian applications and two military types – a 4 x 4 with 4-wheel steering and the LG3000 6 x 4 rigid. During the war the company also built the L701 3-tonner which was, in fact, an Opel built under licence. This, and the L4500, continued after the war, joined in 1949 by the L3250 and in 1950 by the L6600,

1971 Mercedes-Benz 0.302

1974 Mercedes-Benz '2232'-Series 6 x 2 tanker

also offered in forward-control rear-engined form as the 06600H passenger model. A trolleybus version was also listed.

New model designations appeared about this time. The letter 'L' was now carried by all bonneted models and 'LP' by forward-control vehicles. An 'A' suffix indicated all-wheel drive and an 'S' an artic tractor. Passenger models carried the 'O' prefix and, if rear-engined, an 'H' suffix, while all types included a three-number

concentrated at Gaggenau, while Mannheim coped with the lighter types and the 1¾-tonner was built in the former Auto Union factory at Düsseldorf. By 1963 much of the production was concentrated in a new plant at Worth.

In 1963 type designations changed again. New models included the 6-wheeled 2220 and the 9½-ton payload 1620 with 10.8-litre 6-cyl underfloor diesel engine. A new line of diesel engines was now appearing, abandoning the

company's old pre-combustion chamber principle in favour of the injection type. In 1965 the 0321 passenger model was replaced by the 0302 and by 1968 a new lightweight range, comprising the L406, L408, L508 and L606, from 1½ to 2¾ tons capacity, was available along with the 0305 standard city bus. In 1969 new tiltcab "heavies" were introduced, powered by an equally new 320bhp 16-litre V10 diesel engine.

A year later Hanomag-Henschel Fahrzeugwerke GmbH was acquired, although its products continued for a while as Hanomag-Henschel, albeit frequently with Mercedes-Benz engines, and by the early 1970s the lighter Hanomag-Henschels had appeared in the Mercedes-Benz line-up. Euclid Inc was acquired in 1977,

taking the company into the a new field, heavy off-highway dump truck

Models now cover all sizes from 1 to 100 tons gross with 4 x 2, 4 x 4, 6 x 4 and 6 x 6 drive. On the passenger side, the 0305 continues along with the 0307 touring coach, while the 0317 is an articulated bus with underfloor diesel engine, the chassis of which is assembled by Steyr-Daimler-Puch AG. Other more experimental types include the petrol-electric 'Hybrid-Bus' and a hybrid battery-electric trolleybus called the 'Duo-Bus'.

Commercial production is still concentrated at Worth, although passenger types are now built at Mannheim and the Unimog all-wheel drive series at Gaggenau. Mercedes-Benz vehicles are also assembled throughout the world.

Mercedes-Benz 'LAS'-Series 4 x 4 artic tractor c1954

1966 Mercedes-Benz LPS1418 artic tractor

1979 Mercedes-Benz '1719'-Series 4 x 4 tipper

designation representing the engine fitted. Thus, the company's first chassisless rear-engined passenger model was the 0321H and in 1956 a new 1¾-ton truck, with 1.8-litre 4-cyl petrol or diesel engine, was the L319, also offered in 10/18-seat passenger form as the 0319.

Further new type designations appeared in 1961 when semi forward-control trucks received the 'L' suffix and a re-styled bonneted design, used mainly as an artic tractor, appears to have had no suffix at all. Forward-control models continued as 'LP'. One new model was the LP333, a twin-steer 6-wheeled rigid with 10.8-litre 6-cyl diesel engine and a payload capacity of between 8 and 10 tons. Heavy truck production was

1978 Mercedes-Benz '2624'-Series 6 x 4 wrecker

1960 Meili 'Flex-Trac' 6 x 6 truck

1979 Meili MA-4000 4-ton tipper

MA-3000 and 4-ton MA-4000. All had MWM or Perkins diesel engines from 47 to 75bhp, the heaviest having servo-assisted brakes as standard and power assisted steering as an option. The 'Multimobil' is now made in Italy as the Sirmac.

MEILONG/*Taiwan ? to date*
The Meilong is a light truck. One early model was a 3-wheeler with a Perkins 4.99 diesel engine located beneath a locally-built cab incorporating a modified Ford Thames 'Trader' sheet-metal front-end.

MEISELBACH/*USA 1904-1909*
Various types of Meiselbach highwheeler were built by the AD Meiselbach Motor Wagon Co, North Milwaukee, Wisconsin. The original model was a 1-tonner with an opposed-piston horizontal twin-cyl water-cooled petrol engine, friction transmission and chain-drive, but for 1906 double-disc friction-drive was introduced and by 1908 the range comprised 1-, 2- and 3-tonners.

MENARD/*Canada 1910-1919*
The Menard Motor Truck Co, Windsor, Ontario, built trucks with capacities of between 1 and

3½ tons in 1910, the 1½-tonner having a 6-cyl Beaver petrol engine and worm-drive. By the end of production fire appliances were also built, manufacturing rights passing to the Mapleleaf Mfg Co Ltd, who introduced the Mapleleaf range.

MENDIP/*England 1907-1908, 1912-c1913*
C W Harris designed a series of "undertype" steam wagons, building the first in his workshop at Chewton Mendip, Somerset. Called the Mendip, it was a 2- or 3-tonner with top-fired vertical water-tube boiler and a compound horizontal engine with Stevenson's link motion. One example was exhibited at the Bath & West Show but proved unpopular with the judges.

Following a gap of four years, the Mendip was revived by the Mendip Engineering Co which now ran the factory. The new model was a 1½-ton delivery van with a 16hp 4-cyl Aster petrol engine, a 4-speed gearbox and chain and "live" axle final-drive. The business was sold to W H Bateman Hope, MP, JP, and re-constituted as the Mendip Motor & Engineering Co Ltd, moving to Southmead, Bristol, but no documentary evidence of further commercials can be found.

MENOMINEE/*USA c1917-1937*
The Menominee Motor Truck Co, Clintonville, Wisconsin, offered trucks with capacities of up to 3½ tons by 1917, using Wisconsin petrol engines as standard, other components including Cotta or Detlaff transmissions and Columbia, Shuler or Timken axles.

The 1923 range covered models from 1 to 6 tons capacity plus two passenger types for 16/20 and 25 passengers. A 1-tonner was marketed as the 'Hurryton', but in 1928 the Four Wheel Drive Auto Co acquired the business and re-

named it the Utility Supply Co. Menominee production continued and by 1932 included trucks from 1½ to 8 tons capacity and three bus chassis, the largest being suitable for 35-seat bodies. Waukesha engines were introduced one year later.

MERAY/*Hungary c1928-1935*
Meray Motorkerekpargyar RT, Budapest, was a motorcycle manufacturer which also built a forward-control 4-wheeler of about 1-ton capacity, with an underfloor 3-cyl radial engine mounted at the rear.

MERCEDES-ELECTRIQUE/*Austria 1906-1908*
Emile Jellinek, who had developed Mercedes passenger cars, joined Oesterreichische Daimler-Motoren-Gesellschaft GmbH, Wiener-Neustadt, in 1906, replacing Chief Engineer Paul Daimler by Ferdinand Porsche and introducing Porsche's range of battery- and petrol-electric commercials which were sold as Mercedes-Electrique and Mercedes-Mixte.

The battery-electrics were still being sold as Lohner-Porsche by Jacob Lohner & Co, Vienna, so to avoid accusations of similarity, the Mercedes-Electrique range used traction motors in the rear wheels.

MERCEDES-ELECTRIQUE-STOLL/*Austria 1906-1913*
Oesterreichische Daimler-Motoren-Gesellschaft GmbH, Wiener-Neustadt, also built Lohner-Stoll based trolleybuses as Mercedes-Electrique-Stoll. These were near identical to Lohner-Stoll designs, incorporating a current collection system originally developed by Ludwig Stoll at Wiener-Neustadt.

MERK-PULLAX/*Switzerland 1958-1971*
The first Merk-Pullax built by Hans Merk Maschinenfabrik, Dietikon, Zürich, was a multipurpose 4 x 4 vehicle offered as

1903 Merryweather chemical escape fire appliance

the P20 2-tonner and P40 3-tonner, both with single-tube backbone chassis.

Prototypes had 4-cyl petrol engines, although the later P20 had a 20bhp 1.15-litre 4-stroke 'V'-twin diesel engine, and the P40 a 40bhp 2.29-litre V4 diesel, both supplied by Warchalowski, Vienna. The lighter model had a 6 forward and 2 reverse transmission with differential locks on both axles, but the P40 used a 4-speed main box and 2-speed auxiliary.

Both were available with an automatic winch which could be synchronized with the vehicle's traction to enable it to climb a 45° gradient with 1- or 2-ton loads.

1952 Merryweather 'Marquis' motor pump fire appliance

MERRYWEATHER/*England*
1899-c1939 & c1948-c1968

Specializing in fire-fighting equipment, Merryweather & Sons Ltd, London SE10, called its first self-propelled appliance the Merryweather 'Motor Fire King' but it was frequently marketed simply as the Fire King. It was powered by a rear-mounted coal- or oil-fired vertical water-tube boiler driving a 2-cyl vertical engine and a few other commercial steamers such as trucks and cesspool emptiers were also built up to 1910, although these had front-mounted boilers.

The company's first petrol-engined appliance appeared in 1903, this being a chemical unit powered by a 24/30hp 4-cyl engine and using numerous Aster compo-

nents, while again up to 1910 some petrol-engined trucks were also built. Meantime, 1904 saw the first petrol-engined Merryweather motor pump and a battery-electric chemical unit, with two hub-mounted traction motors, was also listed briefly.

The first centrifugal pump appliance was introduced by Merryweather in 1906 and in 1908 a turntable ladder was built, Aster components still being employed. The 1920s and 1930s saw increasing use of Albion chassis and components, although finished vehicles still carried the Merryweather name. One particular model of the late 1920s was a bonneted design powered by a 75bhp 6-cyl petrol engine with 3-plate clutch and 4-speed transmission. It was the

first Merryweather to employ shaft- rather than chain-drive and part of its standard equipment was a 3-cyl rear-mounted pump, driven by shaft and chain from the gearbox, capable of throwing a 45-m vertical jet.

Other proprietary chassis, such as Austin and Leyland, were used during World War II, retaining their original identities, but with a return to peace the dropframe AEC 'Regent' passenger chassis was adopted and sold in various forms as the Merryweather 'Marquis'. AEC chassis continued to be used right up to about 1968 with identification simplified by the used of a Merryweather triangular motif in place of the famous AEC logo on the front of each vehicle. Since then only proprietary chassis have been used, still carrying the original manufacturer's name.

MESERVE/*USA 1901-1903*
Based at Canobie Lake, New Hampshire, W F Meserve constructed steam lorries, using wooden frames and a boiler and vertical 2-cyl engine supplied by Edward Clark, Dorchester, Massachusetts. The Meserve had a capacity of 2 tons and double chain-drive. Later, the business moved to Methuen, Massachusetts, where it became known as the

Meserve Auto Truck Co, building a few petrol-engined trucks.

MESSENGER/*USA 1913-1914*
Although railroad cars were the speciality of the Messenger Mfg Co, Tatamy, Pennsylvania, an experimental 2-ton truck was also built, powered by a 30hp 4-cyl petrol engine.

METRO/*USA 1926-1927*
The Metropolitan Coach & Cab Corp, New York, built taxicabs and larger capacity passenger vehicles as Metros or Metropolitans. These included an unusual 4-axle bus chassis.

METROBUS/*England 1977 to date*
Metro-Cammell-Weymann Ltd, Birmingham, began experimenting with Gardner and Rolls-Royce engines while still offering the Metro-Scania passenger range. This led to the termination of the company's agreement with Scania Bussar AB and the announcement of the Metrobus double-decker. Specification comprised a transverse rear-mounted Gardner or Rolls-Royce diesel engine, a Rockwell-Thompson semi-frame and Voith self-changing gears or GKN-SRM automatic transmissions. A giant 6-wheeled double-decker was developed for use in

1922 Merryweather turntable-ladder fire appliance

1961 Merryweather turntable-ladder fire appliance

1967 Merryweather 'Marquis' pump escape fire appliance

1978 Metrobus double-deck bus

Hong Kong in 1981.

METRO-SCANIA/*England 1970-1977*
The Metro-Scania 'Metropolitan' was a chassisless single- or double-decker constructed by Metro-Cammell-Weymann Ltd, Birmingham, using a rear-mounted 11.1-litre 6-cyl Scania diesel engine and running units and a fully-automatic electro-hydraulic transmission. It was listed as a 63-passenger single-decker or as a single- or dual-door double-decker with respective capacities of 75 and 74 persons.

Few were single-deckers, and experiments with alternative designs led to the termination of the agreement with Scania Bussar AB and the introduction of the Metrobus double-decker.

METROVICK/*England 1934-1942*
The Metropolitan-Vickers Electrical Co Ltd, Trafford Park, Manchester, offered a four-model range of Metrovick battery-electrics, each with a single traction motor driving the rear axle via a short propeller shaft, and worm- or spiral-bevel axles. Heaviest in the range were an 18/22cwt version with a 191-cm wheelbase, and a 3-tonner with 336amp/hr batteries and a 330-cm wheelbase, but the latter was withdrawn in 1938.

METZ/*USA 1916-1917*
The Metz Co, Waltham, Massachusetts, built a 1-ton bonneted truck with a 4-cyl petrol engine, shaft-drive and pneumatic tyres.

MFO GYROBUS/*Switzerland 1950-c1960*
Possibly the most unusual bus ever built was the MFO Gyrobus, developed by Maschinenfabrik Oerlikon, Oerlikon, Zürich, using the gyroscope principle to generate electric power for its traction motors. The prototype could carry 70 passengers but in the centre of the chassis was a horizontal gy-

1974 Metro-Scania BR11DH double-deck bus

ro weighing some 1496kg. To start the gyro an electric charge was taken from overhead poles spaced at suitable intervals along the route, this being passed to a traction motor which launched the gyro at 3000rpm. This stored enough energy to send the bus approximately 6km in flat country, power being transmitted from the gyro to a 100hp traction motor connected to the back axle. The experiment was quite successful.

MGT/*France 1950-1954*
Million-Guiet-Tubauto SA, Argenteuil, Seine-et-Oise, built chassisless MGT single-deck trolleybuses, with body and running units the same as for a petrol-engined model marketed as the Tubauto.

MIAG/*Germany/West Germany 1936-1945, 1949-1955*
Muhlenbau und Industrie AG, Braunschweig, originally built the Miag road tractor using a rear-mounted 10 or 20bhp diesel engine. Following a four year break Miag battery-electric municipals and a Volkswagen-engined load-carrier, both built by the company's successor, Miag-Fahrzeugbau GmbH, Ober-Romstadt, were introduced and a new road tractor, the ID20, announced. With a gross train weight of 12,000kg, this was powered initially by a vertical twin-cyl Benz diesel driving through a ZF box but by 1955, a 3-cyl MWM diesel was fitted.

MICM/*Rumania 1964-1966*
MICM Uzina Maconica, Muscel, Cimpalung, constructed a simple

2-seat utility version of the UAZ 4 x 4. The same 70bhp 4-cyl engine was used but a 2-speed auxiliary gearbox was not fitted. The MICM had a canvas top and was later sold as the ARO.

MIDLAND ELECTRIC/*England c1935-c1958*
Midland Vehicles Ltd, Leamington Spa, Warwicks, marketed Midland Electric forward-control battery-electrics with traction motors behind the driver and shaft-drive to the rear wheels. As well as lighter types, there were the 1¼-ton B25 and 1½-ton B30, either of which could be had in chassis, truck or van form. Of these, only the 1¼-tonner was listed during World War II, but with a return to peace a 5-model range appeared, the heaviest being 1½-tonners.

MIESSE/*Belgium c1904-1972*
Established in 1894, Jules Miesse

et Cie, Brussels, built a number of light delivery models before the introduction of a 1½-ton steamer, using a front-mounted semi-flash vertical paraffin-fired boiler and 3-cyl single-acting engine with mushroom inlet and exhaust valves.

Steam vehicle production came to an end in 1907. Light petrol-engined models and heavier types did not arrive until the mid-1920s when a series of models from 1 to 5 tons capacity was listed. These included both trucks and buses, all with 4-cyl petrol engines, but were joined in 1926 by a new bonneted passenger model using the company's own 100bhp 5.2-litre straight-8 petrol engine with magneto ignition which had double-reduction drive and a 3-speed transmission.

In 1927 a rigid 6-wheeler, again with the straight-8 engine but also featuring a 4-speed transmission, cross-braced chassis frame, 6-wheel servo brakes and worm-drive, was added to the range and developed into a forward-control goods model. Special producer-gas trucks were also produced and by 1929 a straight-8 5-tonner was offered on the home market.

A most unusual machine was the 1930 6 x 4 forward-control 'Double Bus' for up to 100 passengers. It was designed to use either petrol or electric propulsion, current for the latter coming from batteries or overhead lines. Petrol-engined versions were intended to have two 4- or 6-cyl units, each driving one rear axle and mounted transversely across the chassis frame, but in practice only the 4-cyl was tried.

In 1931 2-stroke Junkers opposed-piston diesel engines were fitted in the company's 3- and 5-ton trucks. A licence to build Gardner diesel engines was obtained in 1932, and by 1934 these had become standard. By 1939 4-, 5- and 6-cyl licence-built Gardners were used throughout the range

1939 Midland Electric B.25 1¼-ton battery-electric integral van

which included light forward-control trucks up to a rare rigid 8-wheeler with roof-mounted radiator. Under German occupation, wartime production centred upon vehicles constructed for or converted to producer-gas. With peace, many of the lighter models vanished, and the range encompassed vehicles from 5 to 18 tons capacity, some using an 8-cyl licence-built Gardner.

From 1948 the company assembled Mack and Nash trucks for the European market and in 1949 a forward-control 6-cyl engined passenger chassis with preselect transmission was announced. This was followed by a 6-speed underfloor-engined model in 1951; by 1955 this had been replaced by a vertical front-engined design.

Association with Ets Brossel Frères and FN resulted in a series of military trucks in the mid-1950s, but by 1960 standard goods models comprised 10/13-ton 4 x 2s and a twin-steer 6-wheeler, using the new 10.4-litre Gardner 6LX diesel. The 8-cyl Gardner re-appeared in a heavy tractor, and vehicles also began to be marketed as Automiesse. A 210bhp 11.4-litre Büssing diesel engine was used in some goods models, but passenger types were still Gardner-powered, some with front vertical engines and others with horizontal underfloor units.

By the late 1960s production had dropped although a new rear-engined passenger model, with 5.2-litre V6 diesel engine and 6-speed Allison automatic transmission was introduced, as were redesigned forward-control trucks and tractors for up to 18 tons GVW and 38 tons GCW.

MILDE/France 1896-1909
The first battery-electric Mildé commercial was a 1-ton van based on a Panhard passenger car chassis by C H Mildé et Cie, Levallois-Perret, Seine. This was followed by a 1¼/1½-tonner. An electric-powered fore-carriage was developed in 1900 to convert horse-drawn vehicles to self-propulsion and the forward-control battery-electric series was expanded. The fore-carriages were discontinued by 1902, and in 1903 forward-control petrol-electrics were listed, the 1-tonner having a 10hp Mildé engine. After 1904 most Mildés had shaft-drive. Certain Mildé patents are understood to have been used in the later Mildé-Kreiger.

MILDE-KREIGER/France 1946-1947
A front-wheel drive 1/1¼-ton forward-control battery-electric van called the Mildé-Kreiger was exhibited at the 1946 Paris Salon by Le Conducteur Electrique Blinde Incombustible SA, Courbevoie, Seine. It is believed to have used both Mildé and Kreiger patents although it was based on the Peugeot-built Chenard-Walcker D3A model.

MILITOR/USA 1917-1918
Both the Militor Corp, Jersey City, New Jersey, and the Sinclair Motor Corp, New York, were responsible for the production of 150 Militor trucks and tractors to designs by the US Army. The Militor was a bonneted 4-wheel drive machine of about 3 tons capacity, powered by a 36bhp 4-cyl Wisconsin petrol engine under a "coal-scuttle" bonnet with radiator between engine and driver. It had 4-speed transmission.

MILLER/USA 1907-1908
The Miller Garage Co Inc, Bridgeport, Connecticut, advertised both goods and passenger models, the most popular of the latter being sightseeing buses. These had a 40/45hp 4-cyl Continental petrol engine, 3-speed transmission, chain-drive and a claimed maximum speed of 32 km/h.

MILLER METEOR/USA 1949
The Miller Meteor was a passenger model constructed on a Hercules-engined Biederman chassis by the Fort Pitt Commerce Corp, Washington, DC.

MILLOT/Switzerland 1904-1906
The Millot bus was ahead of its time, having full weather protection for both driver and passengers. Designed by Eugen Kaufman of Zürich, it was a normal-control vehicle with honeycomb radiator and chain final-drive.

MILNES/England 1901-1902
The first Milnes commercial was a 2-ton lorry, powered by an 8hp 'V'-twin Daimler engine, exhibited by G F Milnes & Co Ltd, Wellington, Salop, at the Automobile Club Show, Islington, in 1901 and which, it transpired, was really a German-built Marienfelde.

It had Simms-Bosch magneto ignition, a "coal-scuttle" bonnet, front-mounted honeycomb radiator and four forward speeds with gear-changing effected by two levers. Drive was transmitted to a chassis-mounted differential via a cardan shaft, with all-gear drive to the rear wheels, making this one of the noisiest commercials ever built! Braking comprised a double-block loco-type system on the 1st gear drive shaft, two screw-down brakes on the rear wheels and a sprag acting on the back axle.

One month later, an agreement was signed between Milnes and the German manufacturer whereby the British company was to be sole agent in the British Empire for ten years. A showroom was opened off London's Oxford Street, managed by Henry George Burford who was later to make his name importing the American Fremont-Mais and ultimately building Burford trucks, and consulting engineers responsible for the specification of the Milnes lorry were F R Simms & Co.

That June, two Milnes lorries were the first petrol-engined vehicles to take part in the Liverpool Heavy Vehicle Trials, receiving a Gold Medal, and later that year they were also the only petrol-engined machines in the War Dept trials at Aldershot. In October a Milnes lorry became the first petrol-engined vehicle in Britain to carry the Royal Mail.

By 1902 a 16hp 4-cyl model with a capacity of 2½ tons had ap-peared and 1½- and 1¾-tonners with 2-cyl engines were also built. One of these became the first passenger-bodied Milnes when it received a 16-seat single-deck tramcar-style body.

Towards the end of 1902 Motorfahrzeug und Motorenfabrik AG, Marienfelde, the company that supplied Milnes with its chassis, was taken over by Daimler-Motoren-Gesellschaft, Cannstatt. This invalidated the Milnes agreement and a new arrangement was finalized whereby the German factory would supply chassis only to a new company called Milnes-Daimler Ltd, these vehicles being sold as Milnes-Daimler.

MILNES-DAIMLER/England 1902-1916
With the merging of Motorfahrzeug und Motorenfabrik AG and Daimler-Motoren-Gesellschaft GmbH, Milnes commercials became Milnes-Daimlers, offered throughout Britain by Milnes-

Milnes-Daimler open-top double-deck bus c1903

Milnes-Daimler open-top double-deck bus c1909

Daimler Ltd, Wellington, Salop. Among the first were five 16hp 22-seaters for the Great Western Railway with Milnes-Daimler bodies but the closure of the firm's bodybuilding plant led to the supply of chassis only.

By 1904 the first Milnes-Daimlers had appeared in London with the London Road Car Co, followed by others with Thomas Tilling and Birch Bros. Later, the London Motor Omnibus Co acquired priority on Milnes-Daimler output, delaying deliveries to its competitors. Most of these vehicles were open-top 34-seaters with 24hp petrol engines.

The 1905 range included a 9hp 2-cyl 2-ton goods model and a 4-tonner powered by an 18hp 4-cyl petrol engine. Both had single-piece "coal-scuttle" bonnets that lifted off for maintenance and a single transmission brake was fitted. By 1908 shaft-drive was standard and goods models from 2 to 5 tons capacity were listed, while the 1913 range included a 20hp 1-tonner and 45hp 6-tonner. However, due to interest shown in passenger cars the company was now known as Milnes-Daimler-Mercedes Ltd.

Relying upon German imports, the business was doomed when war broke out and brought about the company's downfall.

MILWAUKEE/USA 1901-1902

The Milwaukee Automobile Co, Milwaukee, Wisconsin, built a few heavy steam trucks designed by W L Bodman. These had a capacity of 1814kg, employed a seasoned oak frame and were powered by a paraffin-fuelled fire-tube boiler connected to a 3-cyl single-acting engine providing speeds of 6 and 16km/h.

MINERVA/Belgium 1913-1957

Minerva Motors SA, Antwerp, entered the commercial vehicle field with a forward-control 2½-tonner, using a 4-cyl sleeve-valve petrol engine, 4-speed constant-mesh transmission and overhead-worm final-drive. Production ceased during World War I, and it was not until 1923 that a new 2/4-tonner appeared. Meanwhile, Minerva engines were used in the Auto-Traction heavy tractor, which was acquired in 1925, and Auto-Traction models joined the range. New commercials were developed, and by 1927 the heavier types had double-reduction drive and 4-wheel servo brakes.

The first passenger model, the 'CR', was introduced in 1926, using a 5.3-litre 4-cyl petrol engine. Another model, the 'HTM', arrived in 1927 while 1929 saw new 20/24-seaters and a 2½-ton truck. For a short time, direct-injection

Minerva refuse collector c1927

Minerva artic tractor c1931

1936 Minerva single-deck passenger chassis

sleeve-valve diesel engines were tried but replaced by more conventional types of 60 and 95bhp output. By 1936 the commercial range embraced bonneted petrol-engined vehicles from 1¾ to 4½ tons capacity, a normal-control 6½-tonner with Knight petrol engine, and a series of forward-control diesel trucks and tractors.

After World War II the 'HTM' passenger model was re-introduced but attention was given over to the 1½-ton C15 forward-control truck which had a 4-cyl Continental engine and remained in production until 1953. Few other commercials appeared after this, apart from the chassisless 4 x 4 C20 fitted with a 2.3-litre 4-cyl Continental side-valve engine and 4-speed synchromesh transmission.

MINIBUS/USA 1963 to date

The first Minibuses built by the Passenger Truck Equipment Co, Huntington Park, California, were used on a shopper's shuttle route in Washington. Specifications soon included Dodge or Chrysler V8 engines for petrol, diesel, propane or natural gas fuel. In 1967 the business was re-

named Minibus Inc, production moving to Pico Rivera, where vehicles have since been assembled to customers' particular requirements.

MINNEAPOLIS/USA 1910-?

A 3-cyl 2-stroke engined truck was exhibited at the 1910 Minneapolis Auto Show by the Minneapolis Motor & Truck Co, Minneapolis, Minnesota. It was announced that 1-, 3- and 6-ton models were to be built but these never materialized.

MINSEI/Japan 1938-1960

The Nippon Diesel Engineering Co Ltd, Kawaguchi, licence-built a 2-stroke opposed-piston 4-cyl Krupp-Junkers diesel engine fitted in a 7-ton truck which was the basis of production for a number of years. In 1942 the business was re-registered as Kanegafuchi Diesel Industries Ltd and in 1946 Minsei Sangyo Ltd, becoming Minsei Diesel Industries Ltd in 1950, by which time the original 7-tonner had acquired a 4-speed transmission, air/hydraulic or full air servo brakes and a spiral-bevel rear axle. Bonneted 'Condor' passenger models were listed during this period; there was even a chassisless rear-engined version followed by derivatives for up to 70 passengers.

In 1955 the original licence-built engine was replaced by the company's own design, a 155bhp 4.9-litre 4-cyl 2-stroke, and arrangements made to collaborate with the Tokyo-based Nissan Diesel Motor Co Ltd. Air suspension appeared on Minsei passenger types in 1957 and by 1960, as part of the Nissan Diesel Motor Co Ltd, the first forward-control trucks had appeared as Nissan Diesel or Minsei Nissan.

MITCHELL (1)/USA 1905-1908

The Mitchell Motor Car Co, Racine, Wisconsin, built a "cabover" 1½-tonner powered by a horizontally-opposed twin-cyl petrol engine. This had a 3-speed transmission, shaft-drive and spiral-bevel rear axle and the same chassis is believed to have been used as the basis for a battery-electric hotel bus.

MITCHELL (2)/USA 1906

The J Henry Mitchell Mfg Co, of Philadelphia, Pennsylvania, built a few 1-tonners of bonneted layout. Powered by 12/14hp 2-cyl petrol engines, these had a wheelbase of 250cm and a 3-speed transmission.

MITSUBISHI/Japan c1955 to date

Following dismembering of the Mitsubishi engineering empire in

1950, Mitsubishi Heavy Industries Reorganized Ltd, Nagoya and Mizushima, took over light commercial production under the Mitsubishi name. Most were 3-wheelers, the later 'TM' model being a 1½/2-tonner with 2-cyl air-cooled petrol engine, transverse rear suspension and wheel-steering. The first conventional truck was the 2/3-ton 'Jupiter', announced in 1959, using a 2.2-litre 4-cyl petrol or diesel or a 3.3-litre 6-cyl diesel, 4-speed synchromesh transmission, hypoid rear axle and hydrovac brakes.

In 1964 the company joined with the manufacturer of heavier Mitsubishi Fusos as Mitsubishi Heavy Industries Ltd, introducing the 2-ton bonneted 'Jupiter Junnior' with torsion-bar independent front suspension and the 2/3-ton forward-control 'Canter' powered by 2-litre 4-cyl petrol or diesel engines. Passenger models were represented by the 'Jupiter'-based 25-seat 'Rosa' with 6-cyl diesel engine and synchromesh transmission.

By the early 1970s the 'Jupiter' and 'Canter' ranges covered payloads of up to 6½ tons, while the 1966 T620 forward-control 6-tonner had been up-rated to join the Mitsubishi Fuso line as the T650. 'Jupiters' were withdrawn towards the end of the 1970s, with forward-control types forming the backbone of the range, 'Canter' models being sold in Australia as Dodge Canter and in Switzerland as MMC-FBW.

MITSUBISHI FUSO/*Japan 1930 to date*
When commercial vehicle production got underway at the Mitsubishi Shipbuilding & Engineering Co Ltd, Kobe, models were marketed as Mitsubishi Fuso or simply Fuso, starting with a series of US-style bonneted buses. By 1935 the company had developed its own diesel engines, fitting these in

Mitsubishi Fuso mobile home 1959

a series of 2½/3-ton trucks and the existing bus range.

Vehicle production was transferred to Kawasaki in 1941, but few machines were built during the war. With a return to civilian production in 1946, a series of bonneted 6/7-ton trucks and buses with 6-cyl diesel engines was announced. In 1950 the business was dismembered, Mitsubishi Heavy Industries Reorganized Ltd taking over the lighter models, and Mitsubishi Nippon Heavy Industries Ltd the heavier Mitsubishi Fusos.

By 1958 a 7/8-tonner, based on the 1946 model, was also in production, using a 155bhp 8.6-litre 6-cyl diesel engine, 4-speed transmission and air brakes, while passenger types were represented by a similarly-based 40-seater and a new rear-engined 45-seater with automatic transmission and power-steering. A prototype 1½-decker constructed in 1959 got no further.

The company was also producing more specialized machines, including a 1-man halfcab dump truck, a 6-wheel drive bonneted truck with a 10-ton payload and a 6 x 6 20-ton artic tractor powered by a 200bhp 13.7-litre diesel engine coupled to a 10-speed transmission. Lighter bonneted models were re-styled in 1961 and joined by new tiltcab forward-control models for up to 11 tons payload, the heaviest being the T390 6 x 2 rigid.

The re-uniting of the two companies in 1964 as Mitsubishi Heavy Industries Ltd gave the business a comprehensive vehicle range, although "heavies" continued to be sold either as Mitsubishi Fuso or Fuso, and lighter types simply as Mitsubishi. Mitsubishi Fuso passenger types were now all rear-engined with air brakes and conventional leaf spring suspension although air suspension was listed as standard for the MAR750L motorway coach, its 210bhp V8 diesel engine producing a maximum speed of 125km/h.

By the early 1970s the lightest Mitsubishi Fuso was the T650, originally part of the lighter Mitsubishi line, while the heaviest were bonneted 6 x 6s in rigid and tractor form. All forward-control models had tiltcabs and new engines included a 310bhp turbocharged V8 diesel and 190bhp V6. Other new types included various crane-carriers, fire appliances and construction trucks as well as off-road dump trucks for up to 100 tons GVW.

Re-styling and additional models appeared in 1972, some 6 x 4 rigids now having gross weights of up to 30 tons. This range is much the same now except that most medium- and heavy-duty models are of forward-control layout. Exceptions include the 6 x 6 T330, the 6 x 4 NV and the 4 x 4 W82 dump truck. Generally, only in-line diesel engines are used, the largest being a 430bhp 18.4-litre 8-cyl model fitted in the largest dump trucks. The largest passenger model is now the 50-seat rear-engined MS, with V8 engine and air suspension. Certain models are sold in Australia as Dodge Fuso and in Switzerland as MMC-FBW.

M & J/*England 1908*
Using a 4-cyl petrol engine, 4-speed transmission and chain-drive, Martin & Jellicoe Ltd, Thames Ditton, Surrey, offered 1- and 2-ton M & J or Martin & Jellicoe vans.

MK/*Netherlands/Spain 1953 to date*
NV Motorkracht, Haageveen, built six trucks powered by 4-cyl Deutz diesel engines. Although these were the only vehicles actually built by the company, the MK name which they carried can still be found on Magirus-Deutz models imported into Spain by this company, which is now owned by and acts as a distributor for Magirus-Deutz AG.

MLT/*France 1900*
The MLT was a 12-seat passenger wagon powered by compressed

air. It was a product of Molas, Lamielle et Tessier, Paris, and carried its fuel in 11 tanks with a total capacity of 0.5cu m. Gas burners heated the air which was then directed into the engine's four cyls at varying pressures to provide power outputs of anything from 1 to 35hp. Transmission comprised a countershaft with double chain-drive to the rear wheels.

MMC/*England c1898-1908*
Better known for its passenger cars, the Motor Mfg Co Ltd was established in Coventry. Its products were sold as MMC, and comprised a number of light delivery models and larger goods and passenger types. Charabancs were particularly popular and led to the development of John Maltby's range in 1905. Commercial MMCs were powered by licence-built De Dion petrol engines, initially located in a horizontal position at the rear but later fitted in a vertical front-mounted position. In August 1905 the factory was sold to the Daimler Motor Co (1904) Ltd and MMC production was moved to another location. In 1907, however, the company was re-registered as the Motor Mfg Co (1907) Ltd, moving to London SW4, where production continued half-heartedly.

MMC-FBW/*Switzerland ? to date*
In order to gain sales in the lighter truck market, heavy vehicle manufacturer Franz Brozincevic et Cie Automobiles Industrielles FBW, Wetzikon, Zürich, markets the Mitsubishi 'Canter' 2-tonner and Fuso or Mitsubishi Fuso 6½-tonner in Switzerland, using the MMC-FBW brand name.

MOAZ/*Soviet Union c1964 to date*
The Magilev Lift & Hoist Plant, of Magilev, constructs two heavy commercial models under the MOAZ brand name. These comprise the MOAZ-529E, a 2-axle 20-ton artic dump truck, and the MOAZ-6401, a 200bhp 4 x 2 bonneted tractor.

MOBILE/*USA 1901-1903*
As well as light commercials, the Mobile Co of America, Tarrytown-on-the-Hudson, New York, built a 3-ton steam truck, also known as the Mobile Steamer. This had double chain-drive.

MOC/*England 1906-1907*
Similar in appearance and specification to passenger models built by Sir W G Armstrong, Whitworth & Co Ltd, the MOC was constructed by Motor Omnibus Construction Ltd, a subsidiary of the London Motor Omnibus Co, at Walthamstow, London. Using

1974 Mitsubishi Fuso 'FU'-Series 6 x 4 tipper

a 32hp 4-cyl petrol engine supplied by traction engine manufacturer Richard Hornsby & Sons, and with axles (and, later, engines) by Armstrong-Whitworth, a cone clutch and 4-speed transmission, these went into service with the London Motor Omnibus Co.

In 1907 the operating divisions of the London Motor Omnibus Co amalgamated to form the Vanguard Motor Omnibus Co with MOC production curtailed and the company's requirement for complete Armstrong-Whitworth chassis halted.

MOC-CROMPTON/*England 1909*
Using an MOC chassis, the MOC-Crompton was an experimental battery-electric bus carrying nearly 2 tons of batteries and two 7½hp Crompton traction motors. Unusual was the use of a generator instead of circuit breakers between batteries and traction motors, this located transversely under the bonnet. The vehicle's speed was pedal-controlled but passenger operation was not forthcoming as regulations stipulated that the unladen weight of such vehicles was to be no more than 3½ tons, and the MOC-Crompton weighed nearly 6½. A lighter type was later developed as the Crompton.

MODERN (1)/*USA 1911-1912*
A 2-ton stakeside truck with 4-cyl petrol engine was built by the Modern Motor Truck Co, St Louis, Missouri. This had a wheelbase of 295cm, a governed maximum speed of 24km/h, a 3-speed transmission and double chain-drive.

MODERN (2)/*USA 1914-1919*
Replacing lighter designs, the Bowling Green Motor Car Co, Bowling Green, Ohio, introduced the Modern worm-drive 1-tonner and double chain-drive 1½-tonner adding 2- and 3½-tonners two years later. From 1917 only the 1½-tonner was offered.

MOELLER/*USA 1910-1914*
The first Moeller trucks were 5-tonners built by M L Moeller & Co, New Haven, Connecticut. Available in normal- and forward-control form, both had a 4-cyl petrol engine. A 3-tonner was launched in 1912, when the company was re-named the New Haven Truck & Auto Works, and by 1913 a 1½-tonner was also available. From 1912 trucks were often referred to as New Haven.

MOGUL/*USA 1911-1916*
Built by the Mogul Motor Truck Co, Chicago, Illinois, the Mogul was listed as a 2-, 4- or 6-ton forward-control truck with 4-cyl petrol engine, 3-speed transmission and double chain-drive. In 1914 production moved to St Louis, Missouri, where one of the largest types built was the Model 'U', designed for hauling timber.

MOGURT/*Hungary c1955 to date*
The Hungarian Trading Co, Budapest, uses the Mogurt name for any Hungarian-built vehicles sold for export.

Mol 6 x 6 dump truck c1976

MOL/*Belgium 1966 to date*
Starting with a municipal chassis, Gebroeders Mol Pvba, Hooglede, introduced other specialist types under the Mol name. The municipal had a low-silhouette cab, air-cooled Deutz diesel engine, Allison automatic transmission and Kirkstall axles, while others included both normal- and forward-control trucks of similar specification but with ZF manual transmission. Later re-named Mol NV, the company now concentrates on heavy-duty 4 x 4, 6 x 4 and 6 x 6 trucks, fitted mainly with Deutz diesels, Spicer or ZF transmissions and Timken axles, while Silver Eagle bus production is now handled at the same plant.

MOLINE/*USA 1920-1922*
Agricultural implement manufacturer the Moline Plow Co, East Moline, Illinois, marketed a 325-cm wheelbase Model '10' 1½-ton truck with 4-cyl petrol engine and 3-speed transmission aimed at the agricultural market.

MONITOR/*USA 1908-1914*
Using a 4-cyl petrol engine, the 1-ton Monitor truck was built by the Monitor Automobile Works, Janesville, Wisconsin. It had selective transmission and double chain-drive as standard although some had shaft-drive and, occasionally, forward-control.

MONTPELIER/*USA 1958*
The Montpelier '75' was a delivery vehicle built by the Montpelier Mfg Co. Power came from a 70bhp air-cooled Hercules V4 petrol engine, with engine, clutch, gearbox and front axle removable as one for maintenance. A water-cooled power unit was optional and other features included one-step entry and a flat floor line enabling the driver to stand full height.

MOON/*USA 1912-1917*
As well as passenger cars and a light commercial, the Joseph W Moon Buggy Co, St Louis, Missouri, offered the 1½-ton Model 'B' truck, latterly as the Moon Motor Car Co. This had chain-drive and a variety of body styles.

MOORE (1)/*USA 1911-1916*
The F L Moore Co, Los Angeles, California, built a series of trucks with capacities of 2, 3, 5 and 6½ tons. By the end of the first year the F L Moore Motor Truck Co had been formed to handle assembly, all types being of bonneted layout. In 1913 the business was acquired by the Pacific Metal Products Co, Torrance, California, and production transferred. A typical specification was the 5-tonner which had a 4-cyl petrol engine, 4-speed transmission and countershaft.

MOORE (2)/*USA 1914*
A light commercial built by the Moore Motor Truck Co, Philadelphia, Pennsylvania, was joined by similar models with capacities of 1½, 2, 3, 4 and 5 tons. Most were of bonneted layout, the largest having a 4-speed transmission and a wheelbase of 490cm.

MORELAND/*USA 1912-1941*
Starting with 1½-, 3-, 3½- and 5-ton bonneted and forward-control trucks with Hercules or Continental petrol engines, Brown-Lipe transmissions and chain-drive, the Moreland Motor Truck Co began in Los Angeles, California, later moving to Burbank. By 1924 the largest model, a 6-tonner had been joined by a prototype 6 x 4 dropframe double-deck bus with 6-cyl Continental petrol engine, Westinghouse air and Lockheed hydraulic brakes, Gruss air suspension at the front and an open-top all-metal 60-seat body. This was an expensive vehicle and the company's attention turned to a load-carrying 6-wheeler called the TX6.

The bogie fitted to this model was unique to Morelands, incorporating axles located by equalizing rocker beams pivoting from the centres of the semi-elliptic leaf springs. It had a capacity of 10 tons, but was soon joined by a 6-ton version. The company also constructed trailers and various types of commercial bodywork, later introducing the 1723-kg capacity 'Ace' and the 7-ton 'Californian', powered by Continental and Hercules petrol engines respectively.

At the start of the 1930s, the company became more involved in the manufacture of trailers and commercial bodywork, the few Morelands built being more customized than before. Hercules or Cummins diesel engines were used, such as the 125bhp Cummins unit fitted in the 19,050kg GVW or 30,844kg GCW TA-420CD listed until 1941.

MORETTI/*Italy 1954-c1961*
Already a specialist manufacturer of sportscars, Fabb Automobili Moretti SpA, Turin, also built a forward-control 1-tonner, with 62bhp 1.2-litre double overhead-cam petrol engine and 8 forward speeds.

MORGAN/*USA 1903, 1908-1913*
Ralph L Morgan founded the R L Morgan Co in 1903, and a forward-control petrol-engined truck went into production. This had a 40hp 4-cyl engine, planetary transmission and double chain-drive. Rated at 5 tons capacity, it was joined by new 2- and 3-tonners in 1912 and the company renamed the Morgan Motor Truck Co. Later production was taken over by W M Steele and vehicles renamed Steele.

MORGAN STEAM/*USA 1902-1903*
Ralph L Morgan , Worcester, Massachusetts, developed the heavy Morgan Steam truck, using a 600psi vertical water-tube boiler and 2-cyl compound engine. In

1903 the R L Morgan Co was formed and the petrol-engined Morgan truck introduced.

MORRIS (1)/*England c1956-1968*

In the 1950s the Morris-Commercial range became abbreviated to Morris, although the company itself was still Morris Commercial Cars Ltd, Birmingham. Following a merger with the Leyland Motor Corporation Ltd in 1968 all models were marketed as Leyland.

MORRIS (2)/*Turkey 1968 to date*

As well as building its own brand of Austin truck, BMC Sanayi ve Ticaret AS, Izmir, offers a 3-model series of locally designed Morris trucks with diesel engines of between 68 and 120bhp output.

MORRIS-COMMERCIAL/*England 1924-1954*

In a bid to enter the mass produced light truck market, W R Morris acquired the Soho, Birmingham, factory of E G Wrigley & Co, registering Morris Commercial Cars Ltd to assemble a 1-tonner as the Morris-Commercial. This used Morris passenger car components such as a 1.8-litre 4-

Morris-Commercial 1-ton truck c1928

1949 Morris-Commercial FV9/5 5-ton refuse collector

1930 Morris-Commercial 'Imperial' double-deck bus

cyl side-valve petrol engine, wet-plate clutch and 3-speed transmission, with pneumatic tyres and electric lighting as standard. Known as the 'T'-Type, it was claimed to be the first mass-produced British truck.

By 1925 an extensive range of standard bodies was available and in 1926 a Roadless Traction half-track derivative was offered. A new 2.5-litre petrol engine was fitted in the 1¼/1½-ton 'Z'-Type truck, which also had a dry-plate clutch, 4-speed gate-change transmission and servo brake option. The 1½/2-ton 'D'-Type 6 x 4, also

announced in 1926, was intended for the military. Powered by a 35bhp 4-cyl side-valve petrol engine, the standard 'D'-Type had a single dry-plate clutch, 4-speed main transmission with auxiliary spur-gear reduction box and servo-assisted rod brakes.

A revolutionary passenger model, the 'Dictator' H, appeared towards the end of 1929. Intended for 28 passengers, power was provided by a 110bhp 6-cyl petrol engine mounted in unit with a single dry-plate clutch and a gearbox incorporating handwheel adjustment of a band-type clutch stop.

Specification also called for 4-wheel braking and removable front-end assembly comprising wheels, axle, springs, engine, clutch and gearbox, to aid maintenance. Also at the end of 1929 a trailing-axle 6-wheeler called the 'RD'-Type entered production for a payload of 2½ tons using the same engine as the 'D'-Type 6 x 4, while Stoewer-Werke AG, Stettin, Germany, attempted licence production of a 2-tonner, possibly based on a new 2½-ton model called the 'P'-Type 'Leader' which had a 3.7-litre 4-cyl side-valve petrol engine.

A new series of "heavies" was developed in Adderley Park, led by the 4/5-ton 'Courier' with 85bhp 5.1-litre overhead-valve high-cam petrol engine and 4-wheel vacuum-servo brakes. Only a few 'Dictator' H models were built before being replaced by the forward-control 'Dictator' HT, another passenger type being the double-deck half-cab 'Imperial' HD, announced in 1931. Both models were powered by a 6-cyl version of the 'Courier' engine although, unlike the 'Dictator', the 'Imperial' had a twin-plate clutch and an offset transmission to pro-

**1953 Morris-Commercial
'PV'-Series 1-ton integral van**

'LD' replacement of the 'PV' were fitted with a 2.2-litre Austin petrol engine, and by 1956 the Morris-Commercial name was replaced by those of Austin, Morris or BMC.

MORRIS-LEON BOLLEE/ *France 1929-1931*

W R Morris of Morris Motors Ltd, Cowley, Oxford, acquired Automobiles Léon Bollée, Le Mans, Sarthe, forming Morris Motors Ltd Usines Léon Bollée at Le Mans. It was not until 1929 that a true commercial model – the 1½-ton 'T'-Type, aimed primarily at the French colonies, was built. It had a high ground clearance and was powered by a 15.9hp Hotchkiss petrol engine. Other features included a 4-speed transmission, worm final-drive and servo 4-wheel brakes. This model was listed until 1932, but in 1931 W R Morris disposed of the business to

A Dunlop Mackenzie and Henry Smith, who continued manufacture under the Léon Bollée name.

MORRISON/ *England 1933*

Although A E and A C Morrison planned to add 1¼-, 1½- and 2-ton battery-electrics to their light delivery range, it is believed that these did not appear until 1934 when A E Morrison & Sons had been formed in Leics. They were marketed as Morrison-Electric.

MORRISON-ELECTRIC/ *England 1934-1941*

A E and A C Morrison, Leicester, founded A E Morrison & Sons in 1934, continuing the Morrison range of battery-electrics under the Morrison-Electric name. In 1935 the business moved to South Wigston where a new range, called the '600'-Series, was introduced. Heaviest of these were 1-, 1½-, and 2-ton models and at

vide a low floor line. Despite the double-decker's advantages, few were sold, the largest number going to Birmingham Corp with Lockheed hydraulic brakes and a Simms magneto. A 5.3-litre 6-cyl side-valve petrol engine was used in the lighter 20-seat 'Viceroy' bonneted model.

In the truck line, new 8- and 12-tonners were planned but only prototypes built. A major development was the bonneted or semi forward-control 'C'-Type for payloads of 1½ to 3 tons with spiral-bevel drive, 4-wheel hydraulic brakes and a choice of engines. The 'C'-Type restored the company's confidence and there was soon a 4/5-ton 'Leader' designed to operate within the new 2½ tons unladen weight limit, and in 1937 the semi forward-control 'Equiload' was launched, continuing until the company merged with the Austin Motor Co Ltd in 1952. By 1938 these had been re-styled to keep pace with rival models, incorporating full normal-control and using the old 3.5-litre petrol engine, although a 1¼-tonner employed a new 2.1-litre overhead-valve 4-cyl unit.

A forward-control 5-tonner and a 20/26-seat coach chassis arrived in 1939 and, as the war started, so the 'PV' 1-tonner appeared, a vehicle that was to become one of the first factory-produced delivery vans to utilize full-height internally-sliding doors. During the war a 4 x 4 artillery tractor was developed, using a 72bhp 4-cyl petrol engine and 10-speed transmission. A fascinating experiment conducted at this time was the fitting of Saurer diesel engines in two 'Equiload' chassis. These engines were subsequently developed into a 2-valve per cyl

1953 Morris-Comercial 'NV'-Series truck

layout from their original 4-valve per cyl design and fitted as standard in the 1948 forward-control FVO 5-tonner. This unit proved unsatisfactory and was replaced by a 4-cyl Morris-Commercial unit bored out to 3.8 litres, although some export models had 6-cyl Oerlikon diesels. A passenger chassis was also announced along similar lines.

Re-styled 2/3- and 5-ton 'Equiloads' appeared in 1951, with petrol or diesel engines and hydrovac brakes, and in 1952 the business merged with the Austin Motor Co Ltd to form the British Motor Corp Ltd, some models now being marketed as BMC. Collaboration between the two manufacturers was soon evident in other ways, such as when the new 1½-ton 'Equiload' 'LC'-Type and the

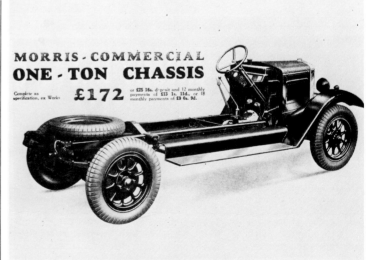

**MORRIS-COMMERCIAL
ONE-TON CHASSIS**
£172 Complete as specification, ex Works or £25 16s. d-p'sit and 12 monthly payments of £13 1s. 11d., or 18 monthly payments of £9 0s. 9d.

1925 Morris-Commercial 1-ton chassis

about the same time special streamlined bodies such as the 'Airline', 'Airstream' and 'Airflow' were announced. In 1936 the business merged with Electricars Ltd, Young Accumulators and Hants Electric Chassis to form Associated Electric Vehicle Manufacturers which continued until 1941 when Crompton Parkinson Ltd took control and models were re-named Morrison-Electricar.

MORRISON-ELECTRICAR/
England/Wales 1941-c1972

When Crompton Parkinson Ltd took control of Associated Electric Vehicle Manufacturers, South Wigston, Leics, the brand name for battery-electric delivery models changed from Morrison-Electric to Morrison-Electricar and a number of heavier types in the 2/3-ton payload bracket were based on former Electricar designs. The range was gradually cut back until only a 1-tonner was available, but in 1948 50% of the company's shares were acquired by the Austin Motor Co Ltd and the company re-named Austin Crompton Parkinson Electric Vehicles Ltd. A new factory was opened in Birmingham, while the old South Wigston premises remained in production, and a range of 1-, 2- and 3-ton capacity vehicles announced, sold in Britain as Morrison-Electricar or abroad as Austin-Electricar.

In the early 1950s a pedestrian-controlled 1-tonner and a 4-wheeled artic tractor called the GT were announced. The SD and MD dairy ranges followed and by 1958 there were even battery-electric mobile shops on a wheelbase of 201cm. When T H Lewis went out of business in 1963 its Electruk range was absorbed into the Morrison-Electricar stable and in 1966 the business was transferred to Tredegar, South Wales. In 1968 Crompton Leyland Electricars Ltd was formed following the merger of the British Motor Corp Ltd and Leyland Motor Corp Ltd. Later types were known as Crompton Leyland Electricar.

MORRISS/*England 1899-c1901*

Frank Morriss, King's Lynn, Norfolk, specialized in improving the performance and design of German-built Daimlers. He also operated a local bus service using a 10-seat Morriss wagonette powered by a 5½hp Daimler petrol engine. Other examples were sold in the locality over the next couple of years and a later development was the Sandringham hotel bus.

MORS/*France 1900-1915*

The earliest Mors truck appears to have been an 8hp chain-drive

1964 Morrison-Electricar Model D/FG 1/1½-ton battery-electric milk float

1969 Morrison-Electricar battery-electric boxvan

model for the French Army. It was built by Soc d'Éléctricité et d'Automobiles Mors, Paris, and was followed by a 12hp 4-cyl petrol-engined truck. By 1905 a 2-tonner, with 5.5-litre 4-cyl 'T'-head petrol engine, 3-speed transmission and pressed-steel, rather than the earlier armoured timber frame, was listed, a 4-speed double-deck bus with compressed air starter joining it almost immediately.

By 1906 models ranged from 1½ to 5 tons capacity, the lightest being of "cabover" layout, while heavier types had dropframes, 6.2-litre petrol engines, transverse rear suspension and extra-long wheelbases. Re-named Soc Nouvelle des Automobiles Mors in 1908, the company began to drop commercial types in favour of passenger cars and, although four commercial models were listed in 1914, all were discontinued.

MORTON (1)/*USA 1912-1916*

Built in the Harrisburg, Pennsylvania, factory of the Harrisburg Mfg & Boiler Co, the Morton or Morton Tractor range was designed and marketed by the Morton Truck & Tractor Co Inc. A 5-model range was offered by 1913 with capacities between 1½ and 5 tons. One model had 4-wheel drive, but all had 30hp 4-cyl petrol engines, 4-speed transmissions and chain-drive. By 1915 4-wheel drive and 4-wheel steer 3- and 6-tonners were also being built. From 1914 many vehicles were exported to Russia.

MORTON (2)/*France 1929-1930*

A 6-ton Morton truck was announced by Moteurs Morton, Su-

resnes, Seine, who had previously manufactured stationary diesel engines. This had a 40bhp 2.6-litre diesel unit constructed partly of aluminium, compressed air starter, double-reduction final-drive and air brakes at the rear, but production does not appear to have followed. A number of 1-ton diesel lorries are believed to have been built, these being the smallest diesel-engined vehicles of the day.

MOTALA/*Sweden 1933-1938*
Motala integral buses were built by Motala Verkstads AB, Lindholmen, Motala. With a choice between Chrysler or Reo petrol and Daimler, Deutz or Hercules diesel engines, this marque was unusual in that engines were generally mounted vertically on one side of the vehicle. The exception to the vertical side-mounted engine position was a fleet of vehicles with horizontal 6-cyl Hall-Scott petrol engines supplied to Stockholm Tramways in 1935.

MOTOCART/*England 1953-c1959*
When the 3-wheeled Opperman Motocart was re-named Motocart, all marketing was handled by Transport Materials Supplies Ltd, London SW1. Specification appears to have been as before but towards the end of the 1950s all design and manufacturing rights passed to Transport Equipment (Thornycroft) Ltd, Basingstoke.

MOTO-GUZZI/*Italy c1935-c1940, 1945-c1967*
Developed from an earlier series of lightweight 3-wheeled commercials employing motorcycle components, the first Moto-Guzzi 3-wheelers for payloads in excess of 1 ton employed 4-speed transmissions and shaft-drive. Built by Moto-Guzzi SpA, Como, these were discontinued during World War II but re-introduced in the form of the 1500kg payload 'Ercole' with 5-speed transmission. Hydraulic brakes were employed from 1955 and coil-ignition from 1957. In 1967 the company was re-organized as Soc Esercizio Industrie Moto Meccaniche SpA but the only "heavy" model was still the 'Ercole', now with fully-enclosed 1-man cab but retaining its 500cc horizontal power unit and handlebar-steering with un-coupled 3-wheel brakes.

MOULTON/*England 1974-1976*
One of the most revolutionary passenger vehicles was the 8-wheeled Moulton coach, brainchild of Alex Moulton. Of chassisless design, it had small-diameter wheels and a front-mounted underfloor engine.

The single prototype, built by Moulton Developments Ltd, Bradford-on-Avon, Wilts, had an unladen weight of only 7¼ tons, and was constructed of welded square-section steel tubing to provide a near perfect rigid spaceframe. Integral roll-over hoops were capable of withstanding 2¼ times the vehicle's own gross weight should it overturn. Luggage lockers with a total capacity of 49cu m ran beneath the floor for almost the entire length of the

1980 Moxy D16B 6x6 artic dump truck

vehicle and the 'Hydragas' suspension was inter-connected to enable the vehicle to cross all surface undulations with no perceptible change in attitude. Brakes were power-hydraulic and many mechanical parts derived from those used in mediumweight British trucks of the period. The Perkins 6.354 V6 diesel engine could be removed on a special trolley for major maintenance.

This design was taken one stage further when plans were laid down for an 8-wheeled rigid goods model for operation at 16 tons GVW. This also employed space-frame technology, contained below floor level apart from the cab structure. Neither design reached production although Moulton's ideas have had considerable influence other projects.

MOWAG/*Switzerland 1950 to date*
Commencing vehicle assembly in 1950, Mowag Motorwagenfabrik AG, Kreuzlingen, later known as Mowag Motorenfabrik AG, has concentrated on the manufacture of special-purpose vehicles using components supplied by other manufacturers, such as SLM diesel engines and ZF gearboxes. The company now concentrates on smaller and lighter models, using Chrysler components, mainly for fire-fighting, police, military and similar applications.

MOWAG/*Switzerland 1951 to date*
A 6-cyl Chrysler-engined 2-ton 4 x 4 was the first mediumweight Mowag, built by Mowag Motor-

wagenfabrik AG, Kreuzlingen, for use as a military or civilian truck or fire appliance. There was also a series of cab-forward trucks with horizontal underfloor SLM diesel engines and ZF transmissions. for up to 9 tons payload. A similar range was offered towards the end of the 1950s, comprising 4-, 5- and 9-tonners using both Chrysler and SLM underfloor diesel engines; a special narrow-cab steel-carrier with SLM 8-cyl horizontal engine; a 5-cyl Büssing-engined 4 x 4 tipper; and various passenger models for up to 80 persons.

By 1965 the underfloor-engined models were joined by front-engined 4- and 5-tonners with Chrysler straight-6 or V8 engines, underfloor types now having Büssing or Perkins power

units, while a vertical 5-cyl in-line 2-stroke diesel powered a new 9-tonner. Petrol engines were rarely used after 1967, but a new series of 4 x 4 V8-engined fire appliances was developed and civilian commercials discontinued. Occasionally, however, there were new civilian models such as an 8 x 4 rigid announced in 1977 powered by a new 8-cyl diesel engine and employing Chrysler components. Production at Mowag Motorenfabrik AG, as it is now known, continues along similar lines.

MOXY/*Norway 1974 to date*
The 6 x 6 Moxy articulated-frame dump truck was developed from a prototype built by Glamox A/S, a subsidiary of the Glamin A/S industrial group. Moxy A/S was formed at Molde later that year to

1964 Multicar Model 22 2-ton tipper

Multiwheeler 'Anaconda' tractor c1934

pursue series production, the vehicle being called the D15. In 1975 the improved D16 was launched and during 1978 the D16B appeared. With a maximum payload of 26 tons the Moxy has a 235bhp Scania DS8 industrial diesel engine ahead of the front axle and one-man cab, a Clark 'Powershift' torque-converter transmission and balance beam rear suspension similar to the old DAF-Trado and Scammell systems. Front-wheel-drive can be disengaged if not required.

MTN/*England 1951-1956*
Motor Traction Ltd, Croydon, Surrey, was registered to continue Manton production under the MTN brand name, but with a move to new premises at New Addington, Surrey, the Rutland name was also introduced, being used generally for all home market models. Seventy-five per cent of Rutland production went to Spain and Portugal as MTN, other export markets including South America, West Africa, Rhodesia, India, Pakistan and Turkey.

MUCHOW/*Germany 1928-1931*
Muchow & Co Fahrzeug und Geratefabrik GmbH took over the Berlin plant of Elitewagen AG and continued Elitewagen production under the Muchow brand name. One new model was a battery-electric conversion unit for coupling to un-powered trailers,

while other new types included a 5-ton truck and 10-ton tractor.

MUIR-HILL/*England 1931-c1972*
E Boydell & Co Ltd, Old Trafford, Manchester, designed and assembled a line of construction machinery under the Muir-Hill brand name, introducing a series of petrol- and diesel-engined dump trucks using Fordson tractor engine/transmission units. These had 1-man half-cabs and 2-way drive, often with a reversible seat and steering column. Production later moved to Gloucester where one of the most popular models in the early 1960s was the 10B machine powered by a 52bhp 3.6 litre Fordson diesel engine driving through a dry-plate clutch and 6-speed constant-mesh transmission. Towards the end of the 1960s the company was re-named Muir-Hill Ltd, becoming a distributor for heavy-duty Mack dump trucks and heavy haulage tractors, gradually running down Muir-Hill production.

MULAG/*Germany 1909-1913*
When Scheibler Automobil Industrie GmbH, Aachen, manufacturer of Scheibler trucks, was re-named Motoren und Lastwagen AG, vehicles became Mulag. These were mainly 3-tonners, renamed Mannesmann-Mulag when the company was re-organized as Mannesmann-Mulag Motoren und Lastwagen AG.

MULTICAR/*East Germany 1964 to date*
Manufactured by VEB Fahrzeugwerk Waltershausen, the first Multicar 2-tonner was a 1-man half-cab truck offered with a variety of bodies and a 13bhp 2-cyl air-diesel engine. Intended mainly for internal works use or as a site dumper, it was replaced in 1974 by a more powerful version, using a 45bhp 4-cyl diesel engine.

MULTIWHEELER/*England 1933-1941*
Multiwheelers (Commercial Vehicles) Ltd was set up at South Harrow, Middx, to resume production of the Beardmore-Multiwheeler road tractor series as Multiwheeler. Only a few were

built, using AEC and Gardner diesel engines, before the company turned to trailer manufacturing for the war effort.

MURTY/*USA 1949 to date*
Specializing in the manufacture of logging equipment, Murty Bros, Portland, Oregon, developed one of the world's first specialist 8-wheeled crane-carriers, and in 1952 produced an unusual rigid load-carrier called the 'Flat-Top'. Available in 10-ton 4- and 15-ton 6-wheeled form, this had a 1-man "sentrybox" cab and was capable of hauling long logs. A 150bhp 6-cyl White engine and Clark 5-speed main transmission were standard for both types, the smaller having a 2-speed Eaton axle and the larger a Brown-Lipe auxiliary transmission providing a further ten ratios. Crane-carriers are now the main product line.

MUSKER/*England 1898-1905*
The first Musker wagons developed by Charles and Arthur Musker, Bootle, Lancs, comprised a vertical coke-fired flash boiler type and an oil-fired flash boiler model. Engine, boiler and transmission of the oil-fired model were all slung under the wagon, driver, controls and chimney being located in one corner of the load-carrying area, while the coke-fired model had a fuel hopper positioned over the boiler.

Both wagons had a 4-cyl single-acting engine with cyls cast in pairs with automatic injection of air to the fire and water to the boiler. Both were unsuccessful but new a factory in Liverpool introduced an improved wagon with vertical semi-flash coke-fired boiler and 25hp cross-compound engine, again slung beneath the frame. Four examples were built, three of which were shipped to New Zealand, but later wagons had vertical fire-tube boilers. All designs and components were eventually sold to Savage Bros.

1901 Musker "undertype" steam wagon

N

NACKE/*Germany 1901-1929*
The first commercials built by Automobilfabrik Emile Nacke, Coswig, Saxony, were chain-drive trucks and buses, although shaft-drive was quickly adopted. World War I saw production of a 5-ton bonneted "subsidy" truck and after the war a 3-tonner was added. Later, a 4-cyl 2½-tonner and a 6-cyl 5-tonner, both with worm-drive, were standardized.

NAG/*Germany 1903-1931*
Following the takeover of Kuhlstein Wagenbau, Neue Automobil GmbH, Berlin, introduced the NAG road-train, this having a capacity of 20 tons for use in the African colonies. The following year a 16-seat bus was produced, and by 1906 various other passenger types had been built. The first double-decker in Berlin, again an NAG, and 2-, 3½- and 6-ton trucks, with 2- or 4-cyl petrol engines, were added to the range in 1907. The company's first cardan shaft-drive bus arrived in 1909 and substantial quantities of NAG buses were delivered to ABOAG, the leading Berlin operator.

The company became Neue Automobil AG in 1912, and Nationale Automobil AG in 1915, but when civilian production resumed after World War I the range was slimmed down. It now comprised 3½- and 5-ton 45hp trucks and buses, joined by a drop-frame bus chassis with 75 hp petrol engine in 1924, the same year that a 6-wheeled model was announced. Lighter commercials of about 1-ton capacity were built on a 12/65PS 6-cyl petrol-engined passenger car chassis, while others, based on AEG designs, included bonneted battery-electrics.

Presto-Werke AG was acquired in 1927 and a light truck introduced into the NAG stable as the NAG-Presto. By 1930 other models included a 3.6-litre 2¼-tonner, 4-litre 2½-tonner and 10.8-litre 5-tonner, plus a 2½-ton 6-wheeler and various single- and double-deck buses, but early in 1931 the company was itself taken over by Automobilwerke H Büssing AG and all vehicles were marketed as Büssing-NAG.

NAIRN/*Scotland 1870-1871*
Andrew Nairn, Leith, Midlothian, constructed a 50-seat double-deck steam bus with Field-tube boiler capable of up to 25km/h. This ran briefly in Edinburgh, while a second vehicle operated over a 4.8-km route between Edinburgh and Portobello. Legal action closed down the service.

NAM/*West Germany 1949-1950*
Using 4- or 6-wheeled ex-WD GMC chassis, Niedersachsicheas Auto und Motoren Instandsetzungswerk built forward-control NAM passenger models. These had either their original engines or Henschel or Deutz diesels.

NAMI/*Soviet Union ? to date*
Nautshno-Issledovatelskii Automobilnoi i Automotornoi Institut, Moscow, is a motor industry research and design establishment which also has the only vehicle test track in the Soviet Union. Over the years, certain specialist and experimental vehicles have carried the Nami name while undergoing development trials, one such being a large cargo truck developed for crossing the vast un-made regions and construction sites of the USSR.

NANCEIENNE/*France 1900-1903*
Using Brillié and Gobron-Brillié patents, the Nanceienne truck was built by Soc Nancéienne d'Automobiles, Nancy. It used a 2-cyl opposed-piston engine, designed to run on petrol or alcohol fuel, located vertically under the seat, a 3-speed transmission and chain final-drive. The standard model had a capacity of 2 tons and one example won a Gold Medal at the 1901 Alcohol Trials. Short-lived 3- and 4½-ton tippers were announced in 1902.

NAN-FANG/*China 1970 to date*
A rear-engined bus called the Nan-Fang (Southern) is built in the Kuangehou Motor Vehicle Plant, Kuangehou, Kwangtung Province.

NANYANG/*China ? to date*
The Nanyang Motor Vehicle Plant, Honan Province, is responsible for building the Nanyang 7-ton dump truck. This has a 160bhp 6-cyl diesel engine and is similar to the Huang-He or Huang-Ho (Yellow River) 7-ton dump truck.

NAPIER/*England 1902-1920, 1931*
Already building light commercials, D Napier & Sons Ltd, London SE1, developed a bonneted 5-ton truck, using a 4.9-litre 4-cyl petrol engine and twin water-cooled transmission brakes. Nothing came of this and in 1903 a chain-drive passenger model, with 35hp 6.4 litre 4-cyl 'T'-head dual-ignition petrol engine was announced, selling only in small quantities. Until 1912, when a Truck Dept was set up, most other commercials were of the lighter variety.

By 1913 1½-, 2- and 3-tonners were listed as standard, all with 4-cyl petrol engines, magneto ignition, unit transmission and worm-drive. A 2¼-tonner announced in 1915 was intended for military use, while a new 4¼-tonner had a 6.2-litre petrol engine. After World War I only a 2-tonner was briefly listed, although later development work led to the construction of a 3-wheeled "mechanical horse" in 1931, but design and construction rights were sold to Scammell Lorries Ltd.

1931 Napier prototype mechanical horse

NAPOLEON/*USA 1917-1923*
The Napoleon Motors Co, Traverse City, Michigan, built 1- and 1½-ton Napoleon trucks, sold in Britain by the Seabrook Bros as Seabrook-Napoleon. Powered by 4-cyl overhead-valve Gray petrol engines, both had 3-speed transmissions and bevel-gear rear axles, production being continued by the Traverse City Motor Co from 1921.

NASH/*USA 1918-1930, 1947-1955*
The Nash organization took two separate bites at the truck market. First, as the Nash Motors Co, Racine, Wisconsin, it acquired the Thomas B Jeffery concern and its 4 x 4 Jeffery Quad, which became the Nash Quad. Second, in 1918 it added shaft-drive 1½- and 2-ton Nash trucks, employing 4-cyl side-valve petrol engines, coil ignition and 3-speed transmission. Four-speed transmissions were listed by 1921, but all commercial types

1948 Nash Model 3248 3-ton truck

were gradually withdrawn.

After World War II, as the Nash-Kelvinator Corp, Detroit, Michigan, the company introduced an export-only 2/3-ton bonneted chassis/cab powered by a 3.8-litre 6-cyl 'Ambassador' passenger car engine, production of this continuing under the American Motors Corp, Kenosha, Wisconsin, until the mid-1950s.

NASH QUAD/*USA 1917-c1919*
The 2-ton 4 x 4 Nash Quad succeeded the Jeffery Quad following the takeover of the Thomas B Jeffery Co by the Nash Motors Co, Racine, Wisconsin. Specifications were as before and the model was so popular that the company claimed to be the world's largest truck producer in 1917.

NATCO/*USA 1912-1916*
The Natco was a 2-tonner with a 285-cm wheelbase built by the National Motor Truck Co, Bay City, Michigan. It had a 4-cyl petrol engine and was of forward-control layout with four body styles available.

NATIONAL (1)/*England 1909-1919*
Thomas Clarkson founded the National Steam Car Co Ltd, Chelmsford, Essex, to construct and operate steam buses. At first these were renovated Clarkson steamers, but soon 34-seat open-top National double-deckers were entering service and by 1913 some 173 examples were in service in London. Each had a lightweight chassis frame with semi-elliptic plate springs and, in the centre of

the chassis, one paraffin and one water tank. A water-tube type boiler was housed under a front bonnet and a small pump drew fuel from the paraffin tank into an air chamber where the air was compressed to an oil pressure of 30psi. The oil was then passed to the burner beneath the boiler and exhaust gases emitted through openings in the bonnet sides. The engine was a 32hp 2-cyl double-acting type located across the centre of the chassis, but all other mechanical units were more conventional. Unusually electric interior lighting was provided by a DC dynamo powered by a vertical 2-cyl steam engine alongside the driver.

A coke-fired version, the Coke National Motor, was developed during World War I due to oil shortages. This was of different frontal appearance and used only in the Chelmsford area. After the war they were converted back to oil and known as National Motors. By 1919 the National Omnibus & Transport Co Ltd was finding maintenance increasingly expensive and the decision was taken to operate only petrol-engined vehicles. Thomas Clarkson later designed and constructed his own Chelmsford steam wagon.

NATIONAL (2)/*Canada 1915-1925*

Although the National Steel Car Co Ltd, Hamilton, Ontario, specialized in the manufacture of railway rolling stock, it also built a number of 1 to 5 tons capacity National trucks. Most had shaft-drive.

NATIONALE/*France 1899-1900*

Built by La Cie Nationale des Courriers Automobiles, Paris, the Nationale steam bus had a flash boiler and 2-cyl compound engine with a divided crankshaft enabling each cyl to drive one rear wheel via a heavy roller chain. Fifteen passengers and 12cwt of luggage could be carried.

NAYLER/*England 1903-1909*

Nayler & Co Ltd, Hereford, concentrated on the manufacture of steam vehicles, starting with a short-lived 5-ton vertical fire-tube compound "undertype" wagon. This proved impractical and a series of "overtypes", both in wagon and tractor form, were produced. Because these were said to have infringed upon Foden patents, legal action by the Sandbach company led to the end of production.

NAZAR/*Spain 1957-1967*

Factoria Napoles SA, Zaragoza and Valencia, built a number of trucks and buses ranging in capacity from 1½ to 9 tons. All were of forward-control layout, with 3-cyl Perkins diesel engines in the lightest models and, with one exception, 4-cyl Matacas or 6-cyl Henschel diesel engines in the heavier types. Most were constructed from Henschel components. The exception was the 7-ton 'Super 7', which had a 6.305 Perkins 6-cyl diesel engine. Passenger models varied from 14 to 50 seats capacity, one Nazar bus being the first Spanish passenger model to feature air-conditioning. After production ceased, the Zaragoza factory was bought by Barreiros.

NAZZARO/*Italy 1914-1916*

Founded by Felice Nazzaro, a famous racing driver of the time, Nazzaro & Cia Fabb. Automobili, Turin, built fifty trucks. These may have been for military use and were fitted with 4-cyl Anzani petrol engines.

1946 NCB 1-ton battery-electric

NCB/*England 1945-c1955*

The manufacture of battery-electric delivery vehicles was a sideline of Northern Coachbuilders Ltd, Newcastle-upon-Tyne, Co Durham, both light- and medium-duty types being sold as NCB or NCB Electric after World War II. In the heavier category were 1- and 1½-tonners, joined in 1949 by a 2-tonner and by the 1/1¼-ton 'Percheron' 3-wheeler. At this time the company also built a battery-electric version of the Pagefield 'Paragon' refuse collector as Walker-NCB and quickly moved to the Team Valley Trading Estate, Gateshead, where the 1- and 1½-ton 'Commuter' battery-electric went into production in 1953. Later the company was re-organized as Smith's Electric Vehicles Ltd, and vehicles marketed briefly as Smith's NCB Electric.

NEFAG/*Switzerland c1943 to date*

In 1937 Elektrische Fahrzeuge AG, Oerlikon, Zürich, was re-organized as Neue Elektrische Fahrzeuge AG, replacing EFAG battery-electrics by the NEFAG range. The first heavy models were battery-electric conversions of former petrol-engined trucks created during World War II, but since then the company has concentrated on 3- and 4-wheeled battery-electric delivery types with payloads of up to 2 tons. The most powerful traction motors have an output of 6hp, providing a working range per charge of up to 56km.

NELSON-LEMOON/*USA 1913-1927*

Prior to 1913, the products of Nelson & LeMoon, Chicago, Illinois, were marketed simply as LeMoon, the first major change of specification being the replacement of chain-drive on all but the heaviest Nelson-LeMoon — a 3-tonner. Continental petrol engines were normal, except for a Buda-engined 5-tonner announced in 1918, and models remained much the same until the LeMoon brand name was re-introduced following the registration of the Nelson-LeMoon Truck Co.

NEOPLAN/*West Germany 1953 to date*

Specializing in the manufacture of rear-engined chassisless passenger models as Neoplan or Auwärter, Gottlob Auwärter KG, Stuttgart, started with models powered by a 110bhp Kamper diesel engine, introducing air suspension in 1957 and the revolutionary 'Hamburg' series in 1961. This had independent front air suspension and a longitudinal wishbone system with auxiliary pneumatic springing at the rear. Numerous other special features were included, such as forced-air ventilation.

1979 Neoplan 'Spaceliner' N117

The first 'Skyliner' double-deck coach appeared in 1967 using a 340bhp air-cooled Deutz V12 diesel engine, and in 1971 the high-floor 'Cityliner' was launched. The replacement of the old single-decker by the 'Jetliner', built in a new factory at Pilsting, soon developed into a "tropical" version in 1973. This subsequently went into production alongside other German-designed models in a factory at Kumasi, Ghana, where a special version aimed at the local market was also built.

Breaking the company's traditional rear-engined layout, a mid-engined city bus was announced in 1974, and the first articulated Neoplan, the 'Longliner', again with mid-mounted engine, arrived the following year. At the 1975 Frankfurt Show the 144-seat double-deck artic 'Jumbocruiser', fitted with a 440bhp Mercedes-Benz diesel engine, made its debut. Considerable re-styling has taken place since then and licence production has taken place since 1977 in the Hayward, California, factory of the Gillig Bros, such models being sold as Gillig-Neoplan. The German company, meanwhile, has introduced special airside buses for moving up to 133 passengers between aircraft and terminal buildings.

NEPPER/*USA 1961 to date*

Richard C Nepper, a former employee of the Ahrens-Fox Fire Engine Co, acquired all assets, machinery, components, etc, of the Ahrens-Fox operation from Mack Trucks Inc, which had inherited these from the C D Beck Co, Sidney, Ohio. Using proprietary chassis, Nepper now hand-builds fire appliances and services existing machinery at his works in Cincinnati, Ohio. It is uncertain whether his appliances are sold under the chassis manufacturer's names or his own.

NETCO/*USA 1914-1938*

Netco trucks were assembled from proprietary components by the New England Truck Co, Fitchburg, Massachusetts, starting with a 4-cyl Continental petrol-engined 1½-tonner with worm-drive. This was joined by a 2-tonner in 1916 and by the early 1920s a series of 2/2½-tonners was built, using Continental petrol engines, Brown-Lipe transmissions and Timken axles. In 1927 a Hercules-engined 4-tonner arrived and by the mid-1930s an extensive range of models up to 10 tons capacity, with Waukesha or Lycoming in-line petrol engines, was advertised. The most popular vehicles were fire appliances and sewer- and drain-cleaning lorries.

NEUSTADT/*USA 1911-1914*

Although the Neustadt Motor Car Co, St Louis, Missouri, is said to have constructed self-propelled fire-fighting equipment as early as 1905, little evidence can be found and it was not until 1911 that the company's first true commercials appear to have been built. The first were the Model 'A' 1- and Model 'B' 2-ton chassis, both of bonneted design, with 4-cyl petrol engines and solid or pneumatic tyres. Production is accredited to the E L Epperson Commercial Truck Co, also of St Louis, during 1912 but this was probably only a sales organization, despite the fact that Epperson trucks were also listed at this time. From 1912 manufacture was again carried out by the Neustadt Motor Car Co.

NEVADA/*USA 1913-1916*
Design and manufacturing rights for Kato trucks were bought from the Four Traction Auto Co, Mankato, Minnesota, by the Nevada Mfg Co, Nevada, Iowa. Marketed as the Nevada, the new model was listed only as a shaft-drive forward-control 3-tonner. From 1914, production was handled by a new company — the Nevada Truck & Tractor Co.

NEW EASYLOADER/*England 1932-1933*
New Easyloader Motors Ltd, Islington, London N7, continued production of Easyloader low-loading vehicles as the New Easyloader. The first new model was the 3½-ton 'T-Type with increased power and a 4-speed transmission, followed by a short-wheelbase 2-tonner. Three wheelbase lengths were available.

NEW STUTZ/*USA 1931-1940*
The New Stutz Fire Engine Co was founded in Hartford City, Indiana, to take over production of the Stutz fire truck range. Generally, vehicles were custom-built, one of the most noteworthy being the first diesel-engined appliance produced in the US – a Cummins-engined job supplied to the city of Columbus, Indiana, in 1939. Unfortunately the business failed to compete with larger manufacturers.

NEW YORK (1)/*USA 1912*
Using the motto "made in the East for the East", the New York Motor Works, Nutley, New Jersey, offered New York trucks with capacities of 1360, 2721 and 4359kg. The lightest model had a 4-cyl petrol engine, while heavier types were powered by 6-cyl units, making these amongst the earliest 6-cyl-engined commercials in the US. All employed double chain-drive.

NEW YORK (2)/*USA 1913-1921*
The Tegetmeier & Riepe Co, New York, started production with the 1½-ton New York Model 'L', using a 4-cyl side-valve petrol engine, 3-speed transmission and double chain-drive. Worm-drive was optional from 1915 and in 1917 became standard for a new 2-tonner. Both models continued unchanged until the end of production.

NEWTON-DERBY/*England 1920-1926*
Electrical equipment manufacturer Newton Bros (Derby) Ltd announced the first battery-electric Newton-Derby truck as a 2½/3-tonner with two traction motors, each geared direct to a rear wheel. Other unusual features included

both foot- and handbrakes acting on the rear wheels and cab access via a door in the front bulkhead. Particularly popular as a municipal vehicle, the T2, as it was called, was soon joined by the 1/1½-ton T1 and 5½-ton T3, later variations employing a worm-drive rear axle.

1938 NGT SE4 single-deck bus

NGT/*England 1933-1939, 1951-1953, 1972*
To carry the maximum number of passengers in a 10-m 3-axle vehicle, the Northern General Transport Co Ltd, Gateshead, Co Durham, designed and constructed its own model using a side-mounted 6.3-litre Hercules petrol engine located beneath the floor between front axle and rear bogie. Known as the NGT SE6, but occasionally referred to as the Northern General, it had a seating capacity of 45 and was of single-drive layout, transmitted to the leading rear axle via a Fuller transmission.

The first example had its entrance behind the front axle, but subsequent versions had forward entrances. Only six SE6s were built by the operator, all others coming in both bus and coach form from the Associated Equipment Co Ltd, West London, with AEC petrol engines and David Brown transmissions. Between 1936 and 1939 more SE6s, and 13 4 x 2 SE4s, were built in Gateshead, and after World War II some of the original 6-wheelers received diesel engines.

During the early 1950s a few 10-m x 3.5-m buses and coaches were also built, with 43- and 28-seat bodies, respectively, and AEC diesel engines. Finally, a re-built Leyland 'Titan' and similarly treated AEC-PRV 'Routemaster' became the 'Tynesider' and the 'Wearsider', both of normal-control layout with entrance alongside driver for one-man operation, but neither was continued.

NIIGATA/*Japan 1934-1937*
Powered by 4- or 6-cyl diesel en-

gines, Niigata trucks were built by the Niigata Engineering Co Ltd. Little is known about them, but the 2½-tonner may have had a 40bhp 3.9-litre 4-cyl engine.

NILES/*USA 1916-1926*
Assembled from a variety of proprietary components, the Niles truck range was introduced by the Niles Car & Mfg Co, Niles, Ohio, and continued by the Niles Motor Truck Co, Pittsburgh, Pennsylvania, and finally by the South Main Motor Co, also of Pittsburgh. One-, 2- and 3-tonners were listed initially, with Continental or Buda petrol engines, shaft-drive and long radius rods, but after 1918 only the two heaviest models were available.

NISSAN/*Japan 1934 to date*
The Nissan Motor Co Ltd, Yokohama, was established to continue Datsun production, also introducing new designs as Nissan. The first new model was the semi-forward-control 1½-ton '80'-Series, with 3.7-litre 6-cyl side-valve petrol engine, 4-speed transmission and hydraulic brakes, which was joined by the bonneted '180'-Series. Production continued through World War II, and by 1952 the largest model was an 85bhp 4-tonner, also available in passenger form.

Collaboration with Minsei Diesel Industries Ltd in 1955 led to the fitting of a 100bhp 3-cyl 2-stroke Minsei diesel engine in a 6-ton Nissan, and the setting up of a joint marketing operation which led to the establishment of the Nissan Diesel Motor Co Ltd in 1960 and a separate Nissan Diesel range. Meanwhile, 1956 saw the arrival of the 1¾-ton Nissan 'Junior' with Austin-derived 1.5-litre overhead-valve petrol engine and hypoid final-drive. By 1959 this was also available as a forward-control 2-tonner, while other new models included a 1½-ton 4 x 4 and a fire-fighting version of the

'Junior'. In 1960 the NUR690 rear-engined bus, with 3-cyl Minsei diesel engine and 5-speed transmission was announced, bonneted 'Juniors' received independent front suspension and forward-control 'Juniors' were renamed the 'Caball'.

A new '80'-Series, with semi forward-control, 120bhp 3-litre petrol engine, 4-speed synchromesh transmission and hydrovac brakes, was introduced six years later as a 3½-tonner and the designs and assets of Prince Motors Ltd were acquired towards the end of 1967, complicating the lighter end of the range even more. Apart from the 'Junior', all models now had forward-control, the 'Clipper' and 'Caball' having semi-elliptic leaf springs and vacuum-servo brakes, while the 1-ton E20 had torsion-bar independent front suspension. Among heavier models was a 3½-tonner and a mediumweight "heavy" with 4-litre 6-cyl petrol or 6.8-litre 6-cyl diesel engine. By the late 1970s all heavy models had been discontinued, the Nissan range including only lighter types, a number of which are now built under licence by the Yue Loong Motor Co Ltd, Taipei, Taiwan.

NISSAN DIESEL/*Japan 1960 to date*
Collaboration between Minsei Diesel Industries Ltd and the Nissan Motor Co Ltd in the mid-1950s led to the formation of the Nissan Diesel Motor Co Ltd, Tokyo, manufacturing Nissan Diesel trucks and buses. The company's first forward-control trucks quickly developed into a tiltcab 8-tonner, while a bonneted 6 x 4 with 230bhp 6-cyl engine handled a 15-ton payload. A new series of 4-stroke diesel engines began to appear in 1962 although, even as late as 1970, the old 2-stroke design was still available and some passenger models used a turbocharged 9.9-litre V8. However, standard 4-wheelers for over 14 tons GVW were soon fitted with a 10.3-litre 6-cyl 4-stroke unit.

About this time, bonneted types were re-styled using fibreglass bonnets, optional power-steering and exhaust brakes, one special order comprising more than 2000 30-ton 6 x 6 tractors for log-hauling in Siberia. The 4-stroke engines were standard by 1972 and a new tiltcab 6-tonner, using a 135bhp 6.8-litre 6-cyl engine, 4-speed transmission and air/hydraulic brakes, was announced.

By 1976 a slimming of mediumweight models at the Nissan Motor Co Ltd led to the introduction of lighter types at Nissan Diesel. One of the first was the forward-control 8½ tons GVW CM90, with 145bhp 5.7-litre 6-cyl engine, 5-speed synchromesh transmission, hypoid-drive and hydrovac brakes. By the late 1970s many more heavy models were listed, including both 4 x 2 and 6 x 4 forward- and normal-control types, also available as artic tractors and dump trucks; crane-carriers and fire appliances; and passenger models of both front- and rear-engined layout, some with 5-speed transmissions and air suspension. Certain models are also licence-built by the Yue Loong Motor Co Ltd, Taipei, Taiwan, while others are assembled in Australia as the UD.

NOBLE/*USA 1917-1931*
The Noble truck was available in capacities from 1 to 5 tons, all models having Buda petrol engines. Built by the Noble Motor Truck Co, Kendalville, Indiana, these had 6-cyl petrol engines from 1929.

NORD-VERK/*Sweden 1969 to date*
Built by AB Nordverk, Uddevalla, the Nord-Verk 6-wheeled off-highway truck or dumper is powered by a Volvo diesel engine with 4-speed torque-converter transmission. With a payload of 22½ tons, the vehicle articulates and is steered by actuating hydraulic rams which act upon the forward section carrying the cab and power unit. Most popular as a dump truck, it is also used for other load-carrying activities on unmade ground and for handling ISO containers.

NORDE/*England 1961-1962*
Hauliers Toft Bros & Tomlinson Ltd and subsidiary the North Derbyshire Engineering Co Ltd, Darley Dale, Derbys, developed a unique artic which was considered to be the most powerful and fastest of its day. Called a Norde, it was for operation at 28 tons gross, but restricted by legislation to 24 tons and capable of sustained motorway running at up to 112km/h. Using a number of semi-trailers, the operator planned for one driver to undertake two Derby-London trips per day within regulation hours. In practice, only one semi-trailer was built and this feat was never achieved.
Power came from a Cummins NTO-6 12.2-litre turbocharged diesel. This drove a heavy-duty double-reduction AEC axle through a Self Changing Gears RV30 semi-automatic 8-speed box. Suspension was by semi-elliptic leaf springs at the front, a rubber-sprung system at the drive axle and Hendrickson tandem rubber arrangement for the semi-

1962 Norde Mk 4 x 4 tanker

trailer. The cab was a wrap-round screen structure by Bowyer Bros (Congleton) Ltd with dual headlamps and rearward extension to enclose the large engine. Full Westinghouse air braking was employed.
Other models included 6-wheeled rigids with Bedford TK cabs and, usually, a Perkins engine. The company now concentrates on the design and manufacture of semi-trailer suspensions and running units.

NORMAG/*Germany/W Germany 1938-1952*
Normag-Zorge GmbH, Zorge, Harz, and Hattingen, Ruhr, built Normag agricultural tractors and road-going machines. First of the latter was a chassisless design, powered by a 22bhp diesel engine. A new model appeared in 1948 but was relatively short-lived.

NORTHFIELD/*England 1961-c1965*
With load capacities of between

1961 Northfield F7 11-ton artic dump truck

11 and 14 tons, the Northfield was a 4-wheeled fully-articulating dump truck with front-wheel drive, power steering and a one-man half-cab. Available as the F7 or F9, with wheelbases of 310- and 340-cm respectively, it was built by Northfield Industrial Fabrications Ltd, Osset, Yorks, mainly for off-highway use. Power came from either a Ford or a Perkins diesel engine.

NORTHWAY/*USA 1919-1923*
Using its own 4-cyl overhead-valve petrol engine, the Northway Motors Corp, Natick, Massachusetts, offered 2- and 3½-tonners with the unique feature of fully-enclosed and heated cabs. Two years after production ceased, this company offered a "speed truck" called the Rocket.

NORTHWESTERN/*USA 1915-1930*
The Star Carriage Co, Seattle, Washington, advertised Northwestern trucks as "built in Seattle for Seattle's hills", starting with a 1360kg model but offering 1½- and 2-tonners from 1919 and a 2½-tonner in 1923. Continental petrol engines, Covert transmissions, Sheldon axles and Bosch ignition systems were used in all models.

NOTT/*USA 1911-c1914*
Well-known for its horse – drawn steam fire trucks, the Nott Fire Engine Co, Minneapolis, Minnesota, also built 4- and 6-cyl petrol-engined pumpers and tractors for converting horse-drawn appliances to self-propulsion. In 1912 a worm-drive appliance of modern appearance was introduced.

NW/*Austria 1898-1918*
The first NW or Nesselsdorfer truck was a rear-engined 2½-tonner with tiller-steering developed from the 'President' passenger car, manufactured by Nesselsdorfer Wagenbau-Fabriks-Gesellschaft, Nesselsdorf.
Power came from a 4-cyl Benz petrol engine assembled from two twin-cyl units and a 3-speed transmission was employed. By 1900 it had been re-built with a 2-cyl petrol engine and wheel-steering, and was joined by a steam passenger model built under licence from De Dion Bouton.
The next appeared in 1906, this being a 25/30hp 4-cyl petrol-en-

gined bus, followed by two fire appliances in 1911. A series of 2-ton shaft-drive trucks, with 35hp overhead-cam petrol engines, entered production in 1915, followed in 1916 by a similarly powered 4-tonner for use with a drawbar trailer or as a 22-seat bus. Towards the end of 1918, Nesselsdorf found itself in the new country of Czechoslovakia, and from the beginning of 1919 all models were sold as Tatra.

NWF/*West Germany 1952-1955*
Nordwestdeutsche Fahrzeugbau GmbH, Wilhelmshaven, built the NWF rear-engined forward-control chassisless buses and road-rail buses. These were available with Ford petrol or diesel engines.

NYBERG/*USA 1912-1914*
The Nyberg Automobile Works, Anderson, Indiana, built a 1½-ton Nyberg truck as well as passenger cars.
Designed by the company's founder, Henry Nyberg, this had a 4-cyl petrol engine, 3-speed transmission and chain-drive from a rear countershaft. The vehicle was of bonneted layout on a wheelbase of 310cm, with production undertaken at Chattanooga, Tennessee, before the model was withdrawn.

NYE/*USA 1920-1921*
Sometimes referred to simply as the Hood, the Nye was a 5- or 7-ton tractor aimed at the American logging industry. It was built by the Hood Mfg Co, Seattle, Washington.

NYSA/*Poland 1958 to date*
Zaklady Budowy Nadwozi Samochodowych Nysa introduced the forward-control Nysa series of vans, minibuses and ambulances, using a 57bhp 2.1-litre 4-cyl petrol engine with Warszawa transmission and rear axle.
By 1962 a de-luxe minibus version was being built in the Sanocka Fabryka Autobusow factory at Sanock, and in 1969 an updated series, known as the 521, was announced by Fabryka Samochodow Dostowczych, as it is now known. The same engine now produces 70bhp and a kombi version is also available.

1969 Nysa Model 521 minibus

OAF/*Austria 1948 to date*

Previously marketed as Austro-Fiat and AFN, the OAF truck range was introduced by Oesterreichische Automobilfabrik AG, Vienna, using numerous MAN components. Built alongside OAF-Electro battery-electric models, these were mainly bonneted types until about 1963, when the 'Tornado' series of forward- and normal-control trucks was announced. Using its own or a Cummins, Leyland or MAN diesel engine, these were for 16 tons GVW, with ZF 12-speed transmissions, the forward-control cab being common to the Gräf & Stift.

1966 OAF 'Hurricane' L7-130 truck

The semi forward-control 13-ton GVW 'Hurricane' arrived in 1966 with a 130bhp diesel engine, although a military 4 x 4 derivative had a 90bhp MAN multi-fuel engine. By 1974 all models were similar to the German MAN range, often using the same cabs, and a 6 x 6 military truck built for the Austrian Army bore an even closer resemblance. Lighter Saviems were offered at the bottom end of the OAF range in 1976, while at the top there was an 8 x 4 crane-carrier with low-line MAN cab introduced in 1978.

OAF-ELECTRO/*Austria 1948-c1956*

The OAF-Electro battery-electric delivery van was supplied mainly to the Austrian postal authorities, employing numerous components common to the OAF diesel truck range built by Oesterreichische Automobilfabrik AG, Vienna.

OEHLER ELEKTRO/*Switzerland 1928 to date*

Oehler Elektro battery-electric trucks, when introduced by Eisen und Stahlwerke Oehler & Cie AG, Aarau, had capacities of between 1 and 5 tons. After World War II particular emphasis was laid on the 1/1½ tons payload category, such models having a tubular backbone frame and independent suspension. In 1971 the company was re-organized as Oehler Aarau AG and now offers one 2- and one 4-tonner with top speeds of between 16 and 32km/h.

OETIKER/*Switzerland 1928–1936*

The Oetiker 3-ton bonneted truck with 6-cyl Maybach petrol engine succeeded the Arbenz commercial range, production of which passed from Arbenz AG, Albisrieden, Zürich, to E Oetiker & Cie Motorwagenfabrik in 1923. Other features of this model included a 3-speed overdrive transmission, shaft-drive and 4-wheel mechanical brakes. Four and 5-ton versions were later offered.

1963 OAF 'Tornado' 9.200 truck

A forward-control half-cab passenger model was developed in 1929, and by 1934 a 55bhp 4.9-litre 4-cyl Mercedes-Benz diesel engine was offered in the company's 4-tonner and a 95bhp 7.4-litre 6-cyl diesel, also by Mercedes-Benz, in the 5-tonner. Commercial production ceased when the company began to concentrate on exhaust brake mechanisms.

O & K/*Germany/West Germany 1938 to date*

The first O & K commercial, built by Orenstein-Koppel und Lubecker Maschinenbau AG, Berlin and Dortmund, was a 30bhp diesel road tractor which, by 1953, was powered by a 100bhp diesel engine. Meanwhile, 1951 saw the first O & K double-deck bus, this being constructed mainly from Büssing components for Berlin operation. In 1954 the company was re-named O & K Orenstein und Koppel AG, continuing bus and some tractor production but introducing in 1971 a series of truck-cranes with air-cooled Deutz diesel engines.

OK/*USA 1917-1928*

The first OK trucks, also marketed as OK Truck or Oklahoma, were worm-drive 1½- and 3-tonners with 4-cyl Buda petrol engines built by the Oklahoma Auto Manufacturing Co, North Muskogee, Oklahoma. Production later moved to Okay, Oklahoma, and in 1921, under the direction of the Nolan Truck Co, 1½-, 2½- and 3½-tonners were listed, joined by a 1-ton model in 1923. A 2½-ton "oil-field special" was added briefly to the range in 1926 but for the last two years only a 3-tonner was offered.

OLD RELIABLE/*USA 1911-1927*

The first Old Reliable truck was a chain-drive forward-control 3½-tonner built by the Henry Lee Power Co, Chicago, Illinois, which was re-organized in 1912 as the Old Reliable Motor Truck Co. Two-, 4- and 5-tonners were listed by 1913, and by 1915 there were eight models, from 1½ to 7 tons capacity. The lightest types now had worm-drive, and by 1917 the line also included a bonneted lightweight. The range was trimmed in 1924, by which time the company is believed to have been renamed Reliable Trucks Inc.

OLDS/*USA 1905-1907*

Although the first Olds commercial was built by the Olds Motor Works, Detroit, Michigan in 1904, this was only a light car-based model, and it was not until the following year that a chain-drive 1½-ton truck or 18-seat bus was introduced, using a vertical 2-cyl petrol engine. This lasted only a short time, the next truck offered being the 1918 Oldsmobile.

1936 Oldsmobile artic tractor

OLDSMOBILE/*USA 1918-1924, 1936-1939*

By the end of World War I, the Olds Motor Works had moved to Lansing, Michigan, and a new 1-ton truck or 14/16-seat bus introduced as the Oldsmobile. This had a 4-cyl Northway overhead-valve petrol engine, cone clutch, 3-speed transmission and full electrics, and was offered until 1924. A final batch of Oldsmobile trucks appeared in 1936 for export only, using a 3.5-litre 6-cyl side-valve petrol engine, enlarged to 3.8-litres for 1937, when forward-control models were also introduced. Heaviest were 5- and 6-tonners with 2-speed rear axles and hydrovac brakes.

1905 Olds 1½-ton truck

OM/*Italy 1928-c1978*

Following its takeover of Fabbrica Automobili Zust, Brescia, in 1917, Officine Meccaniche SpA concentrated on the manufacture of passenger cars until acquiring a licence to construct Saurer commercials. All were of bonneted layout with payloads of between 3 and 7½ tons, civilian types generally using 5.7-litre 4-cyl or 8-litre 6-cyl diesel engines, while military models were petrol-engined. The heaviest at this time was the 'Titano', using a 137bhp 11.5-litre diesel engine, 5- or 8-speed transmission and full air brakes. An unusual military model announced in 1932 was the forward-control 4-wheel drive 'Autocarretta' with independent suspension, 4-wheel steering and, until 1936, solid tyres.

Civilian forward-control models did not appear until 1946 when the 'Super Taurus' 5-tonner, with 5.8-litre 4-cyl diesel engine, 8-speed transmission and air/hydraulic brakes, was announced. Another forward-control type was the 1950 2½-ton 'Leoncino', powered by a 58bhp 4-cyl diesel engine and fitted with a 5-speed synchromesh transmission and hydraulic brakes. On the passenger front, a 6-cyl transverse rear-engined model with the same transmission system had already been in production since 1948, and was quickly joined by bonneted versions of the 'Leoncino' range, which was also built in France as the Unic and in Switzerland as OM-Berna and OM-Saurer. Oth-

1961 OM 'Titano' 4 x 4 dump truck

1961 OM 'Titano' truck

er 'Leoncino' variations included bonneted and forward-control military 4 x 4s and a front-wheel drive low-loader.

The early 1950s saw both chassised and chassisless passenger types, some OM horizontal diesel engines also being supplied to Bianchi for use in trucks and Viberti for buses. By 1954 the 2-ton air-cooled 'Lupetto' and 3½-ton 'Tigrotto' had joined the company's truck range as had the 'Tigre', with 150bhp 6.9-litre 4-cyl supercharged diesel engine, and the 4- or 6-wheeled twin-steer 'Super Orione', using an 11.6-litre V8 diesel, 8-speed transmission and air brakes.

The 'Super Orione' was replaced in 1960 by a new version of the 'Titano', using a 230bhp 6-cyl turbocharged diesel engine, and by the mid-1960s OM SpA was also building bonneted 6 x 6 trucks of Fiat design. In 1967 the 8½-ton OM 150, with 8.1-litre 6-cyl Unic diesel engine, 10-speed transmission and air brakes was announced, and the following year Fiat and OM merged to form Fiat Azienda OM, introducing Fiat diesel engines and cabs to the OM range.

By 1973 all types from 1½ to 22 tons payload were available, the heaviest models using a 306bhp Unic V8 diesel engine and lighter types a 4.9-litre OM unit. Pass-

enger requirements were catered for by a few truck-based forward-control models, while the only commercial to retain its OM cab was a 4-wheel drive version of the 'Tigrotto'. Within two years the only OM trucks were in the 3 to 10 tons GVW range, also sold as Fiat. Saurer-engined models were assembled by Adolph Saurer AG and marketed as OM-Saurer. With the founding of the Industrial Vehicles Corp, the Brescia factory appears to have been given over almost exclusively to the manufacture of mediumweight forward-control trucks using Deutz air-cooled diesel engines and sold as Magirus-Deutz.

OMT/*Italy 1963-1967*

Officine Meccaniche Tortonesi Srl, Tortona, was an established trailer manufacturer and axle conversion specialist which introduced a standard rigid 8-wheeled truck for the home market.

Using a Fiat cab, AEC AV690 6-cyl diesel engine, 8-speed transmission and air brakes, this was marketed as the OMT and was later joined by a series of twin-steer 6-wheeled tractors. These, and later versions of the 8-wheeler, were offered with 11.5-litre 6-cyl Fiat diesel engines.

ONEIDA/*USA 1917-1930*

Initial models built by the Oneida Motor Truck Co, Green Bay, Wisconsin, comprised four sizes from 1 to 3½ tons capacity, using 4-cyl Continental petrol engines, 3-speed Cotta transmissions and Timken worm-drive. A 5-tonner arrived in 1919 by which time Hinkley petrol engines and Wisconsin axles were used throughout the range.

One year later a 2-ton forward-control battery-electric truck was

1963 OMT 8 x 2 truck

marketed as the Oneida Electric, but only until 1922 when financial problems set in, leading to the company's re-organization as the Oneida Manufacturing Co in 1924 and as the Oneida Truck Co in 1928. Throughout this time goods models from 1 to 5 tons capacity and passenger types for between 25 and 42 passengers were offered, with Continental or Hinkley engines or, from 1927, Hercules units.

OPEL/*Germany 1910-c1921, 1926-1931*

Although light commercials were available from Adam Opel AG, Rüsselsheim-am-Main, as early as 1899, the first 1-ton truck did not appear until 1910, this having a 45hp 5-litre petrol engine. A 3-ton "subsidy" truck was also built but phased out after World War I in favour of lighter types. A new 1-tonner, with 10/40PS 2.6-litre 4-cyl petrol engine, was introduced

in 1926 and up-rated to 1¾ tons capacity, but in 1931 became known as the Opel Blitz along with other new models.

1960 Opel Blitz 1¾-ton

OPEL BLITZ/*Germany/West Germany 1931-1975*

New models announced by Adam Opel AG, Rüsselsheim-am-Main, in 1931, as Opel Blitz, included a 2½-ton truck with 61bhp 3.5-litre 6-cyl petrol engine. The old 1¾-ton Opel was also re-named. This model was replaced by a 1-tonner, using a 2-litre 6-cyl passenger car engine in 1934, and a brand new factory was set up at Brandenburg

Opel Blitz 1½-ton motor pump fire appliance c1950

where full mass-production got underway.

A 3-ton bonneted truck was developed into a 3½-ton 4 x 4, also built by other manufacturers, while a 2-tonner became the basis of a half-track for military use during World War II. The end of the war saw this manufacturer back in its original plant, and in 1946 a new 1½-tonner was introduced, using a 2.5-litre 6-cyl petrol engine. By 1952 this had been uprated to 1¾ tons capacity and in 1959 became a semi forward-control model.

The Opel Blitz range disappeared early in 1975 and has now been replaced by certain Bedford models which are marketed as Bedford Blitz.

Opperman Motocart tipper c1953

OPPERMAN MOTOCART/
England 1947-1953
Originally developed for agricultural use, the Opperman Motocart was a large 3-wheeler powered by an 8bhp single-cyl JAP petrol engine mounted on the front wheel. It had a capacity of 1½ tons and standee driving position. Built by S E Opperman Ltd, Borehamwood, Herts, chassis were also supplied to Lacre Lorries Ltd as a basis for its 'T'-Type road-sweeper. Later production

appears to have been carried out by Transport Equipment (Thornycroft) Ltd.

ORION/Switzerland 1900-1910*
Zürcher und Huber Automobilfabrik Orion, Zürich, developed the first Swiss single- and twin-cyl petrol engines for commercial vehicles, fitting a horizontal single-cyl unit amidships in the first chaindrive Orion. This engine, which developed about 20hp, had a single camshaft operating both inlet and exhaust valves. By 1903 a twin-cyl horizontal engine was offered in a similar model, and by 1905 a whole range of vehicles was available, using 7 or 9hp single-cyl units or twin-cyl types providing up to 24hp. Orders were plentiful and the company, which was now known as Zürcher Automobilfabrik Orion AG, moved to a new factory and allowed licence production to take place in Italy.

About 1907 the London General Omnibus Co experimented

1904 Orion open-top double-deck bus

with Orion buses but no orders followed, although the design was now improved, using an amidships-mounted horizontal 4-cyl petrol engine, front-mounted radiator, 4-speed transmission and chain-drive. The company's competitors were now well ahead, and the marque soon disappeared.

ORWELL/England 1915-1928*
Ransomes, Sims & Jefferies Ltd, Ipswich, Suffolk, was manufacturing steam and agricultural equipment when it began to develop battery-electric commercials under the Orwell or Ransomes Electric names. A few prototypes were built before a series of trucks and municipal types, believed to include models of up to 5 tons capacity, were launched in 1920, with two traction motors driving the front wheels. By 1924 the company's first trolleybus, a single-decker for the local council with tram-type hand controller, had been built, but such vehicles were later sold as Ransomes.

OVERLAND (1)/USA 1911-1913*
A 1-ton "cabover" introduced by passenger car and light van manufacturer Willys-Overland Co, Toledo, Ohio, was marketed as the Overland, although it was

OSHKOSH/USA/South Africa 1918 to date*
Following the success of the Wisconsin Duplex 4 x 4 truck, the Wisconsin Duplex Auto Co set up a new factory at Oshkosh, Wisconsin, re-organized itself as the Oshkosh Motor Truck Manufacturing Co and introduced the normal-control Model 'A' 2-tonner, marketed as the Oshkosh. Featuring thermo-syphon cooling, this had a 72hp 4-cyl Herschell-Spillman petrol engine and a pre-ignition fuel heating system to overcome problems created by the use of low-grade fuels. A 3½-tonner arrived in 1920, and a 5-tonner in 1924, by which time the company was supplying many trucks which were used the growing construction industry.

1950 Oshkosh Model W-703D

The Model 'H', with a 6-cyl petrol engine and double-reduction final-drive, went into production in 1925, and by 1932 machines of up to 19,957kg GVW were available. Now called the Oshkosh Motor Truck Inc, the company announced its 4-wheel drive and 4-wheel steer 'TR' model in 1933, for use with a bottom-dump semi-trailer or as an earth scraper, making it the first rubber-tyred earthmover, and in 1935 certain models were offered with Cummins diesel engines. One of the lightest Oshkosh trucks of modern times also appeared in 1935, this being the 2-ton 'J'-Series, soon joined by the similar 'FB'-Series.

Re-styling in 1940 saw the introduction of the long-running 'W'-Series and large numbers of standard Oshkosh trucks were supplied to the armed forces during World War II, mainly for airfield snow-clearance and wrecker duties. The first 6 x 6 Oshkosh appeared in the late 1940s and was joined in the early 1950s by the 35-ton payload W-2800 of usual probably built by the Federal Motor Truck Co, Detroit, Michigan. Power came from a 40hp 4-cyl petrol engine.

All subsequent commercials were re-named and sold as Willys-Overland.

OVERLAND (2)/*England 1926-1928*

Willys-Overland-Crossley Ltd was established in 1920 to assemble Willys-Overland commercials in Britain, but later introduced its own 1¼-ton Overland truck, using imported 2.5-litre 4-cyl side-valve petrol engines, 3-speed transmissions and axles.

Unusual features for a British-built truck included coil-ignition, a spiral-bevel axle and demountable-rimmed wooden wheels, which were replaced by the detachable steel type in 1927. Based in Stockport, Cheshire, this company was an offshoot of the Crossley brothers' empire. who changed the marque's name from Overland to Manchester in 1928.

1979 Oshkosh 'F'-Series 6 x 6 artic tractor

"conventional" appearance with set-back front axle, but including planetary gearing and a torque-proportioning differential within the transfer box. A new line of airfield snow-clearance vehicles, headed by the WT-2206, was also announced.

The first 50-50 Series 4 x 4 "conventionals" appeared in 1955, designed for use as truck-mixers with load distribution divided equally between front and rear axles, but as load capacities grew so did the number of rear axles fitted, leading to drive configurations of up to 10 x 6 layout. From 1956, certain models used International cabs, but in 1960 an all-steel cab with forward-angled windscreen was introduced. The largest Oshkosh at this time was the Model 3000 60-ton "cabover" tractor with 1-man offset cab for off-highway operation, usually with a dump semi-trailer.

The U-44-L was a normal-control all-wheel drive utility vehicle with 2-man tandem offset cab introduced in 1962 for the transport of drilling and similar equipment. The multi-axle versions of the 50-50 Series had now led to the 'D'-Series truckmixer, another bonneted design, with twin front steering axles and 12 x 10 drive.

As the Oshkosh Truck Corp, the company's first standard "cab-overs" appeared in 1971, when the tiltcab 'E'-Series was announced in 4 x 2 and 6 x 4 rigid or artic form. These are now built only in the factory of Oshkosh Africa (Pty) Ltd, Paarl, near Capetown. By 1973 the first Oshkosh airfield fire crash tenders were under construction. Known as the 'M'-Series, the first was the 4 x 4 M-1000, followed by the M-1500 6 x 6 powered by a 510bhp diesel engine. For civilian fire-fighting, the 6 x 4 cab-forward 'A'-Series and low-silhouette 'L'-Series are supplied to various fire equipment manufacturers who sell finished appliances under their own names. The ultimate, however, is the 8 x 8 P-15, one of the world's largest airfield fire crash tenders, powered by two 430bhp Detroit Diesel engines.

The most popular Oshkosh "conventional" for some years has been the 'F'-Series with 6 x 4, 8 x 6 and 10 x 6 drive, again aimed mainly at the construction industry, with the similar 'R'-Series 6 x 4 available as a rigid or articulated model. However, the 6 x 6 'J'-Series of 1974, based on the 'F'-Series, was intended for desert use, having an extra large capacity radiator, sand tyres and other modifications.

A new range of mixer chassis arrived in 1975, in the form of the 'B'-Series, using a centrally-placed 1-man cab and forward-discharge drum. Unusually, this model is rear-engined with 6 x 4, 6 x 6 or 8 x 6 drive. Another new range is the 'H'-Series for snow clearance duties. Power comes from two Caterpillar diesel engines, a 225bhp unit providing forward and reverse motions and a 425bhp unit powering the rotary plough. Some long-standing customers, however, prefer to have older models re-engineered by the company and sold back to them at two-thirds the price of a new vehicle. Most unusual of all current Oshkosh models is the 'V'-Series school bus chassis using a 210bhp diesel engine.

1949 Oshkosh Model W-1600-BD 6 x 6 artic tractor

1933 Oshkosh Model FDL 8-ton 4 x 4 tipper

1978 Oshkosh 'F'-Series 6 x 6 tipper/snowplough

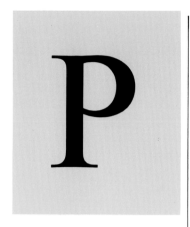

P

PACIFIC (1)/*USA 1942-1945*
Because the Pacific Car & Foundry Co, Renton, Washington, had more spacious production facilities than the Knuckey Truck Co, the Fruehauf Trailer Co, which had been commissioned by the US Government to supply the 40-ton capacity M25 articulated tank transporter, sub-contracted the construction of motive units to the Washington company. The TR-1 tractor was of fully-armoured 6 x 6 forward-control layout, powered by a 240bhp 6-cyl Hall-Scott petrol engine, making it one of the most powerful trucks built during World War II. Transmission was via a 4-speed main box and 3-speed transfer, with shaft-drive and chains between the Knuckey bogie's rear wheels. Three power winches were fitted, one at the front to haul the vehicle out of difficulties, and two at the rear to ease loading and unloading.

In 1944 the semi-trailer was up-

for quarry, oilfield or heavy haulage work and for fire-fighting.

Now a subsidiary of International Harvester, the company offers four basic models, on which a multitude of special requirements can be based. Of these, the P-16 is by far the largest and the most powerful. In 1973, one of the most interesting orders went to the Abnormal Loads Divn of South African Railways. This comprised a number of P-12 heavy haulage tractors, each powered by a 540bhp turbocharged Cummins V12 diesel engine coupled to a Clark 1600-Series torque-converter transmission with 8-speed power-shift box. One thousand litres of fuel were carried and cabs offset to the right to provide maximum visibility.

PACKARD/*USA 1905-1923*
The Packard Motor Car Co, Detroit, Michigan, was already building passenger cars when it constructed its first commercial – a forward-control 1½-tonner with 15hp horizontal twin-cyl petrol engine. This used a Packard touring car back axle and 3-speed sliding-mesh transmission with chains between countershaft and rear wheels. Semi-elliptic leaf springs were used throughout with a single transverse spring at the rear. Some of these were equipped as fire appliances and one even acted as official baggage car for the American Automobile Association's first Glidder Tour.

In 1908 this model was joined by the 3A 3-tonner, using a 30hp 4-cyl petrol engine with water-

1905 Packard 1½-ton truck

coupled via a multi dry-plate clutch and 3-speed gearbox to an overhead-worm rear axle with spur-gear differential. A 12-cyl passenger car known as the 'Twin Six' was also announced in 1915 and a number of these were fitted as 18-seat buses.

Chain-drive Packards were discontinued in 1920 in favour of worm-drive models for between 1½ and 7 tons capacity. The 2-ton Model 'X', also introduced at this time, was the first Packard built to take pneumatic tyres, using also a 40bhp 4-cyl petrol engine, multiplate clutch and 4-speed transmission, with a twin-cyl tyre pump mounted on the front of the gearbox. Until the end of production 2-, 3-, 5- and 7½-tonners were built, some in passenger form. Four trolleybuses built by the Brill Car Co, Preston, Ontario, were based on the 3-ton chassis, complete with Westinghouse traction equipment, single-deck bodies and false radiators.

PACKERS/*USA 1910-1913*
Packers trucks were built by the Packers Motor Truck Co, Pittsburgh, Pennsylvania, until 1911 but then at Wheeling, West Virginia. Standard models were 3- and 4-tonners, although 1- and 2-ton models were available to order. All were of bonneted layout, with a 4-cyl petrol engine, Hele-Shaw multi-plate clutch, 3-speed transmission and double chain-drive.

PAGE/*USA 1916-?*
The Page was a front-wheel drive load-carrier offered briefly by the Page Bros Buggy Co, Marshall, Michigan.

PAGEFIELD/*England 1907-1951*
Walker Bros (Wigan) Ltd set up Pagefield Commercial Vehicles Ltd to construct Pagefield commercials. The company's first at-

1943 Pacific (1) TR-1 6 x 6 armoured artic tractor

rated to 45 tons capacity and a more rugged version of the TR-1, known as the M26A1, appeared using a "soft-skin" cab. Many of these machines later saw service with overseas armed forces and as civilian heavy haulage tractors.

PACIFIC (2)/*Canada 1947 to date*
Based in North Vancouver, British Columbia, Pacific Truck & Trailer Ltd was set up by three former executives of the Hayes Mfg Co Ltd to design and build log-haulers for the home timber industry, later offering other types

jacketed cyls cast in pairs. The engine was controlled via a throttle lever fixed to the steering wheel and a foot accelerator. A 3-speed transmission and chain-drive were used. Two- and 5-tonners, designated Models 2B and 5A, arrived in 1912 and the first 3- and 4-ton worm-drive trucks appeared in 1914, by which time the chain-drive 3-tonner had been militarized, some even receiving half-track conversions. One and one-half and 2½-ton worm-drives and a 6-ton chain-drive went into production in 1915, the former having 4-cyl monobloc engines

tempt was a 2-tonner powered by a 2-cyl petrol engine, replaced by a 28hp 4-cyl unit in 1911 when a similarly-powered 3-tonner was introduced.

During World War I over 500 "subsidy" 3-tonners, known as the 'N' Model, were built, using 40hp Dorman 4J 4-cyl petrol engines, separately-mounted 4-speed gearboxes, shaft-drive and double-reduction axles. Three and one-half and 5-ton versions were constructed after the war but sales were poor until 1923 when an enquiry led to the development of "the Pagefield system" of refuse collection.

A few forward-control half-cab passenger models with dropframe chassis were built from 1927, using a 6-cyl Dorman petrol engine which could be wheeled from the front of the chassis for maintenance. At the same time it was announced that Walker Bros was to merge with the Lacre Motor Car Co Ltd and all Pagefield production would move to the latter's Letchworth factory. This, however, did not happen.

In 1929 a prototype 6-ton 6-wheeled truck-crane was developed for the LMS Railway. This used Tilling-Stevens petrol-electric transmission for both travelling and crane movements and was supplied to other railway companies, often under the Walker name. By the end of the 1920s a Gardner marine diesel engine had been fitted experimentally in a Pagefield truck chassis, leading to the introduction of the Gardner-Pagefield in 1930, this being joined in 1931 by the 4-ton 'Pegasus' and 10/12-ton 'Plantagenet' 6-wheeler.

Another design was the 'Prodigy' low-loader of 1932 which originally had a Meadows petrol engine, but from 1934 could be had with a Perkins diesel. Axles and other components previously manufactured in the same factory

Pagefield demountable container refuse collector c1929

were now of proprietary make and during World War II and the late 1940s only a few truck-cranes and a few municipals were built. In 1947 Pagefield Commercial Vehicles Ltd ceased trading, vehicle manufacture being continued by the parent company under the Pagefield name until 1951.

PAIGE/*USA 1918-1923*
As well as producing a number of Jeffery Quads, the Paige-Detroit Motor Car Co, Detroit, Michigan, built its own 2-ton truck, which it marketed as the Paige or Paige-Detroit. This had a Continental petrol engine, 3-speed transmission, shaft-drive and worm rear axle. For 1919, this model was up-rated to 2½ tons capacity and joined by a similar 3½-tonner, while for 1921 a 1½-tonner appeared and all three models were fitted with Hinkley engines. Later only passenger cars were built but in 1928 the business was acquired by the Graham brothers, who introduced a new light Paige commercial.

PALLADIUM/*England 1914-1925*
Passenger car manufacturer Palladium Auto-Cars Ltd, West London, entered the commercial vehicle ·market with a 3/4-ton shaft-drive truck fitted with a Dorman petrol engine. In 1915 production moved to Putney, London SW15, and five years later the 3/4-tonner was replaced by a 4-ton model with Continental petrol engine, 4-speed transmission and a much publicized double cantilever rear suspension as an option, mainly for passenger use.

PALMER-MEYER/*USA 1914-1918*
Based on an earlier lightweight design, the Palmer or Palmer-Meyer started as a 1- or 1½-tonner, built by the Palmer-Meyer Motor Truck Co, St Louis, Missouri. These had 4-cyl side-valve petrol engines, 3-speed transmissions and double chain-drive.

1936 Pagefield 'Pompian' boxvan

Shaft-drive appeared in 1915 and from 1917 only 1- and 2-tonners were built.

PALTEN/*Austria 1954*
The Palten was a short-lived 1-ton forward-control delivery van built at Rottenmann, Styria. Power came from a 991cc 2-stroke 'V'-twin air-cooled diesel engine built by Warchalowski of Vienna. Other features included a pressed-steel chassis frame, aluminium body and full independent suspension.

PANHARD/*France 1895-1959*
In 1895 Panhard et Levassor, Paris, offered a light truck and entered a 12hp 3.3-litre 4-cyl petrol-engined bus in the 1897 French Heavy Vehicle Trials. For 1898 a 1-ton van, with wheel-steering and 8hp 4-cyl petrol engine, was listed and a 1½-ton truck took part in the Military Trials of 1900. Early designs had front-mounted vertical engines, armoured timber frames and chain-drive, lighter models employing 3-speed transmissions and a bonneted layout while heavier types had 4-speed transmissions and an underseat engine.
Registered SA des Ans Ets Panhard et Levassor, the company exhibited a shaft-drive 20hp bus at the 1905 Paris Salon, later offered also as a 2-ton truck. By 1910 most Panhard trucks were of chain-drive design, available in both normal- and forward-control form and using a variety of 4-cyl 'T'-head petrol engines. The company's first military model was the 1911 Chatillon-Panhard artillery

tractor, a number of variations being built during World War I.
With the resumption of civilian production only bonneted 1½- and 3-tonners were built, using 4-cyl poppet- and sleeve-valve petrol engines, 3-speed transmissions, bevel final-drive and full electrics. Models up to 4 tons payload were listed and by 1925 all had 4-wheel brakes. Knight sleeve-valve engines were now used and long-wheelbase coaches were added. For colonial use, 1½-, 2½- and 4½-ton producer-gas trucks were available from 1927 and until 1929 there were also battery-electric 2-tonners with Oerlikon traction motors mounted on the rear axle, coil front suspension and 4-wheel brakes.
Models from 1¼ to 8 tons capacity were listed for 1930 and by 1931 certain heavy models had servo brakes and two new diesel engines had been developed. The smallest was a 60bhp 4.4-litre 4-cyl unit and the largest a 90bhp 6.8-litre 6-cyl unit, both of sleeve-valve design. By 1933 the 6-cyl unit had been enlarged to 8.9 litres and joined by new 6.3-litre 4- and 9.5-litre 6-cyl petrol engines.

1899 Panhard 1½-ton truck

Lighter trucks were now rare, most models being concentrated in the 4 to 8 tons category by 1937, and by 1939 forward-control derivatives were also listed. The only petrol engines available in the commercial range were now 4-cyl units, while regular diesels had now been joined by a 5.6-litre 4-cyl Bernard as an option. Collaboration between Panhard, Somua and Willème led to the formation of the Union Française Automobile but little came of this apart from a 1949 Panhard-Somua bus.
In the late 1940s, production centred upon a 5-ton forward-control range available as a rigid, tractor or passenger chassis. There was a choice of three engines, petrol or diesel. Other features included a 5-speed overdrive transmission, double-reduction back axle and air/hydraulic brakes. In 1951 this range was up-rated to 7 tons capacity and by 1952 4 x 4

1955 Panhard 7-ton tipper

and 6 x 6 versions were advertised, while various Panhard components were incorporated in Floirat and Tubauto passenger types. An association with Citroën in 1954 boosted light van production as well as introducing a Type 55 Citroën bonneted truck under the Panhard name, powered by a 6.8-litre Panhard diesel engine. Only lightweight delivery models were offered after this and the 7-tonner was withdrawn.

PANTZ/*France 1899-1907*
Using premises at Pont-à-Mousson, Meurthe-et-Moselle, Charles Pantz developed the 1½-ton Pantz truck. An unusual feature was the 8hp 2-cyl horizontal petrol engine and 3-speed pulley transmission, all of which could be removed as

one and re-installed in an identical vehicle, thereby enabling one engine to be used in two or more vehicles.

PARAGON/*England c1913*
Developed by W P Durtnall, the Paragon petrol-electric bus was intended for London operation. It had a 40hp flat 6-cyl engine driving on an alternator mounted on the outer casing of an electric motor whose ends terminated in slip rings. One end of this motor's rotor was connected to the rear axle and the other to a magnetic clutch. Controls were mounted on top of the steering wheel with only the brakes pedal-operated. Despite its advantages, the system failed to be successful.

PARKER (1)/*England 1898-1899*
Designed by Thomas Parker, an 8- to 10-passenger steam bus went into production at the Wolver-

hampton factory of Parker Bros Ltd. Powered by a vertical oil-fired boiler and two 2-cyl compound engines, it was unusual in that it had 4-wheel steering.

PARKER (2)/*USA 1918-c1933*
Using Continental, Waukehsa or Wisconsin petrol engines, the Parker Motor Truck Co, Milwaukee, Wisconsin, started with a range of trucks in the 1- to 5-ton capacity range. In 1924 the business was re-organized as the Parker Truck Co Inc, and models slimmed down to capacities of between 1 and 3½ tons. The lightest had a Buda engine while the others remained much as before.

PARVILLE/*France 1928-c1930*
Edouard Parvillé et Cie, Paris, offered 1½- and 3-ton Parvillé commercials. Both were front-wheel drive battery-electrics, the lighter having a "coal-scuttle" bonnet and the heavier forward-control.

PATHFINDER/*USA c1913-1914*
The Pathfinder Motor Car Mfg Co, Indianapolis, Indiana, occasionally used its larger passenger car chassis as a basis for van, ambulance or hearse bodywork. The largest was a 1-ton delivery van with 4-cyl petrol engine, 3-speed transmission and shaft-drive.

PATRIOT/*USA 1917-1926*
Patriot or Hebb trucks were built by the Hebb Motors Co, Lincoln, Nebraska, and actually marketed under a combination of marque and model names, thus the 1½-ton 'Lincoln' was called the Patriot-Lincoln and the 2½-ton 'Washington' the Patriot-Washington. Both had 4-cyl Buda petrol engines and 4-speed transmissions, while the Patriot-Lincoln had internal-gear final-drive and the other worm-drive.

Most components were built by the company which also supplied chassis frames, radiators and bodies to other manufacturers. By the middle of 1918 Continental petrol engines were being used and in 1920 the company was reformed as the Patriot Motors Co. By 1921 Hinkley engines were fitted in the largest models and a year later the business was purchased by the Woods brothers, who continued production as the Patriot Mfg Co, building 1-, 2- and 3-ton Patriots with Buda or Hinkley petrol engines, Covert transmissions and Empire or Wisconsin worm axles. Models later became known as Woods.

PATTON/*USA 1899*
Built by the Fischer Equipment Co, Chicago, Illinois, the 8-ton Patton petrol-electric truck was actually developed by the Patton

Motor Vehicle Co, Chicago. It had a vertical 3-cyl engine supplied by the American Petroleum Motor Co driving an 8kw Crocker-Wheeler dynamo which, in turn, provided electric current to two 7½hp traction motors, one powering each rear wheel. It resembled a horse-drawn wagon of the period, with the engine mounted above the fore-carriage and the traction motors located ahead of the rear axle.

PAULDING/*USA 1913-1916*
Paulding trucks were listed with capacities of up to 2721kg. Built by the St Louis Motor Truck Co, St Louis, Missouri, early models were of forward-control chain-drive layout but for 1916 a shaft-drive bonneted layout was adopted.

PAYMASTER/*USA 1973*
Designed by Dean Hobgenseifken, the Paymaster was a streamlined prototype tractor unit. Intended as a design exercise, it had an aerodynamically-constructed cab and air spoilers to reduce drag when coupled to a semi-trailer, while the engine was mounted under the fifth wheel coupling, with twin radiators, transmission and rear axle removable for maintenance. Towards the end of 1973 design rights were purchased by Ryder Systems, Miami, Florida, and ten production models constructed by the Hendrickson Mfg Co, these being known as Ryders.

PAZ/*Soviet Union 1970 to date*
Built by the Pavlov Autobus Works, Pavlov, the PAZ passenger range was originally based on GAZ truck chassis. Current models use the company's own chassis and comprise the PAZ-652 23/32-passenger city bus with 84bhp 6-cyl engine and the PAZ-672 46-passenger bus with 130bhp V8 engine and 4-speed transmission.

PECARD/*France c1900-1929*
Well-established as a manufacturer of agricultural steam engines and road rollers, L et A Pecard Frères, Nevers, also built the Continent's only "overtype" steam wagon, a double high-pressure 2-speed type with chain-drive and rear axle differential.

PEDRAIL/*England 1913*
Pedrail Transport Ltd, West London, built a forward-control tracked lorry with a capacity of 5 tons.

PEERLESS (1)/*USA 1911-1918*
The first trucks built by the Peerless Motor Car Co, Cleveland, Ohio, were rugged bonneted

models from 3 to 6 tons capacity. All had 4-cyl petrol engines built by the company, cone clutches, 4-speed transmissions and chain final-drive, and many were used by the Allied Forces in World War I. A worm-drive 2-tonner was added in 1916 and two truck-tractors, with capacities of 3 and 6 tons, were also built. Many war-surplus 4- and 5-tonners were re-conditioned for civilian use in the British Isles, eventually leading to a new Peerless marque.

PEERLESS (2)/*England 1925-1933*
War-surplus 4- and 5-ton American-built Peerless trucks were reconditioned and sold on the civilian market by Slough Lorries & Components Ltd, Slough, Berks, later developing into a line of complete vehicles assembled by the Peerless Trading Co Ltd from spare parts and British-made proprietary components. Generally known as Peerless, models were also marketed as Peerless Trader or Trader to avoid confusion with the American-built model.

Specifications were similar to the original Peerless although by 1930 options included a reinforced chassis frame for 8-ton payloads, pneumatic tyres at the front with solids at the rear and 4-cyl Gardner diesel engines. In 1930 the 8-ton Tradersix with 115bhp 8-litre 6-cyl overhead-valve Meadows engine and chain-drive was announced. This was followed by the Tradersix 90 with power unit mounted well ahead of the front axle and chain- or worm-drive.

A trailing-axle 12½-ton 6-wheeled rigid, with Dewandre servo brakes, appeared the following year, and in 1933 a 4/5-ton normal or forward-control range was introduced, using Gardner 4LW diesel engines, Meadows transmissions and Kirkstall worm-drive axles. These never actually entered production.

PEGASO/*Spain 1949 to date*
A 6-cyl diesel-engined forward-control 8-ton truck was the first offering of Empress Nacional de Autocamiones SA, Barcelona, following the 1946 takeover of La Hispano-Suiza Fabrica de Automoviles SA. Fitted with an 8-speed transmission and air brakes, this first Pegaso was joined in 1950 by a 125bhp diesel- or 145bhp petrol-engined bus chassis and chassisless 1½-deck coach.

During the early 1950s various 4- and 6-wheeled trucks, buses and trolleybuses were added to the range, and in 1955 new 5- and 6-tonners went into production at Barajás, Madrid. Leyland Motors Ltd acquired a major sharehold-

ing in 1960 and Leyland diesel engines and other components were adopted for a range of medium-weight trucks. New models based on this range included the 1063 twin-steer 6-wheeled rigid and the 1066 single-drive 8-wheeler, while passenger requirements were catered for by a number of rear-engined chassis. Towards the end of the 1960s new models included a 26-ton dump truck and various 4 x 4 military types.

Pegaso artic tractor c1963

A 5-ton 4 x 4 military truck of DAF design entered production in 1970, followed by Pegaso's own 6 x 6 design, and after the debut of a new angular cab in 1972 new truck models were announced, with gross vehicle weights of up to 38 tons and engine outputs of up to 350bhp. Various vertical and horizontal-engined passenger chassis are now listed and the same company also builds SAVA commercials.

1974 Pegaso Model 6031-N coach

PEKING/*China 1968 to date*
Powered by a 75bhp 4-cyl 4-stroke petrol engine, the 2-ton forward-control Peking BJ-130 truck is built by the Peking Erh Li Kou Motor Vehicle Plant. An hydraulic clutch is used in conjunction with a 4-speed transmission.

PEKOL/*Germany/East Germany 1938-1951*
Oldenburger Vorortbahnen GmbH, Oldenburg, was a bus operator that began building its own bus. Called the Pekol, this was a forward-control design using a rear-engined Mercedes-Benz chassis. From 1947 Mercedes-Benz or Henschel diesel engines were employed.

PEMFAB/*USA ? to date*
Pemberton Fabrications Inc specializes in constructing Pemfab custom fire truck apparatus for direct

sale or for supply to the many small custom fire truck builders. In addition to the "Cincinnati" type cab, a low-profile cab is now offered and a wide range of engines, transmissions, pumps and fire-fighting equipment available.

PENA/*Mexico 1956 to date*
Trailers del Norte SA, Monterey, Nueva Leon, builds Pena trucks and trailers. Only heavy-duty types are available, early examples being assembled mainly from imported components. Current models use many Mexican parts.

PENINSULA/*Canada 1961-1962*
Only about ten examples of the Peninsula "cabover" truck-tractor were built. Constructed by the Peninsula Truck Divn of Switsen Industries Ltd, a vacuum cleaner manufacturer, Welland, Ontario, these were available in 4- and 6-wheeled form, had a prominent front overhang and were powered by Cummins, Rolls-Royce or Detroit Diesel engines, with Fuller transmissions and Shuler, Eaton or Timken axles. They were for on- and off-road use and intended for gross weights in excess of 16,330kg. The last example was a 55/60-ton off-highway dump truck.

PENN/*USA 1923-1927*
H W Sofield, designer of the Keystone truck left the Keystone Motor Truck Corp, Oaks, Pennsylvania, in 1921 to found the Penn Motors Corp, Philadelphia. In 1923 this company bought out the original firm and the Keystone range was subsequently re-named Penn.

PENTON CANTILEVER/*USA 1928*
Often referred to simply as the Penton, the 4-cyl petrol-engined Penton Cantilever truck was so called because of its chassis construction, having a light frame supported by truss rods below the sidemembers. Built by the Penton Motor Co, Cleveland, Ohio, it also had an unusual front-drive arrangement employing large-diameter spur-gears inside the front wheels. Designed for local deliveries, it had a centre door.

PEOPLE'S/*USA 1900-1902*
The People's Automobile Co was founded in Cleveland, Ohio, to construct and operate motor buses in opposition to the city's tramway system which was suffering from a prolonged strike. Passenger cars and light commercials were also built.

PERKINS/*England 1871-1902*
The Perkins was a 3-wheeled steam tractor for converting horse wagons to self-propulsion. Built by Perkins & Sons, London, it had a water-tube boiler and compound engine. The single powered front wheel was carried in a circular sub-frame along with boiler and engine, the whole rotating within the mainframe to provide steering. Although a prototype appeared and the design was listed for many years it is doubtful that further examples were built.

PERL/*Austria 1907-c1960*
Automobilfabrik Perl AG, Lies-

1932 Perl D4 light fire appliance

ing, Vienna, entered the commercial field with petrol-engined motors quickly adding battery-electric lorries and tractors. By 1920 both goods and passenger types were offered and in 1927 modified chassis were used as a basis for the Czechoslovakian FRAM passenger range.

Diesel engines were introduced during the 1930s, and following World War II production was narrowed down to diesel-engined passenger models and the company re-named Perl-Auhof Karrosseriefabrik. By 1959 one model was based on a welded frame of steel tubing, carrying a 6-cyl Henschel diesel engine at the rear. With a claimed maximum speed of 117km/h this had semi-elliptic leaf springs and hollow rubber suspension units. The ZF gearbox had a secondary reduction providing ten ratios, and the entire space between the wheels was taken up by a full-width baggage area.

PERLINI/*Italy 1958 to date*
Already a manufacturer of trailers, semi-trailers and third axle conversions, Officine Meccaniche Costruzioni Roberto Perlini, Verona, has built up a good line of on- and off-road dump trucks and airfield fire crash tenders.

The largest Perlini crash tender was announced in 1971, using two 8-litre BPM or 8.7-litre American-built Ford V8 petrol engines mounted horizontally at the rear, an automatic transmission, air-conditioning and power-steering. Dump trucks are 4-wheeled half-cab designs, the heaviest having a V16 Detroit Diesel engine and Allison automatic transmission for a payload of 75 tons, while the smallest, the T15, is for highway operation with a Fiat, Scania or Detroit Diesel engine, 6-speed transmission, power-steering and air-hydraulic brakes.

1969 Perlini T15 dump truck

sharing a cab with the Kenworth Truck Co which, like Peterbilt, is now a subsidiary of the Pacific Car & Foundry Co. An unusual vehicle developed in association with Pacific Intermountain Express in the mid-1950s was the 'Dromedary', comprising a long-wheelbase 4-, 6- or 8-wheeled tractor with horizontal diesel engine and van body between cab and fifth wheel coupling.

Production moved to Newark, New Jersey, in 1960 and a second plant was opened in Nashville, Tennessee, in 1969. Standard Peterbilts now used Cummins NH220 diesel engines, Spicer 12-speed transmissions and fully-floating hypoid or double-reduction rear axles, while gross weights ranged from 15,422 to 113,397kg. Caterpillar and Detroit Diesel engines were becoming popular and by the early 1970s Peterbilts were virtually custom-built, often using a 15-speed Fuller transmission.

The cab-forward '200'-Series for refuse collection was announced in 1971, sharing its cab with Kenworth, and from 1973 Kenworth cabs also appeared on Peterbilt "conventionals" with the exception of the Model 383 off-road type. The inevitable construction truck, the Model 346 with set-back front axle, arrived in 1973. Some ten models, including "conventional", "cabover" and cab-forward types, are now listed with gross weights of up to 56,698kg for on-road operation. Caterpillar, Cummins and Detroit Diesel engines from 210 to 450bhp output are offered.

Peterbilt 6 x 4 tipper c1956

PETERBILT/*USA 1939 to date*
When the Fageol Truck & Coach Co's Oakland, California, factory was purchased by T A Peterman, the Peterbilt Motors Co continued truck production under the Peterbilt brand name. These were similar to the bonneted Fageols, but with the option of aluminium alloy frames and other weight-saving parts. Cummins, Hall-Scott and Waukesha engines were used.

In 1944 the business passed to a group of employees who concentrated on "conventional" models, including some 6 x 6 off-road trucks, until 1950, when a prototype "cabover" was assembled. This entered series production in 1952 as the Model 350, was replaced by the Model 351 and is still offered as the Model 352,

Peterbilt 6 x 4 artic tractor c1959

PETROL PONY/*England 1935-1936*
Designed by Frank Waring, the prototype Petrol Pony 3-wheeled "mechanical horse" had a tubular backbone frame, a single-cyl petrol engine mounted behind the rear wheels and a lever-operated motorcycle-type kick-change gearbox. A second prototype, powered by an Austin 7 engine, appeared in 1936 and was said to be capable of hauling a 1/1½-ton load, but series production did not follow.

PEUGEOT/*France 1898 to date*
Among the earliest commercial types built by SA des Automobiles Peugeot, Audincourt, was a short-lived 8hp 1-tonner using a rear-engined chain-drive chassis. Just as rare was a chain-drive 1½-tonner with front-mounted 1.8-litre 2-cyl petrol engine introduced in 1905.

By 1909 there was also a 3½-tonner powered by a 3.8-litre 4-cyl petrol engine.

For 1913 a new 7-model range of commercials was offered in capacities of up to 5 tons, using 4-cyl side-valve petrol engines and chain-drive. All except the heaviest were of normal-control layout, while a 1914 3-tonner introduced worm-drive.

By 1917 heavy Peugeots were restricted to worm-drive 3- and 4-tonners, a 22-seat passenger model being based on the latter after World War I.

Medium-duty types were still advertised in the mid-1920s, but the emphasis was on lighter delivery models. The heavier designs included the 1923 1½-ton low-loading 1543 with 3-litre 4-cyl Latil petrol engine and the 1929 1¼-ton 1593 with a 6-cyl unit.

Lighter types predominated throughout the 1930s but in 1941 the 2-ton DMA entered production, this being of forward-control layout with Cotal 4-speed electrically-selected transmission and transverse independent front suspension. This model continued after the war, receiving a new 1.3-litre overhead-valve Peugeot petrol engine in 1948. Assembly of the forward-control Chenard-Walcker D3 van, with a payload in excess of 1¼ tons and side-loading, was taken over by the company in 1950, now using a Peugeot engine, 4-speed transmission, hydraulic brakes and torsion-bar independent suspension all round. By 1955 this became the D4, which was replaced in 1965 by the 1½-ton J7 which was offered with independent suspension and front-wheel drive.

In 1980 the company acquired Chrysler's European interests, including the Dodge and Karrier

Peugeot DMA 1½-ton truck c1947

commercial ranges and early in 1981 merged with Renault to provide a nationalized commercial range.

PFANDER/*Switzerland 1946 to date*
Pfander AG, Dubendorf, Zürich, specializes in the manufacture of light battery-electric and petrol-powered commercials for municipal, hotel bus, local delivery and internal works use. The majority are lightweight types but the present series includes both rigid and tractor models with capacities of up to 2000kg. Among these are the EKB 900 1-tonner with a 48 volt 7hp traction motor, the EKB 1000 with two 48 volt 4½hp traction motors, and the EKB 2000 for 2-ton payloads, powered by two 80 volt 7 or 9hp traction motors.

PFS/*England 1922-1924*
Following development of the Tilling-Stevens petrol-electric system, Percy Frost-Smith constructed PFS petrol-electric passenger models. Also known as the FS, these had 4-cyl White & Poppe engines driving 24kw dynamos with worm-drive to the rear wheels. Only six were built for London passenger service with 48-seat open-top double-deck bodies.

PHÄNOMEN/*Germany 1927-1945*
Known also as the Granit, the Phänomen was a light bonneted truck introduced by Phänomen-Werke Gustav Hiller, Zittau, Saxony, to replace its Phänomobil 3-wheeler. The first was the Model 15 powered by a 1.5-litre 4-cyl petrol engine with compressed-air cooling. In 1931 this was followed by the Model 25 with a 2.5-litre capacity engine suitable for payloads of between 1500 and 1700kg and later by the Model 30, powered by a 3.05-litre unit and with a capacity of between 2300 and 2500kg.

Many styles of factory-produced bodywork were available, particular attention being given to ambulances and other emergency or municipal types. Three years

after production ended, a range of air-cooled commercials appeared as IFA, IFA-Granit and Robur.

PHILLIPS/*England c1903*
Charles D Phillips built a 3-ton "undertype" steam wagon with vertical water-tube boiler and 45hp compound engine.

PHONIX/*Hungary 1905-1915*
The Phonix Automobile Works, Budapest, built a series of buses based on the German Cudell 'Phonix' model. These had 4-cyl overhead-valve petrol engines and chain final-drive. The factory became known as the Machinery, Mill & Automobile Works in 1911, Phonix production continuing until the premises passed to Magyar Altalanos Gepgyar and MAG, Magomobil and Magosix models were introduced.

PHP/*USA 1911-1912*
Introduced by the PHP Motor Truck Co, Westfield, Massachusetts, the PHP was a 1-tonner with a wheelbase of 288cm. Called the Model 28, it had a 30hp 4-cyl petrol engine, 3-speed transmission and shaft-drive. The company was called the Westfield Motor Truck Co for the last few months of production.

PIAT/*France 1899-1900*
The first Piat steam wagon, a 5/6-tonner using a rear-mounted vertical water-tube boiler and double compound engine, was built by A Piat et Fils, Paris. Eight metres in length, it had Gooch single eccentric valve gear, all-gear drive and a load-carrying platform at the front with steersman ahead and driver at the rear. Coal, coke or wood fuel was used.

PICKERING/*Scotland 1905-1906*
F G Pickering & Co Ltd, Tweedmouth, built a 2/3-ton lorry which was entered in the 1905 Liverpool Trials and exhibited at the Agricultural Hall Show. It had a 20/24hp 4-cyl Simms petrol engine, Simms-Bosch ignition and radiator between driver and engine. Drive was by way of a 3-speed Soames constant-mesh gearbox to countershaft and side chains, providing road speeds of 6, 12 and 18km/h.

PICKWICK/*USA 1927-1933*
After 1920 the Pickwick Stages System, Los Angeles, California, converted a number of standard commercial types to suit operating requirements on long-haul routes, but within seven years it was constructing complete vehicles. The first of these was the all-metal chassisless 'Nite Coach' which was a low-silhouette double-deck de-

sign with intermediate gangway leading to 13 twin-berth compartments. A front-mounted Sterling petrol engine was fitted.

A factory was set up at Inglewood, California, but only four more examples were built although plans were made for a day coach version called the 'Duplex', of which forty were built by the end of 1931. The firm entered receivership at this time and built 18 more 'Nite Coaches' of modified design using a transverse rear-mounted Waukesha petrol engine.

PIE/*USA c1956*
Several experimental vehicles were built directly or in collaboration by transport operators Pacific Intermountain Express. Carrying the name PIE, one was an 8-wheeled truck-tractor which, together with a tandem semi-trailer, was 18m long and carried 1814kg more than a normal road-going artic of the day. Special features included a slimline cab with engine mounted amidships and additional load-carrying space on the tractor unit. Subsequent models were built by Kenworth and Peterbilt.

PIE-FRUEHAUF/*USA 1956*
A joint venture in advanced vehicle design to explore frameless tanker construction resulted from collaboration between transport operators Pacific Intermountain Express and trailer manufacturers Fruehauf Inc. This was a drawbar trailer exercise using a modified White 3000 cab and engine mounted on rails so that it could slide out for maintenance. Vehicle and trailer had a combined capacity of 34,060 litres of petroleum products.

PIEPER/*Belgium 1905-1910*
Soc des Ets Pieper, initially of Nessonvaux, but later of Liège, was a pioneer in the petrol and battery-electric vehicle fields. Henri Pieper developed a petrol-electric drive system, based on the ideas of the Fischer Motor Vehicle Co, New Jersey. Within less than a year a new company, SA Auto-Mixte, was established at nearby Herstal-lez-Liège and the new transmission became known as the Auto-Mixte system, eventually being developed into the British KPL system. Manufacture of Pieper petrol and battery-electric vehicles continued until 1910.

PIERCE/*USA ? to date*
Pierce Mfg is one of the more prolific builders of custom fire truck apparatus. Using chassis provided by Ford, International Harvester, Kenworth, Dodge, Mack or other special fire truck fabricators, Pierce produces pumpers, ladder

trucks, aerial ladders and medic vehicles under the Pierce name.

PIERCE-ARROW/*USA 1910-1932*

An established producer of passenger cars, the Pierce-Arrow Motor Car Co, Buffalo, New York, constructed a forward-control 5-ton chain-drive truck in 1910 but abandoned it in favour of a bonneted worm-drive 5-tonner called the Model 'R'. The 2-ton Model 'X' went into production in 1914 and both types saw extensive military service as did a number of Class 'B' "liberty" trucks.

Six models, from 2½ to 7½

1919 Pierce-Arrow R-9 5-ton truck (left-hand vehicle)

1933 Pierce-Arrow 5-ton truck

tons capacity, were listed during the early 1920s, all of bonneted layout with 4-cyl petrol engines and 4-speed transmissions, and in 1924 the 6-cyl 'T'-head engined Model 'Z' passenger chassis was announced. The 'Fleet Arrow', introduced in 1927, was a lighter commercial range using many passenger car components, and was available for a number of years despite a takeover by the Studebaker Corp in 1928. By 1929 there were three 'Fleet Arrow' models and six heavier trucks, and by 1931 models from 2 to 8 tons capacity were listed.

For 1932 a high speed dual-ignition straight-8 2-tonner was advertised, but by the end of that year all commercial production had been transferred to the associated White Motor Co factory, Cleveland, Ohio, where all were produced as Whites. Between 1933 and 1934, however, some 15-seat buses were built in the Pierce-Arrow factory as Studebaker Pierce-Arrows.

PIERCY/*USA 1915-1916*

Two and one half-ton petrol-electric trucks were marketed as Piercy or Hub by the Hub Motor Truck Co, Columbus, Ohio. Of bonneted layout, these had a 4-cyl petrol engine driving a generator which, in turn, supplied electric current to a traction motor mounted in each rear wheel hub.

PIERREVILLE/*Canada 1969 to date*

Founded by the sons of Pierre Thibault, builder of Thibault fire appliances, Pierreville Fire Engines Ltd was established in Pierreville, Quebec. All appear to use various chassis makes but are generally sold as Pierreville.

PIGGINS/*USA 1912-1913*

The Piggins Motor Car Co, Racine, Wisconsin, built Piggins trucks, quickly establishing the Piggins Motor Truck Co to continue production. One-, 2- and 3-tonners were offered, the smallest having normal-control, a 4-cyl petrol engine, 3-speed transmission and shaft-drive. Two- and 3-tonners were of forward-control layout. The factory was eventually purchased by the Racine Motor Truck Co for the manufacture of Reliance trucks.

PIONEER (1)/*England 1902*

Using mainly American components, the Pioneer Power Co Ltd, London, built an experimental 10-ton steam wagon. Intended for one-man operation, the Pioneer wagon had a vertical boiler of the horizontal fire-tube type fed automatically from a fuel hopper. The driver sat alongside the front-mounted boiler which supplied steam to a 4-cyl swashplate engine powering the front wheels independently. Ackermann steering acted on the rear wheels.

PIONEER (2)/*USA 1920-1921, 1924*

A 4-cyl Continental petrol-engined 2-tonner was announced by the Pioneer Truck Co, Chicago, Illinois. Production continued into 1921 when a 1-ton model was introduced. No further commercials appear to have been built until 1924 when the 1-tonner returned briefly, powered by a 4-cyl

Golden, Belnap & Swartz petrol engine.

PIONEER STAGE/*USA 1923-1930*

Developing from a San Francisco taxicab business, the California Body Building Co constructed rugged bonneted buses, initially on stretched White chassis, introducing the Pioneer Stage brand name. A 6-wheeled version was constructed in 1923, by which time the operating side of the business had become the California Transit Co and its trade name Pioneer Stages. Although much of production was for the company's own use, many were sold and a larger factory was opened at Oakland, California, in 1927. In 1929 the business merged to form Pacific Greyhound Lines and the manufacturing subsidiary became the Pioneer Motor Coach Manufacturing Co. Only a few coaches were built before the company was taken over by the C H Will Motors Co.

PIPE/*Belgium c1905-c1917, 1921-1931*

By 1907 SA des Usines Pipe, Zuen, Brussels, was constructing a 16hp goods and passenger model and a 25hp bus, production of which appears to have continued until World War I. The factory resumed production with both trucks and passenger cars but the latter were dropped in favour of commercials, starting with a 4-cyl petrol-engined 2-tonner. The range quickly expanded to include types up to 5 tons capacity with an option of producer-gas engines and a line of heavy road tractors for operation at up to 20 tons GTW. In 1931 the business was taken over by Ets Brossel Frères which merged with SA des Automobiles Industriels Bovy to manufacture the Bovy-Pipe range.

PIRET/*Belgium 1936*

Using mainly American and British components, Ets Piret, Brussels, built a few Piret trucks. These had 4.6- or 5.2-litre engines.

PIRSCH/*USA 1926 to date*

Experienced in mounting fire-fighting apparatus on proprietary chassis, the Peter Pirsch Co, Kenosha, Wisconsin, introduced its first complete machine in the mid-1920s. These included a series of pumpers from 150 to 750gpm capacity powered by 6-cyl Waukesha petrol engines, although chemical and hose units were also built. These open-cabbed machines were joined by a closed-cab pumper in 1928 and by 1931 an 25.9-m artic aerial ladder truck was completed.

Some proprietary chassis were

1971 Pirsch Model 41D

used but disguised as Pirsch machines, often carrying General Motors cabs. Mainly Hercules or Waukesha petrol engines were used throughout the 1930s and all vehicles were of bonneted layout until the first cab-forward design arrived in 1961, both were listed throughout the 1960s. Known as the Peter Pirsch & Sons Co, the firm now concentrates on rigid and artic cab-forward appliances as well as supplying bodywork on commercial chassis.

PITTSBURG (1)/*USA 1908*

With a payload of up to 10 tons, the Pittsburg steam truck was built in small numbers by the Pittsburg Machine Tool Co, Allegheny, Pennsylvania. It had a fire-tube boiler, 3-cyl single-acting engine, 2-speed gearing and double chain-drive, other features including an air-operated foot-brake acting on the differential, a handbrake acting on the rear wheels and an engine-operated winding drum.

PITTSBURG (2)/*USA 1908-1911*

Soon after the Shady Side Motor Vehicle Co, Pittsburgh, Pennsylvania, introduced the Pittsburg battery-electric commercial range, the company was re-registered as the Pittsburg Motor Vehicle Co to handle series production. Most were lightweight models and by 1910 no less than six types were listed, with capacities of up to 2721kg. All had double chain-drive and the three largest carried two traction motors.

PITTSBURG (3)/*USA 1909-1910*

A 3-ton forward-control truck was built by the Parr Wagon Co, Huff Station, Pennsylvania, normally marketed as the Pittsburg, but sometimes known as the Parr. It had a 36hp 4-cyl Waukesha petrol engine, friction transmission and double chain-drive.

PITTSBURGHER/*USA 1919-1923*

Announced by the Pittsburgher Truck Mfg Co, Pittsburgh, Pennsylvania, the Pittsburgher started as a 2½-tonner powered by a 4-cyl Continental petrol engine and fitted with a 4-speed transmission and worm final-drive. A 5-tonner, with Midwest petrol engine was added in 1921 and when production came to an end other Midwest-engined models were available for 1½- and 3-ton payloads.

PLYMOUTH (1)/USA 1909-1914

The Commercial-Motor-Truck became the Plymouth in 1909 when the Plymouth Motor Truck Co was formed. The existing range was continued, but by 1912 only 1- and 2-tonners, with 25.6 and 40hp petrol engines, respectively, were offered.

PLYMOUTH (2)/USA 1937-?

The Plymouth light commercial range was introduced by the Chrysler Motors Corp, Detroit, Michigan. The heaviest model was based on a light Dodge truck chassis powered by a 3.3-litre 6-cyl side-valve Plymouth petrol engine.

PODEN/Portugal c1961

For the Portuguese market, Foden trucks built by Foden Ltd, Sandbach, Cheshire, were sold as Poden.

PODEUS/Germany 1905-1918

Designed by Joseph Vollmer, Podeus trucks were rugged vehicles built by Paul Heinrich Podeus at his works in Wismar, Mecklenburg. Production appears to have centred upon 3- and 5-ton models with 45 and 55hp 4-cyl petrol engines and the bulk of production went to Eastern Europe. Later, Maschinenfabrik Podeus AG was founded to continue production.

POHL/Germany 1924-1930

Gustav Pohl-Werke, Gössnitz, was a manufacturer of motor ploughs and agricultural tractors that also built the Pohl road tractor. Based on the company's existing agricultural model, this had a 30bhp 4-cyl Deutz diesel engine from 1926.

POLE/USA 1913-1920

Introduced by the Commercial Truck Co, Philadelphia, Pennsylvania, the Pole battery-electric delivery range was never a good seller.

PONTIAC/USA 1906

Although 1-, 1½- 2- and 3-ton trucks were announced by the Pontiac Motor Car Co, Pontiac, Michigan, only one prototype appears to have been built. Designed by Martin Halfpenny, the range was fitted with his patented auxiliary springs.

PONY CRUISER/USA 1938-1951

The bus operator People's Rapid Transit Co, Kalamazoo, Michigan, constructed a 16-seat body on a forward-control front-engined Ford chassis called the Pony Cruiser. By 1940 a larger engine was fitted and a 19-seat model built by Kalamazoo Coaches Inc,

which now handled the vehicle-building side of the business. By 1947 Chevrolet and International chassis were used and in 1948 a larger design went into production as the Kalamazoo Cruiser.

POPE-HARTFORD/USA 1906-1914

As well as passenger cars, the Pope Mfg Co, Hartford, Connecticut, built Pope-Hartford commercials and emergency service vehicles three years after the company's founder, Colonel A A Pope, had acquired the International Motor Car Co, Indianapolis, Indiana. Early Pope-Hartfords were fairly light models, larger 3- and 5-ton stakeside trucks being introduced later.

POPE-WAVERLEY/USA 1903-1908

Colonel A A Pope of the Pope Mfg Co, Hartford, Connecticut, acquired the International Motor Car Co, Indianapolis, Indiana, re-naming it the Pope Motor Car Co and changing its battery-electric vehicle brand name from Waverley to Pope-Waverley. This range comprised battery-electric commercials of up to 5 ton capacity, and for 1906 included 1-, 3-, and 5-tonners. In 1908 the business again became independent, being re-named the Waverley Co with Waverley as the brand name.

POWER/USA 1917-1923

The Power 2-tonner went into production in the Detroit, Michigan, plant of the Power Truck & Tractor Co, and by 1918 had been joined by 1-, 3½- and 5-ton models. All had 4-cyl Continental petrol engines and worm final-drive, with wheelbase lengths of up to 450cm. By 1922 production had moved to St Louis, Missouri, where only 2- and 3½-tonners were built, both with 4-cyl Hinkley petrol engines and 4-speed transmissions.

POWERTRUC/England c1963

The Powertruc was a special adaptation of the Dagenham-built Ford 400E chassis/cab with a Ford diesel engine mounted amidships in place of the regular power unit. This engine was used both to propel the vehicle and to power jetting equipment for cleaning drains and sewers.

PRAGA/Czechoslovakia 1910 to date

With capacities between 1½ and 6 tons, the first Praga trucks built by Automobilni addeleni Prvni Ceskomoravske tovarny na straje, Prague, had petrol engines and shaft-drive. These were not as successful as the 4/5-ton Type 'V', announced in 1911. This had a

1936 Praga TN single-deck coach

6.85-litre 4-cyl side-valve petrol engine and chain-drive and was adopted as a "subsidy" vehicle until 1923.

In 1912 the 2½-ton Type 'L' using a 3.8-litre petrol engine was added, followed in 1913 by the 4/5-ton Type 'T' and in 1916 by the 5-ton Type 'N'. Production continued along similar lines through-

1965 Praga S5T2 5-ton tipper

out the 1920s, new models including the 'MN' 2-tonner and a 3-ton version of the 'L', the 2½-tonner being replaced by the 'RN'-Type, using a 3.47-litre 6-cyl petrol engine.

From 1930 the 'N'-Type could be had with a 7-litre capacity air-cooled Deutz diesel engine, and in 1933 the 6-wheeled 'TO'-Type bonneted passenger chassis, powered by an 11.5 litre 6-cyl petrol engine entered production, variations including the 'TOT' 7-tonner and 'TOV' 100-passenger city bus.

Licence production of many models was undertaken in Yugoslavia forming the foundation of the TAM series, also sold as Orava.

After World War II the 'RN'-Type received an all-steel cab and hydraulic brakes, an innovation on other models being the Praga-Wilson 5-speed pre-select transmission.

Prototypes, including forward-control 4- and 5-tonners, were also constructed but developed no further. The first new model for series production was the 3/5-ton 6 x 6 V3S, introduced in 1952 with an air-cooled Tatra 6-cyl engine and current today, although now built in the former Avia factory at Letnany. It was joined in 1957 by

1944 Praga RN 2½-ton truck

a 4 x 2 rigid or tractor version, the S5T, but this was withdrawn in 1973.

PRESTO/Germany 1926

When Presto-Werke AG, Chemnitz, Saxony, acquired Dux Automobilwerke AG, Wahren, near Leipzig, production of the 22/80 PS Dux truck or bus continued as the Presto.

Presto-Werke AG was itself taken over by Nationale Automobil AG, Berlin, and manufacture of the Dux-designed Presto continued as the NAG-Presto.

PRETOT/France 1900

The Prétôt was a front-wheel drive bus. The name of the manufacturer is uncertain but it is known that production was carried out in Paris.

PREVOST/Canada 1947 to date

Prevost Car Inc, Ste Claire, Quebec, was an established bus bodybuilder which introduced an all-steel bodied coach called the Prevost. By 1959 the specification had been up-dated in the form of

1962 Prevost 'Le Normand' single-deck coach

1970 Prevost 'Panorama' TS-47 high-floor single-deck coach

the air-suspension 'Le Normand' coach, followed by the 'Le Travelair' airport bus in 1962 and the 'Le Panoramique' touring coach in 1966. A high-floor 6-wheeler called the 'Champion' was introduced in 1967 and in 1968 the first super-luxury 6-wheeled 'Panorama' coach was built, entering series production in 1971 as the 'Prestige'. Current versions use rear-mounted V8 Detroit Diesel engines, 4- or 6-speed manual or automatic transmissions and a single-tyred trailing axle.

PRIMUS/*Germany 1935-c1941*
Primus Traktoren GmbH, Lichtenberg, Berlin, designed and constructed a number of diesel-engined agricultural and road haulage tractors. In its earliest form, the haulage version had a 10hp single-cyl Deutz engine mounted just ahead of the rear axle. In 1937 the company was re-organized as Primus Traktoren Gesellschaft Johannes Kohler und Co KG, introducing 2-cyl diesel engines. A shortage of diesel engines during World War II is believed to have resulted in a number of battery-electric models being built.

PRINCE/*Japan 1952-1967*
As well as passenger cars, the Prince Motors Co, Tachikawa, offered a bonneted 1-tonner powered by a 45bhp 1.5-litre 4-cyl overhead-valve petrol engine. In 1954 the company was re-named the Fuji Precision Machinery Co Ltd with some models sold as PMC. In 1956 the original model was up-rated to 1¾ tons capacity and called the 'New Miler', and a forward-control derivative was introduced as the 'Clipper'. Renamed Prince Motors Ltd in 1961, 83bhp 1.9-litre petrol engines were fitted in the heaviest models

and by 1966 these were carrying a 2-ton payload. By this time the Nissan Motor Co Ltd had taken over and in 1967 the Prince range was absorbed into Nissan.

PRINCESS/*England 1906*
The Century Engineering Co Ltd, Willesden, London NW10, built a 2-ton van known as the Princess, powered by a 2-cyl petrol engine.

PROCTOR/*England 1947-1952*
Proctor Springwood Ltd, Norwich, Norfolk, hauliers since the mid-1930s, built a Perkins P6-engined diesel 4-wheeler known as the Proctor Mk I, sometimes referred to as the Proctor Diesel. Capable of carrying a 5/6-ton payload this had a Moss 5-speed box, spiral-bevel final drive and 410-cm wheelbase. Three examples were shown at the 1948 Commercial Motor Show, comprising a Mk I, a Mk II tipper, and a Mk III 8-ton tractor with Scammell coupling. Both this and the Mk II had 5-speed David Brown boxes but were otherwise mechanically similar to the Mk I. In 1949 Praill's Motors Ltd, Hereford, previously a distributor for the marque, took over the manufacturing rights and assembly moved to Hereford later in the year. Within three years the business was sold to Oswald Tillotson, Burnley, Lancs.

PROGRESS/*USA 1911-1914*
The Universal Machine Co, Milwaukee, Wisconsin, built Progress commercials in three sizes of which the largest were 1½- and 3-tonners. All were of forward-control layout, with 4-cyl petrol engines, 3-speed transmissions and double chain-drive.

PROSPECT/*USA 1923-1924, 1930-1934*
The Prospect Fire Engine Co was

founded in Prospect, Ohio, quickly introducing the Prospect 'Deluge' rotary fire pumper on Ford or Reo chassis. This model was replaced by the Prospect-Biederman fire pumper but six years later a new Prospect machine, employing a Mors chassis, was announced, remaining on the books until the plant closed and Keenan Hanley, Chief Engineer, left to set up the Hanley Engineering Service to build Hanley appliances.

PROSPECT-BIEDERMAN/*USA 1924-1930*
Following production of the Prospect 'Deluge' rotary fire pumper, the Prospect Fire Engine Co, Prospect, Ohio, announced the Prospect-Biederman 'Deluge Master Fire-Fighter' using a specially constructed Biederman chassis. This was listed until a new Prospect machine, mounted on a Mors chassis, was introduced.

PROTOS/*Germany 1914-c1918*
Passenger car manufacturer Siemens-Schuckert-Werke GmbH, Nonnendamm, Berlin, added a 4-ton forward-control truck to its light commercial range but production was short-lived.

PRUNEL/*France 1906*
Soc des Usines Prunel, Puteaux, Seine, added a large chain-drive commercial to its light delivery range powered by a 30/33hp 4-cyl petrol engine. Towards the end of 1906 a 3-tonner took part in the Industrial Vehicle Trials in Paris and a double-deck bus also appeared, some examples of the latter being exported to Great Britain. Within a couple of months all models were marketed merely as UDPX.

PTC/*New Zealand c1935-1940*
The Passenger Transport Co Ltd, Otahuhu, was a passenger transport undertaking that began building vehicles of its own design, calling these PTCs. Using Kirkstall axles, David Brown steering gear and Lockheed brakes, these included two Meadows petrol-engined models, a Gardner-engined 36-seater, and a couple of 40-seaters with Leyland 'Cub' engines.

PULL-MORE/*USA 1914-1917*
The Pull-More Motor Truck Co, Detroit, Michigan, is said to have built a number of 3-ton trucks.

PULLCAR/*England 1906-1909*
A 12/14hp twin-cyl Fafnir petrol engine located under the footboard powered the Pullcar 2-wheeled conversion unit for adapting horse-drawn wagons to self-propulsion. The brainchild of

Horace Viney, who owned the Pullcar Motor Co Ltd, Preston, Lancs, early versions had a 2-speed epicyclic gear system, chain-drive and pneumatic tyres. By 1907 the company offered complete 4-wheeled delivery vans incorporating the conversion new unit.

Amongst employees working on the project was Edward Atkinson, who left the Pullcar Motor Co Ltd in 1907 to found Atkinson & Co. By the time Pullcar production came to an end, a 15.9hp White & Poppe petrol engine was standard equipment.

PUMA/*Brazil 1978 to date*
The first Puma trucks to leave the Sao Paulo factory of Puma Veiculos e Motores Ltd were medium-capacity 4-wheelers with fibreglass cabs and were offered with Perkins 4.236, MWM or Detroit Diesel engines.

PURREY/*France 1898-1913*
Tramcar manufacturer Valentin Purrey, Bordeaux, also built single-speed steam wagons using a vertical cross water-tube boiler and compound "undertype" engine. Capacities ranged from 4 to 10 tons and included a number of large passenger types. About 1908 the business was re-named Purrey et Exshaw and, after Exshaw acquired the firm in 1913, it was known as H Exshaw et Cie and all models sold as Exshaw.

PYRENE/*England c1970-c1971*
An established manufacturer of fire equipment, Pyrene Ltd mounted its products on truck chassis such as Dennis, Bedford and Commer. Their "swansong" was a powerful airfield fire crash tender mounted on a Reynolds Boughton 6 x 6 cross-country chassis and marketed under the Pyrene name.

During the 1970s the company was acquired by the Chubb organization.

PYRODYNE/*England 1904-1908*
John Solomon Vivian Bickford ran the Bickford Burners Co, Camborne, Cornwall. He concentrated on the development and production of motor vehicle components, particularly carburettors, but later introduced an oil-fired steam wagon known as the Pyrodyne (sometimes incorrectly spelt Pyrodyen). Intended for a 1 ton payload, this had a most unusual automatic oil feed system. Performance of the 12 or so examples that were completed is said to have been excellent, 4.5 litres of oil taking the wagon some 6km with a 1-ton payload at a maximum speed of 32km/h.

Q ELECTRIC/*England 1938-1952*

The Sunderland, Co Durham, Q Electric Vehicle Co Ltd offered mediumweight battery-electrics with interchangeable components based on the German Bleichert range. It was a subsidiary of the Steels Group, sharing manufacturing premises with Coles Cranes. The first Q Electrics were re-named Bleicherts, comprising a 2-ton low-loader, municipal tower wagon and 5-ton 6 x 4, but few true Q Electrics were built before the end of World War II.

In 1943 Steels Engineering Products Ltd was founded and a 1-ton bonneted van with dummy radiator went into production soon after, quickly followed by a forward-control version and later by a forward-control 2½-tonner. All used the same traction motor, drive, controller, battery and rectifier, smaller vehicles having one traction motor and the larger two. The 1-tonners had a range of about 56km and larger types a range of 80km.

QH/*England c1961 to date*

Specializing in the construction of hydrostatically-driven load-carrying vehicles for the mining industry, Qualter, Hall & Co Ltd, Barnsley, South Yorks, offers QH low-silhouette shuttle cars and supply vehicles. Shuttle cars are divided into two categories – a non-flameproof series including diesel-electric and battery-electric types, and a flameproof series, using diesel-hydraulic and battery-electric drive.

All have 4-wheel hydrostatic drive with a hydraulic motor built into each wheel. Other features include power-assisted 4-wheel steering and a flexible round-link scraper chain through the length of the hopper-style body.

QIAO-TONG/*China c1958 to date*

Qiao-Tong or Ch'iao-Tung (Communication) trucks are built in the Shanghai Cargo Vehicle Plant and include the 4-ton SH-141 with 90bhp 6-cyl engine, 5-speed transmission and a top speed of 70km/h and the SH-361, a 15-ton dump truck with either a 210 or 220bhp diesel engine.

QMC/*USA 1926-1927*

The US Army Motor Transport Corps conferred with the Goodyear Tire & Rubber Co, Akron, Ohio, with a view to developing a militarized version of its multi-wheeled vehicles.

A prototype was constructed using a World War I Class 'B' 3½-tonner, re-designated a Class 'C' 5-tonner, and in 1926 the first 6 x 6 QMC TTSW 1½-tonner was constructed by the US Quartermaster Corps.

QMC 7½/9-ton 6 x 6 military truck c1934

Components were common to the World War I Class 'B' truck. Towards the end of 1927 a 5-ton petrol-electric 6-wheeler was also constructed, featuring an electric motor in each of the six wheels.

QUADRAY/*USA 1904-1905*

The Commercial Motor Vehicle Co was founded in Detroit, Michigan, to build large battery-electric commercials under the Quadray name. Four-wheel drive and, sometimes, 4-wheel steer were characteristics of all models. Goods vehicles were listed for capacities of up to 6¼ tons and passenger models for up to 50 passengers, the largest chassis using one 3½hp traction motor in each wheel and 4-wheel steering.

QUADRU/*USA 1911*

A 15-ton 4-wheel drive petrol-electric truck called the Quadru was exhibited at the 1911 Detroit Auto Show by its designer, R Fuller. It was only experimental, powered by a 32bhp engine which provided electric current for four traction motors, one in each wheel.

QUEST 80/*England 1980 to date*

Export only side-engined passenger chassis, diesel-electric and battery-electric trolleybus hybrids are built at Telford, Salop. The first was a diesel-electric trolleybus for operation on or off overhead lines in Johannesburg, South Africa. This was followed by a number of high-floor diesel buses for Johannesburg, with Mercedes or Gardner engines located behind the driver at a slight angle to the offside chassis frame side-member. Some had conventional leaf springs and others air suspension.

A low-floor design forms the basis of an articulated model for operation in Belgium, while a further hybrid is a twin-steer 6-wheeled battery-electric trolleybus carrying 3 tons of batteries. Trucks are now under development.

RABA/*Hungary 1904, 1912-1941, 1961-1963, 1970 to date*

The first Raba truck was built by Magyar Vagon és Gépgyár Resvehitarsasag, Raab, only briefly before the company turned to lighter commercials. Later, however, 5-ton Praga trucks were built under licence. In 1920 a similar licence agreement was made with Fried Krupp AG of Germany, leading to the assembly of the first Raba passenger models.

Re-named Ungarische Waggon und Maschinenfabrik, the company introduced the 3-ton 'Super' truck following the signing of another licence agreement, this time with the Austro-Fiat concern. Production slowed during the early 1930s but in 1936 Raba-Maros military trucks were introduced and a licence to manufacture MAN diesel engines in 1937 resulted in a MAN-engined passenger model. In 1938 Raba-Botond cross-country vehicles entered production, but the Occupation led to the factory being dismantled. When production resumed it had little to do with truck or bus manufacture.

In 1961, however, as Wilhelm Pieck Vagon és Gépgyár, a 4 x 4 10-ton forward-control half-cab dump truck was developed, sold abroad as Mogurt, production of which passed to the Dutra works in 1963. To replace this, the company came to another licence agreement with MAN covering the manufacture of diesel engines and axles which, by 1970, included trucks. The first was a 4-wheeled rigid design and this was joined by a 6-wheeled rigid and an artic tractor model. All are still available.

RAE/*England 1910-1911*

"Undertype" steam wagons with vertical water-tube boilers and horizontal cross-compound engines were manufactured by John Rae, Huddersfield, Yorks. One unusual feature was that drive was taken from the engine crankshaft via a short chain to a rear countershaft and differential carrying gear wheels at each end that meshed with annular gears bolted to each wheel.

RAF/*Austria 1908-1913*

Although Reichenberger Automobil Fabrik GmbH was founded in 1907 to build luxury passenger cars at Reichenberg-Rosenthal, Bohemia, it was soon building commercials. The first was a flat truck, later offered as a van or 12-seat bus, powered by a 30hp 4.5-litre petrol engine located under the driver's seat. In 1911 the company began building Knight sleeve-valve engines, using them in its own vehicles and selling units to Laurin & Klement and Puch. This led to a close association between RAF and Laurin & Klement and in 1913 the latter bought the former and Laurin & Klement designs continued briefly as RAF. These comprised lorries from 1½ to 6 tons capacity and buses for 10 to 35 passengers.

RAGHENO/*Belgium 1929-c1940*

Usines Ragheno, Malines, built railway rolling stock and bus bodies when it constructed a number of trolleybuses for Antwerp Tramways. These had ACEC traction units. The company also built chassis for Ets Brossel Frères throughout the 1930s as well as Gardner-engined vehicles under its own name. After the war the company appears to have been involved in the production of Iso bloc buses for the Belgian market but these were sold as Isobloc.

1911 Railless trolleybus

RAILLESS/*England 1909-1927*

The Railless Electric Traction Co Ltd was set up to promote trolleybuses in Britain, marketing complete systems under the Railless or RET brand names, although having no vehicle manufacturing facilities of its own. The first Railless, demonstrated at Hendon, London, comprised a James & Browne chassis and Hurst Nelson body, but the first to enter service, in Leeds and Bradford in 1911, employed chassis constructed by the Alldays & Onions Engineering Co Ltd.

Re-named the Railless Electric Construction Co Ltd in 1912, the company continued to use Alldays & Onions chassis, introducing its first open-top double-decker in 1913. In 1918 the business was acquired by Short Bros (Rochester & Bedford) Ltd who re-registered the company as Railless Ltd and began to construct complete chassis and bodywork in its Seaplane Works, Rochester, Kent. Covered-top double-deckers appeared in 1922, doing much to influence the development of the British trolleybus.

RAINIER/*USA 1918-1927*

John T Rainier set up the Rainier Motor Corp, New York, to build passenger cars and light commercials, and introduced a 1½-ton worm-drive truck with front-mounted engine and 3-speed Brown-Lipe transmission. By 1921 an expanded range included 2-, 2½-, 3- and 5-tonners and by 1925 Rainier Trucks Inc, as it was then known, offered various types up to 6 tons capacity using 4-cyl Continental petrol engines.

RALPH/*South Africa 1967-1971*

The only heavy commercial to be designed and built entirely in South Africa, the first Ralph was an American-style "cabover" artic unit, the brainchild of Ralph Lewis. The Ralph enterprise was based at Ophirton, Johannesburg, the first "cabover" acting as a demonstrator. Most early Ralphs were powered by Detroit Diesel engines and each vehicle was regarded as a "one-off" constructed to the customer's requirements.

Rolway Enterprises (Pty) Ltd was soon registered and the company's first order received from the South African Government, for a massive 105 tons GCW tank transporter powered by a 12V71 Detroit Diesel driving five axles. The first multiple order was for four 6 x 4 heavy haulage tractors for the Abnormal Loads Divn of South African Railways, followed by two separate batches of heavy-duty bonneted artic ore carriers each capable of hauling 50 tons of ore at up to 80km/h and powered by V12 Cummins diesels developing 700bhp and driving through an 8-speed torque-converter transmission. Specifications now included Allison, Clark, Fuller or Spicer transmissions, Rockwell-Standard or Hendrickson axles and Cummins or Detroit Diesel engines. Gross weights of up to 72,000kg were catered for.

By 1970 only a dozen trucks had been built and additional finance was necessary. An approach was made to the Industrial Development Corp which agreed to purchase 51% of Rolway's share capital. Production shifted to larger premises at Alrode, and many employees were taken on. The company's former individualism changed overnight and Ralph Lewis found the new organization top-heavy with personnel and expenditures. Closure came after only 42 Ralphs had been built.

RAM/*Netherlands 1968 to date*

R A Mimiasie NV, Rotterdam, was an army surplus dealer that began selling 6 x 6 ex-US Army trucks with DAF engines under the RAM name. In 1970 these began to assume their own identity following the introduction of a semi forward-control MAN cab, 186bhp MAN diesel engine, ZF transmission and other new components. Four years later a 4 x 4 version, with 126bhp MAN diesel engine, was announced but current production utilizes DAF engines.

RAMIREZ/*Mexico 1959-1961, c1974 to date*

Along with Sultana buses, Trailers de Monterey SA, Monterey, Nuevo Leon, introduced Ramirez trucks employing Cummins diesel engines of up to 320bhp output in conjunction with 12- or 15-speed transmissions. A new range of tractor-trucks up to 36,000kg capacity was introduced during the 1970s, also using Cummins diesels.

RANDOLPH/*USA 1908-1913*

The Randolph Motor Car Co, Flint, Michigan, introduced a variety of commercial types, sometimes marketing these as 'Strenuous Randolph'. By 1912, when production came under the jurisdiction of the Randolph Motor Truck Co, Chicago, Illinois, these were headed by a 4-ton flat truck, all models having 3-speed transmissions and double chain-drive.

RANGER (1)/*USA 1908-1910*

The Ranger was a buggy-type 2-seater with rear load platform. Introduced by the Ranger Motor Works, Chicago, Illinois, it had a 2-cyl air-cooled petrol engine, planetary transmission and tiller steering.

RANGER (2)/*USA 1920-1923*

The 2-ton Ranger, with 4-cyl Wisconsin petrol engine, Timken worm-drive rear axle and Detroit chassis frame, went into production at the Southern Motor Mfg Assn's plant in Houston, Texas. It had a 340-cm wheelbase and was carried on pneumatic tyres but in 1923 was de-rated to 1½ tons capacity.

RANSOMES/*England 1920-1942, 1946*

A development of the steam and agricultural equipment built by Ransomes, Sims & Jefferies Ltd, Ipswich, Suffolk, was a 2-speed "overtype" wagon, construction of which was sub-contracted to Ruston & Hornsby Ltd, Lincoln. It was a chain-drive machine with a pressed-steel chassis and Ackermann steering but was discontinued following spasmodic production.

Meanwhile, Orwell battery-electrics had continued to be built

1970 Ralph Model C12C3 6 x 4 artic tractor

1928 Ransomes trolleybus

by the company, the first trolley-buses of 1924 also being sold under this name. By the late 1920s these were sold as Ransomes, featuring electric servo braking with relay switch beneath the foot pedal, a foot-operated motor controller and 60hp underfloor traction motor. The first 6-wheeled Ransomes trolleybuses were delivered to Maidstone in 1928 but the majority were 4-wheelers of single- and double-deck layout. Production ceased during World War II, but in 1946 fifty trolleybuses were shipped to Singapore.

1907 Rapid (1) 1-ton integral van

RAPID (1)/USA 1906-1912
By 1906, commercials built by the Rapid Motor Vehicle Co, Pontiac, Michigan, included various trucks and buses with forward-control and underseat petrol engines. By 1907 there was a 1-ton delivery model, two 1½-tonners and various passenger types for between 12 and 24 persons. In 1908 designer Max Grabowsky left to set up the Grabowsky Power Wagon Co and by 1909 the General Motors Corp showed an interest in the business, which now offered some 17 models. Only 1-, 2- and 3-tonners were advertised for 1910/11 and in 1912 the company became part of the General Motors Truck Corp, subsequent models being sold as GMC.

RAPID (2)/Italy 1907-1918
The first commercials built by Soc Torinese Automobili Rapid, Turin, included a 20-seat bus but the company's most popular model was its motor water cart powered by a 25/30hp 4.6-litre 4-cyl 'T'-head petrol engine and equipped with a 4-speed transmission and shaft-drive. This and other commercials had a capacity of 4 tons, production continuing along similar lines until the end of World War I.

RAPID (3)/Switzerland 1962 to date
Introduced by Rapid Maschinen und Fahrzeuge AG, Dietikon, Zürich, the 'Alltrac' 400 was a 1¼-ton payload light 4 x 4 powered by an 8½hp 391cc air-cooled single-cyl MAG engine located ahead of the front axle. It was popular in the Swiss agricultural field and

was joined by heavier models such as the 1966 'Alltrac' 1500 for 3 tons payload with a 1.5-litre 2-cyl MWM diesel engine.

Another model was the 'Alltrac' 550, available with a single-cyl Lombardini diesel engine, while the 'Alltrac' 1000 had a 2-cyl unit of the same make. The largest current model is the 4-ton payload 'Alltrac' 1750, using a 40bhp 4-cyl Perkins diesel engine, 8 forward and 4 reverse constant-mesh transmission and disengageable front-wheel drive.

RASSEL/USA 1910-1912
The E C Rassel Mfg Co, Toledo, Ohio, offered 1- and 2-ton open delivery vehicles. Both had 4-cyl petrol engines, selective transmissions and double chain-drive. At the end of 1911 the company was re-named the Rassel Motor Car Co, adding 3- and 5-ton models.

RATHGEBER/Germany/West Germany 1909-1912, 1951-1952
Joseph Rathgeber AG, Munich, was building railway and tramcar bodies when it introduced licence-built Büssing trucks under the Rathgeber name. This arrangement continued until the company returned to bodybuilding. In 1951 the firm's own chassisless coach, powered by an air-cooled Deutz or water-cooled Steyr engine went into brief production. This ended when the company returned once more to bodybuilding.

RAYNER/England 1907
T J Rayner & Sons Ltd, Rayleigh, Essex, took over production of the short-lived Standard "over-type" steam wagon for only a few months and at the end of this period constructed a few petrol-engined trucks and buses. All were marketed as Rayner.

RECTORY/England 1905-1909
The "undertype" Rectory steam wagon employed a vertical fire-tube boiler, smokebox superheater and totally-enclosed compound engine. It was built in the Sunderland, Co Durham, premises of the Rectory Engineering Co Ltd. Other features included a countershaft differential and double chain-drive. Only prototypes were built, and in 1909 the company offered for sale all patterns and designs.

RED WING/USA 1912
The Wallof Motor Truck Co, Red Wing, Minnesota, built prototype Red Wing trucks. Expertise gained in building these was later used to develop the Canadian Redcliffe truck.

REDCLIFFE/Canada 1913-1914
Developed from the earlier Red

Wing, the Redcliffe was a Continental-engined 1½-tonner, available either as a truck or bus. Few were built, the manufacturer being then Redcliffe Motors Co Ltd, Redcliffe, Alta.

1963 Redler Mk II mobile crane

REDLER/England c1960-c1965
Using a specially prepared Seddon chassis, Redler Conveyors Ltd, Stroud, Glos, introduced a 5-ton truck-crane with crane movements controlled from the vehicle's cab. Later up-rated to 6 tons capacity, this vehicle employed heavy-duty Seddon 15/10 front and rear axles, Perkins 6.354 diesel engine and Albion transmission. A reversible driver's seat provided access to crane controls.

All crane movements were hydraulically-controlled and additional 2.5-m lattice jib sections for converting the standard 7-m boom to 17-m could be carried on the slewing superstructure even when in use. For travelling, the shortest boom length was projected towards the rear.

REDMUND/England 1833
David Redmund was Engineer of the London & Paddington Steam Carriage Co, formed in 1832 to operate Hancock's steam carriages. Following a dispute with Hancock, Redmund constructed his own steam carriage on cast-iron wheels, using Hancock's 'Enterprise' as a model, but calling his carriage 'Alpha'. The boiler was to Redmund's own design and unfortunately proved to be a total failure.

REFORM/Switzerland ? to date
A light high-mobility 4000kg GVW truck powered by a 3-cyl Perkins diesel engine is manufactured by Reformwerke and marketed as the Reform. Designed for cross-country work or municipal duties, provision is made for attaching additional equipment such as cutters and sweepers.

With 4-wheel drive, the vehicle has a gradient ability up to 60%.

REHBERGER/USA 1923-1938, c1946
Arthur Rehberger & Son, Newark, New Jersey, offered a range of assembled trucks from 1½ to 7 tons capacity. Using Buda petrol engines, Brown-Lipe or Fuller transmissions and Timken axles, these were joined by a low-loading bus chassis in 1925 using front air springs. Passenger models soon predominated. A gap in vehicle production was filled by heavy trailers. Soon after World War II a new 1½ to 3½ tons payload export range was planned but never reached production.

RELAY/USA 1927-1933
With considerable capital, the Relay Motors Corp acquired the Commerce Motor Truck Co, the Garford Motor Truck Co and Service Motors Inc, concentrating truck production at Wabash, Indiana, and Lima, Ohio, but soon only the Lima plant was used. While the three former marques continued, a Relay range was also announced from 1 to 4 tons capacity, using 6-cyl Buda petrol engines, 4-speed transmissions and internal-gear drive.

1931 Relay 'Duo-Drive' truck

By 1931 a Continental-engined 3/4-tonner, a 5-tonner and a 7-ton 6-wheeler had appeared but the most interesting Relay was the 6 x 4 'Duo-Drive' "conventional", which used two Lycoming straight-8 petrol engines located side-by-side with a total output of 275bhp, each driving a rear axle via separate air-operated 5 forward and 2 reverse Fuller transmissions.

Other features included an hydraulic clutch system and a single sleeper bunk.

The liquidation of the Relay Motors Corp led to the withdrawal of all Commerce and Service trucks, but a few Relays and Garfords were built by the Consolidated Motors Co in an unsuccessful attempt to save the firm in 1933.

RELIANCE (1)/USA 1906-1911
The Reliance Motor Car Co, Owosso, Michigan, built a variety of commercial types which, by

1908, included a 22-seat bus and a 5-ton truck. All types had 2-, 3- or 4-cyl 2-stroke engines and were mainly of "cabover" layout. The commercial range was so successful that the company was re-named the Reliance Motor Truck Co, moving to larger premises in Detroit, where the General Motors Truck Co took an interest, acquiring the business in 1911. All remaining models were sold as GMC.

RELIANCE (2)/USA 1917-c1927
The Reliance name was also used for 1½- and 2½-tonners, built in the Appleton, Wisconsin, plant of the Racine Motor Truck Co. Both had 4-cyl Buda petrol engines, 3- or 4-speed transmissions and Badger external-gear final-drive. The company was re-constituted as the Reliance Motor Truck Co in 1918 and in 1922 became the Appleton Motor Truck Co, but Reliance production continued until about 1927.

RELIANCE (3)/England 1936-1957
A 2-ton industrial truck running on full-size pneumatic tyres was introduced by Reliance Trucks Ltd, Heckmondwike, Yorks. Production continued with modifications into the 1950s, the last models featuring a standee driving position.

Much later the company acquired manufacturing rights for the Dennis-Mercury industrial truck and tractor and formed Reliance-Mercury Ltd.

RELIANCE-MERCURY/England 1972 to date
Following the acquisition of the Dennis-Mercury industrial truck operation, Reliance Trucks Ltd was re-organized as Reliance-Mercury Ltd, Halifax, West Yorks, marketing its products as Reliance-Mercury. Among these is the 'Haulmajor' terminal tractor with lifting fifth wheel coupling and 155 or 180bhp turbocharged Leyland diesel engine driving the hub-reduction rear axle via a Clark 'Powershift' transmission with 3 forward and 3 reverse speeds.

A 1-man cab can be mounted on the left or right of the chassis and optional duplicate controls are available for forward and reverse.

REMINGTON/USA 1911-1913
The Remington Standard Motor Co, Charleston, West Virginia, offered 5-, 7½- and 10-ton trucks. All were of forward-control layout, with 4-cyl petrol engines, dual spark plugs and unusual hydraulic transmissions.

1961 Renault 'Voltigeur' 1-ton integral van

RENAULT/France 1905-1965, 1980 to date
Using a 10hp 1.9-litre 2-cyl petrol engine of its own make, Renault Frères, Billancourt, Seine, constructed its first 1-ton truck seven years after the first Renault passenger car was built, but it was not until 1909 that the first heavy-duty model, in the form of a 4-cyl petrol-engined 3-tonner, was produced. This was joined by a 6.1-litre 4-cyl petrol-engined 5-tonner with 4-speed transmission, fitted briefly with chain-drive, and by a forward-control 21-seat single-deck bus with radiator behind the driver, exhaust gas interior heater and pneumatic tyres. A forward-control 3-ton truck appeared in 1910, while a more specialized machine, built shortly before World War I, was a 4-wheel drive and 4-wheel steer artillery tractor.

By then registered SA des Automobiles Renault, the company was closely involved in military production for the next few years, but when civilian types re-appeared after the war these ranged from 1 to 7 tons capacity and were based on pre-war designs. By the early 1920s all models up to 2 tons capacity had pneumatic tyres as standard which were optional for heavier models. All types were fitted with the company's own 4-cyl petrol engines hidden beneath "coal-scuttle" bonnets. A popular model of this period was the 1½-ton 'MH'-Type 6x4, using a 2.1-litre monobloc petrol engine, which sold well on the export market with twin tyres all round.

By 1924 the company was supplying many of Paris's buses, often in association with Scemia and thus also known as Renault-Scemias. The company's driver-over-engine layout was now being replaced by a driver-beside-engine design incorporating 4-speed transmission, double-reduction final-drive and servo-assisted 4-wheel brakes. Experimental buses included a 6 x 2 single-decker and a 65-seat double-decker. Between 1925 and 1927 some battery-electric buses were also built and at the end of this period a 55mph bonneted coach, with 4.8-litre 6-cyl petrol engine and servo 4-wheel brakes, was constructed.

All trucks now had 4-wheel brakes also but 6-cyl types did not arrive until 1929. Some medium-weight models now had frontal radiators, a feature that was to become standard throughout the range by 1930 when the first Renault diesel trucks appeared using a 7.25-litre 4-cyl direct-injection engine. A year later a 10.5-litre 6-cyl diesel was announced, and by 1933 a 45bhp 4.3-litre 4-cyl model was offered in medium-duty models.

The heaviest trucks now had 5-speed transmissions as standard, and for 1934 servo-assisted steering was added. New forward-control trucks were introduced the same year and a new 5.3-litre overhead-valve petrol engine replaced the earlier 4- and 6-cyl side-valve units. By 1938 the heaviest vehicles were now 12/15-tonners with 12.5-litre 6-cyl diesel engines, while buses were listed in both forward- and normal-control form with capacities of up to 45 passengers.

Nationalization came in 1945 when the company was re-organized as Régie Nationale des Usines Renault, now offering only forward-control trucks and buses. The latest model was a 7-tonner using an 8.4-litre 4-cyl diesel engine and it was this design that acted as prototype for the Polish Star range. The first entirely new passenger model for some time was a chassisless single-deck bus announced in 1949. This had a 6.2-litre 6-cyl horizontal underfloor diesel engine, 5-speed overdrive transmission, auxiliary coil spring suspension at the rear and air brakes. New 5- and 7-ton trucks arrived the following year. At the lighter end of the range a forward-control 1-tonner was now listed with 4-wheel drive and hydrovac brakes were applied to a 2½-tonner in 1953.

In 1956 the business was merged with that of Floirat, Latil and Somua to form SA de Véhicules Industriels et Equipements Mécaniques, and from late 1957 all heavy Renault trucks and buses were sold as Saviem or Saviem-LRS. Medium-duty models such as the 'Voltigeur', 'Goelette' and 'Galion' continued as Renault but were themselves absorbed into the Saviem programme in 1965, leaving only light vans and pick-ups under the Renault name.

In 1977, however, Renault Véhicules Industriels was formed, taking under its wing all Berliet and Saviem production, which continued under these names until 1980 when new corporate models were announced as Renault for 1981. At the bottom end of the range is the 1½/1¾-ton payload 'Master' panel van, available in front- or rear-wheel drive form with a variety of alternative specifications, while at the opposite end are the TF231, TR280 and TR305 tractor units, the first two carrying Berliet cabs and the latter a "Club of Four" structure. Other more specialist models as well as normal medium-duty types are also advertised.

1958 Renault 2-ton truck

RENARD/*France 1903-1908*

The Renard road-train system was developed by Col Renard and marketed by Soc Française des Trains Renard, Paris, although the first was built by Soc A Darracq. This first model had a 60hp 4-cyl Darracq petrol engine in front of a 4-wheeled tractor with a series of universally-jointed shafts running aft through the train of 6-wheeled wagons, and driving the centre set of wheels on each wagon via a countershaft and double chains. Each front set of wheels tracked automatically after the tractor.

Aimed largely at under-developed regions, production got underway using 4-wheeled trailers and a 72hp Filtz petrol, or even a steam engine, but manufacturing rights were sold to the Daimler Motor Co (1904) Ltd, Coventry, England, which continued production as the Daimler-Renard.

RENNOC-LESLIE/*USA 1918-1919*

Using components common to the company's agricultural tractor, the shortliyed 2½-ton Rennoc-Leslie was built by the Rennoc-Leslie Motor Co, Philadelphia, Pennsylvania.

It had a 360-cm wheelbase, a 4-cyl Buda petrol engine, 4-speed Warner transmission and worm-drive rear axle. Production ended in 1919.

REO/*USA 1911-1967*

In late 1904 R E Olds left the Olds Motor Truck Works, setting up the Reo Motor Car Co, Lansing, Michigan, and producing the first true Reo truck in 1911. This had a 4-cyl underseat petrol engine and chain-drive, and was joined in 1913 by the 2-ton bonneted Model 'J', one of the first trucks to have electric lighting and starting as standard.

The 1-ton 'Speedwagon' made its debut in 1915, its model name sometimes used as a marketing name. This had a 30hp 4-cyl petrol engine, 3-speed transmission and bevel-drive. The Model 'J' was discontinued in 1916 and production centred upon the 'Speedwagon' range, some of which by 1925 had 6-cyl engines. A special passenger model, also with 6-cyl engine, was announced but replaced in 1927 by a modified series comprising the 'FB' and 'GB' models.

By 1928 Reo trucks were listed in capacities of up to 3 tons, all with 4-wheel internal-expanding brakes, and a 6-cyl 'Junior Speedwagon' was advertised in 1929. The company's products were now popular on the export market, and by the end of 1929 Reo Motors (Britain) Ltd was formed to handle import and assembly of vehicles for Britain.

A 1932 4-tonner had a straight-8 petrol engine, and in 1934 the 'Gold Crown' 6-cyl petrol engine was offered in various chassis ranging from 1½ to 6-ton capacity. An agreement between Reo and Mack Trucks Inc that year led to the introduction of the Reo-built Mack Jr line through Mack

1937 Reo 'Speed Wagon' tipper

distributors, while the first Reo "cabover" was announced and the last bonneted Reo passenger model in the form of the 3L6H appeared. The company's first full-front city bus, and its first rear-engined model the 3P7, also appeared that year.

Particularly significant in 1939 was the building of the last 'Speedwagon', ousted by a heavy-duty "conventional" range. The manufacture of chassisless buses known as the 'Flying Cloud' also got underway. Finances were far from good and production reached an all-time low by the time the business was re-organized in 1940 as Reo Motors Inc. Much of World War II was spent in bus manufacture using proprietary sectional bodies, but there were also the inevitable military trucks.

In 1945 another new passenger model with underfloor 6-cyl Continental petrol engine, went into production. A revived 'Flying Cloud' chassisless range appeared in 1947, also with underfloor Continental units but coupled to Spicer torque-coverter transmissions. Meanwhile, a 93bhp overhead-valve version of the 6-cyl 'Gold Crown' engine arrived and new Model 30 and 31 "conventional" trucks for gross weights of up to 16,329kg were announced. These had 170 and 200bhp Continental petrol engines, Warner transmissions and Timken axles.

The early 1950s saw a number of new light urban delivery models, while engine developments included a 1pg unit in 1953, a heavy-duty V8 petrol in 1954, and the first diesel-engined Reos in 1956, using turbocharged Cummins

units. During the 1950s the company joined with GMC and Studebaker to construct military 2½-ton 6 x 6s, often referred to as Reo-Studebakers, using Reo 'Gold Crown' or Continental petrol engines.

The White Motor Co acquired the business in 1957, re-designating the Lansing plant as the Reo Divn, and moving Diamond T assembly to the same plant in 1960. 'DC'-Series "cabovers", with hydraulic tiltcabs and 207 or 235bhp 'Gold Comet' engines were announced in 1958 for gross weights of up to 19,500kg, joined in 1962 by the 'E'-Series "conventional" powered by a new 200bhp 6-cyl engine. A wide range of 4 x 2, 6 x 4, 6 x 6 and 8 x 6 trucks were now offered, with petrol or diesel engines of up to 335bhp output, but in 1967 the Reo and Diamond T operations were combined and all models re-named Diamond Reo.

1946 Reo '19'-Series bus

REPCO/*Australia 1965 to date*

With a standee driver location at the rear, the Repco 'Trademaster' milk-float is built by PBR Pty Ltd, East Bentleigh, Victoria, using a Ford 'Cortina' petrol engine, Voith automatic transmission and front disc brakes.

REPUBLIC/*USA 1914-1929*

The Republic Motor Truck Co, Alma, Michigan, was established to take over the business of the light truck builder Alma Motor Truck Co. They quickly introduced bonneted types with capacities of up to 3150kg, offered in Britain as Whiting by importer Whiting (1915) Ltd. These had Lycoming, Continental, or Waukesha petrol engines and Torbensen internal-gear axles. The company was incorporated in 1916 and became one of America's largest truck builders, producing over 10,000 vehicles annually with Timken or Eaton worm-drive axles, but by the 1920s financial problems had curtailed much of production.

By the mid-1920s the heaviest Republic was a 5-tonner. As well as trucks, numerous dropframe passenger models were listed for up to 32 persons. In 1927 6-cyl petrol engines, usually Continentals, arrived and in 1928 the Linn Manufacturing Corp was acquired. A year later Republic merged with the American LaFrance Truck Co to form the LaFrance-Republic Corp, constructing trucks as LaFrance-Republic.

REX/*USA c1976 to date*

The Rexnord Engineering Co, Milwaukee, Wisconsin, specializes in the assembly and marketing of construction trucks based on Diamond-Reo, Hahn, Hendrickson and Rite-Way chassis under the Rex brand name. Truckmixers are particularly popular, and to compound this activity the company acquired the Arlan Manufacturing Co, builder of the Rite-Way, in 1978. These models are still sold as Rite-Way.

REX-SIMPLEX/*Germany 1910-1921*

Using its passenger car models as a basis, Automobilwerk Richard und Hering AG, Ronneburg, offered Rex-Simplex light trucks. These were based on the 9/16, 10/28 and 17/38 PS chassis.

REYNOLDS/*USA 1920-1923*
Listed in four sizes from 1½ to 5 tons capacity, Reynolds trucks were built by the Reynolds Motor Truck Co, Mt Clemens, Michigan, using 4-cyl Hinkley petrol engines, 4-speed transmissions with power take-off facilities and worm-drive. Apart from the 5-ton model, all were pneumatic-tyred and fitted with an engine-driven tyre pump. Only 1½- and 2-tonners were advertised during the last two years of production.

REYNOLDS BOUGHTON/
England 1970 to date
For many years Reynolds Boughton Ltd, of Amersham Common, Bucks, concentrated on the design and manufacture of specialist bodywork. In 1970 the first complete Reynolds Boughton chassis, known as the 'Griffin', was built with a massive rear-engined 6 x 6 for use as an airfield fire crash tender. Power was provided by a super-charged V16 Detroit Diesel developing 635 bhp and driving through a 6-speed transmission with 2-speed auxiliary. This model is the heaviest in production, but has since been joined by lighter 6 x 6 models, again with rear engines.

Towards the end of the 1970s chassis assembly was transferred to Winkleigh, Devon, and the company re-named Reynolds Boughton Chassis Ltd. Numerous new models of 4 x 4 configuration, ranging from the 7 ton GVW 'Pegasus' to the 27 ton GVW 'Phoenix', all with rear engines, were launched, followed by the 'Scorpio' 4 x 2 for 10 tons GVW. Latest in the series is the RB 44, a 4-wheel drive model but with Ford 'A'-Series cab and modified bonnet. Early production models were fitted with Ford's 3-litre V6 developing 100 bhp, but later versions have been offered with the 2.8-litre V6 producing 133 bhp, normally coupled to a Ford C3 automatic gearbox, as a rapid intervention fire appliance.

RFW/*Australia 1969 to date*
The first multi-axle RFW truck was an 8-wheeler with Scania diesel engine and Bedford KM cab. It was built at the Chester Hill, NSW plant of the RFW Truck Mfg Corp.

Trucks are built only to special order, using Caterpillar, Cummins, Nissan, Rolls-Royce or Detroit Diesel engines and other proprietary components. Concentrating entirely upon heavy-duty models, recent deliveries include single and twin-steer 8 x 4 rigids, a 6 x 4 passenger model and cross-country 4 x 4 and 6 x 6 airfield fire crash tenders.

RICHARD/*Germany 1926-1928*
Richard & Co GmbH, Ronneburg, Saxony, built a substantial truck chassis for a payload of 3300kg. Power came from a 6-litre 4-cyl petrol engine driving through a 4-speed transmission, all components were manufactured in the same factory.

RICHELIEU/*Canada 1938-c1946*
Since 1918 fire equipment manufacturer Pierre Thibault (Canada) Ltd, Pierceville, Quebec, had been fitting out proprietary chassis as fire appliances when it introduced its own machines under the Richelieu brand name. An airfield fire crash truck was amongst the types developed during World War II. Soon after the war, models were re-named Thibault.

RIKER/*USA 1917-1921*
Following a period as Locomobile-Riker, trucks built by the Locomobile Co of America, Bridgeport, Connecticut, were re-designated Riker. Only 3- and 4-tonners were built, using the company's own 4-cyl 'T'-head petrol engines, 4-speed transmissions and worm-drive rear axles. Production passed briefly to the Hares Motors Co Ltd in 1920.

RIKER ELECTRIC/*USA 1898-1903*
Medium- and heavy-duty battery-electric trucks went into production at the Riker Electric Motor Co, Brooklyn, New York, as Riker Electric, covering capacities of up to 5 tons. Typical models had full-length bodies with driver mounted high at the front. In 1899 A L Riker sold the business and his name to the Electric Vehicle Co, Elizabethport, New Jersey, which re-organized the Elizabethport factory under the Riker Electric Vehicle Co. In 1900 production moved to the Electric Vehicle Co's Hartford, Connecticut, plant but Riker Electrics were eventually withdrawn as they competed with the same company's Columbia series.

RIMPULL/*USA 1975 to date*
The off-highway range of Rimpull rigid and articulated dump trucks is built by the Rimpull Corp, Olethe, Kansas, using 'Quad-Reduction' axles incorporating a double-reduction differential and double-reduction planetary transmission. Normal and bottom-dump models are listed with engines of up to 1200bhp output and capacities of more than 170 tons.

RITE-WAY/*USA c1961 to date*
The Rite-Way was one of the first front-discharge truckmixers to use a centre-mounted 1-man cab and

rear engine. Developed by the American Rite-Way Corp, Dallas, Texas, early types were 2 and 2.5cu m machines with three or four axles and 4- or 6-wheel drive powered by Cummins or Detroit Diesel engines. The company moved to Fort Wayne, Indiana, becoming Rite-Way of Indiana and introduced 2.2, 2.5 and 2.8cu m versions on up to five axles. Production eventually passed to the Arlan Manufacturing Co, Arlington, Texas, and was marketed by the Rexnord Engineering Co which took over the business in 1978 and now manages it as a subsidiary.

ROBERTS/*England 1862*
Designed by William Roberts, the 7½-ton Roberts steam fire engine was built in Millwall, South London, by Brown, Lennox & Co, and may have been the first self-propelled appliance in Britain. Unusually, it was a 3-wheeler with a coal-fired vertical boiler, 2-cyl vertical engine and chain-drive, and was intended for works use with a local shipbuilder. It was said to be capable of producing a 450gpm output and could travel at up to 22km/h.

ROBERTSON/*England 1903-c1912*
The Robertson steam wagon, manufactured by James Robertson & Son Ltd, Fleetwood, Lancs, had a vertical boiler and 2-speed compound "undertype" engine with countershaft differential and chain-drive. Unusual features included rear wheel internal-expanding brakes and hydraulic tipping gear activated by a steam pump.

ROBEY/*England 1905-1934*
Steam traction engine manufacturer Robey & Co, Lincoln, constructed its first steam wagon along "undertype" lines, using a vertical fire-tube boiler and all-gear drive, followed by a similar model employing a Belvedere boiler. These served as prototypes for the true Robey range, which arrived in 1914 in the form of an "overtype" design, re-styled in 1919 by Frank Bretherton, who had also been responsible for the Bretherton "undertype".

The new version was again an "overtype", employing a pistol-type boiler and stayless firebox and a 2- or 3-speed gear system. Introduced as a 5-tonner, it was up-rated to 6 ton capacity in 1923 and there were also a few 10-ton 6-wheelers and artics. Few specification changes were effected.

ROBINSON (1)/*USA 1912-1920*
The Robinson Motor Truck Co's Robinson truck succeeded the

Gopher range which was also built in Minneapolis, Minnesota. Initially, 1½- and 2-ton models were offered, but for 1913 a 5-tonner was also advertised, using a 50hp petrol engine. Most types were of forward-control layout with an underseat engine, but production waned in favour of truck equipment.

ROBINSON (2)/*USA 1915-1920*
Originally marketed as the Golden West, the Robinson had a capacity of 2 tons and was known as the Model 'D'. Built by the Golden West Motors Co, Sacramento, California, it had 4-wheel drive effected by enclosed chains running between gearbox and driveshafts. Underslung springs were also fitted. Later the company became the Big Four Truck Co, subsequent models being sold as Big Four.

1967 Robur LO2500 charabanc

ROBUR/*East Germany 1956 to date*
The Robur 'Garant' was a development of the IFA-Granit and built by VEB Robur-Werke Zittau Lastkraftwagen und Motoren, Zittau, Saxony. This began as a bonneted truck of about 2 tons but was joined in 1960 by the forward-control LO2500 with 3.4-litre 4-cyl petrol engine and compressed-air cooling. This was succeeded by the LO3000 which is still built.

ROCHET-SCHNEIDER/*France 1906-1914, 1919-1951*
Founded in 1894, passenger car manufacturer Ets Rochet-Schneider, Lyons, used a 4-cyl petrol engine from its passenger car range in its first trucks and buses, which were built until World War I. Some were re-introduced after the war, but in 1922 new 1½- and 2½-tonners were introduced, the latter with an 18bhp 4-cyl petrol engine.

In the early 1930s, the company experimented with pre-combustion diesel engines built under an Austrian licence, and soon both 4- and 6-cyl versions were available, the larger listed in the heavy-duty 'Ajax' series. The model 425 was a diesel-powered truck which used one of these engines and a ZF overdrive transmission. By the end of 1937 the Rochet-Schneider range included the 3-ton Model 420, the new 425, the 'Ajax' and a 6-wheeled derivative known as the 'Centaure'.

The company was now well known for its development of alternative fuels, offering producer-gas conversion units for its own and other marques, but also producing a compressed gas system with fuel held in 12 cyls located along the chassis frame. Meanwhile, many Rochet-Schneiders had been delivered as passenger models and in 1938 the 'Marathon', 'Mercure', 'Phebus' and 'Phenix' were announced for urban and inter-city operation. A concerted effort was made after World War II to keep the factory going with these models, but this failed and the business was acquired by Automobiles M Berliet.

ROCKFORD/*USA 1914*
The Rockford Motor Truck Co was set up by the Rockford Automobile & Engineering Co, Rockford, Illinois, to develop a series of trucks. The company built 1-tonners as chassis only for customers to add their own bodies.

ROEBUCK/*England 1930-1934*
The Roebuck began as a bonneted 4-cyl petrol-engined truck built by the Roebuck Engineering Co Ltd, Smethwick, Birmingham, but was joined in 1931 by a forward-control rigid-6, using an 8-litre 6-cyl Meadows petrol engine and 4-speed transmission. A bonneted version was also available, both having a payload capacity of 12 tons.

ROFAN/*Switzerland ? to date*
Manufactured by Jenbacher Werke, Rofan light trucks and tractors are intended mainly for internal works use or for haulage around docks and warehouses. Capacities range from 1000kg for rigids up to 30,000kg for tractors.

ROGERS UNA-DRIVE/*USA 1919-c1922*
The Rogers Una-Drive was a 3-ton 4-wheel drive truck built by the Rogers Una-Drive Motor Truck Corp, Sunnyvale, California. Powered by a 4-cyl Buda petrol engine, drive was carried to a central transfer box and then transmitted by drive-shafts to front and rear axles.

ROKKO/*Japan 1932-1942*
The Rokko was a bonneted 1½-ton truck built by the Kawasaki Rolling Stock Co Ltd, Kawasaki, a subsidiary of the Kawasaki Dockyard Co. Diesel engines were introduced in 1941.

ROLAND/*USA 1914-1915*
Superseding the Hexter truck was the petrol-electric Roland, listed in 3- and 3½-ton forms by the Roland Gas-Electric Vehicle Co, New York. It was also understood to be available in passenger form.

ROLLS/*England 1904-1905*
Various commercials built by Cie de l'Industrie Electrique et Mécanique, Secheron, Geneva, Switzerland, were offered in Britain by C S Rolls & Co under the Rolls brand name.

ROMAN/*Rumania 1971 to date*
Intreprinderea de Autocamioane Brasov, Brasov, builder of trucks under the Bucegi, Carpati and SR brand names, added the Roman to its line after a licence agreement with the French Saviem concern. Initially, the Roman range used the MAN forward-control cab and an imported Raba-MAN diesel engine, but later models had 135 or 216bhp MAN-Saviem units. Both 4- and 6-wheeled rigids and tractors were listed as well as certain 4 x 4 and 6 x 6 "specials". From 1973 the DAC brand name was used for certain models and the latest Roman is a rear-engined city bus with full air suspension.

1976 Roman R-10-215 tractor

ROMEO/*Spain 1959-1972*
Based on Alfa-Romeo designs, the 1-ton Romeo was a forward-control van, pick-up or minibus manufactured by Fabricacion de Automoviles Diesel SA, Avila. Offered initially with an Alfa-Romeo 'Giulietta' petrol or Alfa-Romeo-List diesel engine, it was advertised from 1962 with a Spanish-built Perkins diesel or the original petrol unit. From 1967 these vehicles were marketed by Motor Iberica SA which introduced the F108 Romeo-Ebro in 1972.

ROOTS & VENABLES/*England 1898-1905*
The Roots Oil Motor & Motor Car Co Ltd, South London, pioneered the development of oil-engined vehicles in Britain, introducing a 1-ton van with 6hp 2-cyl engine, double chain-drive and tiller-steering. Certain models are believed to have been sold as Roots Petrocar, but after 1902 all were built on the company's behalf by Sir W G Armstrong, Whitworth & Co Ltd.

ROSS AUTO/*England 1950 to date*
Specializing in the design and

1960 Ross Auto milk float

manufacture of light battery-electric delivery vehicles, Ross Auto & Engineering Ltd, Southport, Lancs, introduced a 1¼-tonner initially with a range of up to 80km per charge. This design was modified over the years and by the 1960s the 1¼-tonner had become the 1½-ton 'Major' and a smaller model the 1-ton 'Beaver'. By 1970 the 'Stallion' 1½-tonner had taken the place of the 'Major', and later three new models were announced, comprising one lightweight, the T3000 1½-tonner and the T6000 3-tonner.

ROTINOFF/*England 1952-1960*
Rotinoff Motors Ltd, Colnbrook, Bucks, was set up to design and construct heavy bonneted tractors for heavy load hauling. The most successful model was the GR.7 'Atlantic', a 6 x 4 drawbar outfit for 140 tons GTW which entered production in 1954. This had a 250bhp 6-cyl Rolls-Royce supercharged diesel engine, 4-speed constant-mesh David Brown gearbox with 3-speed remote auxiliary, and a fully-floating double-reduction bogie.

Overseas enquiries led to the development of the 8-cyl engined 'Super Atlantic' and the rigid 'Viscount' for road-train operations. With an overall length of 12m and hypoid rather than the 'Atlantic''s worm and epicyclic rear axles, the 'Viscount' was sold as the GR.37/AU. The company was re-named Lomount Vehicles & Engineering Ltd in 1960 and subsequent models sold as Lomount.

ROWE/*USA 1912-1925*
Following an attempt on the light commercial market, the Rowe Motor Co, Coatesville, Pennsylvania, introduced a series of 4-cyl Wisconsin petrol-engined trucks of up to 5 tons capacity with 4-speed transmissions and worm- or chain-drive. In 1912, when a 5-ton 6-cyl engined "cabover" was built, the company was known as the Rowe Motor Manufacturing Co, moving to Downington at the end of 1913.

During its relatively short life, this company built a number of interesting vehicles, introducing

one with an early form of air suspension in 1913 and another with hydraulic transmission in 1921. Production moved to Lancaster in 1918 where a 3-tonner with V8 Herschell-Spillman petrol engine went into production both as a truck and as a bus.

ROWE-HILLMASTER/*England 1953-1962*
The coach-operating and garage business of Rowe's Garage Ltd, Liskeard, Cornwall, entered the vehicle building business with a prototype passenger chassis called the Rowe-Hillmaster, using a vertical front-mounted 5.43-litre 4-cyl Meadows diesel engine, 5-speed Meadows transmission and Moss rear axle. In 1954 a horizontal underfloor-engined derivative was developed and two or three others built before the company concentrated on goods versions. The first was a 7-ton forward-control rigid using mechanical units similar to the prototype passenger model. To finance the operation both the coaching and garage businesses were sold, M G Rowe (Motors) Ltd set up, and a new works opened at Doublebois.

1959 Rowe-Hillmaster tipper

A 9-ton rigid powered by a 135bhp 6-cyl Meadows diesel engine was announced in 1956, and within two years a range of trucks from 6-ton rigids to 15-ton artics was listed, using AEC, Gardner, Leyland and Meadows diesel engines. A 6 x 4 rigid with AEC or Meadows diesel engine, Hendrickson bogie suspension and Eaton axles was announced in 1959 and advertised alongside other rigid models until the end of production.

c1961 Rowe-Hillmaster 15-ton

RUBBER RAILWAY/*Canada 1970-c1980*
The Rubber Railway or RRC was an articulated-frame bonneted 8-wheeler introduced by the Rubber Railway Co, Cambridge, Ontario. It had hydraulic steering and a 320bhp Cummins VT0903 diesel engine driving all except the front

axle, via a Fuller transmission to the second axle and back through the central pivot point to third and fourth axles. All wheels were fixed, suspended on hollow rubber springs and walking-beam suspension systems and shod with twin tyres throughout.

Aimed at the construction industry, manufacture was taken over by the Care Equipment Co for 1976 but production rights later passed to Flextruck Ltd, which developed a rear-engined version known as the Flextruck.

RUGGLES/*USA/Canada 1921-1928*
The Ruggles Motor Truck Co, Saginaw, Michigan, and London, Ontario, offered a series of bonneted trucks up to 3 tons capacity powered initially by its own 4-cyl petrol engine. From 1924, Hercules and Lycoming engines were mainly used, a 29-seat passenger model listed in 1926 and 1927 having a Wisconsin unit. Canadian production ceased in 1926.

RUMELY/*USA 1919-1928*
Agricultural machinery manufacturer the Advance-Rumely Thresher Co, LaPorte, Indiana, also assembled a 1½-ton bonneted truck for agricultural communities. Specification included a 4-cyl Buda petrol engine, Fuller 3-speed transmission and Sheldon worm-drive back axle. Towards the end of production the firm was renamed the Rumely Products Co.

RUMPLER/*Germany 1926-1931*
Rumpler Vertriebs GmbH, Berlin, turned from passenger cars to unusual front-wheel drive commercials. Although a prototype appeared in 1926, not until 1930 did small-scale production get underway. One particularly interesting model was a 5-ton rigid lowloader with forward-mounted petrol engine driving the front axle which also steered. All axles were independently sprung and the close-set rear bogie ran on small-diameter wheels to provide low deck height.

RUSH/*USA 1915-1918*
The Rush was an assembled delivery truck built by the Rush Delivery Car Co, Philadelphia, Pennsylvania. It was powered by a 17hp 4-cyl Lycoming petrol engine and fitted with a cone clutch and bevel-drive. In 1916 the Rush Motor Truck Co was formed to continue production, but a series of price rises put the firm out of business.

RUSHTON/*England 1929-1935*
George Rushton was Works Manager for the Associated Equipment Co Ltd during its move from Walthamstow to Southall, Middx. Unofficially, he began building a series of road and industrial tractors of Fordson design, using mainly Fordson components, with the 'General' name. Power came from a 4.4-litre 4-cyl engine running on petrol, diesel or paraffin. When using the latter it reached a maximum speed of 20kmh with an 8/10-ton payload. Later, George Rushton left to set up the Rushton Tractor Co (1929) Ltd, Walthamstow, London, building a pneumatic-tyred road tractor, a steel-wheeled agricultural model, and a full crawler version. Production was later transferred to St Ives, Hunts, where it continued under the name Agricultural & Industrial Tractors Ltd.

RUSSELL/*Scotland 1833-c1835*
Scott Russell designed six carriages for the use of the Steam Carriage Co of Scotland. Built in Edinburgh, these had light multitubular copper boilers with heavily stayed sides, twin-cyl vertical engines and all-gear-drive to the rear axle. Fuel was carried in a separate tender, enabling this to be exchanged for a full tender when needed. Each carriage carried 26 passengers. Operations were closed down by the authorities.

RUSSOBALT/*Russia 1908-1915*
Three capacities of truck were offered by the Russko-Baltyskij Waggonyj Zavod, Riga, as the Russobalt or Russo Baltic. One of the first types was the bonneted Model 'M' 2-tonner with chain final-drive. Another was the Model 'T' of 1913, powered by a 60hp petrol engine and also fitted with chain-drive.

RUSTON/*England c1920*
An old-established traction engine and steam tractor manufacturer, Ruston Hornsby & Co Ltd, Lincoln, never built a steam wagon of its own but did supply boilers for Ransomes wagons, one of which carried the Ruston brand name.

RUTLAND/*England 1952-1956*
Built by Motor Traction Ltd, the Rutland brand name was brought in for home market sales of the MTN commercial range following a move to New Addington, Surrey. Vehicles could be built to any specification, incorporating Perkins, Gardner or Meadows diesel engines, David Brown or Moss transmissions and Moss or Eaton axles. Chassis frames, suspension systems, drive-lines and controls were all assembled in Motor Traction's factory using bolted construction, with spring hangers, prop shaft supports and engine mountings of steel plate welded

Rutland 'Condor' 6 x 2 truck chassis-cab c1959

into position.

By 1956 the range included 2/3-, 5/6-, 7/8-, 9/10-, 12- and 15-ton payload trucks, special 4 x 4 and 6 x 6 types, a rear-engined passenger model and a 50-ton 6-wheeled crane-carrier. The 'Clipper' passenger chassis had appeared in prototype form in 1953. The 6-cyl Perkins R6 diesel was mounted longitudinally with drive transmitted via a single dry-plate clutch and 5-speed David Brown synchromesh gearbox to a transfer box halfway along the chassis. It then returned via a single propeller shaft to the 2-speed Eaton axle. A second 'Clipper', using a 4-cyl Meadows diesel, was constructed in 1954 but it is unlikely that any others were built.

RUTTGER/*Germany 1920-1922*
Carl Rüttger Motoren Vertriebs GmbH, Berlin, specialized in the manufacture of tractors for agriculture and road use.

RYDE/*England 1904-1905*
Light commercials built by Ryde Motors Ltd, London W13, were joined by a commercial chassis for truck or bus use, powered by a 30/32hp 4-cyl petrol engine.

RYDER/*USA 1973 to date*
Following the 1973 launch of the aerodynamically-styled Paymaster tractor, design and manufacturing rights were acquired by Ryder Systems, Miami, Florida, and ten "production" models ordered from the Hendrickson Mfg Co. Various engines, including the Cummins VT 903 and Detroit Diesel 6-71, 6-71T or 8V-71T were fitted, while transmissions were of the Fuller RT910 type.

RYKNIELD/*England 1903-1911*
The Ryknield Engine Co Ltd, Burton-upon-Trent, Staffs, re-

1957 Rutland pantechnicon

1954 Rutland 'Clipper' coach

ceived considerable encouragement from local brewery interests when it began building commercials. Initially, only a 1-tonner was built, using a 10hp 2-cyl engine, magneto ignition, 2-speed transmission and shaft-drive. In 1905 a 35hp bus was announced, having an 8.1-litre 4-cyl 'F'-head petrol engine with dual ignition and twin carburettors. Shaft-drive was employed and special features included a screw-down clutch hold control and a conductor-controlled auxiliary brake at the rear.

The company was re-named the Ryknield Motor Co Ltd in 1906 and a forward-control version of the bus appeared soon after. There was also a new 4-cyl petrol-engined chassis available in 2-, 3- and 5-ton forms and a side-valve range was introduced in 1909, the 1½-ton model having a 20hp 3-litre 2-cyl unit and the 3-tonner a 9.8-litre unit and 4-speed box. Later that year some forty Ryknield buses were sold to Brussels.

S

1927 Safeway Model 64 single-deck coach (right-hand vehicle)

SACHSENBERG/*Germany 1943-1944*
An unusual steam tractor, similar in design to the later Lowa tractor, was built in the Rosslaw, Dessau, factory of Gebr Sachsenberg AG.

SACHSENRING/*Germany/East Germany 1945-1948, 1956-1960*
After World War II Horch Werke AG became VEB Kraftfahrzeugwerke Horch and a new bonneted 3-tonner powered by a 100bhp 4.2-litre 6-cyl engine was marketed as the Sachsenring. Between 1948 and 1956 this was sold under the IFA brand name but was re-named the Sachsenring under VEB Sachsenring Kraftfahrzeug- und Motorenwerk. Models were similar although re-styled and available as an artic tractor unit, the last new model being the 90bhp S 4000-1 which was introduced in 1959.

SADRIAN/*Spain 1956-1962*
Largest of the motorcycle-based Sadrian commercial range built by Adrian Viudese Hijos, Murcia, was an artic for 1000kg payloads. This had a 197cc Hispano-Villiers petrol engine and open-sided one-man cab.

SAF/*Germany 1905-1911*
SAF trucks and buses were built by Suddeutsche Automobilfabrik GmbH, Gaggenau, and also sold as Gaggenau, Safe and SAG. The company supplied early post buses for the German Imperial Mail, as well as some of Berlin's earliest double-deckers, most of underseat-engined layout. Fire appliances and tractors were another speciality, the latter including some heavy models of up to 25 tons capacity.

A number of these vehicles had Benz petrol engines, and in 1907 this firm acquired the business, allowing it to continue independently until 1910, when it was re-named Benz-Werke GmbH vorm Suddeutsche Automobilfabrik. Some steam trucks and buses may have been built under

Stoltz licence, and from 1911 all vehicles were sold as Benz or Benz-Gaggenau.

SAFEWAY/*USA 1926-1928*
Founded to construct and sell the Six Wheel Truck, the Six Wheel Co, Philadelphia, Pennsylvania introduced the 6-wheeled Safeway coach. This had single or twin rear wheels mounted on a bogie to the design of Ellis W Templin, pioneer of the American-built 6-wheeler with the Goodyear Tire & Rubber Co.

The Model 64 city-type coach, with 6-cyl Continental petrol engine, and the Model 66 double-decker became extremely popular and one of these was used by the Nairn Transport Co on its 1046/1126km cross-desert routes from Damascus, Iraq, to Baghdad, Syria.

SAFIR/*Switzerland 1907-1908*
The Safir was available as a 30hp shaft-drive or 50hp chain-drive truck, built under Saurer licence by Automobilfabrik Safir AG, Zürich. Both were of bonneted design with an exhaust brake and compressed air starter but, despite developing the world's first small diesel engine for use in road vehicles, the company closed down.

SAGE/*France 1908-1909*
Based on German Stoltz designs, SAGE steam vehicles were built by SA des Génératerus Economiques, Lyons. The first, a steam bus, appeared at the Paris Salon alongside a 5-ton truck, both having a 4-cyl compound 'V'-engine with cam-operated poppet valves.

SAIM/*Italy 1967-1968*
Officine SAIM SpA, Rome, was a commercial bodybuilder specializing in tippers which also built an 8-ton forward-control low-loader called the SAIM. Using a 6-cyl Fiat diesel engine and OM running units, the forward section was of normal truck appearance while the rear axle was much lower and air-sprung. Fitted with the company's own 5-speed gearbox, this vehicle incorporated a chassis

frame stepped down immediately behind the cab. Designed gross weight was 13,000kg.

ST CLOUD/*USA 1920*
Founded by L R Brown the St Cloud Truck Co was based in St Cloud, Minnesota, introducing a 2½-ton truck assembled from proprietary components. A 1-tonner, also using proprietary components, was announced.

ST LOUIS/*USA 1921-1922, 1929-1951*
Well known for its tramcars, railway rolling stock and bus bodies the St Louis Car Co, St Louis, Missouri, built a few prototype trolleybuses and production models during the early 1920s, also constructing an experimental 6-wheeled petrol-electric bus in 1929. Although other prototypes were built after World War II, few production types appeared.

ST PANCRAS/*England c1903-c1914*
The St Pancras steam wagon was introduced as a vertical fire-tube boilered "undertype" by the St Pancras Ironworks Co Ltd, Holloway, North London. In 1907 the design was radically altered when Toward high-pressure water-tube boilers were fitted to some examples, but the majority were equipped with a new design of short horizontal fire-tube type. All models had a totally-enclosed twin-cyl compound engine with Stephenson's link motion driving the rear wheels via two countershafts and double chain-drive. By 1911 the design was out-of-date and manufacturing rights were acquired by the Steam Car Syndicate Ltd, London NW10. Few examples were sold after this.

ST VINCENT/*Scotland 1903-1910*
Also known as the Scottish Aster due to its use of 2- and 4-cyl Aster petrol engines, the St Vincent was built at the Wm McLean Co's St Vincent Cycle & Motor Works, Glasgow. Most were medium-sized passenger models, such as the 12-seater charabanc with 14/

16hp 2-cyl engine exhibited at the Edinburgh Show in 1908.

SALVADOR/*USA 1915-1916*
The brand name of the Mansur Motor Truck Co, Haverhill, Massachusetts, was changed from Mansur to Salvador, the sole model being a 2-tonner with two seats mounted on top of the engine, worm final-drive and a choice of three wheelbase lengths.

SAME/*Italy 1963*
Agricultural tractor manufacturer SAME, Bergamo, exhibited a short-lived series of all-wheel drive trucks and tractors at the 1963 Turin Show.

Advertised as the SAME or Samecar, all had rear-mounted air-cooled SAME diesel engines ranging from a 2.5-litre 2-cyl unit up to a 7.5-litre V6. The lightest was the 4 x 4 2½-ton 'Toro', and the heaviest was the 6 x 6 'Elefante' for 32 tons GVW.

SAMPSON/*USA 1905-1913*
The Alden Sampson Mfg Co, Pittsfield, Massachusetts, replaced its passenger car line by a series of Sampson or Alden-Sampson trucks. Most early models were chain-drive forward-control 5-tonners with 40hp 4-cyl petrol engines, although by 1909 1-, 2-, 3- and 4-tonners were also being made.

In 1908 the company began building petrol-electric road-trains, hauled by a bonneted tractor with a 40hp petrol engine driving a generator supplying current to traction motors driving the centre wheels of each of two 6-wheeled trailers. Maximum speed was said to be 12km/h. Road-train production ended in 1910 when the factory moved to Detroit, Michigan, and the low-priced 'Hercules' model was introduced. Apart from this, which had a 30hp 4-cyl Continental petrol engine, all Sampsons used the company's engines. By 1912 the company had been acquired by the United States Motor Co, but Sampson production continued on a small scale.

SAMSON/*USA 1920-1923*
Another firm controlled by W C Durant was the agricultural tractor manufacturer Samson Tractor Co, Janesville, Wisconsin, which introduced a few light "cabover" trucks for agricultural users. The heaviest was a 1¼-tonner, available with extension wheel rims for field operation.

SAN/*Poland 1952-1968*
Sanocka Fabryka Autobusow, Sanock, based San passenger models on Star chassis with 100bhp diesel or 105bhp petrol engines. Some

were sold as SFA's and most were front-engined forward-control types. From 1968 front-engined buses and rear-engined integral coaches were sold as Sanok.

SANBERT/*USA 1911-1913*
The 1-ton Sanbert was built in the Syracuse, New York factory of the Sanford-Herbert Truck Co. Called the Model 'J', this had a 3-cyl air-cooled 2-stroke engine under the seat, driving the rear wheels via a 2-speed transmission system and double chains. In 1913 it was replaced by new 1- and 1½-tonners, both powered by a 4-cyl petrol engine and fitted with a 3-speed transmission, but these were re-named Sanford when the company became the Sanford Motor Truck Co.

SANDOW/*USA 1915-1928*
Introduced by the Moses and Morris Motors Corp, Chicago Heights, Illinois, the first Sandow trucks were 1½-, 2- and 3-tonners, the lightest with worm- and the rest with chain-drive. These were sometimes sold as Moses & Morris but soon the Sandow Motor Truck Co was formed to continue production and in 1921 new 1- and 5-ton models were advertised. All appear to have had 4-cyl Buda or Continental petrol engines.

SANDRINGHAM/*England/ Wales 1979 to date*
While the standard long-wheelbase bonneted Land-Rover does not come within the scope of this volume, a 6 x 6 conversion marketed as the Sandringham 6 certainly does, as it can handle 50% more payload. Undertaken by SMC (Engineering) Ltd, Hambrook, Glos, the conversion has two axles located centrally beneath the load-bed and uses mainly standard Land-Rover components.

The V8 petrol-engined model has a payload capacity of 2000kg and employs a 4-speed synchromesh main gearbox with 2-speed transfer, permanent 6-wheel drive and a lockable central differential. Six-cyl models have no lockable central differential and can be had with 6 x 4 drive if required. Most versions of the long-wheelbase bonneted Land-Rover can be had in this form and the Ministry of Defence is sponsoring development of an armoured gun-hauling version. Plans are now underway to produce such conversions in quantity in a Welsh factory.

SANDUSKY/*USA 1908-1914*
The 1-ton Sandusky was built by the Sandusky Auto Parts & Truck Co, Sandusky, Ohio. This company was also variously described as the Sandusky Auto Parts & Motor Co and the Sandusky Auto Parts & Motor Truck Co. Fitted with an enclosed express body, the Sandusky became a 1½-tonner in 1912.

SANFORD/*USA 1913-1937, 1969 to date*
The Sanford Motor Truck Co, Syracuse, New York, took over the Sanford-Herbert Co and this company's Sanbert trucks were re-named Sanford. By 1916 various models up to 2 tons capacity were advertised, all of "conventional" layout with worm-drive, and by the 1920s Continental petrol engines were listed as standard in an expanded range from 1 to 6 tons capacity.

Typical models included a 1½-ton "speed truck" which was called the 'Greyhound' and a special bus chassis.

Six-cyl petrol engines were available from 1924, spiral-bevel final-drive introduced in 1926, and a number of fire appliances were also listed. Although these became popular during the early 1930s, in 1937 vehicle production ceased in favour of fire-fighting equipment.

As the Sanford Fire Apparatus Corp, the company began building complete diesel-engined cab-forward appliances in 1969 and these are still available, sometimes on Duplex chassis.

SANOK/*Poland 1968-1972*
San or SFA front-engined buses and rear-engined chassisless coaches were later re-named Sanok. These also used numerous Star components and were powered by a 105bhp Star petrol or 125bhp Wola-Leyland diesel engine. The Sanok was later replaced by the Autosan.

SANTANA/*Spain c1972*
Based on the British Land-Rover, the Santana range included certain military types, one of which was a 1¼-ton forward-control cargo and personnel carrier known as the 1300. This was built by Metalurgica de Santa Ana, SA, Linores, a company which had previously handled the marketing of British-designed Commers in Latin American countries as the Commer-Santana.

SARACAKIS/*Greece 1970-1973*
Using Volvo components, for whom they acted as agents, Saracakis Bros SA, Athens, constructed medium-capacity city buses on ladder-type chassis frames. Designated Type SB55, these had front-mounted 6-cyl Volvo diesel engines.

SAURER (1)/*Switzerland 1903 to date*
Using a short-lived shaft and pinion drive system, the first truck built by Adolph Saurer AG, Arbon, was a 5-tonner with 25/30hp 4-cyl 'T'-head petrol engine, cone clutch and 4-speed transmission. The company's first bus arrived the following year, employing chain-drive, and later that year the company developed the world's first exhaust brake. By 1905 1½-, 2½- and 3-ton trucks were also being built and Saurer passenger models became increasingly popular, particularly with the Swiss Postal Authorities.

One year later the 5-tonner was up-dated, receiving a new 30hp 4-cyl petrol engine, rear drum brakes and a lower chassis, and in 1907 Safir AG, Zürich, began to assemble both goods and passenger types under Saurer licence. Oesterreichische Saurerwerke AG was already doing this in Austria and in 1910 other assembly plants were opened in France and Germany, quickly followed by one in the US. Production now comprised four models, with capacities of 1½, 2, 3 and 3½ tons, the two largest using the 30hp engine and chain-drive, the smallest a 16hp 3 litre 4-cyl unit and shaft-drive while all models had 4-speed transmissions.

1903 Saurer (1) 5-ton truck

Saurers were already popular in many less hospitable parts of the world, and accordingly a special reinforced chassis with improved ground clearance was used for a new colonial truck with a 3/4-ton payload. Powered by a 30, 36 or 45hp 4-cyl petrol engine, this could be had with an extra radiator for tropical use and was easily identified by its wide large-diameter wheels. In 1912 the company became the leader for supplying commercial vehicles on the home market, a position which it has never lost. Exports suffered badly during World War I, much of production being taken up by military orders. Among these was the 'A'-Type, a 3-ton shaft-drive, often with canvas tilt body, also built under licence from 1915 by MAN of Germany. By 1918 the 'A'-Type was available to civilian users also and by 1921 2-, 3-, 4- and 5-tonners were listed. Four-cyl 'L'-head petrol engines of 32, 40 or 48bhp could be fitted, while other features included a 4-speed transmission. By 1927 these power units had increased outputs of 42, 52 and 62bhp and were available in a variety of 'A'-Type models from light- to heavy-duty load-carriers, buses to coaches and municipal vehicles to fire appliances.

Earlier diesel engine experiments were revived in the mid-1920s, and in 1926 the 'B'-Type commercial was developed, using a 4- or 6-cyl petrol engine. First of these was the 1½/2-ton 2B Model fitted with a new 42 or 55bhp 4.7-litre 4-cyl unit. Two years later the first diesel-engined Saurers appeared in the form of 4- and 6-cyl options on the 'B'-Type and by 1930 the 'B'-Type range included models from 2 to 6 tons capacity or, in the case of passenger models, for up to fifty passengers. The most well known and most typical was the 5BLD with 80bhp 7.8-litre 6-cyl overhead-valve diesel engine, multi-plate clutch, 4-speed transmission and cardan-drive to spiral-bevel rear axle. Meanwhile, Motorwagenfabrik Berna AG, Olten, had been acquired in 1929 and has continued as part of the Saurer empire until today.

Continuing its experiments with diesel power, Saurer introduced a cross-flow engine in 1932 but that same year the Swiss authorities clamped down on vehicle size and weight resulting in a new 6 x 4 Saurer becoming illegal and leading to its production being transferred to the company's French factory. Diesel developments went a step further in 1934 when Saurer's direct-injection system was announced, this being hurriedly incorporated in all the firm's existing diesels and overseas production rights sold in numerous countries.

Later that year the 'C'-Type made its debut for payloads between 1 and 6 tons. The lightest were the LC1 and LC1.5 models, still offered with a choice between petrol and diesel power. Medium-weight requirements were catered for by the 1C and 2C 1- and 2-tonners using CRD or CR1D 4-cyl diesels of 4.5 and 5.3 litres respectively.

1934 Saurer (1) 'C' Type truck

During this period the company also developed forward-control all-wheel drive military vehicles featuring a backbone chassis and 4, 6 or 8 independently-suspended wheels connected to the chassis by coil springs, and by the time World War II got underway examples of these were in full production. Producer-gas ver-

1978 Saurer (1) Type D330N 4 x 4 tipper

sions of civilian models were now available also, and by 1946 a new artillery tractor — the 4-wheel drive forward-control M4H with a capacity of 1½ tons — was coming off the production line, using a 70bhp rear-mounted 4-cyl diesel engine. Forward-control versions of the 'C'-Type also appeared and the heaviest model could now haul a 7-ton load. All were available in passenger form if required.

Each model in Saurer's 1950 range could be had with any one of 11 different diesel engines, including a 250bhp V12 and a 300bhp turbo-supercharged V12. New on the passenger scene were the rear-engined 3H and 4H models for thirty and seventy passengers respectively. Six or 8-cyl diesel engines drove the rear axle via an 8-speed transmission. With payloads of 3½, 5½ or 6½ tons, a new line of all-wheel drive forward-control trucks known as the 'CM'-Series was announced in the early 1950s, employing a 5-speed main transmission and 2-speed auxiliary with dis-engageable Tracta-type front-wheel drive. A derivative of this was the 1953 6CM military 6 x 6.

1944 Saurer (1) U8 military truck

By the late 1950s the 'C'-Type range included the S4C for up to 10 tons payload and the 6C for up to 11 tons. At the opposite end of the range the LC1 offered a capacity of nearly 3 tons and was built under licence by OM of Italy.

In 1965 the 'D'-Type Saurers arrived in the form of the 2D and 5D models, offered with a bewildering array of specifications. They could be had as normal- or forward-control front-engined vehicles or even with rear underfloor engines, headed by a 6-cyl diesel of up to 240bhp output. Generally, semi-elliptic leaf springs were used apart from on the buses, which had air suspension, and the familiar Saurer exhaust brake was fitted as standard on all types. Most variations had 8-speed transmissions, with city buses using pre-select systems. Payloads ranged from 6¾ to 10 tons for trucks, 22 to 180 persons for buses.

1955 Saurer (1) L4C postbus

In 1971, 2D models were replaced by the 4D, using a new 200bhp 8.8-litre 6-cyl diesel engine. A derivative of the 4D was the 4DM 4 x 4 type, which had a 6-speed ZF synchromesh transmission with 2-speed auxiliary. The heavier 5D was similar, but available with engines of up to 330bhp, a unit fitted as standard in the bonneted 5DM 4 x 4. Heaviest of all was the 6 x 4 5DF until 1974, when an 8 x 4 version was launched. This had a capacity of 18 tons. Co-operation on the bus front also came in 1974, with Leyland and DAB to develop the underfloor-engined Leyland-DAB-Saurer series.

In the light- to mediumweight range the company offers the Saurer-OM series ranging from the 2½-ton payload Type 35 to the 8-ton payload Type 130R. A new heavyweight for 1975 was a twin-steer 6-wheeled tractor using the turbo-supercharged 330bhp 6-cyl diesel engine. All other medium- to heavyweight models are now of 'D'-Series extraction, covering layouts of 4 x 2, 6 x 2, 6 x 4 and 8 x 4 drive. All-wheel drive models include both 4 x 4 and 6 x 6 types,

the lightest being derivatives of the Saurer-OM Types 75 and 90. On the passenger side, the company now offers its own underfloor- and rear-engined models.

SAURER (2)/*Austria 1906 to date*
When Adolph Saurer AG could not keep pace with demand for its early trucks and buses, Oesterreichische Saurerwerke AG was set up in Vienna to construct vehicles for the Austrian market. Most, it is believed, were of normal Saurer specification. This arrangement continued until 1937 when the Austrian plant went independent, continuing to licence-build Swiss-designed models under the Saurer name, many of which were supplied to the German Armed Forces during World War II.

In 1959 the business was acquired by Steyr-Daimler-Puch AG and continues to build vehicles under the Saurer brand name, identical in every way to the Swiss-built Saurers.

SAURER (3)/*France 1910-1956*
Adolph Saurer AG, Arbon, Switzerland, began building Saurer trucks and buses in the former Darracq-Serpollet factory in Suresnes, Seine, to cater for the French market. Chain-drive trucks of 3½ and 5 tons, and a light bus, were shown at the Paris Salon in 1910 and subsequent sales led to rapid expansion of the new plant.

In 1917 the company became Soc des Automobiles Industrielles Saurer, by which time it was supplying large numbers of trucks to the French Army. However, a slump followed the war and the company offered only French-built equivalents of the Swiss range. By the early 1930s articulated derivatives of these were offered by the French factory, and when a new 6 x 4 Swiss-built truck was outlawed by the Swiss authorities, production was taken up by the French factory.

After World War II all models were largely indistinguishable from their Swiss counterparts and in 1956 the factory was sold to SA des Automobiles Unic.

SAURER (4)/*USA 1911-1918*
Previously imported from Switzerland, manufacture of Saurer trucks got underway in the Plainfield, New Jersey, factory of the Saurer Motor Co. Initially, only a 4-tonner was available but by 1912 5- and 6½-tonners were also listed. In 1911 the company became a member of the short-lived International Motor Co, which also handled Mack and Hewitt sales, but by 1918 the Saurer range had been largely eclipsed by increasing demand for Macks.

SAURER (5)/*England c1927-1931*
Saurer trucks were also built in Britain by the Saurer Commercial Vehicle Co Ltd which introduced one of the first practical diesel-engined trucks into the country in 1928. Two years later Sir W G Armstrong Whitworth & Co Ltd, Newcastle-upon-Tyne, Co Durham, took out a licence to build Saurers under the Armstrong-Saurer brand name, and this precipitated the end for British Saurers.

SAVA 'WE'-Series truck c1959

SAVA/*Spain 1957 to date*
Starting with the 2000-kg payload P.54 3-wheeler, Soc Anon de Vehicules Automoviles, Valladolid, was soon building heavier models based on the British-designed Austin, Morris and BMC commercial series. Others were built under Berliet licence. Marketed as SAVA, SAVA-Austin, SAVA-Morris and SAVA-BMC, these had Spanish-built cabs until 1963, when the S-76 model brought the BMC 'FG' cab into the range. Later models, based on the bonneted 'WF' 3-tonner, forward-control 'FF' 5-tonner and on a 7-ton version of the 'FG', were identical to their British counterparts. The business was acquired by Empresa Nacional de Autocamiones SA, builder of Pegasos, in 1966 and continues to build trucks up to 6 tons capacity and light buses.

SAVA single-deck coach c1965

SAVAGE/*England 1903-1913*
General engineering and traction engine manufacturer Savage Bros Ltd, King's Lynn, Norfolk, built a small number of "undertype" steam wagons following acquisition of patent rights for the Musker vertical water-tube boiler. The company also used a top-

fired loco-type boiler and a vertical cross water-tube design in some wagons, but all were powered by the same 2-cyl compound engine with a piston-valve to the high-pressure cylinder and a slide-valve to the low.

Saviem JL25 artic tractor c1963

SAVIEM/*France 1955-1980*

SA des Véhicules Industriels et Equipements Mécaniques was established in Surersnes, Seine, to market Saviem commercials following the merger of Floirat, Latil, Renault and Somua interests. For the first couple of years an assortment of models was offered under such brand names as Saviem-Floirat, Saviem-Latil, Saviem-Somua or Saviem-LRS, although with rationalization the Saviem name was itself becoming established by 1957. Models continued along much the same lines until 1960, joined by Chausson passenger types in 1959 which introduced mid-mounted under-floor-engined chassisless passenger designs to the line.

Early rationalization came in the form of engines, many of the older designs being replaced by the company's own 4.6-litre 4- and 6.8-litre 6-cyl 'Fulgur' diesels and in 1961 an engineering and marketing deal was signed with the German Henschel concern to produce the short-lived Saviem-Henschel. A new diesel engine plant was set up in a former French government factory at Limoges in 1964 and later that year new 5- and 7-ton forward-control trucks using Renault 4- and Perkins 6-cyl diesels were developed. On the lighter front, Renault's 'Galion' and 'Goelette' models were absorbed a year later and by 1969 had developed into an up-dated series with new 85bhp 3.3-litre diesel engine, hydrovac braking and coil spring independent front suspension.

The most important move of this period, however, was a technical and marketing agreement with MAN whereby this German manufacturer would supply 6- and 8-cyl diesel engines for Saviem's heaviest models while Saviem would supply transmissions and a new tiltcab for MAN's use. The new Saviem heavyweights were to be known as Saviem-Renault. The company liaised with Alfa-Romeo of Italy, in 1968, resulting in the launch of a new 2-ton forward-control van known as the FC20 and providing an Italian sales outlet for light- and medium-duty Saviems.

By 1971 Saviem had become a member of the European "Club of Four" along with DAF, Magirus-Deutz and Volvo, leading to the introduction of the standardized Saviem 'J' model in 1975 with forward-control tiltcab, Limoges-built 5.5-litre 6-cyl diesel under MAN licence and a 5-speed ZF box.

In 1974 the Berliet truck and bus operation passed from Citroën to Renault, eventually leading to some integration, although by 1978 this was reflected only in the grouping of all commercial vehicle production under the management of Renault Véhicules Industriels. The under-5-tons GVW category was now catered for by the forward-control 'S'-Type, also listed in 4 x 4 form, while the lightest 'J'-Type was now the JK60 for 6 tons gross. The heaviest models could now be had as Saviems or Saviem-Renaults for gross combination weights of up to 40 tons, while normal-control models from 4 x 2 to 6 x 6 layout were really MAN's for up to 48 tons gross. Crane-carriers with up to six axles were also listed.

For 1980 all rationalization was complete. The Berliet marque had now disappeared and all trucks and buses were known henceforward as Renault.

1964 Saviem S7 7-ton truck

SAVIEM-HENSCHEL/*France/Germany 1961-1963*

An agreement signed by SA de Véhicules et Equipements Mécaniques of France and Henschel-Werke GmbH of West Germany enabled certain models to be sold in the respective countries as Saviem-Henschel. However, this was a short-lived arrangement and few examples can be traced.

1974 Saviem Renault SM 32 240 Artic tractor

SAVIEM-RENAULT/*France 1968-c1976*

Co-operation between MAN of Germany and Saviem of France led to the introduction of Saviem-Renault heavyweights using MAN diesel engines and a new Saviem tiltcab. Heaviest of the series was the SM32.240 tractor for 32 tons GCW, of which some were also sold in the United Kingdom. As the 1970s passed the Renault suffix was dropped and by about 1976 all models were apparently sold simply as Saviem.

SAYERS & SCOVILL/*USA 1907-c1912*

Founded in 1876, the Sayers & Scovill Co, Cincinnati, Ohio, was a well known carriage builder that also constructed a 2-ton chain-drive truck of forward-control design with a 4-cyl air-cooled petrol engine mounted vertically under the seat. Production of this model continued until a series of factory-built ambulance and hearse prototypes were built.

SCAT/*Italy c1914-1918*

Established in 1906 by Giovanni Ceirano, Soc Ceirano Automobili Torino, Turin, offered 2- and 4-ton SCAT trucks during World War I. Fitted with 4-cyl petrol engines, most went to the Italian Air Service. In 1918 the business passed out of the family's hands but in 1924 was re-acquired and the following year Ceirano trucks made their debut.

SCHACHT/*USA 1910-1938*

The Schacht Manufacturing Co, Cincinnati, Ohio, began truck production with a series of bonneted Continental or Wisconsin petrol-engined models of up to 4 tons capacity, increasing this to 7 tons by 1922, by which time the business was known as the G A Schacht Motor Truck Co. When, in 1926, the low-loading 'Super Safety Coach' was announced, various proprietary units were employed. This had a 6-cyl petrol engine, 8-speed transmission and Gruss air springs at the front.

An injection of capital led to the founding of the LeBlond-Schacht Truck Co in 1927 after which vehicles were sometimes referred to as LeBlond-Schacht. Towards the end of 1928 the Armleder Truck Co, Cincinnati, was acquired and models integrated with the Schacht line.

By the early 1930s all vehicles had 6-cyl petrol engines and were available in capacities from 1½ to 10 tons, using Continental engines in lighter types and Hercules or Wisconsin units in the others. Tractor versions appeared in 1932, and in 1936 the local Ahrens-Fox Fire Engine Co was

1974 Scania 110 8 x 4 tipper

SCANIA/*Sweden c1903 to date*

In the early 1890s the English cycle manufacturer Humber Ltd set up a small factory in Malmö to cope with increasing sales in Sweden and Denmark. Known as Swedish Humber AB, this became independent in about 1900 and was re-named Scania Maskinenfabrik AB, constructing a series of cycles and motorcycles.

A true commercial model with forward-control, engine beneath the driver's seat and chain-drive arrived in 1903 and by the end of that year Scania vehicles were being fitted with the company's own engines. In 1911 the company merged with Vagnfabriks Aktiebolaget i Södertälje to form Scania-Vabis Aktiebolaget to rationalize both models and facilities and compete with the many imported American marques.

In 1969 the Saab group acquired the company, re-named the conglomerate AB Saab-Scania, and continued production under the Scania name. Models included the successful 110-Series, and the 140-Series with 350bhp 14-litre V-8 engine. In 1971 a quiet version of the CR111 single-deck bus was introduced, with rear engine compartment fitted with sound-absorbent panels, and in 1972 a new heavy-duty cross-country vehicle with automatic transmission entered production. Known as the SBAT, it is in production today in both 4 x 4 and 6 x 6 forms.

In 1973 a special arrangement was made with British body-builders Metro-Cammell-Weymann Ltd, Birmingham, whereby Scania supplied engines and running units for a new range of British-built single- and double-deck buses. The result was the Metro-Scania which, although short-lived, did much to establish a new force in the British double-decker market. In 1975 the up-dated 81-Series replaced the earlier 80 and the 86 the 85-Series 6-wheeler. Similarly, the 110- and 140- Series are now replaced by the 111 and 141 Series and the bonneted 'T'-Range is offered in 6 x 4 rigid or tractor form.

1977 Scania 111 artic tractor

SCANIA-VABIS/*Sweden 1911-1969*

In 1911, Scania-Vabis Aktiebolaget was formed from a merger between vehicle manufacturers Scania Maskinenfabrik AB, Malmö, and Vagnfabriks Aktiebolaget i Södertälje, to rationalize

models and facilities and provide a united front against increasing US-built vehicle sales. The first Scania-Vabis trucks were based on the Type 5 Vabis, a 20 hp chain-drive model, discontinued in 1913. Towards the end of 1912 a new commercial range, from 1.5 to 6 tons capacity, was launched, entering full production by 1913. These had chain-drive, engines from 30 to 70 hp output, and were of bonneted layout. Examples were sold both abroad and at home.

By the end of World War I the company had developed a 4-wheel drive and steer system, supplied to the Swedish Army, civilian users and, later, fire-fighting organizations. This incorporated a separate propeller shaft to each wheel from a centrally-located gearbox, and an engine located ahead of the front axle to place as

much weight as possible on the front wheels.

The company's first 6-wheeler was a double-drive model launched in 1923. In the same year a special attachment for Scania-Vabis tippers whereby road-making materials could be spread evenly to various depths, controlled by a drive system from the vehicle's rear wheels was developed. Another idea was a double-reduction axle, joined in 1924 by a new 36 bhp overhead-valve engine and, later, by a 50 bhp side-valve unit.

Car production was discontinued in 1928 and the Malmö plant closed, but the company was still ahead on new developments.

1927 Scania-Vabis type 3251 truck

One was the patent progressive spring which guaranteed stability and smoothness under load. This, combined with the double-reduction axle with its small casing and low-loading chassis, led to a new generation of passenger vehicles. Another major step in the passenger field came in 1929 when special "narrow" engines were fitted in the company's chassis, leading to the development of the full-front "bulldog" type bus in 1931.

Until this time, the Swedish Post Office had not used large vehicles on long-distance runs, preferring the rail network. Following consultations with the Scania-Vabis design team, a unique vehicle was devised. Based on a 36bhp bonneted chassis, it was the first all-weather post bus, employing removable rear tracks and front skis. Truck production took a back seat during this period, but both the double-reduction axle and the patent progressive suspension were used in this area.

In 1927 experiments with heavy fuel oil were made and by 1930 the Hesselman-Scania engine was developed, providing a 65bhp output, which could be petrol-started and switched to heavy oil. The first production Scania-Vabis diesel engine did not appear until 1936. This 7.75-litre unit developed 120bhp at 2000rpm and was an immediate success. In 1939 a new series of direct-injection diesels of 4-, 6- and 8-cyl layout was developed. Production com-

1975 Scania 81 truck

menced in 1949 when these became known as the 'D'-Series. Turbocharging was applied by 1951, with the 8-cyl D815 which developed 205bhp and was the first production turbocharged diesel in Europe.

Although Sweden was not involved in World War II, Scania-Vabis developed a few heavy armoured tanks and an armoured truck known as the SKP, often referred to as the "Panzer Truck", some 250 being constructed, many of which are still in service with the United Nations. By 1946 production of commercial vehicles had reached 1500 chassis a year and the company's technical knowledge of engines and transmissions was much sought after with information exchanged with Leyland Motors Ltd and American Mack. Such arrangements were relevant to bus technology, resulting in the development of the Scania-Vabis C50 'Metropol' bus in 1953. For many years, Mack gearboxes bore signs of Scania-Vabis ancestry and Mack still uses Scania-Vabis engines for special applications. A new bonneted truck range appeared in 1954 with air brake reservoirs mounted on the axles. This was spearheaded by the L51 4-wheeler with B420 diesel engine and by 1956 some 4,500 chassis a year were built at Södertälje, just over one half being exported.

The need for more powerful engines in 1958 led to the announcement of the 10.25-litre normally-aspirated D10. This had 165bhp, and was followed in 1959 by the smaller D7, the D11, D8 and, eventually, the turbocharged DS11 and DS8. The introduction of the D10 also heralded a revised truck range, the 75-Series, another bonneted range which was highly successful. Similarly, the D11 and DS11 engines led to the 76-Series in 1963, both bonneted and forward-control, and known, respectively, as the L76 and LB76. By the mid-1960s Scania-Vabis sought expansion and in 1969 it merged with the Saab group, the new organization being known as AB Saab-Scania and vehicles reverting to the Scania name.

purchased. By 1937 the range was segregated into 'A'-Series "conventionals" for 1½ to 3½ tons payload, and 'CU'-Series "cabovers" for 2½ to 5 tons payload. With decreasing commercial sales, efforts were concentrated on the Ahrens-Fox operation.

SCHEELE/*Germany 1899-1925*
Heinrich Scheele, Lindenthal, Cologne, launched a range of battery-electric vans and trucks. In 1906 the business was re-organized as Kolner Elektromobil-Gesellschaft Heinrich Scheele, continuing to manufacture battery-electric models.

SCHEIBLER/*Germany 1899-1909*
Fritz Scheibler Gesellschaft, Aachen, produced Scheibler vans and light buses. In 1903 the company was re-named Scheibler Automobil Industrie GmbH and vehicles of up to 3 tons capacity were constructed. Later the company was re-named Motoren und Lastwagen AG and all vehicles sold as Mulag.

SCHIEMANN/*Germany 1901-11*
Germany's first trolleybus system was set up at Konigstein, Saxony, by Max Schiemann of Gesellschaft für Gleislose Bahnen Max Schiemann & Co, Wurzen, Saxony, using vehicles built by Siemens und Halske AG with front-wheel drive and bogie steering. When production began in Schiemann's own factory, using Siemens und Halske traction equipment, rear-wheel drive was employed. Towards the end of production goods vehicles were constructed, for operation on a trolley system, the firm's most unusual machine being a heavy tractor working on the same principle.

SCHILTER/*Switzerland 1958 to date*
The first Schilter was a 1-ton payload rear-wheel drive agricultural truck built by Schilter AG, Schaffhausen. Powered by a horizontal air-cooled 2-cyl petrol engine, it was joined in 1959 by a 4 x 4 version for a payload of just under 2 tons using a 9 or 12bhp MAG petrol engine in unit with transmission and rear axle. Currently, 1-, 2-, 3- and 4-tonners are advertised, the lightest being the Model 1000 with tubular backbone chassis, 10bhp front-mounted single- or 16bhp twin-cyl MAG air-cooled petrol engine or a 14bhp single-cyl Lombardini diesel unit, transmission using a 6 forward and 2 reverse system.

SCHINDLER/*Switzerland 1957-c1959*
A manufacturer of railway wag-

ons and lifts, Schindler acquired the manufacturing rights for the German-designed Orion bus in 1957. Re-named the Schindler, it re-appeared at the Geneva Motor Show with 34 seats, an 8-litre rear-mounted Kamper diesel engine and Continental air suspension. Also on show was a large-capacity integral trolleybus with pneumatic suspension intended for operation with a passenger-carrying trailer.

SCHLEICHER/*USA 1911-1919*
The Schleicher Motor Vehicle Co was set up at Ossining, New York, to manufacture large-capacity trucks to special order. Three, 5-, 6-, 8- and 10-tonners were available, the two lightest models having a 45hp 4-cyl Continental petrol engine and all types 4-speed transmissions and double chain-drive.

SCHMIDT/*USA 1911*
The 1-ton FCS truck built by the Schmidt Bros Co, Chicago, Illinois, was re-named the Schmidt in 1911. Despite a move to new premises at Grand Crossing, production ended after a few months.

SCHNEIDER/*France 1908-1920*
Following the bankruptcy of Soc des Automobiles Eugène Brillié, Ets Schneider, Le Havre, which had been assembling vehicles of Brillié design, began to sell under the Schneider or Brillié-Schneider names. Most were passenger types but some trucks using similar chassis were constructed under the Schneider name. One interesting vehicle was a 1914 military tractor, where engine, radiator and driver were mounted high behind the front axle. Later that year the company was taken over by Soc d'Outillage Mecanique et d'Usinage Artillerie, continuing production as CGO-Schneider until the Somua name was introduced in 1920.

SCHURMEIER/*USA 1910-1911*
The Schurmeier Wagon Co, Minneapolis, Minnesota, built horse-drawn wagons until 1910 when the first Schurmeier trucks were built. A truck plant was opened at St Paul and about 100 vehicles built. All were forward-control types, listed as 1-, 2- and 3-tonners, and powered by 2-stroke engines with chain-drive. A vertical twin unit powered the lightest model while a vertical 3-cyl type was used in the other two.

SCHUTZE/*Germany 1900-1902*
Based at Oggersheim, Giesserei und Maschinenfabrik Paul Schütze built 10-ton battery-electric lorries of unusual design with a powered front bogie.

SCHWARTZ/*USA 1918-1923*
H B Schwartz founded the Schwartz Motor Truck Corp, Reading, Pennsylvania, to build 4-cyl worm-drive Schwartz trucks. By 1920 1½-, 2½- and 5-tonners were listed, the two lighter models using Continental petrol engines and the heavier a Buda. A Lycoming-engined 1½-ton "speed truck" was announced in 1922 but in 1923 the business was purchased by the Clinton Motors Corp and all subsequent models sold as Clinton.

SCHWARTZKOPFF/*Germany 1897-1907*
John I Thornycroft & Co Ltd, London W4, granted the Schwartzkopff Loco Works, Berlin, a licence to build Thornycroft steam wagons for the German market. This arrangement continued under the direction of L Schwartzkopff Berliner Maschinenbau AG.

SCOT/*Canada 1972 to date*
The first Scot truck was a bonneted 6 x 4 tractor built by the Atlantic Truck Mfg Co Ltd, Debert, Nova Scotia. Powered by a Cummins NTC335 diesel engine, it had a Ford 'Louisville' cab and was joined by a 6 x 4 "cabover" dump truck. A new 6 x 4 "conventional", with the company's own cab and bonnet, appeared in 1976 as the A2HD model. Other types include fire appliances and off-road designs with a wide choice of engines, transmissions and other components. Engines are mostly Cummins or Detroit Diesels from 180 to 600bhp output, the heaviest trucks having capacities of up to 181,436kg.

SCOTT (1)/*England 1903-1904*
G D Scott, Duffield, Derby, constructed prototype 3- and 5-ton steam wagons. These had Field-tube boilers with concentric rear wheels and crankshaft, and equalizing gear.

SCOTT (2)/
England 1952
Already well-established as a manufacturer of industrial and railway platform trucks, Scott Electric Vehicles Ltd, Kidderminster, Worcs, also introduced a 1-ton battery-electric delivery vehicle. This was a 3-wheeler with a single driven front wheel and a 2hp traction motor.

SCOTT-STIRLING/*England 1905-1908*
Built in Scotland as the Stirling, the Scott-Stirling was later built in Scott, Stirling & Co Ltd's Twickenham, Middx, factory. The first new model was a 24hp 4-cyl petrol-engined design suitable for 36-seat open-top double-deck bus

1921 Scammell (1) 7-ton artic tractor

SCAMMELL (1)/*England 1919-1921, 1933*

G Scammell & Nephew Ltd, Spitalfields, London, E1, was a body-building and repair business that began experimenting with a bonneted artic tractor unit using a trailer coupling developed from the American Knox-Martin system. This was carried on semi-elliptic leaf springs attached to the tractor's rear axle, enabling the wheels to take the semi-trailer's weight rather than the chassis frame. This was one of Britain's first "matched" 6-wheeled artics, capable of hauling a 7-ton payload at up to 19km/h.

A new factory opened in 1922 at Watford, Herts, where Scammell Lorries Ltd was set up to handle series production. G Scammell & Nephew later developed a forward-control rigid low-loader with 4-cyl Meadows petrol engine, 4-speed transmission and a claimed top speed of 64km/h.

SCAMMELL (2)/*England 1922 to date*

Ten-ton versions of the Scammell "matched" artic 6-wheeler were soon in production at the Watford, Herts, factory of Scammell Lorries Ltd and the world's first "matched" artic tanker, for 9092 litres of fuel oil, was shown at the 1922 Olympia. Fifteen-tonners were listed by 1926, the same year that the company's first 'Pioneer' 6-wheeler, with centrally-pivoted non-powered front axle and rocking balance-beam rear suspension was built. Other developments included a "frameless" tank semi-trailer for use with the company's artic tractor units, and the experimental 'Auto-Van' for local deliveries, powered by a 3-cyl air-cooled radial petrol engine mounted vertically over the gearbox/differential unit.

The Scammell range was expanded in 1928 with the introduction of a 6-ton 4-wheeled rigid, using an 80bhp version of the company's own 7-litre 4-cyl petrol engine and optional worm drive back axle. In 1929 two examples of the world's largest lorry, a 100-ton artic for heavy machinery transport, were built to special order, again using the 7-litre petrol engine, employing a 4-in-line rear wheel arrangement on the tractor. The 'Pioneer' was militarized by the provision of 6-wheel drive, and new 'Pioneer' prototypes included a half-track and armoured car.

The Depression brought fire appliance orders from the local council and in 1932 a "mechanical horse" prototype was purchased from D Napier & Son Ltd, leading to Scammell's own 1933 version, offered as a 3- and 6-tonner with 1.13- and 2.04-litre 4-cyl petrol engines, respectively, and 4-speed transmissions. Two years later two special 6 x 4 tractors, with 160bhp Parsons petrol engines, 10-speed transmission, double-reduction rear axles and Gruss air springs, were supplied to the Anglo-Iranian Oil Co, while a 6 x 2 'Rigid-6' and a diesel-engined rigid 8-wheeler joined the series.

was a series of tropically-equipped 4-wheeled rigid and artic oilfield units.

New additions at the heavier end of the market included the 6 x 4 'Junior Constructor' and 6 x 6 'Constructor', followed by the 6 x 6 'Super Constructor', all offered as rigids or tractors. The mainstay of production continued to be 4 x 2 tractors, these being re-named 'Highwayman'.

Earth-moving requirements were catered for by dump trucks using Edbro or Telehoist equipment on the 'Mountaineer' chassis and, later, on the 'Constructor', these being joined by the 1-man cabbed 4 x 2 'Sherpa' and 6 x 4 'Himalayan'.

In 1955, the company was acquired by Leyland Motors Ltd, but retained its individuality. The forward-control 4 x 2 'Handyman' tractor was introduced in 1960 to cope with increased trailer lengths and the first 'Routeman' rigid 8-wheelers, using cabs common to the 'Handyman', were announced. Pride of place at the 1960 Commercial Motor Show went to the "truck of the future" a 6 x 4 forward-control "matched"

1949 Scammell (2) 'Scarab' mechanical horse

World War II saw the 'Pioneer' in use as a tank transporter, artillery tractor and recovery vehicle, a 4 x 4 heavy tractor, using 'Pioneer' components and a 6 x 6 experimental version. Peacetime brought the 20-ton 'Showtrac', a drawbar/generating tractor into the range, and in 1949 the first 4 x 4 'Mountaineer' appeared. A new military model, developed from the experimental 6 x 6 'Pioneer', was the Meadows-engined 6 x 6 'Explorer', some examples being supplied to overseas heavy haulage operators. Also for export

artic known as the 'Trunker', designed for 30 tons gross operation, the maximum permitted weight at the time being 24 tons. Only three were built.

Presented at the next Commercial Motor Show was the re-designed 'Routeman' with fibreglass cab. Another new model was the 4-wheeled 'Scarab-Four' "mechanical horse". The 3-wheeled 'Scarab', a descendant of the original "mechanical horse", was soon replaced by the fibreglass-cabbed 'Townsman', and by 1965 the 'Routeman' cab had also ap-

1928 Scammell (2) 6-ton truck

1963 Scammell (2) 'Highwayman' artic tractor

1950 Scammell (2) 'Rigid-8' 8 x 2 trucks

peared on the 'Handyman' and on a new version of the 'Trunker', now of twin-steer 6 x 2 layout with a load transfer device on the second steering axle to aid traction. A brand new "heavy", replacing the 'Constructor' for heavy haulage, was the 6 x 4 'Contractor' for operation at up to 240 tons gross, followed by the forward-control 'Crusader' in 4 x 2 and 6 x 4 form.

In the early 1970s the Watford plant was absorbed into British Leyland's Special Products Divn and re-named Scammell Motors, resulting in numerous overseas orders carrying the Leyland brand name. Production of Scammell semi-trailers was transferred to Hoveringham, Notts, and eventually acquired by the York Trailer Co Ltd, while some Thornycroft production, such as the 'Nubian

Major' and LD55 dump truck, was transferred to Watford. In recent years the plant's experimental dept has figured prominently in the development of new Leyland models, particularly for military use. Typical are the 'Commander' tank transporter tractor, the rear-engined 4 x 4 and 6 x 6 'Nubian' fire crash tender chassis, and the 6 x 4 'Amazon' heavy haulage version of the 'Crusader', all announced at the 1978 Motor Show, plus the T43 'Landtrain' and T45 'Roadtrain' truck and tractor ranges. Current production includes T45-cabbed 6- 8-wheeled rigids called 'Constructors' now marketed as Leyland, the 6 x 4 'Amazon', 'Commander', and 'Nubian', and the heavyweight S24 6 x 4 and 6 x 6 series for gross weights of up to 300 tons.

bodies. One hundred were ordered by the London Power Omnibus Co Ltd but the operator went out of business in 1907 and, as the Scott-Stirling Motor Co Ltd's largest customer, this led to the closure of the Middx plant.

SCOTTE/*France 1894-c1914*
A 14-seat "overtype" steam bus was developed by Soc des Chaudières et Voitures à Vapeur, Paris, under the Scotte brand name, using a coal-fired vertical Field-tube boiler and 2-cyl vertical marine-type engine with chain-drive to differential countershaft and double chain-drive to the rear wheels. By 1897 a Scotte postbus was used with a passenger-carrying trailer and, by 1905, a heavy haulage tractor had also been built. Later, special road-trains were developed for military and colonial use.

SCOUT/*England 1909-c1914, 1920-1921*
The heaviest of a series of light commercials introduced by Dean & Burden Bros Ltd, Salisbury, Wilts, under the Scout brand name was a 1-ton payload shaft-drive machine with 4-cyl petrol engine. The company was renamed the Scout Motors Ltd, adding chain-drive 2- and 3-ton bonneted chassis using 32 and 38hp 4-cyl petrol engines in 1910. By 1914 worm-drive was standard but vehicle production was discontinued in favour of armaments, and not resumed until 1920, when a few commercials similar to the pre-war range were built.

SD/*England 1923 to date*
The SD 'Freighter' also known as the S & D or Shelvoke & Drewry was a small-wheeled, short-haul goods model introduced by Shelvoke & Drewry Ltd, Letchworth, Herts. Powered by a 35bhp 2.2-litre 4-cyl petrol engine located transversely it had a 3 forward and 3 reverse epicyclic transmission driving the worm rear axle via bevel-gearing and propeller shaft.

1959 SD 'W'-Type refuse collector

The vehicle was controlled by two tram-type controllers, the right-hand actuating steering and the left working the transmission and rear wheel brakes. A 2-ton version appeared in 1928, and in 1929 enclosed cabs were fitted and the company's own 38bhp 2.4-litre petrol engine used. From 1932 this was offered with the option of a 44bhp 3-litre unit when licence production of Latil road tractors got underway, using the Traulier and Loco-Traulier brand names.

In 1933 the company acquired municipal equipment patents, and later that year wheel-steering was introduced on 'Freighter' buses. The first front-radiatored SD was the 'E'-Type of 1938 which had a transverse front-mounted petrol engine and wheel-steering. This was built in municipal, goods and passenger form, re-designated the 'N'-Type after the war. In 1946 it was joined by the larger single- or crew-cabbed 'W'-Type using a 55bhp 3.9-litre SD petrol engine, mounted in a longitudinal frontal position. Most 'W'-Types were municipal but a number of 3-ton low-loaders were also supplied to the service industries.

The 'N'-Type was withdrawn in 1950, and from 1954 Perkins P4 4-cyl diesel engines were optional for the 'W'-Type, which continued to be built until the introduction of the 11 tons GVW 'TW'- and 14 tons GVW 'TY'-Series in

1929 Scammell (2) 'Pioneer' 6 x 4 artic tractor

1926 SD 'Freighter' single-deck bus

1963 SD 'TY'-Type 'Pakamatic' refuse collector

Seagrave artic aerial ladder fire appliance c1960

1960. The former had an SD petrol or Perkins P6 diesel engine, while the latter used a Leyland 0.350 diesel. Both carried a restyled cab, and a series of refuse collection bodies with capacities of up to 6 cu m were listed with 5-speed transmissions and air-actuated hydraulic brakes. 'Pakamatic' compressing refuse collection bodies were announced in 1961 for both chassis, and in 1963 a "mini" version appeared in the form of the 8½ tons GVW 'TN'-Series powered by a 4-cyl Perkins diesel.

1979 SD 'PN'-Series

The first multi-wheeled SD was a 3-axle street washer and by 1970 refuse collection bodies with compressed capacities of up to 15 cu m were joined by the 'Revopak' ejector discharge model. In 1973 the first Motor Panels cabs were fitted to most models, and in 1975 the company constructed the 'CSD' fire appliance in collaboration with Carmichael, Worcester. Power units included a Cummins V8, Perkins V8 and Rolls-Royce straight-8, models comprising a water tender and 4 x 4 airfield fire crash tender. Interest led to the development of the 'NY'-Series 4 x 4 chassis for 16 tons GVW in 1976 using a Leyland diesel engine, 6-speed transmission and Motor Panels tilt-cab.

Current municipal models include tankers and fore-and-aft, 'Pakamatic' and 'Revopak' refuse collectors, the largest being the 6 x 4 'NT'-Series. Non-standard models comprise the 'SPV'-Series constructed to customer requirements. Common in this series are 4 x 4s and 6 x 6s, but there is also the 'PSD' Model designed for urban deliveries, as well as a new passenger model.

SDS/*Belgium 1938-1940*
SA des Automobiles SDS assembled a series of long-bonnetted truck chassis aimed at the general haulage market. These had Hercules petrol or Gardner diesel engines, Timken axles, Clark transmissions and Lockheed hydraulic brakes with Dewandre servo-assistance.

SEABROOK/*England 1913-c1917, 1919-1924*
Seabrook Bros, London ECI, were vehicle importers who frequently sold other marques as Seabrook. Among these was the Standard range of 1-, 1½-, 2- and 3½-ton trucks built by the Standard Motor Truck Co but marketed as Seabrook or Seabrook-Standard. Manufacture of these ceased in 1915 although imported models were available in Britain until about 1917. Seabrook Bros began marketing the American-built Napoleon range in the UK, as Seabrook or Seabrook-Napoleon in 1919. These were built by the Napoleon Motors Co, later re-named the Traverse City Motor Co, and although manufacture ceased in 1922, models were available in Britain until 1924.

SEAGRAVE/*USA/Canada 1907 to date*
In 1909 the first self-propelled fire appliances with underseat 4-cyl air-cooled petrol engines built by the Seagrave Co, Columbus, Ohio, were joined by a tractor using the same engine for hauling artic ladder trucks. Production got underway in Walkerville, Ontario, in 1910 and the first water-cooled Seagraves appeared in 1911 as bonneted chain-drive cen-trifugal pumpers with 6-cyl petrol engines. Meanwhile, Couple Gear electric tractors were supplied with Seagrave ladder trucks as the Seagrave-Couple Gear, and by 1915 some were available with front-wheel drive.

The company's first self-propelled water tower appeared in 1917 and by 1922 a shaft-drive pumper was introduced, pump outputs of between 350 and 1300gpm being listed the following year. Now called the Seagrave Corp, the company closed its Canadian plant and in 1932 announced a 240bhp V12 petrol engine based on Pierce-Arrow designs. Some Ford and Reo truck chassis were used during the Depression, but in 1936 the first limousine Seagrave, called the 'Safety Sedan Pumper', was introduced as was the smaller 'Sentry' series. Meanwhile, a Canadian licence had been taken out by Bickle Fire Engines Ltd.

The bonneted 'Anniversary' series of 1951 was a completely new style, although still using the old V12 engine, now up-rated to 300bhp.

This was joined by the first cab-forward Seagrave in 1959 which, like the 'Anniversary' range, was offered in open and closed form. Another first was the development of an aerial platform unit in 1961.

Heralding the demise of the V12 engine, Hall-Scott and Waukesha units were made available in 1962, and in 1963 the business was acquired by the FWD Corp eventually transferring it to its own plant at Clintonville, Wisconsin. One casualty was a rear-mounted turntable ladder which had been designed for the cab-forward chassis. The Columbus plant was retained, however, and production again got underway, this time using ordinary commercial chassis sold as Seagrave Commercial-by-Timpco. Following the withdrawal of the 'Anniversary' series in 1970, a new cab-forward range powered by Detroit Diesel engines was developed for use as a combination pumper and artic ladder truck.

SEARS/*USA 1909-1912*
The Sears was a high-wheeled wagon powered by a 2-cyl horizontally-opposed air-cooled petrol engine located under the seat. Built by Sears, Roebuck & Co, Chicago, Illinois, it had tiller steering, chain final-drive and full-elliptic leaf springs all round. Production was taken over by the Lincoln Motor Car Works and models marketed as Lincoln.

SEDAN/*France c1901-c1910*
The Sedan was a front-wheel drive lightweight vehicle popular as a delivery model during the early 1900s. Built by Procédés Bertin et Cie, it was powered by a 22hp flat-twin petrol engine located un-

1910 Seagrave chemical engine fire appliance

der a "coal-scuttle" bonnet with radiator mounted between driver and engine and rear wheel brakes available for "emergency" use. Capacities of up to 2 tons were available. The range was also built for the British market by the Sedan Auto-Car Syndicate Ltd, Wolverhampton, Staffs, in 1909 and 1910.

SEFA/*Spain 1931-1936*
Sociedad Espanola de Fabricacion de Automoviles, Madrid, was founded to build Sefa passenger cars and commercials but only the latter were produced. Only 35 examples were built, these being in the 3- to 5-ton payload class, with 4-cyl engines.

SEITZ (1)/*USA 1908-1913*
Forward-control petrol-engined Seitz trucks were built by the Seitz Automobile & Transmission Co, Detroit, Michigan, using a double friction transmission system which, it was claimed, could be used as an emergency brake by putting it into reverse. Models included 2-, 3- and 5-ton trucks, the 3-tonner having a 40/45hp 4-cyl engine, and double chain-drive.

SEITZ (2)/*Germany/West Germany c1940-c1949*
Fahrzeugfabrik Seitz & Co AG, Kreuzlingen, built Seitz battery-electric delivery vehicles to combat the lack of liquid fuel during World War II. In the last year of production, models comprised the forward-control Type 'A' for 1½-ton payloads, using a 4.5kw traction motor and the bonneted Type 'E', a 2-tonner with 8kw traction motor. Both had a range per charge of about 80km. Before production ceased a new company, Mowag Motorwagenfabrik AG was established to manufacture Mowag commercials.

SELDEN/*USA 1913-1932*
Introduced as bonneted 1-, 2- and 3½-tonners, the first trucks built by the Selden Motor Vehicle Co, Rochester, New York, were of shaft-drive layout with 20 or 40hp 4-cyl Continental petrol engines, 3- or 4-speed Brown-Lipe transmissions, and Russel or Timken axles. In 1912 the Selden Truck Sales Co was founded to market the range, introducing a deferred-payment plan which led to increasing sales and later to exports.

There were six models, comprising worm-, chain- and internal-gear types, the only chain-drive model being a 2-tonner, while internal-gear versions were listed in 1- and 2-ton forms. The original 1-, 2- and 3½-tonners had worm-drive.

When the US entered the war, the company was called upon to

1921 Selden 'A'-Series 2½-ton truck chassis

build 3700 examples of the standardized 'B'-Class "liberty" truck, resulting in considerable expansion. Models now included the 1½-ton Model 1½A; a 2-ton worm-drive; and 2½-, 3½- and 5-ton Models 2½A, 3½A and 5A. All had Continental petrol engines, the lightest using a 25bhp unit mounted on 3-point suspension, a 4-plate clutch, 3-speed Brown-Lipe transmission and single-piece Timken rear axle. The 2 2½- and 3½-tonners were identifiable by radiator brush guards and finned radiator tops.

In 1922 the company merged with the Atlas Motor Truck Co to form the Industrial Motors Corp, the Atlas name being discontinued by 1923. By 1925 Selden production was also on the wane but despite this, the 1½- and 2½-ton 'Pacemaker' and the 3/4-ton 'Roadmaster' were announced in 1928, all using 6-cyl LeRoi petrol engines. The business was acquired by Hahn Motors Inc in 1929, continuing under the Selden or Selden-Hahn name until 1932 when the Selden-Hahn Motor Truck Corp ceased operation.

SELVE/*Germany 1920-1929*
Specializing in the manufacture of light commercials and fire appliances, Selve Automobilwerke AG, Hamelin, Hanover, also designed and constructed an unusual 6-wheel drive 1½-tonner in 1928. With twin rear tyres, a 50 PS 3-litre 6-cyl engine and an 8-speed transmission, this on/off-road machine also had independent suspension all round. The lighter models all used a common chassis, powered by a 1.5- or 2-litre petrol engine.

SEMEX/*West Germany ? to date*
As well as importing Liaz, Skoda and Tatra trucks, Semex Nutzfahrzeuge GmbH, Dorsten, constructs 6 x 6, 8 x 8 and 10 x 8 trucks under the Semex brand name. These use Tatra or Deutz air-cooled diesel engines, and apart

from the 26.256 6 x 6 model, which has a semi forward-control Motor Panels tiltcab, have low-mounted forward-control cabs. Transmissions and axles are usually of Tatra origin and models are specially popular in the construction industry as dump trucks, crane-carriers and concrete pumpers.

SERPOLLET/*France 1894-1899*
Léon Serpollet was an automotive pioneer, who specialized in light- and mediumweight steam-powered vehicles. Using a flash boiler, his vehicles were paraffin-fuelled by 1898 with chain-drive to the rear axle. From 1899 he collaborated with Frank Gardner, constructing heavier Gardner-Serpollet commercials.

SERVICE/*USA 1911-1932*
Starting with its Model 'A' high-wheeler, using a 22hp 4-cyl petrol engine, friction transmission and chain-drive, the Service Motor Car Co, Wabash, Indiana, moved to more conventional models when, as the Service Motor Truck Co, it announced a 5-model series of bonneted trucks from 1 to 5 tons capacity in about 1915. Employing 4-cyl Buda petrol engines, 3- or 4-speed transmissions and Timken worm-drive rear axles, these were joined during World War I by 'B'-Class "Liberty" trucks.

A lighter "speed truck" was announced in 1923, the company now being known as Service Motors Inc, but in 1927 it was acquired by the Relay Motors Corp and production merged with Commerce, Garford and Relay trucks of Lima, Ohio. A new range of Service trucks, identical with Relays apart from worm-drive and steel disc wheels, was announced but production ceased with Relay's liquidation.

SETRA/*West Germany 1950 to date*
The coachbuilding and engineering concern, Karl Kässbohrer GmbH, Ulm, developed a chassis-

1915 Selden 2-ton integral van

less rear-engined coach marketed from 1951 as the Setra, referred to as the Kässbohrer at prototype stage.

A series of buses based on the same design was also offered and in 1956 the Eagle, Golden Eagle and Silver Eagle passenger types were developed using similar construction techniques.

1956 Setra prototype coach

Re-organized as Karl Kässbohrer Fahrzeugwerke GmbH, the company developed a series of Setra passenger types, all with rear-mounted diesel engines and standard mechanical and body components. Current production uses MAN or Mercedes-Benz diesel engines and includes a high-floor 6-wheeler and an artic city bus.

SHAKESPEARE/*England 1915-1916*
Built by the Kalamazoo Motor Vehicle Co, Kalamazoo, Michigan, Kalamazoo trucks were sold in the UK by the Shakespeare Motor Co, London EC4, as the Shakespeare.

SHAKTIMAN/*India 1958-1963*
Built under licence by the Indian Ordnance Factories, Jabalpur, the 5-ton Shaktiman normal-control 4 x 4 truck was based on a military model built by Maschinenfabrik Augsburg-Nürnberg AG. The design utilized an easily-replaced all-steel cab with flat angular surfaces to aid repairs. Some 5000 were built, all powered by a 130bhp multi-fuel engine.

1964 Setra S10 single-deck coach

1951 Seddon 3-ton boxvan

SEDDON/*England 1938-c1940, 1946-1980*
Foster & Seddon, Salford, Lancs, were transport contractors and commercial vehicle distributors who introduced a 6-ton payload forward-control Perkins P6-engined diesel truck for legal operation at up to 48km/h. Production ceased in favour of military trailers, but resumed after the war. In 1947 production was transferred to Oldham, the company re-organized as Seddon Lorries Ltd, and passenger versions offered on the export market. In 1950 a 3-ton rigid using a 4-cyl Perkins diesel engine was added and the business re-named Seddon Diesel Vehicles Ltd, and in 1952 a new passenger chassis with mid-mounted 6-cyl Perkins diesel engine was introduced. In 1954 the 1¼-ton bonneted '25' model was announced and fibreglass introduced in cab construction.

models included a 14 tons GVW version of the Mk 15 and the 'Pennine' Mk 19 passenger chassis powered by a 98bhp horizontal underfloor AEC diesel engine. For 1959 trailing-axle 6-wheeled rigid goods models were also advertised and a 30-ton version of the 'Sirdar' offered, while a bonneted 6 x 4 artic for up to 45 tons GCW was added in 1961.

Radical changes occurred in 1964 when the '13:Four' rigid, using a new Motor Panels cab and Perkins 6.354 diesel engine, set the pattern for the future. In 1965 the '16:Four' was announced, this time with a Perkins V8 diesel producing 170bhp. By 1967 a V8-engined artic tractor, the SD4, had been up-rated to 28 tons gross and was joined by Gardner and Rolls-Royce engined versions for 32 or 38 tons gross.

In 1970 the company was re-organized as Seddon Motors Ltd

Vehicles Ltd led to its takeover in 1970, the two ranges remaining separate. An unusual liaison was with Magirus-Deutz (Great Britain) Ltd which led to a single Seddon-Deutz goods model. Meanwhile, experimental work led to a new heavyweight range.

In 1974 the business was taken over by the International Harvester Corp, becoming Seddon Atkinson Vehicles Ltd. The new heavyweight introduced in 1975 was available in 4-, 6- and 8-wheeled form as the Seddon-Atkinson '400'-Series. Although all goods models were now sold as Seddon-Atkinson, one Seddon, using the old Motor Panels cab, was marketed as a refuse collector until 1980.

1973 Seddon 'Pennine IV' bus

SEDDON-ATKINSON/*England 1975 to date*
Using Cummins, Gardner and Rolls-Royce diesel engines, the Seddon-Atkinson '400'-Series, introduced by Seddon Atkinson Vehicles Ltd, Oldham, Lancs, comprised 4-, 6- and 8-wheeled rigids and a 4 x 2 artic tractor unit for operation at 32/38 tons GCW. A 17-ton GVW 4-wheeled rigid, the '200'-Series, using a 134bhp International 6-cyl diesel engine, was added and in 1978 the first rigid '300'-Series 6-wheeler for 24 tons GVW was constructed. This carried a lower-mounted version of the current Motor Panels cab adopted for the '400'-Series and was powered by a 200bhp International diesel engine driving

through a 6-speed ZF transmission. Later, a '300'-Series artic tractor unit was also offered. The smaller '200'-Series could only be had in this form as a conversion.

A single Seddon municipal was advertised but was replaced by a municipalized '200'-Series with high-roofed crew-cab in 1980. More significant is the '401'-Series artic tractor, a modified version of the '400'-Series, employing lightweight components.

SEDDON-DEUTZ/*England 1971*
Co-operation between Seddon Motors Ltd, Oldham, Lancs, and Magirus-Deutz (Great Britain) Ltd resulted in a prototype goods model using a Seddon '13-Four' rigid, powered by a 120bhp Deutz F6L912 air-cooled V6 diesel engine. Transmission was via a ZF 5-speed constant-mesh gearbox and 2-speed Eaton axle.

1971 Seddon-Deutz truck

SEDDON VAN TWIST/*Netherlands c1952-1955*
During the 1950s Kemper en Van Twist Diesel NV, Dordrecht, Dutch distributor for the British-designed Seddon goods and passenger range began assembling these marketing them as Seddon Van Twist. The normal-control 1¼-tonner retained the bonnet and scuttle of the home proudct, but larger models were fitted with Dutch-built cabs. From 1955 the company built its own trucks under the Van Twist name.

1960 Seddon DD8 8 x 4 truck

By 1956 wraparound windscreens had begun to appear and in 1957 new lightweight plastics cabs were advertised for Mk 12 and Mk 15 models. The first "heavy" Seddon was the 24 ton gross DD8 8 x 4 rigid, offered in single-drive form as the SD8, but heavier was the 40 tons GTW 'Sirdar' bonneted 6 x 4 tractor for export. Other new

and the 32/38-ton tractor, carrying a version of the standard Motor Panels cab, could be had with a turbocharged Rolls-Royce diesel engine. The 'Pennine' passenger chassis was now built by Pennine Coachcraft Ltd, and a new version, the 'RU', with rear-mounted Gardner engine.

Negotiations with Atkinson

1977 Seddon-Atkinson '200'-Series tipper

Sentinel DG6 "undertype" steam wagon c1928

SENTINEL/*England 1917-1957*

When the Sentinel Waggon Works Ltd, Shrewsbury, Salop, was founded, the Alley & McLellan steam wagon range was re-named Sentinel, production of the 'Standard' model continuing along the same lines. Financial problems forced the company to re-organize in 1920 as the Sentinel Waggon Works (1920) Ltd, and in 1923 the "undertype" 'Super' series was announced, using a vertical inclined water-tube boiler, a modified and up-rated single-speed engine and double chain-drive.

The company's first rigid 6-wheeler, the DG6, was announced in 1927, using a cross water-tube boiler with 2-speed gearing between engine and countershaft. The bogie was of double-drive layout with chains connecting second and third axles. In 1929 the DG8, one of the first production rigid 8-wheelers, was introduced along with a 4-wheeled version.

Pneumatic tyres were available from about 1930.

The 'S'-Type arrived in 1934, using lightweight components and shaft-drive. Pneumatic tyres were now standard. The "undertype" engine was a 4-cyl single-acting in-line unit with camshaft-operated poppet-valves, while the vertical cross water-tube boiler was mounted at the back rather than at the front.

Four, 6- and 8-wheeled versions were advertised but lost popularity in the face of government legislation.

The company had already shown interest in internal-combustion engines but shortly before World War II the Sentinel Waggon Works (1936) Ltd improved on its 'S'-Type steamers by introducing electric speedometer drive, cylinder lubrication and tyre pump, a self-stoking boiler and pto-driven dynamo. During the war, prototype underfloor petrol-engined truck chassis were constructed with series production beginning in 1945, using an 85bhp 5.7-litre 4-cyl horizontal petrol engine, 4-speed transmission and worm-drive, followed by a diesel-engined 7/8-tonner in 1946. Both had 3-man cabs, and the diesel version had a 90bhp 6.08-litre Sentinel-Ricardo engine, 5-speed Meadows transmission and also hydraulic servo brakes.

By 1948, models included the 4-cyl engined 4/4 DV rigid and the 4/4 DVT tipper or tractor unit; a new 10-ton payload 6/4 DV rigid 6-wheeler with 9.1-litre 6-cyl Sentinel-Ricardo engine and 5-speed

1950 Sentinel S6T "undertype" steam tipper

transmission; and a chassisless underfloor-engined bus. The company's last steamers were 100 6-wheelers exported in 1950.

Another change of name, to Sentinel (Shrewsbury) Ltd, was followed by the introduction of direct-injection diesel engines and vacuum-servo brakes in 1952, by which time the 6-wheeled model was listed as a lightweight 4-cyl engined 6 x 2 or as a 6-cyl engined 6 x 4.

By the mid-1950s the company was concentrating on railway work but the diesel vehicle range struggled on until manufacturing rights and all components were acquired by Transport Vehicles (Warrington) Ltd.

SENTINEL-GARNER/*England 1933-1936*

When Garner Motors Ltd failed in 1933 the Sentinel Waggon Works (1920) Ltd, transferred production to Shrewsbury and introduced a range of Sentinel-Garner vehicles, using Austin and Meadows petrol engines or a Perkins 'Leopard' diesel. With the front crossmember un-bolted, engines could be removed using a built-in roller system.

Despite such innovations, the Garner activity was sold to a group of ex-Dodge employees who set up business in North London, registering the name of Garner Motors Ltd.

SHAND-MASON/*England c1899-1900*

Shand, Mason & Co was an established builder of manual and horse-drawn fire-fighting equipment which also constructed a number of self-propelled steam appliances. The business was being bought by Merryweather & Sons Ltd.

SHANGHAI (1)/*China ? to date*

Using Jay-Fong truck chassis, Shanghai buses built in the Shanghai Bus Factory, Shanghai, include 23-, 36- and 48-passenger city buses, the largest being of 6 x 4 layout.

SHANGHAI (2)/*China ? to date*

Built alongside Qiao-Tong or Ch'iao-Tung (Communication) trucks in the Shanghai Cargo Vehicle Plant, Shanghai, the SH-380 is a 32-ton off-road dump truck powered by a 400bhp V12 diesel engine.

SHANGHAI (3)/*China ? to date*

Building a number of light commercials since the mid-1950s, the Shanghai Motor Vehicle Plant, Shanghai, currently offers a 1-ton 3-wheeler with 27bhp air-cooled 'V'-twin petrol engine and a forward-control 2-tonner using a 75bhp 4-cyl petrol engine, designated the 58-1 and the SH-130.

SHEFFIELD/*England 1899*

Although 1-, 2- and 4/5-ton Sheffield steam wagons were offered by the Sheffield Motor Dray & Engineering Co, Hillsborough, Sheffield, few were actually sold. The Sheffield had a rear-mounted vertical Field-tube boiler supplying steam to a vertical 3-cyl single-acting engine with Wilkinson's patent valve gear.

SHEFFLEX/*England 1921-1937*

During World War I the Sheffield-Simplex Motor Works Ltd, Sheffield, Yorks, was sub-contracted to assemble 1½-ton Commer Cars. With the cancellation of this arrangement at the end of the war, the company was left with quantities of components from which it began to construct its own Shefflex trucks. Due to a financial crisis, the project was abandoned and all components and finished vehicles were sold to R A Johnstone, who operated some and sold the remainder. Using the profits, he re-commenced production as Shefflex Ltd. The old fixed-head 3.8-litre 4-cyl petrol engine was built by the new company which, in 1926, became the Shefflex Motor Co Ltd at Tinsley, Sheffield. Models comprised 1½- and 2-tonners, up-rated to 2- and 2½-tonners by 1929 when they were joined by a 24-seat pas-

1949 Sentinel STC4 single-deck bus

senger model and a low-loading refuse collector. A semi forward-control layout was adopted the same year to provide extra load space.

In 1930 trailing-axle 6-wheelers of 4 and 5 tons capacity were offered, using a 4-litre Dorman petrol engine. The following year a 3-cyl 2-stroke Petters diesel engine was offered but this was unsuccessful. By 1935 Gardner diesels were sometimes offered and refuse collection bodies were being mounted on Shefflex chassis. A Meadows-engined refuse collector called the 'Ideal' was built later that year and the last Shefflex supplied to Sheffield Corp in 1937. After this, the company used other chassis such as 6-wheeled Electricars, AEC 'Monarchs' converted by Shefflex to battery-electric and petrol-engined Fordsons with crewcabs.

SHEPPEE/*England 1905-1914*

Founded by Col F H Sheppee, the Sheppee Motor & Engineering

1980 Shuntmaster demountable body transporter

access door, power-steering and an alternative rear axle. The heaviest model currently listed, again using an Atkinson chassis, is a 32/40-tonner, available also in kit form, retaining its original 180bhp Gardner 6LXB diesel engine, Kirkstall axles and suspension, but fitted with a hydraulic lifting fifth wheel coupling, Allison automatic transmission, 1-man all-steel tiltcab, power-steering, heavy-duty front bumper and op-

Sheppee steam charabanc c1906

Co was set up in York to perfect the Colonel's ideas of steam power for road vehicles. Only a few experimental types were built but they left a mark on the industry. The Sheppee was of bonneted layout, using a liquid-fuelled boiler producing steam at 900psi. The totally-enclosed engine, which was slung beneath the chassis, incorporated double high-pressure single-acting cyls with push-rod-operated poppet-valves.

SHUNTMASTER/*England* c1976 to date

Lyka Cranes Ltd, Preston, Lancs, offers the Shuntmaster terminal tractor using new or time-expired tractor chassis. Among the first was a series of 16-tonners based on old Atkinson tractors with Scammell auto-couplings. These couplings were retained, but new equipment included a 1-man all-steel tiltcab with rear jack-knife

erator walkway behind the cab.

Towards the end of 1980 a demountable body shunter was developed, using an old Ford D1110 truck chassis extended at the front to take a low-line 1-man cab ahead of the front axle. This has single tyres all round and incorporates a lifting subframe of 8128kg capacity using a hydraulic equalizing system to counteract uneven weight distribution.

SICARD/*Canada 1938-1968*

Sicard Inc, Ste Thérèse, Quebec, developed a line of snow-removal equipment before constructing its first semi forward-control trucks. The first incorporated a cable-actuated scraper within the body to eject the load from the rear. Later, conventional tipping bodies were offered plus a line of refuse collection vehicles and street sprinklers, while development of snow-clearance machines con-

tinued. Confusion arose when Kenworth and KW-Dart trucks were built, occasionally carrying the Sicard brand name, but in 1967 the business was acquired by the Pacific Car & Foundry Co and the Sicard range was phased out.

SIEBERT/*USA 1911-1916*

The Shop of Siebert, Toledo, Ohio, introduced a 1-ton Siebert truck, using a 4-cyl petrol engine and wheelbase of 320cm. Later, as

1968 Sicard gritter/snowplough

the Siebert Motor Truck Co, a bonneted 1-tonner, also with a 4-cyl engine, plus a 3-speed transmission and double chain-drive, was added to the line.

SIEMENS-HALSKE/*Germany 1882, 1899-1900*

Siemens und Halske AG, Berlin, is said to have experimented with a trolleybus system as early as 1882, but little appears to have come of it. Towards the end of the 19th century a road/rail bus was developed, running off current taken from overhead tram lines. Two flanged wheels at the front ensured that it followed the track but when required to leave this route, these could be retracted and the vehicle operated off batteries charged from the overhead system. After this the company concentrated on electric traction systems, constructing the earliest Schiemann trolleybuses.

SIGNAL/*USA 1913-1923*

A 1½-tonner with 4-cyl petrol engine, 3-speed transmission and double chain-drive was the first model built by the Signal Motor Truck Co, Detroit, Michigan, replaced in 1915 by new 1-, 2- and 3-

tonners. Worm-drive was offered the following year and a 1½-tonner re-introduced. Although a 5-ton model was announced in 1917, the Signal Truck Corp, as it was now known, gradually withdrew all models.

SILENT DODGE/*England 1979 to date*

Using a Dodge '50'-Series chassis the Silent Dodge is an experimental battery-electric vehicle originally developed by Chrysler United Kingdom Ltd and Chloride Technical Ltd. Based on the earlier Silent Karrier, only one example was built under this arrangement, with a 26-seat personnel carrier body. Further examples are now being built by the Renault and Pengeut - owned Karrier Motor Co Ltd.

SILENT KARRIER/*1975-1979*

Based on a modified Karrier K60 'Walk-Thru' model, the Silent Karrier was an experimental 1¾-ton battery-electric developed

1975 Silent Karrier K60 van

jointly by Chrysler United Kingdom Ltd, National Carriers Ltd and Chloride Technical Ltd. The prototype was capable of speeds of up to 64km/h and had a range per charge of 40km. A 25kw DC electric traction motor and high output lead-acid batteries were fitted. The Clayton Dewandre power-hydraulic braking system also obtained energy from these batteries, using a separate electric motor and hydraulic cylinders. It was intended to develop this into a 2½-ton machine using new sodium-sulphur batteries, but only 71 vehicles, all with lead-acid batteries, were built.

SILENT RIDER/*England 1973*

As an experiment into the feasibility of battery-electric buses, the SELNEC Passenger Transport

Executive put a 41-seat battery-electric bus in service. Based on a strengthened Seddon 'RU' chassis with bodywork by Pennine Coachcraft Ltd, it was called the Silent Rider and fitted with electrical equipment by Chloride Technical Ltd, Swinton, Manchester. Batteries were distributed around the chassis to aid weight distribution and a 72kw Electro Dynamic Construction traction motor drove the rear axle. This was the only vehicle of its type.

SILVERTOWN/England 1904-c1910
The Silvertown Co, London, built an unusual battery-electric delivery vehicle called the Silvertown. It had driven axles at both front and rear, powered by a traction motor mounted in the centre of each. To facilitate steering, a differential distributed the drive between the two front wheels.

SIMCA/France 1954-1958
Known for its passenger cars and light commercials, Soc Industrielle de Mécanique et de Carrosserie Automobile, Nanterre, Seine, found itself with a ready-made truck factory when it acquired the Ford SAF operation at Poissy, Seine-et-Oise. A 5-ton forward-control model continued as the Simca 'Cargo', with 1½- and 3-ton military derivatives employing both 4 x 2 and 4 x 4 drive. A bonneted 5-tonner with Ford V8 petrol engine was the 1957 'Caboteur' with Unic front-end, and in 1958 a 25-seat forward-control coach called the 'Iseran' was introduced. Production of all commercials was transferred to the associate company of SA des Automobiles Unic during 1958.

SIMMS/England 1904-1907
The Simms Manufacturing Co Ltd, London NW6, manufactured automotive components but also constructed motor vehicles, occasionally referred to as the Simms-Welbeck. Heaviest of the early range was a 12hp 1-tonner powered by the company's own 2-cyl petrol engine, but this was joined in 1905 by 2- and 5-ton trucks using 25 and 35hp 4-cyl petrol engines, 3-speed transmissions and chain-drive.

Some engines were also supplied to T Coulthard & Co Ltd for use in the 1905 4-ton Simms-Coulthard truck.

SIMONIS/England c1921-c1935
Henry Simonis Ltd used proprietary chassis as a basis for its firefighting equipment, sometimes removing the chassis manufacturer's name and substituting its own or occasionally marketing the finished product under another name, of which the most common was Commer-Simonis. The company also undertook self-propulsion work on horse-drawn equipment and imported certain German-built appliances under the Simonis name.

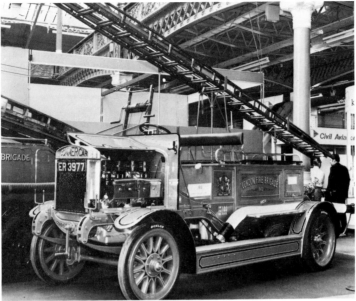

1913 Simonis 'YC'-Type motor pump fire appliance

SINGER/England 1929-1932
In an attempt to compete against other light mass-produced truck builders, Singer Motors Ltd, Coventry, Warwicks, introduced a 2-tonner in 1929 using a 57bhp 3.1-litre 4-cyl petrol engine, 4-speed transmission, foot-operated lubrication, overhead-worm final-drive and servo-operated brakes. Also listed in 20-seat passenger form, this was marketed as the Singer or Singer Industrial Motor and joined in 1930 by a short-wheelbase version. The debut of the 1¾-ton 'Prosperity' model fitted with a 3.4-litre overhead-valve 6-cyl petrol engine was in 1932. By this time there was also a 1¼-tonner assembled from passenger car components but this, too, was short-lived.

SINPAR/France ? to date
Sinpar Equipements Spéciaux are specialists in the conversion of commercials to all-wheel drive configuration, often marketing these under their own name. Many are based on medium-weight Renault trucks but the company also adapts the Continental-built Ford 'Transit' to 4 x 4 layout using a 'Transit' differential assembly mounted in a specially designed front axle which has locking hubs.

SIRECOME/Italy 1946 to date
Sirecome snc, La Spezia, began re-building military vehicles under the Sirecome brand name. At first only the 2½-ton 6 x 6 GMC was used, fitted with an 89bhp Perkins diesel engine, but later types were based on the Reo-Studebaker and similar 'M'-Series 2½- and 5-ton 6 x 6, using 120bhp 6-cyl Perkins diesels. Components from these were later used in the construction of forward-control 4 x 4 and 6 x 6 models, fitted with Fiat or Perkins diesel engines of up to 230bhp output. Now called Sirecome SpA, the company still offers vehicles of this type, also custom-building to specific requirements.

SIRMAC/Italy 1978 to date
Developed from the 4 x 4 Meili 'Multimobil', the Sirmac is a 2500-kg payload forward-control truck powered by a Fiat V6 or Ford V8 petrol engine or by a 6-cyl in-line Fiat diesel. Built by Sirmac SpA, Bologna, it has a 10-speed transmission and independent suspen-

1979 Sirmac 6 x 6 truck

sion all round. A 6 x 6 derivative appeared in 1979.

SISU/Finland 1931 to date
Although involved in tramcar production, Oy Suomen Autoteollisuus AB, Helsinki, began to build Sisu trucks such as the bonneted 'SH' 3-tonner, using an 85bhp 6-cyl side-valve petrol engine and 4-speed transmission. Similar models were assembled in both truck and bus form until 1943 when the business merged with Vanajan Autotehdas Oy to build military trucks under the Yhteissisu name.

Throughout 1948 Sisu trucks remained available, most post-war models, such as a 5-tonner with 90bhp 5-litre 6-cyl engine, 5-speed overdrive transmission and hydrovac brakes, running on wood gas. By 1949 a 110bhp petrol engine was listed along with 80 and 100bhp diesel units and a forward-control passenger model. By 1953 the heaviest trucks, for up to 13 tons GVW, were powered by 140bhp 8.7-litre 6-cyl diesel engines, and by the late 1950s Leyland diesel engines were standard. The company introduced a huge 6 x 6 bonneted tractor for operation at up to 180 tons GTW, and an off-highway dump truck fitted with a Rolls-Royce engine and 10-speed transmission. Road-going vehicles were now listed for up to 20 tons gross, using a variety of Leyland engines and 5- or 6-speed

Sinpar 4 x 4 oilwell servicing unit c1970

1972 Sisu terminal tractor

transmissions, while single-drive 6-wheeled rigids were equipped with an electro-hydraulically lifted third axle for use when unladen.

By 1965 the company's first horizontal underfloor-engined passenger chassis had appeared, and in 1964 the 9/10-ton KB117 forward-control truck brought a tiltcab into the range, soon offered on other models. Bonneted trucks were re-styled and fitted with fibreglass bonnets. The most powerful engine was now a 330bhp unit, and by 1968 a forward-control 3½-ton 4 x 4 powered by a 160bhp 6.5-litre turbocharged diesel engine located behind the cab had been developed into a 6 x 6 truck.

In 1967 Sisu and Vanaja merged, the latter being absorbed into the Sisu range, and by 1970 passenger models included chassis with front-, amidships- or rearmounted engines. New models included a 1-man cabbed terminal tractor with Allison automatic transmission, the 4- and 6-wheeled forward-control 'Bulldog' based on Vanaja designs, and the 4-wheeled bonneted 'Bear'. The 'Bulldog' had an AEC, Leyland or Rolls-Royce diesel engine of up to 295bhp output, while the 'Bear' was powered by a 165bhp Leyland unit. Heavi-

er models currently available are for gross weights of up to 33 tons, with 312bhp 12.2-litre 6-cyl Rolls-Royce diesel engines, Fuller range-change transmissions and dual-circuit air brakes.

SIVERS/*England 1930*

The 5/6-ton Sivers lorry was based on Peerless designs and built by haulage contractor Thomas Sivers, London W3.

SIX WHEEL TRUCK/*USA 1924-1928*

The Six Wheel Co was set up in the former factory of the Hall & Kilburn Co, Philadelphia, Pennsylvania, in 1923, the new company being a subsidiary of the American Motor Body Corp. A series of trucks with single or dual rear wheels mounted on a bogie was marketed as the Six Wheel Truck and later passenger versions as Safeway. These bonneted trucks were in the 4/5-ton class, with 6-cyl Continental petrol engines, and some were being exported.

SKODA/*Czechoslovakia 1925 to date*

Following the introduction of Skoda-Sentinel steam wagons, Skoda Závody AS, Plzen, acquired Laurin & Klement AS, Mlada Boleslav, continuing prod-

1963 Sisu KB117 tractor

wheeled rigid truck and 6 x 4 passenger model announced.

By the mid-1930s diesel and producer-gas types were advertised in all classes and from 1936 4- and 6-wheeled trolleybuses developed. Production of an experimental chassisless 6-wheeled bus with rear engine and streamlined body stopped because of the war, but trucks from 1 to 7 tons capacity with petrol, diesel or producer-gas engines, were built at Mlada Boleslav, and 6 x 4 and 6 x 6 military models at Plzen.

The business was nationalized as Liberecké Automobilové Závody in 1946 and all truck and bus production centred on Plzen. The 706 8-tonner was moved to the Avia factory at Letnany, Prague, which led to the Liaz range in 1951 which also built badge-engineered Skodas. These are still built, as are Skoda trolleybuses based on the Karosa SM11 bus chassis which are assembled in the Ostrov nad Ohri plant.

uction of this company's 1½- and 4/5-tonners under the Skoda brand name. By 1930 trucks from 1½ to 5 tons and buses from 12- to 35-passenger capacity were listed and in 1932 the first diesel models were built and the 8-ton 706N 6-

Shrewsbury, England, to construct its own version of the 'DG'-Series Sentinel steam wagon. These were known as Skoda-Sentinel and were built as 4-, 5- and 6-tonners.

SLEEPER COACH/*USA 1937*

Paul W Seiler was a former president of the General Motors Truck Co who registered the shortlived company, Sleeper Coaches Inc, Detroit, Michigan. Using a rear-engined Reo chassis, a 16-berth Sleeper Coach was constructed but series production did not follow.

SLM/*Switzerland 1906-1907, 1924-1932*

Schwitzerische Lokomotiv- und Maschinenfabrik, Winterthur, was a locomotive builder that also built 3½- and 5-ton SLM steam wagons. The lightest was a chain-drive design with vertical boiler and front-mounted engine while the other, which also had a vertical boiler, used an "undertype" engine with gear-drive to the rear wheels.

Some years later the company developed a transmission system whereby gear-changing took place by oil under pressure, using no levers, forks or dog-clutches as in the usual gearbox. A number of prototype front-wheel drive vehicles were constructed, mainly for municipal operation, including 2- and 3-ton bonneted trucks with 35bhp 4-cyl petrol engines and hydraulically-operated combined 3-speed transmission and differential. These were advertised in Britain as Modern Wheel Drive.

SM/*England 1910*

The SM or Shave-Morse was a

Skoda 706RTO single-deck coach c1964

SKODA-SENTINEL/*Czechoslovakia 1924-c1932*

Skoda Závody AS, Plzen, made a licence agreement with the Sentinel Waggon Works (1920) Ltd,

shaft-drive steam lorry built by the Steam Car Syndicate Ltd, London NW10. It had a paraffin-fuelled semi-flash boiler under the driver's seat and a 2-cyl vertical

1965 Sisu K138 tanker

engine located in front. Proprietary components were used, the front axle by Butler and the worm-drive rear axle by Dennis Bros. Few were built and although the company constructed a few St Pancras wagons in 1911 it never made an impact on the steam vehicle market.

SMIT/*Netherlands 1970 to date*
Carrosseriefabriek Smit BV, Joure, is a bodybuilder that also builds Smit mobile shops. Using a Citroën ID engine and Ford D400 transmission system, these are similar to others built in the Netherlands.

SMITH/*England 1906-1907*
A short-lived bonneted 3-tonner with 42hp 4-cyl petrol engine and chain-drive was built by Frank Smith, Manchester, Lancs. A passenger model was announced soon after but appears never to have been built.

SMITH FLYER/*USA 1917-1920*
An unusual 5-wheeled buckboard-type vehicle called the Smith Flyer was built by the AO Smith Co, Milwaukee, Wisconsin. The company was better known for its earlier Smith-Milwaukee range.

SMITH FORM-A-TRUCK/*England 1921*
During the early 1920s there were a number of British companies offering long-wheelbase conversions on the Ford Model 'T' chassis. Smith Form-a-Truck Ltd offered a long-wheelbase conversion of the Model 'T' Ford called the Smith Form-a-Truck.

SMITH-MILWAUKEE/*USA 1912-1915*
As well as building the later Smith Flyer, the A O Smith Co, Milwaukee, Wisconsin, built the 3-ton Model 'A' and 6-ton Model 'B' Smith-Milwaukee trucks. The Model 'A' had a wheelbase of 420cm, twin-ignition 4-cyl petrol engine, 3-speed transmission and worm-drive. For 1913 it was uprated to 3½ tons capacity and joined by the Model 'B'.

SMITH'S ELECTRIC/*England 1956 to date*
After a short period as Smith's NCB Electric, the former NCB and NCB Electric battery-electric urban delivery range became known as Smith's Electric, now built by Smith's Delivery Vehicles Ltd in the Gateshead, Co Durham, factory. The existing range continued, joined in 1959 by a battery-electric version of the Karrier 'Bantam' artic tractor unit called the Electric Karrier.

A new delivery model of about

1964 Smith's Electric CG65 integral van

the same period was the 1/1¼-ton 'Suburbanite' which joined existing 'Commuter' models. By 1964 the company had joined forces with an American consortium to supply battery-electric chassis for use in the Battronic vehicle series. Meanwhile, Smith's Electrics of up to 2 tons capacity were built in Britain.

The debut of the revolutionary 'Cabac' took place in 1969. This, for safety reasons and to assist the driver, featured driver access via the back of the cab and through the load-carrying area.

SMITH'S NCB ELECTRIC/*England c1955-1956*
Previously sold as NCB or NCB Electric, Smith's NCB Electric battery-electric urban delivery vehicles were marketed briefly by Smith's Delivery Vehicles Ltd, Gateshead, Co Durham, before they were re-named Smith's Electric.

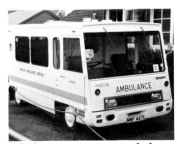

1936 SOS 'SON'-Series single-deck bus

SOS/*England 1923-1944*
The Birmingham & Midland Motor Omnibus Co Ltd, trading as Midland Red, drew up plans in 1923 for the company's own single-deck vehicle which became known as the SOS. The prototype was a light bonneted pneumatic-tyred 32-seater known as the 'S'-Type, and when series production got underway some early examples were apparently built on Tilling-Stevens chassis.

Over 500 'S'-Types were in service by 1925, with engines and transmissions supplied by Wolseley Motors Ltd, when the forward-control 'FS'-Type appeared and, in 1927, the first 6-cyl petrol engines were fitted. A double-deck prototype was constructed in 1931, production of which got underway as the REDD in 1932, and in 1934 this developed into the front-entrance FEDD double-decker using the company's 'K'-Type diesel engine from 1937.

Another prototype was a 1935 rear-engined single-decker, which used one of the company's petrol engines mounted transversely at the back of the chassis. Four were built, all re-fitted during the war with underfloor diesel units. In 1944 a prototype BMMO double-decker was built and all subsequent models known as BMMO.

SOULES/*USA 1905-1908*
The Soules was a 1-ton shaft-drive truck built by the Soules Motor Car Co, Grand Rapids, Michigan. Power came from a 22hp horizontally-opposed twin-cyl petrol engine.

SOUTH BEND/*USA 1913-1916*
The South Bend Motor Car Works, South Bend, Indiana, introduced 2- and 4-ton chain-drive trucks.

These were listed until, the last year of production when they were replaced briefly by 1½-, 2- and 3½-tonners with worm- or internal-gear drive.

SOUTHERN/*USA 1919-1921*
The Southern Truck & Car Corp, Greensboro, North Carolina, built 1- and 1½-ton Southern trucks.

Later production was undertaken by the Carolina Truck & Car Corp.

SOUTHERN COACH/*USA 1945-1961*
Southern Coach 32-seat underfloor-engined transit buses entered series production in the Southern Coach Manufacturing Co's Evergreen, Alabama, plant following some years of bus rebuilding work.

Using Waukesha petrol engines and Spicer transmissions, vehicles were built in capacities of up to 50 persons, some using Fageol Twin Coach petrol engines while others had Cummins or Leyland diesels. After 1956 production dropped and the plant was eventually acquired by the Flxible Co.

SOVAM/*France 1961 to date*
Sovams were originally only light models but over the years SA Morin Automobiles Sovam, Parthenay, has developed a range of heavier types for use as mobile shops, libraries, showrooms and emergency vehicles.

1973 Sovam prototype ambulance

The heaviest model to be announced up to 1968 was a 6-wheeler for 9 tons gross using a Perkins 6.354 diesel engine. The 1971 range, from 3½ to 7 tons GVW, had petrol or diesel Peugeot engines, Peugeot transmissions and Etalmobil bodies. These designs remain, but with Renault engines.

SPA/*Italy 1908-1947*
The first SPA commercials were entered in the 1908 Industrial Vehicle Trials and comprised two passenger types and a 1½- and 2/3-ton truck. They were built by Soc Ligure Piemontese Automobili, Crocetta, Turin, and were reasonably successful, leading to series production.

By 1910 these early chain-drives had been joined by a shaft-drive 2-tonner with 3.4-litre 4-cyl 'T'-head petrol engine and a 4-speed transmission, and by 1914 various shaft- and chain-drive trucks up to 3½ tons payload were also available.

World War I saw 1½-, 2½- and 3½-tonners built for the Armed Forces as well as a 10-ton forward-control prototype, but with peace the 1½-tonner appears to have been replaced by a 1¾-ton model with 2.7-litre monobloc petrol engine and bevel-drive. The company went into liquidation in 1925, but was revived by Fiat SpA which continued the existing truck line, most of which had 4.4-litre petrol engines, 4-speed transmissions, pneumatic tyres and full electrics.

Production of the Pavesi artic tractor was now being handled by the company, and by 1931 Ceirano trucks were also built. Licence production of SPA trucks, meanwhile, was taken up by Základow Mechanicznych Ursus SA, Poland, as Ursus, and the SPA factory was concentrating on military truck production. Most well known of these was the 'Dovunque' which started as a 3-ton 6 x 4 with 4-cyl SPA or 6-cyl Fiat petrol engine, but which later developed into a 108bhp 6 x 6 diesel truck. Another all-wheel drive model was the AS37 1-tonner, with 4-wheel steering and 6-cyl Fiat diesel engine. After World War II the SPA name was dropped and the factory given over to the manufacture of heavy Fiats.

SPANGLER DUAL/*USA 1947-1949*
The unconventional Spangler Dual 8-wheeled truck was the brainchild of the D H Spangler Engineering & Sales Co, Hamburg, Pennsylvania. Particularly unusual were the two 100bhp Ford V8 petrol engines, each of which drove one of the rear axles. Assembled entirely from Ford components, the vehicle had twin tyres all round. Flat trucks and fire appliances were built on this chassis and there was also a 3-axled version.

After production ceased the company continued to offer Spangler twin-steer conversions for standard truck chassis.

SPARTAN (1)/*USA 1946-1949*
To provide an inexpensive passenger model, the Spartan Coach & Manufacturing Co Inc, Sturgis, Michigan, introduced the 21-seat Spartan, using an International Harvester engine, 5-speed transmission and a welded steel tube body frame. By 1949 25- and 29-seat versions were also offered, but comfort rather than economy was the priority, and the business closed through lack of sales.

SPARTAN (2)/*USA 1975 to date*
Spartan Motors Inc was founded in Charlotte, Michigan, by a group of former employees of Diamond Reo Trucks Inc. Spartan trucks include the '2000'-Series, popular as a fire appliance, the HH-1000 6 x 4 40-ton coalhauler, and a series of truck-tractors similar to the old Diamond Reo range. Engines are by Cummins and Detroit Diesel.

SPAULDING/*USA 1913*
The Spaulding Mfg Co, Grinnell, Iowa, offered the Model 'T' 1-tonner using the same 4-cyl petrol engine fitted in the Model 'E' passenger car. The Model 'T' had a wheelbase of 385cm, 3-speed transmission and double chain-drive.

SPEEDWELL (1)/*Scotland 1900*
The Speedwell was a 3-ton capacity "undertype" steam wagon with a 200psi Toward boiler and compound engine providing road speeds of 4 and 8km/h. Built by the Speedwell Motor & Cycle Co, Aberdeen, only one such wagon can be traced.

SPEEDWELL (2)/*USA c1908-1915*
The Speedwell Motor Car Co, Dayton, Ohio, developed a series of forward-control trucks and by 1912 both 2- and 3-tonners were being built, both with 4-cyl petrol engines and double chain-drive. A power winch was available for mounting behind the cab. For 1913 and 1914, a 6-tonner was also listed, with a stakeside body.

SPYKSTAAL/*Netherlands c1965 to date*
Up to the mid-1960s a range of battery-electric trucks built by Spykstaal NV, Spijkenisse, was aimed at municipal and industrial users, many being of lightweight 3-wheeled construction. Then the company began to construct complete mobile shops, using Ford or Opel engines, and other proprietary components, but assembling the chassis itself. By 1975 a series of front-wheel drive low-loading models, now with 115 or 152bhp Ford diesel engines and Allison automatic transmissions, was

1970 Spykstaal Model 6000 6 x 2 mobile shop

launched and the range currently includes 3- and 4-wheeled battery-electrics and 4- and 6-wheeled diesel-engined mobile shops.

SPORTSCOACH/*USA 1974*
When Gillig Bros, Hayward, California, ended production of its front-engined 'Microcoach', manufacturing rights were sold to Sportscoach. It is not known whether any Sportscoach versions were actually built.

SPYKER/*Netherlands 1921-c1923*
Nederlandsche Automobiel en Vliegtuigenfabriek, Trompenburg, constructed a purpose-built Spyker commercial in the form of a 264-cm wheelbase 2-tonner with a 4-cyl side-valve monobloc petrol engine, 4-speed transmission and worm-drive.

SR 4 x 4 truck c1964

SR/*Rumania 1954 to date*
Based on the Soviet ZIL-150 4-tonner, the first SR truck built by Uzina Steagul Rosu, Brasov, was a rugged bonneted 3-tonner powered by a 95bhp 5.5-litre petrol engine and known as the 101. Production continued almost unchanged until the introduction of the Bucegi and Carpati ranges during the 1960s, although even these are often referred to as SRs. Now called Uzina de Autocamioane Brasov, the factory also offers DAC and Roman trucks, some of which are built under licence in Yugoslavia as the Torpedo.

STANDARD (1)/*England 1906-1907*
The Standard was a 5-ton loco-boilered compound "undertype" steam wagon built by the Standard Steam Lorry & Omnibus Co, Rayleigh, Essex. It had a top-fired boiler, countershaft differential, double chain-drive and sometimes Rayner patent wheels. The latter had a series of cyls each containing a piston arranged around the hub with a rod carrying a hardwood shoe attached to each piston, each shoe forming the wheel tread. In this way the air trapped in each cyl was expected to cushion the vehicle's ride.

In practice, however, the idea was a failure. Only a few were built until 1907 when production passed briefly to T J Rayner & Sons Ltd, the wheel manufacturer. Some late wagons are believed to have been sold as Rayner.

STANDARD (2)/*USA 1907-1908*
An unusual drive system was adopted for the Standard petrol-electric truck built by the Standard Gas & Electric Power Co, Pennsylvania. This had a horizontally-opposed twin-cyl engine under the driver's seat which drove a shunt-wound generator. This, however, did not drive the vehicle. When the engine speed dropped below 1000rpm, the generator became a motor, drawing current from the batteries and boosting the engine to its normal speed. If the vehicle ran out of petrol, the batteries enabled the truck to continue for re-fuelling.

Other features included a 3-speed transmission and double chain-drive.

STANDARD (3)/*USA 1912-1930*
The Detroit, Michigan built Stan-

dard truck used Continental petrol engines, Brown-Lipe transmissions and Timken worm-drive axles. It was a product of the Standard Motor Truck Co, the heaviest models having chain final-drive. By 1925 vehicles ranged from 1¼ to 7 tons capacity, all models over 2½ tons having 4- or 9-speed transmissions. By 1930 all were known as Fisher-Standard and for a while were sold in the UK as Seabrook-Standard.

STANDARD (4)/USA 1913-1915
The Standard Motor Truck Co, Warren, Ohio, apparently had no connection with any other business of the same name. Again marketed as Standard, its trucks comprised 1-, 1½-, 2- and 3½-tonners. Certain examples were sold in the UK as Whiting by Whiting (1915) Ltd. The manufacturer appears to have had some connection with the Warren Motor Truck Co.

1961 Standard (5) '20' integral van

STANDARD (5)/England 1961-1963
The Standard Motor Co Ltd, Coventry, Warwicks, built only passenger cars and light commercials until an up-rated version of its Standard 'Atlas Major' ¾-tonner was announced as the 1-ton Standard '20'. Powered by a 2.1-litre 'Vanguard' petrol engine or 2.3-litre Leyland diesel, this was listed until 1963 when it was absorbed into the Leyland range as the Leyland '20'.

STANDARD (6)/India c1965 to date
As well as a light commercial, Standard Motor Products of India Ltd, Madras, builds a chassis/cowl version of the old 1-ton Standard Atlas or Leyland '20' commercial, powered by a 68bhp 2-litre petrol engine.

STANDARD TRACTOR/USA 1915-1916
Built by the Standard Tractor Co, Brooklyn, New York, the Standard Tractor, sometimes known as the Standard, was a forward-control machine for drawbar work. It had an unusual final-drive arrangement whereby the countershaft was located behind the rear wheels with roller chains between, enabling the vehicle to

have a short wheelbase. Unusually, full air brakes were fitted and there were air connections for trailers.

STANELECTRIC/England c1963-c1969
Production of Manulectric battery-electric delivery vehicles passed from Sidney Hole's Electric Vehicles, Brighton, Sussex, to the Stanley Engineering Co Ltd, Egham, Surrey, the brand name changing to Stanelectric or Stanley. Five rider-controlled models, from 1 to 1½ tons capacity were listed, production being transferred to Exeter Airport before closing down.

STANLEY (1)/USA 1909-1916
The Stanley brothers, Estes Park, Colorado, constructed a 12-seat light bus which they called the 'Mountain Wagon'. Others showed interest and the Stanley Motor Carriage Co, Newton, Massachusetts, began assembling 'Mountain Wagons' with 30hp 2-cyl petrol engines. Trucks of 1 and 1¼ tons capacity were also built.

STANLEY (2)/USA 1935-1936
Using patents of the old Stanley Motor Carriage Co, the Stanley Steam Motors Corp, Chicago, Illinois, advertised a series of steam buses but few appear to have been built.

STANLEY STEAMER/USA 1924
The Steam Vehicle Corp of America was set up at Newton, Massachusetts, and Canastota, New York, to produce passenger cars and commercials under the Stanley Steamer brand name, also using patents of the old Stanley Motor Carriage Co. Production did not follow.

STAR (1)/England 1907-1931
Starting with passenger cars and light commercials, the Star Cycle Co, Wolverhampton, Staffs, offered a 1¼-ton payload car-derived van or light truck by 1907 and by 1909, a range of chain-drive commercials from 1 to 4 tons capacity, the largest of which had a 6.2-litre 4-cyl petrol engine and a 4-speed transmission. The business was now called the Star Engineering Co Ltd and by 1914 the 4-tonner was the only chain-drive Star, others featuring double-reduction back axles which, during World War I, were used on 2½/3- and 4/5-ton models.

After the war the company advertised worm-drive 1½- and 2½-tonners and a double-reduction 3-tonner, the two lightest models having a 3.8-litre 4-cyl petrol engine and the 3-tonner a 4.1-litre unit. From 1926 all models had

1927 Star (1) 'Flyer' bus

front- as well as rear-wheel brakes and in 1927 a low-loading 20-seat passenger chassis with 3.4-litre 4-cyl petrol engine, twin-plate clutch and full electrics was announced. This developed into the company's most famous product, the Star 'Flyer' with 3.2-litre 6-cyl overhead-valve petrol engine capable of producing 80km/h. Later, the 'Flyer' was fitted with a 3.6-litre unit and vacuum-servo brakes.

In 1928 the business was sold to Guy Motors Ltd and, although a 1¼-ton model with reinforced chassis frame and 6-cyl 'Flyer' engine was developed, there were few heavier types.

STAR (2)/USA 1913-1914
One and 1½-ton Star trucks were built by the Star Motor Car Co, Ann Arbor, Michigan. Both were of bonneted layout, powered by a 4-cyl side-valve petrol engine driving through a 3-speed transmission and double chains. The larger of them had a wheelbase of 325cm.

Star (3) (Rugby) truck c1928

STAR (3)/USA 1926-1932
Using its passenger car chassis, Durant Motors Inc, Lansing, Michigan, offered a series of light commercials under the Star brand name, but also sold as Rugby in certain markets. Later, a 2.8-litre 6-cyl Continental petrol engine was fitted in a new chassis and the first Star truck, also marketed as the Star Six Compound Fleettruck or Star-Fleettruck, was introduced. This was a 1/1½-tonner with high-ratio 4-speed transmission which sold only as the Rugby from 1927. Another model was also a 1-tonner, but with an option of either a 4- or 6-cyl petrol engine. By 1929 this had a 3-speed

main transmission and 2-speed auxiliary, although heavier models of the 1931/2 period reverted to a normal 4-speed system.

1960 Star (4) single-deck coach

STAR (4)/Poland 1948 to date
Prototype Star trucks were built in the Ursus factory, Warsaw, but series production got underway in the Storahovice factory of Fabryka Samochodow Ciezarowych. With a payload of 3½ tons, the first Star, the rigid Model 20, was powered by an 85bhp petrol engine. Later, artic and tipper versions using 87 and 105bhp petrol units were developed.

In 1958 a 6 x 6 forward-control model was introduced for both military and civilian customers, and in 1961 a 100bhp diesel engine was offered in most models. Original models were now out-of-date despite modifications, so the 28/29 series was developed for a 5-ton payload using the company's own 100bhp diesel or 105bhp petrol engines and a cab from Chausson, France. Even the 6 x 6 model was re-vamped to take this cab, and a new 4 x 4 vehicle powered by a 150bhp petrol engine became the basis of a fire appliance fitted with Jelcz bodywork.

As well as supplying mechanical components to other manufacturers, the company currently offers the '200'-Series on-highway range using the 150bhp 6-cyl diesel engine and 5-speed transmission.

STAR-TRIBUNE/USA 1914-1916
Michigan-built OK light delivery trucks were marketed as the Star-Tribune by the Star-Tribune Motor Sales Co, Detroit. This was listed only as a 1¼-tonner and is believed to have had a 4-cyl side-valve petrol engine.

STARBUCK/USA 1912-1913
A 1½-ton forward-control open express truck was the sole commercial model listed by the Starbuck Automobile Co, Philadelphia, Pennsylvania. It had a 4-cyl petrol engine, 3-speed transmission, double chain-drive and platform rear springs.

STEAM-O-TRUCK/*USA 1918-1920*

Introduced as the Stokesbary, the Steam-o-Truck was a 5-ton steam lorry built by the Steam Automotive Works, Denver, Colorado. It had a front-mounted boiler located under a conventional bonnet and a 2-cyl engine geared directly to the rear axle. Initially, the boiler operated at 700psi, but was later reduced to 600psi.

STEAMOBILE/*USA 1919*

The Steamobile was one of America's last steam trucks, having a high-pressure boiler and Uniflow V4 engine. Built by the Winslow Boiler & Engineering Co, Chicago, Illinois, it had a capacity of 5 tons and shaft-drive.

STEAMOTOR/*USA 1917-1920*

The Steamotor Truck Co built the 2-ton Steamotor. This had a 600psi boiler and 45hp 2-cyl Doble engine, the former mounted in a conventional position and the latter under the driver's set. Other features included a 360cm wheelbase and shaft and worm final-drive.

From 1919 production was handled by the Amalgamated Machinery Corp.

STEARNS/*USA 1911-1913, 1915-1916*

The Frank B Stearns Co, Cleveland, Ohio, launched a chain-drive 44hp 4-cyl petrol-engined bonneted 3-tonner, offering only a 5-ton version after 1912. This had a 3-speed transmission but was discontinued to concentrate on passenger car production. A new 5-tonner with Knight sleeve-valve 4-cyl petrol engine appeared in 1915, also marketed as the Stearns-Knight. It was unusual in that the engine was spring-mounted using a subframe and inverted semi-elliptic leaf springs.

STEELE/*USA 1914-1919*

Previously sold as the Morgan by the Morgan Motor Truck Co, Worcester, Massachusetts, 2-, 3-, 4- and 5-ton Steele trucks were built by W M Steele in the same factory. These were "cabover" models with Steele-built petrol engines, Cotta 3-speed transmissions, countershafts and double chain final-drive.

STEGEMAN/*USA 1911-1917*

Stegeman trucks had capacities up to 5 tons and were built by the Stegeman Motor Car Co, Milwaukee, Wisconsin. Most had 4-cyl petrol engines, the lightest running on pneumatic tyres and all models over 1-ton capacity having chain-drive. Shortly before production ceased, a 6-cyl engine with electric starting was used in some

models and a new 7-tonner with fully-floating worm-drive added to the range.

STEINKOENIG/*USA 1926-1927*

The Steinkoenig Motors Co, Cincinnati, Ohio, offered a series of Waukesha-powered "conventional" trucks. In 1927 the company was re-organized as the World Motors Co, introducing World trucks.

STEPHEN/*England c1966-c1968*

Alexander Stephen & Sons constructed the Stephen terminal tractor for handling semi-trailers in docks and warehouses. Fitted with a one-man half-cab, this was also available with a matching frame semi-trailer complete with winching equipment.

STEPHENSON/*USA 1910-1913*

Stephenson trucks were available as forward-control 1- and 3-tonners with 4-cyl petrol engines, friction transmissions and double chain-drive. Built by the Stephenson Motor Car Co, Milwaukee, Wisconsin, these had respective wheelbase lengths of 280 and 330cm. Production was later handled by the Stephenson Motor Truck Co.

STERLING (1)/*USA 1909-1910*

The Model 'C' Sterling truck was built by the Sterling Vehicle Co, Harvey, Illinois. It had a 2-cyl petrol engine, 3-speed transmission, shaft-drive and a wheelbase of 220cm.

STERLING (2)/*USA 1916-1951*

The Sterling Motor Truck Co, Milwaukee, Wisconsin, took over the Sternberg Motor Truck Co, concentrating on a range of 1½- to 7-ton "conventionals", also build-

ing some Class 'B' "Liberty" trucks. Five- and 7-ton civilian models were still chain-driven and the distinctive wood-lined bolted chassis frames were patented by the company in 1922.

The company built its own 4-cyl petrol engines and used 4-speed sliding-mesh transmissions on its lightest models; 3-speed constant-mesh on its medium-duty types; and 6-speed constant-mesh on the 5- and 7-ton chain-drives. A worm-drive 1½-tonner made its debut in the mid-1920s, about the time that the company's 6-cyl petrol engine appeared in some models. Chain-drive continued to be available for heavy applications or where extra ground clearance was required. The heaviest models were now 12- and 20-ton tractors.

Multiple transmissions were announced in 1928 and in 1929 a 1-tonner was launched and some of the heavier types advertised as 6-wheelers using a central differential unit and chain-drive system to all four bogie wheels. By 1930 the company's 6-cyl petrol engine was producing as much as 185bhp, and in 1931 the "conventional" 'F'-Series was announced. To increase sales and production facilities, the LaFrance-Republic Corp was acquired in 1932, becoming the LaFrance-Republic Divn of the Sterling Motor Truck Co.

With the Depression, sales continued to drop. Despite this the company was one of the first to offer Cummins diesel engines as an option, adding a new "cabover" series in 1935 with unusual rear-tilting cab. By 1937 these were joined by 'G'-Series "cabovers" with forward-tilting cabs and 125bhp Cummins diesel engines. In 1939 the former distributors of

the Fageol Truck & Coach Co were bought out, and in the same year chain-drive Sterlings became the 'H'-Series and 6-wheelers the 'J'-Series.

During World War II, as well as military vehicles, a 6 x 4 chain-drive heavy wrecker, 6 x 6 medium and heavy wreckers, a 6-ton 6 x 6 airfield fire crash truck, and a 6-ton 6 x 6 swinging-boom crane were developed. The firm also collaborated with the US Army to design and construct a heavy 6 x 6 chain-drive which appeared in prototype form as the T-28. Powered by a 291bhp Continental engine, this was fitted with fifth wheel coupling. By 1947 it had developed into the T-29, a 20-ton tractor powered by a 525bhp Ford

1943 Sterling (2) DDS 235 6x6 artic tractor

V8 tank engine, and by the 1940s had become the T-35 25-ton 6 x 6, and finally the T-46 for use with a 75-ton heavy equipment trailer.

Although based on pre-war designs, some post-war models dispensed with the famous wood-lined bolted frame construction. In 1951 the business was acquired by the White Motor Co, becoming its Sterling Divn, and all vehicles being sold as Sterling-White.

Sterling (2) 6 x 4 artic tractor c1950

STERLING (3)/*USA 1973 to date*
Using the same trademark as the old Milwaukee-based Sterling operation, Sterling Custom Built Trucks Inc, Kansas City, Kansas, has revived the Sterling name on a series of trucks, tractors, cranes, trailers and other specialist types.

STERLING-WHITE/*USA 1951-1953*
The takeover of the Sterling Motors Corp, Milwaukee, Wisconsin, by the White Motor Co led to the formation of the Sterling Divn of the White Motor Co. Marketed as Sterling-White, the company's heavy custom-built models were similar to earlier Sterlings. Sterling-White production was transferred to the White Motor Co's Cleveland, Ohio, base in 1952 where it continued until it was replaced by that of Autocar.

STERNBERG/*USA 1907-1915*
The Sternberg Motor Truck Co, Milwaukee, Wisconsin, designed and constructed a series of "cabovers" of 1, 1½, 3½ and 5 tons capacity using various 4-cyl 'T'-head petrol engines of between 29 and 44hp output. Apart from the 1-tonner, which had friction-drive transmission providing an infinite number of speeds, all had cone-and-disc transmissions providing 2 forward and 1 reverse speed and chain-drive. An unusual feature was the wood-lined chassis frame of solid oak pressed into the channel frame sidemembers to deaden road shocks. Apart from the 1½-tonner, which had platform springs at the rear, all used semi-elliptics.

In 1914, a chain-drive 7-tonner was announced and followed by the company's first bonneted models with worm-drive. The old "cabovers" were gradually replaced by these with the exception of the 7-tonner. Increasing anti-German feeling forced the company to change its name to the Sterling Motor Truck Co, and its models to Sterling.

STEVENS/*England 1972-c1975*
Employing a 4-cyl Ford petrol engine of up to 2-litres capacity as well as Ford running units, the 1-ton Stevens delivery van was a bonneted Edwardian looking vehicle doubling as a promotional vehicle. Built by Anthony Stevens Automobiles Ltd, Warwick, it was available in several lighter sizes as well as a 12-seat minibus and was assembled from sheet aluminum panels mounted on a welded steel frame. One option included an automatic transmission.

STEWART (1)/*Scotland 1902-1910*
Steam engineers Duncan Stewart & Co (1902) Ltd, Glasgow, built steam wagons of Thornycroft design. Most were loco-type "undertypes", also known as Stewart-Thornycrofts. When Thornycroft steamers ceased, the company developed a vertical water-tube boilered colonial wagon with chain-and-bobbin steering and cast steel wheels.

STEWART (2)/*USA 1912-1916*
The Stewart Iron Works, Covington, Kentucky, offered a single commercial model known as the Model 1. This was of forward-control layout with a 2-cyl 4-stroke petrol engine and double chain-drive. The wheelbase was 240cm and the chassis frame incorporated steel sidemembers with cross-members of hickory wood.

STEWART (3)
USA c1912-1941
The founders of the Lippard-Stewart Motor Car Co formed the Stewart Motor Corp, Buffalo, New York, introducing a light commercial similar to the Lippard-Stewart. This was joined by the Model 'K' 1-tonner with 2-cyl underseat petrol engine, 2-speed transmission, double chain-drive and solid tyres. Lighter models were built in quantity, but in 1917 a 4-cyl Buda-engined 2-tonner was announced, followed, in 1918, by a 3½-tonner. Milwaukee and LeRoi petrol engines were used, and in 1921 a "speed truck" was developed, joined by a 6-cyl petrol-engined passenger model in 1925.

Although a 4-cyl petrol engine was listed as an option for 1- and 1½-tonners after 1926, 6-cyl units were now standard. By 1930 the range comprised six models from 1½ to 7 tons capacity, using Lycoming and Waukesha petrol engines. In 1931 a 130bhp straight-8 Lycoming was fitted in a 3½-tonner, popular for long-distance work, and soon available with third axle conversion.

All models were re-styled in

Stewart (3) 2-ton truck c1918

the mid-1930s, the largest being a 7/8-tonner, and by the late 1930s only Waukesha petrol and Waukesha-Hesselman diesel engines were fitted. In 1938 the first Stewart "cabovers", from 1½ to 3 tons capacity were advertised, but in 1939 new management took over, concentrating on models from 3 to 7 tons capacity. Production gradually came to an end.

Steyr Type 40 1½-ton truck c1931

STEYR/*Austria 1922 to date*
The 2½-ton Steyr Type III bonneted truck was introduced by Oesterreichische Waffenfabriks Gesellschaft AG, Steyr, using a 12/34 PS 6-cyl petrol engine, its replacement being the Type 40 with an 8/40 PS 6-cyl petrol unit. In 1926 the company was re-named

Steyr-Werke AG and by 1935, when it became known as Steyr-Daimler-Puch AG, various 6 x 4 models were also listed. In 1937 the Type 640 6 x 4 was developed, using a 2.26-litre 6-cyl petrol engine, and in 1941 a V8-engined 4 x 4 was developed for military use. This model formed the basis for post-war vehicles such as the 3-ton Type 370, later offered with a 4-

and, finally, a 6-cyl diesel engine.

During the 1950s new 4-, 5-, 6-, 7- and 8-tonners were announced, and in 1959 the revolutionary Steyr-Puch 'Haflinger' appeared. The forward-control 'Plus' truck range arrived in 1968 for payloads of between 5 and 16 tons, the largest using a 320bhp diesel engine. A few all-wheel drive versions were offered, and in 1975 an 8 x 4 rigid joined this range.

In the passenger line, new models were based on Austrian Saurer designs with diesel engines

1974 Stevens 1-ton integral van

1965 Steyr Type 680 fire appliance

1979 Steyr Type 1291.320 artic tractor

producing up to 230bhp. An interesting design was the 1973 chassis-less Type 'L' using the 'Haflinger' engine and other common components. Capable of carrying up to twenty passengers, it had a rear entrance. It was replaced in 1975 by the larger Type 'S', using a 55bhp 2-litre Mercedes-Benz diesel engine and 28-passenger body.

1979 Steyr-Puch 'Pinzgauer' 6 x 6 integral van

STEYR-PUCH/*Austria 1959 to date*

Series production of the Steyr-Puch 'Haflinger' light 4 x 4 truck got underway in the Graz plant of Steyr-Daimler-Puch AG using a 27bhp 643cc twin-cyl opposed-piston underfloor petrol engine. It was succeeded by the 4 x 4 or 6 x 6 'Pinzgauer', also using an air-cooled petrol engine but now with an 87bhp 2.5-litre 4-cyl unit. Like the 'Haflinger', this has a central tubular backbone chassis.

STILL/*West Germany 1950-1955*
Hans Still AG, Hamburg, marketed 1½-ton capacity battery-electric trucks as either Still or Hans Still.

STILLE/*Germany 1930*
Maschinen und Fahrzeugfabrik Stille, Munster, built a massive 8-wheeled bonneted bus of chassis-less construction powered by a 7-litre 6-cyl Maybach engine. A few were equipped to run on producer-gas.

STODDARD-DAYTON/*USA 1911-1912*
Motor car manufacturer the Dayton Motor Car Co, Dayton, Ohio, entered the commercial vehicle field with 1- and 2½-ton forward-control trucks. Marketed as Stoddard-Dayton, these had chain-drive and solid tyres but were replaced in 1912 by short-lived van and truck versions of the company's 28hp passenger car chassis.

STOEWER/*Germany 1900-1927, 1931*
The first Stoewer commercials were built by Gebr Stoewer Fabrik für Motorfahrzeuge, Neutorney, Stettin, and comprised a 3-ton truck and a 15-seat bus, both using a 10/20 PS 2-cyl petrol engine. However, the company concentrated on battery-electric types until 1905, when a 24hp 4.6-litre 4-cyl petrol engine was introduced for some models and a 30bhp 5.9-litre unit in 1906 for others.

In 1912 a new range was announced, many of the trucks being of "subsidy" type. After the war, only low-key production was carried on until a 1½-tonner with 28bhp 2.6-litre 4-cyl petrol engine went into series production. Known as Stoewer-Werke AG, the firm also built a few 3-tonners using a 40bhp 5.7-litre petrol engine, but production tailed off. A brief revival was made in 1931

with a licence-built Morris-Commercial, but nothing appears to have come of this.

STONEFIELD/*Scotland 1974-1980, 1981 to date*
Stonefield Developments, Paisley, Renfrewshire, was established to develop a new concept in off-road vehicles. The result was a light rugged machine of 4 x 4 or 6 x 4 configuration with as many as 64 different options. A number of pre-production vehicles were completed prior to 1978 with cabs of flat-panelled steel by Jensen Motors Ltd, special attention being given to chassis and transmission arrangements. With investment from the Scottish Development Agency, the operation was re-named Stonefield Vehicles Ltd and a factory set up at Cumnock, Ayrshire, with a capacity of some 2,500 units per year.

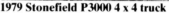

1979 Stonefield P3000 4 x 4 truck

With a 1½-ton payload rating, the 4 x 4 is sold as the P3000 or P5000, with 3-litre V6 or 5.2-litre V8 petrol engines, respectively. The 6 x 4 is rated at 3 tons capacity. The unique feature of the Stonefield is its spaceframe design, eliminating the need for a conventional chassis. By combining this with one of two powerful engines, a 3-speed fully-automatic transmission and the Ferguson 'Formula' 4-wheel drive system, the company offers a unique range of on/off-highway vehicles. The industrial recession at the end of the 1970s forced the firm's closure in 1980. However, it was rescued early in 1981 by Gomba Motors Ltd.

STRAKER/*England 1901-c1912*
Consulting engineer Sidney Straker had an interest in Owen, Brazil & Holberrow, Bristol, which became Brazil, Holberrow & Straker Ltd in 1899. With the break-up of the Bayley-Straker consortium in 1901, it was again re-named as the Straker Steam Vehicle Co Ltd. While modifications were carried out to the old Bayley design, L R L Squire joined the company and it was re-named Sidney Straker & Squire Ltd. Modifications to the Bayley wagon included single chain final-drive and

the re-location of the vertical De Dion-type boiler over the front axle. An off-set chimney was provided and the compound engine incorporated cyls of 10 and 17.5 x 17.5cm. Wagons from 2 to 12 tons capacity were sold as Straker and petrol-engined vehicles as Straker-Squire.

In 1903 a 7-ton colonial wagon appeared, this having a compound engine with 30hp more than the earlier 25hp and Straker's 3-point suspension using a transverse semi-elliptic front spring was employed. The final design was an "overtype" which appeared in 1905, having a loco-type boiler and the same compound engine as was fitted in the 1903 colonial model. Traction engine style chain steering was specified and steam wagon production took a back seat until about 1912 when it ceased altogether.

STRAKER-CLOUGH/*England 1921-1927*
Also sold as Clough-Smith, the Straker-Clough trolleybus was marketed by Clough, Smith & Co Ltd, London SW1, using a Straker-Squire chassis. The first was a single-decker based on the 'A'-Type 5-tonner, one of the earliest British trolleybuses to use a foot-operated rather than tram-type controller. The Clough-Smith traction motor was located at the front of the chassis with shaft-drive to the rear wheels.

STRAKER-McCONNELL/*England 1905-1906*
A short-lived arrangement between Motorwagenfabrik E Arbenz & Cie, Switzerland, and motor dealer Straker & McConnell Ltd, London, resulted in the Straker-McConnell truck. It was a re-named Arbenz which was supplied in small numbers, mainly in passenger form.

STRAKER-SQUIRE/*England 1906-1926*
As well as Straker steam wagons, Sidney Straker & Squire Ltd, Bristol, arranged with the manufacturer of German Büssing commercials to sell these in Britain as Straker-Squire. The first were 3-tonners with 28/30hp 4-cyl petrol engines supplied both as goods and passenger models. The new marque found favour as London buses where some 356 double-

1903 Straker steam bus

1914 Straker-Squire 3/4-ton truck

deck versions were operating by 1908. By 1907 new models included a worm-drive 1-tonner and a petrol-electric chassis, while a 1¼-ton 2-cyl petrol-engined van was added in 1908.

Vehicles were now assembled mainly from British components to the company's own design, and in 1910 a 5-ton chain-drive truck was advertised for colonial use, followed in 1912 by a number of trolleybus chassis. Now known as Straker-Squire (1913) Ltd, the firm soon introduced a 3/4-tonner which was used extensively for military service during World War I.

The company suffered from the post-war slump, but managed to invest in the development of a new semi forward-control model called the 'A'-Type which went into production in 1919. This was a 5-tonner powered by a 55bhp 4-cyl monobloc petrol engine and fitted with a 4-speed transmission and worm-drive. By 1920 4-, 6- and 8-ton versions were listed but none was popular due to design faults. Another model, the 2½-ton 'BW'-Type, arrived in 1922 but this did nothing to improve the situation. Despite dabbling in the trolleybus market with the Straker-Clough, the company was forced into liquidation.

STRAUSSLER/*England 1935-1940*

Nicholas Straussler was a consulting engineer who designed and developed military vehicles during the 1930s, often arranging for other manufacturers to construct them. In 1935 he formed Straussler Mechanization Ltd, Brentford, Middx. The first design was a 15-ton 8-wheeler which was a complete departure from conventional ideas, with tandem front-drive bogie and independent semi-elliptic leaf spring suspension throughout. Power came from a 150bhp 7.2-litre twin overhead-cam V8 petrol engine located under a low-mounted forward-control cab. The 6-speed transmission was worked by two gear-change levers

1913 Straker-Squire trolleybus

and the chassis comprised two pressed-steel channel-section sidemembers located back to back with interspersed crossmembers. It was designed for transporting petrol and carried a 16,820-litre tank.

In 1937 three 4 x 4 vehicles using Ford components and driven front axles derived from normal non-steering drive axles were produced. These were 1-, 2- and 3-tonners, a prototype twin-engined 3-tonner being built by H Manfred Weiss RT, and prototypes of the other two by Garner Motors Ltd which subsequently built 53 3-tonners as the Garner-Straussler. A number of other military types were also built under the name of Alvis-Straussler. During World War II Straussler Mechanization built a few specialized military types, including a

prototype self-propelled 6pdr gun carriage using Standard components in 1943, and a heavier version based on the Bedford QL 3-tonner.

STREICHER/*Germany 1950-1962*

M Streicher Fahrzeugbau, Stuttgart, concentrated on municipal vehicles, specializing in refuse collectors and street sweeper/sprinklers.

Typical was the 'Cannstatt' sweeper/collector with one Mercedes-Benz diesel engine providing propulsion and another powering two circular brushes. Introduced early in 1959, this carried a fibre brush at the rear which directed the sweepings to a suction point through which they were drawn into a fully-enclosed side-tipping body.

STRICK/*USA 1978 to date*

An unusual form of artic tractor unit is the Strick 'Cab Under', a twin-steer outfit with 1.2-m high cab and Cummins 903 turbocharged V8 engine located behind. A 13-speed Fuller 'Roadranger' transmission is fitted. Built by trailer manufacturer, the Strick Corp, Fairless Hills, Pennsylvania, it is intended to provide maximum payload capabilities within a given length.

1957 Studebaker integral van

STUDEBAKER/*USA c1913-1917, 1927-1964*

Studebaker Electric commercials,

built by the Studebaker Automobile Co, South Bend, Indiana, were soon replaced by petrol-engined passenger car derivatives, some of more than 1-ton capacity. In 1913 a "heavy" model was developed, but failed to reach series production. This was a 3-tonner with 4-cyl 'T'-head petrol engine, 4-speed transmission and spur-gear final-drive. By 1917 only passenger cars and very light commercials were being built but as the Studebaker Corp the company began to build larger models in 1927, starting with a 14/18-seat coach based on the 'Big Six' passenger car. By 1929 this had been replaced by a larger model, now powered by a 118bhp 5.5-litre straight-8 petrol engine.

New 1- and 3-ton trucks, powered respectively by a 4-litre 4- and 5.9-litre 6-cyl petrol engines appeared in 1928. These were the first Studebaker trucks to sell in quantity. Towards the end of 1928 the company compounded its truck-building activities by merging with the Pierce-Arrow Motor Car Co, after which some vehicles were sold as Studebaker-Pierce-Arrow.

By the early 1930s 4-speed transmissions were used extensively on larger models and 2-speed back axles on the 3-tonner, all types having the company's own 6-cyl petrol engines. Both normal- and forward-control models were listed for 1936 but only up to 3 tons payload, the largest model now using a 6.3-litre 6-cyl Waukesha petrol engine and 5-speed transmission. Hercules engines were introduced in 1938 and a new 2/3-ton model was added. In 1941 all models were revamped as the 'M'-Type, again using the company's own engines, but a series of bonneted 6 x 4 and 6 x 6 2½-ton military trucks used Hercules engines.

'M'-Types continued to be

1935 Straussler 15-ton 8 x 4 tanker

1961 Studebaker artic tractor

built, and were joined by the '2R'-Series in 1949, powered by the firm's own 6-cyl petrol engine. By 1954 1½- and 2-tonners used a 3.8-litre V8 unit, increased to 4.3-litre by 1955, but there were no significant changes until 1962 when a diesel-powered tractor for 18 tons gross appeared using a 130bhp 3.5-litre 4-cyl 2-stroke coupled to a 5-speed transmission. For 1963 V8 petrol engines were standard with Detroit Diesels optional, even for a 1-tonner, but production lasted only a few months.

STUDEBAKER ELECTRIC/
USA 1902-c1913
Starting with battery-electric passenger cars, the Studebaker Automobile Co, South Bend, Indiana, gradually introduced commercial models, the largest being a 5-tonner advertised in 1906. Apart from the lightest types, all were wheel-steered with a forward-control driving position and chain-drive. Gradually these battery-electrics were discontinued in favour of petrol-engined types sold as Studebaker.

STUTZ/*USA 1919-1928*
The Stutz Fire Engine Co was founded in Indianapolis, Indiana, and could have been connected with the Stutz Motor Car Co. The company's first fire appliances included pumpers, ladder trucks and combinations powered by 4- or 6-cyl Wisconsin petrol engines. Examples were sold throughout the US and abroad, and in 1926 the company's own 175bhp 6-cyl overhead-cam petrol engine was used in certain models. In 1931 the New Stutz Fire Engine Co was established in Hartford City and models sold as New Stutz.

SUBURBAN/*USA 1912-1913*
The 1½-ton Suburban worm-drive truck had a 29hp 4-cyl petrol engine and disc clutch. It was built by the Suburban Truck Co, Philadelphia, Pennsylvania, and was followed in 1913 by a 2-tonner with cone clutch.

1952 Studebaker ambulance

SULLIVAN/*USA 1916-1923*
One and 2-ton Sullivans were added to the light commercial range of the Sullivan Motor Truck Corp, Rochester, New York, using 4-cyl Buda petrol engines, Brown-Lipe 3-speed transmissions and Timken worm-drive axles.

SULTANA/*Mexico 1953 to date*
Trailers de Monterrey SA was founded in Monterrey, Nuevo

Leon, in 1952 and production of the Sultana bus began the following year. Using an imported Detroit Diesel engine and various other imported components, a whole range of passenger models was developed which today include nearly all Mexican components. Since 1959 the Sultana range has been built alongside Ramirez commercials.

SUMIDA/*Japan 1923-1936*
Ishikawajima commercials, built by the Ishikawajima Jidosha Works Ltd, Tokyo, were renamed Sumida after which much of production was military. The Jidosha Kogyo Co Ltd was formed in 1933 following a merger with the manufacturers of Dat and Chiyoda trucks, and although bonneted Sumida models continued to be built, these were eventually absorbed into the Isuzu line when the Kyoda Kokusan Jidosha KK organization joined with Jidosha Kogyo.

SUMNER/*England 1880-1882*
James Sumner, of Leyland, Lancs, constructed a largely unsuccessful 5-ton steam wagon as an experiment but later turned his attention to steam lawn mowers. This ultimately led to the formation of the Lancashire Steam Motor Co which first introduced its own steam wagons in 1896.

SUN (1)/*Germany 1906-1908*
A number of goods and passenger vehicles were built by Kraftwagen Gesellschaft Roland GmbH, Ber-

lin, under the Sun brand name. These were powered by 4- or 6-cyl Argus petrol engines of up to 70hp output.

SUN (2)/*England 1948-c1953*
The British-built Sun was a large 3-wheeled open truck with tipping body designed primarily for agricultural or construction work. It was introduced by Sun Engineering Ltd, Scunthorpe, Lincs, and had a power unit mounted over the small single front wheel whilst the rear wheels were of larger diameter.

SUNBEAM/*England 1929-1963*
The Sunbeam Motor Car Co Ltd, Wolverhampton, Staffs, entered the heavy passenger vehicle market with the Sunbeam or SMC 'Pathan' 4-wheeler and 'Sikh' 6-wheeler. Both used a 142bhp 8-litre 6-cyl petrol engine and were intended for single-deck operation.

Few were built but one 6-wheeled chassis was re-constructed for trolleybus use in 1931, leading to the introduction of a series-produced Sunbeam trolleybus.

Sunbeam Commercial Vehicles Ltd was set up to market the product which it continued to build for many years. Following a takeover by Rootes Securities Ltd, and the merging of Karrier trolleybus production with that of Sunbeam, some were sold as Karrier.

In 1948, following a further takeover by Guy Motors Ltd, the company was re-named the Sun-

1966 Sultana 8 x 4 1½-deck coach

1931 Sunbeam MS2 double-deck trolleybus

1961 Sunbeam S4A double-deck trolleybus

1946 Sunbeam W4 double-deck trolleybus

beam Trolleybus Co Ltd, moving to the Guy factory where production continued spasmodically.

Lake, Wisconsin, built a 6-wheeled commercial known as the Super-Traction. Production did not last long as the business was acquired by the Wisconsin Truck Co, Loganville, in 1923 and the Super-Traction absorbed into the Wisconsin range.

SUPER TRUCK/*USA 1919-1936*
As well as the Manly truck, the O'Connell Motor Truck Corp, Waukegan, Illinois, constructed the Super Truck, also described as the Super or the O'Connell. The most interesting version was aimed at the construction business and was unusual in that the driver's seat was reversible, pivoting around the steering column to enable the vehicle to be driven easily in either direction. Called appropriately the 'Two-Way Drive', it was advertised in various sizes from 2½ to 7½ tons capacity using a Wisconsin petrol engine and the manufacturer's own transmission system.
More conventional machines included 4- and 6-cyl Wisconsin petrol-engined trucks from 2½ to 7 tons capacity fitted with Fuller transmissions and Timken or Sheldon axles.

SUPERIOR (1)/*USA 1912-1914*
The Superior Model 'A' 1-tonner was listed by the F G Clark Co, Lansing, Michigan. It was powered by a 4-cyl petrol engine and had a 3-speed transmission, double chain-drive and solid tyres.

SUPERIOR (2)/*USA 1938-c1940, 1946-1948*
Founded in about 1930, the Superior Coach Corp, Lima, Ohio, concentrated on the manufacture of school bus bodies until a complete integral model called the 'Avenue' was introduced. This had a rear-mounted Ford V8 engine and was joined in 1931 by the

SUPER-TRACTION/*USA c1922-1923*
The Six Wheel Truck Co, Fox

'Rocket', a long-distance model. Production ceased during World War II but in 1946 a new transit bus went into production.

SUTPHEN/*USA 1967 to date*
A well-known manufacturer of fire-fighting equipment, the Sutphen Fire Equipment Co, Amlin, Ohio, now builds complete vehicles under the Sutphen brand name. The first were 6-wheelers with "Cincinnati" cabs and diesel engines with outputs of between 265 and 525bhp, intended for use with the company's aerial tower equipment. In 1972 an experimental 2000gpm pumper powered by a Ford 3600 gas-turbine engine was also built, but production still centres upon the 6-wheeler.

SWISSCAR/*Switzerland 1958-?*
In a joint project, Swiss coach-builder Ramseier & Jenzer and Tüscher combined resources and experience to design and construct a rear-engined integral coach aimed at the international touring market. Called the Swisscar, it had a Perkins P6 diesel engine located longitudinally between the chassis frame side-members with fan and radiator offset to one side. It was first shown to the public at the 1959 Geneva Motor Show.

SWITCHMASTER/*USA ? to date*
Affiliated to the Hendrickson Mfg Co, Lyons, Illinois, the White Machinery Corp, Joliet, Illinois, builds the Switchmaster road/rail shunter which can move from road to track and back by operating a single lever. Conforming to existing road regulations, the Switchmaster has a 6-cyl petrol or 4-cyl diesel engine with respective outputs of 143 and 123bhp. Other features include a full torque-converter transmission with 3 forward and 3 reverse speeds and a unique weight transfer system where the weight of a rail wagon can be transferred to the steel rail wheels of the Switchmaster to boost tractive effort.

SYMES/*Canada 1912-1914*
The Symes Motor Truck Co, Chatham, Ontario, built the 1-ton Symes bonneted truck. Three and 5-tonners could be had on special order.

SYNNESTVEDT/*USA 1904-1907*
The last year of manufacture for the battery electric Synnestvedt built by the Synnestvedt Machine Co, Pittsburgh, Pennsylvania, saw the Type 'F' 3- and Type 'D' 5-tonners. Both had double chain-drive, the former having a wheel-base of 214cm and the latter 256cm.

T

TALBOT (1)/England c1918-c1930

A 20-seat passenger model sold as Talbot or Clement-Talbot introduced by passenger car manufacturer Clement Talbot Ltd, London W10, was based on an earlier 3/4-tonner using a 4.5-litre 4-cyl petrol engine. In 1923 a 1½-ton "subsidy" truck was developed. This used a 54bhp 4-cyl overhead-valve petrol engine and 4-speed transmission but was unsuccessful.

The 20-seater was still listed in 1926 and a new 1½-tonner with 3-litre 4-cyl side-valve petrol engine, 3-speed transmission and worm-drive was announced two years later. About 1930 the company was acquired by Rootes Securities Ltd and subsequent Talbots were often sold as W & G by associated company W & G Du Cros Ltd.

TALBOT (2)/Germany 1937-1939

Talbot battery-electrics were of bonneted layout for capacities of up to 2½ tons. Built by Waggonfabrik Talbot GmbH, Aachen, they were often based on passenger car chassis and sometimes sold as Talbot Elektrisch.

TAM/Yugoslavia 1947 to date

Tovarna Automobilov Maribor, Maribor, based its first TAM truck, a bonneted 3½-tonner, on a Praga model. Called the 'Pionir', it was also available as a bus but in 1955 a licence agreement was signed with Klockner-Humboldt-Deutz AG to build certain Magirus-Deutz models. The first was a 4½-tonner powered by an imported 85bhp 4-cyl Deutz air-cooled diesel engine.

This arrangement led to considerable expansion with licence-built Deutz air-cooled diesels in V4 and V6 configuration manufactured at Maribor as well as numerous trucks, buses and chassisless passenger types. In 1960 the factory was re-organized as Tovarna Automobilova in Motorjev Maribor and the first TAM de-

signed and constructed entirely in Yugoslavia appeared as the 2-ton 2000. This had a licence-built 55bhp 4-cyl Perkins diesel engine and was of forward-control layout.

The factory now constructs air-cooled V8s under licence as well as all Klockner-Humboldt-Deutz's in-line air-cooled diesels, current truck and bus production including a modified 2-tonner known as the 2001, mediumweight bonneted trucks of up to 6½ tons capacity using an out-of-date Magirus-Deutz cab, and various 4 x 4 chassis, buses and coaches.

1924 Taskers 3-speed 6-ton "overtype" steam wagon

TASKERS/England 1909-1925

W Tasker & Sons Ltd, Andover, Hants, was a well-known manufacturer of steam and agricultural equipment when it constructed a prototype steam wagon of compound "overtype" layout using four crank shaft discs in place of a flywheel. This led to a series of 3- and 5-tonners and one 10-ton artic, all using chain-drive to the rear wheels, but the Tasker was never as popular as other makes.

TATA/India 1971 to date

Previously sold as Tata-Mercedes-Benz, the Tata range is built in the Tata Engineering & Locomotive Co's Jamshedpur factory. These are actually licence-built Mercedes-Benz commercials, some of out-dated design.

TATA-MERCEDES-BENZ/India 1954-1971

Mercedes-Benz trucks and buses were assembled in India by the Tata Engineering & Locomotive Co, Jamshedpur, and sold as Tata-Mercedes-Benz until the Tata name was adopted.

TATE/Canada 1912-1914

Tate Electric Ltd, Walkerville, Ontario, built various Tate battery-electrics up to a 2-ton chain-drive stakeside.

TAYLOR/USA 1917-1918

When the Burford Motor Truck Co, Fremont, Ohio, was taken over by the Taylor Motor Truck Co, a series of 1-, 1½-, 2½-, 3½-

and 5-ton Taylor trucks was introduced. Wheelbases ranged from 325 to 400cm and all models had 4-cyl Continental petrol engines, Covert transmissions and Timken worm-drive axles.

TAYLOR HYDRACRANE/England 1945-c1956

Using an unknown make of tipper chassis, F Taylor & Sons (Manchester) Ltd developed a self-propelled yard crane for its own use featuring a non-slewing jib. This became the prototype for a new concept in lifting equipment, early versions of which were mounted on ex-WD Morris-Commercial chassis. Called the Taylor Hydracrane, these had twin hydraulic rams raising and lowering the non-slewing jib. When the supply of ex-WD chassis came to an end, the company built its own chassis, renaming these Taylor Jumbo.

1961 Taylor Jumbo Series 42 3-ton 4 x 4 mobile crane

TAYLOR JUMBO/England c1956-c1964

Taylor Jumbo hydraulic cranes succeeded the Taylor Hydracrane range of F Taylor & Sons (Manchester) Ltd. Marketed as the 'Jumbo' and 'Jumbo Junior', it in-

corporated hydraulic operation but now with full slewing motions. Acquired by Steels Engineering Products Ltd in 1959, the company introduced telescopic boom systems three years later and segregated production into the 4 x 4 Series 42 and 4 x 2 Series 50, the latter being a 4-ton diesel hydraulic outfit. Over the next few years the hydraulic principles developed by Taylor were incorporated into the designs of another Steels subsidiary manufacturing Coles cranes which within a year was taken over.

TCAVDAR/Bulgaria ? to date

Using Czechoslovakian Skoda chassis, engines and components, Uzina Tcavdar, Botevgrad, built both medium- and large-capacity Tcavdar passenger models up to 1975 when agreement with Karl Kassbohrer Fahrzeugwerke GmbH, manufacturer of Setra passenger models, led to the development of the 11M3. This is still based on the Skoda 706 chassis powered by a 160bhp front-mounted diesel engine.

TECHNO/USA 1962

The Techno was an unusual front-drive 6-wheeled container truck built by the Techno Truck Co, Cleveland, Ohio. It was based on an International bonneted model converted to front-wheel drive and with no conventional chassis frame behind the cab. Instead, the single-tyred tandem rear wheels were suspended on a steel framework which also held a hydraulic lifting mechanism designed to take a loaded container within. Although a 6-ton prototype was built, 4-, 5-, 6- and 8-ton models never left the drawing board.

1919 Tatra TL2 military truck

TATRA/
Czechoslovakia 1919 to date
Initially, Tatra Werke Automobilbau AG, Koprivnice, offered a couple of Nesselsdorfer or NW designs under the Tatra name but following the development of a unique tubular backbone passenger car design, introduced a commercial derivative in 1923. The tubular backbone contained the propeller shaft and the wheels were independently suspended through the use of swinging half-axles attached to the tube. The lightest version appears to have been the Type 26 6-wheeler with a capacity of approximately 1½ tons, powered at first by a 1.05-litre horizontally-opposed 2-cyl petrol engine and later by a 1.68-litre 4-cyl unit of similar design.

The first heavy model, however, was a 4 x 2 3-tonner with 7.48-litre 4-cyl petrol engine, soon joined by the 10-ton 6-wheeled Type 24, using an 11-litre 6-cyl petrol engine and available from 1935 with diesel option. Meanwhile, the Type 26 was replaced by the Type 72 in 1933, which used a 1.9-litre petrol engine, but this was withdrawn in 1937 and the company concentrated on the heavier models.

The Tatra design was specially popular in military circles where its high mobility was a welcome asset and by 1939 the 10-ton 6-wheeler had become the Type 81 powered by a 160bhp 12.46-litre V8 diesel or 120bhp 14.73-litre V8 producer-gas engine. In 1942 a range of air-cooled diesels from 4- to 12-cyl layout was developed, the 4-cyl unit being fitted in subsequent 3-tonners and the 12-cyl model in the Type 111 10-tonner.

Apart from the re-naming of the company as Tatra np in 1945, there were few important developments until the mid-1950s when the Type 138 6-wheeler supplemented the Type 111, eventually replacing it and still in production today, now itself supplemented by the even heavier Type 148. Other developments of the 1950s included a 4 x 4 vehicle fitted with a de-tuned version of the company's 2.5-litre V8, the Type 500HB integral bus with rear engine and a series of 6-wheeled trolleybuses available until 1960.

In 1967 the forward-control Type 813 was announced in 4 x 4, 6 x 6 and 8 x 8 form, mainly for use as a military truck or as a heavy haulage tractor for up to 300 tons gross. Like the Types 138 and 148, this has a 270bhp air-cooled diesel engine.

1938 Tatra T86 single-deck trolleybus

TEIJO/*Finland ? to date*
The Teijo is a forward-control truck for gross weights of 2560kg incorporating a Volkswagen engine, wheels and front suspension.

TEMPO/ *Germany/ West Germany 1936-c1940, 1949-1968*
During the late 1920s and early 1930s Vidal und Sohn GmbH, Hamburg, developed a popular range of light 3-wheeled commercials marketed as Tempo. The first 4-wheeler was a 1-tonner, however, powered by a 600cc 2-cyl Ilo petrol engine. Production was interrupted by World War II, but in 1949 a new forward-control 1-tonner with underseat Volkswagen petrol engine and front-wheel drive was constructed as the 'Matador', replaced three years later by the 'Matador' 1000 using the company's own 672cc 3-cyl 2-stroke engine and the 'Matador' 1400 with a 1.09-litre 4-cyl Heinkel unit.

In 1958 these were superseded by the Austin-engined Tempo 1500 range for 1¼-ton loads which, with its independent suspension and front-wheel drive, not only eliminated the need for a normal propeller shaft but also enabled one model to be fitted with a hydraulically-elevating floor to aid loading. The range was an immediate success with licence production taken up in various parts of the world, one of these being Jensen Motors Ltd, West Bromwich, Staffs.

Since 1955 the company had been partly owned by Rheinstahl-Hanomag AG, Linden, near Hanover, and in 1963 it was taken over completely and re-named Tempo-Werke GmbH. Production continued as Tempo for three more years before the design became part of the Hanomag commercial range.

TEN CATE/*Netherlands 1935-1939, 1945-1947*
Fa. J & I Ten Cate, Automobiel en Trailerfabriek, Almelo, began operations building trailers for use with Chenard-Walcker tractors imported into Holland by Adr Beers NV. In 1934 the company began building chassis as a basis for the Beers 'Trambus' and one year later introduced Ten Cate bonneted artics, complete with semi-trailers, using Deutz diesel engines, central tubular chassis and four or six wheels. Discontinued on the outbreak of World War II, these were replaced when peace returned, by a series of reconditioned dump trucks, some with White engines, sold as Ten Cate.

TENTING/*France 1898*
The only commercial built by Soc Nationale de Construction de Moteurs et Automobiles H Tenting, Boulogne-sur-Seine, was a 22-seat bus powered by a 16hp 4-cyl petrol engine. It also had electric or tube ignition, friction-drive and a roof-mounted exhaust.

TERBERG/*Netherlands 1965 to date*
One of numerous ex-military vehicle dealerships set up after World War II was Automobielbedrijf en Machinefabriek W G Terberg & Zonen Benschop NV, Benschop, which by the mid-1960s was rebuilding ex US Army Diamond T and Reo 6 x 6s and selling them as Terberg. Soon complete vehicles were constructed using Diamond T and Reo components and the

1971 Terberg concrete pumper

company began to manufacture some of its own parts.

The first Terberg was the 6 x 6 N800 using a DAF diesel engine. This was joined by the semi forward-control SF1200 with Mercedes-Benz diesel engine and cab and by a bonneted 6 x 4 designated the SF1400.

Now registered Terberg Automobielfabriek BV, the company continues to offer some of these models but its latest machines include vehicles of up to 8 x 8 layout employing numerous Volvo components including cabs which are offered through some Volvo dealers outside the Netherlands.

1972 Terberg SF1200 artic tractor

TEREX/*Scotland/USA 1969 to date*
Although the General Motors Corp had been forced to sell its Euclid Divn to the White Motor Corp in 1968, General Motors (Scotland) Ltd, Motherwell, Lanarcks, continued to build earthmoving machinery as Terex. Various heavy dump trucks were offered and in 1972 the General Motors Corp set up a Terex Divn in

1975 Terex 'Titan' 350-ton 6 x 6 dump truck

Hudson, Ohio, to construct similar models under this name.

Within a couple of years vehicles from 17 to 150 tons capacity were available, using Cummins and Detroit Diesel engines, but by 1975 one of the world's largest dump trucks, the 350-ton 'Titan' 33-19, had been built in Ohio. Power came from a 3300bhp locomotive engine and this electric-drive 6-wheeler operated at a gross weight which was in excess of 600 tons.

TERMINAL TUG/*USA ? to date*
The Terminal Tug is a special yard shunter for handling semi-trailers, manufactured by the Bulk Transport Systems Divn of the FMC Corp. It has a V6 petrol engine, Allison transmission and unusual swinging cab.

TGE/*Japan 1917-1931*
The TGE 1-tonner was the first mass-produced truck in Japan, built by Tokyo Gasu Denki KK, Tokyo. It was constructed along American lines and later up-rated to 1½ tons payload. One was supplied to an Imperial residence in Tokyo and was so successful that in 1931 the brand name was changed to Chiyoda, the name of the residence.

THAMES/*England 1905-1913*
The Thames Ironworks, Shipbuilding & Engineering Co Ltd, Greenwich, London, began building the Thames "undertype" steam wagon as a sideline. It was a 2-speed 5-tonner with loco-type boiler, transverse compound engine and shaft-drive. Soon after it was introduced it was joined by a 1-ton van powered by a 10/12hp 2-cyl Aster petrol engine, a 24/30hp passenger model and a 25/40hp design using a 6-cyl petrol engine. By 1911 some models were being sold as Kerry-Thames and in 1911 an unusual stage coach style double-deck bus was developed. This particular vehicle was made in collaboration with Motor Coaches Ltd, London.

1977 Terex 33-07 dump truck

THIBAULT/*Canada c1946 to date*
Previously sold as Richelieu, fire appliances built by Pierre Thibault (Canada) Ltd since World War II are marketed as Thibault. Among custom-built machines is the 'Tribocar' enclosed pumper and various rigid and articulated appliances, all using Detroit Diesel engines.

THIRION/*France 1902-1904*
A Thirion et Fils, Paris, built fire appliances using a 2-cyl horizontal petrol engine under the driver's seat, driving the rear wheels via a 3-speed transmission and driveshaft. It had accommodation for five men and was fitted with two pumps, one at the front, the other at the back, both chain-driven from the propeller shaft.

THOMAS (1)/*USA 1905-1911*
The ER Thomas Motor Car Co, Buffalo, New York, built mainly light commercial chassis with 4-cyl petrol engines rated at between 14 and 16hp. One was used by the Maxim Motor Co as a basis for its first fire appliance.

THOMAS (2)/*USA 1906-1908*
The Thomas Wagon Co, Vernon, New York, began fitting air-cooled 2-cyl engines in its horse-drawn farm wagons. Other features included wheel steering, a friction transmission and double chain-drive. These were 3-tonners, their production was moved to a new factory in Lititz, Pennsylvania, for the last few months.

1904 Thornycroft 2-speed 3-ton "undertype" steam wagon

THORNYCROFT/*England 1896-1977*
John Isaac Thornycroft of John I Thornycroft & Co Ltd, Chiswick, West London, was a steam launch builder who constructed a 1-ton steam van with chain-drive to the front wheels and centre-pivot rear wheel steering. A marine-type vertical boiler was used and it was first publicly shown at the Crystal Palace Motor Show of 1896.

To handle series production the short-lived Thornycroft Steam Wagon Co Ltd was set up and the second Thornycroft wagon, an opposed-cyl tipping refuse truck, supplied to Chiswick Vestry the following year, making this one of the world's first true municipal vehicles and certainly one of the earliest tippers. Production moved to Basingstoke, Hants, in 1898 where one of the world's first articulated commercials was constructed, using a marine-type water-tube boiler and a compound engine with cyls located side-by-side driving the rear wheels by chain. This won the Premier Award at the Liverpool Self-Propelled Traffic Association's Trials later that year.

In 1900 a passenger version of the "undertype" wagon was exported to Burma and by 1902 a double-deck bus with vertical water-tube boiler and opposed-piston compound engine was on trial in London. Thornycroft wagons were specially popular overseas and a number of licence agreements were signed for overseas and even Scottish assembly. The Basingstoke company, however, was now becoming interested in internal-combustion engined vehicles, its first models being paraffin-fuelled and aimed particularly at the Colonies. Some were also supplied for military use.

By 1907 steamers had taken a back seat and petrol-engined commercials were rapidly gaining ground. The first were 4-tonners, soon joined by 1½-, 2- and 2½-ton types of which the latter were supplied in passenger as well as goods form. A new range, with 16hp 2- or 30hp 4-cyl petrol engines, went into production and in 1913 the 3-ton 'J'-Type "subsidy" model with 'T'-head petrol engine was introduced.

Sales slumped after the war but a 2- to 6-ton range was offered and

Thornycroft 'Q'-Type artic tractor c1924

from 1922 various new passenger models, including the 24-seat BZ, 30-seat 'Boadicea' and 34-seat 'Patrician' were listed. Soon after this, complete articulated trucks were built in various capacities from 4 to 12 tons. By 1923 prototype producer-gas vehicles were running and the following year a new "subsidy" type, the 1½-ton A1, was introduced incorporating engine, clutch and gearbox as one unit. This could also be had as a 20-seat bus or coach.

Britain's first production 4-wheel drive truck, the Thornycroft 'Hathi', appeared in 1924, developed from a War Office prototype, but few were built and the majority were exported. The A1 had now been joined by the 2-ton A2 and in 1926 a 6-wheeled version for 3 tons became the A3. Meanwhile, an earlier 2½-tonner was now called the KB, also having a unit engine and gearbox, and the long-running 'J'-Type became the JJ 5/6-tonner.

In 1927 the first 6-cyl engines were fitted in Thornycroft passenger models, with the debut of the 'Lightning' coach which also had 4-wheel servo brakes. The BC, a re-designed chassis for 32-seat bus or coach bodywork, appeared in 1929 and the HC 6-wheeler also announced that year employed a dropframe chassis with no front brakes, available as a double-decker for up to 68 persons. Another significant 1929

1948 Thornycroft SG/NR6 coach

being replaced by vehicles of forward-control layout, such as the 'Handy' and 'Dandy' for 2- and 3-ton payloads respectively, while the most popular mediumweight model was now the 4-ton 'Sturdy'. Heavier requirements were catered for by the 'Strenuous', 'Mastiff', 'Taurus' and 'Iron Duke', while the diesel-engined 6 x 4 'Amazon' with set-back front axle became popular as an off-road 6-tonner. A brand new model was the lightweight forward-control 'Stag' 6-wheeler with 6-cyl petrol or diesel engine and 8-speed transmission.

Another important development was the 7½/8-ton 'Trusty', also a lightweight, using a 4-cyl diesel engine. The first proprietary-engined Thornycroft was the 'Bullfinch', a 3-tonner with Dorman-Ricardo diesel engine. Gardner 6LW diesels were offered in certain passenger models. In 1935, a new version of the 'Sturdy', now with a 62bhp 4-cyl petrol engine, appeared and two

1955 Thornycroft 'Trident' truck

ton 8-wheeled version of the 'Trusty' even listed with petrol-injection from 1946. A 12-ton 6-wheeled export model was announced two years later as the 'Trident' but did not actually enter production until 1950. Another new model was the 'Sturdy Star', using a 4.18-litre 6-cyl direct-injection diesel engine. By the end of 1948 the company had been re-named Transport Equipment (Thornycroft) Ltd to differentiate it from John I Thornycroft & Co Ltd's boat-building firm.

A significant 1950 development was the 85-ton 6 x 4 'Mighty Antar' tractor powered initially by a 250bhp 18-litre Rover 'Meteorite' diesel engine driving the rear bogie through a 4-speed main and 3-speed auxiliary transmission. Although developed for oilfield use, it was soon adopted for use as a tank transporter tractor by the services. As well as the 'Sturdy Star', by 1952 there was also a 'Nippy Star' 4-tonner, and the 'Mighty Antar' was also being supplied in 4 x 2 artic tractor form. The 'Nubian' could now be had in 6-wheeled form. Developed from this was the 'Big Ben', which gradually became an intermediate model between the 'Nubian' and 'Mighty Antar', specially popular for oilfield use.

The 'Nippy Star' and 'Sturdy Star' were replaced by the 'Swift' and 'Swiftsure' about 1957, and a year later the plastics-cabbed 'Mastiff' 4-wheeler was announced. The 'Trusty' was also available in bonneted form and both the 'Big Ben' and 'Antar' (as a new lighter version was known) could be had in 'Sandmaster' desert versions.

A 4 x 4 dump truck was built

briefly in 1960, but increasing specialization in heavy-duty overseas models led to the company's take-over by AEC Ltd to form Associated Commercial Vehicles Ltd in 1961 and the gradual withdrawal of more conventional models in favour of AEC designs some of which were even built at Basingstoke.

Many Thornycrofts now had AEC diesel engines and spare production space was taken up with the manufacture of AEC transmissions. The product line was slimmed down to include only 4 x 4, 6 x 4 and 6 x 6 'Nubians' and the 'Big Ben' and 'Antar' types, the latter now having a 333bhp 16.2-litre supercharged 8-cyl Rolls-Royce diesel engine.

In 1964, the 6 x 6 'Nubian Major' fire crash tender chassis was introduced, which was to be the last Thornycroft to be built. The 1962 takeover of Associated Commercial Vehicles Ltd by the Leyland Group led to increasing model rationalization and by the late 1960s Thornycroft models were becoming increasingly associated with Scammell Motors, whose semi-trailers and light "mechanical horses" were built at Basingstoke for a while. In 1969, however, the Hampshire plant was sold and 'Nubian Major' production moved to Watford, Herts.

A year later the last "new" Thornycroft was announced. This was the 6 x 4 bonneted LD55 'Bush Tractor' based on the Aveling-Barford AB690 dump truck chassis, but often sold abroad under the Leyland name. Eventually, the 'Nubian Major' was replaced by the rear-engined Scammell 'Nubian' and the Thornycroft name vanished.

1935 Thornycroft 'Stag' 10/12-ton boxvans

model was the JC 10-ton 6-wheeled truck.

For 1931 new models included the 32-seat 'Cygnet' single-decker and a 4 x 2 double-decker called the 'Daring'. On the goods front, there was the 2-ton 'Bulldog', 2½-ton 'Speedy' and the bonneted 'Jupiter' which was the company's heaviest 4-wheeler at that time. By 1932 there were forty civilian models and although the company was now experimenting with diesel engines, these did not enter full production until at least 1933. Many bonneted designs were now

years later the 26-seat 'Beauty-ride' was its passenger derivative.

Production was now being concentrated increasingly on goods models which led naturally to numerous military orders during World War II. Some 20,000 military Thornycrofts were supplied during hostilities, including over 5000 3-ton 'Nubian' 4 x 4s, numerous versions of the 6 x 4 'Amazon' and 'Tartar', and militarized derivatives of the 'Sturdy'.

After the war, the 'Nippy', 'Sturdy' and 'Trusty' formed the backbone of the range, with a 15-

THOMAS (3)/*USA 1916-1917*

Charles K Thomas was the former Vice-President of the Federal Motor Truck Co when he founded the Thomas Auto Truck Co in New York. The sole product was a 2-ton assembled truck with 4-cyl Buda petrol engine, Covert-Brown-Lipe 3-speed transmission and Timken-David Brown overhead-worm back axle. Later, this company became part of the Consolidated Motors Corp.

THOMPSON/*USA 1905-1906*

The Thompson steamer was available as the Model 'A' delivery van and Model 'B' 10-seat wagonette. Both had a Stanley burner and 10hp Fitzhenry engine with drive via a single roller chain. They were built by the Thompson Automobile Co, Providence, Rhode Island.

THREE POINT/*USA 1919-1926*

The Three Point Truck Corp used the New York Air Brake Co's plant at Watertown, New York, to manufacture the unusual Three Point truck with its pivoting front axle. This marque also had radius rods at front and rear axles and a radiator similar to that of a Rolls-Royce. It was purely an assembled truck, available only as a 6-tonner after 1922. Although listed until 1926, production may have ended in 1924.

TIAO-JIN/*China 1958 to date*

Little is known of the early products of the Nanking Motor Vehicle Plant, Nanking, Kisngsu Province, which are sold as Tiao-Jin or T'Iao-Chin (Leap Forward). Current production includes the 2½-ton NJ-130, powered by a 79bhp 6-cyl engine, and the 1½-ton 4 x 4 NJ-230, with an 88bhp 6-cyl unit. The Wei-Xing (Satellite) bus range is also built here.

TIENTSIN/*China ? to date*

The Tientsin Bus Factory, Tientsin, Hopei Province, builds three passenger models as well as a 4 x 4 utility vehicle. Lightest of the buses is the 10-seat TJ-620 with 67bhp engine, while the intermediate design is the 23-seat TJ-644C with a 95bhp unit. The largest is the 41-seat TJ-660 articulated model with 110bhp engine and 5-speed transmission.

TIFFIN/*USA 1913-1923*

The first trucks to be built by the Tiffin Wagon Co, Tiffin, Ohio, comprised models of up to 1800kg capacity. Specifications included 4-cyl Buda or Continental sidevalve petrol engines, Hartford clutches, Bosch magnetos, 3-speed transmissions, Timken axles and double chain-drive.

For 1916 1½-, 5- and 6-tonners were added, all three having the option of double chain-drive or internal reduction gearing contained in drums mounted on the rear wheels, with electric lighting and starting fitted to all, except the 5- and 6-tonners. By about 1922 vehicle construction was being handled by the Tiffin Art Metal Co.

TITAN (1)/*USA 1917-c1932*

The first American-built Titan truck was a 5-tonner built by the Titan Truck & Tractor Co, Milwaukee, Wisconsin, using a 4-cyl petrol engine, 4-speed constant-mesh transmission and internal-gear final-drive. As the Titan Truck Co during the early 1920s, 2-, 2½- and 3½-ton trucks were introduced, using 4-cyl Buda engines, and by 1925 the smallest Titan was a 1-tonner.

TITAN (2)/*West Germany 1971 to date*

Titan Stahl und Geratebau GmbH, Berghaupten-Gengenbach, builds Titan special vehicles for logging, yard shunting, earthmoving and heavy haulage. Current production centres upon multi-axle chassis for crane-carrier and other duties with configurations of 6 x 4, 6 x 6, 8 x 4, 8 x 6, 10 x 4, 10 x 6 and 10 x 8, and other types of 4 x 4, 6 x 6 and 8 x 8 layout for use as dump trucks and heavy haulage tractors, the latter often derived from forward-control Mercedes-Benz models with strengthened chassis frames and ZF transmissions.

TMC/*USA 1975 to date*

A subsidiary of the Greyhound coach organization, the Transportation Mfg Corp, Roswell, New Mexico, has built almost all this operator's new vehicles since 1975, using the TMC name. This company also assembles the Orion city transit bus, designed by Ontario Bus & Truck Industries Inc, Missisauga, Ontario, marketing this also as the TMC or Citycruiser.

TMU/*Spain c1965*

Built by Thomas, Mintegue Uniguen, the TMU was a heavy-duty dump truck or tipper assembled from Mack, Pegaso and other vehicle components.

TOLEDO (1)/*USA 1901*

A manufacturer of light steam cars, the American Bicycle Co, Toledo, Ohio, also built a Toledo steam wagon. This had a water-tube boiler running on paraffin, a horizontal cross-compound engine with piston valves and Stephenson's link motion and internal-gear final-drive. With a capacity of about 2 tons, it was used daily

1925 Tilling-Stevens TS6 open-top double-deck bus

TILLING-STEVENS/*England 1911-1953*

Developed from the Hallford-Stevens petrol-electric bus, the Tilling-Stevens TTA1 was a joint venture of bus operator Thomas Tilling Ltd and engineers W A Stevens Ltd, Maidstone, Kent. Unlike its predecessor, the TTA1 had one traction motor obtaining current from a 20kw DC generator and driving the rear wheels via a shaft and overhead-worm rear axle. A distinguishing feature was its "coal-scuttle" bonnet and radiator behind the engine. A number of TTA1s, built by the newly formed Tilling-Stevens Ltd, entered passenger service but in 1913 the 40hp TTA2 appeared, some with single- and others with double-deck bodies.

1921 Tilling-Stevens charabanc

The re-designed TS3 arrived in 1914, sporting a conventional front-mounted radiator, and this was quickly joined by the improved TS4. After World War I the 2½-ton TSB4 and 4-ton TSB3 introduced conventional transmissions to the range but these were to remain in the background until at least the mid-1920s. Meanwhile, various other petrol-electric designs were announced, including the TS5, also available as a 4-ton truck, with 4-cyl twin-block 'L'-head petrol engine. The last petrol-electrics of this series were the TS6 and TS7 of the late 1920s, the former being offered as a normal- or forward-control type and the latter only in forward-control form.

By 1926 the conventional transmission range was increasing in popularity, particularly among passenger operators, leading to the introduction of the 'Express' single-decker. In 1929 the company attempted unsuccessfully to revive interest in the petrol-electric system and in 1930 Thomas Tilling Ltd disposed of the company which was re-named TS Motors Ltd, some models now being sold as TS or TSM. Sales were far from satisfactory, despite the launch of a new passenger range in 1932, but in 1938 the company managed to acquire the Vulcan Motor & Engineering Co Ltd, moving production to Maidstone.

Petrol-electric transmissions returned in the late 1930s with a special series of military trucks for use as mobile workshops, searchlight units, etc. Designated Types TS19 and TS20, these had Vulcan engines and incorporated a 2-speed Cotal gearbox on the rear axle to assist the vehicle on unmade ground. Soon after the war a 5-ton payload battery-electric truck got no further than prototype stage, but the 'K'-Series passenger range announced in 1947 was luckier, appearing in various forms using Gardner or Meadows diesel engines. The company's final offering was the 'Express' Mk II coach with 4-cyl Meadows engine offered until 1953, despite a Rootes Securities takeover in 1949.

1950 Tilling-Stevens coach

within the manufacturer's own factory.

TOLEDO (2)/*USA 1912-1913*
The Toledo truck range was announced following the takeover of the Rassel Motor Car Co by the Toledo Motor Truck Co, Toledo, Ohio. The Model 'A' was a 1-tonner with forward-control, a 4-cyl petrol engine, 3-speed transmission and double chain-drive.

TOMLINSON/*England 1947-1961*
The heaviest Tomlinson battery-electric was a 1-tonner built by Tomlinson (Electric Vehicles) Ltd, Minster Lovell, Oxon. It was a pedestrian-controlled model supplied either as a chassis or with bread van or milk float body.

TOWER/*USA 1915-1923*
The first Tower trucks were worm-drive 2-tonners, replaced in 1921 by a series of 2½- and 3½-tonners. Built by the Tower Motor Truck Co, Greenville, Michigan, the later models had 4-cyl Continental petrol engines, Fuller transmissions and Timken worm-drive axles.

TOWNMOBILE/*Australia c1965*
As an answer to Sydney's rapid transit problems, experiments got underway with battery, trolley and dual-mode passenger vehicles. Developed by Elray Engineering Pty Ltd, and known as the Townmobile system, designs were drawn up for a series of battery-powered buses (of which at least one was built) for up to 116 passengers, trolleybuses for faster operation and greater range and dual-mode vehicles capable of re-charging their batteries while running on the overhead wire system.

TOYOTA/*Japan 1935-1944, c1946 to date*
The Toyota Automatic Loom Works Ltd, Kariya City, entered the commercial vehicle business with a 1½-ton bonneted truck called the G1 with a 65bhp 3.4-litre 6-cyl petrol engine and 4-speed transmission.
Vehicle building activities were re-organized under the Toyota Motor Co Ltd in 1937 and by 1938 the G1 had been replaced by the 'GB'-Series. A 6-cyl diesel engine was developed in 1937 but did not enter production. A revised model was the 'KB' of 1942, which was assembled until 1944 when there was a short break before it re-appeared after the war. The 'BX' 4-tonner arrived in 1951 in both bonneted and forward-control form, gradually evolving into the 5-ton 'FA'- and 'DA'-Series, the latter having a diesel engine. By the late 1950s 4 x 4 and 6

1972 Toyota 'Hi-Ace' 1600 1-ton truck

x 6 military trucks were also in production.
Increasing numbers of lighter types were now being assembled, particularly up to 1½ tons payload, while the larger civilian models were now up-rated to 6 tons capacity with 4- or 5-speed synchromesh transmissions and optional 2-speed axles. By 1970 the forward-control 'Hi-Ace' had appeared for weights of up to about 1 ton, sometimes sold as Toyo-Ace, becoming the first Japanese commercial to be sold in Britain. Meanwhile, 'FA'-Series 6-tonners were now available with a 128bhp 4.2-litre petrol engine, but the heavier field was catered for by Hino Motors Ltd, which had become an associate company in 1966.
'FA' and 'DA' ranges are still offered, with the bottom end of the truck and bus market covered by the 2-ton semi forward-control 'Dyna' and delivery vans by the 1-ton 'Hi-Ace'.

TRABOLD/*USA 1911-1932*
The first truck built by the Trabold Truck Mfg Co, Johnstown,

Pennsylvania, was a chain-drive "cabover" powered by a 4-cyl petrol engine. By 1913 a range of bonneted commercials with 4-cyl Buda petrol engines had been launched and by 1915 bevel-gear drive was available on certain types with worm-drive adopted in 1923.
In 1922 the firm was re-named the Trabold Motors Co and in 1924 moved to Ferndale. Most popular were the 1½- and 2½-tonners, but standard trucks were not listed after 1929 when the firm became the Trabold Co, returning to Johnstown. Some of the last Trabolds had Lycoming straight-8 petrol engines and hydraulic 4-wheel brakes.

TRACKLESS/*England 1921-1924*
Although Trackless Cars Ltd was set up in Leeds, West Yorks, to build trolleybuses, only four were actually built. Many components were supplied by the nearby Kirkstall Forge and vehicle assembly undertaken by the Blackburn Aeroplane & Motor Co Ltd, also in Leeds. The four vehicles were

1921 Trackless trolleybus

double-deckers built for Leeds Corp, the most interesting feature being a front-wheel drive system enabling each vehicle to have a low floor height in the lower saloon. The front wheels were each driven by a traction motor mounted in a special fore-carriage which actually pivoted when the vehicle was cornering.

TRACKMOBILE/*England ? to date*
The Trackmobile is a special shunting tractor constructed by Strachan & Henshaw Ltd with both road and rail wheels for working in railway yards. It can manoeuvre across railway tracks to reach the wagons required and transfer to the track to move them. The most unusual feature is that the sets of road and rail wheels are set at 90° to each other, enabling the vehicle to move north-south for road work and east-west for rail.

TRAFFIC/*USA 1918-1929*
For a number of years the Traffic was a "one size" truck built by the Traffic Motor Truck Corp, St Louis, Missouri. It was an assembled 1800-kg vehicle with a 4-cyl Continental petrol engine, Covert 3-speed transmission and Russel internal-gear final-drive. Pre-1925 Traffics had a distinctive semi-circular crossmember at front and rear, the former serving also as a bumper, while post-1925 examples used conventional crossmembers.
By 1927 the range included 1½-, 2- and 3-ton models, using a larger 4.15-litre Continental petrol engine and a heavier Clark internal-gear rear axle while 1929 saw a short-lived 6-cyl engined 4-tonner.

TRANSICOACH/*USA 1948-1950*
The Crown Coach Corp, Los Angeles, California, was a distributor for Wayne passenger models after World War II but quickly combined with the Wayne Works, Richmond, Indiana, to build the Transicoach, based on C J Hug's sectional bus body system. Assembly took place in the Richmond factory, most vehicles having Hercules engines and 5-speed Fuller transmissions.

1970 Toyota Model 8000 DA115 6-ton truck

TRANSIT (1)/*USA 1902*

The manufacturer of Steamobile and Keene Steamobile steam passenger cars was the Steamobile Co, Keene, New Hampshire, which also built the Transit steam truck. This had a 6hp vertical double-acting 2-cyl engine, single chain-drive and a driver positioned at the rear with the load ahead.

TRANSIT (2)/*USA 1912-1916*

Built by the Transit Motor Car Co, Louisville, Kentucky, the first Transit truck was a chain-drive 3-tonner, using a 32hp petrol engine and 3-speed transmission. For 1913 1-, 2-, 3½- and 5-ton models were available, all with forward-control and double chain-drive. The company was re-organized as the Transit Motor Truck Co and for 1914 2- and 3½-ton rigids and a 5-ton dump truck were advertised. A 1-tonner was introduced for 1915, this having an underfloor engine, while all other types had the engine between the seats.

TRANSPORT (1)/*USA 1919-1925*

Using proprietary components, the Transport Truck Co, Mount Pleasant, Michigan, built 1-, 1½- and 2-ton trucks. These had Buda or Continental petrol engines and Fuller transmissions. When production ended, six models were offered, the company being known as the Transport Motor Truck Co.

TRANSPORT (2)/*England 1946-1948*

Glover, Webb & Liversidge Ltd, London SE1, manufactured refuse collection equipment, introducing the short-lived Transport front-wheel drive low-loading moving-floor refuse collection vehicle. Of integral construction, this had a 4-cyl Meadows petrol engine, David Brown transmission and a set-back steered and driven Moss front axle.

TRANSPORT TRACTOR/*USA 1915-1917*

The Transport Tractor Co Inc, Long Island City, New York, built the Transport Tractor, powered by a 25hp 4-cyl petrol engine, for handling 5-ton trailers. The driver was seated over the engine and other features included a 3-speed transmission with a bottom gear ratio of 45.8:1 and worm final-drive.

TRANTOR/*England 1977 to date*

Combining the functions of agricultural tractor, cross-country vehicle and commercial load carrier, the Trantor was developed by W H S Taylor Engineering Developments Ltd, Stockport, Cheshire. It resembles a conventional

1979 Trantor drawbar tractor

agricultural tractor but is fitted with a fully enclosed cab integral with the chassis/spaceframe, front and rear wings and a full complement of legal lighting, three cab seats and a folding ½-ton capacity load space. It is capable of speeds of up to 96km/h, and all wheels have air-assisted dual-line brakes. A special conversion kit enables cable-braked trailers to be hauled.

Power comes from a 78bhp Perkins 4.236 4-cyl diesel engine mounted at the front of the chassis/spaceframe which utilizes independent front suspension and rear leaf springs. A 2-speed non-live power take-off is provided at the front and the transmission for this vehicles is via an Eaton twin-range 10-speed box.

TRAULIER/*England 1932-1939*

Shelvoke & Drewry Ltd, Letchworth, Herts, took out a licence to manufacture the French Latil 4-wheel drive and 4-wheel steer tractor as the Traulier. Previously, sales had been handled by Latil Industrial Vehicles Ltd.

Some Trauliers were specially equipped for road/rail work and were known as Loco Trauliers, but a typical road-going Traulier of 1933 would have a 50bhp 4-cyl Latil side-valve petrol engine, a choice of low or high gear ratios and could cope with gross weights of up to 22 tons. The use of internal gearing in each of the four wheels unfortunately resulted in only a 823cm turning circle. Postwar production was handled, again under the Latil name, by a company called US Concessionaires Ltd, Ascot, Berks.

TRAYLOR/*USA 1920-1928*

Traylor trucks of 1¼-, 2-, 3- and 4-

ton capacity went into production in the Cornwells Heights, Allentown, Pennsylvania, factory of the Traylor Engineering & Mfg Co, using 4-cyl Buda petrol engines, Brown-Lipe 3- and 4-speed transmissions and Sheldon worm-drive rear axles. From 1925 the range comprised 1-, 1½-, 3- and 5-tonners.

1940 Triangel artic tractor

TRIANGEL/*Denmark 1918-1950*

The merger of H C Frederikson & Son with Automobilfabbriken Thrige and another automotive manufacturer resulted in the formation of Die Forenede Automobili Fabriken A/S, Odense, which launched Triangel commercials using, initially, the company's own 50bhp 4-cyl monobloc petrol engine. Models ranged from 2 to 5 tons capacity, one of the best-sellers of the 1920s being the 2½-ton 'Mignon'.

The first forward-control Triangel was the 'Special' of 1930, and other models of the period included the T35 3-tonner of 1936, T62 5-tonner of 1938 and a half-track 6-wheeler specially devel-

oped for the Danish Army. Diesel engines were first fitted in 1936, early types being Hercules units and later ones Danish-built Bur-Wains. One of the last trucks was the T50X 4½-tonner of 1941.

TRIANGLE/*USA 1917-1924*

The Triangle truck was built by the Triangle Motor Truck Co, St John's, Michigan. The first model was a 1½-tonner called the Model 'A' with a 4-cyl Waukesha petrol engine and 3-speed transmission. In 1920 this was joined by the 2½-ton Model 'B', with Rutenber petrol engine and 4-speed Fuller transmission, and in 1922 by the 1-ton 'AA' and 2-ton Model 'C', the former using a Herschell-Spillman petrol engine.

TRIBELHORN/*Switzerland 1902-1919*

One of the first commercials built by A Tribelhorn & Cie, Feldbach, was a 5-ton truck and by 1907 a battery-electric bus with a top speed of 14km/h was advertised. By 1917 various battery-electric models for up to 5 tons payload had been constructed, usually with forward-control layout and with chain final-drive. Specially popular for municipal use, they were re-named EFAG when the business was re-organized as Elektrische Fahrzeuge AG.

TRITRACTOR/*England 1925*

The Tritractor was a short-wheelbase 3-wheeled tipper built by Tritractor Ltd, London EC2. It had a capacity of 6½ tons and in prototype form was powered by a rear-mounted Continental petrol engine with the tipping body ahead of the driver. What appeared to be a single wheel at the front was in fact two located side by side. Production models had a one-man cab and an AEC engine located at the front, with tipping body behind. Many other components were also of AEC origin, including both the transmission system and radiator.

TROJAN (1)/*USA 1937-1940*

The first heavy dump trucks built

by the Trojan Truck Mfg Co, Los Angeles, California, were powered by 190bhp Caterpillar V8 engines with conventional sliding-gear transmissions and an auxiliary box. Nine forward and 3 reverse speeds were available and final-drive to the tandem-drive bogie was effected by a central drive-shaft and sprockets inside the wheels. The massive chassis frame was assembled from four channel-section side-rails located inside each other. The 14cu m scow-end body had a capacity of approximately 70 tons.

TROJAN (2)/*England c1949-1962*
After World War II light commercials built by Trojan Ltd, Croy-

1960 Trojan minicoach

don, Surrey, were superseded by a new 1-tonner, with 24bhp 2-stroke engine. Customer resistance to the unorthodox power unit led to the announcement of an electric version called the Electrojan in 1951. By 1956 a 32bhp Perkins P3 diesel was optional and production of the electric model ended. The 1-tonner was·also available as a passenger vehicle or, in conjunction with Carrimore Six Wheelers Ltd, as a 1¼-ton payload artic up to 1959, when it was replaced by a forward-control model offered in 1¼-ton chassis/scuttle, chassis/cab, 9cu m van or 12-seat personnel carrier form. Again powered by a Perkins P3 diesel, this had independent suspension all round and was later sold in artic form.

TSINGHUA/*China ? to date*
The Tsinghua University Machine Shop, Tsinghua, near Peking, builds 2-ton "cabover" trucks as a training exercise for students.

TUBUS/*Spain 1940-1952*
La Hispano de Fuente en Segures SA, Castellon de la Plana, was a

bus operator which also built Tubus buses due to losses incurred during the Spanish Civil War. Initially, these were based on Bedford chassis but later the company built its own chassis and fitted engines by AEC, Cummins and Perkins.

TUDOR/*England 1979 to date*
Tudor Vehicle Imports (UK) Ltd offers the Rumanian-built Aro and TV ranges on the British market as the Tudor. Both have common components and are available in a number of different forms such as chassis/cab, pick-up, van and minibus form.

TULSA/*USA 1913-1916*
The Tulsa Automobile and Mfg Co, Tulsa, Oklahoma, built 1- and 1½-ton Tulsa trucks. It is believed that this company was formed from the Harman Motor Truck Co, Chicago, Illinois, and the Pioneer Automobile Co, Oklahoma City, Oklahoma.

TURBINE/*USA 1904*
The Turbine was a unique and unusual vehicle built briefly by the Turbine Electric Truck Co, New York. It had a Roberts water-tube boiler supplying steam to a 24hp engine which in turn drove a generator. This then supplied current to two General Electric traction motors which drove the rear wheels. It was a huge machine with a wheelbase of 287cm, track of 183cm, and with an unladen weight of 6 tons. Both of its axles were centrally pivoted for suspension purposes.

TURGAN/*France 1900-1907*
The first commercial built by Turgan, Foy et Cie was a steam omnibus, which was entered in the Paris Commercial Vehicle Trials. By 1905 3- and 6-ton single-speed steam wagons had been built, us-

ing a coal-fired double-drum water-tube boiler ahead of the driver and two compound engines under his seat, each driving a rear wheel via a long chain. Later that year a 24hp 4-cyl petrol-engined chassis was developed and adopted both for goods and passenger work, followed in 1907 by a forward-control 4-tonner with circular radiator and double chain-drive.

TURNER-MIESSE/*England 1906-c1909*
Thomas Turner & Co, Wolverhampton, Staffs, licence-built Belgian-designed Miesse steam vehicles, marketing these as Turner-Miesse. The steam wagons were intended for payloads of about 1½ tons, employing a paraffin-fired vertical boiler and a horizontal 3-cyl single-acting engine under the body. Transmission was via a countershaft differential and double roller chains.

By 1909 the company had been re-named Turner's Motor Mfg Co Ltd, moving to larger premises, although steam wagon production is said to have finished at about this time.

TUTTLE/*USA 1913-1914*
The 1½-ton Tuttle was built by the Tuttle Motor Co, Caneastota, New York. It had a 4-cyl Hazard petrol engine, Sheldon axles and Sheldon spoked wheels. Wheelbase was 330cm and worm final-drive was used.

TV/*Rumania 1960 to date*
Uzina Autobuzul Tudon Vladiminescu, Bucharest, originally built buses and trolleybuses using SR components but later introduced a light- to mediumweight forward-control commercial range based

on the even lighter Soviet UAZ. Numerous Aro components, including engines, transmissions and axles, were used. These were up-dated in 1969 and a 4 x 4 derivative announced. Three capacities now covered payloads of up to 1250kg. Current models are powered by a rear-mounted 140bhp V8 petrol engine and sold as Aro in some countries but Tudor in Britain.

TVW/*England c1956-1962*
Transport Vehicles (Warrington) Ltd, Warrington, Lancs, fitted Commer TS3 2-stroke engines in 6-wheeled Sentinel goods models, calling these TVWs. Instead of using the normal under-chassis position, these were front-mounted and when Sentinel production ceased in 1957, the Warrington firm acquired all remaining components and commenced full assembly the following year of 4-, 6- and 8-wheeled rigid goods models, using Commer, Leyland and Meadows engines.

As stocks of Sentinel cabs were exhausted, so Boallay cabs were fitted, and models cut down to one 4- and one 8-wheeler. The 4-wheeler used the TS3 engine and a Meadows transmission, while the 8-wheeler had a 6-cyl Gardner diesel and David Brown main and auxiliary boxes. Most were used by local hauliers.

TWIN CITY (1)/*USA 1913-1914*
Frank R Brasie of the Brasie Motor Truck Co, Minneapolis, Minnesota, developed a forward-control chain-drive 2-ton truck which he marketed as the Twin City, although it was often known as the Brasie. However, he decided to concentrate on lighter types and

1958 TVW 7-ton truck

293

the company was re-named the Brasie Motor Car Co, light commercials being sold as Packet.

TWIN CITY (2)/USA 1917-1922

Built simultaneously by the Twin City Four Wheel Drive Co Inc, St Paul, Minnesota, and the Four Wheel Drive Mfg Co, Minneapolis, Minnesota, the 4 x 4 Twin City truck was based on designs laid down by J L Ware who had previously built Ware trucks. The Twin City was a 2- or 5-tonner, both powered by a 4-cyl petrol engine and fitted with a 3-speed transmission and 4-wheel brakes.

TWIN CITY (3)
USA 1918-1929

The Minneapolis Steel & Machinery Co, Minneapolis, Minnesota, built "conventional" shaft-drive trucks which it sold as the Twin City. Available in various capacities between 2 and 3½ tons, they were joined by passenger models such as the DW parlour coach, a low-slung 25-seater with 60bhp petrol engine and air springs at the front.

TWISTER DRAGON WAGON/
USA 1972 to date

The Twister Dragon Wagon started life as an experimental 8 x 8 on/off-road machine built by the Lockheed Missiles & Space Co Inc, Sunnyvale, California. Of forward-control layout, it has a 225bhp Caterpillar diesel engine, Allison 6-speed transmission with 2-speed transfer box driving the rear four or all eight wheels.

Models use Rockwell-Standard tandem bogies at front and rear, with independent walking-beam suspension throughout, steering being effected by a universally-jointed fully-articulating chassis frame. Maximum speed is claimed to be 88km/h and the vehicle is capable of climbing a 60° gradient.

TWYFORD/USA 1906

The Twyford Motor Car Co, Brookville, Pennsylvania, introduced a 16hp truck powered by a vertical 2-cyl petrol engine, but this is likely to have been built only as a prototype, and a series of 6-, 10- and 15-seat buses may not have been built at all.

TWIN COACH
USA 1927-1953

Frank and William Fageol registered the Twin Coach Corp, Kent, Ohio, to construct a revolutionary single-deck passenger model powered by two 55bhp 6-cyl Waukesha petrol engines located behind the front axle and under the seats. Thus, the vehicle's entire length was free of any mechanical intrusion and entry/exit doors could be positioned ahead of the front axle and behind the rear axle if required.

In 1929 a much lighter single-engined version was introduced, also sold as Twin Coach, and a series of multi-stop delivery vans, mainly 1-tonners, with front- or rear-wheel drive developed. These could be had with petrol or battery-electric propulsion from 1930. Both twin- and single-engined passenger models were replaced by a new rear-engined series about 1935, some of the lightest models using an engine-over-axle rather than engine-behind-axle layout.

In 1936 the light delivery range was sold to Continental-Divco to provide greater capacity for new diesel-electric city buses announced the previous year, while 1938 saw the debut of the unique 'Super Twin' with four axles and seating for 58 passengers. This was not a true articulated model as it was only hinged vertically between the close-spaced second and third axles to reduce road shocks and handle gradients and both 1st and 4th axles steered. Two 3-axle versions were also built but the 'Super Twin' developed no further.

After World War II a new design incorporated an underfloor 6-cyl high-compression petrol engine of the company's own make coupled to a Spicer torque-converter transmission. Some 41- and 44-seaters again had two engines but this idea was short-lived. So far, the company had never used diesel engines, preferring to rely

1930 Twin Coach single-deck bus

upon the economics and flexibility of twin petrol units, but now operators were crying out for good diesel-engined vehicles and the company could offer none. Sales declined rapidly and in an attempt to save the business an lpg-fuelled engine was developed. This fuel was easy to obtain and relatively cheap, so some operators began converting existing twin-coach vehicles, while others placed new orders. One customer ordered 500 lpg engines. In 1953 the business was sold to the Flxible Company.

The Kent, Ohio, plant was eventually purchased by the Highway Products Co, which announced new passenger models as the Twin Coach Highway.

1947 Twin Coach 41-S single-deck bus

U

UDPX/*France 1906*
Prunel commercials, built by Soc des Usines Prunel, Puteaux, Seine, were re-named UDPX in 1906. These used a new 35hp 4-cyl petrol engine and some producer-gas versions were built both in normal- and forward-control form. Production was short-lived.

UERDINGEN/*Germany/West Germany 1930-1958*
Using Krupp components, railway wagon builder Waggonfabrik Uerdingen AG, Uerdingen, Krefeld, constructed the first modern German trolleybus, marketing this as the Uerdingen. Later the company's first chassisless model appeared, and by 1949 a new range based on Henschel running units was announced. An unusual feature was a Volkswagen petrol engine which could be used to run a generator to provide current to the traction motor so that the vehicle could operate over short distances without relying on its overhead supply. The 1950s saw a number of chassisless rigid and artic vehicles using Büssing components, but with decreasing interest in trolleybuses, production ended.

ULTIMATE/*USA 1919-1925*
Sold as the 2-ton Model 'A', 3-ton Model 'B' and the AJL and BU passenger models, Ultimate commercials were built by the Vreeland Motor Co Inc, Hillside, New Jersey, powered by a 4-cyl Buda petrol engine. Passenger versions had capacities of between 25 and 30, with Westinghouse electric lighting and starting, while the larger of the two was the only Ultimate commercial built after 1923.

UNIMOG/*West Germany 1948 to date*
Gebr Bohringer GmbH, Göppingen, developed the 4 x 4 Unimog for agricultural use. It could be operated as a 1½-ton truck or as a farm tractor, powered by a 1.7-litre 4-cyl Mercedes-Benz diesel engine. Manufacturing rights were bought in 1951 by Daimler-Benz AG, which set up production in its

Unic 'Izoard' artic tractor c1964

UNIC/*France 1909 to date*
Starting with taxicabs and light commercials in 1905, Soc des Ans Ets Georges Richard, Puteaux, Seine, later introduced shaft-drive petrol-engined Unic commercials from 1¼ to 2½ tons capacity with a chain-drive option on the heaviest. Large-scale production began in 1911 with the 2-ton 'O'-Type, also available as a 15-seat coach and fitted with a 3.3-litre 'L'-head monobloc petrol engine by 1913.

Re-named SA des Automobiles Unic in 1914, an up-dated range was available by 1919, employing full electrics, 4-speed transmission and pneumatic tyres, and by 1925 the company's first 3-tonner, the 3-litre M5C, was advertised. In 1929 a dropframe passenger model was listed. The first true Unic "heavies" were developed in 1931, these being the bonneted CD2 and CD3 4- and 6-wheelers, using a licence-built 8.6-litre 6-cyl Mercedes-Benz diesel engine, double-reduction final-drive and vacuum-servo brakes.

By 1934 Unics were available from just under a ton to 11 tons capacity, all of bonneted layout, including a half-track powered by a 2.2-litre petrol engine. During World War II the company joined with Bernard, Delahaye, Laffly and Simca, but this arrangement was short-lived and in 1946 the normal-control ZU range was launched with 4- or 8-speed transmissions. The heaviest version, a 7-tonner, was powered by a 110bhp 9.8-litre 6-cyl diesel engine and lighter models had a 6.8-litre 4-cyl unit.

In 1951 the company began to collaborate with Simca but there were few new models up to 1955 apart from some all-wheel drive derivatives. The firm was now building smaller OMs under licence, and in 1956 took over Saurer's French interests, introducing

Unic cabs on French-built Saurers which were sometimes sold as Unic-Saurer. Considerable re-styling took place in 1957, and in 1958 the company became SA Unic, the heavy vehicle division of Simca.

By 1960, when forward-control models went into full production, a 5-ton bonneted model used Fiat front-end metal, and by 1964 the company's most powerful 6-cyl diesel engine was a 210bhp turbocharged unit. Tractors for gross weights up to 65 tons were soon offered, and a new 10.8-litre V8 diesel engine produced up to 270bhp in standard form. Meanwhile the Unic-Willème was a Willème tractor unit with a Unic diesel engine. By 1966 synchromesh transmissions were standard, and by the end of the year Fiat SpA had acquired the business, re-naming it Fiat France SA; some models were sold as Unic-Fiat.

A new tiltcab made its appearance in 1968, and 7.4-litre OM diesel engines were fitted in certain models. More integration had

occurred by 1970 when regular Unics were identical to some Fiats now that the bonneted Unics had been withdrawn, and the latest Unic diesel engine, a 340bhp 14.9-litre V8, was fitted in some of the heavier Fiats.

A brand new truck plant had been constructed in 1973 at Trappes and production moved there. Since then, the company has taken over assembly of all Fiats in the 10 to 16 tons GVW sector but the Unic name is used only on vehicles sold in France and Belgium. Among these are a number of 4 x 4 and 6 x 6 normal-control models for the French construction industry using Magirus-Deutz cabs and components as a result of Fiat's IVECO connection.

Unic 'Vosges' truck c1969

1926 Unic C9L6 1¼-ton truck

UNIC-WILLEME/*France c1965*
A short-lived merger between the French manufacturers SA Unic and Ets Willème brought about the Unic-Willème, a Willème tractor unit fitted with a Unic diesel engine.

1960 Unic-Willème artic tractor

1979 Unimog U1300L water tender fire appliance

Gaggenau plant. A more powerful version, using the company's 2.2-litre 6-cyl petrol engine, arrived in the form of the Unimog 'S'-Type in 1954, making it even more versatile.

The Unimog is now advertised in a variety of forms for a wide range of applications, using engines from 34 to 150bhp output. There is even a 6 x 6 conversion and a 4 x 2 front-drive conversion with hydraulically-lifted low-loading body.

UNION (1)/*USA 1901-1904*
The Union, built in Philadelphia, Pennsylvania, had a high centre of gravity with a 2-cyl petrol engine slung beneath the chassis frame. Built by the Union Motor Truck Co, it had a "reversible roller ratchet and movable crank-pin" transmission.

UNION (2)/*USA 1912-1914*
The Model U-1 Union was a 1½-tonner built by the Union Motor Truck Co, San Francisco, California. A 2-tonner was introduced later.

UNION (3)/*USA 1917-1925*
Assembly of a 2½-ton truck using proprietary components got underway in the Union Motor Truck Co's Bay City, Michigan plant. In 1921 it was joined by 4- and 6-ton models which had Wisconsin petrol engines, Fuller transmissions, and bevel-gear axles. By 1925 the line comprised 1½-, 2½- and 4-tonners.

UNION (4)/*England 1935-1939*
Specializing in the haulage of

drawbar trailers around London's dockland, the Union Cartage Co Ltd, London E3, built its own heavy road tractors, fitting Gardner 5LW diesel engines. The Union tractor was of bonneted layout, incorporating components taken from withdrawn vehicles, although some had Fowler 'Warrior' tractor chassis. The last Union incorporated both Foden and Fowler components.

UNITAS/*Scotland 1919-1924*
The Unitas truck was built only for the Scottish Co-Operative Wholesale Society Ltd, Glasgow, by Belhaven Engineering & Motors Ltd, Wishaw, Lanarks, using a normal Belhaven chassis sporting a radiator bearing the Unitas name. All Unitas trucks were bodied by the operator, some finding their way into the fleet of the United Co-operative Baking Society.

UNITED (1)/*USA 1915-1930*
A United truck range was built by

1966 Unimog 'S' 4 x 4 drawbar tractor

1939 Union (4) drawbar tractor

the United Motor Truck Co, Grand Rapids, Michigan, in capacities of 1½, 3 and 5 tons. All had 4-cyl Continental petrol engines, the two smaller having worm-drive, the larger chain-drive. In 1916 the company was re-named the United Motors Co and by the early 1920s various models from 1 to 5 tons capacity were listed.

In 1922 the business became the United Motors Products Co, and from 1923 Herschell-Spillman, Waukesha and Wisconsin engines were fitted, although a 1/1½-tonner of 1926 used United's own engine and later versions had Hercules units. In 1927 the firm was taken over by the Acme Motor Truck Co, although the United name continued.

UNITED (2)/*USA 1917-1920*
The United Four-Wheel Drive Co, Chicago, Illinois, built 4 x 4 United trucks, but no information is available. Some claim the firm took over the Lamson Truck & Tractor Co, Chicago, in about 1919, continuing Lamson truck manufacture until 1920.

UNITED STATES/*USA 1909-1930*
The first United States or US truck, built by the United States Motor Truck Co, Cincinnati, Ohio, had a 20hp flat-twin engine located under the seat and double chain-drive. By 1912 this had been joined by a 1½-ton "cabover" and 3-ton "conventional", both using 4-cyl petrol engines, and in 1916 new 3½-, 4-, and 5-tonners, with worm- or chain-drive, were added. During the 1920s, the company became the United States Motor Truck Co Inc. Continental and Hinkley engines were used but Buda units were later adopted.

UNIVERSAL/*USA 1910-1920*
The first Universal was a forward-control 3-tonner with a 330-cm wheelbase. It was built by the Universal Motor Truck Co, Detroit, Michigan, and fitted with a 30hp 4-cyl petrol engine and double chain final-drive. One- and 2-tonners were announced in 1913, the smallest having shaft-drive, and by 1915 the 1-tonner had been up-rated to 1½ tons payload. Production was taken over by the Universal Service Co in 1916.

UPPERCU/*USA 1924-1927*
With the acquisition of Healy & Co, Inglis M Uppercu's Aeromarine Plane & Motor Corp, Keport, New Jersey, began building ambulances, hearses and other special types on Cadillac passenger car chassis and in 1924 front-wheel drive single- and dou-

1968 Unipower 'Invader' prototype 4 x 4 truck chassis-cab (left-hand vehicle)

UNIPOWER/*England 1937 to date*

The 4-wheel drive bonneted Unipower tractor was built by Universal Power Drives Ltd, Perivale, Middx, for industrial and forestry use in 1937. Early models were petrol- or diesel-powered, the former using an 85bhp 6-cyl Hercules unit and the latter a 4LW Gardner. Standard components included a single dry-plate clutch, 5-speed main and 2-speed auxiliary box and Rzeppa high-angle constant-velocity joints driving all four wheels. Girling wedge-operated brakes were actuated by a Clayton Dewandre vacuum-servo system.

The 'Hannibal' and 'Forester' models were the most popular, with only a few 4-wheel steer 'Centipedes' produced from 1956. In addition to assembling complete vehicles, the company also did third axle conversions on Commer goods models, marketing these as Commer-Unipower.

Re-named Unipower Ltd, in 1968 the company launched a new forward-control 4 x 4, the 'Invad-

Unipower 'Hannibal' 4 x 4 drawbar tractor c1961

er', using a 170bhp Perkins V8 diesel. In 1972 this model was redesignated the P44 and offered with Cummins or Rolls-Royce diesel engines. Subsequent versions have been supplied as airfield fire crash tenders, more recently by AC Cars Ltd, Thames Ditton, Surrey, who acquired the business in 1977.

ble-deck buses were developed as the Uppercu. Only two double- and thirty single-deck models were built before production ended. These had quickly removable Continental petrol engines and transmissions, although examples built after 1925 are said to have had 6-cyl Waukesha units.

UPTON/*USA 1902-1903*

The Upton Machine Co's "bread and butter" was the manufacture of planetary transmissions, although some trucks were also built. The company's factory was at Beverly, Massachusetts. Models included a 2-tonner with 10hp 4-cyl petrol engine and a 3-tonner with 20hp 4-cyl petrol engine, both having planetary transmis-

sions, wheel steering and double chain-drive.

URAL/*Soviet Union c1960 to date*

The earliest Urals were based on the Ural-ZIS, but of far more rugged construction. One of the first was the Ural-375D 5-ton 6 x 6. Built by Ulyanovska Automobile Zavod, Ulyanovska, this has a 200bhp V8 petrol engine and 5-speed transmission. A 6 x 4 model, the Ural-377, was developed in

1971 Ural-375 6 x 6 tanker

1965 and is now offered in both tractor and rigid form or as a dump truck.

URAL-ZIS/*Soviet Union c1942-c1960*

To protect ZIS truck production during World War II, part of the assembly operation was moved from the Zavod Imieni Stalina factory, Moscow, to Ulyanovska where a new plant was opened to build the Ural-ZIS range. Although based on the ZIS, models were not similar.

One of the first was a normal-control 3-tonner using a 76bhp 6-cyl petrol engine, followed by a 2½-ton producer-gas truck sold as the Ural-ZIS-352. These continued after the war but the 3-tonner was replaced by the Ural-ZIS-355 in 1956 and in 1958 by the 355M 3½-tonner. Later, the marketing name was shortened to just Ural.

URBAN/*USA 1911-1918*

Built by the Kentucky Wagon Mfg Co, Louisville, Kentucky, the Urban battery-electric had Edison alkaline batteries and double chain-drive. Both open and closed bodies were offered on wheelbases up to 325cm, with capacities up to 2 tons.

URSUS/*Poland 1924-1939*

Zaklady Mechaniczne Ursus SA, Czechowice, Warsaw, built Ursus goods and passenger models powered by imported Citröen or locally-built Fiat petrol engines. Most popular was the 1½/2-ton payload Type 'A', based on Italian SPA designs. Prototype Star chassis were built in this factory but World War II terminated commercial vehicle production. Since then only agricultural tractors have been built.

UTIC/*Poland 1967*

The coachbuilding firm of Uniao de Transportadores Para Importacao e Comercia Ltd, Lisbon, acted as agent for AEC and Leyland commercials, later assembling chassisless passenger models with AEC or Leyland underfloor diesel engines and running gear, marketed as UTIC. AEC-based models have been withdrawn, but Leyland-based types are still available. These are being built in factories which are at Lisbon and Porto.

UTILITY/*USA 1910-1912*

Available in 1- and 3-ton form, the Utility was a forward-control truck with a 4-cyl petrol engine. It was built by the Stephenson Motor Car Co, South Milwaukee, Wisconsin, both models having friction transmissions and double chain-drive.

V

VABIS/*Sweden 1903-1911*

The first truck built by Vagnfabriks Aktiebolaget i Södertälje was a 1500kg payload design with 15hp 'V'-twin engine and front-mounted radiator. Influenced by early Benz types, this had semi-elliptic leaf springs, shaft-drive and bonnet. A 4-cyl engine was developed soon after and in 1906 a 2-ton shaft-drive lorry appeared, followed by a chain-drive 3-tonner. Fire appliances were also built but by 1910, management was realizing that both models

1903 Vabis 1½-ton truck

and facilities were similar to those of Scania Maskinenfabriks AB and discussions with that company led to their merger to form Scania-Vabis AB, vehicles being sold as Scania-Vabis.

VALLEY/*USA 1927-1929*

Also known as the Valley-Dispatch, the Valley truck range was previously sold as Huffman, changing when the Huffman Bros Motor Co, Elkhart, Indiana, became the Valley Motor Truck Co. With capacities of between 2½ and 4 tons, trucks had mainly Her-

cules petrol engines but production lasted only until the Elkhart Motor Truck Co was formed and the product was then renamed Elkhart.

1978 Valmet Model 1542 6 x 4 aircraft towing tractor

VALMET/*Finland 1945 to date*

Valmet Oy, Helsinki, built diesel and agricultural engines and railway locomotives when it introduced a single-deck trolleybus. This was short-lived, but since then the company has developed a range of all-wheel drive timber tractors and military vehicles. The majority are of 4 x 4 configuration, powered by the company's own 82bhp diesel engine. Articulated steering is used and a derivative is a military gun tractor and troop-carrier, powered by an uprated Valmet diesel engine of 90bhp output and equipped with a front-mounted power winch. Another development is a 6 x 6 timber tractor with a 135bhp Scania diesel engine.

VANAJA/*Finland 1948-1967*

Vanajan Autotehdas Oy, Helsinki, collaborated with Oy Suomen Autoteollisuus to build Yhteissisu military trucks during World War II, and broke away to develop its own Vanaja range. Early versions were powered by a 5-litre 6-cyl petrol engine, but by 1954 a 5.7-litre diesel unit was standard. Both normal- and forward-control passenger models were listed, and by the late 1950s Vanaja trucks used AEC diesel engines of 7.7-, 9.6- and 11.1-litre capacities. Both 4- and 6-wheeled trucks were advertised, the 6 x 4s being unusual in that drive was taken to the front steering axle, and it had only one bogie

1970 Vanaja TTB 8 x 4 truck-crane

In 1958 an underfloor-engined passenger model called the VLK500 was announced, but before 1968 the business was acquired by Oy Suomen Autoteollisuus and the Vanaja name was discontinued.

VAN-L/*USA 1911-1912*

One-, 1½- and 2-ton Van-L trucks

1961 Vanaja 4 x 4 artic tractor

were offered by the Van-L Commercial Car Co, Grand Rapids, Michigan. All were of forward-control layout, with 4-cyl petrol engines, 3-speed transmissions and double chain-drive.

VAN TWIST/*Netherlands 1955-1967*

Gaining vehicle construction experience by assembling the British-designed Seddon range for the Dutch market, Kemper en Van Twist Diesel NV, Dordrecht, announced the Van Twist series. These were based on the Seddon, having a Perkins diesel engine, Moss transmission and Kirkstall axles. Five models were listed, including one normal-control type, but were never successful.

V-CON/*USA 1971 to date*

Built by the Vehicle Constructors Divn of the Marion Power Shovel Co Inc, Dallas, Texas, V-Con dump trucks are available in four sizes from 250 to 270 tons capacity. All are diesel-electric models using turbocharged 8- or 12-cyl Alco or 12- or 16-cyl Detroit Diesel engines of up to 3000bhp output, mounted amidships and driving a generator which passes current to General Electric traction motors mounted in the wheels. The eight wheels are positioned 4-abreast and normally six are driven. The four front wheels steer in pairs, providing a 15-m turning circle. Brakes are hydraulic, with electronic actuation, using disc units on all powered wheels and internal-expanding drums on the non-powered. Because of their size, V-Con dump trucks are usually assembled on site.

VEC/USA 1901-1906
The Vehicle Equipment Co, Brooklyn, New York, built goods and passenger battery-electrics, selling these as VE, VEC, or even Vehicle Equipment Co. In 1902 an ambulance was supplied with batteries slung beneath the chassis frame. Tiller steering was employed and an electric motor drove the rear wheels direct. Many of America's early sight-seeing buses were supplied by the company, which also built brewer's drays, coal trucks and specialist vehicles. In 1905 production moved to Long Island City, but the company was soon known as the General Vehicle Co, marketing its products as GV.

VEERAC/USA 1910-1914
The Veerac Motor Co was founded in Minneapolis, Minnesota, to build the 1-ton Veerac delivery model. The Veerac name was derived from the company's own 20hp 2-cyl 2-stroke air-cooled engine which was described as "Valveless, Explosion Every Revolution, Air-Cooled". It had a planetary transmission and chain-drive, speed being governed to a maximum of 24km/h. For the final year, production continued at Anoka, Minnesota.

VERITY/England 1899
EA Verity, of the Verity Motor Co, Bradford, Yorks, built a single "undertype" steam wagon, using his own design of flash boiler. It was coke-fired with final-drive by roller chains running on sprockets inside each rear wheel.

1964 Verro 'City' road-sweeper

VERRO/Sweden ? to date
Verro produces a range of pur-pose-built street sweepers employing brushes and suction. The larger models follow the accepted practice of cab-over-engine layout and are based on mediumweight truck components, while lighter types use a rear cab layout and rear-wheel steering for greater manoeuvrability.

VETERAN/Canada 1920
Designed by ex-servicemen, the Veteran was built at Sherbrooke, Quebec. It was a 3½-tonner with a 4-cyl Buda petrol engine, Cotta 3-speed transmission, overhead-worm drive and fully-enclosed all-steel cab. Some were supplied to the Canadian Post Office.

VETTER/West Germany 1980 to date
Walter Vetter, Fellbach, has developed a 12-m single-drive 6-wheeled chassisless double-deck passenger model for use as a service or school bus during the week and as a private coach at weekends. Powered by a rear under-floor OM 407HA diesel engine, it incorporates a toilet and galley and for normal bus operation caters for 102 seated and 17 standee passengers.

The rearmost lower saloon seats and two tipping courier seats in the forward step well are all removable to provide an alternative seating plan for weekend running, when the rearmost downstairs section can be transformed into a baggage hold. The main entrance is located just ahead of the rear bogie, with direct access to the 7-step staircase to the upper saloon.

A series of articulated single-deckers is also being developed.

1961 Viberti CV64 double-deck bus

VIBERTI/Italy 1953-1966
Officine Viberti Torino SpA, Turin, was principally a vehicle body-builder but also constructed chassisless large-capacity city buses with Fiat, Lancia, OM or Pegaso engines and running units, as well as airfield fire crash tenders, fuel tankers and heavy dump trucks.

Also known as the 'Monotral', the first passenger Vibertis were based on 4 x 2 and 6 x 4 running units using horizontal rear-mounted engines and air suspension. In 1956 a luxury coach was shown in prototype form, and in 1960 6 x 4 double-deckers were built for use in Turin, each having a capacity of 140 persons and using a 250bhp front-mounted diesel engine and 4-speed automatic transmission. Another high-capacity model was the artic CV60, which carried 130 passengers when hauling a 4-wheeled trailer.

1970 Vickers-AWD Model V518 8 x 4 crane-carrier chassis-cab

VICKERS-AWD/England 1966-1971
Although called Vickers All Wheel Drive since 1962, the crane-carriers built by this company, based in Swindon, Wilts, did not carry the Vickers-AWD brand name until 1966. Both 6- and 8-wheelers were built, one of the most unusual being the V531 6-wheeled twin-steer unit used as a basis for the Iron Fairy 'Zircon' 10-ton hydraulic telescopic boom model. With the exception of the V518 8 x 4 carrier, all models carried a low-silhouette version of the Motor Panels cab, and in 1971 the business was acquired by the 600 Group with all subsequent models sold as Crane Travellers.

VICTOR (1)/USA 1910-1914
The Victor Motor Truck Co, Buffalo, New York, offered five de-livery vans as well as ambulances, police patrol vans, fire appliances and buses during its first production year. By 1912 seven trucks, from 1 to 10 tons capacity, were listed but from then until the line ceased only 3- and 5-tonners were offered.

VICTOR (2)/USA 1918-1920
With a wheelbase of 350cm, 1½- and 2-ton Victor trucks were built by the Victor Motor Truck & Trailer Co, Chicago, Illinois. Both had 4-cyl Continental petrol

1971 Vickers-AWD 8 x 4

engines, Fuller 3-speed transmissions and Clark internal-gear rear axles.

VICTOR (3)/USA 1923-c1928
Trucks from 1¼ to 5 tons capacity were offered by Victor Motors Inc, St Louis, Missouri. The smallest had Hercules petrol engines but the 3½- and 5-tonners, plus a short-lived 6-tonner announced in 1925, had Continental units. A Continental-engined 35-seat passenger model was offered in 1926 and 1927.

VIM/USA 1918-1923
The Vim Motor Truck Co was set up in Philadelphia, Pennsylvania in 1915, adding 1½- and 3-tonners to its light commercial line in 1918. For a while the company built its own engines but Continental or Hercules units were fitted after 1919. In 1921 the business was acquired by the Standard Steel Car Co.

1969 Volkswagen 1-ton integral van

1947 Volvo (1) LV150 3-ton truck

VOLKSWAGEN/West Germany c1952 to date

Based on a lighter model launched in 1949, the 1-ton Volkswagen appeared during the early 1950s, using a rear-mounted 1.19- or 1.49-litre 4-cyl horizontal air-cooled petrol engine. It was of chassisless design with rear-wheel drive and assembled in the Wolfsburg, Brunswick, plant of passenger car manufacturer Volkswagenwerk GmbH.

Engine capacity gradually increased to 1.8 litres, but in 1975 this long-running design was replaced by the 'LT' range, using a front-mounted water-cooled 2-litre petrol engine and shaft-drive to the rear wheels. Available with diesel power, the 'LT' is also offered in various capacities with alternative body styles up to 4½ tons, and has been joined recently by the medium-duty MAN-VW range which was developed from the 'LT'.

VOLTZ/USA 1915-1918

Three- and 5-ton Voltz trucks were listed by the Chicago-based Voltz Bros. Final-drive was by countershaft and double chains to the rear wheels and electric lighting was standard.

VOMADA/Belgium c1964 to date

A subsidiary of the Berry Co, Wichita, Kansas, since 1971, Vomada SA builds multi-wheeled crane-carriers, none of which carries the Vomada name as the company supplies finished units to established crane manufacturers.

VOMAG/Germany 1915-1944

Textile and printing machinery specialist Vogtlandische Maschinenfabrik AG vorm J C & H Dietrich, Plauen, Vogtland, turned to truck-building during World War I, introducing 3- and 4-tonners with chain- or cardan-drive. After the war, a 1½-ton truck and a shaft-drive bus went into production, and by 1924 6-wheelers were advertised, including a rear-steer passenger design.

1979 Volkswagen LT31 truck

By the mid-1920s 3-, 4-, 5-, 6- and 7-ton trucks with 4-cyl petrol engines up to 65bhp output were listed, and by 1928 an unusual front-wheel drive bus had been added. The company's first diesel engine was installed in 1930 and in 1932 Vomag Betreibs AG was established to continue production. By 1935 2- and 3-axle trucks for up to 9 tons payload were available, and a 100bhp diesel road tractor offered in 1937. Re-organized as Vomag Maschinenfabrik GmbH in 1938, the company's activities were curtailed by the war.

Vomag single-deck bus c1925

VORAN/Germany 1928-1929

The first Voran commercial was a 2-ton 6-wheeled truck. Built by Voran Automobilbau AG, Wilmersdorf, Berlin, this was joined by a series of buses, including front-drive double-deckers, for ABOAG, the leading Berlin bus operator. One operated in England in London.

VOLVO (1)/Sweden 1928 to date

The first commercial assembled by AB Volvo, Gothenburg, was the 1½-ton payload LV40 utilizing many components common to the company's passenger car. A 6-cyl model was the LV60 2-tonner with 55bhp 3-litre side-valve petrol engine and 4-speed transmission. By the early 1930s the first 6 x 2 truck had appeared as the LV64LF. The first forward-control model was the LV75 'Bulldog', which became popular as a bus chassis.

Hydraulic braking arrived in 1933, and a Hesselman-type spark-ignition oil engine capable of running on various fuels was developed for heavier models. The LV70B was a special version of an earlier goods chassis adapted for passenger work, while lighter trucks included the LV76 and LV78 1½-tonners of 1934. Another new passenger type could carry 34 persons, using either a 4.1-litre petrol or the Hesselman-type diesel engine.

At the heavy end of the truck range the LV93 4-tonner was advertised from 1936, but was soon overtaken by the 5-ton LV290, available as a 6½-tonner in 6-wheeled form. The largest city bus was the B50, with 7.6-litre Hesselman diesel engine and Lysholm-Smith torque-converter transmission, but was not successful. With World War II, the company was quick to counteract a fuel shortage with producer-gas versions which carried the producer unit on the front bumper. Despite the war, a new 5-tonner designated the LV140 appeared in 1944, along with the forward-control B40 bus which shared its engine, a 5.7-litre overhead-valve petrol unit, with the 5-tonner. Volvo's first diesel was a 95bhp 6.1-litre 6-cyl unit fitted in the heaviest truck so far, the 1946 LV150. Exports boomed after the war and in 1951 the 8/12-ton L395 was available as a 4- or 6-wheeler with a variety of mechanical specifications including hydrovac or full air brakes. By 1954 this had developed into a military 6 x 6 with turbocharged output of 195bhp.

Passenger types were improved, comprising the B658 with horizontal underfloor diesel en-

1965 Volvo (1) FB88 6 x 4 tipper

gine and the B635 and B727 rear-engined models. The heavy-duty L495 introduced ZF power-steering, while at the opposite end of the range the L2304 'Laplander' was a 4 x 4 high-mobility vehicle with a 2½-ton payload for use with a powered-axle trailer developed for the Swedish Army. A new departure was the steel-cabbed forward-control L420 and L430 models for 3 and 5 tons payload respectively. These had 3.6-litre overhead-valve V8 petrol engines coupled to a 4-speed synchromesh transmission and 2-speed rear axle.

When announced in 1963, the 7½-ton forward-control tiltcab L4751 used a 97bhp 4.7-litre die-

gined coach chassis with manual transmission.

Another heavy tractor was the 6-wheeled FB88, and new on the 1974 Swedish market was a rigid 8-wheeled version of the F86 imported from the Scottish plant. A significant development was the formation of the "Club of Four" (DAF, Magirus-Deutz, Saviem and Volvo) to develop a new model in the 6/13 tons GVW class. The first appeared a few years later, but meanwhile the heaviest bonneted models had been re-organized as the N10 and N12 in 4 x 2, 6 x 2 or 6 x 4 form. The 'Laplander' was now known as the C30, using a 6-cyl overhead-valve Volvo petrol engine and available as an op-

1972 Volvo (2) F86 8 x 4 tipper

1978 Volvo (1) F1217 artic tractor

sel engine, 5-speed synchromesh transmission and hypoid back axle. Options included a 2-speed axle, air and exhaust brakes and turbocharging to produce up to 123bhp. The heaviest bonneted model was now the L4951 tractor for 35 tons gross. The passenger series had also changed, in that the largest horizontal underfloor-engined design could now carry up to 51 passengers.

The debut of the famous F86 and F88 ranges was seen in 1965, the largest version of the latter being a 6 x 4 rigid utilizing a 9.6-litre diesel engine and an 8-speed twin-ratio transmission. By 1969 16-speed splitter and torque-converter transmissions were not uncommon and both the F86 and the F88 were available on the UK market. Volvo's most powerful truck in 1970 was the turbocharged 330bhp F89. For 1971, the chassis-less B59 city bus was launched using a horizontal rear engine, semi- or fully-automatic transmission and self-levelling rear suspension. The B58 was an underfloor-en-

tion with 6-wheel drive, some examples also being built by the Hungarian manufacturer of Csepel trucks.

In 1977 the last F88/F89 models were replaced by the F10/F12 series, with independently sprung tiltcabs and optional air-conditioning. The F614 "Club of Four" series used a turbocharged 6-cyl diesel and a new F4 for 6½/7 tons gross was introduced for urban delivery requirements.

Current passenger models comprise the front-engined B57, the underfloor-engined B58, also available in artic form, and the recently introduced BIOM. On the truck side, the ageing F86 has been replaced by the F7 with modified "Club of Four" cab also shared with the mediumweight F6 rigid.

Recently the company has suffered poor returns, and has negotiated with its rival, SAAB-Scania, in the hope of a merger. Financial assistance was eventually given by the Norwegian government.

VOLVO (2)/*Scotland c1971 to date*

A Scottish haulier introduced Volvo trucks to the UK in 1967, setting up Ailsa Trucks Ltd, Glasgow, to manage the operation. In addition to its own Ailsa passenger model, the company developed a rigid 8-wheeler based on the F86 model. Aimed at the UK tipper market, this was originally available only in 8 x 4 form, but a single-drive version was later developed. Gradually, instead of importing complete vehicles from Sweden, a manufacturing and assembly operation was set up at Irvine, Ayrshire, as Volvo Trucks (Great Britain) Ltd. Virtually all heavy Volvo multi-wheelers are now manufactured at Irvine using mainly British components, and some 8-wheelers are being exported back to Sweden where they originated from.

VOLVO BM/*Sweden 1973 to date*

Previously marketed as the BM-Volvo, the DR860 artic frame 6-wheeled dump truck became the Volvo BM DR860, when the maker (previously Bolinder-Munktell-Volvo) was re-registered Volvo BM AB. The plant at Eskilstuna quickly introduced a general-purpose model, known as the TC860, again using a pivoting main frame but with a load capacity in excess of 18 tons. This is suitable for log- or pipe-hauling, cement-mixing or cable-laying.

1979 Volvo BM artic tanker

1979 Volvo (2) F731 8 x 4 tipper

VULCAN (1)/*USA 1913-1916*
American versions of the British-designed Commer Car range were produced by the Driggs-Seabury Ordnance Co, Sharon, Pennsylvania, but this company eventually announced the Vulcan truck with capacities of 3 to 7 tons. The 4-cyl petrol engine, cone clutch, chain final-drive, pressed-steel chassis frame and many other components were all by Driggs-Seabury. With the onset of World War I, the range was slimmed down to three models from 2 to 5 tons capacity and soon discontinued. The company also built vehicles under the Driggs-Seabury, DSO, Ritz, Sharon and Twombly brand names.

VULCAN (2)/*England 1914-1953*
Previously concentrating on passenger cars and light vans, the Vulcan Motor & Engineering Co Ltd, Southport, Lancs, built a 1½-ton truck as its first venture into the commercial vehicle field. This had a 3.3-litre 4-cyl 'T'-head petrol engine, cone clutch, 4-speed transmission and worm-drive. After World War I, production continued, although now with a 4-cyl 'L'-head engine. In 1919 the company joined A Harper, Sons & Bean Ltd, becoming this company's truck division.

By the early 1920s various models from 1¼ to 4 tons capacity were advertised, all with 4-cyl side-valve petrol engines, magneto ignition and worm-drive, and a light artic model appeared in 1922. Various military types were built, including a 1½-ton 6 x 4, a 2-ton Vulcan-Kégresse half-track, and the 4-wheel drive Holverta-Vulcan.

Financial difficulties led to new management in 1928 and ideas began to take shape. One was the 3-ton 'Runabout', due to the company's desire to enter the lucrative world of small-wheeled low-loading vehicles. Another was the 6.6-litre 6-cyl petrol-engined 'Brisbane' bus with 4-speed transmission, a cruising speed of 72km/h and 4-wheel servo brakes, which was mounted on a dropframe chassis similar to the slightly earlier 'Manchester' model. By 1930 the 'Emperor' double-decker appeared but was short-lived.

In 1931 the company went into liquidation and the factory was placed in the hands of the Receiver. Activities centred upon the 1½-tonner, but by 1933 many passenger models had gone and new forward- and normal-control trucks from 1½ to 4 tons capacity were announced with plate clutches and enclosed cabs. A forward-control 5/6-tonner appeared in 1934, when 4-cyl Dorman and Gardner diesels began to be fitted. Bonneted and forward-control 2-tonners announced in 1935/6 had spiral-bevel drive and hydraulic brakes, and in 1937 the line-up at Earls Court included a 1¾-ton bonneted model, two 2½-tonners and three 5-tonners.

Due to continuing financial problems, the company was bought by Tilling-Stevens Motors Ltd, re-named Vulcan Motors Ltd and moved to Maidstone, Kent, in 1938. Now using more bought-in components, the company concentrated on forward-control medium-duty models. The war curtailed production, but 6-ton trucks were still supplied to civilians.

The 1948 range comprised a 6/7-ton rigid, a short-wheelbase tipper, and an artic tractor, all with

1919 Vulcan (2) 'VSC'-Type 1½-ton truck

Vulcan (2) single-deck bus c1925

similar specifications and Vulcan petrol or Perkins diesel engines. The parent Tilling-Stevens concern was taken over by Rootes Securities Ltd in 1950 and although a 7-ton Gardner-engined truck was announced, the marque gradually disappeared.

W

WABCO/*USA 1968 to date*
Introduced by the Construction Equipment Divn of the Westinghouse Air Brake Co, Peoria, Illinois, the Wabco range of heavy-duty off-highway dump trucks replaced the Haulpak marque. The

1972 Wabco 3200 235-ton 6 x 6 dump truck

company now builds models up to 235 tons capacity. All are of semi forward-control layout using Cummins or Detroit Diesel engines of up to 700bhp output in models up to 85 tons capacity, driving through 6-speed Allison power-shift transmissions to a double-reduction rear axle.

Diesel-electric models are the 120-, 170- and 235-tonners, the smallest of which has a Caterpillar, Cummins or Detroit Diesel V12; the second a V12 or V16 Detroit Diesel; and the largest a General Motors V12 producing up to 2475bhp. In each, the engines power hub-mounted traction motors running through a spur.

WACHUSETT/*USA 1922-1930*
Trucks produced by Wachusett Motors Inc, Fitchburg, Massachusetts, included vehicles in the 1- to 2½-ton payload range, with "conventional" layouts assembled from Continental petrol engines, Brown-Lipe transmissions and Timken rear axles.

WALKER (1)/*USA 1906-1942*
The Walker Vehicle Co, Chicago, Illinois, was a prolific builder of battery-electric road vehicles, developing its first 1-tonner in the first year of production and offering derivatives until production ceased 36 years later.

The Walker carried its batteries on each side of the chassis. In the case of the 1-tonner, the single 4hp traction motor was built into the back axle with one end of the armature shaft connected to a dif-

1919 Walker (1) Model 'K' van

ferential gear, from which drive shafts carried power to a small pinion which engaged with the wheels through a sun and planet gear. Following conventional battery-electric practice, it was of forward-control layout with the driver operating a drum-type controller. This system was used for most Walker battery-electrics with the exception of the 1915 Model 'G' of normal-control layout. Batteries were carried beneath the chassis and under the bonnet, but the same drive system was employed.

To consolidate production and lessen competition, the rival CT Electric Commercial Truck Co, Philadelphia, Pennsylvania, was taken over in 1928, but with battery-electric sales dropping during the mid-1930s the last model was a petrol-electric panel van powered by either a 4- or 6-cyl Chrysler engine.

WALKER (2)/*England 1947-1955*

Apart from a 6-wheeled mobile crane developed from a Pagefield prototype around 1930 and a series of battery-electric vehicles sold as Walker-NCB between 1945 and 1947, the first Walker commercials did not appear until the company was acquired by Walmsleys, a large engineering concern. Immediately, some Pagefield municipal types were re-named Walker, and in 1951 the first true Walker, a Perkins P6-engined 5-ton export model, was assembled from bought-in components and supplied mainly as a refuse collector. For a while, the company joined forces with County Commercial Cars Ltd, Fleet, Hants, forming Walkers & County Cars Ltd to construct municipal bodies on various chassis, but in 1955 both vehicle assembly and body-building activities were closed down.

WALKER-JOHNSON/*USA 1919-1923*

The Walker-Johnson Truck Co, East Woburn, Massachusetts, built a 2½-ton truck with a wheelbase of 375cm. Marketed as the Walker-Johnson, this had a 4-cyl Buda petrol engine, 4-speed Brown-Lipe transmission and Timken worm-drive axle. In 1920 production was transferred to Boston, and for 1922 a shorter 1-tonner with a 4-cyl Midwest petrol engine replaced the earlier model, also known as the WJ.

WALKER-NCB/*England 1945-1947*

Walker Bros (Wigan) Ltd, whose subsidiary, Pagefield Commercial Vehicles Ltd, had been building commercial vehicles since 1907, came to an arrangement with Northern Coachbuilders Ltd, of Newcastle-upon-Tyne, in 1945 whereby Walker were permitted to build battery-electric delivery vehicles employing NCB electrical equipment, marketing these as Walker-NCB.

WALLACE/*England 1919-1922*

Richmond Motor Lorries Ltd, London W12, built the 1½-ton Wallace truck using mainly American components. Production was supervised by SA Wallace, and the specification included a 4-cyl Continental 'Red Seal' petrol engine, 3-speed transmission and bevel-drive rear axle. There was also a charabanc model but few were sold.

WARD/*England 1980 to date*

An unusual mid-engined coach chassis for 11-m bodywork has been developed by coach operator Ward Bros (Lepton) Ltd, Lepton, Huddersfield, West Yorks, using a Perkins V8-640 diesel engine and ZF transmission.

Fitted with a Plaxton coach body, the prototype chassis returned an amazing top speed of 148km/h in trials, but to avoid problems on windy motorways is not equipped with power-steering.

The company intends to produce such chassis in quantity, eventually fitting Rydewell rubber suspension units at the rear, and possibly also at the front, to improve ride characteristics and cut down on suspension repairs.

WARE/*USA 1912-1915*

Designed by J L Ware, the 4-wheel drive Ware truck went into production in the Ware Motor Vehicle Co's St Paul, Minnesota, factory. Drive was transmitted from the 4-cyl petrol engine by shaft to the rear axle, where power dividers each side of the differential transmitted it back to the front axle via two long shafts. Available in three sizes up to 3 tons, the Ware was superseded by the Twin City, built by the Twin City Four Wheel Drive Co.

WASHINGTON/*USA 1909-1912*

The Washington Motor Vehicle

1950 Ward LaFrance pumper fire appliance

WARD LaFRANCE/*USA 1918 to date*

The Ward LaFrance Truck Corp was set up at Elmira, New York, by a member of the LaFrance family which was already producing the American LaFrance fire appliance. Early Ward LaFrance trucks were assembled types in the 2½ to 7 tons payload category, using Waukesha petrol engines, Brown-Lipe transmissions and Timken axles, a noteworthy feature being an automatic lubrication system. By 1920 the 2½-tonner had pneumatic tyres and an engine-driven 2-cyl air pump for keeping them inflated. Six-cyl models arrived in 1926, followed by the first passenger types in 1929 and by the highly adaptable 'Bustruk' of 1930.

1969 Ward LaFrance 'Ambassador'

petrol or Cummins diesel engines, but by the mid-1950s production was centred almost entirely upon fire appliances. The company's first cab-forward appliance appeared in 1959. Offered with a multitude of alternative specifications, this was available in both 4- and 6-wheeled form and the line has been repeatedly up-dated

1979 Ward LaFrance prototype pumper fire appliance

During the 1930s custom-building took precedence and the company was one of the first in the USA to adopt diesel power on a large scale. Much heavier models were now being built, with particular emphasis on bonneted tractors for gross loads of up to 20 tons and fire-fighting vehicles were being built in increasing numbers.

World War II saw the company constructing numerous wreckers for the military, using a 10-ton 6 x 6 chassis, as well as 6 x 4 and 6 x 6 rigid load-carriers. In 1945 the Ward LaFrance 'D'-Series was introduced for GCWs of 40,000 to 60,000lb, powered by Continental

since then.

The largest appliance is now a twin-engined 4-wheel drive airfield fire crash tender capable of speeds up to 60mph while a special 8 x 8 heavy-duty forward-control military truck powered by a 600bhp diesel engine is also built.

1942 Ward LaFrance wrecker

Co, Washington, DC, offered four battery-electric models with capacities of up to 2 tons. Each had Edison alkaline batteries and double chain-drive. Operating range was said to be 80km per charge.

WATEROUS/USA 1906-c1923
A builder of horse-drawn fire-fighting equipment, the Waterous Engine Works, St Paul, Minnesota, also built self-propelled fire trucks, the first of which was also the first petrol-engined appliance in the US. It had one engine for traction and one for pumping, and was of forward-control layout. This was followed by the company's first single-engined motive and pumping unit, with a 4-cyl petrol unit ahead of the driver.

WATSON (1)/USA 1917-1925
Originally a wagon and trailer builder, the Watson Wagon Co, Conastota, New York, was an early exponent of the drawbar and artic trailer, introducing a series of heavy truck-tractors, often using 4-cyl Continental petrol engines, 4-speed Brown-Lipe transmissions and Timken worm-drive with a capacity of about 5 tons. In 1919 the company was re-organized as the Watson Products Corp, and by 1923 as the Watson Truck Corp, by which time a series of "conventionals" from 1 to 3 tons capacity was also listed. These often had Buda or Waukesha petrol engines.

WATSON (2)/England 1918-c1929
Previously responsible for the British Berna range, Henry Watson & Sons Ltd, Newcastle-upon-Tyne, Co Durham, built the bonneted Watson truck. Standard was a 3½/4½-tonner, joined later by a 6-ton version, both with rack-and-pinion final-drive. The 32hp 5.3-litre 4-cyl petrol engine with cone clutch and 4-speed box was mounted on a subframe which extended along the rolled channel chassis frame. A passenger version, with a more powerful bored-out engine, was also offered. The 1922 6-tonner had a 6.3-litre petrol engine ahead of the front axle, and although advertised until 1929, actual production may have finished earlier.

1911 Waterous hose wagon

WEI-XING/China c1958 to date
The Wei-Xing (Satellite) is a large-capacity single-deck bus built by the Nanking Motor Vehicle Plant, Nanking, Kisngsu Province. Production is carried out alongside that of Tiao-Jin or T'iao-Chin (Leap Forward) trucks.

WEIDKNECHT/France 1896-1898
The Weidknecht vertical-boilered steam tractor was used to convert horse-drawn wagons and carriages into self-propelled artic machines. It was built by F Weidknecht, Paris, which was re-named Weidknecht Frères et Cie. Another steam commercial built around the same time was the Weidknecht & Bourdon.

WEIDKNECHT & BOURDON/France 1897
Builder of Weidknecht steam vehicles, Weidknecht Frères et Cie, Paris, also built the twin-cyl Weidknecht & Bourdon steam bus. Only a few were constructed, these featuring Soims valve gear, countershaft differential and chain-drive.

WELLS (1)/USA c1905
Captain Wells made several attempts at motorizing horse-drawn fire-fighting equipment. He converted steam pumpers to self-propulsion by removing the fore-carriage and placing the front end on modified passenger car chassis. He also designed a custom-built 3-wheeled tractor to haul escape carriers.

WELLS (2)/England 1915
A 3-ton "subsidy" lorry powered by a 4-cyl Dorman petrol engine, and with a 3- or 4-speed transmission and worm-drive, was built in small quantities by Wells Motors Ltd, Kings Cross, London.

WENDAX/Germany 1949-1951
The Wendax tri-van was joined by a 4-wheeled forward-control truck powered by a front-mounted 1.1-litre Volkswagen petrol engine in 1949. Built by Wendax Fahrzeugbau GmbH, Hamburg, this had front-wheel drive.

WERKLUST/Netherlands 1974 to date
Using a British Motor Panels cab the Werklust is an unusual 6-wheeled container truck with front-wheel drive. It is built by BV Machinefabriek Werklust, Apeldoorn, using a Mercedes-Benz diesel engine and Allison fully-automatic transmission. Its single rear wheels are suspended on a specially designed framework which can be reversed around a container for loading by a hydraulic ram gear system.

1931 White Model 65K boxvan

WHITE/USA c1906 to date
In 1906 the White Sewing Machine Co, Cleveland, Ohio, which had been assembling steam passenger cars and light commercials, was re-named the White Co, by which time heavier commercial models were also built. Supplied mainly as buses and fire appliances, these were fitted with front-mounted compound engines, radiator-type condensers and shaft-drive, although heavier 2½- and 3-tonners soon employed vertical boilers, double compound engines and chain-drive.

An internal-combustion engined series arrived in 1910, using a 4-cyl 'L'-head monobloc petrol engine, 4-speed transmission and double-reduction shaft-drive on a 1½-tonner, and chain-drive on a 3-tonner. By 1912 all steamers had ceased and a chain-drive 5-tonner was added, this range, plus a 1-tonner, being offered until the end of World War I.

1961 White 'Compact' Model 1500 boxvan

In 1917 the company, by then known as the White Motor Co, constructed a fleet of sightseeing buses. Known as the 'YP'-Type, these were developed from an earlier truck chassis and led to the company's involvement in the design and manufacture of "people movers". In 1918 chain-drive was abandoned for double-reduction bevel-drive, and detachable-head engines were introduced for all models. The Model 50 of 1921 was the company's first specifically passenger model, still using the popular 4-cyl petrol engine but fitted with air brakes from 1925. For 1926 the 4-cyl Model 53 and 6-cyl Model 54 were announced, the latter being the company's first 6-cyl engined commercial, using dual coil-ignition and a 4-speed transmission. This developed into the 1928 54-A with set-forward dashboard and engine over the front axle to provide for up to 38 passengers. As an experiment, the firm constructed a 6-cyl petrol-electric model equipped with two rear-mounted GEC traction motors.

Trucks were up-dated, with pneumatic tyres and electric lighting regularly supplied by 1928, and new models included the 1¼-ton Model 57 and 3½-ton 58 available with air brakes. Other models took the White range up to a maximum capacity of 7½ tons. A heavy tractor of 1929, called the Model 59, was added to these, using the 6-cyl petrol engine from the 54 bus. At the opposite end was the 1-ton Model 60 with a 54bhp 4.3-litre 6-cyl side-valve unit, spiral-bevel drive and hydraulic 4-wheel brakes.

The early 1930s saw the launch of heavy-duty trucks known as the 620 and 640 Series for gross weights of up to 16 tons and the introduction of the 'K'-Series with engines encroaching into the cab to provide increased body space. The company's first 6 x 4 rigids, using Timken worm-drive back axles, were also built.

1943 White 6 x 6 recovery vehicle

During 1932, the company took over the Indiana Truck Corp and became involved with Studebaker-Pierce-Arrow, assembling some Pierce-Arrows at Cleveland. Vehicle development work continued, particularly on the passenger front, and by the end of 1932 a 143bhp horizontal 12-cyl petrol engine had been manufactured for a line of passenger chassis with capacities of up to 100 passengers. These had a dual starting system, wet-plate clutch and 5-speed constant-mesh transmission. Although they initially sold well they had a poor reputation.

The re-styled 1934 '700'-Series normal-control truck used coil-ignition 6-cyl petrol engines and 5-speed transmissions in the over 3 tons class, and by 1935 a heavy forward-control range began to appear, using a derivative of the old 12-cyl horizontal engine. Even bonneted models had streamlined cabs, and in 1937 the old flat-12 engine was dropped from the passenger line and a new selection of underfloor-engined types introduced.

Although a few 1937 custom-built heavy trucks assembled for export had Cummins diesel engines, most still had petrol units. The range now covered payloads from 1½ to 16½ tons, all with 6-cyl engines up to a maximum of 130bhp output with air brakes and 5-speed transmissions in heavier types. The 704 model school bus was introduced on a 2-ton bonneted truck chassis, and by 1938 a new bus plant was building both chassis and bodies. Multi-stop delivery vehicles such as the underfloor-engined 'Merchandor' and 'White Horse' 2-tonner were introduced, and by 1939 bonneted 6-wheel drive trucks were built for military use.

Wartime production centred upon 4 x 4, 6 x 4, 6 x 6 and half-track military models, many of standardized design, but civilian production resumed in 1945, with the same line-up as offered before the war. By 1947 torque-converter transmissions and air-conditioning were listed for the heavier trucks, while buses were re-styled in 1949. A new forward-control design was the 1949 'Super Power'

300 truck line using tiltcabs, 2-speed rear axles and other options. A 12.2-litre 6-cyl Cummins diesel engine was available but came too late to save the bus line, the last of which was assembled in 1953. Both the Sterling Motors Corp and the Freightliner Corp were acquired in 1951, followed by the Autocar Co in 1953. By 1955 heavy White tractors for up to 45,360kg gross were listed, usually with turbocharged Cummins diesels, but also available with White petrol engines up to 215bhp output.

Reo Motors Inc was acquired in 1957, and by 1959 new forward- and normal-control models were offered as the '5000'-Series and 'TDL', respectively, both employing lightweight features. Cummins diesels were standard, and mechanical options included Clark, Fuller or Spicer transmissions. The Diamond T Motor Truck Co was added in 1960, while special Whites were included in a new line, amongst them a twin-steer 6-wheeler and the 'Constructor' on/off-highway bonneted 6 x 4 aimed at the construction business with a wide choice of petrol and diesel engines. Urban delivery requirements were catered for by the 11,793kg GVW 'Highway Compact' series with Chrysler or Ford

petrol, Perkins or Detroit Diesel engines. A special version of the '3000'-Series was the half-cab 'Utilideck' for the movement of steel girders, while other urban delivery models included the low-cab '1500'-Series.

By 1964 6-cyl Perkins diesel engines and the company's own V8 petrol unit were available, but the latter was apparently only a re-worked Cummins diesel and not generally adopted.

For 1967 the range covered models from the '1500'-Series, also available in 6-wheeled form, up to 4 x 2, 6 x 2, 6 x 4 and 6 x 6 rigids and tractors, both in forward- and normal-control form, using Caterpillar, Cummins, Detroit Diesel, Diamond Reo and Perkins engines. To supply the West Coast market, the bonneted diesel-engined Western Star line was announced in 1968, assembled at Ogden, Utah, and Kelowna, British Columbia. By the late 1970s, the White range covered all basic capacities from the low-tiltcab 'Road Xpeditor 2' to the forward-control 4 x 2 and 6 x 4 'Road Commander', and its bonneted sister the 'Road Boss', for gross weights of up to 56,919kg. The Western Star series continues, the largest being a bonneted 6 x 6, while the 'Constructor' is now marketed as Autocar.

1964 White 'Compact' artic tractor

1966 White Model 4564TD 6 x 4 artic tractor

WESTERN/*USA 1917-1923*
The Western Truck Mfg Co, Chicago, Illinois, built the 7-ton capacity Western truck using a 4-cyl Wisconsin petrol engine, 4-speed transmission and double chain-drive. It had a wheelbase of 362cm and was in production until 1920 when it was replaced by new trucks with capacities of 1½, 2½ and 3½ tons. All three had Timken worm-drive rear axles, the smallest having a 3-speed transmission and the larger models 4-speed.

WESTLAND/*England 1906*
The Westland was a 1½-ton delivery model built by F W Baker Ltd, Stourbridge, Worcs. It had a 15hp 4-cyl White & Poppe petrol engine, shaft-drive and circular radiator.

WESTMAN/*USA 1912-1914*
The forward-control 1½-ton Westman had a dual-ignition 4-cyl petrol engine, 3-speed transmission and shaft-drive. It was built by the Westman Motor Truck Co, Cleveland, Ohio.

WHITE HICKORY/*USA 1917-1921*
A 1½-ton wagon with 4-cyl Continental petrol engine, 3-speed transmission and Timken worm-drive back axle, the White Hickory was built by the White Hickory Wagon Mfg Co, Atlanta, Georgia. In 1921, 2½- and 3½-ton versions were offered.

WHITESIDES/*USA 1911-1912*
The Whitesides truck was built by the Whitesides Commercial Car Co, initially at Franklin, Indiana, but during 1912 at Newcastle. It was powered by a 30hp petrol engine and supplied with closed van, open dray, or stakeside bodies.

WHITING/*England 1915-c1920*
Whiting (1915) Ltd, London NW1, was a vehicle importer that marketed several US-built trucks in Britain under its own name. Among these were vehicles built by the Clydesdale Motor Truck Co, the Denby Truck Co, the Federal Motor Truck Co, the Hall Motor Car Co, the Republic Motor Truck Co Inc and the Warren Motor Truck Co. Federals were sold as Whiting-Federal.

WICHITA/*USA 1911-1932*
Wichita trucks were built initially by the Wichita Motor Co and later by the Wichita Falls Motor Co, both of Wichita Falls, Texas. Ranging from 1½ to 5 tons capacity, these were intended for oilfield use and fitted with Waukesha petrol engines and Timken or Wichita axles.

1976 White Freightliner 6 x 4 artic tractor

WHITE FREIGHTLINER/USA 1951-1977

A takeover of the Freightliner Corp, Portland, Oregon, by the White Motor Co led to the introduction of the White Freightliner marque comprising mainly lightweight heavy-duty "cabover" trucks and tractors. The first few years of production saw the company in the forefront of truck design, introducing a short-cab model, roof-mounted sleeper compartment and America's first 4-wheel drive tractor specifically for on-highway operation. A revolutionary new forward-control cab appeared towards the end of 1953 which, with up-dating in 1958, is similar to many produced by this and other US manufacturers.

Half-cabs appeared in 1964 on 6 x 4, 6 x 6 and 8 x 6 construction models and in 1974 a lightweight

1968 White Freightliner

"conventional" was added in tractor form only. Eighty per cent of the components were interchangeable with those of the long-standing "cabover", both types using Cummins diesel engines, Fuller 'Roadranger' 10-speed transmissions and Rockwell axles. Both were offered in 4 x 2 and 6 x 4 form. In 1977 the brand name reverted to that of Freightliner.

WILSON/USA 1914-1925

The J C Wilson Co, Detroit, Michigan, was a manufacturer of horse-drawn wagons who introduced the Wilson 2-tonner with double chain-drive. From 1916 worm-drive was used and the following year new 1- and 3-tonners were added, joined by a 3½- and a 5-tonner in 1918, the latter with a 4-speed transmission. For 1920 1½-, 2½-, 3½- and 5-ton models were listed, all with 4-cyl Continental petrol engines, 4-speed Brown-Lipe transmissions and Timken worm-drive axles.

WILLEME/France 1930-1978

The early 1930s saw new Willème models beginning to replace the Liberty-Willème range, one of the

first being the LH 1-tonner with single-cyl petrol engine and 3-speed transmission. By 1935 new heavier models were being produced, particularly for heavy haulage work, and in 1937 Etablissements Willème was established at Nanterre, Seine, to continue production. Most of the new models were in the 8 to 15 tons class with 8-speed transmissions and air brakes, comprising both bonneted and forward-control models and some 6-wheelers.

By the end of World War II even larger vehicles were under construction, including a 50-ton tank transporter and a 150-ton 8 x 4 tractor. Engine capacities increased considerably during the 1950s and by 1959 full forward-

1956 Willème 5471-CG 8 x 4 aircraft recovery truck

control was available as an option. For 1962 the company became connected with AEC Ltd of Britain, offering AEC alternatives to its own engines, and soon after was assembling BMC trucks as Willème-BMC.

Tiltcabs were listed for some models from 1968 but financial problems brought production to a halt the following year. By 1971 a manufacturing licence had been acquired by Perez et Raimond, Villeneuve-la-Garenne, which re-launched the Willème name on a series of heavy haulage tractors of 6 x 4, 8 x 4 and 8 x 8 layout for loads of up to 1000 tons. In 1978 these were re-named PRP.

Willème-BMC tanker c1964

WILLEME-BMC/France 1963-1965

Camions Willème SA marketed certain British-built Austin, Morris and BMC trucks in France as Willème-BMC. Typical was the forward-control 8-ton payload G160 rigid, sold as the FH K160 in the UK and other markets.

WILLYS-OVERLAND/England c1926-1928

Willys-Overland was the marketing name for American-built Willys commercials imported into the UK by Willys-Overland-Crossley Ltd, Stockport, Cheshire. Though highly-priced, a few were sold but to increase their appeal, a greater percentage of UK components was introduced. Thus came about the Manchester, sometimes known as the Willys-Manchester.

WISCONSIN DUPLEX/USA 1917-1918

The Wisconsin Duplex Auto Co developed a 1-ton 4 x 4 using numerous proprietary components in its Clintonville, Wisconsin, factory. Powered by a 32hp 4-cyl Reo petrol engine driving through a 3-speed transmission, this incorporated a Dorr-Miller automatic

Willème wrecker c1951

positive-locking centre differential in the front axle with roller bearings on the axle steering pivots.

Later the company moved to Oshkosh and in 1918 was re-organized as the Oshkosh Motor Truck Manufacturing Co.

WMW/Germany 1909-1910

Feodor Siegel Automobili und Maschinenfabrik, Schönebeck, Elbe, built a 1-ton version of its light WMW or Siegel delivery van using the same 9hp 2-cyl petrol engine. A 12hp 4-cyl unit was also available.

WOLFWAGON/USA 1956-c1964

Developed by the Wolf Engineering Corp, Dallas, Texas, the Wolfwagon was an integral box-van with driving compartment at the front which could be driven as a single unit or coupled to others of its kind and operated as a drawbar or road-train combination. When acting as a trailer, the Wolfwagon was controlled by the driver of the drawing unit. The design concept was such that vehicles could be assembled into road-trains and handled by one driver on long runs but split into individual units for urban delivery. Series production appears to have been undertaken by the St Louis Car Co, St Louis, Missouri, and both 2- and 3-axle models advertised. The engine was mounted either at the front or beneath the body.

WS/USA 1915-1918

The WS or Weier-Smith was built by the Weier-Smith Truck Co, Birmingham, Michigan, as a 1½-ton truck but replaced for 1917 by a 2½-ton model. For 1918 the company, then known as the WS Truck Co, offered a 3½-tonner powered by a 4-cyl Continental petrol engine. Other features included an 8-speed transmission and a worm-drive rear axle.

Y

YA/*Soviet Union 1925-c1945*
Yaroslavl Automobilova Zavod, Yaroslavl, Volga, introduced the 3-ton YA-3, powered by a 35bhp 4-cyl AMO petrol engine. Also known as the JA and sometimes referred to as the Yaroslavl, this was replaced by the 3½-ton YA-4 in 1928 using a 70bhp 6-cyl Mercedes-Benz petrol engine. Between 1929 and 1934 a 4½-tonner called the YA-5 was produced. This had a 93bhp engine and became a basis for other marques such as the YAG and YAS. Passenger models included the YA-1 70-seater and YA-2 city bus. Later, the marque name was changed to YAAZ, YAZ or YAAZ.

YAG/*Soviet Union c1930-c1941*
The 8-ton 6 x 4 YAG-10, powered by an American Hercules engine, was built by Yaroslavl Automobilova Zavod, Yaroslavl, Volga, based on the YA-5 design. About 1932 it was joined by the YAG-12, a 12-ton 8 x 8 cargo truck with 4-wheel steering powered initially by a 93bhp 6-cyl Continental engine. Later versions could be had with a 105bhp unit.

YALE/*USA 1920-1922*
Named after the famous university, the Yale was a 1½-ton bonneted truck built by the Yale Motor Truck Co. Power came from a 4-cyl Herschell-Spillman petrol engine.

YAS/*Soviet Union c1934-c1945*
Certain dump trucks based on YA chassis and running gear by Yaroslavl Automobilova Zavod, Yaroslavl, Volga, were known as YAS.

YAAZ/*Soviet Union c1945-1959*
YA trucks built by Yaroslavl Automobilova Zavod, Yaroslavl, Volga, were later called YAAZ, YAZ or JAAZ. Products included the 7-ton YAAZ-200, powered by a 110bhp engine, the YAAZ-210 series and the YAAZ-214 7-ton 6 x 6, YAAZ-219 12-tonner and YAAZ-222 10-ton dump truck. All had 6-cyl diesel engines. Vehicle production eventually moved to the new KRAZ plant at Kremenchug and the Yaroslavl factory used for diesel engine production.

YELLOCAB TRUCK/*USA c1924-1927*
The Yellow Cab Mfg Co, Chicago, Illinois, built the 1-ton Yellocab Truck. Production of this Continental-engined model continued after the takeover of the business by General Motors in 1925 and its re-organization as the Yellow Truck & Coach Mfg Co.

YELLOW COACH/*USA 1922-1942*
The Yellow Motor Coach Co, Chicago, Illinois, began production of passenger vehicles in 1922. In 1925 the nearby Yellow Cab Mfg Co merged with Yellow

1964 YAAZ-451D 1-ton truck

Coach to form the Yellow Truck & Coach Co, a subsidiary of General Motors. A fleet of 71 revolutionary double-deckers, all with transverse petrol engines mounted at the rear, was delivered to the Fifth Avenue Coach Co in 1936. These were one-man operated and some were converted to diesel.

Also in 1936, Pacific Greyhound Lines placed the first Yellow Coach 'Super Coaches' in service. These seated 37 passengers and were powered by an 11.6 litre petrol engine transversely mounted at the rear. Baggage was stowed beneath the floor. Designated Model 719, some 329 examples were built in the first year, with another 1,256 of the similar Model 743 from 1937 to 1939. The last few 743s were powered by Detroit Diesel engines, superseded in 1939 by the Model 744. When the company ceased, production

was continued by the parent GMC concern as GM Coach.

YELLOW-KNIGHT/*USA 1925-1927*
Soon after General Motors took over the Chicago-based Yellow Cab Mfg Co, the Yellow-Knight truck was announced. Offered alongside the smaller Yellocab Truck, this brought the maximum capacity of goods models up to 4 tons, using a Knight or Buick petrol engine.

YERMAK/*Soviet Union ? to date*
Designed by the Automobile Research Institute of the USSR, the Yermak has a capacity of 25 tons and is intended for operation in remote areas. Features include full double-glazing and air-conditioning for operation in extreme cold, tyre pressures that can be varied while the vehicle is in motion, and 6-wheel drive. Power is provided by a 320bhp diesel engine.

YOUNG (1)/*USA 1920-1923*
One and one-half and 2½-ton Continental-powered trucks were built by the Young Motor Truck Co, Geneva, Ohio. These were assembled from numerous proprietary components.

YOUNG (2)/*USA ? to date*
Young Spring & Wire builds the Young terminal tractor for handling semi-trailers in docks and marshalling yards.

YOUNG (3)
USA 1970 to date
The 4-wheeled Young 'Bison' and 6-wheeled 'Crusader' 22.5-m snorkel fire appliances have Caterpillar or Detroit Diesel engines and low-profile cabs. They are built by the Young Fire Equipment Corp, Lancaster, New York.

Yellow Coach c 1945

ZABO/*Netherlands 1957 to date*
NV Carrosseriefabriek Zabo, Ridderkerk, was a coachbuilder which also built a 60-passenger integral city bus called the 'Junior'. This had an 83bhp Perkins diesel engine, Bedford clutch and gearbox and Clark axles. In 1973 the company introduced a new chassisless model, using DAF running units.

ZEITLER & LAMSON/*USA 1914-c1916*
The Zeitler & Lamson Motor Truck Co, Chicago, Illinois, introduced a 5-model range of trucks from 1 to 5 tons capacity. All had Continental petrol engines but production ended, models being re-introduced as KZ and King-Zeitler.

ZELIGSON/*USA 1946*
The Zeligson Truck & Equipment Co, Tulsa, Oklahoma, converts and re-conditions military trucks for the civilian market, re-selling these as Zeligson. Other products include custom-built models, using military and civilian components, aimed at oilfield operators and special clients, normally with Detroit Diesel engines and power winches.

ZETTELMEYER/*Germany 1936-1939*
A former traction engine builder, Maschinenfabrik Hubert Zettelmeyer, Konz, near Trier, built a 20bhp diesel tractor of integral construction.

ZIL/*Soviet Union 1957 to date*
The Zavod Imieni Stalina factory, Moscow, was re-named Zavod Imieni Likhacheva in 1956 and vehicles previously sold as ZIS became ZIL. By the end of 1957 the ZIS-designed ZIL-150 normal-control 4-wheeler had been replaced by the ZIL-164, and in 1958 the 6 x 6 ZIL-151 was succeeded by the 4½-ton ZIL-157.
The ZIL-164 was ousted by the ZIL-130 in 1964, using a 170bhp V8 petrol engine and 5-speed transmission, and an associated

1961 ZIL-130 6½-ton truck

factory uses this as the basis for a dump truck. Heavy-duty 6 x 6 bonneted trucks are the ZIL-131 and ZIL-131A, which replace the ZIL-157 and use numerous components from the ZIL-130 range.
Since 1964 the factory has also built the twin-engined ZIL-135 8 x 8 forward-control range with a total power output of 360bhp from two V8 petrol engines located across the chassis behind the cab. Buses for up to 62 passengers are also built, and the factory was used to develop the Kamaz truck range, now built at the Kamske Auto Zavod factory.

ZIMMERMAN/*USA 1915-1916*
A ½-ton high-wheeler built by the Zimmerman Mfg Co, Auburn, Indiana, was later re-rated for 1½-ton capacity. It had a 2-cyl petrol engine, planetary transmission, and double chain-drive.

ZIS/*Soviet Union 1932-1956*
Several thousand of the 3-ton ZIS-5, built by the Zavod Imieni Stalina factory, Moscow, were sent to Spain for use in the Civil War in 1936. When the factory was re-named, all vehicles became known as ZIL.

1965 ZIL-130 truck

ZIU/*Soviet Union to date*
Zavod Imieni Unitzki assembles single-deck ZIU trolleybuses.

ZUBR/*Poland 1960-1968*
The 8-ton Zubr forward-control truck, the A-80, went into production at the Jelezanskie Zaklady Samochodow plant in Jelcz. It was powered by a 155bhp Wola diesel engine and in the mid-1960s was

joined by a 4-wheel drive version. Production of both continued until the Jelcz range was introduced.

ZUST/*Italy 1910-1917*
Built by Ing Roberto Zust Fabbrica Italiana di Automobili SA, Brescia and Milan, the first Zust truck was a bonneted chain-drive 2-tonner powered by a 4-cyl 'L'-head petrol engine, which was soon joined by a 4-tonner of similar layout. In 1912 the company was re-named Fabbrica Automobili Zust, and by 1916 models ranged from 2 to 5 tons, using 4-cyl side-valve monobloc engines. Light models had shaft- and heavy models chain-drive. In 1917 the business was bought by Officine Meccaniche SpA.

1960 Zwicky runway sweeper

ZWEIRAD/*West Germany ? to date*
Zweirad Union AG converts existing vehicles into road/rail machines, marketing these as Zweirad. Most are based on small Mercedes-Benz and Unimog models.

ZWICKY/*England 1910-c1970*
Zwicky Ltd, Slough, Berks, built its first vehicle, a massive motor pump fire appliance with fixed monitor, for the Tottenham Fire Brigade, and from then on manufactured only special vehicles. After World War II the company concentrated on the construction of airfield vehicles, including refuellers, aircraft starting equipment, fuel metering machines and runway sweepers. Many were powered by Ford petrol or diesel engines.

ZYPHEN & CHARLIER/*Germany 1925-1926*
A 4-ton truck powered by a 45/60 PS 4-cyl BMW petrol engine was developed by Eisenbach und Maschinenfabrik van der Zyphen und Charlier GmbH, Cologne-Deutz. A passenger version was also listed but both were withdrawn.

Zwicky fuel metering unit c1962

1936 ZIS-5 3-ton truck

Marques of trucks and buses

Over the years a great number of marques have been recorded apart from those already listed in the A-Z part of this book. This section covers these as comprehensively as possible along with brief data; in general vehicles under 1 ton have been omitted.

A

ABAM
Germany   1898-1905

ABBOTT-DOWNING
USA   1916-1917

ACE
USA   1923

ACEC
Belgium   1929

ACME
USA   1903

ACME WAGON
USA   1916

ACOMAL
Belgium   1972

ADAMS
England   1903-1906

ADAMSON
England   1912-1924

ADMIRAL
USA   1914

ADVANCE
USA   1918

AJAX
USA   1911

AJAX
USA   1920-1922

ALAMO
USA   1912

ALCO
USA   1905

ALENA STEAM
USA   1921-1922

ALL-AMERICAN
USA   1926-1928

ALLEN
Ireland   1907

ALLEN & CLARK
USA   1908-1910

ALLEN-KINGSTON
USA   1907-1909

ALLFOUR
USA   1918-1924

ALLIANCE
USA   1916

ALLIED TRUCK
USA   1920

ALPENA
USA   1910-1914

ALTMANN
Germany   1905-1907

AMALGAMATED
USA   1913-1917

AMBLARD
France   c1912

AMERICAN
USA   1921-1924

AMERICAN BRASS
USA   1907-1908

AMERICAN BUS
USA   1926

AMERICAN COMMERCIAL
USA   1918-1923

AMERICAN ELECTRIC
USA   1914-1916

AMERICAN FOUNDRY
USA   1906

AMERICAN MACHINE
USA   1906-1909

AMERICAN MACHINE
USA   1916

AMERICAN NAPIER
USA   1906-1909

AMERICAN STEAM TRUCK
USA   1918-1922

AMERICAN STEAMER
USA   1903

AMERICAN TRUCK
USA   1910-1912

AMES
USA   1911

AMTORG
USA   1930-1935

ANCHOR
USA   1911

ANDERSON
USA   1909-1912

ANDOVER ELECTRIC
USA   1914-1917

ANHEUSER-BUSCH
USA   1911-1912

ANSUL
USA   c1973

ANTHONY-HATCHER
USA   1909

APEX
USA   1917-1923

APOLLO
Germany   1914-1922

APPERSON
USA   1905-1920

APPERSON-LEE
USA   1911

APPLETON
USA   1922-1934

A & R
USA   1913-1915

ARANDSEE
USA   1920

ARBENZ
USA   1911-1916

ARIEL
England   1911-1912

ARIES
USA   1911-1912

ARMORED
USA   1915

ARRAS
France   c1904

ARTANA
USA   1912-1915

ASTER
France   1901-1910

ATKINSON & PHILLIPSON
England   c1905

ATLANTA
USA   1911

ATLANTIC
USA   1913-1915

ATSUTA
Japan   c1930-c1935

AUBURN WAGON & BUGGY
USA   1911-1912

AULTMAN-TAYLOR
USA   1906-1923

AUROCH
France   1964-?

AUTO-DYNAMIC
USA   1901

AUTO-ELECTRIC
England   1935-1939

AUTO-LUX
Italy   1945-1950

AUTO TRACTOR
USA   1930

AUTO-TRUCK
USA   1915-1916

AUTOCAR EQUIPMENT
USA   1904-1909

AUTOMATIC
USA   1912-1922

AUTOMOBILE
USA   1900-1911

AUTOMOTOR
USA   1901-1904

AUTORAILER
USA   1946

AUTOTRUCK
USA   1916

AYRES
USA   c1911-c1912

B

BABCOCK ELECTRIC
USA   1911-1912

BACHNI
Switzerland   c1902

BACON
USA   1901-1910

BADENIA
Germany   1912-c1925

BAILEY
USA   1914

BAILEY-PERKINS
USA   1919

BANTAM
USA   1912

BARBER
USA   1906

BARBER
USA   1912

BARGER
USA   1918

BARRE
France   c1920-c1930

BARRON
USA   1918

BARTHOLEMEW
USA   1911-1912

BARTLETT
USA   1921-1922

BARTLETT
USA   1926-1930

BATTON
USA   1898-1899

BAUCHE
France   c1927-?

BAUER
USA   1925-1927

BAUMI
Germany   1925

BB COMMERCE
USA   1912

BCK
USA   c1911-c1912

BEAN
USA   1973 to date

BEARDSLEY
USA   1915-1917

BEARDSLEY ELECTRIC
USA   1914

BEAVER
USA   1911

BEAVER
USA   1915-1920

BEAVER
USA   1920

BECRAFT
USA   1911

BEGGS
USA   1918-1928

BELDEN
USA   1911

BELGA
Belgium   1968

BELGICA
Belgium   1901-1909

BELLMORE
USA 1911

BELMONT
USA 1923-1926

BERLINER
Germany 1898-?

BESTEVER
USA 1917

BICKNELL
England 1905

BIEHL
USA 1911

BIGGAM
USA 1917

BILGERI
Austria c1900-c1908

BINDEWALD-ALBRECHT
Germany 1905

BINGHAMTON
USA 1922

BLACK DIAMOND
USA 1905

BLACKER
USA 1910-1912

BLAISDELL
USA 1905-1909

BLAW KNOX
USA c1968

BOBBI WAGON
USA 1946

BONEY
USA 1911-1912

BORBEIN
USA 1903

BOSNJAK
Australia 1980 to date

BOULTON
Canada c1929

BOUR-DAVIS
USA 1919

BOWLING GREEN
USA 1912-1916

BOWMAN
USA 1921-1922

BOYERTOWN
USA c1972-?

BOYLE
USA 1911

BRADFIELD
USA 1929-1930

BRADFORD
USA 1919-1920

BRANDON
USA 1911-1912

BRAUN
Austria c1900-c1910

BRAY
England c1955-c1964

BRENNAN
USA 1907-1909

BRENNAN
USA 1912

BREZE
USA 1903

BRISTOL
USA 1909

BRITISH
England 1905-1907

BRITTON
USA 1911-1912

BRITTON-STEVENS
USA 1916

BROCKVILLE-ATLAS
Canada 1909

BROMFIELD
USA 1930

BROOKE
England c1903-1913

BROOKS-LATTA
USA 1912

BROWN & SAUTER
USA 1912

BROWNE
USA 1907

BRUNN
USA 1907

BRUNNER
USA 1910

BUCKEYE
USA 1911-1916

BUCYRUS-ERIE
USA ? to date

BUDA
USA 1920

BUGNON
France 1911

BUHRER
Switzerland c1950-c1965

BURLINGTON
USA 1917

BURROUGHS
USA 1914

BURSTALL
England 1824

BYRON
USA 1912

BYRON
USA 1933

C

CADOGAN
England 1904-?

CALDWELL
USA 1912

CALEY & NASH
USA 1912

CALIFORNIA
USA 1911

CAMPAGNE
France c1906

CANNON
USA 1912

CANTON
USA 1906

CANTON BUGGY
USA 1912

CAPITAL
USA 1912-1922

CAR
Italy 1905-1906

CARGOMATIC
England 1980 to date

CARL
USA 1915-1916

CARLSON
USA 1911-1916

CARROL
USA 1912

CARTER
USA 1911

CASADAY
USA 1905

CASCO
USA 1924-1930

CASE
USA 1920-1923

CASEY
USA 1912-1914

CAZES
France 1910-?

C-B
USA 1914-1915

C & D
USA 1907

CEDAR
USA 1921

CEDAR RAPIDS
USA 1910-1914

CHAMPION
USA 1912-?

CHAMPION-ROTARY
USA 1922-1923

CHARLON
France 1906

CHATTAQUA
USA 1912

CHESTER
USA 1916

CHICAGO MOTOR BUGGY
USA 1908

CHIEF
USA 1910

CHILDS
USA 1909

CHING-KAN-SHAN
China c1958-?

CHRISTOLHOMME
France 1907-1908

CHRISTOPHER BROTHERS
USA 1911-1912

CHURCH
England 1908

CINCINNATI
USA 1912

CITY CARRIAGE
USA 1910

CK-DUMPER
Switzerland 1959-?

C de L
USA 1913

CLARK
USA 1912-c1914

CLARK-HATFIELD
USA 1909

CLARK TRUCKTRACTOR
USA 1921

CLARKE
England 1902-1903

CLARKSPEED
USA 1926-1931

CLASSIC
USA 1917

CLEMIC-HIRSCH
USA 1905-1906

CLERMONT-STEAMER
USA 1923

CLEVELAND
USA 1960-1961

CLEVELAND ELECTRIC
USA 1955-1960

CLIFFORD
USA 1905

CMC
USA 1920

COCKERILL
Belgium 1904

COHES
USA 1912

COLERIDGE
USA 1911

COLES
USA 1955

COLLINS
USA 1901

COLPITTS
USA 1911-1912

COLUMBUS
USA 1902-1907

COMET
USA 1916-1925

COMMER
USA 1911-1912

COMMER
USA 1913

COMMER WOOD
USA 1905

COMMERCE
USA 1907-1921

COMMERCIAL STEAMER
USA   1903

CONCORD
USA   1933-1938

CONDOR
USA   1917-1918

CONSOLIDATED
USA   1934

COOK
USA   1920-1922

CORLISS
USA   1917-1918

CORTLAND CART
USA   1916

CORWIN
USA   1905-1906

COTE
France   c1900-c1914

COTTINGHAM BROTHERS
USA   1911-1912

COUNTY
England   1916-1921

COURIER
USA   1909-1912

COVEL
USA   1916

CRAM
USA   1911-1912

CRARY
USA   1912

CRESCENT
USA   1912-1913

CRESCENT
USA   1917

CRESTMOBILE
USA   1901-1905

CROWN
USA   1923

CROWTHER
USA   1911-1912

CROXTON
USA   1913-1914

CUMBACK
USA   1910

CURRAN
USA   1928

CYCLONE
USA   1920

CYCLONE
USA   1922-1923

CYPHERS
USA   1911-1912

D

DAT
Japan   1926-1932

DAVENPORT
USA   1902-1903

DAVIS
USA   1914-1916

DAVIS & THOMPSON
USA   1911-1912

DAY
USA   1902

DAYTON
USA   1917

DE MESMAY
France   c1911

DE WITT
USA   1911-1912

DELIA
USA   1915

DELLA STANGA
Italy   c1968

DEMAG
West Germany   ? to date

DENEGRE
USA   1920-1922

DESBERON
USA   1900-1904

DESMARAIS
France   1906-c1907

DETROIT-WYANDOTTE
USA   1913-1916

DEVON
USA   1911-1916

DIAMOND
USA   1911

DIAS
West Germany   1946-?

DIRECT DRIVE
USA   1907

DISPATCH
USA   1921

DOLFINI
USA   1900

DORNFIELD
USA   1911-1912

DOWNE
USA   1911

DOWNING
USA   1915

DOWNS
USA   1911-1912

DOYLE
USA   1911-1915

DRAUZ
West Germany   1951-1962

DRAYMASTER
USA   1931-1933

DRIER
USA   1929

DRIGGS-SEABURY
USA   1916

DSF
Austria   c1922

DUBOIS
France   1905-?

DUERR
USA   1911-1912

DUHAMEL & BRUECHNER
USA   1911

DUPERRUT
France   1908

DUPLEX
USA   c1972

DURIEZ
France   c1950

DUSSEAU
USA   1912

DUTY
USA   1909-1927

DYKE
USA   1900-1904

DYLE & BACALAN
Belgium   1906

DYNAMIC
USA   1920

E

EAST DAVENPORT
USA   1912

EASTERN POWER
USA   1909-1912

EASTON
USA   c1912

ECKHARD
USA   1917

ECKLAND
USA   1931

ECW
England   1950-1957

EDWIL
USA   1934-1940

EHRLICH
USA   1920

EIMCO
USA   1957 to date

ELBURT
USA   1915

ELBURTO
USA   1920

ELECTRIC
USA   1911-1912

ELECTRIC
USA   1923

ELECTRIC MOTIVE
England   1894-?

ELECTRICAL STREET CAR
England   c1899-1901

ELECTRO-COACH
USA   1917

ELECTROMOBILE
USA   1920

ELECTRUCK
USA   1916-1925

ELECTRUCK
USA   1925-1928

ELKHART
USA   1917-1920

EMANCIPATOR
USA   1909

EMBREE McLEAN
USA   1911

EMERY
USA   1950-1952

EMF
USA   1912

EMPIRE STEAM
USA   1901-1903

EMRESS
Belgium   1906-1907

ENGER
USA   1909

ENGLISH ELECTRIC
England   1926-1931, 1939

ENKEL
USA   1915

EPPERSON
USA   1912

ERIE
USA   1914-1920

ETUDES DE MATERIAL ET DE TRACTION
France   c1923

EUGOL
USA   1922-1923

EUREKA
USA   1903

EVERETT-KING
USA   1899

EVERITT
USA   1911-1912

EWBANK
USA   1916-1917

EX-CEL
USA   1912

EXETER
USA   1909-1913

F

FAIRBANKS
USA   1906-1911

FAIRFIELD
USA   1927

FAIRMAN
USA   1915

FAKA
West Germany   1956-1957

FALCK
Denmark   c1973

FAMOUS
USA   1914

FAWICK
USA   1913-1916

FERON & VIBERT
France   1905

FFG
West Germany   1979

FIDES
Italy   1908

FIELD
USA   1920

FIFTH AVENUE COACH
USA   1916-1925

FINNAGAN
USA   1913

FIREBAUGH
USA   1947

FISHER
USA   1901-1905

FITZJOHN
Canada/USA   1938-1958

FLECKWICK
USA   1933

FLINT
USA   1924-1927

FLOIRAT
France   1948-1956

FLXETTE
USA   c1963 to date

FLYER
Canada/USA   c1955-1971

FORME
USA   1917

FOUR TRACTION
USA   1911

FOX
USA   1913

FOX
USA   1959

FRANCISCO
Philippines   1948 to date

FRANKFURTER
West Germany   c1919-c1925

FRAT
Syria   ? to date

FREEMAN
USA   1921

FREMONT
USA   1919-1925

FRONT DRIVE
USA   1921-1929

FULLER BUGGY
USA   1909

G

GALLOWAY
USA   1911

GALLOWAY
USA   1917-1918

GANDON
France   1900

GARDNER-SERPOLLET
France   1899-1907

GEFRAT
Germany   1930-?

GLOBE
USA   1920-1922

GOLDEN STATE
USA   1928-1935

GOLDEN WEST
USA   1919-1920

GOLDENGATE
USA   1927

GOLIATH
USA   1920

GORDON
England   1824-1830

GOTTWALD
West Germany   ? to date

GOULD
USA   1954-1955

GOVE
USA   1921-1922

GP
USA   1929-1935

GRAND RAPIDS
USA   1913

GRASSI
Brasil 1961-c1964

GRAVELY
USA   c1972

GRAY
USA   1916

GREAT EAGLE
USA   1920

GREAT LAKES
USA   1949-1956

GREEN
England   c1914

GREENVILLE
USA   1926-1928

GREYHOUND
USA   1975 to date

GROVE
USA   ? to date

GROVE ALLEN
England   1972 to date

GUMPRICE
USA   1912

H

HABERER
USA   1911-1912

HALL
USA   1921-1923

HALLER BROTHERS
USA   1911

HAMILTON
USA   1917-1921

HAMPDEN
USA   1922

HANDI-KAR
USA   1914

HANNAY
USA   1917

HANOVER
USA   1922-1926

HARMON-YOUNT
USA   1913

HASBROUCK & SLOAN
USA   1912

HASKALL
USA   1916

HATFIELD
USA   1916-1918

HATHAWAY-PURINTON
USA   1924-1925

HAVERS
USA   1911

HAWTHORN-LESLIE
England   1900

HAYES
USA   1916-1918

HAYES-LEYLAND
Canada   1936-?

HEILUNGKIANG
China   c1970 to date

HELLMANN
Germany   1902-1904

HENDERSON
USA   1915-1927

HENDY
USA   1913

HENNEGIN
USA   1914

HERCULES
USA   c1911

HERCULES
USA   1961

HERTNER ELECTRIC
USA   1934-1936

HERTZ
USA   1925-1928

HERWAYTHORN
France   1949-?

HIBERNIA
USA   c1904

HICKS-PERRETT
USA   1922

HILTON
USA   1913

H & M
USA   1919

HOADLEY
USA   1914-1922

HOADLEY
USA   1916

HOCKÉ-SEDDON
Belgium   c1965

HOHNSBEHN
USA   1913

HOLLAND
USA   1901

HOLMAN
USA   1922

HOLT
USA   1912-1925

HOOSIER
USA   1913

HOPKINS
USA   1911-1912

HORNER
USA   1913-1914

HORNER
USA   1914-1917

HORNWOOD
England   1906-1907

HOUGHTON
USA   1915-1917

HOUSE COLD TIRE SETTER
USA   1919

HRL
USA   1921

HUAINAN
China   1970 to date

HUEBNER
USA   1914

HUNT
USA   1920

HUNTER-WECKLER
USA   1909

HUNTINGDON
USA   1912

HUPMOBILE
USA   1920-1925

HURLIMANN
Switzerland   c1928-?

HURON
USA   1912-1923

HURON RIVER
USA   1912

HURTU
France   1922-1929

HUSELTON
USA   1913

HYDRAULIC TRUCK
USA   1916-1917

HYRADE
USA   1916

I

ICE
USA   1913

IDEAL
Switzerland   1900

IDEAL
USA   1912

IMBODEN
USA 1877-1878

IMMEL
USA 1911

IMPROVED
USA 1905

INDEPENDENT
USA 1911

INDEPENDENT
USA 1914-1921

INDEPENDENT
USA 1915

INDEPENDENT
USA 1915-1918

INDEPENDENT
USA 1927-1934

INDUSTRIA
France 1909-c1914

INDUSTRIAL
USA 1921-1922

INLAND
USA 1919-1920

INTERSTATE
USA 1908-1918

IOWA
USA 1919

IRON FAIRY
England ? to date

ITALIA
USA 1922-1925

IVES
USA 1914

IVEY
USA 1913

J

JACCARD
USA 1911

JACKSON
USA 1891

JACKSON
USA 1902-1929

JAMES
England 1824-1832

JARMS MACHINERY
USA 1911

JARVIS
USA 1906

JEEP
USA 1963-c1965

JENBACH
Austria c1947-c1950

J & H
USA 1920-1921

J & J
USA 1920-1921

JMH
Switzerland c1969

JOERNS-THIEN
USA 1911

JOHNSON
USA 1912

JOHNSON
England ? to date

JOHNSON SERVICE
USA 1909

JOHNSTON
England 1935-1955

JONES
England 1938-?

JONZ
USA 1911-1912

K

KANKAKEE
USA 1918-1920

KARDELL
USA 1918-1920

KARRY LODE
USA 1920

KARWISCH
USA 1911

KASTORY
USA 1924

KAUFMANN
Germany c1901-1905

KAWS QUALITY
USA 1922-1925

KEETON
USA 1908

KELDON
USA 1919

KELLEY
USA 1903

KELLY
USA c1905

KELLY STEAM
USA 1902-1903

KEMNA
Germany 1926

KEMP
USA 1912

KEMPER
USA 1909

KENAN
USA 1915

KENDALL
USA 1911

KENEN
USA 1913-1915

KENOSHA
USA 1918

KENTUCKY WAGON
USA 1914

KESTOTANKKI
Finland ? to date

KISSELKAR
USA 1916-1919

KJELLBURG
Sweden 1909-?

KLAG
USA 1912

KLONDIKE
USA 1918-1920

KNAPP
USA 1911-1912

KNELLY'S
USA 1911-1912

KNIGHTSTOWN
USA 1933

KOENIG & LUHRS
USA 1916-1917

KOPF
USA 1911

KOTERBA
USA 1912

KRANZ
USA 1911

KRATZNER
USA 1912

KRESS
USA 1911-1912

KRICKWORTH
USA 1912-1917

KRONENBURG
Netherlands ? to date

KUANGCHOU
China 1966 to date

KUEHNE
USA 1911-1912

KUHN
USA 1918-1920

KUNKEL
USA 1911

K - Z
USA 1921-1923

L

L'ELECTROMOTION
France 1900-1909

LA BRUGEOISE & NIVELLE
Belgium 1960-c1964

LA CROSSE
USA 1914

LADERER
USA 1911

LAMBERT-MORIN
USA 1912

LAMMERT & MANN
USA 1922

LANCHESTER
England 1915

LANE
England 1900

LANG
USA 1912-1931

LANG & BUTTON
USA 1890-1900

LANGBRIDGE
England c1914

LANGE & GUTZEIT
Germany 1899-?

LANGERQUIST
USA 1911

LANSING
USA 1917-1920

LAUREL
USA 1916-1921

LAURENT
France 1907-1908

LAURENT-RIKER
France c1939

LAYZELL
England 1900

LEAR
USA 1909

LEASE
USA 1921-1922

LEHMBECK
Germany c1901-1905

LEHNE
USA 1911

LEON MAX
France 1927-1934

LEUSCHNER
USA 1911

LIAONING No 2
China c1971 to date

LIEBHERR
West Germany ? to date

LIMA
USA ? to date

LINDSEY
USA 1909

LINER
England 1955-?

LION
USA 1921

LITE WAY
USA 1953-1955

LITTLE GIANT
USA c1921

LMV
France ? to date

LO TRUK
USA 1940

LOMAX
USA 1913

LONE STAR
USA 1920-1922

LORAIN
USA 1901

LORAIN
USA ? to date

LOS ANGELES CREAMERY
USA   1913-1914

LOUISIANA
USA   1919

LOWELL
USA   1917-1918

LUCK TRUCK
USA   1912-1914

LUDERS
Germany   1930

LUDLOW
USA   1914

LUITWEILER
USA   1912

LUXOR
USA   1924-1927

LWC
USA   1916

LYON
USA   1911

LYONS
USA   1919-1921

M

McCARRON
USA   1927-1929

McCREA
USA   1906-1908

McCULLOUGH
USA   1899

MacINNIS
USA   1911

McKEEN
USA   1912

MACK
France   1978 to date

MAGNARD
France   1906

MAJESTIC
USA   1925-1927

MALICET & BLIN
France   c1908-1912

MANAHAN
USA   1911

MANITOWOC
USA   ? to date

MAPLE BAY
USA   1911-1912

MAREMONT
USA   1916

MARINETTE
USA   1909

MARKERT
USA   1911

MARKEY
USA   1912

MARKS
USA   1901

MARSHALL
USA   1919-1921

MARTIN
USA   1929-1932

MARTIN-PARRY
USA   1920-1921

MARWIN
USA   1918

MARX
USA   1911-1912

MASTER
USA   1907-1920

MATERIEL DE VOIRIE
France   c1951

MATHESON
USA   1906-1907

MATTILE
Switzerland   1959

MAXIM
USA   1912-1916

MAYBRATH
USA   1949

MD
USA   1908

MECHANICS
USA   1926-1928

MEECH-STODDARD
USA   1922-1927

MEGOW
USA   1909-1911

MENGES
USA   1921

MERCEDES-MIXTE
Austria   c1908

MERCHANTS
USA   1912

MERCURY
USA   1913-1914

MERCURY
England   1920-1964

METALLURGIQUE
Belgium   c1900-c1916

METENS
USA   1911-1912

METEOR
USA   1941

METZ
USA   1909

MEYER-ULM
Germany   1923-?

MGT
USA   1947-1950

MHC
USA   1915

MICAMPBELL
USA   1909-1915

MICHIGAN
USA   1907, 1910

MICHIGAN
USA   1960 to date

MID WEST
USA   1925

MIDDLEBORO
USA   1913-1914

MIDDLETOWN
USA   1911

MIDLAND
USA   1918-1919

MIEUSSET
France   1918-1925

MILFORD
USA   1946

MILLARS
England/France   1927-1936

MILWAUKEE
USA   1951

MIN SHENG
China   1934-c1937

MINER
China   1970 to date

MINNEAPOLIS
USA   1920

MINNEAPOLIS STEEL
USA   1910-1928

MITCHELET
USA   1923

MITCHELL
USA   1903-1922

MITCHELL-LEWIS
USA   1910-1916

MITSUBISHI
Japan   1920

MOBIL
USA   c1969

MODAG
Germany   1925-1926

MODERN WHEEL DRIVE
England   1924-1932

MOHICAN
USA   1920-1921

MOLDENHAUER
USA   1911

MOLLER
USA   1919-1937

MOLZEN
USA   1916

MONARCH
USA   1909

MONARCH
USA   1916

MONOTRAL-VIBERTI
Italy   c1966

MORITA
Japan   ? to date

MORRIS
USA   1899-1909

MORRIS & SALOM
USA   1896-1897

MORTON
Scotland   c1900-1907

MORTON
USA   1917-1920

MOSELEY
USA   1919

MOSLER
USA   1913

MOTIL
England   1980 to date

MOTOR BUGGY
USA   1908-1910

MOTOR CONVEYANCE
USA   1911

MOTOR PRODUCTS
USA   1914

MOTOR RAIL
England   1948-?

MOTOR STORAGE
USA   1905-1908

MOTOR TRUCK
USA   1902

MOTOR WAGON
USA   1910-1911

MOTOX
USA   1921

MOYEA
USA   1904

MPC
USA   1925-1928

MT
Spain   1940-1950

MUELHAUSER
USA   1912-1914

MUIR
USA   1903

MULLER
Germany   1908-1911

MULLER
USA   1911

MULLER
USA   1912

MUNCEY
USA   1911

MUNCIE
USA   1906-1909

MUNSING
USA   1913

MUNSON
USA   1899

MURPHY
USA   1914

MUSKEGON
USA   1917-1920

MUTEL
France   1905-c1906

MUTUAL
USA   1919-1926

MWD
Germany   1911-1912

MWF
Germany   1924-1928

MWM
Germany 1923-1931

MYERS
USA 1916-1918

MYERS
USA 1918-1919

N

NAG-PRESTO
Germany 1927-c1931

NAGANT
Belgium 1900-1914

NAM
England c1972 to date

NAMAG
Germany 1906-1914

NAPCO POWER PAK
USA 1955-1956

NASON
USA 1912

NATIONAL
USA 1899

NATIONAL
USA 1926

NATIONAL
USA 1948

NEGRE
France c1906

NEILSON
USA 1906-1907

NELSON
USA 1919

NER
England c1907

NESTOR
USA 1911-1912

NEUMEISTER
USA 1912

NEVILLE
USA 1909

NEVIN
USA 1927-1934

NEW ENGLAND
USA 1915

NEW YORK
USA 1900

NEW YORK AUTO-TRUCK
USA 1920-1921

NEWCOMER
USA 1926-1930

NICOLAS
France ? to date

NIELSON
USA 1906

NILSON
USA 1921

NILSON-MILLER
USA 1909

NOHAB
Sweden 1928-c1935

NOLAN
USA 1924

NONPARELL
USA 1913

NORDISK
Denmark c1948-?

NORDYKE & MARMON
USA 1913

NORRGBER
Sweden c1900

NORTH PACIFIC
USA 1911

NORTHERN
Canada c1912

NORWALD
USA 1911-1922

NORWALK
USA 1918-1920

NUSCO
USA 1916

O

OAKLAND
USA c1907-c1931

OB
USA c1921-1931

OB TRUCK
USA 1923-1933

OFELDT
USA 1900

OGDEN
USA 1919-1929

OH
England c1967

OHIO
USA 1892-1898

OHIO
USA 1911

OHIO FALL
USA 1913

OHIO MOTOR TRUCK
USA 1909

OK
USA 1914-1916

OKONOM
Germany 1921-1928

OLD HICKORY
USA 1914-1915, 1919-1923

OLIVER
USA 1910-1913·

OLNEY
USA 1911

OLSEN
USA 1921-?

OLYMPIAN
USA 1918-1919

OLYMPIC
USA 1922-1923

OLYMPIC
England 1950

OMAHA
USA 1921

OMASKA
USA 1911

OMORT
USA 1923-1934

ONAN WESTCOASTER
USA c1955-c1965

ONLY
USA 1912

OREN
USA 1949-1974

ORIENT EXPRESS
Germany 1895-1905

ORION
West Germany 1952-1956

ORION
Canada 1977 to date

ORLEANS
USA 1920-1922

OS
USA 1914

OSGOOD-BRADLEY
USA 1930-1932

OSMERS
USA 1911-1912

OTTAWA
USA 1960 to date

OVERTIME
USA 1915-1924

OWEN
USA 1912

OWEN-SCHOENECK
USA 1914

OWOSSO
USA 1910-1914

P

PACIFIC METAL
USA 1915

PACKET
USA 1910

PACKETT
USA 1916-1917

PAIGE
USA 1908-1927

PAK-AGE-KAR
USA 1927-1941

PAN
USA 1920

PARSONS
USA 1913

PATENT HOLDING
USA 1911

PATRICK
USA 1916

PATTERSON-OLSEN
USA 1912

PATTISON
England c1935-?

PAVESI
Italy 1915-c1930

PECQUEUR
France 1828-?

PEET
USA 1923-1926

PEKRUN
Germany c1905-c1914

PENDELL LOW BED
USA 1925-1928

PENNFORD
USA 1924

PENNSYLVANIA
USA 1909

PERFECTION
USA 1924-1926

PERKINS
USA 1909

PETERS
USA 1924

PETROLEUM
USA 1923

PETTIBONE
USA ? to date

PFEIL
Germany c1931-c1935

P & H
USA ? to date

PHOENIX CENTIPED
USA c1909-1918

PIC-PIC
Switzerland 1906-1920

PICK
England c1905-1924

PICKARD
USA 1912

PICKWICK SLEEPER
USA 1936

PIEDBOEUF
Belgium 1906

PIEDMONT
USA 1917-1920

PIERCE
USA 1955

PILAIN
France c1906-1929

PILOT
USA 1922

PIONEER
USA 1909-1911

PITMAN
USA 1957

PITT
USA 1913

PITTSBURGH
USA   1920-1925

PLAINS
USA   1923

PNEUMATIC
USA   1896-1905

PONTHIEU
France   c1920-c1925

POPE
USA   1905

PORT ALBANY
USA   1929

POWELL
USA   1912

POWER TRUCK
USA   1919-1925

POYER
USA   1911-1915

PPM
France   1972 to date

PRATT
USA   1911

PREMIER
USA   1903-1925

PREMIER
USA   1906

PREMIER
India   1972 to date

PRESTON
USA   1920-1923

PRICE
USA   1909

PRITCHETTS & GOLD
England   1903-c1906

PRT
USA   1927

PRUDENCE
USA   1902-1906

PRUDENCE
USA   1912

PUBLIC
USA   1914

PUNGS-FINCH
USA   1911-1912

R

RACINE
USA   1917

RAF
Soviet Union   c1955 to date

RAMBLER
USA   1904-1913

RASTROJERO
Argentina   1952 to date

RAUCH & LANG
USA   1905-1923

RAULANG
USA   1922-1928

RAVENNA
USA   1913

RAWLINSON
England   1912

R & B
USA   1929-1941

RCH
USA   1913

READING
USA   1920

REALLORRY
England   1921

REBOUR
France   1903-1908

RECH-MARBAKER
USA   1911

RED BALL
USA   1924-1927

RED HUAI
China   1969 to date

RED STAR
USA   1912

REEVES
USA   1897-1898

REGENT
England   1905-?

REICHSTELTER
USA   1912

REILAND & BREE
USA   1924-1931

RELIABLE
USA   1921

RELIABLE-DAYTON
USA   1906-1909

RELIANCE
England   1915-?

RENVILLE
USA   1911

REOMIE
Netherlands   ? to date

REPUBLIC
USA   1901

REX
USA   1914

REX VIAPLANE
USA   1932

REX-WATSON
USA   1925

REYA
USA   1917-1919

RHODE ISLAND
USA   1900-?

RICHARD
USA   1914-1917

RICHARDSON
England   1900

RICHMOND
USA   1914

RIDEALGH
England   1917

RIDLEY
Scotland   1917

RILEY
USA   1875-1895

RIVALLANT
France   c1910-c1926

R & L
USA   1923-1924

ROAD KING
USA   1956-1957

ROAMER
USA   1927-1929

ROBERTS MOBILE TRUCK
England   1928-1929

ROBINSON & AUDEN
England   c1870

ROBINSON-LOOMIS
USA   1911

ROCCO
USA   1917

ROCHESTER-MAIS
USA   1913

ROCK FALLS
USA   1920-1923

ROCK HILL
USA   1910

ROCKERMAN
Sweden   1958-?

ROCKLIFF
USA   1902-1906

ROCKNE
USA   1932-1933

RODEFELD
USA   1916-1917

ROGERS
USA   1921

ROGNINI & BALBO
Italy   c1926-c1929

ROLBA
Canda/Switzerland   ? to date

ROLLS-ROYCE
England   1914-1927

ROMANOFF
Russia   c1902

ROMEO
Italy   1930-?

ROSLER & JAVERNIG
Austria   c1908

ROSS CARRIER
USA   1933

ROTH
Germany   1907-?

ROTHWELL
England   1905-?

ROTO
USA   1916-1917

ROVAN
USA   1914

ROYAL
USA   1914-1919

ROYAL
USA   1923-1927

ROYAL REX
USA   1921-1923

ROYAL SCOT
Scotland   1923

ROYAL TOURIST
USA   1912

ROYAL WINDSOR
England   1906-1908

RUCOCO
Germany   1930-?

RUDELL
Canada   c1928

RUGGERI
Italy   1967-1968

RULER
USA   1917

RUMI
Italy   1952-c1958

RUSSELL
USA   1912

RUZICKA
USA   1911

S

SAFETY
USA   1926-1928

SAFETY FIRST
USA   1914-1916

SAGE
France   1902-1906

ST LOUIS
USA   1912

SANDRINGHAM
England   1903

SANN
USA   1912

SAUNDERSON
England   1896,1902-1924

SAUTTER
USA   1910-1911

SAUTTER-HARLE
France   1907-c1910

SAVAL-KRONENBURG
Netherlands   ? to date

SB
Germany   1921-?

SBF
Norway   1921-1923

SCANIA
England   1974, 1980 to date

SCHAEFER
USA   1912

SCHEID BROTHERS
USA   1911

SCHIERBAUM
USA   1911

SCHLEICKER
USA 1912

SCHNADER
USA 1911

SCHOEPFLIN
USA 1914

SCHOONMAKER
USA 1921

SCHUBERT
USA 1911-1912

SCHWENKE
Germany c1921

SCLOTO
USA 1911

SCOTT
Scotland 1905-?

SCOTT & CLARK
USA 1911-1912

SCOWEN
England 1905-?

SEAL
England 1922-1930

SECURITY TWIN-DRIVE
USA 1921-1923

SEITZ
USA 1911-1912

SELLEN
USA 1912

SEQUOIA
USA 1914

SFB
West Germany ? to date

SHADY SIDE
USA 1904

SHAFER-DECKER
USA 1905-1916

SHARON
USA 1912-1916

SHAW
USA 1918-1920

SHEFFIELD
USA 1912

SHELBY
USA 1912-1923

SHERWOOD
USA 1914

SHETZLINE
USA 1911-1912

SHILLITO
USA 1901-?

SHOWA
Japan 1959-?

SIEMENS-SCHUCKERT
Germany 1906-1913, 1935-1939

SIERVERS & ERDMAN
USA 1911

SIG
Switzerland c1940-1950

SIGMUND
USA 1912

SIMA-STANDARD
France 1929-1932

SIMPLEX
USA 1899-c1914

SIMPSON & BIBBY
England 1896-1902

SING SING
USA 1912

SIOUX HAWKEYE
USA 1931

SITA
France ? to date

SIX WHEELED
USA 1919-1923

SMYSER
USA 1911

SNA
Switzerland 1903-1913

SNELL
USA 1912

SODERBLOMS
Sweden 1903-1909

SOEST
Germany 1909-1911

SOLIDOR
Germany c1906-c1910

SOLLER
Switzerland 1904-1913

SOMUA
France 1916-1955

SOUTH MAIN MOTOR
USA 1922

SOUTHERN
USA 1911

SOVEL
France 1925 to date

SOWERS
USA 1913-1914

SPA
USA 1930

SPEED
USA 1921-1922

SPOERER
USA 1911-1912

SPOKANE
USA 1911-1915

SPRINGER
USA 1903-1904

SQUARE TURN
USA 1916

STAMAG
Austria 1919-?

STANDARD ELECTRIC
USA 1911-1912

STARLING
England 1905-1909

STAVER
USA 1911-1912

STEAM MOTOR
England 1900

STEAMMOTOR
USA 1911-1912

STEAMOBILE
USA 1902

STEARNS STEAM
USA 1901-1903

STECK
USA 1911-1912

STEEL KING
USA 1914

STEHLING
USA 1911-1912

STEINHAUER
USA 1911-1912

STELA
France c1930-?

STEPHENS
England 1900-?

STEPHENSON
USA 1930

STERLING
USA 1908

STERLING
USA 1917

STEVENS
USA 1888-1906

STEWART
England 1900-1910

STIRLING
Canada c1921

STOUGHTON
USA 1920-1928

STRADDLE CARRIER
England 1959-?

STROMMEN
Norway 1929-?

STRONACH-DUTTON
England c1923

STUART
Scotland 1906

STUART
USA 1920

STUEBINN
USA 1926

STURGIS
USA 1900-c1901

STUYVESANT
USA 1911

SUCCESS
USA 1920

SUDDEUTSCHE
Germany 1934

SULTAN
USA 1911-1912

SUMMERSCALES
England 1917

SUMNER TOPP-STEWART
USA c1921

SUN
Germany c1906-1914

SUNGRI
North Korea ? to date

SUNNYSIDE
Canada c1940-c1945

SUNSET
USA 1911

SUPERIOR
USA 1915-1922

SURCOUF
France 1905

SWAMPBUGGY FABCO
USA 1946

SWANSON
USA 1912

SWIFT
USA 1911-1912

SWP
Switzerland 1958-1965

SYDMOND
USA 1911

SYKES
England c1900

SYMONDS
USA 1912

SYNRI
North Korea ? to date

SYRACUSE ELECTRIC
USA 1899-1903

T

TA KRAF
East Germany ? to date

TADANO
Japan ? to date

TAF
Rumania 1972 to date

TAIT
USA 1914-1926

TALLERO
Italy 1905-?

TARRYTOWN
USA 1914

TEC
USA 1922

TEC-TRUCK
USA 1920-1921

TECHELEC
England 1980 to date

TECO
USA 1948

TEEL
USA 1911

TEEL
USA 1913-1914

TEGETMEIR & RIEPE
USA 1913-1915

TEMPELHOF
Germany c1900-c1905

TEMPLE
France   1905

TEXAN
USA   1918-1923

TEXAS
USA   1921

THANISCH
USA   1912

THEIM
USA   1911

THILL
USA   1911

THOMPSON
England   1960-c1963

THRIFT-T
USA   1947

TIDAHOLM
Sweden   1903-1932

TIERSOT
France   1908

TILLING
England   1908

TITAN
USA   1916-1917

TITAN
Germany   c1930-c1935

TITAN STEAM
USA   1916-1917

TKF
Norway   c1936

TODD
Scotland   1869-1872

TOEPPINGER
USA   1910

TOEPPNER
USA   1912

TOPP-STEWART
USA   1919-1928

TOPPINS
USA   1923

TORBENSENS
USA   1923

TORBENSON
USA   1906-1910

TORO
USA   1923

TORPEDO
Germany   1914

TORPEDO
Yugoslavia   1972 to date

TOURIST
USA   1903-1907

TOURIST
USA   1903-1907

TOWARD
England   1897-c1900

TOWNSEND
USA   1912

TRABANT
East Germany   c1961

TRAC-TRUCKS
USA   1934

TRACKSON
Australia   1903

TRACTION
USA   1901

TRACTOR TRUCK
USA   1900

TRACTOR TRUCK
USA   1917

TRANSCOACH
USA   1974 to date

TRANSIT
USA   1948-1949

TRANSPORTATION
USA   1935

TREVITHICK
England   1800-1803

TRI-CAR
USA   1955

TRIPLE
USA   1916

TRIUMPH
USA   1919-1923

TROY
USA   1914-1916

TRUCK-BUILDER
USA   1919-1920

TRUCKETTE
USA   1947-1948

TRUCKSTELL
USA   1937

TRUCTOR
USA   1917-1918

TRUSTY
England   1928-?

TUNG-FENG
China   ? to date

TURCAT-MERY
France   1914-1917

TWIN PARTS
USA   1921

U

UAZ
Soviet Union   1956 to date

UNION
Germany   1914-1917

UNION CONSTRUCTION
USA   1923

UNITED MOTORS
USA   1911

UNITED STATES CARRIAGE
USA   1911

UNIVERSAL MACHINERY
USA   1912-1913

URSUS
USA   1920-1921

UTA
Northern Ireland   1963-?

V

VACUUM & COMPRESSOR
USA   1909

VAGNON & CANET
France   1902-1903

VALIANT
Australia/South Africa   1973 to date

VAN HOOL
Belgium   1955 to date

VAN WAMBEKE
USA   1911

VAN WINKLE
USA   1913-1919

VANDEWATER
USA   1911

VC
USA   1912-1913

VEENHUIS
Netherlands   ? to date

VELIE
USA   1908-1928

VELIE
USA   1911-1915

VELIE
USA   1927-1930

VERHEUL
Netherlands   1948-1971

VERMOREL
France   1908-1932

VERNEY
France·   1937-1975

VERSARE
USA   1925-1931

VETRA
France   1925-1966

VIALL
USA   1913-1926

VICKERS
England   1928-1933

VICTOR ELECTRIC
USA   1913

VICTOR ELECTRIC
England   1927-1961

VICTORY
North Korea   ? to date

VIDAL
Germany   1928-?

VIDEX
USA   1903

VINCKE
Belgium   c1900-c1910

VINOT-DEGUINGAND
France   1902-1925

VIRGINIA
USA   1932-1934

VITCH
USA   1910-1913

VITRAC & DUGELAY
France   1907-1910

VIVINUS
Belgium   1903-1912

VOGEL
USA   1911

VOLKSWAGEN
Brasil   1980 to date

VOLPI
Italy   1901

VULCAN
USA   1920-1922

VULPES
France   1905-1910

W

WACO
USA   1915-1917

WAF
Austria   1914-1926

WAKEFIELD
England   c1962

WALLIS & STEEVENS
England   1906-1924

WALLOF
USA   1912

WALTER
USA   1911 to date

WALTER
Czechoslovakia   1922-1946

WALTER ELECTRIC
USA   1921

WANTAGE
England   1901-1913

WARD
USA   1912

WARD ELECTRIC
USA   1911-1918

WARD ELECTRIC
USA   1912-1934

WARD ELECTRIC
USA   1918-1935

WARE
USA   1913-1920

WARE
USA   1918-1920

WARFORD
USA   1940-1941

WARNER-SWASEY
USA   1955-1977

WARWICK
USA   1913

WASHINGTON
USA   1908-1910

WASHINGTON
USA   1914-1916

WATERVILLE
USA 1911

WATROUS
USA 1907-1917

WAUKESHA
USA 1915-1922

WAVERLEY
USA 1899-1903, 1908-1916

WAYCLEANSE
USA 1912-1918

WAYNE
USA c1931 to date

W & E
England 1945 to date

WEBB
USA 1908-1912

WEDGWOOD
England 1898

WEEDEN
USA 1911

WEGMANN
West Germany 1951

WEIDMANN
Switzerland 1905-1910

WERNER
USA 1912

WERNER
USA 1935

WEST COAST
USA 1916

WESTCOASTER
USA 1927-1975

WESTCOASTER
USA c1955-c1965

WESTERN
USA 1907

WESTERN
USA 1911-1928

WESTERN
USA 1943-c1955

WESTERN CARRIAGE
USA 1912

WESTERN TOOL
USA 1901-1907

WESTFIELD
USA 1911

WESTINGHOUSE
USA 1901

WESTINGHOUSE
France 1905-c1912

WESTRAK
USA 1950

WEYHER & RICHEMOND
France 1903-1912

W & G
England 1920-1936

WHARTON
USA 1921-1922

WHATOFF
USA 1960

WHITCOMB
USA 1927-1935

WHITE
USA 1900-1903

WHITE HORSE
USA 1939-1942

WHITE-RUXTALL
USA c1943

WHITE STAR
USA 1911-1921

WHITING
USA 1904-1905

WHITLOCK
England 1955-1963

WHITWOOD
USA 1914

WIGGERS
USA 1912

WIKOV
Czechoslovakia 1925-1940

WILCOX
USA 1910-1927

WILKEN BURG CARRIAGE
USA 1911

WILKEY
USA 1911

WILL
USA 1927-1930

WILLEMS
Belgium 1934-1940

WILLET
USA 1913-1914

WILLETT
USA 1909-1913

WILLINGHAM
USA 1915-1916

WILLYS
USA 1930-1962

WILLYS-KNIGHT
USA 1924-1931

WILLYS-UTILITY
USA 1913-1914

WILLYS-VIASA
Spain 1956 to date

WILSON
England 1934-1954

WILSON-PILCHER
England 1901-1907

WINCHESTER
USA 1909

WINKLER
USA 1911-1912

WINNEBAGO
USA 1973 to date

WINSLOW
USA 1919

WINTER & HIRSCH
USA 1923

WINTHER
USA 1917-1926

WINTHER-KENOSHA
USA 1923-1927

WINTHER-MARWIN
USA 1918-1921

WISCONSIN
USA 1912-1925

WISCONSIN
USA 1921-1923

WITT-WILL
USA 1916-1932

WITTENBERG
USA 1966 to date

WM
Hungary c1925-c1939

WMC
USA 1927-1930

WOLBER CARRIAGE
USA 1911-1912

WOLFE
USA c1907-1910

WOLSELEY
England 1901-1921

WOLSELEY-SIDDELEY
England c1905-c1912

WOLVERINE
USA 1918-1922

WONDER
USA 1917

WOOD
USA 1902-1905

WOODBURN
USA 1912

WOODKNIGHT
USA 1911

WOODS
USA 1927-1931

WOODWARD
USA c1921

WOOLSTON
USA 1913

WORLD
USA 1927-1931

WORLDS
USA 1927-1930

WORTH
USA 1907-1910

WRIGHT
England 1901-1903

WRIGHT
USA c1921

W-S
USA 1911

WSC
Scotland 1907, 1912-1914

WUHAN
China ? to date

WUHAN
China 1970 to date

WUHAN
China 1970 to date

WUMAG
Germany 1925-1928

WYNDMOOR
USA 1909

WYNER
Austria 1905-1908

Y

YARD HUSTLER
USA ? to date

YHTEISSISU
Finland 1943-1948

YORKSHIRE
England 1903-1938

YPSILANTI
USA 1880

YUE LOONG
Taiwan 1958 to date

YUNOST
Soviet Union 1963-?

Z

Z
Czechoslovakia 1927-1932, 1945-1946

ZBROJOVKA
Czechoslovakia 1926-1939

ZMAJ
Yugoslavia 1969-1971

ZYPEN
Germany 1926-1927

Glossary

AIR-COOLING System by which engine heat is dispersed by convection using rotating fins or a forced draught.

ARMOURED CHASSIS Timber chassis frame strengthened by bolted iron or steel flitch-plates.

ARTILLERY WHEEL Heavy-duty wooden- or steel-spoked wheel popular up to the end of World War I.

ASSEMBLED VEHICLE One which is constructed from proprietary or "bought-in" components.

BHP Brake horsepower. With the development of new power output measuring devices at the end of World War I it became possible to measure this at the output shaft of any engine. This term replaced that of horsepower and eliminated the two-figure nomenclature in the British Isles.

CARDAN SHAFT Universally-jointed shaft transmitting drive to an axle.

CHAIN-DRIVE Connection between gearbox or countershaft to wheels by chain and sprocket.

COMPOUND ENGINE One in which steam passes from high- to low-pressure cylinders to maximize energy effect.

CONE CLUTCH One in which both driving and driven faces form a cone.

CONNECTING ROD Rod linking piston to crankshaft.

CV French unit of horsepower.

DEAD AXLE One on which the wheels rotate but which does not itself revolve.

DISC BRAKE Very efficient brake in which callipers grip the face of a revolving disc.

EPICYCLIC GEARING Internally-toothed drum containing planetary gears rotating around a central shaft by meshing with a sun wheel carried on that shaft.

'F'-HEAD ENGINE One incorporating overhead inlet and side exhaust or side inlet and overhead exhaust valves.

FIRE-TUBE BOILER Tubular steel boiler with thin open-ended tubes carrying hot gases between the end-plates, thus heating the water surrounding the tubes.

FLASH BOILER One in which steam is generated almost immediately.

FLAT-TWIN Horizontal opposed-piston engine.

GCW Abbreviation for gross combination weight which is the maximum weight at which a vehicle can operate with a semi-trailer.

GTW Abbreviation for gross train weight which is sometimes used for the above but usually refers to a rigid vehicle with drawbar trailer.

GVW Abbreviation for gross vehicle weight which is the maximum weight at which a solo rigid vehicle can operate.

HALF-CAB Usually fitted to construction vehicles, this normally has provision for one driver only but some crane-carriers have two seats in tandem.

HP Horsepower. Common unit of power adopted by James Watt in the late 18th century following experiments with dray horses. Used generally until the end of World War I, it was approximately 50% greater than the rate at which a normal horse could operate through a working day, 1hp equalling 33,000ft/lb of work per minute. Some vehicles were advertised with two horsepower figures, the first representing power at 1000rpm and the second being the maximum power output.

'L'-HEAD ENGINE Side-valve unit with both inlet and exhaust valves on the same side.

LIVE AXLE One which contains the shafts that drive the wheels.

LPG Abbreviation for liquefied petroleum gas.

MAGNETO Electricity generator producing ignition power independent of vehicle batteries.

MONOBLOC ENGINE One with all cylinders cast in a single block.
PS German unit of horsepower.

SLEEVE-VALVE ENGINE One with single or double concentric sliding sleeves around each piston which reveal inlet and exhaust ports through slots placed strategically in the sleeves.

SLIDE-VALVE ENGINE Similar to the sleeve-valve type, slide-valves forming part of the cylinder wall, moving up and down to reveal inlet and exhaust ports.

SPLASH LUBRICATION Big-end bearings lubricated by crankshaft rotating in oil troughs.

'T'-HEAD ENGINE Side-valve unit with two camshafts operating inlet valves on one side and exhaust valves on the other.

TWO-STROKE ENGINE One with fuel/air mixture drawn into crankcase and compressed by piston before entering combustion chamber thereby providing power on alternate strokes.

WATER-TUBE BOILER Reverse of the fire-tube boiler in which hot gases circulate around water-bearing tubes.

WORM-DRIVE Final-drive system employing helical worm gears.

Acknowledgements

Key to abbreviations used below:
C centre; R right; L left; B bottom; CT centre top; CR centre right; CL centre left; CB centre bottom; T top; TR top right; TL top left; BR bottom right; BL bottom left; col column

7L Science Museum; 7TR Science Museum; 8T Smithsonian Institute; 9TL Musée Nationale des Techniques, Paris; 10-11 JC Thompson; 12-13 National Motor Museum; 14T Commercial Motor; 15T London Transport; 17L Automobile Manufacturers Association Inc; 18 Commercial Motor; 20T National Motor Museum; 20BL Western Trucking Magazine; 23 no 5 HA Cypher; 23 no 9 EG Walsh; 24 BR A Morland; 24-5 Imperial War Museum; 25 CR Transport Picture Library; 26TL A Morland; 26LC Imperial War Museum; 26BL Seattle Chamber of Commerce; 26-7 A Morland; 28C A Morland; 28B Transport Picture Library; 30R M Decet; 31 A Morland; 32B HA Cypher; 32-3 N Wright; 33BR Transport Picture Library; 33B 'Commercial Car Journal'; 34T National Motor Museum; 34BR National Motor Museum; 35B A Morland; 36-7 Orbis Publishing Ltd; 39B A Morland; 42CR A Morland; 46 BL Transport Picture Library; 58T National Motor Museum; 59CR Transport Picture Library; 59TL A Morland; 60 no 2 CJ Peck; 60 no 4 Transport Picture Library; 61 no 7 PJ Davies; 61 no 5 Transport Picture Library; 68B 'Commercial Motor'; 70B Volvo Trucks (Great Britain) Ltd; 71T Lawrence Sheffer & Associates; 76 BH Vanderveen; 77B AJ

Ingram; 78R G Howarth; 79T MRM New; 79 TR Associated Graphic Arts; 79BR AJ Ingram; 79B DN Miller; 80L Ashok Leyland Ltd; 80B DN Miller; 81T DN Miller; 82B A Kren; 83T GN Georgano; 85T Aveling-Barford Ltd; 85C Aveling Barford Ltd; 85R Advanced Vehicle Systems Ltd; 87T 'Commercial Motor'; 87TR HJ Snook; 88T AJ Ingram; 89T Fotokronika Tass; 92CL 'Commercial Motor'; 93B Swiss Transport Museum; 95T Transport Picture Library; 95B 'Commercial Motor'; 97CT 'Commercial Motor'; 97BL 'Commercial Motor'; 100T Transport Picture Library; 101TL Transport Picture Library; 101CT Transport Picture Library; 109C Bus History Association; 111CL Transport Picture Library; 114BL Transport Picture Library; 114TR JC Thompson;

The Encyclopedia of Trucks and Buses Picture Credits A-Z section—

126C Transport Picture Library; 129BL Transport Picture Library; 130T MC Beamish; 137C Transport Picture Library; 137B Brad's Truck Photos; 141 'Commercial Motor'; 143CT PJ Davies; 143BR Transport Picture Library; 144R John Harrington; 146T Commercial Motor'; 148R Transport Picture Library; 149BR Bus History Association; 152T Bob Graham; 153BL Transport Picture Library; 154T Transport Picture Library; 154TR 'Commercial Motor'; 155TL Central Office of Information; 155TR F Gainsbury; 155CL Transport Picture Library; 155BR J Wilkinson; 157B Quarto; 159T Bob Graham;

159 col 2 & 3 centre British Fairground Society; 159CR Transport Picture Library; 160T PJ Seaword; 161T AJ Ingram; 163T TA Davies; 163BR Transport Picture Library; 164 WHR Godwin; 165TL M Dryhurst; 166T Bus History Association; 166B Wm A Luke; 166C M Dryhurst; 166B Transport Picture Library; 168B A Kren; 176R AJ Ingram; 176CB Transport Picture Library; 179B T Agland; 180R BH Vanderveen; 184T Transport Picture Library; 184BR Transport Picture Library; 187C Bob Graham; 197T John Wicks; 197L AJ Ingram; 198 'Commercial Motor'; 200TL HJ Snook; 200BL Transport Picture Library; 201R 'Commercial Motor'; 202TL Transport Picture Library; 202C Transport Picture Library; 210T BH Vanderveen; 211BL Transport Picture Library; 211TR Bob Graham; 211BR Transport Picture Library; 212L 'Commercial Motor'; 214L 3rd down Transport Picture Library; 217TR Transport Picture Library; 218 'Commercial Motor'; 221BL Transport Picture Library; 221 2nd col 3rd down Transport Picture Library; 222BL M Dryhurst; 222TR 'Commercial Motors'; 222CR 'Commercial Motors'; 223C Bus History Association; 223B BH Johnson; 224TL Transport Picture Library; 224BR Transport Picture Library; 224TR Transport Picture Library; 225TL AJ Ingram; 226TL 'Commercial Motor'; 226BR Transport Picture Library; 227TR Transport Picture Library; 228TL Transport Picture Library; 228TR Transport Picture Library; 232TL Transport Picture Library; 232C CR Salaman; 234 WHR Godwin; 236BR David Scott; 236T 'Truck' magazine; 237T AJ Ingram; 238B BJ Vanderveen; 240 JC

Gillham; 241C 'Commercial Motor'; 242BL 'Commercial Motor'; 243TR 'Commercial Motor'; 243BR Transport Picture Library; 246L Transport Picture Library; 247C DH Busley; 249TL A Kren; 250 AJ Ingram; 252BR Bus History Association; 260T 'Commercial Motors'; 261CR Transport Picture Library; 261BR South Riding Motor Services; 264TR Transport Picture Library; 265L AJ Ingram; 266B Transport Picture Library; 266R Transport Picture Library; 267 Transport Picture Library; 272C Transport Picture Library; 272BL Transport Picture Library; 274BR Transport Picture Library; 275B 'Commercial Motor'; 275TL Transport Picture Library; 276TR 'Commercial Motor'; 276BR Transport Picture Library; 277BR Transport Picture Library; 278B David Scott; 279T HJ Snook; 279TR 'Commercial Motor'; 279B BH Vanderveen; 281BL WHR Godwin; 281BR A Krew; 283 3rd col C AJ Ingram; 285BL Transport Picture Library; 290BR GOP Pearce; 293TL 'Commercial Motors'; 293BR RS Kenney; 294T Bus History Association; 294B Bus History Association; 295T 'CommercialMotor'; 295B 'Commercial Motor'; 295TR AJ Ingram; 295BR Transport Picture Library; 296C Transport Picture Library; 296B 'Commercial Motor'; 300 TL Transport Picture Library; 300TR AJ Ingram; 301L Transport Picture Library; 301BR Transport Picture Library; 302T Transport Picture Library; 303TL Transport Picture Library; 306CR AJ Ingram; 306TL CJ Peck; 306BR AJ Ingram; 307TL David Scott; 308TL 'Commercial Motor'; 308 BL Transport Picture Library